Writing Your Journal Article in Twelve Weeks

A Guide to Academic Publishing Success

SECOND EDITION

Frain Denio

Printed in the United States of America

28 27 26 25 24 23 22 21 20 19   1 2 3 4 5

ISBN- 9798860865655 Paperback

LIBRARY OF CONGRESS CATALOGING-IN-PUBLICATION DATA

Names: Belcher, Wendy Laura, author.

Title: Writing your journal article in twelve weeks : a guide to academic publishing success

Contents

INTRODUCTION: Using This Workbook 1

The workbook's goals, field-tested nature, pragmatic emphasis, radical audience, revision focus, and disciplines.

General instructions: *Using the print or electronic version. Completing tasks. Following disciplinary tracks and stage pathways. Using the workbook according to your temperament; by yourself; in a writing group; with a writing partner; with coauthors; or to teach a class or workshop.*

Some publishing terms and processes: *What is a journal? What is an article? What processes do journal articles go through?*

Giving feedback to author

WEEK 1: Designing Your Plan for Writing 14

Instruction: Understanding feelings about writing. Keys to positive writing experiences: *successful academic writers write; read; make writing social; persist despite rejection; and pursue their passions.*

Your tasks: Designing a plan for submitting your article in twelve weeks. *Day 1, reading the workbook. Day 2, designing your writing schedule. Day 3, selecting a paper for revision. Day 4, rereading your paper to identify revision tasks. Day 5, setting up your writing site, citation software, and file backup system; addressing coauthorship; and reading a journal article.*

WEEK 2: Advancing Your Argument 60

Instruction: Myths about publishable journal articles: *being profoundly theoretical, packed with ideas, and entirely original.* What gets published and why: *how publishable articles pair evidence and approaches.* What gets rejected and why: *perfectly acceptable articles and those with no argument.* Understanding and making arguments: *what is an argument; how do you know whether you have one; how do you make strong arguments; and how do you write an argument-driven article?*

Your tasks: Organizing your article around your argument. *Day 1, reading the workbook. Day 2, testing out your argument. Day 3, reviewing your article for argument. Days 4–5, revising your article around your argument.*

WEEK 0: Writing Your Article from Scratch 390

Instruction and tasks: Writing your article from scratch without an idea: *setting up, getting an idea, testing your idea, collecting evidence for your idea, drafting your article, and revising your article using the workbook.* Writing your article from scratch with an idea.

Preface to the Second Edition

When I was writing the first edition of this writing workbook, I conceived of it as a specialized text for a narrow audience: graduate students in the humanities and qualitative social sciences. I did not anticipate that it would become popular in many disciplines and with a much wider range of academics, including junior faculty, postdoctoral research fellows, adjunct instructors, recent PhDs, faculty in the professional schools, and even instructors of upper-level undergraduate courses. So I was delighted that academics came to regard this workbook as the bible of journal article publishing, the one text on the subject that they used. Dozens of articles have been published about the positive results of using this workbook to teach writing.

As a result, in producing this second edition I have kept this broader audience in mind. For instance, although many wrote to tell me how much the workbook had helped them, some readers, often new graduate students with no writing experience, didn't have a paper to revise and needed advice about writing journal articles from scratch. So I have added a chapter to help anyone who wants to use the workbook to write an article from its very inception.

In addition, I hadn't anticipated that the amount of time that scholars needed to complete their article-writing tasks would be so wildly divergent. In the first year after the book came out, a quantitative behavioral scientist said to me, "Twelve weeks?! I don't have twelve weeks; I need to write up research in *one* week." And a literary scholar lamented, "Twelve weeks?! I can't write an article in that short a time; I need at least twelve *months*." So in this second edition, I've better addressed these differing needs. "Twelve weeks" remains in the workbook's title, but you'll now find instructions to aid you in completing articles in different time frames.

I *did* anticipate that I would receive quibbles about chapter sequence: How can readers possibly work on argument until they have selected the journal they'd like to publish their article? How can readers possibly select a journal when they haven't completed their literature review? Unfortunately, not all information can be packed into the first chapter. So in defense of my choices, the order of chapters in the book has nothing to do with what's most important to know or do, and everything to do with what's most important to keep you motivated and feeling good about writing. That said, I did rearrange or add a few chapters: I moved the chapter about argument to the second week, since it undergirds the book and your writing, and I added chapters about analyzing evidence and claiming significance.

I have made other improvements as well. My thanks to all of you who emailed me to note errors in the first edition! I must have received one hundred emails about the typo "Inw writing tasks" in the introduction, and I felt happy when I got each one, knowing that people were reading the workbook with such care. I saved and used all your emails to address such mistakes. Second, I updated the citations on faculty productivity and scholarly writing, guiding you according to the latest research. Third, I updated the workbook according to how journals have changed their publication procedures in the years since the first edition was published. And I improved the flow of instruction within chapters, making the tasks even easier to follow.

Although much about the second edition is new, I have kept what readers liked about the first: its humor, its encouraging tone, its stories, its detailed instructions, its base in the scholarly research on writing, and its rich content about getting journal articles published. I have continued to assume that its main readers are those who have published little or not at all. Although people at different stages of their academic career have used the book, my understanding of graduate students' struggles remains the organizing principle of the advice in its pages.

I hope that you find this second edition even more useful than the first. And keep those comments coming! I love to hear from you; just email me at wbelcher@ucla.edu (my lifetime email).

Acknowledgments

In writing the second edition, I am grateful to all the readers who emailed me feedback about the workbook. Of those who took the time to point out errors or inconsistencies in the first edition, none was more appreciated than Steven Gump, who sent me many pages of thoughtful comments and corrections.

I am also grateful to my beta testers, who over the summer of 2016 used my first draft of the second edition to work on an article for publication. Each Monday, they reported how they had used the book that week and what they thought I could improve about it. Among the beta testers were some of the amazing teachers in Princeton University's Writing Program, including Marina Fedosik, Steven A. Kelts, Maria A. Medvedeva, and George R. Laufenberg; other testers included Princeton faculty members Brian E. Herrera, Desmond D. Jagmohan, and Ruha Benjamin and graduate students Jill Stockwell, Jane C. Manners, Jessica Wright, Melanie Webb, and and Katherine R. Hilliard.

Thanks to all those who posted reviews online or wrote about the workbook on social media—your comments were important to the revision process, whether for keeping what worked or changing what didn't. Special thanks to Lisa Munro, Ellie Mackin, Beatriz Reyes-Foster, and others who blogged about their experiences of using the workbook to write an article in twelve weeks.

I am especially thankful for my marvelous University of Chicago Press peer reviewers—Raul Pacheco-Vega, Tanya Golash-Boza, Regina Dixon-Reeves, Patricia Morse, and Jane Hindman—for their insights on how to improve the second edition, and to the Press's staff members, including the amazing senior editor Mary Laur, the gifted copy editor Sandra Hazel, the exceptional production editor Susan Karani, the meticulous senior production coordinator Joe Claude, the dynamic publicist Lauren Salas, and the talented designer Michael Brehm. It has long been a dream of mine to be published by the best-run press in the world, and now I am.

Finally, I thank my superlative friend Bonnie Berry LaMon for saving me from myself since I was fourteen years old.

In the acknowledgments of the first edition, I thanked many, and I'm still grateful to all of them, including my wonderful parents.

INTRODUCTION
Using This Workbook

ITS GOALS

The primary goals of this workbook are to aid you in revising a classroom essay, conference paper, BA or MA thesis, dissertation chapter, talk, or unpublished article and sending it to the editor of a suitable academic journal. That is, the goals are active and pragmatic. The workbook provides the instruction, tasks, structure, and deadlines needed to complete an effective revision. It will help you develop the habits of productivity that lead to confidence, the kind of confidence it takes to send a journal article out into the world. By aiding you in taking your paper from classroom or conference quality to journal article quality, the workbook also helps you overcome any anxiety about academic publishing. For those who don't have a draft to revise, I provide instructions in the chapter "Week 0: Writing Your Article from Scratch."

ITS FIELD-TESTED NATURE

Nothing quite like this workbook exists. Most books about scholarly writing give advice based on the experiences of only the author or a few scholars in the same field as the author. This workbook isn't the product of one person's experience or thought. It wasn't written over just a semester or a year. This workbook is the product of decades of repeated experimenting, with and by hundreds of scholarly writers. I have revised it repeatedly based on my own experiences of running a peer-reviewed journal and regularly teaching the workbook around the world, as well as the feedback of its thousands of readers. By staying in touch with my students as they submitted articles to scholarly journals, I learned more and more about what actually succeeds in the peer-review process, not what is theorized to succeed. Based on this knowledge gathered from the field, the latest research, and the laboratory of the classroom, I wrote and then revised this workbook to make it as helpful as it could be. Very few books about scholarly writing have undergone the fire of testing among hundreds of scholars across a wide range of disciplines. This one has.

ITS PRAGMATIC EMPHASIS

Most instruction books are prescriptive, setting up an ideal process and demanding that you adhere to it. I see such demands as impractical. My aim is helping graduate students, recent PhDs, postdoctoral fellows, adjunct instructors, junior faculty, and international faculty understand the rules of the academic publishing game so that they can flourish, not perish. Thus, this workbook is based on what works. I don't tell you to write eight hours a day; that doesn't work. I don't advise you to read everything in your field; you can't. I don't describe how to write perfect articles; no one does. Publication, not perfection, is the goal here, so the workbook advises you based on what academics have told me they actually did, and what they were willing to do. This workbook is intended not for academic purists but for those in the academic trenches who sometimes grow discouraged and who fear that they are the only ones who haven't figured it all out.

As a result, the workbook details shortcuts and even a few tricks. And it always tells the truth, based as it is in the real world, however upsetting that world can sometimes be. Some journal editors don't like me saying that publishing in certain types of journals won't serve you well when it comes to getting hired or promoted at research universities and many colleges in the United States. Some professors don't like me saying that pre-tenure scholars should prioritize certain types of articles and research. Some academics don't like me saying that publishing in US journals is more prestigious. But I state these unfortunate truths anyway. And the workbook's advice continues to help academics achieve publishing success.

ITS RADICAL AUDIENCE

Over the history of writing this workbook and teaching my courses, I have noticed that a preponderance of my students were women, people of color, non-Americans, and/or first-generation academics. I would repeatedly hear from them, "No one ever told me this" or "I had no idea!" This workbook fills a gap in graduate education training, and has been responsible for helping many on the margins—racially, economically, internationally, and politically—feel more confident and frame their work in ways that would be acceptable to peer reviewers. That's why several people have told me that I should call this an "underground" guide to entering the profession, since it demystifies Euro-American academic conventions. Sometimes I've struggled with the aim of the workbook, wondering if I'm wrong to be helping scholars succeed in the flawed academic system as it exists, rather than working to change it. Aren't I part of the problem if I aid scholars across the globe in formatting their ideas to be palatable to mostly American white male Protestant and middle-aged peer reviewers (or those trained by them)? But in the end, I always decide that it is right to level the playing field so that everyone can play the game and advance, even those disadvantaged by that very system. I believe that everyone should have access to the rules and a chance to succeed. My hope is that enabling more scholars from the periphery—whether in terms of their scholarship or their background—to publish in scholarly journals will improve (and radicalize) academic fields and disciplines for the better.

ITS REVISION FOCUS

Most books about academic writing assume that the most difficult part of the writing process is arriving at good ideas. But in my experience, most academics, even as graduate students, have good ideas (even if they don't think so). The real problem is how many good ideas languish in unfinished, unpublished articles. What most academics need is a way to make publishable the research they have already conducted, or written about in graduate school, or taught. They know that their classroom essays, conference papers, BA or MA theses, dissertation chapters, or unpublished articles aren't ready for journals, but they don't know how to improve them.

Thus, in my workshops I focused on guiding students through a revision of something they had already written, an exercise new to many. It turned out that revising their drafts was far more effective in training them to be better, more productive, and less anxious writers than having them start writing from scratch. Further, once they learned to diagnose and correct their erroneous tendencies by revising, they wrote their next article from scratch easily. I firmly believe that revision is the heart of good writing, and that many scholars are unpublished because they have never learned how to revise their drafts, not because they have bad ideas. This workbook focuses on revision as a key to publication.

If you think that you have no draft to revise for publication, read the section titled "Selecting a Paper for Revision" in the chapter "Week 1: Designing Your Plan for Writing." You may find that you do have something to revise. It doesn't matter if the draft is poor or little more than an outline—the workbook will still aid you in revising it (although you'll need to allot more time for writing). If you really don't have a suitable draft, please turn to the final chapter, "Week 0: Writing Your Article from Scratch."

Most books about academic writing are also excessively concerned with style. Half their pages are devoted to improving word choice and syntax. In my experience, this was the least of academics' problems. Scholarship about writing supported my own observation that what most authors need is a better grasp of macrorevising (such as making arguments, structuring the whole, and summarizing), not microrevising (such as improving style through better punctuation and the reduction of adverbs). Thus, this workbook is devoted to "deep revision" (Willis 1993), the changes that make the greatest difference to an article's quality and hence its success.

I designed this workbook to help you build both skills and self-assurance. Whether you have neither, one, or both—welcome.

ITS DISCIPLINES

This workbook is useful for those in a wide range of disciplines, including the humanities, social sciences, health sciences, behavioral sciences, professional schools, and some applied sciences. I have divided these disciplines into two tracks. (Many people use the words *field* and *discipline* interchangeably, but I use *field* throughout to mean a subcategory of a discipline.)

Many scholars have used this workbook to write journal articles in the **humanities** or **interpretive social sciences** (abbreviated in the workbook as HumInt). The humanities disciplines include philosophy, religion, history, literature, and the arts (including visual arts like painting and photography; media arts like film and television; applied arts like architecture; and performing arts like dance, theater, and music). Some have used the workbook to write interdisciplinary articles about social constructions such as gender, sexuality, race, culture, ethnicity, nation, region, class, and ethics. And some have used it to write articles in the interpretive social sciences such as cultural anthropology, cultural sociology, human geography, political theory, and so on.

Other scholars have used the workbook to write experimental, quantitative, or qualitative journal articles in the **social, health, and behavioral science fields** (abbreviated in the workbook as SciQua). These include the experiment-based fields in the disciplines of anthropology, sociology, psychology, and geography, and in the qualitative and quantitative disciplines like political science, economics, archaeology, and linguistics. Those in the health sciences have also used it to write up research in all branches of medicine, including public health, epidemiology, nursing, pharmacy, health literacy, medical decision-making, and preventive health behaviors like cancer screening, diet, and exercise.

Still others have used it to write about research in the **social science professions**, such as education, business management, communications, public policy, social welfare, urban planning, library science, criminology, development studies, forestry, or international relations. They follow the SciQua track if the article reports on a qualitative or quantitative study, or the HumInt track if the article is interpretive. Only a few have used it for legal writing.

The workbook was not originally written for those in the **natural sciences**. That's because I have no graduate degrees in the sciences (mine are all in the humanities and social sciences), and I have rarely taught scientists. However, so many scientists have told me that they are using the workbook that I've had to bow to reality and do more to address such readers in this edition. So those writing up research in most of the applied sciences (e.g., engineering, computer science, aerospace, agricultural science, operations research, robotics), most of the life sciences (e.g., ecology, biology, botany, paleontology, neuroscience, zoology), and perhaps even the formal sciences (e.g., mathematics, logic, theoretical computer science) and the physical sciences (e.g., astronomy, chemistry, physics, and the earth sciences) will find the workbook more useful than they had. They follow the SciQua track. However, such readers will have to do more than other readers to adapt the book for their purposes, especially regarding time frames. I still recommend that scientists read and use *How to Write and Publish a Scientific Paper* (Gastel and Day 2016), which is practical and accessible, although rather oriented toward biology; *Writing in the Sciences* (Penrose and Katz 2010), which includes writing grant proposals and conference papers; and the encyclopedic *Scientific Writing and Communication* (Hofmann 2016), which emphasizes sentence and paragraph structure.

GENERAL INSTRUCTIONS

Although I wish it were otherwise, this workbook doesn't work by osmosis. You can't just turn the pages, read the occasional text, and then magically have an article materialize by the time you turn the last page. Reading the workbook is just a fifth of the work you must do to ready an article for a journal. The workbook makes that work easier and more straightforward, but it doesn't do the work for you. If you read the workbook just to pick up some tips, you won't learn nearly as much as you will by completing the related tasks. And you probably won't retain much. Doing is learning.

Using the Print or Electronic Version

Your reading in the workbook each week isn't passive: you must answer its questions, write in its boxes, and check off its forms. If you have the print version, go ahead and write your responses directly on the pages. That's how the book was designed to work. If you don't want to write in your print copy or you have an e-book that you can't write in, you can download some of the forms and checklists as PDFs or Microsoft Word documents from my website, wendybelcher.com, at "Writing Your Journal Article in Twelve Weeks Forms." Then you can fill them out either electronically or by hand after printing them out. Also, check my website to see whether any interactive forms have been posted.

Completing Tasks

Each workbook week consists of some instruction from me as well as specific tasks for you to complete each day for five days of that week.

Daily Tasks

The daily tasks encourage limited but daily writing, so that the revision of your article can proceed steadily despite your other responsibilities, such as teaching, working at a full-time job, caring for family members, or writing your dissertation. That is, I founded this workbook on the research that shows that those who write daily publish more than those who write rarely. They are also happier! I'll tell you a lot more about this philosophy in "Week 1: Designing Your Plan for Writing."

Task Timeline

If you happen to fall behind on the daily tasks, which take one to three hours per day, don't give up or feel guilty! The times listed for the duration of each task are minimums; some tasks may take quite a bit longer. If you fall behind, have a catch-up session or reset your twelve-week calendar accordingly. I have seen many cases where authors took twenty-four weeks or even twenty-four months to send their article to a journal, and were published just the same. Persevering is the key. By contrast, if you find that you have moved through a week's tasks more quickly than anticipated—for instance, if you already had a strong abstract or structure—don't stop working for that week. Either move right into the next week's tasks or spend the extra time reading related articles or books.

Task Types

There are five types of tasks in this book. In *workbook* tasks, you read the workbook and complete the exercises. In *social* tasks, you talk about or share your writing with another academic, a writing partner, or a writing group. In *writing* tasks, you write some part of your article, such as the abstract, or something related to your article, such as a query letter. In *planning* tasks, you document your plans and track your success in achieving them. In *reading* tasks, you read journal articles in your field. The workbook doesn't provide any research tasks, nor does it include them in the total writing time, although you may need to do additional research to complete your article.

Task Examples

Several scholars have blogged online about using the workbook to revise an article—including Lisa Munro (2016) and Ellie Mackin (2013). If you want some sense of how others completed the tasks or how the tasks helped them, check out such blogs.

Following Disciplinary Tracks and Stage Pathways

Since scholars in different *disciplines* need different amounts of time to complete an article, you'll find two disciplinary tracks running through the workbook. Since scholars at different writing *stages* also need different amounts of time, you'll find two pathways running through the workbook as well. These are as follows:

- *Humanities and Interpretive Social Science* track: for scholars working on articles containing few to no statistics. Look for the abbreviation "HumInt."
- *Social, Health, Behavioral, and Natural Science Fields Revision* track: for scholars working on experimental, qualitative, or quantitative articles. Look for the abbreviation "SciQua."

- *Revising* pathway: for those who are revising drafts (e.g., of a classroom essay, conference paper, BA or MA thesis, dissertation chapter, talk, or unpublished article), not writing drafts from scratch. This track assumes that you have a rough draft based on some research, and that you will proceed through the workbook chapters in sequence. Start with "Week 1: Designing Your Plan for Writing."
- *Drafting* pathway: for those who are writing drafts from scratch. Start by reading "Week 0: Writing Your Article from Scratch."

No matter what your track or pathway is, start by reading the week 1 chapter. There you'll find instructions for each.

Using the Workbook according to Your Temperament

Some readers follow the workbook step-by-step. If you like a structured approach and the security of detailed instructions, then proceed through the workbook in sequence. If you do that, you will complete and submit your article to a journal. There's a lot to be said for clear guidance.

Some readers hate to be told what to do, preferring not to follow detailed instructions. That's okay too! Instead, set aside an hour or two every week to read a workbook chapter and note its implications for your revision of your article, and set aside at least five hours a week to work on the actual revising. After reading "Week 1: Designing Your Plan for Writing," you can read the chapters in any order, focusing each week on the overall task of that chapter—for example, improving your argument or selecting a journal. When you have completed all the chapters, you are ready to send off your article to a journal. A warning about this second approach: freedom has its price—inertia. If you have a problem staying focused or haven't written much in a long time, follow the structured approach for the first three weeks.

Using the Workbook by Yourself

Most readers use this workbook on their own. Some of the tasks require submitting parts of your journal article to another academic for comments—but otherwise, you can use this workbook independently.

Using the Workbook in a Writing Group

You can also use this workbook in a writing group. Research shows that writing groups help you stay motivated, because they provide support and friendly pressure (Johnston et al. 2014; Brandon et al. 2015; Nairn et al. 2014). To use the workbook in this way, find three or more people who want to revise an article and are willing to commit to doing so in the same time frame.

Selecting group members. If your department already has a journal reading group or writing group, use it as a base. However, you don't need to be in the same discipline or field to participate in a writing group. In fact, it can sometimes be helpful to work with people who are unfamiliar with your content, which forces you to be clear about your topic. Such colleagues can bring a fresh perspective, getting you to see something from a new angle. Some combinations are good to avoid, though. Placing those in the theoretical humanities with quantitative social scientists probably won't work well. Power dynamics may negatively affect groups composed of graduate students and faculty from the same department, or groups including untenured and tenured faculty from the same university (although I know of some groups in Norway that have done just that with success). If you're a senior faculty member, don't put graduate students or junior faculty in the position of refusing your invitation to join you in a group.

Completing tasks with group members. As individuals, set aside time five days a week to work through that week's readings and tasks. As a group, commit to meeting once a week to talk through those readings and tasks and to hear members' reports on how you have each completed the week's goals as stated in the workbook. It's best to meet in person, but you can try video calls or even instant messaging or email. When the workbook task is to submit your journal article to someone else for review, do so with others from your group.

Giving feedback to group members. Before the first meeting, read the advice about how to give and receive feedback in "Week 6: Crafting Your Claims for Significance." Mainly, make sure that your group is a supportive environment for writing, not a graduate seminar for tearing writing apart. The first focuses on building strengths, the second on identifying limits. You are working together to become productive writers, not perfectionists. Also, be sure to monitor the discussion and make sure that the meeting time is mostly spent discussing writing, not fears and anxieties about the profession. Finally, treat all drafts and discussions as confidential, as the group must be a safe place for people to present their writing at any stage.

Making a commitment to group members. This endeavor will work only if your group takes it seriously. Make a written commitment to work together for an agreed amount of time. Although initially it may seem forced, people who make written commitments to each other find that they are more productive. You may either design your own agreement form or use the one on the next page. You can simply email the text of the agreement to one another in the body of the email, but it's best if every member signs a print copy that each can post as a reminder near a computer, front door, or refrigerator.

Writing Commitment Agreement for a Group

I commit to meeting with _____ [first names of group members] every week on _____ [day] at _____ [time]. During each of the next _____ [number of] weeks, I commit to reading the appropriate work-book chapter and completing the daily tasks. I also commit to spending at least _____ [number of] minutes a day, five days a week, on revising my article until it is ready for submission. If I need to adjust the time frame and order of tasks, I will do so in consultation with the group. I commit to carefully reading and reviewing other group members' articles twice. If I cannot meet any of these commitments because of a prolonged illness or a family emergency, I will inform the group immediately. If I cannot meet any of these commitments for any other reason, I will pay the following penalty: _____ [fee]. If any of us do meet all these commitments, we will gain the following:

_____ [benefit].

_____ [signature] _____ [date]

Designing incentives for group members. Many people have found it useful to promise to pay a penalty for not following through on their commitment. One writing instructor required his students to write a $25 check to a political organization that they abhorred and give the check to him in an envelope addressed to the organization (Boice 1990, 75). For those students who did not meet their commitment, the instructor promptly sent their check to that loathed organization (along with their phone number, so they got on annoying call lists). He claimed that this worked as a great motivator! Other possible penalties can be an act of penance (such as grading exams for the writing partner) or public shame (such as writing about the commitment failure to three friends or on social media). Most of us prefer the carrot to the stick, favoring positive incentives rather than negative ones. In that case, you can collect $20 from each group member, put it in an envelope, and split the total among those who actually send out their article. Alternately, you can use the money toward a group activity when everyone sends off their article, such as a celebratory meal. Of course, the best reward will be your sense of accomplishment when you submit the article. There's no substitute for that!

Using the Workbook with a Writing Partner

You can also use this workbook with a writing partner. This is a wonderfully effective method for completing your journal article. Since most academics' real writing challenge is getting the writing done, having a partner helps ensure that you persevere. Setting up writing partnerships can transform students' educational experiences, creating bonds that help them throughout their degree program and even afterward. The research shows that such partnerships also increase faculty productivity (Geller and Eodice 2013; Moss, Highberg, and Nicolas 2014).

To use the workbook in this way, follow the instructions above for "Using the Workbook in a Writing Group." It's best to pick another academic whose goals and abilities are similar to yours and, just as importantly, is likely to persevere and keep you going. Some do their best with a competitor, others with someone who is supportive. Ideally, your partner will be both: someone who encourages you when you feel discouraged, but whose drive pushes you to keep up. You and your partner complete the tasks independently, but meet in person once a week to go over the assignments and exchange writing. Make a written commitment to each other to work together for an agreed amount of time, and agree on the possible penalties or benefits.

Writing Commitment Agreement for Two People

I commit to meeting with _____ [partner's name] every week on_____ [day] at _____ [time]. During each of the next _____ [number of] weeks, I commit to reading the appropriate workbook chapter and completing the daily tasks. I also commit to spending at least _____ [number of] minutes a day, five days a week, on revising my article until it is ready for submission. If I need to adjust the time frame and order of tasks, I will do so in consultation with my partner. I commit to carefully reading and reviewing _____ [partner's name] article twice. If I cannot meet any of these commitments because of a prolonged illness or a family emergency, I will inform _____ [partner's name] immediately. If I cannot meet any of these commitments for any other reason, I will pay the following: _____ [fee]. If I meet all these commitments, I will gain the following: _____ [benefit].

_____ [signature] _____ [date]

Using the Workbook with Coauthors

If you're writing the article on your own and then sending it to your coauthor (perhaps your advisor) for a brief review before sending it to a journal, follow the instructions in the section "Using the Workbook by Yourself." If you and your coauthors are writing different sections separately and then combining your contributions later, follow the instructions in "Using the Workbook in a Writing Group." If you're working more closely, drafting practically every sentence together, read the workbook together and complete the tasks together as well. Remember that coauthoring requires careful discussion of author order; I will give more advice about this in the week 1 chapter.

Using the Workbook to Teach a Class or Workshop

You can also use this workbook to teach a writing course or a professional development workshop. Hundreds of these have been taught using it—either regularly scheduled courses for students or faculty development workshops in Centers for Teaching and Learning (CTLs). To aid instructors and directors of such centers I have created syllabi based on the workbook, enabling you to teach a course or workshop that will be rewarding and relatively effortless for you. Each syllabus is anchored in discussion and participant peer review and thus does not require more of instructors than to read the workbook, facilitate a two- to three-hour discussion and peer-review session once a week, and provide some feedback on abstracts, introductions, and a draft of each participant's whole article. Fill out my Google Form at goo.gl/forms/TkpPrqGdoUmXxUV32 to request the syllabi in a Microsoft Word document format for 15-week, 12-week, 10-week, or 6-week courses or workshops. Be prepared for yours to be popular!

SOME PUBLISHING TERMS AND PROCESSES

If you're a novice author, you may not know basic information about journals, articles, or the publication processes that articles go through at journals. Here is that information.

What Is a Journal?

A *scholarly journal* is a periodical that publishes original research in one to fifty-two issues each year, with four to twenty research articles per issue. Each issue may also contain book reviews, review essays, response essays, and notes. The journal publishes research in one or more *disciplines* (branches of knowledge covered in university departments, e.g., English or anthropology) or *fields* (a subcategory of disciplines, e.g., eighteenth-century British literature or cultural anthropology). Almost all scholarly journals have a *peer-review* process, a quality control mechanism in which one to four scholars who are faculty experts in the author's field evaluate each article. These *peer reviewers* (also called *referees* or *readers*) identify inadequacies, misinterpretations, and errors; provide recommendations to the author for improvement; and aid the editor in making a decision about the value of the work. A journal's staff includes its *editor*, the faculty member in charge of the direction and intellectual processes of the journal; the *managing editor*, the staff member who manages the logistics of publishing the journal; the *editorial board* members, the faculty who agree to peer-review a certain number of articles per year; and the *advisory board*, the faculty who agree to have their prestigious name associated with the journal but who do not provide any labor for it. Good editors try to ensure that the journal has a short *turnaround* time (the time between your submission of the article and the journal's decision to accept or reject it, sometimes called *review time*) and a low *backlog* (the time between the editorial decision to accept your article and its actual publication date, sometimes called *publication lag*, as it depends on the number of articles the journal has already accepted for publication and are in the queue ahead of yours). You will learn more about journals in "Week 4: Selecting a Journal."

What Is an Article?

A *journal article* is an academic genre of the essay, and it has standard features. It is generally five to forty pages (2,500 to 12,000 words) in length, and contains five to fifty citations. It discusses other scholars' writing, is vetted by other scholars (peer reviewers), and is based in the concerns of a discipline (or two). One of its features is the *literature review*, a brief analysis of those scholarly books and articles on the exact topic of the article; which I call the *related secondary literature* (as explained in the week 5 chapter). Another feature is the *argument*, a stance the scholar takes toward the literature or a problem (as explained in week 2); still another feature is the *claim for significance*, the reason why scholars should be motivated to read the article (as explained in week 6). Other necessary features are the *evidence*, the confirmation for the argument collected by the author from written sources or a study (as explained in weeks 7 and 8); a *macrostructure*, the organization of the argument and evidence into a readable pattern (as explained in week 9); an *introduction*, including the article title, abstract, and initial paragraphs that orient the reader toward the meaning and value of the article (as explained in weeks 3 and 10); a *conclusion*, the final paragraphs that summarize the article's main takeaways and articulate its implications (as explained in week 10); and a *microstructure*, the organization of the article's words into a readable pattern (as explained in week 11). Most social, health, behavioral, and natural science articles also have a *Methods* section, summarizing how the study was conducted; a *Results* section, presenting the findings; and a *Discussion* section, analyzing the findings (as explained in weeks 8 and 9).

What Processes Do Journal Articles Go Through?

The **publication process** that a submitted journal article goes through can vary radically, depending on the journal's mandate, its editor's personality and vision, its editorial board, its peer-review process, its support staff's knowledge and time, and its budget size, as well as whether the article is scheduled for a special issue. Generally, however, a journal article goes through the following stages:

Submission. The author(s) of any article must submit it to one (and only one) *peer-reviewed scholarly journal*. It is forbidden to simultaneously submit the same article to multiple journals. An article's author(s) must wait for each journal to decide whether to publish it before they send it to another journal (*single submission* rule). (The one exception is law journals.)

Editorial review. The journal editor skims all article submissions, evaluating whether an article meets basic criteria (e.g., fitting the journal's topic, citing any scholarship, being at least somewhat grammatically sound, and containing content not too similar to an article the journal just published) and has no massive flaws (e.g., having a problematic methodology or no argument). If the editor identifies basic problems, the journal rejects the article, which is called a *desk rejection*. Journal editors are increasingly exercising their discretion to reject articles without sending them on for peer review.

Peer reviewer selection. If the editor finds that the article has no major problems, that person selects peer reviewers for it. This is not easy. Editors must work hard to find scholars willing to provide reviews, sending out 28 percent more invitations to review in 2016 than they had just five years earlier (Didham, Leather, and Basset 2017, 2). They often ask one member of the journal's editorial board or scholars who recently published in the journal to peer-review the article. Some editors select one or two scholars who an author mentions in the article or who do similar work. Some journals ask the author to name potential reviewers, and they will select one of those candidates (but they will never select *only* those prospective reviewers). Those who agree to peer-review the article are rarely famous. Quite a few are emeriti professors, who have some time and want to keep abreast of the field. Strictly speaking, reviewers are supposed to recuse themselves from reviewing articles they suspect were written by their friends or students. Reviewers are asked to return a written report quickly; they rarely do. Thus, nagging reviewers to submit their review is the main job of any journal editor.

Peer review. The peer reviewers read the manuscript, evaluating it for originality, contribution, clarity, relevance, sound scholarship, convincing findings, solid methods, interesting analysis, and strong argument. Some journals give peer reviewers clear instructions for reviewing (e.g., asking them to answer specific questions, fill out a form, or give a grade). The reviewers then send the editor *readers' reports*, which comment on the strengths and weaknesses of the article and suggest improvements to the author. They also recommend whether the editor should accept the article for publication or reject it.

The systems for that peer review can vary greatly. A *double-anonymous* (or *double-blind* or *double-masked*) peer review is that in which the peer reviewers of an article and its author(s) don't know one another's identities. This form is common in the humanities, the social sciences, and some medical fields. Given reviewers' proven bias against women, people of color, and those at less prestigious institutions, this type of review does the most to protect authors. It also aids reviewers in judging articles frankly, without fear of retribution should the author turn out to be in a position of power over the reviewer. *Single-anonymous* (or *single-blind*) peer review is that in which the peer reviewers know the identity of the author, but the author doesn't know the identities of the peer reviewers. This form is common in the life sciences, the physical sciences, and engineering, as well as for books in the humanities. *Open peer review* is that in which authors and peer reviewers know one another's identities. Some journals have experimented with other forms (such as postpublication review). Lots of research has been conducted on which form is fairest; I discuss it in "Week 4: Selecting a Journal."

Editorial decision. The editor now decides whether to accept the article for publication—based on the reviewers' recommendations and the number of manuscripts already accepted. If the peer reviewers all agree that the article is strong or weak, the decision is easy. The challenge comes when one reviewer recommends publication and another recommends rejection. In that case, the editor will sometimes send the article to yet another reviewer, to split the difference. At other journals, the editor will side with one of the reviewers, often the negative one, given how few articles a journal can accept each year. The editor then sends a *decision letter* to the author. Editors almost never accept the article as is, but rather send recommendations for revision (called a *revise-and-resubmit notice*) or else a *rejection*.

Author response. The author can give a variety of possible responses to the editor's decision. If the article is rejected, the author often sends the article to another journal, either with or without revisions. If the article receives a revise-and-resubmit notice, experienced authors always revise the article according to the editorial instructions and readers' reports, then resubmit the article to the editor with a detailed letter explaining the changes they made. Novice authors often let the process intimidate them; they fail to revise and resubmit their article, even though an article's chances of acceptance upon resubmission double.

Editorial/peer-review second round. If the recommended revisions were minor, the editor alone may vet the article in this second round of submission, without sending it back to the original peer reviewers. If the recommended revisions are major, the article will go back to those reviewers for vetting—or even to new reviewers altogether. Many articles go through multiple *review rounds*, with authors revising and resubmitting to peer reviewers two, three, or even four times.

Copyediting, proofreading, and publication. Once the editor has accepted a resubmitted article, it usually goes through *copyediting*, in which a copy editor edits the article's grammar, punctuation, documentation, style, and factual errors. The edited article is sent to the author for review, usually as a Microsoft Word document in which the Track Changes function has been turned on so that the editing is easy to see. The author usually has three to ten days to answer any questions the copy editor has, approve or reject that editor's suggestions, and ensure that no errors have been introduced. Limited authorial changes could be made at this point, although publishers frown on this and may charge the author if they are deemed too extensive. Next, the author sends the article back to the journal, along with any images, permissions for the publication of those images, and the copyright agreement (in which the author gives up certain rights to the article in return for its publication). Then the article is electronically composed and put into the journal's format, from which the article's next-to-final version, *proofs*, are produced. Sometimes there is a *proofreading* round, in which the author gets a final look at the article to make sure that no errors have entered in. The author usually has forty-eight hours to respond to proofs.

Depending on a variety of factors, journals publish articles one to three years after their initial submission. For more information about these stages, consult *The Chicago Manual of Style*, which is online at www.chicagomanualofstyle.org/home.html.

GIVING FEEDBACK TO AUTHOR

Many readers of the first edition of this workbook sent me comments, which were incredibly helpful in preparing the second edition. Keep them coming! I welcome corrections (e.g., typos or grammatical mistakes that you caught) but also any examples from your work that you want to send me (e.g., how you revised a poor title into a strong one), insights on what makes a journal article publishable (e.g., how it works in your field), and successful exercises (e.g., setting up author-order dialogue). To contact me, please email wbelcher@ucla.edu (my lifetime email). You can also go to my website, wendybelcher. com; follow me on Twitter at @WendyLBelcher; or search for the workbook's hashtags, #12WeekArticle, #WYJA, or #WayofWendy.

WEEK 1
Designing Your Plan for Writing

Task Day	Week 1 Daily Writing Tasks	Estimated Task Time in Minutes	
		HumInt	SciQua
Day 1 (Monday?)	Read the introduction to the workbook and then from here until you reach the week 1, day 2 tasks, filling in any boxes, checking off any forms, and answering any questions as you read.	75	75
Day 2 (Tuesday?)	Design a daily and a weekly writing schedule for twelve weeks, and anticipate obstacles and interruptions.	180	180
Day 3 (Wednesday?)	Select a previously drafted paper (or outline) to develop for publication.	60+	60+
Day 4 (Thursday?)	Reread your chosen paper, discuss it, and then make a list of revision tasks.	150	60
Day 5 (Friday?)	Do some final setting up: addressing your writing site, citation management, backing up, and any author-order issues. Read a journal article.	45+	45+
Total estimated time for reading the workbook, completing the tasks, and writing your article		**8+ hours**	**7+ hours**

Each week, you'll have specific tasks designed to aid you in accomplishing your goal of sending your academic article to a journal in twelve weeks. Above is a brief list of the tasks for your first week, divided day by day for five days of work, and totaling about seven hours of work for the week (including reading the workbook, completing its tasks, and writing). This week has about twice the reading of any of the other weeks, so it will take you longer than normal to move through the chapter.

Note the two **tracks**—one for humanities and interpretive social science scholars revising papers for publication (HumInt **track**) and the other for scholars revising experimental, quantitative, or qualitative papers, including social, health, behavioral, and natural science scholars (SciQua **track**). The first task for day 1 is to read the material that follows.

Note: If you're not revising a paper but instead are drafting one from the beginning, please read this whole chapter and then turn to "Week 0: Writing Your Article from Scratch."

UNDERSTANDING FEELINGS ABOUT WRITING

Writing is to academia what sex was to nineteenth-century Vienna: everybody does it and nobody talks about it. A leading scholar of productivity found that most academics were more willing to talk about their most personal problems, including sexual dysfunction, than about problems with writing (Boice 1990, 1). The prevalent belief among academics seems to be that writing, like sex, should come naturally, and should be performed in polite privacy.

Because of this silence, writing dysfunction is commonplace in academia. A survey of over sixteen thousand full-time faculty in the United States revealed that almost a fifth did not read or write scholarship in the past two years (Eagan et al. 2014, 9, 29–30, 33). In addition, almost a third had not published any piece of writing in that time. Over half of them spent less than an hour a day reading and writing scholarship. Furthermore, these statistics are self-reported and so reflect the activities of only those organized enough to respond to the survey. A large-scale study without this bias, of actual publication rates for all faculty members in a province, found that many did not publish: two-thirds of the humanities faculty and one third of the social science faculty had not published even one article in the past eight years (Larivière et al. 2010, 48). In other words, unproductive academics are common. Since publication is the major marker of productivity in academia, these statistics about low productivity are surprising. Or are they?

You don't have to be Freud to figure out that academia's silence about writing may be repressive. Writing is, after all, a creative process; and like any such process, it depends on human connection. If you try to create in an environment where sharing is discouraged, dysfunction is the inevitable result. Certainly, many have found that talking about their struggles with writing has been freeing. The lesson: learning to talk about writing is an important key to becoming a productive writer.

One of the reasons that academics don't talk about writing is that it involves talking about feelings. Academics tend to be more comfortable with the rational than the emotional. Therefore, even if we do manage to talk about writing, we're more likely to talk about content than process. So the first step to success is for you to acknowledge your feelings about writing. Mindfulness is essential.

Let's start with a broad question. What feelings come up when you contemplate writing? I recommend that you call, email, text, tweet, or instant-message someone to discuss this question before using the box below to jot down your answers. Many also use blogs to complete this task.

My Feelings about My Experience of Writing

(If you skipped this last exercise, do return to it and write down at least one feeling. The following will make more sense if you take the time to write something there or at least silently identify one to yourself.)

When I ask students in my writing courses to describe their feelings about their writing experiences, negative ones usually come up first. Some of these comments, taken verbatim from my class notes, are as follows:

> I feel both terror and boredom . . . I get depressed when I think about having to write . . . I feel discouraged, because I feel like I have never done enough research to start writing . . . I have fun in the beginning, but I really hate revising . . . I enjoy revising, but I hate getting that first draft down . . . My advisor is so critical that whenever I think of writing, I feel inadequate . . . I feel like there are rules that everyone knows but me . . . I feel like procrastinating whenever I think of how much writing I have to do and how little I have done . . . I feel ashamed of my writing skills . . . I wish my English was better . . . I feel that if people read my writing, they will know that I'm a dumb bunny . . . I feel like I work at writing for hours and have so little to show for it . . . I spend so much time critiquing my students' writing that I shut down when I come to my own . . . I get a good idea, but then I feel a fog come over me . . . When I think about the fact that my entire career depends on publication, I feel completely paralyzed.

Guess what? You're not alone! Most writers, even accomplished writers, hear these inner negative voices whispering their fears to them whenever they think about writing. Using this workbook will diminish those voices, but the most effective step is to realize that these feelings are justified. Writing is difficult and scary. Feeling anxious is an entirely appropriate response.

It's worthwhile to spend some time thinking about what links your negative feelings. Do they revolve around one or two anxieties, perceptions, or habits? Do they point to a particular fear, such as what others will think of you? Or to a particular negative self-assessment, such as labeling yourself as lazy? Use the box below to identify these links.

Common Elements in My Negative Feelings about Writing

You'll spend time later in the chapter learning to address your negative feelings, but for now just observe them.

Interestingly, when I ask students to discuss their feelings about writing, some positive feelings usually come up too. Students say things like the following:

> I feel excited when I think up a good idea . . . Sometimes I write a sentence that comes out more coherently than I expected, and I feel great . . . I feel euphoric when I realize that I have a good conclusion that ties the paper together . . . I love the feeling of having just finished a paper . . . When I reread something I wrote a year ago, I'm impressed and I think, "Did I write that?!"

To feel better about your writing, then, try to recall the context in which positive feelings arose. Consider any good memories you have of writing: What made that experience good? What were the common denominators? And what are the lessons you can learn from those experiences? (You'll spend time later learning to use these lessons, but for now just write them down.)

Common Elements in My Positive Experiences of Writing

When I ask this question in my courses, students list common elements of good writing experiences such as the following:

> I had a deadline that forced me to sit down and do the writing . . . I had an advisor/friend/spouse who was encouraging . . . I was working on a paper that meant a lot to me personally . . . My parents took my kids for a week . . . I got into a rhythm of writing every evening after watching an episode of *The Simpsons* . . . I had a part-time job that forced me to use my time more efficiently . . . I read an article that really inspired me and got me going . . . I asked my advisor to meet with me once a week and to expect some writing from me every time.

Interestingly, the lessons students learned from these experiences are similar. Apparently, happy writers are all alike, to paraphrase Tolstoy. Academic writers who are successful share similar attitudes and work habits. I call them the keys to academic writing success.

KEYS TO POSITIVE WRITING EXPERIENCES

I have designed this workbook to help you develop skills in the five keys to academic writing success. Knowing these keys can help you design your own program.

Successful Academic Writers Write

"First and foremost, *get writing!*" is the advice given by the author of several academic classics (Morison 1953, 293).

It may sound tautological, but one key to a positive writing experience is to write. Most academics' negative experiences of writing revolve around not writing (i.e., procrastinating), and most of their positive experiences revolve around actually doing it. That is, when academics write, they feel a sense of accomplishment and the pleasure of communicating their ideas. In this sense, writing is the same as physical exercise. Although it may be arduous at first, it does get easier and more pleasurable the more you do it. A legendary professor of film and Chicanx studies at UCLA, Chon A. Noriega, tells his graduate students when they embark on their dissertation, "One usually gets better at whatever one does on a regular basis. If one does *not* write on a regular basis, one will get better at *not* writing. In fact, one will develop an astonishing array of skills designed to improve and extend one's *not* writing." I saw this myself in graduate school: some students practiced yoga as an aid to writing, while others practiced it to escape writing. Don't develop practices that help you avoid writing.

Now, those who don't write often claim that they are "too busy." Indeed, people today are very busy. Some academics have long commutes, others have heavy teaching loads, and still others have young children. So here's the good news and the bad news. Many busy people have been productive writers. Are they just smarter? No. If you pay close attention to how you spend time, you'll find that you may not be quite as busy as you suppose, and that writing doesn't take as much time as you fear.

Robert Boice, a scholar of faculty productivity whose research informs much of this first chapter, demonstrated this truth by finding faculty members who claimed to be "too busy" to write and then following them around for a week. With Boice staring at them all day, most had to admit that "they rarely had workdays without at least one brief period of fifteen to sixty minutes open for free use" (1997a, 21). His subjects spent this free time in activities that were neither work nor play. Boice also found that those likely to describe themselves as extremely "busy" or very "stressed" did not produce as much as those who were writing steadily (1989, 608–9). In other words, you are not too busy to write—you are busy because you do not write. Busy-ness is what you do to explain your not writing. (If you skimmed over those last two sentences, I recommend that you go back and read them one more time.)

No matter how busy your life is, make a plan for writing. Successful academic writers don't wait for inspiration. They don't wait until the last minute. They don't wait for big blocks of time. They make a plan for writing five days a week, and they strive to stick to it. Much of this workbook will be devoted to helping you develop writing into a habit. Short and steady sessions will win the race: "With but a few exceptions, writers who remained in a schedule requiring an hour or less a weekday of writing mastered a sequence of strategies for remaining truly productive over long periods of time" (Boice 1990, 3). As an anonymous person wisely commented online, "The only thing that improves writing is writing."

Successful Academic Writers Read

The best way to learn to write journal articles is to read journal articles. Unfortunately, many students do not. The famous novelist Chris Abani once grumbled to me, "Everyone wants to be an Author, having written nothing and read less." What they don't realize is that "to be a good writer, you have to read a lot" (interview with Kevin Corley in Cloutier 2015, 75). Something surprising happens when you read a lot: your unconscious brain sees patterns your conscious brain does not, so you internalize the language and conventions of your field. As a result, your writing improves, in both form and content.

I know that reading works as an engine of writing because I have seen it in action. I now teach a course in which graduate students are required to select a different peer-reviewed journal every week and then "read" five years of it (i.e., read the titles and abstracts of all the articles published in that period, some of their introductions, and five to ten of the articles in their entirety). The first time I taught it, one of the students had given a dissertation chapter to her advisor before the course began and then another chapter near the end of the course. The advisor said to her, "Your writing, it's like night and day, it reads so much more professionally than it did just eight weeks ago. What happened?!" She replied, "What happened is that I read a hundred journal articles between now and then; I'm steeped in the form." Her reading many published articles enabled this student to write publishable prose. And not just her form improved, her content did as well. During her journal reading, she kept coming across a new theory in her field, one she thought was wrong-headed, so she began writing up her critique in an article. She went on to become one of the few graduate students to publish in the top journal in her field, because her article spoke directly to very recent field concerns and cited many recent articles. She had gained publishable knowledge through her reading.

If you aren't in the habit of reading, start small. One journalist reports that she started by reading "just one page of a book every night before bed." After she had been doing that for a while, she set a timer for fifteen minutes of reading every night. "Eventually I was reading for 30 minutes before bed and another 30 minutes most mornings. Just starting with one page added up: In 2013, I read seven books. In 2014, 22. In 2015, 33. That's almost five times what I read in 2013" (Cooper 2016).

How much should you read? Different fields have different norms. One study found that social science faculty read an average of five articles per week, while humanities faculty read an average of three articles per week (Ware and Mabe 2015, 58). All faculty combined spend an average of 30 minutes to read one article, so the average faculty member is spending one to three hours a week at least skimming journal articles (7). If you're not spending some time each week skimming journals, you may not be reading enough recent journal articles to write them well.

Successful Academic Writers Make Writing Social

The myth that writing should be a solo activity is just that, a myth. Yet the popular image persists of the writer as someone who works alone for months in a cold garret, subsisting on bread and cigarettes while coughing consumptively and churning out page after page of sui generis prose. It's a lonely, hard life, the myth goes, but that's what writing takes. And academics in the humanities often persist in believing that texts spring fully formed from the mind of their authors.

In the sciences, this myth is not so prevalent, since most science articles are the result of a team of researchers who publish as coauthors. Students in the sciences work as secondary authors, contributing sections or data to faculty members' articles, long before they ever become primary authors. That's why the rate of writing dysfunction in the sciences is so much lower. Scholars in the sciences see writing as collaboration. When this idea of teamwork is lost, many of the prevalent writing problems in the academic community arise—writer's block, anxiety over having one's ideas stolen, obsession with originality, fear of belatedness, difficulties with criticism, even plagiarism. All stem from the myth that writing should be a private and isolated activity.

Yet no writing is the product of just one person. And the best writing is created in community, with a strong sense of audience. One study of productive academic writers found that they were unusually aware of this truth, believing that "their ideas, both in terms of what they wrote and how they wrote it, were largely generated through their conversations with others" (Cloutier 2015, 72). Writing was an ongoing process: they spoke or emailed with faculty and students, then presented at conferences or shared drafts, and then interacted with editors and peer reviewers during the submission process. Many of them noted that their thoughts did not coalesce until they talked with someone else about them.

So work to make your writing more public and less private, more social and less solitary. Commit to writing activities that require you to show up in person. Start a writing group. Choose a writing buddy. Take a writing workshop. Meet a classmate or colleague at the library or a café to write for an hour. Persuade another academic to cowrite an article with you. Join a journal-article reading club.

The more you make your writing social, in person or virtually, the more positive your experience of writing will be. This is partly because others give you ideas and language. But it's also because you must relate your ideas to others'. You must know what theories scholars in your discipline are debating, what their primary research questions are, and what methodologies they consider appropriate. You can know this only if you're an active member of the community.

For instance, participating in an association's annual conference can give you a much better idea of trends. Sometimes a conversation with someone in your field can help you shape your ideas and direction better than reading twenty journal articles. If you present your paper at the annual conference, you can also get a sense of how people in the field respond to it and then shape it accordingly. Journal editors often speak at these conferences, frequently describing the kinds of articles they're tired of seeing and the kinds they'd welcome most. You increase your chances of successfully targeting association journals by attending and presenting at their conferences.

You can also make your writing more social by joining virtual communities. Follow relevant scholars, groups, and discussions on social media, tracking hashtags in your field. Some readers have even found it productive to launch scholarly blogs, saying that writing their research in public gives them a keener awareness of audience, which stimulates them to write more clearly and directly (Munro 2016). When writing a journal article, it can be difficult to make your audience seem real to you, because you know it will be months or even years before your article reaches publication and readers. By contrast, with a blog post you know that someone might read and respond to it today, and that immediacy makes your writing more responsive, more dialogical.

Unfortunately, academics, particularly novice authors, experience several problems with making their writing more social. First, many feel real horror at the prospect of networking. Some feel awkward or invasive when attempting to contact someone they admire. Others view deliberate attempts at befriending someone as too nakedly self-serving or superficial. Certainly, reaching out socially takes courage and tact. Yet you'll find that others are often interested in meeting you, and even grateful to you for taking the first step. Many established scholars enjoy being asked for advice about their field. And social media now makes it easier to initiate contact in low-key ways, such as tweeting thanks to a scholar whose recent article you found useful. So whatever your comfort zone, try to push beyond it.

Second, many academics are hesitant about showing their writing to anyone. The university environment can encourage scholars to regard their colleagues as adversaries rather than advocates. They fear that sharing their work will reveal them as impostors and demonstrate their deep unsuitability for academia. And many classmates and professors will be too busy to read and comment on others' work. Fortunately, if you get up the courage to share your work and find someone who wants to share in return, you'll usually discover that you're not as much of an idiot as you thought you were. Moreover, the fresh eye of an outside reader can quickly identify omissions and logical breaks in your writing that would have taken you weeks to figure out. Of course, some readers will be too critical, and others will give you bad advice. But an essential part of becoming a writer is learning to differentiate useful criticisms from useless ones. The more often you experience others' subjective reactions to your work, the more readily you'll be able to cope with peer reviewers' comments down the road.

Third, some academics are good at sharing their work, but only when they consider the article complete. But waiting until their manuscript is "done" before sharing it doesn't work very well. You'll be disappointed when you don't receive compliments, but instead get recommendations for revision that you're little interested in addressing. The point of sharing your writing, though, is to improve it, not to convince others of your talents. So share your writing in its early stages. Show outlines to other academics. Exchange abstracts. Give out drafts, and ask for specific comments about aspects of your writing that you suspect are weak. Post ideas on social media, and develop those that inspire the most debate or commentary. Learn to share your writing at all stages.

Fourth, academics fear that sharing their work will lead to their ideas being stolen. Like so many of the anxieties named in this book, there is a rational reason for this fear: scholars' ideas *do* get stolen. Stories are always circulating among graduate students about which advisors are likely to steal work. But hiding your work won't solve this problem. In fact, getting your writing out to a number of people will help protect it. A saved email or blog post is evidence that the idea or phrasing had originated with you. Furthermore, no one can articulate your ideas like you can. You may suspect that anyone besides you could do a better job of presenting your ideas, but this workbook will help you see that simply isn't true.

All these social activities will help you counter the myth of the lonely writer. Nothing is as collaborative as good writing. All texts depend on other texts, all writers stand on the shoulders of other writers, all prose demands an editor, and all writing needs an audience. Without community, writing is inconceivable. This workbook will help you develop social writing habits and share your work. If you're using this workbook with a writing partner or in a group, you're making excellent progress already!

Successful Academic Writers Persist despite Rejection

The writing life is filled with rejection. Being scorned by publishers is one of the few shared experiences of great writers and terrible ones. A quick read of *Rotten Reviews Redux* offers the comfort of knowing that most canonical authors (e.g., Herman Melville, T. S. Eliot, and Virginia Woolf) had their work rejected in the strongest possible terms (Henderson 2012). Jack London received 266 rejection slips in 1899 alone (Kingman 1979, 87)!

In academia, these rejections often seem to have no rhyme or reason. Peer review is so subjective that work rejected by one journal is often embraced by another. As just one example, an experienced author reported that an article of his that was brutally rejected by one journal for "lack of substance and lack of originality" was enthusiastically accepted without changes by another (Pannell 2002, 104). And an article eviscerated by reviewers at one journal, which he then altered slightly and submitted to another journal, received an award for the best journal article of the year in his field (105) He is not alone in these experiences. The economist George Akerlof received three rejections for a journal article that later won him the Nobel Prize (Gans and Shepherd 1994, 171). Indeed, studies of Nobel Prizewinners found that many early versions of their award-winning work had been rejected by journal editors (Campanario 1995, 1996, 2009). In other words, if you write, you will be rejected. If you send your articles to journals, they will sometimes be rejected. The important thing is not to let that stop you.

Although it's tempting to let others' criticism be the measure of your writing or even your own worth, don't let it be. Peer review is a subjective process rife with bias and carelessness. The difference between much-published authors and unpublished authors is most often persistence, not worthiness. Published authors just keep submitting their work.

Many have exemplified the importance of persistence. One productive Yale professor papered his office with his article rejection notices, claiming them as badges of honor and writing amid the negative notices of a lifetime. A graduate student in one of my courses, Carrie Petrucci, proved the lengths to which determined authors must sometimes go. She wrote an article she believed in, and was aware that resistance to its argument would be high. She was committed to demonstrating that criminals apologizing to their victims provide real benefits to both victims and perpetrators. When the first journal she had submitted her article to rejected it, Petrucci stopped everything she was doing and took two days to make changes based on the comments she had received from the editor and readers. When the second journal rejected her article, she did the same. "What kept me going through two rejections," she emailed me, "was the fact that I had had several people read it prior to my submitting it to any journal and a handful of those people, who had nothing to gain by it (including yourself), had given me the impression that it was strong. . . . Believe me; I clung to those comments as I got some pretty negative feedback on rounds one and two." Then the third journal accepted her article, stating that "it is quite unusual to have a manuscript accepted without requiring any changes. But yours is a high quality product. Good job!" Petrucci won an award for this article, and later accepted a job in criminal justice reform. In the years since, her article has been cited over 120 times and is a founding text in a then-nascent field—no better evidence that her article has worth (Petrucci 2002).

One student told a writing workshop about a friend who was more fainthearted. When this friend received a response from a journal to which she had submitted an article, she opened the letter with trepidation. The first paragraph included the sentence "The reviewers' reports are in and both agree that your article is severely marred by poor writing." Upset, she flung the letter aside and spent an hour in bed ruing her decision to enter academia. When her husband got home, he picked up the letter from the hallway floor, read it, and entered the bedroom saying, "Congratulations, honey! Why didn't you call and tell me your article got accepted?" Upon reading the letter through, she found that the editors had accepted the article pending major revisions. She hired a copy editor to work with her on her prose and then resubmitted the article. The lesson here is that when starting out, harsh criticism can stop you in your tracks; but if you persist, you often find that things aren't as bad as you fear.

Successful Academic Writers Pursue Their Passions

When academics list positive experiences they've had with writing, they often note their genuine interest in a topic as a real motivator. Successful writers don't write primarily for their colleagues, professors, classmates, or hiring and promotion committees. They must, of course, write for them in part—the structural demands of academia don't allow them to be free of the neoliberal constraints of their job (Gill 2009). But within those constraints, so far as it is possible, successful academic writers focus on the questions that fascinate them. This enables them to write journal articles more quickly and to endure their rejection more easily. For example, a student was writing about the negative effect of welfare reform on Cambodian women. She drafted and revised her article in record time, because she was so angry about the policy's consequences. A Korean student who grew up in Japan persevered despite several obstacles to publish her research showing that Koreans in Japan labor under legally imposed hardships. A student who wrote about pedigreed dogs and another who wrote about food metaphors always worked steadily, because the topics were also lifelong hobbies. Many academics use their own experiences of race, gender, sexuality, or nationality to reinterpret canonical texts, placing the tradition in a completely new light.

The lesson? The world changes quickly, so you're more likely to have positive writing experiences if you follow your deepest interests rather than passing fads. Write because "you think you can make some kind of a contribution to some part of the world that matters to you" (interview with Martha Feldman in Cloutier 2015, 82). My own model for this is an artist whose work I came across in the 1980s while researching street art in Washington, DC (Belcher 1987). The artist had spray-painted huge images of women's dress shoes in alleys, unafraid to depict the feminine footwear of pumps across an entire urban landscape. This artist had taken his or her idiosyncrasy and pushed it. So obsess about things, pursue your passions, don't get bullied. Whatever your pump is, paint it.

DESIGNING A PLAN FOR SUBMITTING YOUR ARTICLE IN TWELVE WEEKS

Of course, simply knowing what the successful academic writer's habits are doesn't automatically put them within reach. Many of us find it especially hard to pick up the most difficult key to success: actually writing. The most important step to developing this habit is making a plan of action. When you design a plan, you set up goals and deadlines. Once they're tangible, you can realize these goals and deadlines. This workbook aids you in designing a plan to send an article to a journal in twelve weeks (or in fewer or more weeks, depending on how far along your article is and how much time for writing you have). So let's move into the planning exercise.

Day 1 Tasks: Reading the Workbook

On the first day of your first writing week, start by reading the introduction to the workbook and continue by reading the week 1 chapter all the way through the next three paragraphs, answering all the questions posed. Write directly in the boxes provided or in your own document.

Tracking Writing Time

Each week, you're going to spend about three minutes a day keeping track of how much time you spent writing. You can use the analog form on the next page or a digital one—a time-tracking phone app, an online tool like Toggl, or a digital calendar. If you use the form on the next page, you can post it—say, on your fridge or inside your office door—so you can easily see your progress and remember to mark off writing time each day. If you use digital tracking, just be sure that you can view the whole week at a glance.

This week, mark down everything you do. That includes a variety of writing tasks, such as time spent writing your article, reading and completing the exercises in this book, discussing your article, and writing other academic works like books, theses, or conference papers (perhaps using separate symbols or colors for each type of task). But it also includes recording what you did with the rest of your time that day. List everything: watching television, attending class, commuting, sleeping, caring for family members, laundry, cooking, and so on. This one-time exercise for finding out where your hours go is a useful tool for helping you use your time more efficiently.

Start by marking down the time you spent today completing the workbook tasks. Then on the following days return to this calendar to record what you did each day.

Week 1 Calendar for **Actual** (Not Planned) Time Spent Writing This Week

Time	Day 1	Day 2	Day 3	Day 4	Day 5	Day 6	Day 7
5:00 a.m.							
6:00							
7:00							
8:00							
9:00							
10:00							
11:00							
12:00 p.m.							
1:00							
2:00							
3:00							
4:00							
5:00							
6:00							
7:00							
8:00							
9:00							
10:00							
11:00							
12:00 a.m.							
1:00							
2:00							
3:00							
4:00							
Total minutes							
Tasks completed							

WEEK 1, DAYS 2–5: READING AND TASKS

Day 2 Tasks: Designing Your Writing Schedule

Welcome to week 1, day 2 reading and tasks! Today you're going to design a writing schedule not only for this week but all the way through to submitting your article. Before you get started, let's address a few myths about writing schedules.

The Pitch for Writing Most Days

Many academics believe that in order to write, they must have long, uninterrupted stretches of time. Nothing will do but to be at their desk eight hours at a stretch, or all night, or all weekend. Only then will they be able to concentrate. Such stretches are elusive, however, so they wait for the weekend, and then for the break between courses, and then for the summer. Waiting becomes a permanent state, with writing becoming something they'll do after their qualifying exams or their first year teaching, for instance.

Others forcefully create blocks of time. As one student put it, "If I wait until the night before the paper is due to write it, I will only be miserable for eight hours!" Such academics believe that containing the writing process by restricting it will reduce the painfulness of the experience. What they don't understand is that this irregular practice is what's producing the painfulness! Imagine deciding that "running marathons is painful; I'm never going to run except on the day of the marathon." The marathon then becomes an excruciating experience you never want to repeat. By contrast, people who run a mile or two every day really enjoy running, and often feel lost without it.

Study after study shows that you don't need big blocks of time to write effectively (Boice 1982, 1992; Krashen 2002). In fact, writers who write a little bit most days produce more manuscripts than those who alternate extended writing sessions with weeks or months of not writing at all. Writing just thirty minutes a day can make you one of those unusual writers who publish several journal articles a year. According to the research,

> those who write in regular, unemotional sessions of moderate length completed more pages, enjoyed more editorial acceptance, were less depressed and more creative than those authors who wrote in emotionally charged binges. (Boice 1997b, 435)

The word *binge* here describes a pathology, not a method, as pointed out by Jo VanEvery, an academic writing advisor who hosts the online Academic Writing Studio, and Pat Thomson, author of *Detox Your Writing* (Thomson and Kamler 2016). *Binge writing* is thus a technical term with a precise meaning (VanEvery 2013; Thomson 2013). It means not merely writing for extended periods but also writing in a mild manic state, after which you feel too anxious and exhausted to write for some time (Boice 1992, 201). Excessive, emotional writing such as this—where you don't write for weeks and then stay up all night (or the whole weekend) writing—is not associated with productivity. Indeed, research on many professions has found that requiring long work hours is counterproductive, and that periods of rest are essential to effective long-term productivity (Schwartz, Gomes, and McCarthy 2010). For instance, top athletes and performers rarely practice more than ninety minutes at a time or more than four and a half hours a day (Schwartz 2013; based on Ericsson, Krampe, and Tesch-Römer 1993; Ericsson 2016). One author proved to himself that less is more. When he spent ten hours a day writing a book, he took a whole year to finish. When he spent four hours a day writing his next book, he took only six months to finish (Schwartz 2013). Rest is essential to the creative process.

The moral? Writing *daily* works. Writing *rarely* doesn't. The less you write, the harder it becomes to write. Part of the reason academics feel they need big blocks of time is because it takes them so long to silence their inner critic. Absent the small but satisfying successes of daily writing, that critic becomes harsher and louder. An author writing most days doesn't have this problem. The more that writing becomes a habit, the more likely you are to complete your writing projects and to enjoy the writing process.

What happens when you commit to daily writing? Writing becomes not a choice but a habit. You might think that disciplined people are better at resisting the temptation to do other (more fun) things, but researchers were surprised to find that productive people are in fact worse at resisting temptation than others. Why? Because they rely on habit (Galla and Duckworth 2015). That is, disciplined people do not debate going to the gym or eating their greens; they do it without even thinking about it. For them, it's not a choice; it's a habit. Having a writing habit, a regular writing time and place, does more to enable you to write than some innate ability to resist the temptation to do other things.

Finally, and this may seem counterintuitive, focusing all your energy on writing won't result in increased productivity. In fact, research shows that whatever goal you make your highest priority will most likely not be attained. That's because "the most valued activity" always "carries demands for time and perfection that encourage its avoidance" (Boice 1997a, 23). (That's my favorite line in Boice.) Therefore, writers who make writing a modest, realistic priority are more productive.

So don't establish self-defeating writing goals that relegate everything else in your life to inferior status. Aiming for a forty-hour writing week will only make you feel guilty, not productive. Furthermore, the feeling that you should always be working will haunt every pleasurable moment. You don't resolve desires by entirely suppressing them. Make time to go to the beach, meet a friend for dinner, or play a game of soccer or bid whist. A well-balanced life—with time allotted for friends and family, games and sports, movies and light reading, as well as writing, research, and teaching—is the best ground for productive writing.

Experiments with Writing Most Days

When I assert that short bursts of writing activity can accomplish much and are a common pattern among very productive individuals, most workshop participants look at me skeptically. It's the most controversial idea that I introduce—simultaneously the most contested and the most embraced. Not surprisingly, many immediately voice their disbelief. "No way!" I hear. "That's impossible!" When I ask why, this is what the participants tell me:

> I need whole days to write; otherwise, I forget what I'm working on . . . I lose track. If I don't stay in one mental space for an entire week, my ideas don't cohere . . . I need to get up a head of steam and just keep on going, because if I stop, I'll never get started again.

I listen to their objections, but then ask them to indulge me. "Just as an experiment," I say, "try writing at least fifteen minutes every day for the next week." I remind everyone that we all manage to get to work, use a microwave, and answer email without forgetting how to do these things from one day to the next. "But writing is different," they argue. "It's intellectual; it's about ideas." "Just indulge me," I reply. If a participant still seems reluctant,

I ask, "You seem very convinced you must have big blocks of time. Have you ever tried it any other way?" To a one, these skeptics admit self-consciously, "Well, no." Be wary of being so firmly against something you haven't tried.

The next week, the person who had protested the most is usually the first to volunteer that wow, the fifteen-minute method really does work. One student told me that he had reorganized his entire life into fifteen-minute chunks arranged around work and child care. Another student told me she had solved an important revision problem while standing in line at the Department of Motor Vehicles. Yet another student set herself the goal of writing a two-thousand-word essay for a trade magazine in her field without ever writing more than fifteen minutes a day. In two weeks, she had submitted the essay. A student explained it like this:

> I'm usually an environmental perfectionist when it comes to writing—I have to be at my computer, it has to be silent, and I must have coffee. But I was stuck waiting at the airport for a flight to a conference, and I thought about what you said. So I decided to try writing for fifteen minutes. It worked fine. Then I worried about having to take the time to type up my penciled notes, but I found that in transcribing them I revised them as well, so it was not wasted time. A busy airport would still not be my writing site of choice, but I can see how, by being flexible, I can ensure that I write a little bit every day and keep my ideas fresh.

Another student told me that writing in short daily bursts was especially helpful if he had time for more writing on the weekend. He found that two writing hours on Saturdays were more productive if he had spent fifteen minutes writing on each of the four previous days. It saved him warm-up time on Saturdays. Some find that the short sessions are best for revising and the long sessions for drafting—discover what works for you.

A faculty member told me that just opening the article file five days a week made a difference:

> I can't do the fifteen-minute thing. But I believe in the concept of writing daily, so the way that I've interpreted that concept for myself is that I always have whatever journal article I am working on open on my computer. That means that every work day at some point, I do something to the article—I add a citation, change the spaces in the table, cut a few words from the Methods section, and so on.

In the same spirit, another person told me that she set up a phone notification to go off during her morning walk to work, to remind her to at least think about her article once a day. Yet another told me that on his drive to campus, he listens to one of the University of Oregon's popular *Research in Action* podcasts about writing, research, methods, and productivity, hosted by the indefatigable scholar and coach Katie Linder.

Almost all my workshop participants who follow the daily writing exercise admit that they got a useful amount of work done in fifteen minutes, and they had no problem remembering where they were the next day. Writing most days keeps the article in the forefront of your thoughts, so that you think about it while driving or washing dishes or taking a shower instead of forgetting about it. Furthermore, if you write a little bit before starting an extremely busy day, the feeling of accomplishment makes the rest of the day more manageable.

Questions about Daily Writing

Is fifteen minutes a minimum or a maximum? It's a minimum. If you have more time to spend on writing most days and can do so without burning out, go for it. The principle of daily writing is that it teaches you to write more smoothly, less anxiously, and without depending on rare and irregular big blocks of time. If you're able to write regularly for three to four hours a day without burning out and while publishing your writing, you don't have a problem. Your writing is focused and productive. If you think about your article for fifteen minutes for four days and then write every weekend from eight o'clock Saturday evening to two o'clock Sunday morning, you don't have a problem. Writing for longer periods once or twice a week or occasionally attending an intensive writing boot camp to kick-start or restart a project are both fine. But your lifelong aim should be to do some writing most days, thus the fifteen-minute minimum.

For many of us, writing more than fifteen minutes a day is preferable; given the choice, we'll set aside one to four hours. If you have financial support and no other obligations, you can ratchet your hours as high as you can stand it. But what if you don't? What if you're a professor teaching three, four, or five new courses? Or a single parent who isn't getting much sleep? Or you have a debilitating autoimmune disorder? Large blocks of time don't exist for you. The good news is that you can get some writing done in the few minutes that do open up, and those minutes will be effective. It means that if you suddenly spend half an hour writing, you can be pleasantly surprised by your diligence, not disappointed that you failed to do more. You can rearrange your thinking to value any and all writing opportunities. Indeed, the scholar Tanya Golash-Boza (2012), at the forefront of the wider movement to return academics to a less frenzied pace, forbids writing more than two hours at a time. On her *Get a Life, PhD*, one of the most successful blogs about academic writing, she recommends everything in moderation. Kerry Ann Rockquemore's faculty mentoring program, the National Center for Faculty Development and Diversity, advises the same.

What do you mean by "writing"? This is one of the most frequent questions I get. People want exact details: "If I spend fifteen minutes reading a journal article and taking notes on it, does that count as my fifteen minutes? What about if I spend fifteen minutes hashing out my argument with a friend? What if I spend my fifteen minutes writing a paragraph that I then delete at the last second?" My answer is, "It depends." If all you ever do with your fifteen daily minutes of writing is take notes, discuss your article, or delete paragraphs, that's not writing. It's procrastination. And as Charles Dickens said, "procrastination is the thief of time," and we must arrest it (Dickens 1850, 131). But if you spend three days on those activities and then on the fourth day write a sentence that you keep in your article, then yes, all of it is writing. What's more—it's a perfectly normal writing process. So long as you keep your article progressing, any related activities are good. Finally, I count reading the workbook and completing its tasks as writing.

How can this advice be good if I only binge-write and yet am productive? Since this book first came out, a few academic authors have outed themselves as proud "binge" writers. They write for rare, intense, long days, and yet they publish regularly. A good example is the productive scholar of gender and sexuality Jane Ward (2016), who writes best on two- to five-day retreats far from home, which she schedules about four times a year. She wrote her last book over the course of six writing retreats. Ward describes her writing retreats as "a pleasure," because their rarity "means that I am often longing for it, and I have so many ideas at the ready that I can't wait to unleash them!" Another example is the literary scholar Michael North, who has published a book about every four years since 1984 and has repeatedly told me that he writes only in the summer (1984, 1985, 1991, 1994, 1999, 2001, 2005, 2008, 2013). The socialist scholar of race Keeanga-Yamahtta Taylor drafted her best-selling book *From #BlackLivesMatter to Black Liberation* in two intensive months (2016). Finally, Helen Sword's interviews with successful authors also revealed that quite a few did not write every single day (2016, 2017).

In my experience, however, such writers have three rare qualities in common. First, unlike most, they quite enjoy these intensive writing periods, and they don't develop a posttraumatic stress response after them of avoiding writing. So the negative word *bingeing* doesn't describe their writing habits. Since they feel joy when writing, and write in bursts, let's call them "spree" writers instead. Second, spree writers are light revisers. They write a draft quickly, read through it once, correct typos and a few infelicities, send it off, and get published. Third, spree writers are "in-head" writers. The classicist Michael Kulikowski told me that he composes large chunks of writing in his head—a habit he acquired by writing popular music reviews that way while walking to school as a teenager. Likewise, the prolific scholar and public intellectual Eddie Glaude constructs detailed outlines in his head for any piece of writing, complete with topic sentences and key turns of phrase, such that typing up those ideas happens quickly. That is, sitting down at a computer to write is a last step for such writers, not a discovery process. They use that time to record already thought-out thoughts. (Often, these are the same people who can give off-the cuff lectures without preparation.) In other words, it's the thinking *between* spree-writing sessions that makes these sessions possible. Ward (2016) says that in the months between her writing retreats, "I do research, take notes as ideas emerge and receive feedback from colleagues" as well as "formulat[e] ideas in my mind during my commute to campus or while doing dishes, designing and teaching courses that animate my next writing project, or, especially now, giving lectures, media interviews, etc., about my writing." In fact, she's not a rare writer but someone who spends most days writing, just in her head. So as the patron saint of scholarly writing Raul Pacheco-Vega (2016) rightly puts it on his terrific academic writing blog, spree writers are in fact "writing every single day." (Many scholars use and follow his popular hashtags #GetYourManuscriptOut and #ScholarSunday.)

So if you're the type of person who can think about your article sporadically all day long, draft it pleasurably on rare writing retreats that actually happen, and then produce publishable prose that gets published, great. As Jo VanEvery (2013) states on her valuable academic writing blog, *Transforming Academic Lives*, "If you have a process that works for you, then you don't need to go out looking for other better processes."

But if you're writing only once in a long while, not publishing regularly, and the very thought of writing makes you anxious, then you're not a spree writer. Your process isn't working, and you need to try writing daily. Similarly, if you're a heavy reviser, going through dozens of drafts before sending your article to a publisher, the spree method won't work for you. You'll spend too much of the spree time revising what you had written the last time. To tell it to you plain, if you use spree writing to produce drafts that need a heavy revision or if your lightly revised prose doesn't get published, then you're not a spree writer—you're a weak writer, and you need to switch over to the daily writing method.

Finally, don't fool yourself into thinking that spree writing takes less time. Ward goes on a lot of writing retreats. If a spree writer spends four days writing eight hours a day four times a year, plus an hour each week taking notes, talking about the work, and getting feedback, that comes to about 180 hours of writing a year, or 8 percent of the total work time (given that a forty-hour-a-week job takes about 2,000 hours per year). That's equivalent to writing about forty minutes a day, five days a week.

Any of these methods can work, but none of them work for everyone. You need to be honest about what does work for you. For many years I was not a daily writer. That's why there are twenty years between my first book and my second. Then I was placed in circumstances where I had to write every day, and my writing habits transformed. I don't always get around to writing every day when I'm teaching, but I never go for more than three or four days without writing. It's my *goal* to write every single day, and that has made all the difference.

Obstacles to Writing Daily (or at All)

Before turning to making a writing schedule, it's wise to anticipate the kinds of interruptions to writing (and excuses for not writing) that are going to arise. What challenges lie ahead for you in becoming a writer with good writing habits?

I have listed some of the more common ones below. As you read them, check off those you think might be obstacles for you, and then write down any solutions you think of (either on the back of your daily writing calendar or in reminder software so that they pop up at your next scheduled writing session).

In the first edition, I listed solutions to common writing obstacles here in the workbook, but the list became too long for this edition, partly because people kept sharing obstacles I hadn't addressed, but mostly because people had so many great solutions. So I moved those solutions online, where you can find them at wendybelcher.com at "Solutions to Common Academic Writing Obstacles." Some of the solutions there are easy, some are tough, and others are tough to hear. Some may surprise you by being valid reasons not to write. They are all useful.

Obstacles to Writing My Journal Article

Motivational obstacles. ☐ I just can't get started writing. ☐ I can't sit still to write. ☐ If I have a long, productive writing day, somehow it's harder to get started the next day, rather than easier. ☐ I will write just as soon as (fill in the blank). ☐ I wish I could write as easily as I [exercise/cook/clean/or . . .].

Emotional obstacles. ☐ I'm not in the right mood to write. ☐ I'm afraid of writing because my idea is very controversial or triggering. ☐ I'm afraid of writing because publication is so permanent. ☐ I feel guilty about not writing. ☐ I feel like I have to amputate significant parts of myself to write. ☐ I feel like I have to suck the life out of my work to squeeze it into the square box of academic writing.

Health obstacles. ☐ I'm too depressed to write. ☐ I have serious health issues; I think I may need a break from writing to deal with them. ☐ When I write, weird things happen with food. ☐ I have terrible insomnia and therefore foggy mornings, so writing is tough. ☐ I get terrible back pain when I sit at my computer writing too long.

Obstacles to Writing My Journal Article (*continued*)

Human obstacles. ☐ Why do all that writing work when my coauthors are going to be listed before me in the author byline? ☐ I really can't move forward on this writing project because of others' inaction. ☐ My advisor is more of an obstacle to my writing than an aid. ☐ I would love to ask someone to read and comment on my writing, but everyone seems so busy and I don't want to bother anyone.

Distraction obstacles. ☐ I really am too busy to write! ☐ I get distracted from writing by web surfing, emailing, and texting. ☐ Teaching preparation takes up all my writing time. ☐ My child care responsibilities are preventing me from writing. ☐ I have to make progress on several writing projects at the same time, and I'm in a panic. ☐ I have to read just one more book before I can write. ☐ I couldn't get to my writing site. ☐ It's so nice outside that I don't want to be inside writing; I need that vitamin D! ☐ My responsibilities at my paying job are taking up all my time and energy for writing.

Confidence obstacles. ☐ I can't write because my idea sucks. ☐ I'm beginning to wonder if being a professor is really the career for me and I probably won't get a job anyway, so what's the point of writing? ☐ I'm so far behind in writing for publication, what's the point of trying now? ☐ I'm not smart enough to do this kind of writing. ☐ I write so slowly that I never seem to get much done. ☐ No one's going to read my writing anyway; why bother?

Resource obstacles. ☐ I'm eager to write, but I don't have access to the material or scholarly resources. ☐ It's so difficult to write in English! ☐ I've heard that editors at journals in North America and Britain automatically reject articles written by nonnative speakers—so why should I even try to write an article for them? ☐ I'm an independent scholar, and I'm afraid that once a journal sees that I'm not affiliated, they will automatically reject my article. ☐ Writing takes forever because I never got around to setting up reference-management software for my citations.

Obstinance obstacles. ☐ I'm sorry, but advice books about writing just don't work for me. ☐ I know my writing habits are bad, but that's just who I am, and I can't/don't want to change. ☐ Come on, the whole publishing process is rigged, so what's the point of writing?

Use the box below to note the major obstacles to your writing goals—whether they're mentioned above or not. Also, note whether each obstacle's expected interference level is high, medium, or low.

Obstacles to Writing My Article	Expected Interference		
	☐ High	☐ Medium	☐ Low
	☐ High	☐ Medium	☐ Low
	☐ High	☐ Medium	☐ Low
	☐ High	☐ Medium	☐ Low
	☐ High	☐ Medium	☐ Low
	☐ High	☐ Medium	☐ Low

Solutions to Writing Obstacles

Now, what can you do to interrupt your interruptions and overcome your obstacles to writing? Check out "Solutions to Writing Obstacles" on my website.

Possible Solutions to My Writing Interruptions and Obstacles

Setting a Realistic Daily Writing and Article Submission Goal

If you're already a daily academic writer, congratulations! If you're not, I can guarantee you dramatic improvement as a writer if you commit to being at your writing site and writing five days a week, for fifteen minutes to two hours per session.

You now have a choice of what to do next. If you would find it helpful, the following will help you set up a reasonable schedule and deadline for sending your article to a journal. However, if you feel that too much is up in the air right now—you're unsure about which article you'll revise or how much revision it will need—you can return to this section in week 3 and make a plan then. I will remind you there.

1. **Find or print the two workbook calendars.** To start setting up a reasonable daily writing schedule, you need to study your current overall schedule. To complete this assignment, you will need two workbook forms: the Week 1 Calendar for Planned (Not Actual) Time Spent Writing This Week and the Twelve-Week Calendar for Planning Article Writing Schedule. You can fill out the ones on the next two pages or print out a copy of each from my website at "Writing Your Journal Article in Twelve Weeks Forms" now. Doing this work by hand, not electronically, is best.

2. **Mark down this week's current daily schedule.** Under each of the seven days in the Week 1 Calendar for Planned (Not Actual) Article Writing Schedule, cross out the times unavailable for writing over the next seven days, such as when you'll be in class, at work, at appointments, eating, sleeping, caring for relatives, and so on. (If this week won't be typical, you might try completing this task twice, once for this week and then for a more normal week.)

3. **Mark down when you will write each day this week.** Now, study the time remaining. What times of day might you use for writing? Under each of the seven days in this same weekly calendar, fill in the exact times when you plan to do your daily writing (which includes reading the workbook and completing the tasks).

   While thinking about what daily times might work, make sure that your goal is realistic rather than ambitious. For instance, research suggests that being a morning or an evening person has deep psychological roots that you ignore to your detriment (Diaz-Morales 2007). If you're not a morning person, don't resolve to get up every

Week 1 Calendar for **Planned** (Not Actual) Time Spent Writing This Week

Time	Day 1	Day 2	Day 3	Day 4	Day 5	Day 6	Day 7
5:00 a.m.							
6:00							
7:00							
8:00							
9:00							
10:00							
11:00							
12:00 p.m.							
1:00							
2:00							
3:00							
4:00							
5:00							
6:00							
7:00							
8:00							
9:00							
10:00							
11:00							
12:00 a.m.							
1:00							
2:00							
3:00							
4:00							
Total minutes I plan to work							
Tasks I aim to complete							

Twelve-Week Calendar for **Planning** Article Writing Schedule

Week	Task	Day 1	Day 2	Day 3	Day 4	Day 5	Day 6	Day 7	Total hours	Note
Example May 1–7	Example	8–9 a.m., June 1	8–9 a.m., June 2	0 minutes grad conf	0 minutes grad conf	8–9 a.m., June 5	1–5 p.m., June 6	1–2 p.m., June 7	8 hours	
Week 1	Designing your plan for writing									
Week 2	Advancing your argument									
Week 3	Abstracting your article									
Week 4	Selecting a journal									
Week 5	Refining your works cited									
Week 6	Crafting your claims for significance									
Week 7	Analyzing your evidence									
Week 8	Presenting your evidence									
Week 9	Strengthening your structure									
Week 10	Opening and concluding your article									
Week 11	Editing your sentences									
Week 12	Sending your article!									

morning at four thirty to write. This isn't realistic. Choose a time of day when you're more alert and energetic. Likewise, if you work full time Monday through Friday, don't decide to write every evening for four hours or to set aside your entire weekend. This isn't a realistic goal; striving for it will only discourage you. Aim instead, for example, to write fifteen minutes a day during the week and for several hours on Saturday or Sunday afternoon. If your schedule is to write one hour on Monday, Wednesday, and Friday, still try to get in fifteen minutes of writing on Tuesday and Thursday so that you get started quickly and smoothly on the longer writing days. If you can schedule the writing for the same time most days, all the better. If you can't, still try to come up with a regular pattern. Some attach their writing activity to another task, such as immediately after driving the kids to school.

Of course, the most unrealistic writing schedule is none at all. Don't believe that somehow, by some miracle, your article will get written in the next couple of months simply because you need it to be submitted. You have to have a plan.

4. **Note the total planned writing time and tasks.** At the bottom of the same weekly calendar, fill in the total number of minutes that you plan to spend writing that day as well as the tasks you hope to complete that day.

5. **Tell someone your plan.** Email someone now—whether a friend, writing partner, writing group member, or classmate—and tell that person about your planned writing schedule for the following week. Ask that person to email you next week to inquire whether you met your writing goals. A little social pressure often helps us!

6. **Mark down the daily schedule for the next twelve weeks.** Now turn to the Twelve-Week Calendar for Planning Article Writing Schedule on the previous page. Look at your own datebook or calendar, and note which days over the next twelve weeks will contain obstacles to writing. For instance, perhaps you are hosting a conference, undergoing surgery, taking a vacation, or meeting a deadline for another piece of writing. Such interruptions are normal and acceptable; you just need to consider them when identifying whether sending an article in the next twelve weeks is realistic. Next, write in these obstacles on the twelve-week calendar (e.g., conference hosting takes two days out of a particular week; a family vacation takes seven days out of another). Then, given the days remaining, write down the amount of time for each date that you can spend writing. Finally, add up the times in the Total Hours column.

7. **Choose a realistic article submission deadline.** Now that you have a more scientific understanding of your daily schedule for the next twelve weeks, you can make an informed decision about whether the workbook's goal of revising and submitting a journal article in twelve weeks is going to work for you. When can you plan to send your submission to a journal?

The workbook estimates that those writing HumInt articles will spend an average of 8 hours per week writing and 92 hours in total to complete and send their article. It estimates that those writing SciQua articles will spend an average of 6 hours per week for a total of 72 hours. However, the amount of time that your article will take depends on a huge number of variables, including your daily and weekly writing schedule, your scholarly field or discipline, and the state of your article. Many of those variables may be unknown quantities to you right now (e.g., the level of revision your paper will need). However, we're going to make some guesstimates to help you set up a plan that you can adjust as you go along.

If your article needs a major revision or you can't write for more than three or four hours a week, you'll likely have to spread out each daily task over several days. If your article needs only minor revision or you can write for more than twelve hours a week, you'll likely be able to complete several daily tasks in one day. Those aiming to submit their article in six weeks will need to complete two chapters per week.

The flowchart below collates some of the variables to give you a very rough estimate of the time it will take you to complete and send your article. Use it to make an educated guess about the number of weeks you're going to devote to revision. Then use it to fill out the My Writing Plan Decisions form that follows it.

Estimated Article Writing Time Flowchart

Is your article in the HumInt track?	Does it require a minor revision?	Will you write 4 hours a week?	Plan on sending it in 20 wks
		Will you write 8 hours a week?	Plan on sending it in 10 wks
		Will you write 16 hours a week?	Plan on sending it in 5 wks
	Does it require a medium revision?	Will you write 4 hours a week?	Plan on sending it in 24 wks
		Will you write 8 hours a week?	Plan on sending it in 12 wks
		Will you write 16 hours a week?	Plan on sending it in 6 wks
	Does it require a major revision?	Will you write 8 hours a week?	Plan on sending it in 48 wks
		Will you write 16 hours a week?	Plan on sending it in 24 wks
		Will you write 24 hours a week?	Plan on sending it in 12 wks
	Are you drafting from scratch?	Will you write 8 hours a week?	Plan on sending it in 54 wks
		Will you write 16 hours a week?	Plan on sending it in 36 wks
		Will you write 24 hours a week?	Plan on sending it in 18 wks
Is your article in the SciQua track?	Does it require a minor revision?	Will you write 3 hours a week?	Plan on sending it in 20 wks
		Will you write 6 hours a week?	Plan on sending it in 10 wks
		Will you write 12 hours a week?	Plan on sending it in 5 wks
	Does it require a medium revision?	Will you write 3 hours a week?	Plan on sending it in 24 wks
		Will you write 6 hours a week?	Plan on sending it in 12 wks
		Will you write 12 hours a week?	Plan on sending it in 6 wks
	Does it require a major revision?	Will you write 6 hours a week?	Plan on sending it in 48 wks
		Will you write 12 hours a week?	Plan on sending it in 24 wks
		Will you write 18 hours a week?	Plan on sending it in 12 wks
	Are you drafting from scratch?	Will you write 6 hours a week?	Plan on sending it in 54 wks
		Will you write 12 hours a week?	Plan on sending it in 36 wks
		Will you write 18 hours a week?	Plan on sending it in 18 wks

8. **Choose start and end dates.** If you've read this far in the workbook, completing all the tasks, in practice you've already set this week as your start date. Congratulations! If you're just skimming and don't feel that this is a good week to begin, choose next week. You could even choose the week after or set the book aside for next summer, but I don't recommend this. Then you'd be falling into the trap of thinking you can write only if you have large, uninterrupted chunks of time. There is no time like the present. Since I designed this workbook to accommodate writing to your life rather than the other way around, you can reach your goal of submitting your article even if it's a busy time. Check off the relevant boxes in the My Writing Plan Decisions form below. Then redo the Twelve-Week Calendar for Planning Article Writing Schedule with your current plan.

My Writing Plan Decisions

Track and pathway	☐ HumInt track ☐ SciQua track ☐ Revision pathway ☐ Drafting pathway ☐ Minor revision ☐ Medium revision ☐ Major revision ☐ I'm not sure yet
Number of weeks	☐ 12 weeks ☐ 10 weeks ☐ 8 weeks ☐ 6 weeks ☐ 5 weeks ☐ 18 weeks ☐ 20 weeks ☐ 24 weeks ☐ 48 weeks ☐ 36 weeks ☐ 54 weeks
Minutes per day	I plan to write _____ hours per week (_____ minutes per day, five days a week).
Start date	I already started, on _____ (month/day/year). I will start on _____ (month/day/year).
End date	I plan to submit my article to a journal on _____ (month/day/year).

9. **Post your decision where you can see it.** Once you have filled out the My Writing Plan Decisions form and the Twelve-Week Calendar for Planning Article Writing Schedule, post them somewhere visible. If you need to change the plan, don't worry—it's perfectly normal. Just revise it and post it again. Keeping it up to date with actual patterns and progress is important.

Tracking Writing Time

Don't forget to mark down the times that you wrote, using your Week 1 Calendar for Actual (Not Planned) Time Spent Writing This Week to do so.

Day 3 Tasks: Selecting a Paper for Revision

Welcome to day 3 of week 1! Today you'll learn about article types and select a paper for revision. Many academics believe that in order to get published, they must start from scratch. Nothing will do but to begin a brand-new article on a brave new topic. This is not true. Most academics, even graduate students, have already written a classroom essay, conference paper, BA or MA thesis, dissertation chapter, or talk that contains the seed of a publishable journal article. The trick is to identify which text provides you with this fertilizable seed. Even if you're convinced that you have no text that contains such a seed, do read the next section: it may prompt you to recall one that does. Nothing will teach you better how to write well than revising a text that you've already drafted.

Before you choose an article to revise, let's look at types of articles. Knowing the types can help you best determine which text to select for revising with this workbook as your guide, especially since not all journals publish all types of articles. I have listed the following types in reverse order of importance, from those carrying the least weight with hiring and promotion committees at research universities and many colleges to those carrying the most. I have also indicated those texts that you shouldn't select for revision using this workbook, while nevertheless including some advice on how to publish them.

Types of Academic Articles Not Suitable for Revision with This Workbook

Interview. For our purposes, a brief introduction to and transcript of an interview with another scholar, political figure, or artist. If you feel that you have an interesting topic and interviewee, submitting the interview for a journal's consideration can be a good experience and establish you as someone who supports the field and has connections. However, interviews require some care and planning. If the interviewee is famous and you're not, you may have trouble getting the subject to agree to be interviewed. This workbook aids those writing articles, and is not suitable for publishing interviews.

Book review. An article that analyzes a recently published scholarly book. Publishing this type of writing gets you in the habit of briefly summarizing and analyzing others' work. So if you can produce book reviews quickly (e.g., reading the book and writing the review all in three or four days), go for it. You can use the advice at my web page "How to Write an Academic Book Review." If you work at a slow rate, however, I regretfully must inform you to avoid them. Depending on your discipline, you must publish six to ten book reviews before you have something equivalent in weight to a research article. In some fields or departments, book reviews never add up, counting for nothing. Further, some professors warn graduate students not to publish book reviews, since the authors you review may turn up on hiring or promotion committees someday. I wouldn't go that far, but I would recommend that novice authors review only books that they think are good, a significant contribution to their field. While it can be satisfying to tear into bad books and warn your field about them, you may not want to go on record lambasting their authors if you're pre-tenure. Finally, if you have never published a book, you're not always aware of their acceptable limits. A professor was complaining to me that a graduate student's book review had castigated him for not citing a book published just six months before his book came out, revealing the student's ignorance of book production timelines. Having said all that, book reviews represent an important service in the humanities, being essential to the growth of fields—and the advancement of scholars, as hiring and promotion committees prefer books that get reviewed.

Trade/professional article. An article that distills academic research for a nonacademic audience. To get the word out about their work, academics sometimes write articles for newspapers, popular magazines, trade journals, practitioner newsletters, or websites. They do so to shape policy, change community practices, advance causes, or decry injustices. Some authors regularly publish a distilled version of their academic article in such journals, efficiently getting two publications out of one idea. Such articles can do a great job of getting your name out there and changing the world we live in, but they don't carry much weight with hiring and promotion committees at research universities and many colleges. If you can produce trade or professional articles quickly and would like your research to have a real-world impact, do so for your own satisfaction. Just don't let them become a substitute for writing a research article or a substitute that's so close to a research article that a peer-reviewed journal wouldn't view a related submission as original (more on this in "Week 4: Selecting a Journal"). Working on such an article with this workbook would be overkill, as trade articles need far less apparatus, citations, and evidence.

Note. A brief article that documents a small finding. A note is a short article, usually around five hundred to one thousand words, and typically takes the form of a case history, a methodological innovation, a single observation about a text, a definition of a term, and so on. Scholars publish a note when they have an insight that's too slight for a full-length article or when they don't wish to spend the time to develop an idea (perhaps because it's unrelated to the rest of their research). I recommend that you not devote time to developing notes for academic journals, and send them only notes that you've already written (say, because it was cut from an article). That is, notes are good for offloading interesting sections that you can't fit into any of your research articles without digressing. If the observation directly relates to your research, consider developing it into a research article. Articles published in journals' note sections won't "count" for as much with hiring and promotion committees at research universities and many colleges, although they frequently count for more than a book review or trade article. Using this workbook to work on note articles would be overkill, because they don't include arguments.

Microarticle. An article that's a new scientific form launched by Elsevier, which publishes hundreds of peer-reviewed journals. This short-format science article is no more than two pages long and is intended for publishing "interesting data that have not grown into a full piece of research. Or to share a follow-up research result to a previously published paper. Or [to provide] a description of a failed experiment, which provides a great new insight" (Elsevier 2016). In other words, microarticles are a way to publish "valuable research results (including intermediate and null/negative results), that might otherwise remain unpublished" (Ware and Mabe 2015, 146). Elsevier is also launching short article forms for materials and methods as well as data. Working on such an article with this workbook would be excessive, as microarticles have slim findings.

Translation. An article translating an article written by someone other than the translator. Again, this is a lot of work for a publication without much weight. Still, if it familiarizes you with another's work or introduces an important work to a new audience, then proceed for your own satisfaction. Translating works of theory tends to provide the most boost to your curriculum vitae. Indeed, many important academics launched their career, and made their name, through translating such: the literary scholars Gayatri Spivak and Barbara Johnson by translating Jacques Derrida (Derrida 1976, 1981), Caryl Emerson by translating Mikhail Bakhtin (Bakhtin 1984), and Daniel Heller-Roazen by translating Giorgio Agamben (Agamben 1998). If you're aiming for a US journal, you'll need to translate into English; if you're aiming for journals outside the United States, you can translate into another language, but such translations won't count for as much with US faculty committees. This workbook aids those writing original articles, not translating articles that others have written.

Response article. An article that provides feedback to a recently published article and is published in the same journal as that article (Parker and Riley 1995, 65). It's usually shorter than a research article and easier to write, since it addresses only one article rather than an entire body of literature. It's like a long letter to the editor. It's also easier to get published, because most journal editors want to spark debate and increase attention to their publication. The drawback is that such an article, precisely because it's easier to write than a full research article, can count for less. Still, it counts for more than the previously listed article types and can be valuable in spreading your name. If you've read an article published in the past year that sparks your interest and you can confirm, contradict, or expand on the author's argument, it can be worthwhile to write a response and send it to the editor of that journal. If you're a pre-tenured scholar, just be careful about using this as an opportunity to firebomb another author. People wait for tenure to publish controversial work for a reason: tenure protects the honest from the sensitive. However, as a final word, graduate students with something timely to say and who can articulate it in a considered manner have done well with this form. The Australian sociologist Noela Davis (2009), a graduate student at the time, published a respectful and well-researched response article in the *European Journal of Women's Studies* that rebutted the claims of one of its recent articles, by the feminist professor Sara Ahmed (2008). Davis's article was successful: her response has been cited over seventy times, and no doubt is part of the reason that Ahmed's article has been cited over 220 times. But here again, working on a response article with this workbook would be overkill, since response articles are generally of a narrower scope than peer-reviewed journal articles, being extended criticism of one piece of work.

Review article. An article that surveys the literature on a particular topic. To be published, such an article can't be just a summary of relevant articles and books. It must also provide a critical perspective, pointing out contradictions, gaps, and enigmas in the literature, and suggesting directions for future research. The ordinary dissertation literature review is insufficient in this instance. In some social, health, behavioral, and natural science fields, review articles (sometimes also called synthesis research or systematic reviews) are multiplying at twice the rate of original research articles (Ketcham and Crawford 2007, 1177), suggesting that many scholars write them and many journals publish them, perhaps because they can garner significant citations (Agarwal et al. 2016). But concerns about quality (Ketcham and Crawford 2007) and the impact on the citation of original research (*NCB* editors 2009; DrugMonkey 2013) remain. Also, many review articles are invited, not submitted; that is, editors solicit them from prominent scholars. While popular with researchers, hiring and promotion committees at research universities and many colleges still consider review articles to be lesser than original research articles. Some people have used the workbook to write review articles, but these don't contain original evidence, so the workbook is not quite apt for the task.

Types of Academic Articles Suitable for Revision with This Workbook

Social science research article. An article reporting on data collected about human behavior. Such articles are the standard in the social, health, and behavioral science fields, including anthropology, archaeology, sociology, psychology, political science, economics, public health, geography, education, and business. They can be classified in many ways, and many of them mix methods, but for our purposes I divide such research articles into four types. I define them below, showing how each would differently approach the question of whether judges have biases against certain defendants.

Experimental research article. An article reporting on a study in which the researcher, under tightly controlled conditions, manipulates a variable to determine what causes an effect in <u>human behavior</u>. Such an article usually includes a literature review, description of methods, and discussion of results. For instance, a researcher may show to fifty randomly selected judges the exact same criminal record document, but with different defendant photographs attached to test whether a certain characteristic of defendants (e.g., their gender, race, or age) leads judges to give different sentences in the same case. The defendant characteristic is the manipulated variable. Most experiments are conducted in laboratories, but some are conducted in the field (in which case they are sometimes called natural experiments or quasi experiments). The collected data are analyzed using statistics (often cross-tabulation), so some call this type of article an experimental quantitative study. It is more common in the behavioral sciences than in the social or health sciences. Follow the SciQua track for writing this type of article.

Quantitative research article. An article reporting on a study in which the researcher observes relationships among variables to identify correlations in <u>human behavior</u>. Such an article usually includes a literature review, description of methods, and discussion of results. The research it details doesn't depend on manipulating a variable, nor does it take place in a laboratory. For instance, a researcher may collect information from a state government database on hundreds or thousands of court trials to measure whether judges give different sentences to defendants of certain genders, races, or ages but charged with the same offense. Or the researcher may ask all the judges in a particular state to answer a survey that includes questions about their perceptions of defendants. This type of research is sometimes called a descriptive study, because it describes variables rather than manipulating them and cannot establish causality, only correlation. Typical quantitative methods include working with government data or publicly available survey data or conducting independent surveys, polls, and interviews (whether online, over the phone, in person, or on paper) with one hundred or more people. Owing to their larger sample size, commonly designed to be representative of the population of interest, quantitative studies can provide more generalizable results than experimental studies. Since the 1950s, this type of research article counts as the most prestigious type to publish in the nonexperimental sciences. Follow the SciQua track for writing this type of article.

Qualitative research article. An article reporting on data collected in natural settings using ethnographic research to understand <u>human behavior</u>. The data are generally not quantified and may be described only in words. Such an article often doesn't have strict Methods or Discussion sections, looking more like a humanities article. For instance, a researcher may conduct interviews in person with six to ten judges about their perceptions of defendants or possibly spend several months in a single courtroom observing whether a judge gives different sentences to defendants charged with similar offenses. Typical qualitative methods are lengthy open-ended or structured interviews with a few individuals or observations of a real-life situation (either in person or through recordings). Such exploratory studies are useful in gaining insight into underlying human motivations and designing hypotheses for larger quantitative studies. For instance, the researcher observing the single courtroom may notice how judges react to defendants' clothing, particularly whether they're wearing a jail uniform. Quantitative researchers could then design an experiment in which they make the manipulated variable defendants' clothing. (Of course, the reverse may happen as well, with the findings of a quantitative study leading to an in-depth qualitative study.)

Despite its tremendous value, some disciplines, scholars, and journals will consider qualitative research less serious or reliable than quantitative research. For writing this type of article, you most likely should follow the SciQua track, but not always. Keep reading both types of examples until it becomes clear which track is most helpful for your article.

Interpretive research article. Some social, health, behavioral, and natural science research articles aren't based on experimental, quantitative, or qualitative studies. They don't involve numerical data or direct observation; rather, they're theoretical. For instance, the researcher may write about the history of bias in the US courtroom or the relation of biopower and sovereignty. Follow the HumInt track for writing this type of article.

Humanities research article. An article presenting a new analysis of <u>human expression</u>. Such an article is the standard in the disciplines of literature, art history, religion, philosophy, musicology, and history as well as architecture, film, television, digital media, and theater; it's also the standard at the intersection of such disciplines (interdisciplinary work). Humanities articles have widely varied structures and objectives, largely because most aren't based on inductive reasoning but are instead devoted to valuing the particular over the general. Unsurprisingly, disciplines that treasure the unique tend to have varied article structures. Follow the HumInt track for writing this type of article.

Humanities theoretical article. An article that reviews and advances theory. Such an article traces the development of a certain theory and then goes on to propose a new theory, lambaste errors in the old one, or suggest that one theory is better than another. It rarely has any concrete evidence; sometimes it includes a brief textual example. Advanced scholars usually write these articles. The weight of a theoretical article depends on the era, the field, and the hiring or promotion committee. In certain times and places, a theoretical article can carry tremendous weight. In others, it can be dismissed as too rarefied. I mention this possible drawback only because so many novice authors feel that they must write theoretical articles. You don't have to. But if you have a strong, original contribution to make to theory building, by all means do so. Follow the HumInt track for writing this type of article.

Natural science research article. An article reporting on data collected about the physical world. Such an article is the standard in the formal, physical, applied, and life sciences, including disciplines like biology, mathematics, chemistry, physics, computer science, and astronomy. As the natural sciences vary quite a bit from the social sciences, this workbook was not originally designed for scientific articles, which have highly specific structures and approaches. However, some have used the workbook to write such articles, adapting the experimental or quantitative research article form described earlier. Follow the SciQua track for writing this type of article.

Deciding My Article Type

Based on what I know so far, what type of article am I likely to be developing with this workbook?	☐ Experimental research article ☐ Theoretical research article ☐ Quantitative research article ☐ Humanities research article ☐ Qualitative research article ☐ Humanities theoretical article ☐ Mixed methods article ☐ Social science interpretive article ☐ Natural science research article	
Given that type, what track should I be following?	☐ SciQua track	☐ HumInt track

Considering a Text You Have Already Written

Now that you know the types of academic articles, you're in a better position to select an article for revision. Answer the questions below by writing in the title of a text that you wrote. If the same text is the answer to more than one question, just write "ditto" in the box and consider it a good one to focus on revising. Parts of papers may work for developing into an article as well. You may find it useful to complete this task with the file folders on your computer open as prompts. Even if you're certain that you want to start writing your article from scratch, read what follows first, just in case it reminds you of a paper that would be a good choice.

Praise. Has a colleague or professor ever suggested that you submit a text you wrote for a prize or publication? If not, has anyone ever suggested that a text you wrote was particularly strong or intriguing?

Title:	

Pleasure. Is there any text you wrote that you enjoyed researching and that you still think back on with gratification?

Title:	

Relevance. Does any text you wrote address some aspect of a current debate in your discipline? In your recent reading or conversations, do you find yourself thinking of something you wrote and its relevance?

Title:	

Research. Is any text you wrote particularly well researched? Did you do substantial reading for one and still have all the sources or data?

Findings. Does any text you wrote have particularly strong or unusual findings? Does any contain an original insight that could carry a whole article?

Argument. Does any text you wrote take a strong stand, trying to persuade your readers to believe something?

Jobs/promotion. Does any text you wrote, if you were to publish it, help you make a stronger case for being hired or promoted in your field? (For example, if you are haven't published much and are positioning yourself as a scholar of early twentieth-century modernism, publishing an article about twenty-first-century realism may not help your case.)

Conference paper. Have you ever given a conference paper? Did you receive a positive response? Did you get useful comments that would help you in revising the paper for publication? (Several studies suggest that about 50 percent of conference papers are later published as articles [e.g., Autorino et al. 2007, 835].)

Thesis. Have you written a BA thesis, an MA thesis, or PhD dissertation? What parts of it are worth revisiting for possible publication?

Rejected article. Have you ever submitted an article for publication and received a revise-and-resubmit notice? If not, have you ever received a rejection notice?

Texts That Offer Particular Challenges

If reading through the above brings several texts to mind, remember the following when making your final choice of which one to work on:

General: BA or MA thesis. It's a great idea to revise your thesis for publication. Indeed, nowadays many social, health, behavioral, and natural science departments have students write their thesis in article style, in which case you're all set. But most humanities departments still have students write long theses, in which case you may struggle with the amount of cutting required to get yours to article length. Of the students I know who've been successful in turning a long thesis into a publication, most of them read through the thesis, opened an empty electronic document, and then typed up what they remembered. It may seem counterintuitive, but they found that starting over took less time than cutting. If you can use this method, theses tend to fare quite well in the peer-review process, as they have an attractive thickness, a distilled density of argument and evidence that impresses reviewers. However, a few editors will have a problem publishing an article that originated from an electronically available master's thesis or dissertation. In 2011, a survey of humanities and social science editors revealed that 83 percent of them would consider publishing theses revised into articles, but 3 percent would not under any circumstances (Ramirez et al. 2013, 372–73). If your thesis or dissertation is or will be available electronically, it would be wise to ask prospective journal editors if this is a problem (regarding contacting editors with query letters, see "Week 4: Selecting a Journal").

General: Completed dissertation chapter. Revising a chapter from a defended dissertation is a standard route to publication. In fact, publication of three journal articles is now accepted as the equivalent of a dissertation in certain disciplines (e.g., political science, geography, sociology) at some universities. Two challenges face you in this regard, however. First, revising a dissertation chapter for publication is not just a matter of cutting the chapter out of the dissertation and sending it to a journal, unchanged. You must both shorten and lengthen the chapter to make it a journal article. You must shorten it because chapters are often twice the length of journal articles; but you must also lengthen it in some places because the article must stand alone, unlike the chapter. When cutting, be ruthless; when adding, be judicious. Readers often need less background information than authors assume they do, and peer reviewers readily ask for more if they need it. Second, if you plan to publish your dissertation as a book, don't publish too much of it as journal articles. Book editors vary in their advice, but at least one prominent editor has said that authors shouldn't publish more than one journal article from any dissertation they want to publish as a book. Some also say that authors shouldn't publish any journal article that contains the argument of their whole book. Because of the ready availability of journal articles along with dwindling library budgets, editors fear that consumers won't buy a book if much of it is available in cheaper forms. Other editors claim that this is alarmist thinking, and that two articles published in reputable journals would make them more interested in publishing the book from which these came, not less (Cassuto 2011). Further, I have seen graduate students, as well as recent PhDs, postdoctoral fellows, and adjunct instructors, obtain tenure-track jobs based on their revised dissertation chapter being published in top journals.

So what should you do? If you're in a book-publishing discipline and have two strong pieces of writing, one of which is a dissertation chapter and the other a classroom essay, choose the classroom essay. It's a safer choice for your book publication prospects, and it indicates that you're a scholar with range. That is, if you're entering the tenure-track job market with one journal article and its topic is clearly the same as that of your dissertation, that application isn't as strong as one with a journal article on a topic different from your dissertation's. In addition, hiring and promotion committees frown on scholars whose published journal articles are only from their dissertation. Having said all that, if you don't currently have a strong second piece of writing or if you really want to publish a dissertation chapter, don't hesitate to select the dissertation chapter. The benefits of publishing any article will always outweigh the risks. Just don't ever publish a summary of your entire dissertation in one journal article (although this advice is moot, since dissertation summaries tend not to fare well in the journal's peer-review process [Bowen 2010]). Additional information about what types of dissertation chapters to choose appears later.

General: Chapter from an incomplete dissertation. If you're in your first years of graduate school and you have a paper that you think is going to be an important chapter in your dissertation, think twice about revising it for publication now. All the reasons given above for not publishing chapters from a completed dissertation apply twice as much for chapters from incomplete ones. Journal articles and dissertation chapters are very different genres, so it won't help you draft that chapter. In addition, your ideas may change radically as you write the dissertation, and then you may wish you had waited to publish on the topic. If you really want to work on a prospective dissertation chapter for publication now, don't let my advice here stop you. But if you're debating which of two pieces of writing you want to revise—a future dissertation chapter or something that won't appear in your dissertation—I recommend the latter. Likewise, if you think you'll be writing your dissertation on a particular author/place/culture and you have one paper about that subject that contains your dissertation argument and another that does not, choose the latter paper for revision. Finally, completed or incomplete chapters that never made it into the dissertation are great choices for revision, since they have no other destiny.

General: Reports. Experts in international development, the environment, public health, and so on often work for public agencies. As a result, they write many reports, whether for funding agencies, policy makers, or internal purposes. While such reports can hold amazing data not available in print, a report is rarely argumentative, something an article must be. But if the data in the paper were carefully collected and support a strong argument, and that argument is relevant to a current scholarly debate, then go ahead and select it, but be prepared to do much revising. In general, reports exist to tell readers what to *do* about a problem; journal articles exist to tell readers how to *think* about a problem. While social, health, and behavioral science articles often offer recommendations and solutions in their conclusion, the analysis of the problem takes up the articles' body.

General: Broad surveys. Peer-reviewed journals rarely publish articles surveying the field or the state of the discipline. When they do, veterans in the field are the authors. The conventional wisdom is that a junior scholar hasn't been following the debates long enough to be able to weigh in on such matters. If you're a novice author and a professor tells you that you're an exception to this rule, go for it. Otherwise, why attempt to scale entrenched obstacles? You don't have to throw the work away—use the survey to write an introduction to an article or a literature review.

General: Purely theoretical. Peer-reviewed journals rarely publish articles that explore only the strengths and weaknesses of a particular theory. Also rarely published are articles that propose a theory without a case study (in the social, health, and behavioral science fields, collected information about human behavior, such as experimental data, government data, interviews, student papers, and so on) or a primary source (in the humanities, a human creation such as a novel, folktale, sculpture, musical score, ship's log, graffiti, and so on). Most important theories were launched with case studies or primary sources. For instance, one of the great theorists of the twentieth century, Michel Foucault, was obsessed with primary sources and spent a huge amount of time in archives (James Miller 1993, 97, 108–9); his reading at the beginning of *The Order of Things* (1966) of the primary source Diego Velázquez's painting *Las Meninas* was his launching case study for theorizing systems of representation.

An article making pronouncements without a case study or primary source fares poorly in the journal-article submission process. Also, novice authors can make the mistake of assuming that writing a paper to help themselves understand a theory will be useful to others. Most often, however, such an article is too rudimentary, its author too unaware of the thousands of articles already published on that theory. It's better to save such writing for a classroom lecture you might wish to give on the topic. If you've never published and truly think that your purely theoretical article is publishable, ask a faculty member in your field to read the article and identify whether it is a fresh contribution. Editors will quickly reject theoretical articles on topics that they think have been exhausted or are virtually unassailable. Also, make sure that if you write a purely theoretical article, you send it to a journal that would be open to such writing.

General: Dated research. If your paper is quite old and subsequent research may have vitiated its findings, you may want to think twice about picking it for revision. Some research articles are "evergreen," as they say in the magazine business, especially in the humanities. But most address an academic concern that has waned or include findings that have been superseded or disproved. Such papers can be updated, but you'll need to do additional research. In SciQua fields, adding a longitudinal component might work—going back to interview or survey the original study subjects. If you're unsure where your paper stands, you may want to ask someone in your field to read it with an eye for its current relevance. It's safe to say that choosing to revise anything you wrote more than ten years ago will take a lot of extra work; for something you wrote five or six years ago, carefully review for relevance.

General: Outside your discipline. It's very difficult to write for a discipline other than your own. Just because you took one film course and wrote a paper for it despite being in the political science department doesn't mean that you know how to write for film scholars. You might know—but be sure that someone in that field has sanctioned your approach. Often, your ideas won't be new enough or clearly enough related to the field to warrant publication. One older study showed that those from outside a discipline were significantly less likely to get published in a journal within that discipline (Goodrich 1945, 722). If you're doing interdisciplinary work, that's okay, but selecting the right journal will be essential to avoiding rejection on disciplinary grounds. Finally, it can even be difficult to write within your own discipline if it's outside your field; for example, writing on eighteenth-century Chinese art if you focus on twenty-first-century French art. You'll need to share your articles that are outside your field or period with scholars in that field before sending those articles to peer review.

General: Polemics. The world is a racist, sexist, homophobic, xenophobic, classist, and (insert your own concern here) place. I agree! But you can't get published in scholarly journals imply by asserting that this is the case, no matter how much the journal editor may agree with you. You must do more than declare that an institution isn't working, that a certain artwork is problematic, that an academic field is biased, or that a social condition is egregious. You must have evidence. Solid academic evidence. Without evidence, you're simply writing a newspaper editorial, sermon, manifesto, or blog post, none of which are genres that scholarly journals publish. So if you've written a classroom essay stating that Latinas in the United States face many obstacles in graduating from college or that welfare is destroying the fabric of US society, you must have evidence other than your own casual observations and experiences. Both can be extremely helpful to you in designing a study to test your hypothesis, but without a study, you have no evidence.

In the humanities, even if you do have evidence, you must have something interesting to say apart from pointing out blatant racist or sexist statements in a famous text. For example, a graduate student was writing on anti-Semitism in a short story by the famous children's author Roald Dahl, but she soon gave it up because she couldn't muster the energy to develop an argument that would surprise no one. Dahl was an unapologetic anti-Semite, a widely known fact; few would find it useful for their own research to read an article pointing out examples of anti-Semitism in his stories. To get published, then, this student was going to have to make a more intriguing argument about how such a text operates. She could, for instance, select some anti-Semitic children's book authors and categorize how anti-Semitism works differently in their books than anti-Semitic elements do in books for adults. She would then be offering a schema based on evidence, not simply pointing to examples of racism. In another case, a student was writing about the bias against spirituality in feminist studies but without examining the classic works of feminism, probing classic formulations of feminism, or quoting feminist arguments against spirituality. The student is undoubtedly right about the bias, but without evidence the article is a screed, not a publishable article. You can sometimes get published by arguing against the common wisdom and asserting that a text widely thought to be racist is actually more tolerant, or that a praised text is covertly sexist. Just be aware that assertions without evidence, without interesting evidence, won't get your work into peer-reviewed journals.

General: Not in English. This workbook aids you in revising an English-language article. If you're planning to revise and submit an article in a language other than English, be aware that non-English-language journals often have publication standards that are quite different from English-language ones. Therefore, you may have to extrapolate quite a bit from this workbook. If, however, you plan to revise in that other language but translate the completed article into English, the workbook can help. A perennial debate in my international workshops is whether nonnative speakers of English are best off drafting articles in their own language and then translating them into English, or whether they should start drafting articles in English from the very beginning. Some authors insist that they find it better to draft in their own language and then translate the article. They like the smoothness and logical flow this drafting process enables, although they find they spend some time rooting out the syntax and structure of the original language when rendering their prose into English. Others say that it's easier to be analytical or argumentative in English than in other languages, because English contains more scholarly terms; consequently, it's better to start from the beginning in English. Some worry, though, that scholars writing in others' languages initially express their ideas in awkward or even naïve ways. Weigh these trade-offs before deciding how to proceed with an article that's not in English.

General: Too introductory or descriptive. To get published, your paper will have to go beyond introducing an object or practice, or merely summarizing the research about an object or practice. Some academics have papers that do little more than describe a geographic feature, agricultural technique, painting style, literary movement, and so on. Without an argument, a theoretical approach, or a study, such a piece of writing is more suited to an encyclopedia or edited volume than a journal.

General: Parts published earlier. Don't select for revision a paper that's too similar to texts that you've already published; if you do, you may be accused of self-plagiarism. Many journals now run all submissions through plagiarism-detection software such as iThenticate or CrossCheck. Rules of thumb vary, but using the exact phrases and sentences that appear in a published article will always be a bad idea. Even just one paragraph repeated without attribution from a previous article will anger editors. You can sometimes repeat three to four paragraphs verbatim from a published work of yours, but only if you clearly state that in the text or in the notes. Even then, such paragraphs must be from minor sections, such as Background, Context, or Methods, which don't contain your argument or evidence. Yet repeating text verbatim isn't the only possible self-plagiarism. Yes, most scholars would consider it unwise to select for revision an article that has the same argument and evidence as a published text of yours. However, you could select an article with the same argument but different evidence from your already published article (or the same evidence but a new argument), so long as you don't use the exact same sentences or paragraphs. Some say that so long as you're correlating different variables or looking at a new dependent variable, the evidence can be the same. Some authors say that 50 percent of the ideas in the article can be the same, but I think that most editors would limit this to no more than 10 percent. Some journals allow you to repeat your Methods section verbatim from previously published work without attribution; other journals consider that a scandal. If you're uncertain, you may get the opinion of a journal editor by writing a brief email providing a concise description of your article and its similarities to your previous work.

Having said all that, I should add that some famous scholars developed their "brand" precisely by repeating their ideas a lot in print. It's very difficult to launch a field-changing idea from just one publication. I once commented to the highly cited feminist philosopher Sondra G. Harding that the prolific globalization theorist Arjun Appadurai had only ever really written or published one article, and that was part of the reason why he was so highly cited. She laughed and said she often felt that she had done the same. When your ideas become admired, particularly if they are broadly useful think pieces such as Harding and Appadurai produce, editors will be constantly asking you to submit articles to their journal issues or edited volumes. But, you simply cannot produce that much prose. So when asked, Harding would open a brand-new electronic document, not even glancing at her previous publications, and then write up her ideas from scratch—some of these she had stated in previous works, although of course all would change slightly in the writing. For many people, the sin of self-plagiarism lies in using the exact same language, not in writing up similar ideas. But if you're starting out, be careful. Err on the side of caution.

General: Summary of others' research. Many novice authors would like to publish as an article a literature review from their dissertation or thesis—that is, a long summary of others' research. "I spent so much time on this section!" they tell me. "It should be good for something." But journals in the humanities rarely publish literature reviews. Editors can spot them a mile away and usually reject them without even sending them into peer review. In some social, health, and behavioral science fields, certain types of literature reviews do get published, but they're not easy to write. You'd need to have read almost everything on a topic for which there is no published literature review, then offer a new and useful critical take on the previous research. Even then, although they are useful for the discipline, they don't count for as much as original research. If you really think that you have something original to offer in the form of a literature review, then proceed, but be sure to ask people in your field first.

General: Weak evidence. If you have a paper that has null findings, few findings, or little evidence to support your argument, you'll need to collect better evidence or select another paper.

General: Rumination on teaching. At some point in their career, scholars want to write an article musing on their teaching experiences in a particular course or on a particular topic. I'm not talking here about those who have produced a scientific educational study with rigorous methods, but rather those who have some personal ponderings and unsystematic observations about what works. A few journals in the field of scholarship on teaching and learning (SoTL) will sometimes publish such articles. (I myself did! Belcher 2009). However, almost no other peer-reviewed journal is interested in publishing such meditations—they want original research. They want articles based on a scientific study of a course, with quantifiable data. If you're not in SoTL, your options are to develop a real study; publish your musings in an academic newspaper, magazine, or blog; or submit that as a chapter to an edited volume.

Humanities: Narrow close readings. As an undergraduate in literature, doing a close reading of a single literary text can gain you admiration and an A. Among peer-reviewed journals, it's likely to gain you a rejection. Journal editors want to see something more than an unpacking of the various meanings of one text. Many journals still publish single-text articles, but they will still expect such articles to speak to disciplinary debates. If you have a single-text paper, make sure that you can take it beyond merely unpacking your chosen text. It helps if you are using the single text as a leaping-off point for broad theorizing, or if that text is obscure but important.

Humanities: Popular text studies. Be wary of choosing a paper you've written on a widely discussed text. I know of one top interdisciplinary journal that used to reject automatically any paper that focused closely on Morrison's extraordinary novel *Beloved*, because it received dozens and dozens of such celebratory articles every year. (Someone needs to launch the *Journal of Toni Morrison Studies* so that such articles can get published!) It isn't easy to know what a popular text is—especially in literary fields that focus on canonical texts—but it probably includes any text that's taught in every literature department in the country and yet doesn't have a journal devoted solely to its author (e.g., *Chaucer Review*, *Shakespeare Quarterly*). If you feel that you really do have a new interpretation of this text that would be of broad interest, go for it: just select your journal carefully.

SciQua studies: Small sample size. If you have based your research article on a qualitative study with just a few subjects, even qualitative journals may reject it. Most social, health, and behavioral science fields are so quantitative nowadays that the sample size of even qualitative studies has become an issue. Speaking to others in your field can be helpful in identifying an adequate sample size for both your field and your argument, but anything under 5 subjects is likely too small. The average number of subjects in qualitative dissertations is 31; so various researchers have argued that any study with fewer than 15, 20, or even 25 subjects is too small (Mason 2010). If you want to publish a study with a small number of subjects, articulate in your Methods section why that number represents saturation (the point when adding additional subjects would not further illuminate the matter under study), including the limited nature of your claim, the high quality of your data, the homogeneous population under study, the difficulties of longitudinal studies, and so on (for advice, see Ritchie, Lewis, and Elam 2003; Green and Thorogood 2009). Another strategy is to focus specifically on the outliers in your study. That is, the goal of small samples is not to achieve a certain frequency for cross-tabulations but rather to arrive at unique small case studies.

As one caution, the sociologist Mario L. Small (2009) has noted the increasing trend, driven by quantitative peer reviewers, of qualitative scholars attempting to present the findings of small-scale qualitative studies as representative of much larger groups. Those defending qualitative methods state that such defenses are unnecessary. For instance, a qualitative study of thirty poor African Americans living on one short Philadelphia street need not say anything about the struggles of all African Americans in the United States; it's enough that it's documenting the reality of a particular group of people in a particular place. Small's article is worth reading in full if you're debating what to do about these issues.

Social, health, behavioral, and natural sciences: No study. In some rare social, health, behavioral, or natural science fields, it's perfectly acceptable to theorize and conjecture without an experiment or quantitative/qualitative study; in most, it's unacceptable. As one senior faculty member impatiently remarked in a workshop, "You cannot sit at home and write up analysis based on conversations with your friends over beer and call it political science. That's just bad journalism." If you have a paper in which you speculate on the causes of social conditions or the motivations of individuals but do not have a study to back up your speculations, find out whether your field is one that accepts such work. Most journals will want to see a study showing that racism is the cause of student failure, sexism is preventing men in nursing from doing their job adequately, or parents would be willing to pay for their children to attend better public schools. You'll need interviews with or surveys of such students, nurses, or parents to back up your claims. As mentioned, some SoTL journals will publish articles about teaching without studies, but usually only by authors with a fair amount of teaching experience.

Prioritizing among Several Paper Choices

The preceding section should have helped you rule out some papers as unsuitable for reworking for publication in a journal, and focus on others as having potential. On the one hand, if reading that section caused you to abandon all the papers you thought might be publishable, don't get discouraged! Keep reading, and then turn to the chapter "Week 0: Writing Your Article from Scratch" when instructed. On the other hand, if you're left with a single good paper, great! Select it for revision. If several papers made the cut and you're unsure which one to pick, consider the following.

Professor approved. If your professor recommended that you think about publishing a classroom paper, consider that paper.

Journal approved. If you received a revise-and-resubmit notice from a journal awhile ago, select this article. It always surprises me how many academics are sitting on articles that journals have asked them to revise. Many novice authors read revise-and-resubmit notices as rejections, but that's not what they are. It's better to think of them as an editing stage in the publication process. Even if a journal rejected your article, you may want to consider it for revision, especially if the reviewers gave you solid recommendations for that process. If the reviewers gave you conflicting advice and you aren't sure how to proceed, you might want to read "Week X: Revising and Resubmitting Your Article" now.

Your energy and enthusiasm. If neither of the situations above is the case, you can choose the paper that you think requires the least amount of work to get ready for publication or the one you feel most excited about working on. For those just embarking on a publication career, it's wise to choose a paper that will provide you with the energy to remain motivated.

Deciding Which Paper to Revise

Keeping all the above in mind, use the box below to identify the paper you'll revise. Feel free to talk this over with others first.

My chosen title

Aspects of my selected text that may provide challenges

☐ Thesis length ☐ Currently a diss. chapter ☐ Currently a report ☐ Currently a broad survey
☐ Purely theoretical ☐ Dated ☐ Outside my discipline ☐ Polemical ☐ Not in English
☐ Too introductory or descriptive ☐ Too similar to what has already been published
☐ Just a summary of others' research ☐ A narrow close reading ☐ A popular text study
☐ Personal musings on teaching ☐ Small sample size ☐ Weak evidence ☐ No study

Tracking Writing Time

Don't forget to mark down the times that you wrote, using your Week 1 Calendar for Actual (Not Planned) Time Spent Writing This Week to do so.

Day 4 Tasks: Rereading Your Paper to Identify Revision Tasks

Welcome to day 4 of week 1! Today you'll work on getting reacquainted with your paper. Upon rereading it, don't worry if it's not quite as good as you remember it. Or just as bad! All you need is a seed.

1. **Locate the latest version of your paper on your computer.** There is little more frustrating than starting to revise a paper, only to realize that you're not working on the

most recent version. If you can't find an electronic document for the paper that you're revising for this workbook, only a print copy, set aside time to type it up. This task isn't a waste of time, as it gives you the opportunity to edit onscreen as you go along.

2. **Save a copy separately.** Make sure to save an electronic copy of your article in its current state so that you can compare it with the final result.

3. **Print out the paper you selected.** This whole assignment works best when using a print copy of your paper, not viewing it onscreen. If you can't print your paper, try to defamiliarize it onscreen by putting it in another color or reading it in reduced size.

4. **Reread the print copy once without touching it.** Reading your article without revising it will give you the best sense of its overall state and ideas. Sometimes it will seem better than you remember: congratulations! Other times it will seem dreadful. Be of good courage. As they say in theater, the worse the dress rehearsal, the better the opening night. Good writing is all in the rewriting.

5. **Reread the print copy with pen in hand.** In the margins (or on a separate piece of paper), jot down what you currently think you need to do to each paragraph to get it ready for publication. Be kind to yourself; keep these notes clinical and not insulting. Some notes might be like the following:

- find page reference
- fix logical break
- provide transition sentence
- state relevance or delete
- delete redundancy
- provide citation

- find additional source
- move paragraph to first section
- beef up evidence
- rewrite introduction
- add conclusion

6. **Make a list of revision tasks.** This workbook takes you through a step-by-step revision of your paper, but each case is specific; so identify what you think you need to do to prepare your paper for publication. You can then assign the tasks to the relevant week. So in the box below, use your margin notes to write down your list of revision tasks. The aim is to identify quickly some of the tasks ahead of you, such as doing additional research, rewriting or cutting sections, completing your literature review, providing an argument, adding evidence, finding exact sources, restructuring the paper, and so on. Don't get discouraged if your list seems daunting. We'll make it manageable.

My Revising Tasks

Day 5 Tasks: Completing Miscellaneous Setting-Up Tasks

Welcome to day 5 of week 1! Today you'll work on some last setting-up tasks for writing.

Setting Up Your Writing Site

Having a customary writing site or two is part of forming the habit of writing regularly. When you enter a space where you usually write, it serves as a cue to write—its distinctive features prompt you (Kellogg 1999, 188). So if you can pick one spot as your writing site, that works best. However, many academics tell me that having one writing site is impossible given their complicated life. Instead, they have a variety of sites—including library stacks, reading rooms, coffee shops, bedrooms, and kitchen tables. Some academics also tell me that they are itinerant writers by choice. Fixating on one writing spot doesn't work for them because, after working in a space for a week or two, the place no longer energizes them or it becomes actively associated with feelings of frustration. The point of writing regularly is to develop a habit of writing, and part of that is having a habitual writing spot (or two or three). Use the box below to indicate your writing sites.

	Mon.	Tues.	Wed.	Thurs.	Fri.	Sat.	Sun.
Regular writing site							
Backup writing site							

In addition to having a regular writing site, you need it to be comfortable, especially since you'll be writing there most days. What changes will you make to your writing site to ensure that it's convenient, conducive, and comfortable? In terms of comfort, chairs and tables (or sofas and beds) that worked when you wrote rarely may not work when you are writing regularly. Make sure that you have a good chair, and place your keyboard and screen at the proper height so you don't develop back problems. If feeling lonely while writing is a problem (as it is for many), you might want to consider writing at a nearby café or university common room. If the distractions of a busy household are a problem, you might want to buy earphones. If you can't afford necessary changes to your writing site, try to think of cheap solutions. For instance, when I wanted to work standing up, I found that placing my laptop on a stack of books that were on top of a medium-height bookshelf worked even better than a standing desk, because it also put my books right at hand. Use the box below to indicate what improvements you'll need to make to your regular and backup writing sites to ensure that they're comfortable and conducive.

Regular writing site improvements	
Backup writing site improvements	

Setting Up Citation Software

If you're not already using dedicated citation software, you must read this section and let me harangue you. (If you've been using this software, great—you can skip this section.)

It's impossible to overemphasize the importance of such software to your productivity, happiness, and ethical obligations. You simply must use reference-management software (RMS). No ifs, ands, or buts! Once set up, these programs are so much easier to use, not to mention more accurate. Simply highlight a title and download. That's it—no typing. While citations used to take five hundred seconds to produce by hand, with errors, with RMS they now take five seconds.

Yes, RMS programs are fiddly to set up, and can be frustrating at times; but over your career, they'll save you hundreds of hours of time and twice that in headaches. Further, they'll increase your chances of publication by ensuring that your citations appear properly. Journal editors see disorderly citations as a bad sign; as one commented, "I've noticed that sloppy documentation almost always signals sloppy reasoning!" (Argersinger and CELJ 2006). If you had tried an RMS program before and didn't like it, try again—many problems with earlier versions have been resolved. For instance, you don't have to type in citations from your old articles by hand. So if you have avoided RMS for a long time, stop! Spend at least fifteen minutes today acquainting yourself with one of the programs or at least signing up for a university library workshop on them, if available.

Now, if you are squirming, saying, "I know, I know! I should have set it up a long time ago," guess what? Per usual, you're not alone in your feelings. The 25 percent of scholars who still have not set up an RMS program (Melles and Unsworth 2015; Francese 2013; Ollé and Borrego 2010; Carpenter 2012; M. Wu and Chen 2012) has failed to do so because they feel guilty that they've put it off for so long. But abandon your guilt about what happened in the past. All that matters today, the day you're reading this paragraph, is the future.

What are your options? You have over thirty RMS programs to choose from—some simple, some complicated; some free, some expensive; some that work with Mac operating systems, some that don't; some web-based, some on your desktop; some easily available in your country, some not; and so on. At this writing, four were the most popular in the United States: Endnote, Zotero, Mendeley, and RefWorks, in that order (Melles and Unsworth 2015; Emanuel 2013; Francese 2013). However, according to Google Trends, regional variation is huge, with the most popular RMS program in France being Zotero; in Germany, Citavi; in Brazil and Italy, Mendeley; and in India and the United Kingdom, Papers 3 (now ReadCube Papers 3). Technology changes quickly, so new software is popping up all the time. All have advantages and disadvantages; checking your university library will likely reveal a useful web page discussing them.

Many in the humanities and social sciences like Zotero because it's free, open source, and user friendly. When a friend's advanced research class tested and critiqued all the RMS programs, they unanimously chose Zotero as the best, which suggests a large uptake among junior scholars and that Zotero could become the most popular in the United States. Those in the sciences use Mendeley more frequently, perhaps because it works best for those who have many PDFs of journal articles, and it has a freemium version, meaning that the program owner tempts you with a free version to try to get you to buy the paid version. It's owned by Elsevier, however, and thus is not open source. RefWorks is best suited for people who have huge databases of citations, since it currently has more storage space than Zotero and Mendeley. Thomson Reuters's Endnote is the most sophisticated and the most powerful RMS program, perhaps because it was launched in 1988 and thus has been developed the longest. It has a freemium version, but many universities have a premium subscription available for free to faculty and students. I've used Endnote since 2001 and have been very happy with it. Precisely because it is so sophisticated, it can be time-consuming. For me, however, it's been worth it.

If after reading up on your options you still don't want to set up an RMS program (say it isn't so!), at least install the Google Scholar button on your browser. With it, you just highlight the title of the work on any web page, and Google Scholar provides you with a citation you can copy and paste into your document. If you're still typing the titles of widely available journal articles and books into your word-processing document, you aren't doing research properly. You must move into the twenty-first century!

If I do not use RMS, which one(s) will I check out (and install) today?	☐ Zotero ☐ Endnote ☐ Mendeley ☐ RefWorks ☐ Citavi ☐ Papers 3 ☐ Other _____

Setting Up a File Backup System

I can't tell you how many people I know who have lost entire articles or even books owing to poor backup systems. I have heard from two people who used a thumb drive for backup purposes and then had someone steal their computer and the backpack with the thumb drive in it. I have heard from someone who experienced an online storage site accidentally synchronizing her files in ways that replaced newer files with older ones. I know someone who used a universitywide automatic backup of his computer, only to find, when he needed the backup, that the computer had been set up improperly and wasn't backing up his files. So you need to have several systems in place, and you should stop and set that up now. One easy solution is one of the most effective: the old-fashioned technique of regularly emailing your article to yourself.

If I don't have adequate backup, which one(s) will I check out (and decide to use) today?	☐ Commercial cloud backup ☐ University cloud backup ☐ Portable hard-drive backup · ☐ Emailing my file to myself ☐ Other _____

Addressing Coauthorship

A dean at UCLA once told me that he spent much of every workday adjudicating author order disputes—that is, deciding which of several coauthors' names would appear first on a publication, as well as second, third, and so on. Coauthors disagree about author order a surprising amount of the time. One study found that two-thirds of the 918 coauthors of two hundred articles published in a medical journal disagreed about their relative contribution (Ilakovac et al. 2007, 43).

Disputes about author order arise in part because it's not that easy to assign author order. What matters more: drafting the article or analyzing the statistics? Developing the hypothesis or designing the experiment that tests the hypothesis? If these matters were crystal clear, there would be no disputes.

The other reason they arise is because of "egocentric bias." That is, everyone tends to overestimate their own contribution and underestimate others', whether these are to a basketball team, a marriage, or a coauthorship (Ross and Sicoly 1979; Caruso, Epley, and Bazerman 2006). We all have an excellent sense of what we do, and a poor sense of what others do, especially out of our sight.

Despite how common author order disputes are, you have some options for staying out of that swamp.

Don't have coauthors. If you're in a field where you don't have to have coauthors but are thinking about it, keep the following in mind. On the one hand, coauthored articles are cited more often and get into top-tier journals more frequently than solo-authored articles (Garbati and Samuels 2013, 363). And coauthors with a good collaborative relationship produce more work and better work together. So collaborations can be a good idea. On the other hand, research shows that in the tenure process, women receive less credit for coauthored articles than men do. "Men are tenured at roughly the same rate regardless of whether they coauthor or solo-author. Women, however, become less likely to receive tenure the more they coauthor. The result is most pronounced for women coauthoring with only men and is less pronounced among women who coauthor with other women" (Sarsons 2015). So women should take extra care when coauthoring.

Have fewer coauthors. If you have control over who coauthors this article with you, don't ask too many to participate: "Smaller teams are more enjoyable and more productive. Large teams can get bogged down with the process of coordination and communication and keeping everybody happy" (Pannell 2002, 102).

Know the conventions. Positions like corresponding author, first author, and last author signal different things in different fields. In some fields, the first author to be listed in an article byline made the largest contribution to the article; in other fields, the last author is the most important. In still other fields, author order is determined randomly, alphabetically, or by seniority. Most associations now have detailed guidelines on authorship order, and some journals require authors to answer a series of questions about who conceived the hypothesis, who designed the experiment, who managed the laboratory, who collected the data, who analyzed the data, who drafted the article, and who revised the article so that editors can accurately determine authorship. An excellent website to consult, with a wealth of information about a variety of ethical issues including author order, is the Committee on Publication Ethics at publicationethics.org. One of the site's more useful documents is "How to Handle Authorship Disputes: A Guide for New Researchers."

Agree in advance. If possible, make a written agreement with the other authors before you even start drafting the article. If you're publishing with peers or a group that you're leading, host individual or group meetings to discuss what constitutes a first-author credit. It will help you avoid author order disputes if you hammer out the duties of a first author or second author in advance. Having a plan, laying out expectations, establishing timelines, and then documenting contributions will also help. Leaving the author order decision to later is inviting trouble.

Learn to ask questions of senior coauthors. If you're a junior scholar working with senior coauthors, such as your advisor, you may not have much room to insist on fairness. But raise the issue of author order now—especially if you're a woman or a person of color—because doing so is what professionals do, and demonstrating that you're a professional is part of advancing in academia. In addition, you need to get used to having such conversations.

If it helps, think about these conversations as not about making demands but building your understanding of conventions. Don't start a conversation with senior coauthors by asking about your specific work together. Rather, ask more generally about their experiences of coauthorship and author order, any disputes that have arisen, and their sense of how author order is determined in your field.

Your senior coauthors may be assertive and say that every article they published as a graduate student had their advisor's name appear first in the byline, and that they won't change the practice now that they are an advisor, are on tenure track, and can insist on appearing first. In response, you can choose to protest this, but you'll probably get further in your career if you nod, say you accept this, and then ask under what conditions your advisor would change his or her mind. Either way, you will have put your advisor on alert that you're aware of these issues. Academia is playing the long game, as the expression goes—sometimes you need to go along to get to a place where you have enough power to get your work recognized.

Of course, if the hypothesis/argument, analysis/experiment, and article drafting are all yours and your advisor claims the honor of most prominent author, that's not right. And you have every right to protest. Indeed, some would call it an obligation. Bringing this theft to the attention of your university's administration will help protect other junior scholars, as I can guarantee you that an advisor who has done this once has done it repeatedly. But if you choose to let this violation go, you will hear no criticism from me. A publication is still a publication; you will publish many more.

Deciding What to Do about Coauthors

> If I have coauthors, do I need to schedule an author order conversation? Do I need to find out the conventions in this regard?

Reading a Journal Article

As noted earlier, to be a good writer of journal articles, you must read journal articles. Next week, you'll go through a guided journal article reading exercise. This week, if you've already set up your workspace, RMS, and author order, find an article published in your field in the last six months and study it. Ignore the content and focus on how it works. For instance, how long is the article and its parts? How many citations does it have? Part of the purpose of this workbook is to get you in the habit of reading journal articles, so today is a good day to start.

Tracking Writing Time

Today don't forget to mark down the times that you wrote, using your Week 1 Calendar for Actual (Not Planned) Time Spent Writing This Week to do so.

Then, here at the end of the week, look at your time tracker and consider your accomplishments. Even if you didn't get as much done as you hoped, you have gained an understanding of your patterns and are poised to do better next week. Remember, feeling too much guilt is counterproductive!

WEEK 2
Advancing Your Argument

Task Day	Week 2 Daily Writing Tasks	Estimated Task Time in Minutes	
		HumInt	SciQua
Day 1 (Monday?)	Read from here until you reach the week 2, day 2 tasks, filling in any boxes, checking off any forms, and answering any questions as you read.	120	120
Day 2 (Tuesday?)	Test a statement of your argument with several others, both in and outside your field, then revise it.	30	30
Day 3 (Wednesday?)	Review your article and note where your argument is disappearing and should appear.	90	60
Day 4 (Thursday?)	Revise your article around your argument.	120+	90+
Day 5 (Friday?)	Revise your article around your argument.	120+	90+
Total estimated time for reading the workbook, completing the tasks, and writing your article		**8+ hours**	**6.5+ hours**

Above are the tasks for your second week. Make sure to start this week by scheduling when you will write, and then tracking the time you actually spend writing (using the Calendar for Actual Time Spent Writing This Week form or online software). Documenting how you spend your time enables you to make realistic plans for the following week, and it motivates you through a sense of accomplishment.

Depending on the state of your argument, you may have to spend extra time writing this week to stay on deadline. If you come across any unfamiliar publishing terms, read the section "Some Publishing Terms and Processes" in the introduction to this book.

WEEK 2, DAY 1: READING AND TASKS

FIRST WEEK IN REVIEW

An important lesson you learned last week was that writing a bit most days is a more effective writing practice than saving up your writing for blocks of time that never come. That's why this workbook breaks down, into manageable chunks, the tasks involved in revising an article for publication. If you manage to get some writing done five days a week for twelve weeks, you'll have done more than submit an article to a journal—you'll have developed writing habits that will carry you for a lifetime. Learning to juggle teaching, service, administration, reading, and writing is a strength that will stand you in excellent stead, whether you're now a professor or want to be one. If you think of a professor's days as often involving all five activities, you will be well on your way.

MYTHS ABOUT PUBLISHABLE JOURNAL ARTICLES

Last week, you selected a paper to revise. But what are the essential ingredients for a publishable research article? Most academics know that their classroom essay or conference paper is not yet publishable, but they're not entirely sure why. Let's debunk some common myths about what makes an article publishable. Then we can turn to what really does make an article acceptable to a journal. This information will aid you in determining how to develop yours.

Myth 1: Only Those Articles That Are Profoundly Theoretical and/or Have Groundbreaking Findings Will Get Published

Novice authors have an exaggerated idea of what publishable quality is, because they rarely read the average journal article. Since graduate seminar readings tend to concentrate on leading thinkers, plus a few articles the professor considers groundbreaking, the characteristics of the great majority of scholarship are something with which graduate students seldom acquaint themselves. Most articles are neither earth-shattering nor published by famous scholars, but instead they're narrow in claims and context and published by people like you and me.

Myth 2: Only Those Articles with Lots of Interesting Ideas Will Get Published

Novice authors think that many interesting ideas make an article publishable. Although it is to be hoped that any article has interesting ideas, their sheer accumulation isn't what gets an article published. A senior scholar put it perfectly when he told me, "A graduate student came to talk to me about the article he wanted to publish. Three continents, fifty authors, and a dozen theoretical paradigms later, I'm wondering where exactly it is that thirty pages can hold one hundred thousand words?" Articles get published not for spraying ideas but for articulating one important idea.

Myth 3: Only Those Articles That Are Entirely Original Will Get Published

Novice authors have an exaggerated idea of what makes something original, thinking that only unique work gets published. They worry too much that their own ideas are "obvious or trivial" (Abbott 2004, xi). When they find, upon doing a literature search, that "someone has written my article," they feel discouraged. Yet almost all published scholarship is not the first on the subject and is openly derivative or imitative. So if originality is so elusive, why do those in academia always harp on its importance? Because it remains true that you must do something "new" to be published. To get a better sense of this point, let's take a closer look at the difference between original ideas and new ones.

WHAT GETS PUBLISHED AND WHY

A publishable journal article is a piece of writing organized around one important new idea that is demonstrably related to the scholarship previously published. In other words, research articles get published because they say something new about something old. If your idea is interesting but not new, your article won't be published. If your idea is new but not related to the old (previous research), your article won't be published. If your ideas are multiple but not organized around one new idea, your article won't be published. As some scholars put it, "Tell me something I don't know so I can understand better our common interest" (Booth, Colomb, and Williams 2009, 24).

Note that I didn't use the word *original*. In contrast to *original*, the strict meaning of *new* is not "the first" or "previously nonexistent" but something that has been seen, used, or known for only a short time. For instance, if you write an article about Vietnamese women's reproductive strategies, some of which have existed for centuries, your information will not be "original," but knowledge of it may be "new" to the field of medical anthropology. Bringing attention to something can be sufficiently original to get an article published.

Something new can also be a variation. For instance, if you write an article about schizophrenia using statistics collected by others but correlating variables that they didn't correlate or interpreting the correlation differently, you'll have written something new. To write a variation on scholarship that already exists can be sufficiently original to get an article published.

So don't get fixated on the idea of originality when revising your article with this workbook (or drafting it). Make your material—whether ancient or invented yesterday—fresh, and you'll be published. How do you accomplish that? And what's considered new for the purposes of publication? Three types of newness mark publishable articles.

Publishable Article Type 1: Approaches New Evidence in an Old Way

An article that provides new evidence in support of an accepted idea represents the best bet for novice authors. In such an article, you don't create a new approach; rather, you present new evidence to support an existing approach. (By "existing approach," I mean accepted theories, common methods, dominant arguments, and so on. So long as someone else has proposed a theory, it's an existing approach for you.) This new evidence can result from your laboratory experiments, field observations, primary source study, or archival research. It can also be evidence recently produced by someone else, such as government data or a new film. (Anything produced in the past ten years is considered new in the humanities, where articles can take five years from inception to publication).

Since graduate students are usually more in touch with new cultural trends and practices, they can often make real contributions by writing this kind of article, testing old ideas in new contexts. Those who have grown up in transnational or subcultural contexts also have an advantage in collecting such data.

Unfortunately, simply having new evidence won't suffice. It's not enough to introduce a new text, draw attention to a movement little discussed, detail the events of a religious ritual, add a note to a historical figure, announce your experiment's results, or fill in the details on a little-known cultural practice. While this is important work (and, I think, sadly underappreciated in academia as an end in itself), it's not the kind of research that tends to get published. You have simply written a report, a paper typical of the classroom but uncommon in journals. To be published, you must relate the new to the old. Indeed, as one scholar explained, the popularity of your article can depend on that relation: "Because new ideas must be situated in relation to assimilated disciplinary knowledge, the most influential new ideas are often those that most closely follow the old ones" (Hyland 2004, 31). In this, scholarship is a little bit like pop songs: "nothing is new; rather everything is a slight variation on the old" (Jones and Rahn 1977, 85).

One advantage of using existing approaches is that many require little explaining or defending—you don't need a section on Marx to do a Marxist analysis, you don't need a review of the history of first-wave feminism to do a feminist analysis, and you don't need lots of quotations from Gayatri Spivak to do a postcolonial analysis. (Some explaining may be needed with relatively new existing approaches, however: meta-cartosemiotics, necropolitics, cognitive-affective mapping, transmedia theory, and so on.)

As an example of this new evidence-old approach article, say that you've written an article about art initiatives in the Zaatari refugee camp in Jordan, one of the largest refugee settlements in the world. If you simply describe where the poetry readings are, who paints what kind of paintings, and how song lyrics relate to current events, you probably won't get published. This is so even if you're providing new data that few have collected or presented in scholarly journals. But if you describe this new evidence and employ it to theorize, say, how individuals use the arts to resolve conflicts and recast national identities, then you're on your way to a publishable article. That is, since conflict resolution and national identity have been wide-ranging theoretical concerns for some time, you will have provided new evidence for the old theory that human beings use culture to construct identity. If you simply report on cultural production in Zaatari, you didn't present your evidence in the context of ongoing academic concerns or the scholarly conversation in your field. You didn't approach the new in an old way.

Your new evidence doesn't have to support the old theory; you can refine it or even disprove it. Of course, taking this strategy is riskier, since readers tend to accept evidence *for* things they believe in and to reject evidence *against* things they believe in. If you decide to contradict existing theories, you must have very strong evidence. An example of an article providing new evidence to contradict an old theory would be your finding that low self-esteem is correlated not with shyness but with vitamin D levels. That is, although other researchers on the topic found a strong correlation among low self-esteem, depression, and shyness, your test administered to undergraduate students did not find a strong correlation. You would be using new evidence to undermine an existing theory.

Publishable Article Type 2: Approaches Old Evidence in a New Way

An article taking a new approach to old evidence is typically not by a novice author. Only an author with a strong grasp of existing theories and methodologies, something the novice is often still trying to attain, can invent a new approach. In such an article, the author develops a new way of approaching old data, such as a new method, a new research design, or a new theory.

Again, just having a new approach won't suffice. It's not enough simply to claim that a new theory has explanatory power or that a new methodology will be more useful than an old one. Rather, you must apply the new approach to something that already exists. If the possible error in writing publishable article type 1 (based on new evidence) is that the article is too bound to concrete data, the possible error in writing publishable article type 2 (based on a new theory) is that the article is too high in the theoretical stratosphere. The new theory must be related to old evidence.

One example of a successful new approach–old evidence combination is the work of Timothy Morton. Taking advantage of object-oriented ontology, itself a relatively new school of thought, he arrived at the idea of "hyperobjects," objects so widely spread and long lasting that they are practically everywhere and always—like global warming or Styrofoam (Morton 2010). He brought something new to an old problem, our ecological crisis, and theorized a new approach to existing evidence. If I may immodestly refer to my own work, I too have theorized in this manner. I invented the term *discursive possession* to talk about how the discourse of a subjugated colonized group could possess the thought of a dominant colonial group (Belcher 2012). I made this argument using old evidence—one of the most canonical European texts ever written, *Rasselas*, Samuel Johnson's eighteenth-century novel about Ethiopia—to show how this problematically orientalist text, by an author who had never been to Africa, was nevertheless animated by Ethiopians' own self-conceptions.

Of course, newness can take many forms. If an approach exists elsewhere in the scholarship but is very hard to find, has not been written about in a long time, has not been articulated clearly, has been discredited, or has not been used in your field, then refurbishing that existing but sidelined idea can constitute a new approach.

Publishable Article Type 3: Pairs Old Evidence with Old Approaches in a New Way

An article that presents a new pairing of old evidence with an old approach represents another good choice for novice authors. It gives neither new evidence nor a new approach; instead, it merely links evidence and an approach that hasn't been linked previously. Since very little in the world is truly new, you can create newness by bringing together things that haven't been brought together before. "The originality of a subject is in its treatment" (Disraeli 1870, 142). Those with strengths in several disciplines are most able to make these kinds of links.

Let's examine some examples of an old evidence–old approach–new link article. Heather Love's work brings two disciplines together, sociology and literary studies, thus bridging the social sciences and the humanities; her argument is for a new "method of textual analysis that would take its cue from observation-based social sciences including ethology, kinesics, ethnomethodology, and microsociology" (2010, 375). Other scholars have been involved in social-psychological research on "implicit racial bias," formerly called "automatic race bias," a concept launched in the 1990s. But the concept of implicit racial bias recently migrated from psychology, where it is old, into philosophy, where it is new, to be used in considering a number of old questions in ethics (Brownstein and Saul 2016). As another example, let's say that you have written an article about the problems of racism and sexism in the Hollywood film industry. If you simply note that many Hollywood movies are racist and sexist, you'll have done nothing new. If, however, you demonstrate how the Federal Communications Commission's policies during the 1960s and 1970s caused film production to shift away from inclusion, away from positive portrayals of women and people of color, you're on your way to getting published, because you have paired an old approach (historical analysis of government media policies) with old evidence (sexism and racism in the movies) in a new way. You brought existing data and approaches together to create a new understanding.

Deciding about Revisions

Now that you have read the section on myths about what makes an article publishable and the section on how publishable articles must link old and new, take a moment to write down what you think is new about your article, and how it links to the old.

What is new about
my article?

What revisions
might I need to make
to my article to link
the old to the new?

WHAT GETS REJECTED AND WHY

Peer reviewers and journal editors reject articles for a range of reasons. Yes, some articles are rejected because they have massive theoretical, analytical, or structural flaws. However, most articles fall in the middle of the range, getting rejected for an accretion of small problems rather than a huge theoretical problem. I've identified ten of the most common reasons that journal articles get rejected. If you can learn how to avoid them, you'll vastly improve your chances of getting into print. Each week of this workbook is devoted to aiding you in overcoming one or more of these ten pitfalls of publication. This week, we are going to focus on just one—and it's the main reason. But, let's address a difficult truth first.

Perfectly Acceptable Articles Get Rejected

Some article rejections have nothing to do with the quality of the article itself. Editors immediately reject up to a quarter of their journal's submissions, without even sending them through the peer-review process, because of *other* articles. First, if the journal has recently published a research article on the same topic and with a similar argument to yours, the editor can't publish your research article. Second, if the journal has published many articles on the same region or with the same methodology, and the editor is working to ensure that many are covered, the editor can't accept your article. Third, if the journal has already accepted quite a few articles for publication, such that the next several issues or more are full (called a backlog), the editor can't accept your article. Fourth, journals just don't have space in their pages for all the good articles that they receive (Dirk 1996).

Unfortunately, editors rarely explain these circumstances to their prospective article authors. I once got a rejection within twelve hours of submitting an article to a top journal. Not long after, I ran into the managing editor and said with chagrin, "Wow, you really hated my article—you rejected it instantaneously." She laughed and responded, "No, it's just that we have such a huge backlog that we are currently rejecting everything. I didn't even read your article." I was lucky; I learned why my article was rejected—but how many other authors aren't so fortunate? While it's tough to avoid these types of rejections because of others' articles, the workbook will address what you can do to prevent such types in "Week 4: Selecting a Journal." Let's turn now to the chief cause of article rejection.

The Main Reason Journals Reject Articles: No Argument

The main reason why editors and reviewers reject articles is because their authors either do not have an argument or do not state it properly. Gary Olson, a journal editor so good that he received a lifetime award for his work, stated that "one of the most common and frustrating problems" that editors experience is scholars' failure to state their argument "clearly and early in the article" (1997, 59). The "single most important thing you can do to increase" your chances of publication, he said, is to sharpen your article's argument (61). When you center your article on a single persuasive idea, you've taken a giant leap closer to publication.

Editors or reviewers may not mention the lack of an argument as a reason for rejection. They may instead state that the article is not original or significant, that it is disorganized, that it suffers from poor analysis, or that it "reads like a student paper." But the solution for all these problems lies in having an argument, stating it early and clearly, and then structuring your article around that argument.

But what exactly is an argument? How is it different from a topic? And how do you go about making one?

Part of the reason that unclear arguments are so common in academia is because the rhetoric of argument is notoriously difficult to teach. One book on the subject, jammed with various teaching techniques, carefully acknowledged that postcourse surveys revealed that each technique failed to improve student papers (Fulkerson 1996, 165). Stephen Toulmin invented a model of argument in the 1950s ([1958] 2003), asserting that a good argument has at least three parts: *grounds* (your data or evidence), a *claim* (what you aim to show), and a *warrant* (the assumptions or principles that link the claim to the data)— but it takes a long time to learn how to use his model. Finally, different fields use different terms for the same rhetorical move: some use *argument* and others use *thesis*, *hypothesis*, or *research question*—or sometimes *findings* or even *conclusion*.

So if you feel confused about what an argument is or how to make one, you're in excellent company. Let's dare to figure it out anyway.

UNDERSTANDING AND MAKING ARGUMENTS

Succinctly, an argument is discourse intended to persuade. You persuade someone by engaging that person's doubts and providing evidence to overcome those doubts. A journal article, then, is a piece of writing that attempts to persuade a reader to believe something (or to believe something more strongly). In other words, a journal article is a coherent series of statements in which the author leads the reader from certain premises to a specific conclusion.

In the sciences, the subjective nature of the term *argument*—which seems to suggest that research is about beliefs, not facts—alarms some scholars. They prefer to talk about testing a "research question" or "hypothesis." However, an argument is merely an answered research question or confirmed hypothesis. That is, if the research question is, "Does *x* affect *y* when *z* is present?" the argument is *yes* (*x* affects *y* when *z* is present), *no* (*x* does not affect *y* when *z* is present), or *sometimes* (*x* affects *y* when *z* is present if . . .). Even in the social, health, behavioral, and natural science fields, aiming for an argument rather than a hypothesis will better enable you to write publishable articles.

In the humanities, the aggressive nature of the term *argument*—which seems to suggest that locked-down conclusions are more important than open exploration—also alarms some scholars. They insist that considering all aspects of a question is more important than answering it, since answers always limit possibilities. They prefer to meditate on a key term (like *beauty* or *shipwreck*), building slowly to some resonance. Increasingly, however, US humanities journals don't publish such meditative articles, perhaps because it's more fun to write an article without an argument than it is to read one. Even if you don't like making arguments, knowing more about them can increase your chances of publication success.

Meanwhile, those in critical theory question the terms themselves. Isn't all discourse an argument? Aren't all texts meant to persuade? Can we know for sure that anything is a fact? Indeed, this is part of what makes argument so difficult to teach. Definitions begin to blur; meaning begins to slip. Therefore, let me say that my interest here is pedagogical, not theoretical. I merely want to provide some useful ways of thinking about writing that enable you to get your work published, so I won't go further into the thorny thickets of argument theory. Instead, I will define it.

Argument Defined

The wonderful essayist Lynn Bloom said long ago that an article is focused "on a single significant idea supported with evidence carefully chosen and arranged" (1984, 481). Adapting that statement, I define the term *argument* as follows:

> An argument is (1) your journal article's single significant idea (2) stated in one or two sentences early and clearly in your article and (3) around which your article is organized, (4) emerging from or linked to some scholarly conversation and (5) supported with evidence to convince the reader of its validity.

What Is Your Argument Currently?

Your revision process is still at the early stage, and you may learn a lot more about argument in the next sections; but it can help if you read these sections with a draft of your argument in mind. For the sake of experimentation, try writing in one or two sentences what you understand your argument to be at this point. (If you're still debating between which of two papers to pick for this assignment, complete this exercise for both. That will help you to pick the best one.) If you're not exactly sure what your main argument is, write in several.

What is my argument?

How Do You Know whether You Have an Argument?

Being able to define the term *argument* is less important than knowing whether the journal article you're working on has one. The following tests can help you identify whether the statement you wrote in the box above is an argument. Your statement doesn't need to pass all these tests, but it should pass at least one of them. Keeping your argument in mind, read each test below and then, in the box that follows it, answer the question (checking the square boxes, rather than the round ones, is ideal).

Argument Tests

Agree/disagree test. One of the easiest ways to distinguish whether a statement is an argument is if you can coherently respond to it by saying "I agree" or "I disagree" (Ballenger 2003, 127). For instance, the statement "Toni Morrison is a feminist writer" is one with which you can agree or disagree. It's possible to imagine two people debating this point, perhaps based on African American critiques of the term *feminism* and Morrison's own claims. On the other hand, the statement "Toni Morrison is a writer" is not a debatable argument. Upon hearing that statement, no one is going to assert loudly, "I agree!" because no one would dispute it. So the evaluation of "feminist writer" requires evidence in order to persuade the reader, whereas the actuality "writer" does not. Likewise, the statement "Many California schoolchildren are bilingual" is not an argument. It is a statistical fact. No one who has lived in or studied California would dispute it. However, the statement "Bilingual children do better in school than monolingual children" is an argument (adapted from Feliciano 2001, 876). (Note that here and later when I say "adapted from," the material within quotation marks is not from the article cited but rather an invention of mine, sometimes leaping quite far from the author's actual arguments.) Many might be inclined to disagree with this statement and would need data to be convinced otherwise. Others might immediately agree and eagerly cite it to others in various discussions. Therefore, the statement passes the agree/disagree test and is an argument.

Does my statement pass the agree/disagree test?   ☐ I think so   ◯ I don't think so   ◯ I'm not sure

Gut test. Another test is emotional. What happens when you make a statement of your argument aloud to others (or imagine doing so)? If you feel calm and serene, your statement probably isn't an argument. If, however, you feel a little on edge or even anxious, then it probably is an argument. That is, your body will tell you whether you're about to take the risk of entering a dispute—elevating your heart rate and making your stomach clench. Someone making an argument is often gearing up to fight, anticipating others' attack, and the body can reflect this fight response.

| Does my statement pass the gut test? | ☐ I think so ◯ I don't think so ◯ I'm not sure |

Immediate dispute test. Another test is relational. When I'm teaching a writing workshop, I often have participants express their argument aloud and ask the others to judge whether it's an argument. Often, the others respond either by nodding and saying, "Yes, that's an argument," or by looking puzzled and saying, "I'm not sure whether that's an argument." However, sometimes the author states the argument and someone immediately responds by saying, "No, no, that's wrong, because..." As soon as someone says that, I cut that person off and announce, "Next!" There's no better evidence that you have an argument than if people immediately start arguing with you. (It can work the other way as well: if people respond with terrific enthusiasm—saying, "That's so true!" or "I couldn't agree more!"—then it's probably an argument.)

| Does my statement pass the immediate dispute test? | ☐ I think so ◯ I don't think so ◯ I'm not sure |

Puzzle answer test. Another test is intellectual. Is your statement the solution to a puzzle, an answer to a question that people have about the world, a human creation, or a human behavior? Is it an explanation, however partial, of something mysterious (Harvey 1994, 650)? For instance, many wonder about the causes of violence, environmental degradation, and human inequality and how best to end them. Many wonder about the nature of gender or sexuality. A few wonder whether Shakespeare really did write all the plays attributed to him or whether yoga helps all back injuries. An argument addresses a question that deserves an answer. If your statement is the answer to something the public or scholars have actively wondered about, you probably have an argument.

| Does my statement pass the puzzle answer test? | ☐ I think so ◯ I don't think so ◯ I'm not sure |

Now, some of these tests may not work for you. The gut test won't work for you if you're supporting the consensus (or preternaturally calm). The immediate dispute test won't work if your argument is subtle rather than blunt. If you didn't get clarity from any of these tests, it may be better to turn from confirming tests to negating tests. Therefore, the following tests will help you determine whether the statement you wrote above is *not* an argument.

Tests for Statements That Masquerade as Arguments

Quite a few statements look like arguments but aren't. Disconcertingly, some statements *are* arguments but not The Argument, not the single significant idea that undergirds your journal article. Further, many times authors deploy the formulation "I argue that . . ." in their published article to emphasize an idea, not mark The Argument (e.g., writing

"Against the first objection, I argue that . . ." or "I argue that researchers still have a lot to learn"). It's all very confusing! The following tests can help you identify whether your statement is *not* The Argument of your journal article:

Topic test. When I ask novice authors to articulate their argument, they frequently state their topic instead (i.e., the subject of their article). Confusing the two is a major problem in classroom essays, which often roam around a topic rather than presenting a clear argument. One dead giveaway is a statement that starts with "I'm looking at," "I'm examining," "I'm exploring," or "I'm interested in." A sentence that begins that way is usually just naming a subject—a problem, solution, theory, object, text, thinker, artist—rather than taking a stand about it. As one small clue, who can disagree that you're looking at something?

Fortunately, if you push the statement of your topic, you can often get to an argument. So for instance, a *topic* is, "I'm looking at the role of carnivals in the life of small Midwestern towns"; an *argument* developed from that statement is, "By portraying a more diverse world, carnivals drove the flight of young people from small Midwestern towns." Similarly, a *topic* is, "I'm interested in the challenges faced by Koreans in Japan over the twentieth century"; an *argument* is, "The lower social position of Koreans in Japan over the twentieth century is due to the decolonization process ending Japan's occupation of Korea and the contradictory policies of the Japanese government toward Koreans in Japan" (adapted from Chung 2004). As these examples suggest, one mark of an argument is specificity.

| Is my statement merely articulating a topic? | ◯ I think so   ☐ I don't think so   ◯ I'm not sure |
| If so, how can I reword it? | |

Observation test. Another mistake often made by novice authors when stating their argument is that they state an observation instead (i.e., what they have noticed about their subject). Authors say things like "I argue that Chimamanda Ngozi Adichie's novel *Half of a Yellow Sun* (2006) has a non-linear chronological structure" or "I argue that many of the older men in our study had lost their ability to hear high frequencies." Distinguishing observations from arguments can be quite tricky, as some observations are very sophisticated and not fully separable from arguments. But one main sign that a statement is only an observation is that it doesn't explain anything. The statement can't stand well alone; rather, it demands interpretation. Why does it matter that the novel has an unusual chronological structure? Or that older men are not able to hear high frequencies (the frequencies of women's and children's voices)?

Fortunately, many arguments start with observations; if authors interpret that observation, they can arrive at an argument. So for instance, maybe you conducted field research in which you studied blogs whose authors are living with lupus and then conducted interviews with them, observing that they "view themselves as a distinct group with an experience so unique that others cannot possibly understand it, and thus they share less with those without the disease." Okay, that's thought-provoking, but what does it demonstrate? How do we interpret this different level of sharing? To get from this observation to an argument, you would have to interpret it, perhaps arguing that

> the quality of information garnered in doctor-patient encounters has long been a region of study. I argue that health practitioners receive the least and worst information possible from those with lupus because of the patients' perception that others cannot comprehend their experience. Further research is needed to determine whether instituting more online communication between health practitioners and those with lupus, approaching them in an environment where they are used to being more disclosing, would yield better and more complete information. (Adapted from Pony 2016)

Is my statement just an observation?	◯ I think so ☐ I don't think so ◯ I'm not sure
If so, how can I reword it?	

Obvious test. Sometimes when articulating their argument, novice authors formulate a statement that is obvious—so broad that any reasonable person would never dispute it. They say things like "I argue that colonialism had a lot of bad effects," "I demonstrate that sexism harms girls," or "I show how the 1915 film *Birth of a Nation* is racist." These statements aren't wrong, but they represent beliefs so common that almost no academic would debate them, or they mention characteristics so apparent that almost anyone could notice them. When you're an undergraduate, it can seem as though the purpose of a paper is to say indisputable things like this, but the purpose of a journal article is the precise opposite: to say things that at least some scholars might contest. Further, as these examples suggest, novice writers wanting to right a social wrong often make such arguments. Righting wrongs is vital work, but the purpose of journal articles is to help us understand injustice better, not simply to declare that it exists. Vast swathes of scholarly research are dedicated to uncovering the roots of and solutions to injustice; to be a part of it, you need to add something new.

Unfortunately, getting from obvious arguments to subtle ones isn't easy. You need to proceed from a vague and general claim to a clear and specific one, which often requires deeper research. For instance, instead of saying "I argue that colonialism was bad and shouldn't have happened," you need to say something like "I argue that British colonizers went to great lengths to portray themselves as Christian civilizers in Kenya during the 1950s and to tarnish the Kikuyu as barbaric primitives, despite committing much greater atrocities during the Mau Mau Uprising" (based on the work of Elkins 2005). The first statement is just an assertion—a vague, general statement with which almost no scholar would disagree—but the second is specific and interesting.

Is my statement obvious?	◯ I think so ☐ I don't think so ◯ I'm not sure
If so, how can I reword it?	

Variable test. When I ask novice authors to articulate their argument, they frequently state their variables instead (i.e., the attributes of the subject that are in relation). They say things like "I'm looking at how x affects z," "I'm arguing that x and z are correlated," or "I contend that factors a, b, and c either facilitate or hinder z." Such statements are close to being arguments, but they aren't arguments. The nature of the variables' relation—positive or negative, helping or hindering, negligible or strong—goes unstated. You must state *how* x affects z. So if a mere statement of *variables* is, "I show how rates of gun ownership affect death rates," an *argument* is, "Gun ownership increases death rates." Or, to state a journal article type of argument, "I argue that gun control is vital to the safety of white Americans, not African Americans, because I found that the high levels of white gun ownership are positively correlated with suicides among whites, but that the low levels of black gun ownership are not correlated with reduced homicides of blacks" (adapted from the work of Reeves and Holmes 2015). One sign that a statement is about variables instead of an argument is whether, as in the preceding examples, it includes the words *how* or *why*. Another sign is people's response; if they respond to your statement with "Oh, interesting, what *did* you find?" or "Oh, interesting, how *does* x affect z?" it's not yet an argument.

Fortunately, you're very close to an argument in such a case; you can get to it by stating exactly how or why the variables are related. So for instance, a statement of *variables* is, "We argue that individuals' psychological state impacts their perception of tinnitus"; an *argument* is, "We argue that [PTSD] affects individuals' ability to cope with painful disorders [more negatively than other psychological states] because of our finding that individuals with tinnitus and concurrent PTSD reported significantly . . . more handicapping tinnitus effects when compared with individuals with other psychological conditions" (Fagelson and Smith 2016, 541). At first, it may seem as though the first statement is an argument. It isn't vague, and it lists variables. But it doesn't specify which psychological state is being studied or how it affects the perception of tinnitus—we don't know whether the argument might be that happy people are more affected by pain or that those with obsessive-compulsive disorder might be better at documenting their pain. The second statement really is an argument, clarifying the variables and their specific relation. One trick to reframing a statement of variables into an argument is to replace words that don't have valence (i.e., a negative or positive charge) with words that do. So instead of saying "US radio station DJs in the 1950s gave certain messages about race and gender," replace the word *certain* with a positive word like *radical* or a negative word like *damaging*.

Finally, note that you can't publish an article arguing that many variables are determinative. A student once said to me that she had read many articles about girls' education in a West African country, and each argued for a different variable as the most important in ensuring that girls had access to education (e.g., class, region, siblings). She said that she wanted to write an article arguing that all of them were important, plus another twenty. I told her that no doubt she was right, but that she'd never be able to publish an original research article stating that. Saying that everything is important is not how research moves forward.

Is my statement just naming variables?	◯ I think so ☐ I don't think so ◯ I'm not sure
If so, how can I reword it?	

Gap/overlooked test. When I ask academics to articulate their argument, they frequently state their claim for significance instead. They say things like "I argue that there is a gap in the literature" or "I argue that x is more important than previously thought." The latter frequently takes the shape of "X is viewed incorrectly and therefore is misunderstood" (or overlooked, understudied, undervalued, overvalued). Yes, such statements are types of argument, and should be included in your article if true—but they're not The Argument. Rather, they're claims for significance, claims about the value of the article as a whole—that it fills a research gap, brings attention to unjustly ignored subjects, rectifies incorrect observations, or examines the right things in the right ways. One sign that a statement is a claim for significance instead of an argument is if it's a value judgment, either about the value of your subject of study or about scholarly gaps and oversights. Another sign is if you don't need your whole article to substantiate your statement. If you can address it in a paragraph in the first few pages and never mention it again, it's not your argument.

Fortunately, it's often just one step from your claim for significance to your argument—just state what backs your claim for significance. What does your fill-the-gap scholarship show? Why is your subject important? For instance, a claim for significance is, "No one has looked at the femme fatale character in film noir, even though she is quite fascinating," while an argument is, "The femme fatale character in film noir is not merely a male prop but a woman who controls her own destiny" (adapted from Bronfen 2004, 106–7). The first statement is about the gap in scholarship (claim for significance); the second is about interpreting content in the film (argument). Likewise, a claim for significance is, "The development of democracy in Malawi over the 1990s illuminates the struggles that states face in democratizing when a significant proportion of the population is illiterate"; an argument is, "This study of 1990s Malawian elections reveals that illiteracy is a major obstacle to voting and thus democratization."

Is my statement a claim for significance?	◯ I think so ☐ I don't think so ◯ I'm not sure
If so, what is my argument?	

Speculative test. Another argument articulation error frequently made by novice authors is that they state speculations, not arguments; that is, they state what they conjecture rather than prove. Your statement should not be, as a professor in one of my workshops once said, "applied wishes." An argument can't be what you think should be done in the world because of your research. One form of this problem is a statement that is a policy recommendation. Having policy recommendations in your article is fine, even good, particularly in the conclusion; but a recommendation emerges from the argument and is speculative. Let me alter some of the preceding examples to demonstrate this. Those writing the article about gun ownership might recommend, "I argue that African American members of Congress should stop drafting gun control bills." That's a policy recommendation, not The Argument. Those writing the article about tinnitus and PTSD might recommend, "I argue that the US government's Veterans Administration should provide better support to soldiers with PTSD being tested for tinnitus." That's also a policy recommendation.

Another form of this argument articulation error is a statement that is a prediction. No human being can provide evidence for something that *will* happen. You can speculate about the future, but you can't prove what will happen—therefore, you can't make arguments about it. One sign that you have a speculative argument is the use of the future tense: "I argue that the United States will be better off if it . . ." or "I argue that if the United States does *x*, then it will have *y*." Another sign is if your statement of your argument contains the words *if*, *must*, or *should*. For instance, "Schools should listen to students more" is not an argument. Again, speculations are fine; they simply can't be your argument.

Fortunately, someone with a speculative statement often does have an argument, but just hasn't stated that argument. Go back to your article and look at what backs your policy recommendation or speculation. The basis of that recommendation or speculation is often your argument.

| Is my statement speculative? | ◯ I think so ☐ I don't think so ◯ I'm not sure |
| If so, what is my argument? | |

How Do You Shape a Nonargument into an Argument?

Here are two imagined examples of authors reshaping their nonargumentative statement into an argument, step by step. Since this shaping often does happen in conversation, I've formatted these examples as skits.

HumInt Reshaping an Argument Skit
AUTHOR: I want to tell you about a new book I'm reading.
FRIEND: That's not even a <u>topic</u>.

AUTHOR: That was just me winding up! Wait a second. . . The purpose of this article is to analyze Jamaica Kincaid's novel *Annie John*.

FRIEND: That's a <u>project</u>, not an argument.

AUTHOR: Oh, right. Um, Jamaica Kincaid's novel *Annie John* is a brilliant postcolonial novel that should be studied more.

FRIEND: So true! But I think that's a <u>claim for significance</u>.

AUTHOR: Right, right. This article uncovers what we can learn about the colonial experience from Jamaica Kincaid's novel *Annie John*, set in 1950s Antigua.

FRIEND: That's a <u>topic</u>, and a vague one.

AUTHOR: You're right. Okay, Jamaica Kincaid's novel *Annie John* shows how the colonial experience shaped familial relations.

FRIEND: Interesting! But I think that's a <u>statement of variables</u>, not an argument.

AUTHOR: Hmm. How about: Jamaica Kincaid's novel *Annie John* shows how colonial education shaped familial relations.

FRIEND: That's just a <u>sharpened statement of variables</u>.

AUTHOR: Aargh! Okay, Jamaica Kincaid's novel *Annie John* details how Annie John's British education increasingly alienates her from her mother.

FRIEND: That's an <u>observation</u> about the book, not an argument.

AUTHOR: (*after a sigh and a long pause*) In Jamaica Kincaid's novel *Annie John*, colonial education breeds generational alienation.

FRIEND: Nice! That's an <u>argument</u>. But it could use a little more detail, right?

AUTHOR: Yes. In Jamaica Kincaid's novel *Annie John*, the contempt for local knowledge that colonial education breeds in the new generation causes familial alienation, as the educated younger generation learns disdain for the older generation.

FRIEND: Now, that's an <u>argument</u>!

SciQua Reshaping an Argument Skit

AUTHOR: I'm interested in studying sexual minorities.

FRIEND: Come on! Didn't you read Belcher's chapter?! That's not even a topic.

AUTHOR: Sorry. Okay, I analyze the mental health of sexual minorities in the United States.

FRIEND: That's a research <u>project</u>, not an argument.

AUTHOR: I'm looking at rates of suicide among US sexual minorities.

FRIEND: Hello? Scholar, meet <u>topic</u>.

AUTHOR: Less of the sarcasm, please!

FRIEND: Sorry. Resetting for supportive friend mode.

AUTHOR: Okay, thank you. How about: rates of suicide among US sexual minorities have been studied before, but always poorly; this article rectifies previous errors.

FRIEND: That's cool! But I think that's a <u>claim for significance</u>.

AUTHOR: Oops. Right. Rates of suicide among US sexual minorities must be addressed by the government.

FRIEND: So true. But that's a <u>policy recommendation</u>.

AUTHOR: Oops. Many lesbian, gay, and bisexual (LGB) individuals join LGB communities looking for support.

FRIEND: Hey, did I tell you that my friend Vinay is trying to start a group for queer students of color here?

AUTHOR: Don't distract me! That's off topic.

FRIEND: Oops. Well, I think that you're just making an <u>observation</u> anyway.

AUTHOR: Aargh. Okay, this article suggests how the percentage of sexual minorities in a community affects that community's suicide rates.

FRIEND: Interesting! How does it affect . . . hey, my question about "how" is a sign that it's a <u>statement of variables</u>.

AUTHOR: Oops. Participation in LGB communities affects LGB individuals' suicide rates.

FRIEND: That's just a <u>sharpened statement of variables</u>. You dropped the "how," but I still have the same question: how does it affect suicide rates?

AUTHOR: LGB communities reduce LGB individuals' suicide rates.

FRIEND: Yes!! That's an <u>argument</u>. But wait, can you say that? Isn't that assuming that correlation equals causation?

AUTHOR: Good catch. LGB individuals with high rates of participation in LGB communities have lower rates of suicide.

FRIEND: Wow, that's really great to hear, but are you sure? How can you prove that? Wait—my questions are a sign it's an <u>argument</u>!

Deciding about Argument

Your revision process is still at the early stage, but given what you know at this point about your article, what is your argument?

> Have I learned anything so far that can help me reformulate my statement as an argument? What is my argument now?

How Do You Create an Argument?

It may be that you got through the previous sections and know that you don't have a clear argument or any argument, but aren't sure how to construct one. In that case, you can try out some argument templates. Of course, all templates are reductive, straitjacketing some possibilities and eliminating others. But I like templates because they give you a norm to play with, recast, and even resist. Without rules, there can be no revolution.

Posusta's and Simpson's Argument Templates

The first person to invent an argument phrasal template, as far as I know, is Steven Posusta. After teaching in a UCLA composition tutoring lab as an English major, Posusta wrote a hilarious sixty-two-page book for undergraduates titled *Don't Panic: The Procrastinator's Guide to Writing an Effective Term Paper (You Know Who You Are)* (1996). The aim of the book, according to its jacket blurbs, is to provide the "cool tricks" and "fast fixes" that can enable a student to read Posusta's text in one evening and "hand in your paper tomorrow." As you can imagine, *Don't Panic* has inspired horror in some corners (R. Davis and Shadle 2000) and admiration in others (some teaching assistants have used it in composition classes after learning about it from me). In it, Posusta provides a phrasal template for creating a one-sentence argument, which he calls the "Formula for an Instant Thesis" (1996, 12). It goes like this (the below is verbatim from his book):

#1. Although (general statement, opposite opinion)

#2. nevertheless (thesis, your idea)

#3. because (examples, evidence, #1, #2, #3, etc.). (12)

Of course, some arguments cannot be expressed using Posusta's thesis maker, which was intended for undergraduate papers, not journal articles. It works better for contesting current theories rather than confirming them. Further, few published articles state an argument in one sentence like this; even fewer use these exact words to signal their argument. All the same, rhetorical structures like this back the arguments of many articles.

I like Posusta's Instant Thesis formula, because it distills the requirements of academic discourse to an easily understood essence. It reminds authors that they must do three things to get published: (1) cite others' ideas (<u>although</u>), (2) take a stand (<u>nevertheless</u>), and (3) provide evidence (<u>because</u>). If you think it could be useful, try it out.

Other scholars have worked on argument phrasal templates, including the literature professor Erik Simpson, who arrived at a "magic thesis statement" for undergraduate literary essays: "By looking at [x], we can see [y], which most people don't see; this is important because [z]" (2013). Simpson's aim with this template is to help authors arrive at what he considers to be the essence of a good argument: saying something "a little strange." His template is a useful alternative to Posusta's, because it doesn't foreground contradicting previous scholarship.

Other templates exist as well. The authors of the best text for undergraduates on argument present many (Graff and Birkenstein 2014). Scholars in the humanities used to be told to choose two theorists and point out how one is better than the other, or how one has the better idea. You may find it interesting to ask some faculty whether they know of any templates like this in your field.

Belcher's Argument Templates

If Posusta's Instant Thesis Maker doesn't seem to fit what you want to say, here's my version of it for journal articles, to make it allow for more possibilities.

#1. Other scholars debate/argue/assume/ignore [a problem].

#2. In relationship to that debate, argument, assumption, or gap, I argue/demonstrate/suggest/agree that [y is the case],

#3. based on my qualitative study/quantitative study/experiment/archival research/fieldwork/textual analysis of [my evidence].

Likewise, if Simpson's "magic thesis" doesn't quite fit, another, broader variation is

Through my study of [topic], I found that [evidence], which suggests that [idea] is true.

Do any of the preceding templates help me articulate my argument better? If so, what is my argument now?

Argument Drawing

Since argument templates can limit thought, some find that sketching ideas out, diagramming them, or storyboarding them can provide authors a better idea of their argument (Buckley and Waring 2013). You can map or diagram your article by writing down key words or phrases and drawing arrows between them to indicate the relationships between various theories, topics, and texts. You can storyboard it by writing your article out like a cartoon, with panels, characters (e.g., portraying problems as villains taken down by you or other scholars), and thought bubbles. You have several options for performing such an exercise. You can make it social by drawing it on a whiteboard with others. You can use some of the online argument-mapping software (e.g., Rationale or Argunet). Or you can try playing with your ideas below.

Drawing My Argument

Being in Argument Crisis

If you have an argument that you can work with, no matter how weak or awkwardly formulated, you can skip this paragraph. Or if you're a little uncertain about your argument but mostly feel that it's okay, you can skip this paragraph. If, however, you're now certain that you don't have an argument and, further, that the draft you're working on can't support an argument, don't get discouraged! When I present an argument in my workshops, at least 10 percent of the participants sneak up to me afterward and whisper, as if confessing to murder, "I don't have an argument!" That's okay, it happens to the best of us. Truly.

You have a couple of options. I recommend that if you haven't done yet done so, talk with someone in your field about your topic and see whether you can work up an argument with that person. If that doesn't work, I recommend turning to "Week 0: Writing Your Article from Scratch" and trying out the instructions there. That chapter gives information about the mysterious process of where we get our arguments and what motivates them, as well as how to spot opportunities for adding to a discipline and cultivating questions that deserve answers. All scholars, whether experienced or inexperienced, do their work haunted by this mystery.

Am I in argument crisis?   ☐ I think I'm okay ◯ I think I don't have an argument ◯ I'm not sure

If I am, what will I do?

How Do You Make Strong Arguments?

Once you learn to recognize what makes a statement an argument, you can learn how to make strong arguments. Certain aspects of a strong argument are surprising.

When some people hear the word *argument*, they think of two people yelling, with neither person listening to the other or conceding legitimate points. This is exactly the kind of argument you don't want in your article. An argument is about the search for answers through exchange, a way of thinking through a problem. To have a successful argument, you don't need to annihilate scholarly opponents. That is, you don't need a bulletproof argument or unassailable evidence. Most authors know of evidence against their argument and proceed to publish it anyway. A difficult truth is that those issues most worth arguing over almost never have all the evidence on one side or the other. If you have taken up an argument that has no compelling evidence against it, you probably haven't chosen a publishable argument. In the humanities, scholars have often preferred interesting wrong arguments than dull right ones. Frederic Jameson's claim (1986, 69) that "all third world texts are necessarily . . . national allegories" exemplifies a generative wrong argument (it's impossible that all these texts are any one thing).

So one technique for constructing a strong argument is to build in a consideration of opposing voices. Use counterarguments to modify and sharpen your argument. Don't ignore those scholars who have published opposing arguments—cite them. You may want to take them on directly and dismantle the architecture of their side. That's fine. But you don't have to. Indeed, you don't need to cite them at length, attack their ideas wholesale, or nitpick over minute problems in their research to prove your point. Sometimes strong arguments can consist of showing how the other side is wrong, but mostly they consist of showing how you are right. Anticipate and vitiate possible rebuttals to your argument.

Another technique is not just to acknowledge the limits of your argument but to put them to good use. This is a mark of the best academic writers. For instance, one of the articles published in the academic journal I managed, *Aztlán: A Journal of Chicano Studies*, is an excellent example of a confidently written article with a clear argument that does not silence all opposition. In it, Eric Avila (1998) analyzes different communities' views of the Los Angeles freeway. The article has three sections: in the first, Avila argues that Anglos loved the freeway, and in the second that Chicana/os (now Chicanx) hate the freeway for destroying their neighborhood. In the third section, however, he notes a group that doesn't fit his argument—gay Chicanos, who largely love the freeway as a way out of the space of patriarchy. This final section is what makes his article great: he shows where his argument breaks down in an interesting manner. In the social, health, behavioral, and natural science fields, such openness often shows in authors' descriptions of the limitations of their study. The authors analyze their data as supporting their hypothesis, but admit that variations in sample or variables might have delivered a different conclusion.

Novice writers sometimes ask me, "Why would I want to include evidence that weakens my own position?" The answer, as these techniques suggest, is that it makes your article stronger. If you ignore research that conflicts with your claims, you must assume that the reader won't know of that research, a risky assumption at best.

In my own experience, some of my best work has emerged from being uncertain about which side of my argument was right. I published an article queer-reading the lifelong partnership between two seventeenth-century Ethiopian women in an early African text (Belcher 2016). As I wrote, I kept imagining the wildly different responses and interpretations of traditional Ethiopians, queer Ethiopians, queer theorists, and American LGBTIQA activists, taking into account their best points. Now, the most common comment I receive about the article is that it is "persuasive." If so, the validity of opposing points pushed me to make the best argument possible.

Have I built in a consideration of opposing viewpoints?	☐ I think so ◯ I don't think so ◯ I'm not sure
If not, how will I do that?	

How Do You Write an Argument-Driven Article?

Once you have an argument, you're still not done. A problem of many unpublished articles is that they're not argument driven. Sure, such articles may have an argument, and even have one announced early and clearly, but that argument isn't connected to what's going on in the rest of the article. Its relation to the data and evidence remains unarticulated and unclear to the reader. So—and this is extremely important—don't fall into the trap of letting your evidence organize your article rather than your argument about that evidence.

The best advice for avoiding this trap is given by Tim Stowell of the UCLA Linguistics Department. He tells his doctoral students that when writing a journal article, they should write not like a detective collecting evidence but like a lawyer arguing a case. A detective's report is long, documenting all the items found at the crime scene, all the interviews with the dozens of persons somehow related to the crime, and all the suspects considered, and then noting that John Doe was arrested. By contrast, a lawyer's brief states, "I argue that the defendant murdered his partner for the insurance money, based on evidence from ballistics and two eyewitness accounts." The detective's report is organized by evidence; the lawyer's brief is organized by argument. A detective is keenly aware of the incompleteness of the evidence; the lawyer is forced to act based on that incomplete evidence. To write an argument-driven article, think like a lawyer and present evidence that supports your case; cross-examine the evidence that doesn't support your case; ignore evidence that neither contradicts nor supports your case; and make sure that the jury always knows whom you're accusing of what and why. One easy test of whether your article is poorly organized by evidence instead of argument is to review it for the following: (1) it presents every bit of evidence you analyzed to arrive at your conclusion, and/or (2) it presents that evidence in the order you found it. In this case, you've written a report, not a publishable article.

Now of course, when conducting your research, you very much need to be a detective. After all, a strong court case cannot be built on slim or shoddy evidence or a failure to make sense of complicated evidence. But you need to know when to be a detective and when to be a lawyer. So perhaps the best way to put this advice is, "Think like a detective, write like a lawyer."

Let's study an example of this point on a small scale, using different drafts of an abstract that two scholars invented for one article. As you can see, the first abstract is organized by the evidence and the second by the argument (Swales and Feak 2004, 282–83). Notice how much easier it is to read and understand the second version.

Evidence organized. A count of sentence connectors in 12 academic papers produced 70 different connectors. These varied in frequency from 62 tokens (*however*) to single occurrences. Seventy-five percent of the 467 examples appeared in sentence-initial position. However, individual connectors varied considerably in position reference. Some (e.g., *in addition*) always occurred initially; in other cases (e.g., *for example, therefore*), they were placed after the subject more than 50% of the time. These findings suggest that a search for general rules for connector position may not be fruitful.

Argument organized. Although sentence connectors are a well-recognized feature of academic writing, little research has been undertaken on their positioning. In this study, we analyze the position of 467 connectors found in a sample of 12 research papers. Seventy-five percent of the connectors occurred at the beginning of sentences. However, individual connectors varied greatly in positional preference. Some, such as *in addition*, only occurred initially; others, such as *therefore*, occurred initially in only 40% of the cases. These preliminary findings suggest that general rules for connector position may prove elusive.

Both abstracts state the argument, but only one is argument driven. The strong second abstract is well organized, announcing its topic and significance in the first sentence, its method in the second sentence, its findings in the three following sentences, and its argument that sentence connectors likely do not have general rules in the last sentence. The weak first abstract is not well organized—providing no context, reams of unexplained data, and an unconnected argument. It is organized by the evidence. Now, imagine having to read article upon article organized as this abstract is. Welcome to a journal editor's life! Many submissions come in that are organized by evidence, not argument. As a result, you can make a huge difference in your publication rate by organizing your article around your argument.

Why is this a common problem? People analyzing texts or conducting ethnographic field studies are particularly likely to write evidence-organized articles. That's because the evidence is more real to these authors than their analysis of it. If you admire a canonical author or artist, you may spend much of your article just summarizing the many beauties of that person's creations. If you spent a year as a participant-observer in a village or a corporation, it seems incredibly reductive to pick some argument and force your evidence to fit that tiny glass slipper. You have dozens of hours of recordings, thousands of hours of observation, and more insights than a lifetime's worth of communication. Such authors when told, "Your article is evidence organized!" often plaintively respond, "But you just don't understand! I have to represent all the extraordinary things about this author/artist/village/corporation. And besides, it took me three months to transcribe these recordings, because voice recognition couldn't deal with the language or accent—it cost me so much time that I've got to use as much of it as I can!" But publishable articles are argumentative, not representative. Don't represent all the information you have collected and abandon the reader to making the links. Evidence must be subordinated.

When I make this point about not writing evidence-organized articles, my social science students sometimes counter with the anthropologist Clifford Geertz's famous insistence on "thick description." A student will say, "In my field, it's okay to give a lot of description in a journal article." I always counter by saying, "Fine; bring me one published in the last year in a US journal." No one has been able to do that yet. And experts have long warned against evidence-organized articles, even Geertz, in his very article about "thick description":

> The claim to attention of an ethnographic account does not rest on its authors' ability to capture primitive facts in faraway places and carry them home like a mask or a carving, but on the degree to which he is able to clarify what goes on in such places, to reduce the puzzlement—what manner of men are these? . . . It is not worth it, as Thoreau said, to go round the world to count the cats in Zanzibar. (Geertz 1973, 16)

So, don't count the cats in Zanzibar. Don't include streams of data without providing any argument. Make sure that your ideas about your evidence are organizing the article, not the evidence itself.

Is my article argument organized?	☐ I think so ○ I don't think so ○ I'm not sure
If not, how will I do that?	

Arguments against Argument

Scholars occasionally tell me that authors in their field don't need to have an argument. Rather, they can explore a series of questions without favoring any answers. Here is my response: use of the phrase "I argue that" has seen a spectacular increase in books ever since 1965, almost doubling in frequency every year, according to Google Books Ngram Viewer. Doubling. Every year. Whatever was true in the past is true no longer. A few social, health, behavioral, and natural science articles may not state an argument in their introduction, but nowadays almost all of them state the argument in their abstract—which is as early as you can get! Further, just because an argument is stated as a question doesn't mean it isn't an argument. Often, the phrasing of the question is argumentative, and it's clear from the outset what the answer is likely to be. For instance, let's say the question posed in an article's introduction is, "Do US students who retain their immigrant culture have lower school leaving rates?" The positive words *retain* and *lower* signal the argument. In the humanities, it can get a bit trickier. In heavily theoretical fields, a premium is placed on asking questions and opening up possibilities rather than tying them off neatly with definitive answers. But many questions are simply masked arguments. Insisting that some text or moment cannot be reduced is often the argument.

ORGANIZING YOUR ARTICLE AROUND YOUR ARGUMENT

Having an argument and stating it early and clearly is essential. So how do you ensure that you have one?

Day 1 Tasks: Reading the Workbook

On the first day of your second writing week, read the week 2 chapter up to this page. Writing directly in the boxes provided or your own document, answer all the questions posed, including those asking you to test your statement to see whether it actually is an argument, and to modify your argument as you go along.

Tracking Writing Time

Each day, use the Calendar for Actual Time Spent Writing This Week form (or digital time-tracking software) to keep track of the time you spent writing this week. (If you want, use separate symbols or colors for time spent writing your article, reading and completing the exercises in this book, discussing your article, and writing other academic works such as books, theses, or conference papers.) Then, at the end of the week, evaluate how you spent your time.

If busy, at least mark the check boxes with how long you wrote today. ☐ 15+ min. ☐ 30+ ☐ 60+ ☐ 120+

WEEK 2, DAYS 2-5: READING AND TASKS

Day 2 Tasks: Testing Out Your Argument

Today you'll try out your argument on other people, as a successful argument must persuade others.

1. **Revisit the argument you constructed yesterday.** Do you still like it? Do you still think it passes most of the tests? If you need to revise it a bit, do so now and record it in the box (print or electronic) below.

   My Argument

   In this article, I argue that

Now, thinking like a lawyer, not a detective, write a short list of your evidence. The list doesn't have to be detailed; just list what you are bringing to bear to support your argument.

My Evidence

2. **Share your argument with others.** Find at least two people to whom you can state your argument—out loud if possible, by email if not. You can send them the bare statement of the argument, or you can send your abstract or introduction if you have stated it there clearly. One of your reviewers should be someone in your field; the other should be someone outside it. If your reviewers say that someone else has already made your argument, ask them for a specific citation. It's not very common to make the exact same argument as someone else. In particular, professors can be dismissive, stating that something has "been done to death" or that "nobody wants to hear about that anymore," when in fact it's a new field targeting dated theories to which professors are wedded. Often, such dismissals are code for "I don't like this new trend." If you get such a response, be sure to get a second opinion. Sometimes it's a general opinion, sometimes it isn't.

Reviewers' Comments on my Argument

3. **Revise your argument based on your reviewers' responses.** You don't need to perfect it, just get it as clear as you can at this point. Often, the writing process is a feedback loop over these twelve weeks, with your argument changing as you shape your article, and your article changing as you shape the argument. That's fine. But having clarity about your argument is essential at every step of the journey, even if, or especially if, that argument changes radically over the course of revision. I have written articles where my argument changed constantly during the writing process, getting locked down only in the final draft of the article. By clearly articulating my argument at each stage, I could test out that version and identify its limits. So a shifting argument is not a problem but a sign of dedicated thought.

Tracking Writing Time

Mark your electronic calendar, the Calendar for Actual Time Spent Writing This Week form, and/or the check boxes here with how long you wrote today. ☐ 15+ min. ☐ 30+ ☐ 60+ ☐ 120+

Day 3 Tasks: Reviewing Your Article for Argument

Today you'll take one of two paths, depending on how much you changed your argument.

New Argument

Many people radically alter their argument while completing the exercises in this chapter. If you did that, you already know that the new argument is not informing the paper draft with which you came to this workbook—but you don't need to go through it sentence by sentence at this time. Rather, a good step to take today is to work on drafting a new, very rough introduction and a new, very rough outline. The point here is not to come up with publishable prose but to reorient your brain around the new argument. Once you've done that, you can read through your article to remind yourself of the evidence and the theoretical frame, and see which parts can be salvaged as is and which need to be discarded and rewritten. If you want, you can use the exercises for altered arguments below as a guide for rereading your article.

If my argument is new, do I need to work on a new intro and outline?	◯ Yes ☐ No ◯ I'm not sure
Also, do I need to discard or rewrite parts of the body?	◯ Yes ☐ No ◯ I'm not sure

Altered Argument

If your argument stayed the same or didn't alter that much, follow the steps below. You need to make sure that your article is more like a lawyer's brief than a detective's report. If the paper draft you're working on is short (e.g., conference-paper length), use the questions below to think through how you can "build out" your article. Also, sometimes it can be difficult to see the answers to these questions on your own. Feel free to share your article with another writer, and ask for help to answer these questions.

Print out your article. This exercise works best if your article is in a locked form, where you can mark it but not change it. This tactic aids you in stepping back from your article, giving you a wider view so you can focus on broader solutions, not line editing. For me, that means printing the article out on paper and using pens or highlighters in various colors. For you, that might mean converting the article into a PDF and marking it up with a stylus on a tablet. If neither of those options works for you, you can mark your electronic document using your computer's Text Highlight Color and Comments tools, but try to defamiliarize your article by viewing it at 50 percent size or in a different font than usual. Once you have your article in locked form, you're ready to complete the following tasks:

Highlight your argument. Using a highlighter in yellow or another bright color, highlight sentences where your argument appears. Then flip through the article slowly. How often does yellow appear? You should see yellow in your introduction, at the beginning and/or end of some paragraphs, and in your conclusion. If you have gone four to five pages without any reference to the argument, you need to revise. Mark the areas where you can do that.

Does my highlighting reveal that my argument disappears?	○ Yes ☐ No ○ I'm not sure

Make sure that the main point comes first. Read your paragraphs and determine whether the main point of the information in each paragraph regularly appears only at the end or not at all. If so, you have an article organized by the evidence. We readers should learn no fact without knowing why we are learning it. The principle is point first, evidence second. On your draft, use arrows (↑) to indicate where you need to drag your point up to the beginning of a paragraph or to handwrite an inserted point.

Do my paragraphs regularly lack clearly stated overarching points?	○ Yes ☐ No ○ I'm not sure

Check for "early and clearly." Read until you reach the statement of your argument. It should appear within the first three pages of the article. A journal editor told me that if he doesn't find an argument stated within the first four pages of a submission, he reads no further and automatically rejects it. He told me that's being generous; an editorial friend of his rejects articles if no argument has been stated by the end of the third paragraph. If your article doesn't state your argument early and clearly, figure out the earliest point where you could state it, and move the argument there. Often, you need to do some restructuring of the introduction to make that happen. Then ask yourself how clear your statement of the argument is. If it isn't clear, handwrite in a clearer version.

Does my argument fail to appear within the first three pages or paragraphs?	○ Yes ☐ No ○ I'm not sure

Refine the introduction. Read your introduction. Does it unnecessarily delay your argument? Moving background material (i.e., material some but not all readers will need) to its own section, with a clear heading, is often a good solution. Alternately, does your article start right in on evidence? In other words, does it lack an introduction? That means you have an article organized by the evidence. Handwrite in what material you'll need for an introduction.

Does background material or evidence clutter my introduction?	○ Yes ☐ No ○ I'm not sure

Organize the body properly. Read the body of your article. If you have divided your article into sections that mirror the chapters of your literary subject, or the chronology of related events, or the order in which you came across the information, it's highly likely that your article is organized by the evidence. You need to organize your evidence according to what you want to argue about it, not how the evidence itself is organized. If the body is organized by the evidence, consider how you might reorganize it. Mark in which paragraphs you need to move, rewrite, or drop. As you go along, also ask whether the evidence you present supports your argument. If any of it doesn't, delete those portions and handwrite in whether you'll need new evidence or an argument.

Does the evidence rather than the argument organize my article?	○ Yes ☐ No ○ I'm not sure

Refine the conclusion. Read your conclusion. If you don't have one, handwrite in some thoughts on what it might say. If you do have one, does your argument appear there, or does it disappear? If it disappears, handwrite it in. Finally, is the argument you stated in your conclusion the same as that in your introduction? It's common for the statements of the argument in the introduction and conclusion to vary so much as to contradict each other. Make sure you standardize them—the words don't have to be the same, but the concept of the argument should be.

Does my article lack a conclusion containing an argument, or does the argument in the conclusion contravene my earlier statements of it?	○ Yes ☐ No ○ I'm not sure

If you answered yes to any of the questions above, you have some revising to do. Follow the accompanying instructions.

Tracking Writing Time

Mark your electronic calendar, the Calendar for Actual Time Spent Writing This Week form, and/or the check boxes here with how long you wrote today. ☐ 15+ min. ☐ 30+ ☐ 60+ ☐ 120+

Days 4–5 Tasks: Revising Your Article around Your Argument

Today and tomorrow, you will revise your article around your argument, using your notes from day 3 and your answers to the questions on day 1 to scaffold your revision. This process can take some real time, but if done well, it can cut your time in later chapters.

Often, when you start revising for argument, you find that your argument shifts subtly as you work through your evidence. That's fine. Your argument will continue to take shape over the twelve weeks, so this is not a final effort. You can work on argument a bit every week if necessary.

Arrange Next Week's Meetings

If you're not meeting once a week to discuss this workbook with classmates, a writing group, or a writing partner, email an academic friend about setting up two appointments next week to discuss your article and abstract respectively. You will need thirty to sixty minutes for each meeting, one of which will happen on your first writing day next week, the other on your fifth writing day.

With whom should I discuss my
topic and abstract next week?
When is this person available?

Tracking Writing Time

Mark your electronic calendar, the Calendar for Actual Time Spent Writing This Week form, and/or the check boxes here with how long you wrote both days. ☐ 15+ min. ☐ 30+ ☐ 60+ ☐ 120+

Then, here at the end of your workweek, take pride in your accomplishments. If you planned to have a top writing week and instead had a poor writing week, compliment yourself anyway. A week with any writing is a good week. Then evaluate what patterns you might change to do a little better.

DOCUMENTING YOUR WRITING TIME AND TASKS

Calendar for Actual Time Spent Writing This Week

Time	Day 1	Day 2	Day 3	Day 4	Day 5	Day 6	Day 7
5:00 a.m.							
6:00							
7:00							
8:00							
9:00							
10:00							
11:00							
12:00 p.m.							
1:00							
2:00							
3:00							
4:00							
5:00							
6:00							
7:00							
8:00							
9:00							
10:00							
11:00							
12:00 a.m.							
1:00							
2:00							
3:00							
4:00							
Total minutes							
Tasks completed							

WEEK 3
Abstracting Your Article

Task Day	Week 3 Daily Writing Tasks	Estimated Task Time in Minutes	
		HumInt	SciQua
Day 1 (Monday?)	Read from here until you reach the week 3, day 2 tasks, filling in any boxes, checking off any forms, and answering any questions as you read.	60	60
Day 2 (Tuesday?)	Read others' strong abstracts, and draft your own abstract.	120+	90
Day 3 (Wednesday?)	Find and study one (or two) strong article(s) in your field.	120+	90+
Day 4 (Thursday?)	Find and study articles to cite in your article.	120+	90+
Day 5 (Friday?)	Get a colleague's feedback on your abstract; revise your abstract accordingly.	60	60
Total estimated time for reading the workbook, completing the tasks, and writing your article		**8+ hours**	**5.5+ hours**

Above are the tasks for your third week. Make sure to start this week by scheduling when you will write, and then tracking the time you actually spend writing (using the Calendar for Actual Time Spent Writing This Week form or online software).

Group work. If you're going through the workbook with others (such as in a class or with a partner), work together on the two tasks this week that depend on your talking and exchanging with others. Since they're scheduled for different days, you can decide which task you'll complete on your meeting day.

Individual work. If you're going through the workbook on your own, last week you were to have contacted one or two people whom you trust to provide feedback on days 1 and 5 of this week. If you haven't done that yet, follow the instructions when you get to the day 1 task in this chapter.

WEEK 3, DAY 1: READING AND TASKS

SECOND WEEK IN REVIEW

If you didn't get as much writing done last week as you hoped, join the club. Very few scholars ever feel that they've done enough. Whether you spent long hours working and don't have much to show for it, or you procrastinated when you had every intention of getting a lot accomplished, avoid feeling guilty and start this new week afresh. After all, you have twelve weeks to get it right! If you managed to fit in fifteen minutes to an hour of academic writing most days—congratulations! You're doing great. If this is the first time you've been writing as a daily practice, you're well on your way to making writing a habit.

No matter what happened with your writing last week, take five minutes now to jot down what you've learned so far about making time for writing. What aided or hindered your writing goals? What were the challenges? What worked? Did you find any solutions? (Remember that you can check out the "Solutions to Common Academic Writing Obstacles" at wendybelcher.com.) What could you continue to do or start doing this week to make time for writing? Was your writing plan for last week realistic or unrealistic? Making this task social helps you absorb these lessons—so email or text someone about what you've learned.

Lessons to Be Learned from My Past Week's Writing Experiences

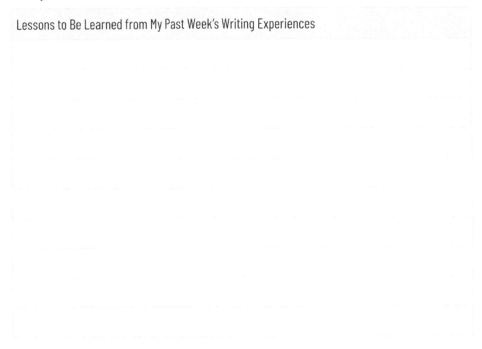

In the first week, you identified your feelings about the writing experience. You learned what makes for a successful academic writer, and you selected the paper you will work on revising. You set a realistic writing goal. In week 2, you learned the myths about what it takes to get published, and the reality that a publishable research article needs to link the new and the old. Most of all, you focused on what an argument is and why it's essential to your success as an academic writer. Finally, you worked on making a list of revision tasks and revising your article around your argument. In other words, you established where you are, where you want to go, and how to get there. This week, you'll study how to use abstracts to conceptualize your article.

ABSTRACTS AS A TOOL FOR SUCCESS

One of the best early tasks you can undertake to improve your journal article is to write an abstract—something that describes your article's topic and argument. In fact, one scholar published an article about how she dramatically improved her writing productivity after learning from this workbook "to write the abstract first," as the task became "the anchor and catalyst for the framing and reframing of writing goals" (Linder et al. 2014, 223). Unfortunately, many scholars see writing an abstract as the *last* step to publication. In the humanities, they may never have to write one! But writing an abstract, regardless of whether journals in your field require one, is an important step in revising your article, not a mere formality. More than one authority has noted that "a well-prepared abstract can be the most important paragraph in your article" (APA 2010, 26).

    Why is writing a good abstract so important?

Solving problems. The act of writing an abstract helps you clarify in your own mind what your article is about. Since an abstract is a miniature version of your article—anywhere from 50 to 400 words, with an average length of 120 words in the social science fields, 150 in the humanities (Lauer-Busch 2014, 48), and 260 in the medical and health sciences—it provides you with the opportunity to distill your ideas and identify the most important ones. It also serves as a diagnostic tool: if you can't write a brief abstract of your article, then your article may lack focus. Finally, it helps you face the problems you'll have to solve in the article itself.

Connecting with editors. Editors who receive a clearly written abstract—allowing them to skim an article—can make quicker and better decisions about whether an article fits their journal's mandates and is worth sending out for peer review. In addition, they can more easily identify the best potential peer reviewers for an article. Or, to put this reality in negative terms, editors often reject an article after reading its abstract alone (Langdon-Neuner 2008, 84). You need to get it right.

Connecting with peer reviewers. When editors ask peer reviewers to indicate their willingness to review an article, most editors attach its title and abstract alone to that email, not the entire article. Thus, your crafting an intriguing abstract is essential to enticing busy scholars to commit to reviewing your article. A weak abstract does the opposite, enabling busy scholars to justify saving their writing time for their own work and refusing to peer-review. Faculty members are neither paid nor obligated by their institutions to write peer reviews, so they do need to be enticed.

Getting found. Most articles are published with abstracts these days, in part because such articles are cited twice as often as those having no abstract (Petherbridge and Cotropia 2014, 23). Most of the time, the abstract is the only part of an article that readers will find online, because most journals place their published articles behind paywalls. Consequently, keywords and proper nouns embedded in your abstract provide an important electronic path to your article for researchers who wouldn't find your work based on its title alone.

Getting read. Your abstract is essential to persuading busy scholars to read your article. It communicates the article's importance and demonstrates whether reading it will add to the scholars' knowledge. It helps potential readers decide whether your methodology is suitable enough or your approach fresh enough to merit the time to read your article instead of the dozens or hundreds of others published on the topic. Your abstract needs to hook the reader, not merely report on your research.

Getting cited. Many readers will never examine more than your abstract—owing to either lack of time and energy or paywalls. In fact, more than one person may cite your article based on reading your abstract alone. (One study estimated that only 20 percent of people who cited an article had read it [Simkin and Roychowdhury 2002].) So, unethical as it sounds, you want to provide an abstract so good that someone could cite your article with accuracy based on that abstract alone. For instance, a scholar writing an article about the efficacy of the women's environmental movement in Senegal may want to state in passing that scholars have published many more articles about the efficacy of a similar movement in Kenya. If your article is about the Kenyan movement, you want that scholar to be able to find and cite your article based solely on your abstract.

INGREDIENTS OF A GOOD ABSTRACT

An abstract is a condensed version of your article, a distillation of its most important information. Common strengths unite good abstracts; common problems plague even published ones. Applied linguists and rhetoricians have studied these strengths, the typical rhetorical "moves" used in a variety of academic genres, including abstracts (Huckin 2001; Swales and Feak 2009, 2010, 2012). Below are some of the main lessons to be gleaned from this diverse research about abstracts. Don't worry; you won't need to memorize these lessons, because there will be a checklist later. For now, just become acquainted with them.
　　An abstract should

- Summarize the article, not introduce it. Novice authors often write abstracts as if they were introductions. Don't—that's what introductions are for.
- Tell a story. State the puzzle or problem that the article is addressing, rather than giving a barrage of data without an argument or a conclusion.
- State the argument and a claim for the significance of that argument.
- Reveal the most valuable findings. People are more likely to read an article if they know what's most interesting about it up front.
- State methods briefly, in no more than a sentence. Don't let your description of how you conducted the study or developed your theoretical frame take over the abstract.
- Use strong verbs, not vague ones. Instead of "exploring" or "examining" a subject, your abstract "argues" or "demonstrates." Instead of "attempts to" or "tries to," your abstract "shows." (One journal editor told me that if she sees the word *explores* anywhere in an abstract, it's a red flag, suggesting that the article is not argumentative.)
- Include all the most relevant keywords, since many search engines search by abstract and title alone.

- Be a self-contained <u>whole</u>. Don't include anything in the abstract that is not self-explanatory; it should make sense to people in your field without their reading the whole article. (This is often difficult to determine on your own; you need others to read your abstract and tell you whether it passes muster.)

- Report what you did do (the <u>past</u>), not what you hope to do (the <u>future</u>). Your abstract should not read like a plan. It should not include statements like "we hope to prove." Those are okay in grant proposals or conference paper proposals but not in a research article abstract, which is a report on a completed study.

Then, for most (but not all) journals,

- Don't include <u>footnotes</u>.
- Don't include <u>citations</u>.
- Don't include <u>quotations</u>.
- Don't include abbreviations, symbols, or <u>acronyms</u>—instead, spell out all terms.

The following sections provide information about abstracts in different metadisciplines. If you're in the humanities, you could skip to your section; but I recommend that you read the next section, because the SciQua fields provide the most assistance in understanding the basic nature of abstracts.

Good SciQua Abstracts

If you're in the social, health, behavioral, or natural sciences or in certain cases a professional school, you're fortunate to have prescribed formulas for writing journal article abstracts. However, trends in scientific abstracts are always changing—perhaps the now rare "graphical abstract" (a single pictorial summary of the article) or five-minute "audio abstract" will become popular (Hartley 2014). Some journals are even asking authors to articulate the main point of their article in a tweet of just 280 characters as a way of encouraging them "to think about the dissemination of their papers when they submit them" (Else 2015). For now, two abstract formulas are common: structured and unstructured.

Sciqua Structured Abstracts

Many journals in experimental or quantitative fields have now moved to a structured abstract format, in which the journal provides five to eight subheadings that structure the order of and information in the abstract. Researchers have grouped the hundred most common subheadings found in structured abstracts under the five most common subheadings; these five they call metacategories: background, objective, method, results, and discussion/conclusion, in that order (Hartley 2014; Ripple et al. 2011; NLM 2015). Authors must provide a sentence or two for each subheading, which thus ensures that all abstracts omit no basic information. Such abstracts are generally longer than traditional ones, serving as more of a précis. According to research, both authors and readers like structured abstracts, as the standardized pattern makes them easier to write and read (Hartley 2014). Therefore, journals are increasingly likely to use them.

Even if you aren't in a field that requires structured abstracts, their standardized pattern can aid you in writing a strong abstract. I have yet to find the perfect abstract, but the structured nature of the following one—on the topic of common words in journal article abstracts—makes the article easy to find, easy to read, and easy to cite:

SciQua Structured Abstract Example

Vinkers, Christiaan H., Joeri K. Tijdink, and Willem M. Otte. 2015. "Use of Positive and Negative Words in Scientific PubMed Abstracts between 1974 and 2014: Retrospective Analysis." *British Medical Journal* 351:h6467.

Objective: To investigate whether language used in science abstracts can skew towards the use of strikingly positive and negative words over time.

Design: Retrospective analysis of all scientific abstracts in PubMed between 1974 and 2014.

Methods: The yearly frequencies of positive, negative, and neutral words (25 preselected words in each category), plus 100 randomly selected words were normalised for the total number of abstracts. Subanalyses included pattern quantification of individual words, specificity for selected high impact journals, and comparison between author affiliations within or outside countries with English as the official majority language. Frequency patterns were compared with 4% of all books ever printed and digitised by use of Google Books Ngram Viewer.

Main outcome measures: Frequencies of positive and negative words in abstracts compared with frequencies of words with a neutral and random connotation, expressed as relative change since 1980.

Results: The absolute frequency of positive words increased from 2.0% (1974–80) to 17.5% (2014), a relative increase of 880% over four decades. All 25 individual positive words contributed to the increase, particularly the words "robust," "novel," "innovative," and "unprecedented," which increased in relative frequency up to 15 000%. Comparable but less pronounced results were obtained when restricting the analysis to selected journals with high impact factors. Authors affiliated to an institute in a non-English speaking country used significantly more positive words. Negative word frequencies increased from 1.3% (1974–80) to 3.2% (2014), a relative increase of 257%. Over the same time period, no apparent increase was found in neutral or random word use, or in the frequency of positive word use in published books.

Conclusions: Our lexicographic analysis indicates that scientific abstracts are currently written with more positive and negative words, and provides an insight into the evolution of scientific writing. Apparently, scientists look on the bright side of research results. But whether this perception fits reality should be questioned. (Vinkers, Tijdink, and Otte 2015)

This clear, useful abstract does what it should—provide basic information about why and how the authors conducted their study and what they found.

SciQua Nonstructured Abstracts

So let's say you're in a social, health, or behavioral science field that doesn't require a structured abstract (or you aren't sure whether the journal to which you will ultimately send your article will require it). How do you go about writing your abstract? Almost no journal with traditional abstracts will allow you a three-hundred-word abstract, the length of the structured abstract example above. Yours will have to be shorter. But you can use the metacategories above to write a solid abstract. Let's look at a nonstructured abstract on inequality that exemplifies making each of these metacategory statements. The numbers in the abstract are mine, added at the beginning of each sentence to make my discussion of the abstract easier for you to follow.

SciQua Nonstructured Abstract Example

Snipp, C. Matthew, and Sin Yi Cheung. 2016. "Changes in Racial and Gender Inequality since 1970." *The ANNALS of the American Academy of Political and Social Science* 663 (1): 80–98.

> [1] [In the United States,] the decades following 1970 to the present were an important period because they marked an era in which measures such as Affirmative Action were introduced to improve opportunities for American minorities and women. [2] Ironically, this also was a period when income inequality dramatically increased in the United States. [3] We analyze Census data from 1970 to 2009 to assess whether inequality in the earnings received by women and minorities has changed in this period. [4] We find a complicated set of results. Racial inequalities persist though to a lesser extent than they did four decades earlier. Asian workers in particular have seen improvements and a lessening of inequality relative to White workers. Gender inequality also persists, though more in some groups than others. [5] Overall, the results of this study underscore the persistence of racial and gender inequality in the United States. (Snipp and Cheung 2016)

Note the efficient structure of this 150-word abstract. The first (1) sentence provides background (the United States has been working toward more equity for people of color and women). The second (2) sentence names a puzzle that the article aims to resolve (the incongruous rise in both opportunity and income inequality), and hints at the objective (looking at earnings inequality in the United States by race and gender). The third (3) sentence describes the method (quantitative analysis of census data) and the topic or question of the article (has earnings inequality in the United States by race and gender lessened?). The fourth (4) sentence presents the results (inequality has diminished for some and not for others). The fifth (5) sentence provides the discussion/conclusion (earnings inequality in the United States by race and gender persists).

To get you started on writing an abstract for your social, health, behavioral, or natural science article, jot down some notes (not full sentences; that will come later) for each metacategory in the form on the next page. If you already have an abstract, use this form to test its soundness.

My SciQua Article Abstract Form

Background/problem: State why I embarked on the project—often some reference to a gap or debate in the literature or a real-world situation or problem.

Objective/aim: State what my project/study was intending to figure out, the topic of the article.

Method/design: State how I accomplished the project; name my data and methodology.

Results/findings: State what I found through the project, my findings.

Conclusions/discussion: State what conclusions I draw from the project, my argument (and recommendations, if that is appropriate).

Keywords: List the keywords or search terms that I definitely want to appear in my abstract.

Good HumInt Abstracts

Humanities and interpretive social science journals are less likely to publish abstracts, but abstracts are still a useful tool for thinking through your article and succeeding in the peer-review process. Your challenge is that HumInt abstracts have much less in common with one another than do SciQua abstracts. In other words, HumInt scholars have more latitude in what information they put in their abstract and how they structure it. This freedom can feel onerous if you like formulas. Fortunately, a solid HumInt abstract has some basic ingredients. It should name the subject under discussion, perhaps give a little background, name some evidence, at least hint at the theoretical framework, make a claim for significance, and state the argument. Let's look at an effective published humanities abstract (written by a graduate student) to get a better sense of those ingredients. The numbers in the abstract are mine, added at the beginning of each sentence to make the discussion of the abstract easier for you to follow.

Humint Abstract Example

Schine, Rachel. 2017. "Conceiving the Pre-Modern Black-Arab Hero: On the Gendered Production of Racial Difference in *Sīrat al-amīrah dhāt al-himmah*." *Journal of Arabic Literature* 48 (3): 298–326.

[1] ʿAbd al-Wahhāb's character in *Sīrat al-amīrah dhāt al-himmah* is but one example of a black hero who figures prominently in a *sīrah shaʿbiyyah*, or popular heroic cycle, the earliest references to which appear in the twelfth century and several of which remain in circulation today. [2] Like several of his counterparts, not only is he black, but he is also alone among his relatives in being so. [3] The explanation supplied in the text of his mother Fāṭimah's eponymous sīrah for his "spontaneous" phenotypic deviation makes use of rhetoric also found in various antecedent and near-contemporary *belles-lettres* sources. [4] Placing ʿAbd al-Wahhāb's case within the context of this literary network illuminates a series of questions concerning the semiotics of race in pre-twelfth-century Arabo-Muslim literature, racially inflected anxieties about control of feminine sexuality, and pre-genetic syntheses of racial and reproductive "sciences." [5] This paper concludes that ʿAbd al-Wahhāb's blackness is produced through a set of scientific and speculative discourses that go beyond the prominent theories of climate influences and Hamitic genealogy, and that posit instead a racial determinacy that occurs spontaneously, regardless of geography or lineage, through a variety of interventions from and against the maternal body. [6] These include the contamination of seminal fluid, "image-imprinting," and divine fiat. [7] The concentration of these theories within a single text makes ʿAbd al-Wahhāb's conception narrative a uniquely apt ground for discussing the broader complex of issues of gender and race in pre-modern Arabic literature.

This is an unusually strong published abstract. The first (1) sentence thoroughly introduces the <u>subject</u> (the text *Sīrat al-amīrah dhāt al-himmah*) and its <u>context</u>, commendably communicating in a short space the text's period, language, and genre (a twelfth-century Arabic language cycle). The second (2) and third (3) sentences specify the <u>evidence</u> under discussion (a black character in this premodern cycle) and the text's intellectual <u>context</u> (its sources and literary network). The fourth (4) sentence gives the <u>theoretical framework</u> (race and gender studies). The fifth (5) sentence declares the <u>argument</u> (blackness in medieval Arabic texts was theorized as due to not climate or genetics but the mother's actions). The sixth (6) sentence provides some specificity regarding the <u>argument</u> (how the mother shapes race). The seventh (7) sentence makes a <u>claim for the significance</u> of the text (it uniquely aids understanding of race and gender in this period). This abstract does everything it should and makes clear the benefit the reader will gain by reading it.

To get you started on writing an abstract for your humanities article, jot down some notes (not full sentences; that will come later) for each guideline in the form on the next page. Don't worry if you leave some parts of this form blank; just put down what you know now.

My HumInt Article Abstract Form

Background/context: Give information about the historical period, the geographic region, the social conditions surrounding the human creations I investigated

Subject: Name the human creations I discussed, their genres, creators, and dates

Claim for significance: Make an announcement about the importance of my subject or my approach to it

Theoretical framework: Suggest the theory I used to discuss the subject, such as feminist or psychoanalytic approaches

Argument: State what my analysis of the subject revealed about the subject, current approaches to the subject, or society

Evidence: Describe my evidence for the argument about the subject, or the elements of the subject I analyzed (e.g., types of textual passages)

Keywords: List the keywords or search terms that I definitely want to appear in my abstract

CRAFTING AN EFFECTIVE ABSTRACT

Day 1 Tasks: Talking Your Way to Clarity about Your Article

On the first day of your third writing week, read this week 3 chapter all the way through until you get to week 3, day 2, answering all the questions posed. Write directly in the boxes provided or in your own document. Also, use the daily writing calendar to schedule your writing time in advance, and then start tracking when you actually wrote.

Your task today aids you in writing a better abstract by helping you attain a clearer sense of audience. Since this is a social assignment, you'll need someone to work with; you were to have set up a meeting with this person last week if you're not meeting automatically in a class or group. A virtual meeting is okay, but emailing or texting won't suffice—you need to talk this through. If the social aspect of this assignment makes you queasy, try to think of the simplest action you could take to satisfy it. Maybe you already discussed the article with someone; if you can recall quite well what you both said about the article, use that in completing the box that follows. Or, if you're having a meal with someone in the next twenty-four hours, describe your article then, even if this person isn't an academic. Or call a friend or a relative and start the conversation by complaining about the assignment; sometimes that can get you over the hump and into the assignment. As a last resort, talk aloud about the article to yourself. The *talking* part is vital.

1. **Describe**. Tell your chosen interlocutor about your article. Start with, "My article is about . . ." or "I am writing . . . ," and follow with a description. Take as much time as you need. Try to give the other person a real sense of your topic, approach, findings, and argument. When you have finished describing the article or idea, ask your listener to relay back to you what they understood you to say, commenting on what was intriguing or unclear. Take notes during this recap, since they can yield improved language for your abstract.

2. **Summarize**. Once your interlocutor has commented, again describe your article, but more succinctly this time. Distill your article into no more than three or four sentences, as if you were giving a brief presentation of your work during an introduction at a conference or chatting in the elevator to an academic you just met.

3. **Write**. Once you've finished summarizing, pick up a pen and use the box below to write one or two sentences starting with "My article is about" or "I am writing." (If you're on the phone with your interlocutor, don't wait to hang up. Do it right then. If you want, you could ask your interlocutor to write down one sentence about your article as well.) The point of the exercise is to get to the clearest, briefest statement of the value and point of the article, and burn off what's not important. It may also help you to sharpen your argument.

What My Article Is About

How did it make you feel to say aloud what you're doing? Did your description change? How? What are the implications for the revision of your article?

What I Learned by Doing This Exercise

By the way, this whole exercise counts as writing time. So congratulations on getting some good writing done!

Setting a Realistic Daily Writing and Article Submission Goal

In week 1, day 3, you had a choice of whether to set up your article submission date then or wait until later. If you didn't do it then, today is a good day to go back and do that, now that you have a better sense of how many hours a week you're working and what level of revision your article needs. Review the section titled "Setting a Realistic Daily Writing and Article Submission Goal" in week 1, day 2.

Tracking Writing Time

Each day, use the Calendar for Actual Time Spent Writing This Week form (or digital time-tracking software) to keep track of the time you spent writing this week. (If you want, you can use separate symbols or colors for time spent writing your article, reading and completing the exercises in this book, discussing your article, and writing other academic works such as books, theses, or conference papers.) Then, at the end of the week, evaluate how you spent your time.

If busy, at least mark the check boxes with how long you wrote today. ☐ 15+ min. ☐ 30+ ☐ 60+ ☐ 120+

WEEK 3, DAYS 2-5: READING AND TASKS

Day 2 Tasks: Reading Others' Abstracts and Drafting Your Own

Today you'll read abstracts and then draft your own as part of getting a better handle on your topic. I know it seems backward to write an abstract now, at such an early stage, but it will help, I promise! The purpose is not to force you to draft the perfect abstract or to lock down your ideas, but to enable you to try out your article-sustaining ideas in a small space before you focus on them in the large space of your article.

1. **Read ten abstracts published in your field in the last year.** Go online to the websites of three or four journals in your field and read the most recently published abstracts. Study how they operate. In the SciQua abstract, does it include sentences about the study's or project's background, objective, method, results, and discussion/conclusion? In the HumInt abstract, does it name the subject under discussion, at least hint at the theoretical framework, perhaps give a little background, make a claim for significance, name some evidence, and state the argument? In particular, how do these abstracts open? What do they always say? What are their strengths? What are their weaknesses? If the workbook's advice contradicts what you found in all ten abstracts in your field, follow the abstracts, not the workbook.

What I Learned by Studying Recent Abstracts

2. **Draft or revise your abstract.** Do so by following the directions for writing your abstract that appear earlier in this chapter. For now, aim for an abstract of two hundred words or less. Don't worry about whether your abstract is short enough for a journal to publish. The point here is to draft a mini-version of your article—you can shorten the abstract later.

3. **Use the checklist to identify weaknesses.** Read each requirement in the checklist that follows. If your abstract meets that requirement, check the box. If you're at an early stage with your article and trying to maintain a creative head space for it, you don't have to fix those weaknesses now. If you're farther along (or returning in later weeks to finalize your abstract), fix the weakness now and then check the box.

My Abstract Checklist

My abstract

- ☐ Is two hundred words or less
- ☐ Names my article's subject or topic
- ☐ Restricts background information to no more than one or two sentences
- ☐ Includes four or five relevant keywords
- ☐ Includes a statement of the hypothesis or argument
- ☐ Makes a claim that the subject or argument is significant and represents something new
- ☐ Makes sense without reading the article (i.e., it can stand alone)
- ☐ Reveals the article's most interesting finding/discovery

- ☐ Doesn't contain future-tense statements (e.g., not "we hope to show" or "we will show" but "we show")

- ☐ Doesn't have weak "attempt" language (e.g., not "this article tries to analyze" or "this study seeks to" or "this article explores" but "this article analyzes" or "this study shows")

- ☐ Uses the present tense to talk about the article (e.g., "the aim of this article is")

- ☐ Uses the past tense to talk about the study (e.g., "the aim of this experiment/reading was")

- ☐ Doesn't include quotations from sources (unless they are just one or two words or the entire subject of your article)

- ☐ Doesn't include abbreviations, symbols, or acronyms

- ☐ Doesn't contain notes or citations

- ☐ Covers each abstract metacategory or humanities abstract ingredient for which I jotted down notes earlier

My SciQua article abstract

- ☐ Doesn't start with data or methods

- ☐ Doesn't omit methods

- ☐ Doesn't have a description of methods longer than one or two sentences

- ☐ Doesn't omit results or findings

- ☐ Doesn't include a description of results or findings longer than two or three sentences

- ☐ Doesn't contain recommendations longer than one sentence

Tracking Writing Time

Mark your electronic calendar, the Calendar for Actual Time Spent Writing This Week form, and/or the check boxes here with how long you wrote today. ☐15+ min. ☐30+ ☐60+ ☐120+

Day 3 Tasks: Reading Strong Articles in Your Field

Today you're going to search for at least one good article that can serve as a model in writing your own. Part of the purpose of this workbook is to get you in the habit of reading journal articles that relate to your work. As mentioned earlier, skimming three to five scholarly articles per week is the average among faculty in some disciplines (Ware and Mabe 2015, 52).

The workbook will lead you through a structured reading exercise in seven steps. You can spend as little or as much time on this task as you want; however, those who spend an entire afternoon or evening finding and reading good articles benefit the most from the task.

1. **Brace yourself.** When reading published articles, you can easily get intimidated. If you start to teeter into anxious feelings of belatedness and insecurity, stop and remind yourself of the following. Your purpose in looking at articles is to study how to write

great articles, not to compare yourself negatively with their authors. Stay focused on your aspirational task. You're just one person—therefore, you don't have to write ten thousand great articles, just one solid one. An editor, two peer reviewers, and a copy editor worked on any article published in a good journal, and yours can look better after all that too. If all else fails, comfort yourself by looking for a bad article. They aren't tough to find!

2. **Search for journal articles in your field that were published in the past two years.** You can do this search in two ways. Search Google Scholar with your search terms, and then skim titles and abstracts to narrow down your finds. Or you can focus only on those articles that come from a journal in which you would like to publish. When selecting articles to read more closely, remember the following. First, don't accidentally pick a bibliographic article, a literature review, a working paper, a report, or a trade article; you must select peer-reviewed journal articles only. Second, the articles you locate don't have to be on your topic, just in your field. In fact, it can be best if the articles aren't on your topic so that their content doesn't distract you. Your aim here is not to conduct research but to find models for your own writing. Third, article styles change, so make sure to select only recent articles; those published in the past one or two years are best. Fourth, checking the work of those scholars you admire can be helpful, but try not to select articles written by people famous across disciplines, like Angela Davis, Noam Chomsky, Judith Butler, or Kwame Anthony Appiah. Articles by the famous tend to be unusual—frequently much better than the majority of articles but sometimes too peculiar to be useful.

3. **Search in more than one place.** First, search Google Scholar using some of the large subject terms important in your field, restricting the search to the past two years. Recent articles haven't been around long enough to be cited or downloaded much, so you probably won't find the Google Scholar citation statistics of much help in identifying worthwhile articles; but if you see one that's already being cited, that's a good one to choose. Once you find some articles, identify for each whether you have access to the whole article, either online or through your university library. If you do, download a few of the interesting ones. If you don't, keep going until you find some that you can download, because you need to read the entire article. Second, go to the websites of the best journals in your field, and read the titles and abstracts of articles published in the past two years. If any articles look interesting, see whether you can download them. Articles already listed on the website as "frequently downloaded" or "most read" can be good choices. And some journals provide highly cited articles for free. Third, check your reference-management software program for recent articles you downloaded but have not read yet. Fourth, if you have a chance to go to a good university library in person and skim articles in recent copies of relevant journals, do so. It can often be easier to skim many articles at the university library's periodical shelves than to skim articles online. Hard to believe, but true! Rows of print journal issues can organize materials in more relevant ways than huge online databases. When I do a shelf search, I never sit down, and that keeps me in skimming mode, not reading mode.

4. **Narrow your choice of articles.** Having completed these searches, you've probably found at least ten articles that interest you and typify how scholars in your field are writing. Now start reading the introductions. If an introduction is strong, keep going; if it seems weak or unclear, discard that article and move on to the next. Keep going until you find one strong article. When narrowing your choices, remember that this article doesn't have to be similar in content to yours; rather, it should provide a sound structure and solutions to some of your writing dilemmas.

My Good Article as Model Checklist

The article I have selected as a model

☐ Was published in the past two years

☐ Is in my discipline and field

☐ Is a peer-reviewed journal article

☐ Is not written by a very famous person

☐ Is available to me in full text and has been downloaded

☐ Has a strong introduction

☐ Is similar to my article in types of methods used (e.g., quantitative, not qualitative)

☐ Is similar to my article in types of subject (e.g., a single-text study, not a multiple-text study)

☐ Is similar to my article in types of structure (e.g., short, not long)

Citation for this good article (author, title, journal, year)

5. **Print out the good article and study its introduction.** When studying journal articles as models, read them not for their content but for their delivery system—how the author presents that content. Look at the first few paragraphs. Can you describe what the author is doing there? What does the article begin with? What kind of background information does the author give you, the reader? Does the article make a claim for significance? How soon does it state the argument? If you read nothing but the first paragraph, what would you know about the article? This is an exercise in thinking about how people set up their article vis-à-vis their audience.

6. **Look at the other sections of the article.** Now examine other aspects of the text. How many citations does the article have? How many examples does it include? Does it cite other scholars throughout or just in the introduction? If your article is SciQua, study how the author has written the Methods, Results, and Discussion

sections. What information has the author relegated to tables? If you article is HumInt, study how the analysis proceeds. What comes first? How has the author organized the material? Grasping how others organize their content will help you organize yours.

7. **Make some notes**. Jot down two or three things that you learned from your model article. You may find that upon closer reading, it isn't as good as you thought. Jot down what you want to imitate and what you want to disregard. These notes don't have to be long, just something for later to remind you what you thought after reading the good article.

What I Learned by Reading Strong Articles

Tracking Writing Time

Mark your electronic calendar, the Calendar for Actual Time Spent Writing This Week form, and/or the check boxes here with how long you wrote today. ☐15+ min. ☐30+ ☐60+ ☐120+

Day 4 Tasks: Reading Articles to Cite in Your Article

Today you'll complete the same task as yesterday, but this time focus on articles whose content will be useful for your research, that is, that you'll cite in your article. It's fine if you have already read the article; this time you will study it for form, not content. How is it organized? How does it present meaning? What does it teach you to do in writing your own article? Sometimes the lesson is negative; you may find problems you want to avoid in your article.

Tracking Writing Time

Mark your electronic calendar, the Calendar for Actual Time Spent Writing This Week form, and/or the check boxes here with how long you wrote today. ☐15+ min. ☐30+ ☐60+ ☐120+

Day 5 Tasks: Getting Feedback on and Revising Your Abstract

Today you're going to share your abstract to get suggestions for revision.

1. **Find someone with whom to exchange abstracts**. Exchanging abstracts is always better than handing yours over alone. When each person is both reviewed and reviewing, it keeps everyone kind. If you're in a writing course or writing group, make sure to work in pairs. If you're not, find someone who has an abstract to share. (PS: All academics have one to share.)

2. **Meet virtually or in person rather than by email**. This is not an exercise in just getting *written* feedback. The talking part is essential so that your exchange partner can work with you to improve the abstract, not just critique it. Often, we're better at explaining things aloud, and your exchange partner can help you bring that language into the abstract. Have your partner take notes as you talk so that you capture your ideas and don't just voice them.

3. **Each read the other's abstract**. Hand a print copy of your abstract over and have your reviewer respond to it right there and then, both in writing and aloud. If you must explain any parts to your reviewer, make sure to note which parts, because an abstract should stand alone. If you need to explain anything, it's not standing alone. When you're done with this exchange, you will have a marked-up draft. Then write down a few notes about what your reviewer suggested would improve your abstract. These may turn out to be key in the revision process as well.

4. **Revise your abstract**. Engage in the revision process with both your reviewer's comments and the various good articles in mind. Your abstract doesn't need to be perfect at this point. You can revise it again later as you proceed with your article revision process, but it will be easier to revise then if you have something solid now.

5. **Post it**. When you're finished with the draft, you can paste a copy above your desk, post it on your blog, or mail it to a friend. But do something to make its completion concrete.

Tracking Writing Time

Mark your electronic calendar, the Calendar for Actual Time Spent Writing This Week form, and/or the check boxes here with how long you wrote today. ☐ 15+ min. ☐ 30+ ☐ 60+ ☐ 120+

Then, here at the end of your workweek, take pride in your accomplishments and evaluate whether any patterns need changing.

Remember that if the work is taking longer or going faster, you can revise your contract and your overall schedule. If your progress is slow, don't allow the demon of discouragement to convince you to give up. The most important work you're doing now is establishing a daily writing habit. That will serve you for a lifetime, years after you've forgotten how long this article took to write.

DOCUMENTING YOUR WRITING TIME AND TASKS

Calendar for Actual Time Spent Writing This Week

Time	Day 1	Day 2	Day 3	Day 4	Day 5	Day 6	Day 7
5:00 a.m.							
6:00							
7:00							
8:00							
9:00							
10:00							
11:00							
12:00 p.m.							
1:00							
2:00							
3:00							
4:00							
5:00							
6:00							
7:00							
8:00							
9:00							
10:00							
11:00							
12:00 a.m.							
1:00							
2:00							
3:00							
4:00							
Total minutes							
Tasks completed							

WEEK 4
Selecting a Journal

Task Day	Week 4 Daily Writing Tasks	Estimated Task Time in Minutes	
		HumInt	SciQua
Day 1 (Monday?)	Read from here until you reach the week 4, day 2 tasks, filling in any boxes, checking off any forms, and answering any questions as you read.	90	90
Day 2 (Tuesday?)	Search for journals in your field.	90+	60
Day 3 (Wednesday?)	Evaluate the journals found, and match your article to them.	90+	90+
Day 4 (Thursday?)	Evaluate the journals found, and match your article to them.	90+	90+
Day 5 (Friday?)	Read relevant articles in the three most suitable journals. Write a query letter. Decide which journal you'll be submitting your article to.	120+	90+
Total estimated time for reading the workbook, completing the tasks, and writing your article		**8+ hours**	**7+ hours**

Above are the tasks for your fourth week. Make sure to start this week by scheduling when you will write, and then tracking the time you actually spend writing (using the Calendar for Actual Time Spent Writing This Week form or online software).

If you've previously made a study of journals in your field or regularly read a wide variety of journals, you can skim this chapter and then move on to the tasks in the next. However, many novice authors remain unpublished simply because they don't select the right journals. If you don't know much about journals, don't have backup journals to send your article to, or plan to submit your article to a journal merely because someone told you to, you need to read this chapter closely and complete the tasks.

WEEK 4, DAY 1: READING AND TASKS

THIRD WEEK IN REVIEW

You have now spent three weeks working on your article. You've worked on setting up better work habits, clarifying your argument, and writing an abstract. If you find that the previous two sentences accurately reflect your recent activities, congratulations! You can move on to the section that follows.

If, however, they don't reflect your circumstances—for instance, you've been reading the workbook and just thinking about working on your article, or you've been neither reading nor writing—stop here for a minute. While procrastinating is perfectly normal and doesn't make you an evil human being, it's not going to help you send a finished article to a journal at the end of twelve weeks. Unfortunately, the method has yet to be invented where you only read and think and still become a published author! So how did you get here, and what are you going to do about it?

You could close this workbook, set it aside, and determine to work on your article later, at a "better time"; but the point of this workbook is to make writing a part of daily life, not a special activity you reserve for some indefinite later. If you can't work on your article right now, at least write down a projected start date. Then put the reminder in your calendar or write it on a note that you post on the back of your front door, on your fridge, or above your writing site to make sure that you do think about this matter again on a particular date.

If you're not ready to give up the ghost of your article, well done! Some diagnosis is in order. Why aren't you working on your article, and what can you do to ensure that you do work on it? You might reread the online advice at my website about solving writing obstacles.

Lessons I Learned from the Third Week's Writing Experiences

Last week, you learned how to use an abstract to think about your article and the challenges that lie ahead in revising it. You're well on your way! This week, you'll learn how to select journals, and you'll be choosing one for your article.

GOOD NEWS ABOUT JOURNALS

Although you might be surprised to learn this, many journals need you more than you need them. Why?

Tens of thousands of academic journals are being published today, more than ever before. According to *Ulrich's Global Serials Directory*, in 2018 the number of active peer-reviewed,

English-language journals with an online version could be broken down by discipline as follows: over 9,000 in medicine and health, over 6,000 in the social sciences, over 3,700 in business and economics, almost 2,000 in education, over 1,500 in arts and literature, and over 1,000 in philosophy and religion. Across all disciplines, there are more than 60,000 peer-reviewed, English-language journals. And the number of journals is always increasing, with the rate of growth having held steady for the past two centuries at around 3 percent a year (Ware and Mabe 2015, 27), thus doubling every twenty years (Mabe 2003, 193). Which means that many editors are looking for material to fill their pages with every year! Indeed, journals published almost two million articles in 2018, according to the bibliographic database Scopus.

The great secret of journal publishing is how often journals go begging for articles. Faculty may discourage graduate students by citing the sky-high rejection rates of leading journals (which aim for 95 percent rejection rates), but such rates aren't the norm. According to a survey of over 5,000 journals, the average rate of rejection in business journals is 70 percent, in education journals 67 percent, in psychology journals 65 percent, and in health journals 54 percent (Sugimoto et al. 2013, 904). In confidential conversations with managing editors at humanities journals, I have found that leading journals in their field can receive as few as twenty unsolicited submissions a year. One small annual journal admitted to a student of mine that it receives only six to eight submissions a year! Some simple calculations with the number of peer-reviewed journals and the number of productive scholars give ample evidence for the theory that many journals do not have 90 percent rejection rates, especially in the humanities. A 60 percent rejection rate is probably more accurate, one that hasn't changed much over the past three decades. Frankly, these odds are much better than your odds of obtaining a fellowship.

In other words, your chances of getting a solid article published have never been better.

THE IMPORTANCE OF PICKING THE RIGHT JOURNAL

Given these facts, why does everyone have the impression that publishing a scholarly article is so hard to do? If we're desperate to publish our articles and editors are desperate to publish articles, why aren't we all published? Because novice authors often send their article to the wrong journal.

Two weeks ago, you learned the most important thing you can do to improve your chances of publication upon sending out your article: stating your argument early and clearly. This week, you'll learn the second most important thing you can do: picking the right journal for submitting your article. I've placed information about selecting an appropriate journal early in this workbook, because you want to make this decision early on and revise your article with a specific journal in mind.

The penalties for choosing the wrong journal are quite high—a perfect article sent to an unsuitable journal won't get published. And the clear majority of journals will be wrong for your article. Indeed, one of the most frequent reasons that any journal rejects an article is because it did not meet that journal's requirements (Meyer et al. 2018; Volmer and Stokes 2016). The editor may couch this in any number of ways—this wasn't for us, or it was too long or too short, too qualitative or too quantitative, too narrow or too broad, too theoretical or too concrete, and so on and so forth—but all these comments really mean the same thing: we don't publish articles of this type. But frequently, other journals specialize in publishing articles exactly like it. That's why it is so important to study actual peer-reviewed journals so that you won't cast your hard work before unappreciative editors or reviewers. It's also why the most frequently given advice to novice authors about choosing a journal—submit to whichever journal is "the best"—is not good advice.

Rejection is not the only cost of choosing the wrong journal. Many novice authors are unaware that <u>authors cannot submit their article to more than one journal at a time</u>. In magazine publishing, you can simultaneously submit your article to dozens of outlets, but in the academic -world this is forbidden. Journal editors consider "shotgunning," the rapid-fire submission of one article to multiple journals, to be an ethical violation, and they ban authors who do so (Rogers 1999; Peer 2016). So if you follow proper protocol, you must wait until you get a decision from the first journal before you can submit the article to another; and since the review process takes three to four months on average (Huisman and Smits 2017, 641), picking the wrong journal can significantly delay publication, perhaps even past the article's relevance. For these reasons and many others, indiscriminately sending articles to the major journal in your discipline without researching your options is not a good strategy.

Furthermore, although many novice authors think that a journal is a journal is a journal, in actuality there are many kinds of journals. Research universities and many colleges reward authors for only those articles that appear in "refereed" or "peer-reviewed" academic journals. Not all academic journals are refereed; that is, not all use the quality control mechanism of peer review in which manuscripts are sent for vetting to scholars in the field, usually anonymously. This process is called anonymous, masked, or "blind" review (if the author doesn't know the reviewer, but the reviewer knows the author) or double-blind or double-masked review (if neither knows the other). Getting published in conference proceedings, anthologies, or other collections often does not meet this refereed criterion and is a frequent error of novice authors aiming for positions at research universities. Given the tremendous variation in periodicals, it's wise to learn the different types of journals out there. This knowledge can help you determine the best journal for your work (and career), and can aid you in revising your article.

So how do you go about selecting the right journal from among tens of thousands? Jot down in the box below any journals you have been thinking about as possible publication outlets. Then keep them in mind as you read the text that follows. Even if you think that you know where you want to publish your article, at least skim the rest of the chapter to ensure that you're not making a mistake.

Journals I Know of That Might Be Suitable for My Article

TYPES OF ACADEMIC JOURNALS

Academic journals evolved from handwritten correspondence during the seventeenth century, when some intellectuals sent missives synthesizing the findings of the day to dozens of other scholars. When such correspondence could no longer keep pace with the scientific developments of the era, in the mid-1660s serials launched all over Europe, periodicals that released numbered issues once a year or more, including the German monthly *Erbauliche Monaths-Unterredungen*, the French *Journal des Sçavans*, the English *Philosophical Transactions*, and the Italian *Giornale de' letterati* (Haveman 2015). By the end of the 1700s, journals had become more specialized, and by the end of the 1800s, illustrations, references, methodologies, and peer review had become standard practices. Journals' origin in letter writing still shapes the form: academic journals are records of scholarly conversations and current concerns. It's wise to remember this background when writing. To submit an article to an academic journal is to begin a correspondence.

Below are some of the standard types of publishing outlets for articles, divided into journals you should avoid, those you should think twice about publishing in, and those you should prefer. If you want, you can skip straight to the "Preferred Publishing Outlets" section and focus on those journals; but since so many scholars do choose to publish in nonrecommended and debatable publishing outlets, I want you to have the full evidence for why I make the recommendations I do.

The gold standard of academic publishing includes several features: journals must be peer reviewed, produced by an academic press (university or commercial), written for scholars, and feature authors who are considered experts in their field, cite their sources, and detail their methodology so that others can replicate or check the research.

Nonrecommended Publishing Outlets

If you're someone with few or no published research articles and you intend on obtaining a university or college position in the United States, I do not recommend that you initially publish in any of the following outlets. They won't lend you the status you need.

Newspapers and magazines. For our purposes, a newspaper or magazine is any popular periodical that never publishes articles containing citations. Newspapers disseminate news on a broad range of topics, magazines on more specific topics. As mentioned in the first chapter, articles in newspapers, magazines, or newsletters can do a great job of getting your name out there and changing the world we live in, but they have little influence on hiring or promotion committees at research universities and many colleges. This is so even though magazines like the *New Yorker* or the *Times Literary Supplement* and newspapers like the *Wall Street Journal* or *Le Monde* can be much more difficult to get published in than any academic journal. The academic judgment against newspapers and magazines—despite the undoubted prestige and exclusivity of some of them—emerges from the perception that many journalists don't have credentials in the field about which they are writing (and so cite information secondhand or thirdhand). Articles in such venues are regarded as too short to do justice to the complexity of the issue and too simple or sweeping in their conclusions. Of course, the antipathy is mutual: newspapers and magazines find full research articles to be too long and complex for their audience. Finally, since newspapers and magazines depend almost entirely on advertisements to stay in business, academics question their impartiality. In short, newspapers and magazines have neither the authority nor the legitimacy sufficient for your purposes.

News and information journals. Periodicals in this category publish news articles and announcements for a specific academic field or profession. Their content may include updates on trends in the field, opinion pieces, review articles, conference reports, book reviews, abstracts of peer-reviewed literature, job announcements, and grant deadlines. They may publish excerpts from forthcoming books (which is useful to remember), but such journals do not publish research articles and are not peer reviewed. The *Chronicle of Higher Education*, for instance, provides news to university faculty and administrators every week; *Scientific American* reports on scholarly discoveries. While such journals are excellent sources for you on scholarly trends, staff writers write the majority of submitted articles. Don't consider such a journal for your article.

Trade and professional journals. Periodicals of this type publish not only news and information, but also articles on the technical or practical aspects of performing in a certain field or profession. Because of their technical bent, these periodicals tend to be more common in scientific or professional fields such as engineering, medicine, business, or architecture, but they can also be found in any discipline with practical elements, such as education, design, film, or archaeology. Their articles are not peer reviewed, have no references, and are written in an informal, more accessible style for practitioners.

Trade and professional journals, which include practitioner newsletters, often include many field-related announcements regarding conferences, calls for papers, job openings, new technology, and so on. For instance, *Communication Arts* is the leading trade journal for the visual communication field, and showcases design work, features profiles on artists, gives advice on the business of design, and reviews relevant conferences and books. It does not publish peer-reviewed articles. Unless you're writing an article intended to instruct others in your field about how to do something well—such as how to record good oral histories or restore water-damaged paintings—such journals are not for you. Occasionally, however, peer-reviewed journals are miscategorized as trade journals, so if you find a trade journal you like, don't dismiss it before checking to see whether it's an academic journal. For instance, *College Composition and Communication* is a trade journal that publishes peer-reviewed articles on writing pedagogy.

Predatory journals. Periodicals considered predatory are not scholarly but designed to make money by charging article-processing fees to authors desperate to make it into print. The business of publishing academic journals is now a billion-dollar industry, and this economic success has attracted scams. So-called predatory journals don't peer-review, edit, or even read the articles submitted to them. Sometimes they don't even publish the submissions. How do you detect such journals? You check the list at predatory-journals.com. (One reason to check is to avoid mistakenly dismissing a journal; Hindawi Publishing Corporation, based in Egypt, and MDPI, based in China and Switzerland, are not predatory publishers.)

If you're still not sure, consult articles that lay out the signs (Arthur 2015; Laine and Winker 2017). The main sign is an email invitation to submit that is rife with grammatical errors and promises of fast publication without having to jump through hoops. Reputable journals don't send bulk emails encouraging authors to submit work to them, much less promising to make the process easy. Other signs that a journal is predatory: not indicating its country of publication; having an email address from a free email provider; or telling you about an article-processing fee only *after* your submission. Checking the editorial board of a suspect journal won't help, as predatory journals sometimes place prominent scholars' names on their board listing without those scholars' permission. Finally, predatory publishers will spoof a real journal occasionally, emailing you while pretending to be that journal and offering to publish your article for a fee. If a journal suddenly asks for a fee when its official website has no mention of fees, it's a spoof scam.

Print-only journals. Periodicals of this type are peer reviewed but do not appear online, only in print. Unfortunately, there's no point in publishing in a journal that doesn't appear online, because "the vast majority of journal use takes place electronically," almost entirely from laptops or PCs (Ware and Mabe 2015, 8, 24, 30, 139). One survey found that only half the health sciences faculty at a large urban research university ever read articles directly in print journals (De Groote, Shultz, and Blecic 2014, 173). That means that you reduce your chances of getting cited by at least half if you publish in a print-only journal. Publishing your article in a journal that appears both in print and online is the only sure way to ensure that scholars find it. Fortunately, print-only journals are becoming rare, with over 90 percent of science journals available online (Tenopir and King 2014, 173).

Debatable Publishing Outlets

I recommend that scholars with few or no published research articles think carefully before choosing to publish their revised research article in any of the following types of outlets. I used to call these questionable outlets, but now I call them debatable outlets, because their value is up for debate (and people do debate with me about them!). In other words, if the particular outlet you're considering falls into one of these categories, that's okay, so long as (1) it doesn't fall into two or more of these categories and (2) it has some prestige or other advantage that carries it out of the debatable category, especially in your discipline. I should note that I have happily published in two of the outlet types below— edited volumes and note journals—so I'm not saying never do it. I'm only saying think twice before you send strong research with a vigorous argument to them.

Working papers series. Periodicals of this type issue preliminary versions of research articles in the applied social sciences. (Such publishing outlets don't exist in the humanities or natural sciences.) Generally published by research institutes, working papers series publish more descriptive and less argumentative work than journals, as their aim is to circulate and thus claim work at an early stage. Institutes view their working papers as a service for novice authors (to help them get the experience of publication) or for the community (to get ideas out quickly to policy makers). But some journals frown upon working papers and regard them as a violation of journals' prohibition on publishing previously published articles. If you're a novice author, check with colleagues in your discipline before committing to publishing a working paper. Hiring and promotion committees at research universities and many colleges will not see a working paper as equivalent to a peer-reviewed journal article. If you have taken the time to write something argumentative, send it to an outlet that counts.

E-print repositories. Known as e-print, preprint, or self-archiving sites, e-print repositories publish research results before these are sent to a peer-reviewed journal. (Such outlets do not exist in the humanities.) In the sciences, it is common to publish results in an open-access e-print repository, as it circulates timely research immediately, rather than after a months-long peer-review process at a journal. Also, many of these repositories allow other scholars to give feedback on your material, enabling you to improve your work before sending it to a journal. E-print repositories have become very popular, and a flurry of them have been created since 2016, including in the disciplines of sports science, law, paleontology, agriculture, library science, sociology, and psychology. The earliest repository, established in 1991 and called arXiv, is massive; it hosts over 1.4 million articles in the disciplines of economics, computer science, physics, mathematics, quantitative biology, quantitative finance, statistics, electrical engineering, and systems science.

Although publishing in such a repository may be fine, you need to check three things before doing so. First, some journals will see e-print publication as violating their prohibition on publishing previously published articles. To find out whether your journal is one of those, go to the online resource SHERPA RoMEO at sherpa.ac.uk/romeo, which provides summaries of every journal's open-access, e-print, and rights policies. Second, find out what kinds of rights the e-print repository requires from you, as it may not automatically allow you to republish the work in a journal. Third, if you're a novice author, check with those in your discipline before committing to publishing in such an outlet.

Society and conference proceedings. Papers presented at some conferences are published by occasional or annual collections known as society and conference proceedings. Although work published in their pages can be as sound as that published in peer-reviewed journals in some fields (Randolph et al. 2007), the perception remains that they are not a trustworthy publishing outlet (Tenopir, Levine, et al. 2015). Too many proceedings are not peer reviewed or even copyedited. Although it can seem like a compliment for an editor to invite you to submit your article to such a periodical after you've presented a paper at a conference, resist. First, many proposed proceedings never make it into print, owing to inexperienced editors running into funding problems or never finding a publisher. Second, unedited, unfinished articles that scholars published in such proceedings have sometimes embarrassed them later. If you've gone so far as to present an article and even receive praise for it, it's far better to focus on revising and submitting it to a journal, where it can go through a serious vetting process. If a peer-reviewed journal accepts your work, it's unlikely that the article will embarrass you later—at least two reviewers thought it was sound. If you're a junior scholar starting out, you want to get as much mileage from your work as you can. Third, US scholars report rarely using conference proceedings in their research: conference proceedings made up only 1.7 percent of their sources, while journal articles made up 62 percent (Tenopir, King, et al. 2015, 97). Fourth, some scholars are under the mistaken impression that they may revise a paper that appeared in a conference proceedings volume and submit it to a peer-reviewed journal. Journals consider this a violation of their rule against accepting previously published articles. If you're certain that the proceedings will be peer reviewed, copyedited, and published, then they qualify as an edited volume, as far as I'm concerned. You should check the next paragraph for a discussion about whether to publish in one.

Chapters in edited volumes. While not strictly periodicals, edited volumes are collections of articles published as a book. Publishing in an edited volume is not equivalent to publishing in a peer-reviewed academic journal. The draw to edited volumes for many novice authors is that it can be quite easy to get into them. Perhaps your advisor or colleague is editing the volume, guaranteeing you a place in it and offering to give you useful and substantive feedback. Perhaps someone approached you at a conference and invited you to submit your article because your topic is on target. While flattering, you run some serious risks if you agree to submit it. First, far fewer people read the average academic book than read an average journal issue. In a widely cited formulation, the scholar Dorothy Bishop wrote of edited volumes, "You might as well write the paper and then bury it in a hole in the ground" (Bishop 2012). Predictably, there have been protests against this analysis, but her point that chapters generally receive less attention than articles is indisputable (although Patrick Dunleavy, in his popular blog *Writing for Research*, at medium.com/@write4research, offers solutions to "radically improve the academic visibility of chapters" once they're published). Second, many edited volumes remain little more than a twinkle in the faculty editor's eye. Faculty underestimate how much effort it takes to put one together, so the enterprise often grinds to a halt somewhere before actual publication. Further, faculty aren't trained copy editors and sometimes will rewrite and publish your article, often for the worse, without even asking your permission.

Therefore, I recommend that you eschew sending your argumentative essays to edited volumes. These volumes are more appropriate for articles that peer-reviewed journals are unlikely to accept because they are too narrow, too descriptive, too speculative, too long, or too educational. For instance, the Blackwell companion series in the humanities publishes edited volumes of informative (not argumentative) essays written by famous scholars about trends in their field; these are used to teach survey courses. Since this workbook is about writing an argumentative article, it won't help you write such a chapter. However, if the editor of an edited volume has a signed book contract with a strong university press and is a well-organized individual with a good reputation as a scholar, then I would not lambaste you for sending that editor an argumentative article. Fortunately, many editors seeking to produce a collection are now turning away from books and toward producing special or themed issues in journals, which solves the problem. Special issues are covered the "Preferred Publishing Outlets" section.

Non-peer-reviewed academic journals. Some scholarly periodicals publish academic articles that are not put through the peer-review process. At such journals, only the editor (or sometimes the editorial board) reads the submissions and determines whether the journal should publish them. You should hesitate before publishing in a non-peer-reviewed journal for two reasons. First, no scholars doing research like yours will review your submission, which means that you won't get their help to make it strong and error free. Second, a review by peers remains the sine qua non of quality in academic publishing—with faculty support for peer review remaining steady at 93 percent (Ware and Mabe 2015, 46). Of course, some non-peer-reviewed academic journals are quite highly regarded within a field; these include *Social Text* and *Harvard Business Review*. Such exceptions prove the rule, however. I do not recommend non-peer-reviewed journals for junior scholars. Since it's not always clear which these are, later in the chapter I will cover how to tell whether a journal is peer reviewed.

Graduate student journals. Some scholarly periodicals are produced and reviewed by graduate students. UCLA, for instance, has approximately twenty-five student-run journals, many of which were established in the late 1960s and have produced seminal articles in their field. Graduate student journals are less likely than their scholarly and faculty-reviewed counterparts to have solid reputations, because the quality of their articles can be low (owing to underpaid and overworked graduate student editors, spotty peer review, unprofessional copyediting, or poor production) and the number of readers few (because their subscription base is shaky or nonexistent and their issues come out irregularly).

Of course, some are great, doing a far better job of reviewing articles carefully and giving detailed responses than faculty-run journals. Journals in business and education include strong student-run journals. For example, the *Harvard Educational Review* is one of the most prestigious journals in education and has been since 1930, and its editorial board is composed of doctoral students. Another prestigious student-run journal is UCLA's *Mester*, which publishes articles on Spanish- and Portuguese-language literature. Both have paid editors and receive strong financial support from their institution. If a graduate student journal has been publishing on time for many years, it's perfectly acceptable for you to consider for publishing your article.

Note journals. Some scholarly periodicals publish very short articles, usually fewer than three published pages and less than two thousand words. Examples of such journals would be the *Explicator, Economics Letters*, and *ANQ: A Quarterly Journal of Short Articles*. Many disciplines do not have note journals. Such journals are perfectly acceptable, but not appropriate for the full-length article you're writing for this workbook.

Review journals. Some scholarly periodicals publish only reviews, whether individual book reviews or reviews that critically appraise research in a subfield. Examples of such journals include *Psychology Review, Annual Review in Anthropology, Annual Review in Public Health, Annual Review of Economics*, and *Reviews in Religion and Theology*. Since this workbook is aiding you in publishing an original research article, review journals are not relevant.

Local journals. Some scholarly periodicals publish only articles by local scholars about a local area. For instance, some universities have journals that publish only their own professors, and some small associations have journals that publish only their own members, such as the *British Journal of Psychodrama and Sociodrama*. Journals of this type may not always announce themselves as such, but a look at their editorial board and recently published authors may show them to be limited. If you're a local author writing about a local area and the journal appears both in print and online, it may be a good outlet for you.

New journals. Scholarly periodicals are considered new if they are planning their first issue or have published only one issue. Unfortunately, the statistics on journal start-ups are dismal. For every 2.5 currently active periodicals, there is one that is defunct—a 40 percent fail rate, according to *Ulrich's Global Serials Directory*. While peer-reviewed journals have a higher survival rate than that—only about one in seven fails—that's still a risk. If a reputable university press is sponsoring it, a leading scholar will be editing it, and it has university-provided funding and staff, the new journal may not be a terrible bet for you; but in general, stick with journals that have been in operation for at least three years.

Electronic-only journals. Some scholarly periodicals have never appeared in print, whether now or in the past. Let me be clear: here I'm not talking in general about online, digital, electronic, or e-journals. I am talking specifically about journals that appear *only* on the internet, especially those that were born digital. Every year since the late 1990s, observers have predicted that journals appearing solely online will achieve parity with journals that also appear on paper. As of this writing, this has yet to happen. In one important sign, almost no journals have dropped their print edition (Ware and Mabe 2015, 30). Further, the explosive growth of electronic-only or solely digital journals since the late 1980s has slowed. Their numbers soared from seven in 1990 to almost four thousand by 2000 (Association of Research Libraries 2000), but since then they have increased more slowly, amounting to only 10 percent of all peer-reviewed journals (according to *Ulrich's Global Serials Directory*).

If electronic-only journals were achieving parity, we would expect to see a much higher percentage of them. In this, journals reflect the overall trend in technology: new media does not entirely replace old media. A journal that appears both in print and online has all the advantages of online access, including communicating ideas quickly, enabling interactive dialogue, and providing immediate viewing of music and film clips. So while some well-established electronic-only journals have excellent reputations, such as *Postmodern Culture*, which was started online in 1990, some in HumInt fields view such journals as less prestigious. Among the signs of imminent change to this viewpoint, however, are statements released by major scholarly organizations directing their hiring and promotion committees to treat peer-reviewed *online* publications as equal to peer-reviewed *print* publications (Committee on Information Technology 2003, 2015). Further, some journals are making the switch to electronic format. In 2016, the Martin E. Segal Theater Center dropped the print edition of all three of its peer-reviewed theater journals, moving them from a traditional subscription-based print and electronic status to free, open-access, electronic-only status. The center had debated the move, worried about junior faculty needing print publications for their tenure file; but then theater research associations issued a white paper stating that publishing electronically should not count against scholars (Bay-Cheng et al. 2013). The journal publisher Wiley has been pressing its life science journals to drop their print edition, perhaps because their full-color illustrations are very expensive to print. So check the norms in your field before submitting your work to journals that appear solely online, especially if you're in the humanities.

Open-access journals. Some scholarly periodicals are available only online and can be read for free by anyone, although authors must sometimes pay to publish in them ("article-processing fees" can be as high as five thousand dollars). Currently, there are almost twelve thousand high-quality open-access peer-reviewed journals, according to the Directory of Open-Access Journals. Most of them are in the sciences, but humanities open-access journals exist, including *Postmodern Culture*, *Transcultural Studies*, and *Digital Humanities Quarterly*, as do social science counterparts, including *SAGE Open*. About fifty of the open-access journals are "megajournals," which rapidly publish many articles in a range of disciplines (Ware and Mabe 2015, 99). The largest megajournal is *Scientific Reports*, which published over twenty-five thousand articles in 2017 (and charges authors a publication fee of US$1,760). Few megajournal articles are produced in the humanities; those that are, tend to be quantitative (e.g., one article in *PLOS ONE* presents algorithms for identifying the authorship of literature written by Shakespeare's contemporaries [Arefin et al. 2014]). The first megajournal in the humanities was launched in 2013: the *Open Library of the Humanities* (which does not charge authors a fee to publish).

In the sciences, open access is commonly celebrated for not concealing research behind unaffordable paywalls; in the humanities, however, the idea of an author paying to get published horrifies (although more than half of peer-reviewed open-access journals do not charge fees) (DOAJ 2015). Further, questions about rigor and originality dog the megajournals, and to some extent smaller open-access journals. Some open-access journals are simply predatory journals that will publish anything sent to them (Bohannon 2013, 62, 64); some depend on online comments as postpublication peer review, the effectiveness of which is debated; and a recent study of open-access nursing journals found them inferior to subscription-based journals in several regards (Crowe and Carlyle 2015). Perhaps as a result, publishing in open-access journals is still not the norm in any field: only 12 percent of all articles were published in these journals in 2013 (Archambault et al. 2014), with the percentage of nonscience articles much lower. At the same time, a growing number of open-access journals are reputable, in part because open access increases the number of times an article gets cited. In 2015, according to Altmetric (2016), 42 of the top 100 most cited articles were published under an open-access model, with most coming from just four publications: *PNAS* (*Proceedings of the National Academy of Sciences*), *PLOS ONE*, the *BMJ*, and the non-peer-reviewed preprint server arXiv. Other research shows that articles that are freely accessible online are read more (P. Davis et al. 2008) and cited more (Hitchcock 2013). But you don't have to publish your article in an open-access journal to receive that benefit. You can post it yourself online at either Academia.edu or ResearchGate (after a certain period mandated by the journal) or your university repository, which is known as "green open access" (publishing in an open-access journal is called "gold open access").

So what's the upshot? Some people can benefit from publishing in an open-access journal, especially if they can write the article-processing fees into their grants and don't have to pay out of pocket. If you have less pressure on where you publish—because you have tenure, for instance, or have already published several articles, work for an institution that doesn't rank journals for hiring and promotion purposes, have a forward-thinking hiring or promotion committee, or live outside the United States and just need an "international" publication on your CV—it may be worth thinking about publishing in an open-access journal. If so, search the Directory of Open-Access Journals at doaj.org for journals that declare themselves to be nonsubscription based, no author payment, full text, and peer reviewed. However, if you don't have funding for the fees, need to publish in prestigious journals for hiring or promotion purposes, or haven't published much, think twice about publishing in open-access journals. A final note: some journals that aren't open access do allow authors to pay a substantial fee to make their particular article freely available; this is known as "optional open access".

Non-US journals. Some scholarly, peer-reviewed periodicals edited outside the United States (i.e., their faculty editor does not teach at a US university) are considered non-US journals. In general, US scholars receive less credit for placing their article in non-US-based journals. Likewise, scholars outside the United States are often given extra credit for placing articles in a journal edited in the United States. Since that nation is the world's largest and wealthiest producer of scholarly knowledge, it tends to dominate the journal market. I don't endorse this ethnocentric reality, but it's my job to tell you that it is a reality. So novice authors planning on academic jobs in the United States should be careful about aiming for journals edited in another country, with the possible exceptions of the United Kingdom and Canada—and even then, only if the journals are prestigious. Three caveats are in order, however. Without local support, local journals will not thrive, and the US dominance of journals will continue, reducing diversity in research. So if you live or do research outside the United States, especially if you're well established, it's an important strike for equity to support local journals by publishing in them and ensuring that vetting committees count them. Second, for those authors conducting case studies on non-US countries, finding a US journal willing to publish your work can be difficult. Many of these journals are interested only in research on US cases—another ethnocentric reality. So you may need to turn to non-US journals. Third, the top journals in many smaller humanities fields are based in Europe. If the top journals in your field are based outside the United States, don't hesitate to publish in them. The *BMJ* regularly tops the list of most-cited journals in any discipline and is published in London; many prestigious theology journals are published in London and Tubingen. Quality trumps location.

Preferred Publishing Outlets

I recommend that you concentrate on the following outlets for getting your article published. Fortunately, these still represent a range of competitiveness and quality, and therefore are not out of reach. I have arranged these types somewhat, from least prestigious to most. I will guide you in researching specific journals later; for now, just write in the box that follows each type, naming any relevant journals that you already know about. If you don't know any, that's fine—you'll search for some later.

Regional journals. Some scholarly, peer-reviewed periodicals publish articles from or about a locale (e.g., metropolis, province, cluster of provinces, nation). If the region is very large (e.g., the Middle East or Asia), such journals can be extremely competitive, but those focusing on smaller regions generally are not. Because of their narrower focus and assumed smaller readership, journals devoted to a region can be rated not quite as highly as other peer-reviewed journals. But a regional journal is a good break-in journal for a novice author whose article falls within its mandate. Some examples are *California School Psychologist*, *Western American Literature*, and *International Journal of the Linguistic Association of the Southwest*. Of course, journals devoted to small regions are sometimes quite prestigious; one example would be the historic *New England Quarterly*.

A regional journal that might be appropriate for my article (if about a region):

Newer journals. Scholarly, peer-reviewed periodicals that are three to seven years old are considered newer. While brand-new journals are a bad bet, newer journals are often a good opportunity. Since newer journals have fewer submissions and fewer already accepted articles, they are often actively searching for submissions, so you have a better chance of getting published quickly in their pages (Sugimoto et al. 2013, 903–4). They also may be more willing to work with novice authors in shaping their work. Further, newer journals are often launched because of new field paradigms that established journals have been slow to accept (Tenopir and King 2014, 161)—good news for you if your research falls within that new paradigm. You can estimate a journal's age by its volume number, which usually proceeds by years; thus, a journal on its eighth volume is generally eight years old (unless it was on hiatus for a few years and thus is older than its volume number would indicate).

A newer journal that might be appropriate for my article:

Interdisciplinary journals. Scholarly, peer-reviewed periodicals that publish work informed by more than one discipline are known as interdisciplinary journals. These journals have been keeping pace with the explosion of interdisciplinary work in academia. It is now common to find journals that either pair two disciplines (e.g., *Philosophy and Literature*) or don't fit directly in any one discipline (e.g., *Human Rights Quarterly*). Such journals are a boon to interdisciplinary scholars, whose work fits uneasily into specific disciplines. That is, if an author writes an article about metaphor in the founding legal texts of the United States, frequently neither the legal scholars nor the literature scholars would be happy with the article's methodology, whereas a journal that combines such approaches would be delighted.

However, you have two challenges when it comes to an interdisciplinary journal. First, you must assess that journal carefully to see whether your brand of interdisciplinary work would fit there. Sometimes you need to beef up your orientation toward one of the disciplines to make your article truly interdisciplinary. Second, the problem with the reputation of interdisciplinary journals is that they tend to be less impressive to hiring and promotion committees (who work strictly within the disciplines). Since this is the problem of all interdisciplinary work, it shouldn't stop you from publishing in interdisciplinary journals, particularly since disciplinary journals can be quite hostile to boundary-crossing work. Just be aware that hiring and promotion committees at research universities and many colleges can view interdisciplinary journals as less relevant. One solution may be to stockpile some statistics about the journal to cite in promotion material, such as its subscription level or rejection rate (if they are high) and the names of prominent scholars who have published in that journal. Another is to ask your department, or any prospective department, about how it weighs publication in interdisciplinary journals. You can use that information to predict whether you and your interdisciplinary work would do well in particular types of departments.

An interdisciplinary journal that might be appropriate for my article (if interdisciplinary):

Field journals. Scholarly, peer-reviewed periodicals that publish work in a field within a discipline are known as field journals. They represent the clear majority of academic journals. For instance, within the discipline of English literature, field journals are focused on regions (e.g., *Research in African Literature*), languages (e.g., *Kiswahili*), periods (e.g., *AMS Studies in the Nineteenth Century*), genres (e.g., *Novel*), ethnicities (e.g., *Amerasia*), theories (e.g., *Postcolonial Studies*), methodologies (e.g., *Feminist Studies*), themes (e.g., *Literature and Medicine*), or authors (e.g., *Emily Dickinson Journal*). Some field journals are devoted to small subfields (e.g., *Harvard Journal of African American Public Policy*), others to enormous fields that resemble disciplines (e.g., *Econometrica*). Overall, field journals are the best option for novice authors submitting their work—they are prestigious, but not out of reach. Hiring and promotion committees never dispute the value of such publications. One additional note: some experts advise novice authors to publish only in those fields in which they plan to apply for tenure-track positions. I disagree— while you certainly should prioritize writing articles for your field, publication in a peer-reviewed journal can never hurt you. However, if you've published several times in other fields and never in the field(s) in which you would like to get hired, think about developing an article in your field(s).

A field journal that might be appropriate for my article:

Themed or special issues. Some journals produce *special issues* (additional issues addressing specific topics) or *themed issues* (regular issues on specific topics). Occasionally these issues are organized by the editors, who propose a theme, select a guest editor, and open submissions to everyone; sometimes scholars propose special or themed issues to journal editors (especially after successful conferences), usually with most authors preselected. Such issues are wonderful opportunities, because they're much less competitive than a usual journal issue. Since journals receive, on average, only a third as many manuscripts for their announced themed issues as for their general issues, submitting work to these reduces your competition by two-thirds (Henson 2007, 784). Indeed, a tenured faculty member mentioned to me that all his articles in top journals had been published in special issues. Many of my students have gone straight into print by carefully looking for such issues and then contacting the editor, even after the deadline had passed. Authors are often dropping out at the last moment by not submitting their final manuscript, thus creating a place for you. So special or themed issues can be your fast track to publication. To find them, you can run a search on Google for "Calls for Papers" or "CFP" and a key term from your research, limiting the results to the past year. To obtain better results, do the same search at H-Net Humanities and Social Sciences online network at networks.h-net.org, limiting your results to CFPs for journals specifically and in the last year. You can also search on Twitter for "CFP" and a key term. Looking at individual journal websites is your best bet if you're trying to get into a specific journal.

One caveat about special or themed issues: thriving journals do not devote most of their issues to them. The problem with regularly publishing themed issues is that it reduces the number of submissions a journal receives. Authors discover the upcoming themed issues, ascertain that their article does not fit, and send their work elsewhere. In turn, journals with declining submissions start doing themed issues as a way of soliciting articles from authors. It can be a vicious cycle. Be sure to use special or themed issues to get your article into a better journal, not a declining one.

> A themed or special issue that might be appropriate for my article:

Disciplinary journals. Scholarly, peer-reviewed periodicals publishing work in a specific discipline (of which there are only about twenty) are known as disciplinary journals. Some examples are *Publication of the Modern Language Association (PMLA)*, the *Journal of Politics*, and *American Anthropologist*. There often is more than one such journal in each discipline; economics has the *American Economic Review*, the *Journal of Economic Theory*, and the *Journal of Economic Perspectives*, to list a few. Disciplinary journals are extremely difficult to get articles into. For one thing, the number of scholars in any discipline is much larger than in any field; thus, the number of submissions received at any disciplinary journal is very high, as is their rejection rate. For instance, the editor of *PMLA* reports that it received 293 article submissions in 2016 and published only about 21 (a 7 percent acceptance rate) (Dimock 2018). That is, for every 100 authors who submit an article there, 93 of them see it rejected. Second, disciplinary journals are, by definition, more general in scope than field journals and consequently must publish work that appeals to a diverse audience, people who aren't working in your exact subject area, period, or region. This means that their articles tend to be broad statements of the big picture, with more complex forms of writing (Shelley and Schuh 2001). Third, such journals often have a reputation for being stodgy or even actively hostile to new ideas (D. Miller 1999; Peplow 2016). Junior scholars often complain about the difficulty of getting their new work published in disciplinary journals. For this reason, I recommend that novice authors not focus on submitting work to these publications unless they have been encouraged to do so by an expert in their field.

> If I really want to aim for a disciplinary journal, which one might be appropriate for my article?

FINDING SUITABLE ACADEMIC JOURNALS

As this review of types of academic journals makes clear, identifying an appropriate journal for submitting your work is essential. But since there are so many journals out there, how do you *find* journals to study? I recommend several approaches, keeping in mind the preferred types of publishing outlets mentioned above.

Day 1 Tasks: Reading the Workbook

On the first day of your fourth writing week, read this week 4 chapter all the way through the next three paragraphs, answering all the questions posed. Write directly in the boxes provided or in your own document.

If you've already selected a journal to which you'll be submitting your article and the journal falls into the preferred category discussed above, you could skip ahead to the chapter "Week 5: Refining Your Works Cited." However, if possible, I recommend that you still use this week to study journals, either as backups (in case your article is rejected by your first-choice journal), as future goals (for other articles you may write), or as conversations (to situate your current article in the scholarly debates). One student spent a weekend using this chapter to study ten different journals in fields that were her career aims—years later, she wrote me to say that she still used the research she conducted that weekend when drafting articles, deciding in advance which journal to aim for. Most journals don't like to publish the same author regularly, so you'll need five to thirty journals for each decade of your publishing career.

If you haven't selected a journal, the guidance below will help you do so. Before getting started, think about your aims in publishing your article. If you're at an early stage of your career and publication is the key to getting your first job, your main goal may be publishing good work in a journal respected by the hiring and promotion committees at your institution. Or perhaps you have an article that represents work you're no longer interested in or can't imagine doing further research on. You know you have some good insights, but it's not the main thrust of your research anymore. In such a case, you may simply want the "points" for publishing in a peer-reviewed journal, so your article can go to a low-tier journal that will be likely to publish it. Finally, some scholars have a particularly timely idea and want to get into print quickly, before someone else beats them to the punch. If that's you, consider choosing a related journal with a quick decision time. Your purpose in getting published should influence which journal you select.

> My aims in publishing this article are
> (e.g., getting a job, getting research
> off my desk, getting promoted,
> communicating to a particular audience,
> timeliness):

Tracking Writing Time

Each day, use the Calendar for Actual Time Spent Writing This Week form (or digital time-tracking software) to keep track of the time you spent writing this week. Then, at the end of the week, evaluate how you spent your time. If you're not getting around to tracking your time, consider setting up time-tracking software. For instance, RescueTime, ManicTime, and other programs monitor and total the minutes spent per day on social media, email, and word processing.

If busy, at least mark the check boxes with how long you wrote today. ☐ 15+ min. ☐ 30+ ☐ 60+ ☐ 120+

Day 2 Tasks: Searching for Journals

Today you'll learn methods for finding a suitable peer-reviewed journal for your article. You don't have to use all the methods if you don't have time, but complete at least the first three tasks that follow. These require a lot of work, but once they're done you can use the results for years to come.

When searching online, remember to use many different keywords. Start with a search on your narrow topic, then on your general subject, and then with keywords reflecting your theoretical approach, your methodology, or your discipline. The latter will reveal journals that aren't necessarily devoted to your subject but might be interested in publishing your article. In other words, topic is not your only way into a journal. Slight variations in keywords (e.g., switching from "woman" to "women") can make a big difference in finding suitable journals.

Ask your advisor and colleagues. Novice authors' most common method of identifying suitable journals is asking people in their field, who will often have a good sense of the major journals. Since there are so many journals to choose from, and sorting through them can be difficult, getting recommendations can be extremely efficient. Furthermore, this is a very easy question to ask in conversation or by email: "what do you consider to be the best journals in our discipline and in our field?" In fact, it's a good idea to spend a moment now sending several emails! The more people you ask, the better.

I plan to contact the following people about suitable journals:

Suitable journals that others recommended:

Unfortunately, people in your field aren't always great sources. If they rarely publish, always publish in the same journals, always publish articles unlike yours, or no longer read journals regularly, they may not be helpful. It's always wise to do some exploring beyond their advice.

Search *Ulrich's Global Serials Directory*. This database is not free, so your institution must be a subscriber for you to access it—but it provides the most comprehensive list of periodicals available, including tens of thousands of peer-reviewed English-language journals published throughout the world. If you have access, you can do all your journal searching here, as it has a very powerful "advanced search" engine. It's particularly useful because it gives a lot of information about each journal, including whether it's still publishing, how often it produces issues, who its editor is, how to contact the journal, what subjects it covers, and whether it's peer reviewed. Furthermore, all these categories can be searched. and reviews of each journal are provided. The latter is particularly useful in getting a sense of the journal's reputation. *Ulrich's* isn't always right and sometimes fails to categorize journals as peer reviewed, but it's the most useful tool we have for tracking down all relevant journals.

Search the *MLA Directory of Periodicals*. This free directory of over six thousand humanities journals provides the most detailed information of any of the databases, so if your research is on modern languages, literature, folklore, or linguistics, this is the only place to go. The directory covers everything, including postal, web, and email addresses; article submission guidelines; frequency of publication and number of articles submitted and published each year; scope and mandate; circulation; and, most unusually, length of time to decision to accept the article and length of time to its publication. The journal editors provide these time estimates, which represent the journals' ideals more often than their realities, but that's still useful information to have.

Check online lists. Lists of journals in various fields are available. For example, see Wikipedia for its Lists of Academic Journals in dozens of fields and disciplines. In the humanities, you can check the Council of Editors of Learned Journals at CELJ.org, an association of US-based humanities journals, which provides links to the websites of over one hundred member journals. In the sciences, Genamics JournalSeek at journalseek.net provides links to over one hundred journals, from all over the world and in many languages.

Check index and research databases. Article index and research databases can help you find suitable journals by searching for relevant keywords in journal titles. In the humanities, these databases include Project MUSE and JSTOR. In the social, health, behavioral, and natural sciences, some of these databases are Pubmed, Ingenta, Web of Science, and Taylor & Francis Online. Your research library also allows you to do searches in article index databases such as Infotrac's Expanded Academic ASAP for journals that publish work like yours. You also can find journals using the free database WorldCat and its advanced search function, setting Format to Journal, Magazine and using your article's subject terms.

Check field- or discipline-specific databases. Fields and disciplines often have databases dedicated to each of them, which thus constitute authoritative lists of journals for a specific field or discipline. In religion, it's Religious and Theological Abstracts. In political science, it's the American Political Science Association's list.

Suitable Journals in *Ulrich's*, the *MLA Directory*, Online Lists, or Online Databases

Check your citations and their bibliography. Reviewing the citations in your own articles, published or unpublished, helps you find journals that regularly publish work on your topic or from your angle. Where were your cited articles published? Do those journals sound like possibilities for you? If you don't find much, pull up the articles you cited and review their bibliography. What articles do they cite, and in which journals were these published? Do any of these journals sound suitable? Finally, you can look up the articles you cite on Google Scholar, and in the Google results list then click on the Cited by link, Web of Science database link, or Related Articles link to find the journals that cite the work you cite.

Check your advisors' CVs. If your research closely aligns with scholars you admire, look up their CV to find where they have published articles. A separate advantage is that if those scholars are in your department, you can then ask them about their experiences with particular journals.

Suitable Journals That Turned Up in My Articles' Citations or My Advisors' Citations

Do an old-fashioned shelf search. Most journal editors will tell you that if you really want to understand their publication's mindset (how the editors think about the journal overall, its range and readership), nothing substitutes for holding a few issues in your hand. For this, you must get up and go to the library if you have access to a good one. Look up the call number of a few journals that you think might be suitable for publishing your article. Go to the section of the library for recent issues of periodicals, and look at not just those journals but also those shelved nearby to find additional journals on your topic. You're guaranteed that these journals are respectable and active ones, because your library is subscribing to them.

Search journal publisher websites. Searching the websites of large academic publishers can also be a good way to find out about journals. Almost all the journals these publishers produce are peer reviewed. They have fewer journals than the databases and so it's not as overwhelming to use their website to learn about each one: the site's relative smallness makes it easier to search by disciplinary category. Since these are university or commercial presses, which must make a return on their investment in each journal, they require their journals to be well run. As a result, these journals are good bets for you. The largest publishers of journals in the world are, in descending order, Springer, Elsevier, Wiley-Blackwell, and Taylor and Francis, which have well over two thousand journals each (Ware and Mabe

2015, 45). More narrowly, those publishers with the most humanities and social science peer-reviewed journals are, according to *Ulrich's* and in order, Springer, Elsevier, Routledge/Taylor and Francis, Wiley-Blackwell, SAGE, Oxford University Press, and Cambridge University Press. An added benefit of searching their website is that massive journal publishers are doing more to provide advice to authors. Some examples are the Springer Journal Suggester web page, where you can enter your title, abstract, and discipline and it will suggest which of their journals might be appropriate for your article, or Elsevier's guide *How to Publish in Scholarly Journals* and its Publishing Connect Training Webcasts. Another benefit of searching such websites is that you can register to receive journals' tables of contents to keep abreast of developments in your field.

Check online evaluation sites.   Other sites not only list journals but also evaluate them. Wikia at humanitiesjournals.wikia.com has thirteen communities evaluating journals in humanities disciplines and fields, including English, Spanish, French, and German literature; history, gender and sexuality, cultural studies, postcolonial studies, and rhetoric; and theater, art history, film, and music. Authors use it to write about their experiences working with journals—how quickly each responded to their submission inquiry, how helpful the reviewers and editors were, and so on. My graduate students and I also publish an evaluative web page called "Reviews of Peer-Reviewed Journals in the Humanities and Social Sciences" at journalreviews.princeton.edu. that you may find helpful. Finally, some scholars publish evaluations of journals, for instance those in the field of education (Henson 2007, 782).

Search method terms in Google Scholar.   Searching for articles with method terms can help you find journals that publish articles featuring those methods. For instance, search Google Scholar for articles published in the last three years that contain the terms "Ghana," "women," "semi-structured interviews," and "logistic regression."

Suitable Journals from My Searches of Library Shelves, Journal Publisher Websites, Online Journal Evaluation Sites, and Google Scholar

Examples of Online Searching for Journals

Let's look at two useful examples of novice authors' searches for journals. A graduate student was looking for a suitable journal for publishing her article about representations of the independence struggle in Congolese film. She started with *Ulrich's* quick keyword search by searching narrowly, using the phrases "Congo film" and "Congo cinema." As she expected, no journals turned up. She then searched using the phrases "Africa film" and "Africa cinema" and got nothing, but then searched with the phrase "African cinema." This slight variation from "Africa" to "African" returned the *Journal of African Cinema*, a newer journal launched in 2009 and edited in South Africa. She then searched on "African cinema" without quotation marks, which yielded 2,664 journals, too many for her to search effectively. So she restricted the search to active, English-language, peer-reviewed US journals available online, and got thirty-eight journals, including *African Arts*, *African Studies Quarterly*, *Cinema Journal*, *Nka*, and *Research in African Literatures*, all suitable for her article. However, since she was in the French department and thought it might be better to publish in a journal closer to her discipline than the African studies journals that had turned up thus far, she then searched for active peer-reviewed journals available online using the term "Francophone." Ten journals turned up, including *Contemporary French and Francophone Studies* (which produces four themed issues a year) and the *International Journal of Francophone Studies* (which has a stated interest in articles on film). After reading the website of the *International Journal of Francophone Studies*, she decided to submit her article to it, the last journal to turn up in her search.

Another graduate student had written an article about conversation analysis and biosemiotics. He was feeling discouraged, because he knew of only three suitable journals for his work, two of which were obscure. Since he wanted a tenure-track position in a philosophy department, he really wanted his article placed in a philosophy journal, not a linguistics journal, so he didn't bother doing searches using the phrase "conversation analysis." But his advanced search on *Ulrich's* Philosophy and Religion subject category for active, refereed, US-based journals available online yielded 383 results. So he narrowed his search to active refereed journals available online and used the term "semiotics," which yielded twelve journals. Then he accidentally came across *Social Epistemology*, a journal that publishes articles about the social production of knowledge. He hadn't really thought about his article as epistemological, but it was definitely about the social production of knowledge. So he started doing searches using the keywords "epistemology" and "knowledge," and found more journals to look at.

Sometimes students will come to me and insist that there are only one or two journals in their field. I used to believe them; now I don't. It's true that some disciplines in the humanities are underrepresented by scholarly journals. Disciplines in which researchers reported difficulties finding appropriate journals for their research included art, design, drama, and music (Sparks 2005, 44). A quarter of scholars in the social sciences and the arts and humanities complained that one of their major difficulties was finding journals in which to publish their interdisciplinary research (43). Nevertheless, if you haven't found at least a dozen journals that might be suitable for your article, you simply haven't searched hard enough.

Tracking Writing Time

Mark your electronic calendar, the Calendar for Actual Time Spent Writing This Week form, and/or the check boxes here with how long you wrote today. ☐ 15+ min. ☐ 30+ ☐60+ ☐ 120+

Days 3-4 Tasks: Evaluating Academic Journals

Today and tomorrow, you will evaluate and rank the journals you found yesterday. From the chapter's section on journal types, you know that your best bet is to focus on publishing in a US-based, peer-reviewed journal that has been around for at least three years, appears both in print and online, and publishes research articles in a particular field rather than a discipline. But what if these requirements hardly narrow your choices? What if dozens of journal choices remain? One approach is to rank the journals you have found. That is, how will a potential employer or dean weigh the importance of the peer-reviewed journal in which your article appeared? Below is some information on how to do that.

Formal Journal Ranking Methods

Reputation ranking. All journals are ranked through general observation and opinion. The intangible of reputation can count for a good deal—especially in the humanities. Do academics in your field or even outside it speak well of the journal? A journal's good reputation in the humanities tends to depend on the prestige of its editor, editorial board, and authors, as well as its past, present, and perceived future impact on the field. If you're on tenure track, ask those in your department about the journals they consider reputable and useful for tenure.

Metric ranking. In the social, health, behavioral, and natural sciences, journals are mostly ranked quantitatively—by rigorously collecting and analyzing data about the influence of each journal. The issue of metrics can be very confusing. So let me start with an easy rule of thumb: if a journal has a JCR (I'll explain this shortly), it has a high-enough rank for your purposes; being tracked is a good sign all on its own. Many metrics now exist for measuring influence, but the oldest is the *Thomson Reuters Journal Citation Report* (JCR), launched in 1975. It arrives at a journal's Impact Factor (IF) by using the Web of Science database of articles to calculate the citations that articles in 11,000 journals accrue over the two-year period after they are published. (It explicitly does not calculate a JCR for arts and humanities journals.) Another popular metric is the SCImago Journal Rank (SJR), launched in 2007, which uses the Scopus database of articles to track the citations that articles in 20,000 journals accrue over a three-year period, along with the prestige of the citing journal. In 2012, Google entered the field, launching Google Scholar Metrics; GSM uses the h5-index, tracking citations over five years to calculate the rank of 40,000 journals, including 4,000 arts and humanities journals, without a bias toward English-language journals (Delgado-Lopez-Cozar and Cabezas-Clavijio 2013, 101, 102, 104, 105, 109).

These metrics can result in wildly different rankings: for instance, in 2012, "*PNAS*, which is ranked sixth according to GSM drops down to position 131 in JCR, whereas *PLOS ONE*, which is positioned as number 52 in GSM tumbles to position 800 when using the JCR" (Delgado-Lopez-Cozar and Cabezas-Clavijio 2013, 111). Further, while one of the top journals in the world, the *New England Journal of Medicine*, had a JCR IF of 55.87 in 2015 (on average, an article published in the journal in 2013 or 2014 received 55 citations in 2015), most journals do not have a rank anywhere near this. Indeed, half of all journals have JCRs of less than 1.00, with lots of respectable journals, especially in the humanities, having impact factors in the .400-to-.600 range. SJR ranks fall into quartiles, from the highest, Q1 (with the highest rank around 38,000), to the lowest, Q4 (with ranks down into the 100s).

In the humanities, it's much tougher to track citations, for a host of reasons. As a result, many journals aren't ranked accurately if at all, even though they are prestigious and influential. For instance, these metrics all depend on the tracked articles having a digital object identifier (DOI), which most humanities articles lack. For instance, I am in the humanities and only one of the articles I've published has a DOI, my article about teaching journal article writing, DOI 10.3138/jsp.40.2.184 (Belcher 2009). It's not surprising that of all my articles, it has been tracked as being cited the most (although other articles of mine might have been cited more often in publications that are tough to track). In other words, if you're in the humanities, it's still best not to rely on metrics.

Altmetric ranking. Meanwhile, many complain that metrics don't capture the true influence of a journal in the world (Basken 2013, para. 2, 4, 9), so alternate indicators have been developed to evaluate that influence. Sometimes known as altmetrics, these indicators result from measuring how many of a journal's articles are viewed online or downloaded as PDFs; discussed on social media, including on blogs and in the journal's Comments section; appear in social bookmarking sites like Mendeley and CiteULike; downloaded as cites to reference-management software programs like Zotero; referenced on Wikipedia; or recommended on literature services sites like F1000Prime. Identifying a journal's ranking by this method is in its infancy, but you can check out Altmetric.com, which provides links to a variety of new online tools calculating impact; Impact Story.com; COUNTER's Usage Factor: Journals (UFJ) measurement tool; or MESUR's scholarly usage database. Some of the large journal publishing companies post Altmetric Attention Scores on journal article web pages; for instance, Taylor and Francis posts Altmetric Attention Scores reflecting how often the article was posted/discussed in the news and on Twitter, Facebook, Google+, Reddit, and Mendeley. You can follow the Altmetrics of individual articles with a widget on your browser. Be aware, however, that older scholars serving on hiring or promotion committees may look askance at candidates who promote their social media stats on their CV, so ask about conventions in your field before you do so.

Other ranking methods. Many other factors can figure into ranking a journal. For instance, the higher the number of subscribers, the better the journal's ranking. In the humanities, journals with more than five hundred institutional and individual subscribers are respectable; journals having a readership of over one thousand are strong. You can find out the number of institutional subscribers at WorldCat, which lists how many libraries subscribe to a particular journal. Other factors in ranking a journal include its funding, publisher, age, authors, and editorial board.

Should You Start at the Top?

One of the hoariest myths about journal article publishing is passed on, from generation to generation, without any real data to back it up. Many faculty tell their graduate students what was told to them—send your article to "the leading journal." If it gets rejected, send it to the second-ranked journal; if it gets rejected again, send it to the third; and so on. You may be eighty before you get published, but at least you started at the top! Clearly, this is terrible advice, for a whole host of reasons. The vagueness of the term *leading* is part of the problem. Leading in which field? In which discipline? Such lack of clarity robs the advice of any practical use.

More important, even where there is agreement on what constitutes a "leading journal"—studies show that as pertains to their own field, professors' opinions on this matter are more similar than their opinions of what constitute the mid- or low-level journals (Weller 2001, 58)—junior scholars may have trouble getting published because of high rejection rates. Indeed, top journals complain that the obsession with impact factors "wastes the time of scientists by overloading highly cited journals such as *Science* with inappropriate submissions from researchers who are desperate to gain points from their evaluators" (Basken 2013, par. 12). That's because most journal articles aren't suitable for top journals, being too narrow in claim, evidence, or argument. For instance, the leading feminist journal *Signs* rarely publishes analyses of single texts. When it does, it's because the single text is a mere stepping stone, a paragraph on the way to making a generalizing claim about all literature or theorizing about a global condition or issue. Yet year after year, *Signs* receives single-text articles, solid but narrower in scope than those it publishes, because the authors are "starting at the top." Such articles might go straight to publication somewhere else, but at *Signs* they won't even go through peer review. With 450 submissions a year (and a 6 percent acceptance rate), the editors are looking for broader work. The editor of a top journal in sociology complained to a colleague of mine that some professors instruct all their graduate students in a particular course to submit their final research paper to that journal, with no regard to fit. This is pure insanity.

Next, statistically, it simply can't be true that hiring and promotion depend on scholars' articles appearing in top journals. If these journals' rejection rates are 90 percent and each discipline or major field publishes only between 200 and 400 articles per year in one or two top journals (Kristensen 2015, 255), they are publishing less than several thousand articles per year. But the US faculty alone numbers 1.5 million, and even if only 10 percent of them are submitting an article in a given year, that still means that the clear majority of them aren't publishing in top journals.

Finally, research does not support the assumption that articles in more selective journals (i.e., journals with high rejection rates) are better reviewed, better copyedited, better written, or better cited than in others (Weller 2001; Shelley and Schuh 2001; Rocha da Silva 2015; Tennant 2016). According to one study, over half the most highly cited articles in the humanities and social sciences were published in nonelite journals (Acharya et al. 2014, 10). Owing to Google Scholar and other search engines, "finding and reading relevant articles in non-elite journals is about as easy as finding and reading articles in elite journals, [therefore] researchers are increasingly building on and citing work published everywhere" (11).

So what should you do? Publishing in a middle-ranked journal, so long as it's peer reviewed, will always be fine. Now, if you research a leading journal carefully, establish that it publishes work like yours, and decide to send your article there, you'll have my full support, but I don't want you to send your article to a journal just because someone told you it was a leading one. This path won't guarantee you early success. At the same time, I've noticed that some of my students—particularly women, first-generation college students, nonnative speakers of English, and US people of color—aim too low. If you tend to undersell yourself, don't.

Evaluating the Quality of Potential Journals

If you're not going to send your article to the highest-ranking journal you can find, what are you going to do? If you took the search process seriously, you have three to ten journals that look like suitable places for your work. Now you must evaluate them, because you should never send your article to a journal you haven't read or closely examined.

For each of the journals you found, use the Belcher Journal Evaluation Form (either in this chapter or on my website) to answer all the questions that follow; each question number corresponds to an item number on the form. Square check boxes on the form indicate positive journal characteristics, diamond check boxes the neutral ones, and round check boxes the negative ones. The more square boxes you check, the better the journal is as an option for you. Some people combine this day's tasks with the next day's and just spend a long afternoon or evening reading. Reading journals is how you become a better writer, so it's never wasted time.

1. **Is the journal peer reviewed?** Oddly enough, finding out the most important piece of information about a scholarly journal—whether it's peer reviewed—can be a difficult task. Confirming that the editor sends submissions to referees for anonymous review often can't be done by looking for this information in the actual journal or sometimes even on its website. But one sure sign of peer review is if the journal's submission guidelines request that articles be stripped of their author's name. That means articles undergo an anonymous peer-review process. Also, look at the acknowledgments in articles and see whether authors thank reviewers. Unfortunately, *Ulrich's* is sometimes wrong about whether a journal is peer reviewed, so you can't use it as a shortcut. If it looks as though the journal isn't peer reviewed, set it aside and start collecting this information for the next journal on your list. On the form, indicate the journal's peer-review status.

2. **Is the journal in the preferred publishing outlet category?** Earlier in this chapter, the section "Types of Academic Journals" addressed at length the nonrecommended, debatable, and preferred publishing outlets. Avoid trade journals, conference proceedings, edited volumes, and brand-new journals. On the form, indicate whether the journal is in a preferred publishing category and, if so, which one.

3. **Does the journal have a solid reputation?** When you asked others about journals in your field, was this journal mentioned? Have you heard it discussed in favorable terms? If you can't find this information easily, it's safe to assume that the journal isn't prestigious. On the form, indicate the level of the journal's reputation.

4. **Does the journal have solid metrics?** If your journal is in the social, health, behavioral, or natural sciences, see whether it's ranked by one of the metric systems. To find out a journal's JCR, go to jcr.incites.thomsonreuters.com; for its SJR, go to scimagojr.com; and for its GSM, go to journal-scholar-metrics.infoec3.es. On the form, indicate whether the journal has a JCR Impact Factor, SJR, and/or GSM and, if so, what that rank is. Also, name any other ranks it has.

5. **Does the journal have a tolerable rejection rate?** As mentioned earlier, journals with sky-high rejection rates aren't good bets for novice authors. It's better to gain the experience of publishing an article than spend a lot of time trying to get articles with a narrow scope into top journals. This rejection rate information is tough to find, however. Usually, only top journals with high rejection rates publish these. *Cabell's Directories of Publishing Opportunities* and the *MLA Directory of Periodicals* provide some statistics, but only in the disciplines of business, education, library science, psychology, psychiatry, literature, language, and linguistics. Some journals do publish the number of submissions they receive each year, which you can divide by the number of articles published per year to arrive at a rejection rate. Sometimes the only way to obtain this information from a journal is to write a query letter to its editor (for instructions, see later in this chapter). But if you can't find this information easily, it's

Belcher Journal Evaluation Form

Journal title _____

Editor's name/email _____

Managing ed. name/email _____

Journal web address _____

1. Peer reviewed ☐ Yes ◯ No ◇ Not sure (find out)

2. Publishing outlet ☐ Preferred ◯ Nonrecommended ☐ Debatable

   Preferred category ☐ Field-based ☐ Interdisciplinary ☐ Regional ☐ Newer ◯ Disciplinary

3. Reputation ☐ Solid ☐ Medium ☐ My department favors it ◯ High ◯ Low

4. Metric ☐ Has a JCR IF _____ ☐ Has an SJR _____ ☐ Has a GSM _____

   Impact Factor ☐ >1 ☐ .5 to 1 ☐ <.5

   Other ranking ☐ _____

5. Rejection rate ☐ <80% ☐ >80% but worth it ◯ >90% ◯ >95% ◇ Don't know

6. Publisher type ☐ Strong (e.g., univ., commercial, assn. press) ◯ Not as strong (e.g., dept.)

   Publisher name _____

7. Longevity ☐ >3 years ◯ <3 years

8. Production ☐ Well produced ☐ Okay, can't tell ◯ Sloppy

9. Punctuality ☐ On time ☐ <1-year delay ◯ >1-year delay

10. Fee-based ☐ No fee to publish ☐ Requires assn. membership ◯ Requires author to pay fee to publish

11. Contributors ☐ Open (often outsiders) ◯ Insular (mostly insiders) ◯ Rarely people like me

    ☐ Mixed ◯ High (profs. only) ◯ Low (mostly grad. students)

12. No. of articles ☐ > 10 articles per year ◯ < 10 articles per year

13. US ed. office ☐ Yes ◯ No, based in _____

14. Available online ☐ Yes ◯ No ◇ Not sure (find out)

15. Available in print ☐ Yes ◯ No ◇ Not sure (find out)

16. Time to publication ☐ <3-month turnaround ☐ >4-month turnaround ◇ Can't tell

    ☐ No backlog ☐ <2-year backlog ◯ >2-year backlog ◇ Can't tell

17. Transition ☐ No ◯ Yes ◇ Can't tell

18. Audience ☐ The right audience for me & this article ◯ Not quite right

19. Themed issues ☐ Sometimes ☐ Never ◯ Frequently ◇ Can't tell

    ☐ Upcoming on my topic of _____

20. Relevant prizes ☐ Yes, for _____ ◯ No

21. Topic match ☐ The journal and article match in topic ◯ No ◇ Not sure (find out)

22. Word/page limits _____ Shortest article: _____ Longest article: _____

    ☐ Match my article ☐ Require a little change ◯ Require big changes

23. Editors/board members I know _____

24. Style ☐ Chicago ☐ MLA ☐ APA ◯ Other

    No./length of notes _____ No. of Cites _____ No. of subheadings: _____

    Other _____

25. Submission ☐ Electronic submission ☐ Email submission ◯ Print submission ☐ Other

    Judgment   Total checked ☐____ Great journal = 22+ checked boxes; Good = 10–21; Bad = 0–9

    Total checked ◯____ Terrible journal = 22+ checked circles; Weak = 7–21; Good = 0–6 safe to assume that the rejection rate is tolerable. On the form, indicate the journal's rejection rate if you can find it.

6. **Does the journal have a substantial publisher?** In general, journals published by a large university or commercial press are more stable than those edited and published by a micropress—a specific scholar, department, or center. Thus, a journal's publication by either a university press (particularly at one of the large public or Ivy League universities) or a large association (such as the Modern Language Association) is a sign that it's here to stay. Commercial presses are also good, although the prestige associated with them is slightly less than that of a university press. On the form, write down the name and status of the publisher.

7. **Has the journal been around for a while?** As noted before, the longer a journal has been around, the more stable it is. If it's been published for more than ten years. you can assume that it's well organized enough to survive the vicissitudes of publishing. If it has been around for more than thirty years, you can assume that its focus is a topic of long-term interest to academia. You can get this information from the journal's copyright page, *Ulrich's* and other databases, the journal's Wikipedia entry, or the number of volumes the journal has produced, which often correspond to calendar years. On the form, indicate how long the journal has been publishing.

8. **Is the journal carefully produced?** A journal with lots of typos and design problems is in danger of collapse. Either it isn't professionally run or it's underfinanced. Journals that have extremely dated websites, poor-quality photographs, mismatched fonts, insufficient publication information, thin print paper, or other signs of neglect are usually not well respected. In general, the more solvent a journal is, the better it looks. On the form, indicate whether the journal looks professionally produced.

9. **Does the journal come out on time?** A journal that does not come out on time may soon not be coming out at all. You don't want to send your work to a journal that may fold in the next year or two. If issues are supposed to come out in the spring and fall and instead come out in the summer and winter, that's not so bad. If the journal is regularly two or three years behind, however, that's a bad sign. How can you tell if a journal is struggling? If it's supposed to come out twice a year and instead publishes a "double issue" at the end of the year, or the date on its cover (say, 2016) is two or more years behind the actual date of publication (2018) it must list on the copyright page, those are clear signs of trouble. On the form, indicate whether the journal seems to be coming out on time.

10. **Does the journal require authors to pay a fee?** HumInt journals rarely require authors to pay a fee to publish in their pages. A few require membership in their association, but that's about it. Fees are common, however, at SciQua journals. I recommend that you avoid journals requiring a fee unless you have a grant that specifically provides for this. On the form, indicate whether the journal requires a fee.

11. **Are the journal's authors varied?** Journals can be quite insular, publishing articles only by those from certain institutions or at certain stages of their career. At the same time, some journals do a great job: although the *Journal of Conflict Resolution* is based at Yale University, only 3 percent of its authors have attended or taught at Yale (Kristensen 2015, 263). So study the authors and editorial board of the journal you have selected to see whether it publishes the work of only a select few. First, compare the names listed on the editorial board with those given in the table of contents. Are the

names frequently the same? That is, does the journal ever publish anyone who isn't on its editorial board? Don't focus on sending articles to journals that publish work by their own board almost exclusively. Second, if the authors and board members aren't always the same, spot-check the status of those who do publish in the journal. Does the journal ever publish anyone ranked lower than a full professor? Are the authors all from research universities? Alternately, are quite a few of the authors graduate students? Journals that publish mostly famous scholars may be hard to break into; journals that publish only graduate students may be too low in status. Third, examine the authors in the past few issues to see whether you can detect their gender, race, or nationality. If authors are more than 75 percent male, more than 85 percent white, or more than 90 percent American, the journal is not varied. On the form, indicate whether the journal is insular or open to writers who are graduate students, women, people of color, or non-American, and the rank of those it publishes.

12. **Does the journal publish many articles per year?** The more often a journal is published and the more articles it publishes a year, the greater its demand for articles. This can mean that a larger or more frequently published journal is a better fit for you. Journals that produce only one issue a year can be very competitive; journals that publish more frequently may not be. On the form, indicate whether the journal publishes more than ten full-length research articles per year (do not count book reviews, editorials, nonscholarly articles, and so on).

13. **Does the journal have a US editorial office?** One measure of a journal's value to hiring and promotion committees at research universities and many colleges is whether it is edited in the United States. If the journal doesn't list an editorial office, use the home institution of the faculty editor as a proxy. The location of the actual publisher isn't relevant. On the form, indicate whether the journal is edited in the United States.

14. **Is the journal available online?** Since electronic access to your work is so important to increasing your reputation, seriously consider publishing only in those journals that have the full content of their articles online (whether behind a paywall or not). On the form, indicate whether the journal is available online.

15. **Does the journal appear in print as well?** Journals that appear both in print and online are the most desirable. On the form, indicate whether the journal is available in print.

16. **Does it take a long time to get published in the journal?** It's an unfortunate truth of academic journal publishing that articles go to print six months to three years after submission and thus one to six years after conception. This gestational period is even longer than that of elephants! The time lag is caused by journals' turnaround (the time between article submission and editorial decision) and backlog (the time between editorial decision and actual publication). The turnaround time is lengthy if peer reviewers aren't prompt in sending editors their recommendation for your article or if authors must go through multiple rounds of revisions. The backlog can also create delays if the journal has accepted articles for several issues in advance, forcing your article to wait in the queue. You can get some sense of how long journals take to evaluate and publish articles. For example, some SciQua journals publish, along with their articles, the dates when the original submission was "received," "resubmitted," "accepted," "published online," and "published in print"—which give you an idea of turnaround time and backlog. Generally, only top journals have statistics impressive

enough to announce. Other methods for determining turnaround times and backlogs are checking the blogs and wikis that crowdsource this type of information at sites like Humanities Journal Wiki, Economics Journal Submission Wiki, Psychology Journals Wiki, or Political Science Journal Submission Wiki. You can also use a comprehensive database like the *MLA Directory of Periodicals*, looking up the turnaround and backlog times listed on the journal website, or ask the editor directly by email using a query letter—although self-reported statistics are often more aspirational than actual. A final but time-consuming method is checking dates in the published articles' bibliographies. That is, if the articles in the journal never have any citations from the last two or three years, that means the journal has a large backlog. On the form, indicate whether the journal seems to have long turnaround times or a large backlog.

17. **Is the journal going through a transition?** If you ever hear that a journal is "going through a transition," avoid sending your article there. New editors, new editorial offices, new mandates, new titles, and new publishers are potential signs of trouble. A student had submitted an article to a journal and received it back in proof form, as it looks when it's about to be printed. But she heard nothing else. She assumed that her article hadn't been published. When I pushed her, she contacted the journal to find out what had happened. The journal admitted that in its transition from one university to another, several manuscripts were lost without its realizing it. Fortunately, it promised to publish the student's article if she could provide the journal with the acceptance letter it had sent! She did, and soon saw her article published. She was lucky; you may not be. On the form, indicate whether you have heard that the journal is going through a transition.

18. **Who reads the journal?** The problem with some of the nonrecommended and debatable publishing outlets described earlier is that they don't reach the right audience—scholars in your field. But even if you've selected a preferred publishing outlet, questions about its audience remain. Who do you want to read your work? If you would like professors in your own country to read it, then pick a journal published in your country. If you would like to get hired in a particular field, pick a journal in that field. You want to get your work in front of those who can most benefit from it—and who can most benefit you. On the form, indicate whether the journal audience consists of those you most want to address with your article.

Evaluating the Match of Your Article to the Journal

Once you've decided that you have located suitable journals of good quality—that are peer reviewed, have solid reputations, are published by a reputable press, have been around for a while, are carefully produced, come out on time, have varied authors, publish more than ten articles a year, appear in print and online, aren't going through a transition, and are read by many in your field or subfield—you're ready to learn a few more things about whether your article will do well at that journal. This information is useful whether you're revising a draft or writing from scratch.

19. **Does the journal have a relevant themed or special issue?** As mentioned above, such issues can be great opportunities. On the form, write down whether the journal produces relevant themed or special issues and if one is upcoming on your topic.

20. **Does the journal offer any relevant article prizes?** Some journals offer prizes for

the best article or the best graduate student article to appear in their pages over the previous year. All other things being equal, selecting such a journal might be to your advantage if you're a graduate student. On the form, write down whether the journal offers a relevant prize.

21. **Does the journal publish articles on topics like mine?** Sometimes, once you begin to study a journal, you realize that your article doesn't fit in terms of topic. The articles in the journal are never about your region, period, or subject, or never feature your method or approach. On the form, write down whether the topic of your article and the topic of the journal match. If you really want to publish in a particular journal and aren't certain about whether it would welcome your article, it's time to write a query letter.

22. **Does the journal have article length limits I can meet?** Some journals never publish articles longer than twelve print journal pages; others will happily publish sixty-page articles. If you've written an article shorter than twenty-five manuscript pages or longer than thirty-five, you need to look carefully at the manuscript length guidelines in the journal. Since article length can be hard to estimate—owing to notes, bibliographies, images, tables, charts, graphs, and varying type sizes—most journals now give word limits. (If they still give the page limit in "manuscript pages," this means double-spaced text with one-inch margins and twelve-point font, usually containing about 250 words to a page. Thus, 20 manuscript pages total about 5,000 words; 36 manuscript pages total about 9,000 words. This translates variously into print journal pages, which typically vary from 300 to 500 words per page.) Some journals have hard limits; other journals don't—you won't know unless you either study the length of the journal's shortest and longest articles (to ascertain whether that journal is following its own guidelines) or email the managing editor. In the other direction, one journal editor claimed that editors of print journals were often looking at the last minute for shorter-than-usual articles that wouldn't push an issue over its allotted page length (Henson 2007, 785). On the form, indicate the journal's word or page limits and whether your article meets them as it currently stands.

23. **Do I know any of the journal's editors?** Study the masthead to find out whether you know anyone on the journal's staff or editorial board. Novice authors are often surprised to find their graduate or undergraduate advisor on the editorial board of their selected journal. Sometimes such insiders can be helpful to you. You can email them to ask whether they think that the journal would welcome an article like yours. Here are two caveats about writing such an email. Editorial board members aren't always well informed about journal mandates, and the extent of their involvement may be reading one or two manuscripts a year. Most editorial boards rotate all their members regularly, with appointments lasting two to three years. If the board members' experience with the journal is limited, their advice will be as well. Furthermore, if the editorial board member you know does research similar to yours, he or she may be selected by the editor to review your article, should you submit it. Asking that person's advice in advance may deny you a sympathetic reader, then, since some scholars feel they should recuse themselves from reviewing an article if they know its author (or at least notify the editor of this knowledge). For these reasons, I recommend that you contact people on editorial boards only if you know them quite well, well enough to have a frank conversation about all these issues. On the form, write down the names from the journal's staff or editorial board masthead of people you know; then add whether you think it's advisable for you to contact them.

24. **Does the style of my article match the journal's style?** You can tell a lot about how your article is going to fare at a journal by studying that journal's style. Is the journal's tone formal or informal, conservative or progressive, playful or serious? For instance, go through the back issues and examine their article titles. Do they seem to be in the same style as your title? If not, you may want to think about choosing another journal or changing your title (see "Week 10: Opening and Concluding Your Article"). Likewise, do the articles tend to have long endnotes and reference lists or short ones? Will you need to alter your documentation if you submit your work to the journal? Are block quotations frequent or absent in the journal? Do the article introductions start with stories or statistics? Are the articles straightforward and clear? Do they have conclusions? Some journals are divided into sections. If so, where would your article fit best? Are there subheadings? Reviewing these small details may seem tedious, but as one blogger commented, checking the length of journal articles' notes and bibliography revealed "one of the most interesting differences in the journals I looked at—some had long, explanatory notes and some were just simple references; likewise some had many pages of bibliography and others had much shorter bibliographies." In turn, this knowledge made "a difference to the place I choose to submit to" (Mackin 2013). On the form, note information about the journal's style, including its style manual, the typical number and length of notes, average number of citations, and presence of subheadings, as well as whether you'd need to change your voice or approach to get your article into the journal.

25. **How does this journal require that articles be submitted?** Journals often have quite strict rules concerning article submission. A few still require you to submit it by email or post, though most require you to use a web form. One frequent requirement is that authors remove their name so that their article can go through an anonymous peer-review process. Other journals require abstracts; many want authors to fill out warrants about ownership, plagiarism, simultaneous submission, and online publication. Quite a few want authors to submit articles with the documentation already standardized according to the *Chicago Manual of Style*, the *Publication Manual of the American Psychological Association*, or the *Modern Language Association Style Manual*. On the form, note any special requirements the journal has for submitting articles.

Deciding on a Journal

Once you have filled out all the information on the Belcher Journal Evaluation Forms, review each one. Which journal looks to be your best bet for submitting your article? Recall that the shapes of the check boxes on this form have meaning: square check boxes indicate positive journal characteristics, diamond check boxes indicate neutral ones, and round check boxes indicate negative ones.

Suitable Journals in Order of Submission

If you've come up with several suitable journals, that's great! If the first journal rejects your article, you can send it to the next journal on your list. Now you have a plan that enables you to respond positively to rejection. By the way, if you want your hard work to benefit others, feel free to email a prose summary of your journal review to me so that I can post it on my page, "Reviews of Peer-Reviewed Journals in the Humanities and Social Sciences," at journalreviews.princeton.edu.

If you're working with coauthors, today is a good day to contact them with your thoughts about which journal would be the best choice, and to get their feedback.

Before you make a final decision about which journal you intend to send your work to, it's wise to send a query letter. Therefore, think about completing the tasks of day 5 before settling on a first-choice journal.

Tracking Writing Time

Mark your electronic calendar, the Calendar for Actual Time Spent Writing This Week form, and/or the check boxes here with how long you wrote both days. ☐ 15+ min. ☐ 30+ ☐ 60+ ☐ 120+

Day 5 Tasks: Reading Relevant Journals and Writing Query Letters

Today you'll read relevant journals and learn how to write a query letter. These two tasks can take up a lot of time, even several days, but both are worthwhile.

Reading Relevant Journals

Now that you have reviewed several journals for appropriateness, spend at least an hour skimming recent issues of the suitable journal(s) you identified, writing any notes on the back of the applicable Journal Evaluation Form. If you spot any articles that relate to your work or come across relevant review essays, attend to them more closely. As you'll recall from last week, part of getting published is citing the relevant literature. Although it's unnecessary to flatter editors by randomly citing articles from the journals to which you intend to send your article, it's necessary to cite directly related articles. Editors want to inspire dialogues in their pages; it helps if you clearly indicate that you're listening to that dialogue, not just speaking to it.

Study the journal's content. First, is there a trend to the articles? Has the journal become a forum for some debate, around which all its articles now revolve? Is it getting away from its mandate? Sometimes journals have an editor's column or introduction, which can give you helpful information about the editorial direction. Second, what are the journal's weak areas? Does your article fill some gap? Sometimes a journal is avoiding publishing certain work, but other times it just hasn't received any good articles on the topic. Third, what articles cover ground similar to yours? How is yours different? If the journal published an extremely similar article in the past three years, this may harm your chances of getting into print there. On the other hand, if that article is older, the journal may feel the need to revisit the issue, particularly if you cite it. On the back of the form, write down trends, debates, gaps, and the titles and dates of similar articles.

Writing a Query Letter to Editors

Some information about a journal you cannot collect by going through its pages or searching online. Indeed, you can obtain some of the most important information only from its staff. That's why emailing the editors of the two or three journals you're most interested in and asking them some questions can go a long way to getting you into print. Such emails are called letters of inquiry or query letters. There are two types: one you send to the journal's managing editor, asking about technical issues like backlog and word limits; the other you send to the faculty editor, asking about content issues regarding your article's fit for the journal.

Emailing the faculty editors of your three top choices is one of the most effective things you can do to increase your chances of publication in a good journal. As the only legitimate way around the single submission rule, it can prevent you from sending your work to a journal that will only reject your article, and it can aid you in finding the journal most likely to accept it. Why wait three to twelve months just to get rejected if you can figure this out beforehand? As one editor put it, "It is wise to contact the editor via email to float a trial balloon, to ensure that the topic and length are suitable (the journal might have already accepted a similar article not yet published)" (Argersinger and CELJ 2006). Another says that such emails "help entice the editor into paying close attention to your article" (Olson 1997, 58). Indeed, some journal publishers are formalizing query letters by setting up websites that allow you to submit an abstract and title to see whether it is a good fit for one of their journals (see for instance Elsevier's Journal Finder).

To Send or Not to Send

Sending query letters is standard practice in newspaper and magazine publishing, but uncommon in journal publishing. Many of us are trying to introduce the practice into academia (Henson 1999, 107–11; Van Til 1986, 19). But some scholars state that journal editors do not welcome query letters and even find them annoying, so you should not send them (A. Day 1996, 83, 93; Rodman 1978, 237–39; Gump 2004, 94). Interestingly, editors themselves are divided on the issue, as a survey shows (Argersinger and CELJ 2006). Meanwhile, most authors, inexperienced or otherwise, don't send query letters. Novice authors feel shy about approaching editors, whom they imagine live on Olympian heights, above us mere mortals, and experienced authors feel confident about their journal choice.

Frankly, though, helping authors is one of the jobs of editors. Therefore, I don't think they have the right to dodge their responsibility. That is, editors don't have the right to get annoyed at authors for asking a few questions before sending their hard work to a journal. It takes no more than five minutes to respond to a query letter, which is the least payment they can render to authors, who receive no money from journals for their articles. But as I promised you at the beginning of this workbook, my aim is to help you survive in the real world, where editors have a lot of power, not to send you as lambs to the wolves.

So before you send a query letter, here are two caveats. First, check the journal submission guidelines to see whether they explicitly invite or discourage query letters. Second, you can't send query letters to top journals. The more submissions a journal receives every year, the more likely it is that it won't respond to query letters—it may even be actively hostile to them. Also, a few rare journals have a triple-blind or triple-masked procedure, in which even the faculty editor doesn't know an author's identity until a final decision has been made about the article's publication. A journal that fits both these criteria is *PMLA*. Once, a student of mine, following my advice about query letters, was rebuked by *PMLA*'s editor at the time, who stated that knowing the name of the student author violated the journal's procedure and affected its ability to judge the article impartially when it arrived. The general lesson here is that you can't send query letters to every type of journal, and the specific lesson is that you shouldn't send these letters to massive journals or top disciplinary journals. Query letters are a technique for use with the other journals in the preferred publishing outlet category: field, regional, interdisciplinary, and newer journals. By the way, you are under no obligation to send the article to that journal just because you sent it a query letter.

Query Letters to the Faculty Editor

The editor (sometimes called the executive editor or editor-in-chief) is the faculty member in charge of the journal's content. This person is the most knowledgeable about what articles are likely to be accepted for publication. When you send a query letter to such an editor, the response will come in one of six ways, which I have arranged loosely from least helpful to most helpful. It should be noted that in no case will an editor's response be "Yes, we will publish it!" Editors will never commit to publishing an article sight unseen, no matter how impressive the query letter is.

No response. A good portion of editors simply won't respond. Although there can be many reasons for this—including being away from email or receiving a large volume of queries—it's not a good sign about the journal's functionality. If you haven't heard back within two weeks, think twice before sending your article to that journal. Chances are that it won't be efficient about getting back to you with a peer review either.

"Send it along" response. If you have done your journal research carefully and written a good query letter, most editors will write back saying, "Sure, send it along" or "I can't tell from a query letter whether this would work for us—send it and let's see." Such a response gives you no information about your chances, and certainly any editor interested in keeping the journal's rejection rate high will encourage you to submit your article. Yet this response is useful in that it lets you know that the journal has an active editor and is likely a solid publication. Further, for many novice authors, even this much encouragement is helpful, creating a kind of deadline or expectation that keeps motivation high. Many novice authors have told me that just knowing that an editor had their work in mind aided them in completing their article and sending it.

"Interesting!" response. Some editors will communicate their excitement about your project. Comments like "This is just the kind of article we are looking for," "In intellectual terms, your manuscript sounds very interesting," or "You don't have to be a 'big' name to publish with us—we are looking for promising young researchers" (direct quotes from emails some of my students have received) are very encouraging.

"Timely" response. A few editors will write back with useful information, such as "It's so interesting that you wrote to me today, because we just had an article drop out of a special issue on *x* and your article sounds like it might fit. Can you send the article immediately?" That is, writing a query letter to editors can gain you access to information you need to make the best decision. Several of my students' articles have been rushed into print because they happened to write a query letter to an editor just when that editor was looking for an article on their topic.

Positive "peer-review" response. A few editors will even give you a bit of a peer review by sending you a response such as "Your article sounds very interesting, although we usually only publish quantitative articles" or "It sounds like your article would be suitable for our journal, although your sample size might be a problem." This kind of response is incredibly useful, and you should thank the editor for giving you such a helpful answer. You may be able to make small changes to your article that will dramatically increase your chances of acceptance. Or you can send it to another journal. A student of mine received three constructive responses to his article about Chinese political economy. All three editors liked his abstract, but each had a different suggestion for what he might change in the article to make it more suitable for that editor's journal. The first noted that the student's article was a single-country study, and the journal tended to publish articles with "a broad comparative (cross-national) content"; the second said the same but recommended that the student include a section on the relevance of his case to other transitional economies; and the third recommended that he be sure to cite the journal's recent articles on the topic. The student, having received these wonderful minireviews, could then decide on the changes he was most interested in making and submit his article accordingly. Adding additional case studies was prohibitive, so he went with the third journal.

Negative "peer-review" response. The most useful editors of all are those who take the time to be negative. This may sound counterintuitive, but getting your query letter rejected is part of what you're trying to do when shopping your article around. Why go through the lengthy peer-review process when you can get it over with in an email exchange? Be grateful for the editor who heads you off at the pass. Editors can tell you that they're no longer interested in publishing articles on your topic, that they never publish articles with your methodological approach, that they already have an upcoming article on your topic, or that they won't be able to publish any new submissions for several years. Such an editor has saved you not only months of time but also the heartbreak of wholesale rejection. It's much easier to accept rejection of your query letter than of your article. You're far more likely to pick yourself up and move on from the first rejection than from the second. One of my students received a very direct and helpful response from an editor, who said, "I would not encourage you to send this along to us. We are moving more and more in [omitted] directions, and consequently publish less and less in more purely [omitted]. In general, we shy away from narrowly [omitted]—especially ones involving very small numbers of subjects. Your work sounds intriguing and I am sure you will be able to place it elsewhere without much difficulty. Indeed, you might think of trying a 'sister' journal of ours, [omitted]." In one day, the student got a peer review that usually would have taken three months at a minimum. She quickly sent an email to the journal the editor had recommended, and moved on.

Elements of the Query Letter to a Faculty Editor.
When drafting a query letter to a faculty editor, make sure to keep it short: no more than two paragraphs. The structure of a query letter is as follows, with no element taking more than a sentence, and the last point being the most important:

- If possible, send the letter from an <u>email</u> account affiliated with a university, not one of your free email accounts.

- Address the editor by <u>name</u> in the salutation.

- Mention any human <u>connections</u> to the editor, if you happen to have them (e.g., scholar so-and-so recommended that you contact the editor).

- State why the editor and the journal readers should be <u>interested</u> in your article (e.g., it will fill a gap, aid understanding, inspire debate, fit a journal theme, is fresh and different from specific articles and/or books already in print, and so on).

- Display <u>knowledge</u> of the journal (e.g., mention any recent articles the journal has published on your topic).

- Give the <u>title</u> of your article.

- State the article's <u>length</u> in words, and note whether this total includes notes, references, or tables.

- State that you have <u>not published</u> this article before (if you have not).

- State that you have <u>not submitted</u> it to any other journal (if you have not).

- Name any prestigious national grants or <u>awards</u> that you received for the research.

- Include your <u>abstract</u>, which can be longer than one sentence but not more than one hundred words. The shorter the abstract, the better.

- Ask a question that will tease out your article's <u>chances of rejection</u>. For instance, "I foresee one potential obstacle to the publication of my article in your journal: I note that my qualitative approach would deviate from the method used in most of the articles that you publish. Please let me know whether this is a problem." Or, "The reason that I am sending you this email, rather than simply sending my article along, is that I am concerned that the regional focus of my article will not quite fit the mandate of your journal. If you have any comments that could help me decide whether to submit my article to your publication, I would appreciate hearing them." Specific questions indicating deep knowledge of the journal will garner a reply from any good editor.

- <u>Thank</u> the editor for taking the time to look at your article.

Sample Query Letter to a Faculty Editor

Dear Dr. [first name, last name]:

Professor [name] recommended your journal, [journal name], as an excellent home for my article titled [title]. I notice that your journal has published articles on [topic] (I am thinking in particular of [author's name] article titled [title] published last year). Since there are few published studies on [topic], my article fills this gap and contributes to the understanding of [some debate or problem]. My article is about [number] words, including notes, references, and tables. I have never published this article, nor have I submitted it to any other journal. Grants from the [name of funders] funded the collection of data for this project.

My article argues that [abbreviated abstract here].

Would such an article interest you? Please let me know whether you feel that my broader focus, on [topic], would pose a problem for acceptance in your journal. As my section on [subtopic] is quite strong, I could recast the article to focus entirely on this [subtopic]. Thank you in advance for your time.

[Name without any title]
[University]
[Department]
[City]
[State/country]

Making the Final Journal Selection

By the end of this week, you should have picked two or three suitable journals and, if possible at this stage in your writing process, the journal to which you plan to submit your article first. If you need to wait for the journal editor to respond to your query letter, don't wait longer than a week. Knowing what journal (or two or three journals) you plan to send your work to makes a psychological difference—it will help you shape the article when you know the conversation you're joining.

Now, if all the foregoing has left you still debating about which journal to choose, here's a shortcut. The journal you select should have four features. It must be peer reviewed, and it must publish articles like yours in topic or field; then, you decide what two other features matter most to you (e.g., print and online availability, turnaround time, advisor's recommendation, rejection rate), and select the journal that seems stronger than the others in all four areas.

Which journal is my best choice for getting this article published?

Which journal is my second choice for getting this article published?

Which journal is my third choice for getting this article published?

Now you need to list what implications your first-choice journal has for the continued writing of your article. For instance, if your article doesn't meet the journal's word limit, you must start aiming for that limit, write a query letter asking how firm that limit is, or choose another journal.

> **What are my first-choice journal's page and/or word limits? What implications do those limits have for the current length of my article?**

Your first-choice journal has additional implications for your revision process. If the journal requires that you list all documentation in the notes, not the text, and you've done the opposite, you may have to switch your article over to that documentation method. If the journal has a special issue that you're aiming for, you'll need to take note of the date and work toward it. If the journal favors particular approaches, you'll need to beef up that part of your article. Use your filled-out Journal Evaluation Form to identify the implications.

> **What are the other writing implications that my first-choice journal has for this article?**

Tracking Writing Time

Mark your electronic calendar, the Calendar for Actual Time Spent Writing This Week form, and/or the check boxes here with how long you wrote today. ☐ 15+ min. ☐ 30+ ☐ 60+ ☐ 120+

Then, here at the end of your workweek, take pride in your accomplishments and evaluate whether any patterns need changing.

DOCUMENTING YOUR WRITING TIME AND TASKS

Calendar for Actual Time Spent Writing This Week

Time	Monday	Tuesday	Wednesday	Thursday	Friday	Saturday	Sunday
5:00 a.m.							
6:00							
7:00							
8:00							
9:00							
10:00							
11:00							
12:00 p.m.							
1:00							
2:00							
3:00							
4:00							
5:00							
6:00							
7:00							
8:00							
9:00							
10:00							
11:00							
12:00 a.m.							
1:00							
2:00							
3:00							
4:00							
Total minutes							
Tasks completed							

WEEK 5
Refining Your Works Cited

Task Day	Week 5 Daily Writing Tasks	Estimated Task Time in Minutes	
		HumInt	SciQua
Day 1 (Monday?)	Read from here until you reach the week 5, day 2 tasks, filling in any boxes, checking off any forms, and answering any questions as you read.	90	60
Day 2 (Tuesday?)	Evaluate your current Works Cited list.	90	30
Day 3 (Wednesday?)	Identify and read any additional works; evaluate other articles' cited works.	120+	0–120+
Day 4 (Thursday?)	Identify your entry point into the related secondary literature.	60+	0–60+
Day 5 (Friday?)	Write or revise your related secondary literature review.	120+	0–60+
Total estimated time for reading the workbook, completing the tasks, and writing your article		**8+ hours**	**5+ hours**

A bove are the tasks for your fifth week. Make sure to start this week by scheduling when you will write, and then tracking the time you actually spend writing (using the Calendar for Actual Time Spent Writing This Week form or online software).

Be aware that this week may take a lot more time or a lot less time than you had anticipated. The time will vary depending on your discipline, drafting stage, research stage, and familiarity with the literature. If you find that you need to take more than a week to complete this chapter's tasks, don't get discouraged! It's extremely common for this chapter to take more time, whether by experienced or novice authors. But for those who are in the constant process of updating their literature review, this chapter may need little more than a skim.

FOURTH WEEK IN REVIEW

You have now spent four weeks designing a writing plan, working on your abstract, developing your argument, and identifying appropriate journals for your article's publication. I don't know you, so this is going to seem weird . . . but I'm proud of you. Do you know how few people in the world have worked for four weeks on a piece of writing? Any piece of writing? You're part of a tiny portion of humanity. Now, maybe you didn't meet all your goals over the past four weeks, but you're still here. So you should be proud too.

And if you're still not writing regularly or getting around to all the tasks you hoped to do—don't feel guilty! Guilt about the past prevents us from action in the present. When we feel bad, it's difficult to get motivated. As a friend once said, you can't hate yourself into changing. Rather, accept that developing good writing habits often takes awhile. Then shake off those negative feelings and focus on today. Today is just as good a day to get started as yesterday, and if you're rereading this tomorrow or in a month or in a year, today is still a good day to get started.

No matter what you did this past week, use the box below to take a minute to write a positive message to yourself about writing. In it, be kind to yourself and be hopeful. Academics tend to deify the hostile and the negative. Dare to be positive! You can also phone or email a friend to complete this exercise in dialogue.

Positive Message to Myself about Writing

In previous weeks, we covered the two main reasons why journals reject articles—because they lack an argument or get sent to the wrong journal. Now we turn to the third main reason that journals reject articles: they're not citing the right bodies of literature. This week, you'll focus on evaluating your sources, that is, works cited, and possibly adding to your literature review of the scholarship directly on your topic.

READING SCHOLARLY TEXTS

When most scholars think about reading in their field, a wave of anxiety sweeps over them. And for good reason: there's so much to read! By some estimates, over 60 million journal articles have been published since the inception of journals in the seventeenth century (Jinha 2010, 258, 261, 262; Ware and Mabe 2015, 27, 28). With another 2.5 million journal articles published annually (Ware and Mabe 2015, 27) and over 120,000 first-edition scholarly books published every year in the United States alone (AAAS and Bosch 2015, par. 2, 3), it's impossible to keep up. Let me prove it.

Let's assume that you're an extraordinary reader, someone who manages to read five books and fifteen articles a week, week in and week out. You'll still read "only" 260 books and 780 articles a year, or about 10,000 books and 30,000 articles over a career. That seems like a lot until you realize that even the smallest humanities discipline publishes over 3,000 books a year in the United States (AAAS and Bosch 2015, indicator IV-12b), and the smallest social science discipline publishes hundreds of thousands of articles each year, so that even extraordinary readers can't keep up with their field. That remains true even though scholars are reading double the amount they read forty years ago, and reading more in less time. One survey shows US faculty reading on average 21 articles per month, or 252 articles per year (about 10,000 articles over a career) (Tenopir, King, et al. 2015, 102). The same faculty also reported spending an average of 32 minutes reading each article and a total of about 11 hours a month, or 132 hours annually, reading articles (102).

What's the upshot? You must abandon the hope of being comprehensive in your reading. No one is reading everything in his or her discipline or field. But fortunately, the bad news is also the good news. If you could keep up with your field, you might feel obligated to do so. But since you can't, you don't have to and instead can make a realistic plan for reading. How do you identify and read enough of the right sources? That's what this chapter is about.

TYPES OF SCHOLARLY TEXTS

All published journal articles cite other texts. And the number of these texts cited in any article is not small. A survey found that US faculty in medicine reported reading 34 texts for their last substantive work, those in the sciences 104, those in the humanities 130, and those in the social sciences 211 (Tenopir, King, et al. 2015, 97). That's a lot of reading!

An important part of strategizing how to get such reading done is to identify your texts by type. Knowing the distinct categories they fall into can help you plan your reading and use the right body of texts for the right purpose. The categories are *primary, original, or exhibit sources* (texts that are your subject of study), *scholarly or secondary literature* (texts that help you think about your subject of study), and *derivative or tertiary documents* (unoriginal texts that should not be cited, like Wikipedia). Another way of typifying texts is according to their authorship. Good scholars ensure that bias has not led to their ignoring strong scholarship by a diversity of authors—I'll have more to say about this later in the chapter.

Primary, Original, or Exhibit Sources

The texts you are analyzing or interpreting in your article are known as the primary, original, or exhibit sources. Joseph Bizup, a prominent scholar of writing, likens such texts to "exhibits in a museum or a trial," which can and are read in a multiplicity of ways in articles (2008, 75). Of course, we subject all texts to analysis, but we analyze only certain sources openly, repeatedly, and carefully in our articles. Primary sources can be written texts, but they can also be images, sounds, or objects. In the experimental sciences, primary sources are any document that describes the experiment. Some examples of what might be your primary or exhibit sources are as follows:

- **archival sources**, such as diaries, letters, email, ships' logs, pamphlets, newsletters, planning documents, court cases, legislation, dictionaries, and corporate reports
- **media sources**, such as magazines, newspapers, news blogs, and television programs
- **ethnographic sources**, such as interview tapes and video, eyewitness accounts, field notes and observations, classroom observations, focus group discussions, and student journals
- **statistical sources**, such as online polls, government censuses, phone surveys, and data sets
- **experiment sources**, such as genome sequences, laboratory notebooks, technical reports, video observations of laboratory experiments with human beings, and student examinations
- **literary sources**, such as novels, short stories, memoirs, and poetry as well as scripts for films, plays, and musicals
- **visual sources**, such as photographs, paintings, sculptures, advertisements, films, videos, television programs, streaming media, and exhibits, but also furniture, buildings, and roads
- **aural sources**, such as pop songs, operas, musicals, scores, concerts, and elevator music, but also alarms and conversation
- **online sources**, such as original material on Facebook, Twitter, Instagram, LinkedIn, Tumblr, and Reddit; Amazon and Goodreads comments; online comment sections; individual blogs; and disease discussion sites

How scholars use a text ultimately determines its category. Some texts not ordinarily treated as exhibit or primary sources become so in certain articles because of how the author applies them. A US history textbook may be an unusable tertiary document to a scholar of the women's suffrage movement, but an essential primary source to a scholar of sexism in educational textbooks.

A common mistake made by novice authors is not citing primary or exhibit sources. If your article proceeds without any, start working to include them in your article. You can't just state your own opinions; you must carefully analyze the exhibit or primary sources as evidence. Even theoretical articles in the humanities cite these sources (e.g., in one of Heather Love's [2010, 385] most cited theoretical articles, she uses a paragraph from Toni Morrison's novel *Beloved* to explicate her theory). When analyzing exhibit or primary sources, there are no shortcuts. You must not skim them; you must read them deeply.

Do I cite primary sources in this article? If not, what's at least one primary source I could include?

Scholarly or Secondary Literature

Most of the texts that scholars cite in their journal article fall into the category of secondary sources, commonly known as "the literature." Such texts are all the books, articles, and chapters written by other scholars and excluding primary sources and tertiary documents.

However, there are several types of secondary literature: *contextual literature* (works that help you describe your subject's context), *methodological literature* (works that aid in your process of studying your subject), *theoretical literature* (works that help you think about your subject), and *related literature* (works that are about your subject exactly). Let's go through each of them.

Contextual Secondary Literature

Scholarly texts containing information about the broader context of your topic are contextual literature; you usually cite them in the introduction of your article or in a dedicated section right after it. Bizup calls these "background" texts, because they are the "materials a writer relies on for general information or for factual evidence" (2008, 72).

Many of us can spend massive amounts of time on this category of literature, tracking down information about the historical, epochal, geographic, economic, demographic, aesthetic, or political context of our subjects. After all, we do need to contextualize. But stay conscious of what contextual literature you're reading, along with how much of it and why. If you're writing an article about Frances Burney's *Evelina*, you may not need to read an entire book about eighteenth-century London. If you're writing an article about risky traditional practices associated with HIV transmission, you may not need to read a book about the biology of disease transmission. Only you can decide what contextual sources are relevant to your work; but if you still have contextual literature to read for this article, try limiting yourself to three texts and then continuing with other article-related tasks. You can always come back to this reading activity. And if you weren't planning to read any contextual literature at all, that's fine by me.

> Do I need to cite more contextual literature in this article? If so, how can I limit that reading?

Methodological Secondary Literature

Scholarly texts supplying you with the *processes* for producing and analyzing your evidence are methodological literature. Bizup describes these texts as "materials from which a writer . . . derives a manner of working" (2008, 72). Most journal articles do not cite methodological literature. If your methodology is common and accepted, you don't need to either. As one senior scholar in the social sciences said to me, "We don't want to see a manual for doing statistics in the Methods section. Would you trust a mechanic who worked on your car with the car's manual in hand?" In the humanities, citing methodological literature is extremely rare. If you're using a methodology that has its challengers, however, you may need to head off the peer reviewers by demonstrating both your awareness of the concerns and your sound reasons for using the method anyway.

> Do I need to cite more methodological literature in this article? If so, how can I limit that reading?

Theoretical Secondary Literature

Scholarly texts supplying you with conceptual approaches to or explanatory frameworks for your evidence are theoretical literature. You most often cite theoretical literature in the introduction of your article or in a theory section immediately following. Bizup describes these texts as the "materials from which a writer takes a governing concept" (2008, 72). The difference between theoretical and methodological literature is slim and depends quite a bit on the discipline: in the humanities, the term *theoretical literature* is more common; in the social, health, behavioral, and natural sciences, the term *methodological literature* is more common. (Indeed, Bizup doesn't differentiate between the two, calling both "method" sources, although he gives a two-part definition of *secondary literature* that maps onto my two terms.) I continue to differentiate them: methods are about how you *do* something; theories are about how you *think* about something. For example, snowball sampling and close reading are methods for collecting data; social cohesion theory and feminist theory are ways of thinking about that data.

Note that, like methodological literature, some theories have become so accepted that they're not always cited these days. Many a Marxist analysis is published without citing Marx's works; many a work of deconstruction is published without citing Jacques Derrida's or Ferdinand de Saussure's works. So you may not need to read or cite any additional theoretical literature. However, if you're working with a new theory, one that might be unfamiliar to many in your field, you'll need to cite some of the literature laying that theory out.

> Do I need to cite more theoretical literature in this article? If so, how can I limit that reading?

Related Secondary Literature

Scholarly texts that analyze and make arguments about the same topic, sources, and/or argument as your article are what I call *related secondary literature* or just *related literature*—scholarship that relates to your article. The previously mentioned types of secondary literature—contextual, methodological, and theoretical—rarely mention your exact topic, sources, and/or argument. Related literature does, and you discuss it in your article's literature review section. Bizup usefully calls these "argument" sources, because they are the "materials whose claims a writer affirms, disputes, refines, or extends in some way" (2008, 75). A literature review is, for him, an exploration of "specific constellations of argument sources" (81).

In the social, health, behavioral, and natural sciences, most scholars are trained to read and cite the related literature as undergraduates. They know that if they are writing about the causes of a social problem, they must discuss the previous research of those who have claimed to identify its causes. If they are challenging the premises of a policy, they know they must analyze the previous research on that policy. But for many novice authors in the humanities, this point—that you must cite the related literature, the constellation of argument sources—is one of the toughest to grasp. Perhaps this is because humanities students can write classroom essays without a professor's ever asking them to cite what has already been argued on the topic. In the classroom, professors rarely assign scholarly articles about a particular novel, poem, or artwork. So humanities students know that they are supposed to reference various theories and theoreticians (like Theodor W. Adorno, Gloria Anzaldúa, or Judith Butler), but they don't know that their interpretation of a work must be related to other interpretations of the work. For instance, if you're writing a class analysis of Stendahl's *Le Rouge et le noir*, you must note who else has written a class analysis of this novel, and articulate how your article relates to the arguments of previous scholarly research on the novel. The task of addressing related literature makes up the bulk of this chapter.

> Do I cite the related literature in this article? If not, what are some keywords of that related literature that I could use to search for it?

Let me summarize the four types of secondary literature by using an example. Say you're writing an article about women's Bible study groups in two Chicago neighborhoods, one predominantly black, one predominantly white. The *contextual* literature might be anything previously published about the history or population of the neighborhoods, Chicago's racial segregation, and/or evangelicalism, among other things. The *methodological* literature might be about the best ways to conduct studies across race or about religious groups, for instance. The *theoretical* literature might be on topics that include feminist theory, intersectionality, and mitigating factors for implicit bias and/or racism. The *related* literature, meanwhile, would be anything published about women's Bible study groups. If nothing has been published on your exact topic, sources, and/or argument, then your related literature would be whatever discusses the next closest thing: for instance, men's Bible study groups, women's Qur'anic study groups, church youth groups, women's bridge clubs, and so on.

Derivative or Tertiary Documents

Popular or reference texts consisting of nonscholarly *summaries* of others' research are known as derivative or tertiary documents ("tertiary" because the research is at third hand, and to align it with the "primary" and "secondary" nomenclature for other texts). Finding out about research through such resources is perfectly acceptable, but then you need to find the actual study, read it, and cite that source. Some examples of derivative documents:

- **magazines, newspapers, and news blogs**, such as *Psychology Today*, the *Atlantic Monthly*, the *Chronicle of Higher Education*, the *New York Times*, *Huffington Post*, *Africa Is a Country* blog, and so on
- **encyclopedias**, such as the *Encyclopaedia Britannica* or Wikipedia, which has an explicit policy of "no original research" (of course, some encyclopedias include original works of research, with information that appears nowhere else, such as many articles in the magisterial *Encyclopaedia Aethiopica*, and therefore must be cited)
- **textbooks**, which depend on original studies but are not themselves original studies
- **websites** that report on scholarship that appeared elsewhere, such as websites for classrooms, CliffsNotes, disciplinary gossip, and scholars' blogs

One common mistake that novice authors make is citing derivative documents instead of the scholarly literature they depend on. For instance, you can't cite the *Washington Post* as a source on inflammation and disease, a classroom website as a source for a quote from the scholar Imani Perry's 2018 book *Vexy Thing*, or an individual's blog as a source of statistics about a nation's car ownership rates. Derivative documents are never an adequate source for experimental data or quotations from scholarship. The real source of the information is not the magazine or website but the articles in journals or the scholarly books that they're quoting.

Of course, sometimes derivative documents are your exhibit or primary sources. That is, if your journal article is about *representations* of inflammation and disease in popular media, or *the spread of quotations* by Imani Perry online, or *popular perceptions* of car ownership, then cite these sources, because for you they're not derivative sources. They're your exhibit or primary sources, the materials you are studying.

> Do I cite derivative documents in this article? If so, do I need to upgrade and/or remove the source(s)?

Advice for Scholars at Resource-Poor Institutions

Let me take a moment to address some challenges in accomplishing the tasks in this chapter. Scholars in many parts of Africa, Asia, and Latin America do not have large libraries or accessible online archives. Neither do Euro-Americans at institutions whose libraries are underfunded. If you're a scholar at a resource-poor university, you're restricted in obtaining the full text of materials, but there are some steps you can take. Many of them depend on having some internet access, but not all of them do.

Search engines. You can use academic search engines to locate peer-reviewed journal articles and books. The best are Google Scholar and Google Books, but multidisciplinary BASE, which searches academic open-access web resources; multidisciplinary JURN, a dedicated journal searcher; and massive multidisciplinary bibliographic databases such as Scopus and WorldCat are also helpful. Discipline-based databases like PsycINFO can be useful as well. Other search engines like Microsoft Academic Search and RefSeek, touted as for "academic research," are aimed at those in secondary schools and so do not provide the precision needed for postgraduate scholarly work, in my experience. Search engines will occasionally locate materials that are freely available online. You simply click on the result and start reading. Many times, however, that search will locate materials that are behind paywalls. There are several techniques for gaining access to these articles.

University library websites. Sometimes, if you do the exact same search at your university library website, you'll find access to the articles through a proxy server.

Academic social networks. Many authors post their articles for free at academic networking websites like Academia.edu, ResearchGate, and Mendeley. If you find a useful article through a Google search but discover that it's behind a paywall, try going to these sites and searching for the same article to see whether the author has posted it there (such posting is called self-archiving or green open access). One side benefit of these networks is that you can set up your own page and follow others' research on topics that interest you.

University open-access repositories. Many universities require their faculty, especially those in the sciences, to post their published materials in open-access repositories. Use a dedicated open-access search engine like BASE to find full-text articles in such repositories. If that doesn't work, you can identify the author's academic affiliation, go to Open DOAR (Directory of Open-Access Repositories) to determine whether his or her university has such a repository, and then search for the full text of that article there.

Disciplinary open-access repositories. Many websites provide full texts in specific fields, including the free full-text archives PubMed Central (PMC), for biomedical and life sciences journal literature; POPLINE, for reproductive health and development literature; and Science.gov, a gateway to government science information as well as scientific databases.

Developing countries' access initiatives. Because of access inequalities, some full-text websites have joined to provide free access to scholarly institutions in Asia, Africa, and Latin America. So long as you're accessing the full-text website through a computer on a campus internet connection in a developing country, you can read the full texts of articles. Websites providing this access include JSTOR, HighWire Press, African Journals Online, and Research4Life, a public-private partnership to provide scholars in developing countries with online access to articles in medicine, economics, law and policy, and other social science fields. You can also use the Open Science Directory, a search tool for finding journals available through such access initiatives. Some open-access sites are specific to a continent, such as Aluka, on African cultural and ecological heritages. So your institution may have access to online archives even though it's resource poor and outside the United States. I have worked with many African scholars who were surprised to find how many useful materials they could access through their campus internet connection.

Authors. If all else fails and you really need an article that you absolutely cannot get access to, you can find the author's email address online and contact him or her to request a copy. So long as authors aren't receiving hundreds of such requests, it isn't difficult for them to send a PDF of their article, and many are happy to do so. Indeed, scholars working in resource-rich environments are obligated to aid those who are not. This contact may even start a helpful conversation, and the author may be able to provide other materials and identify current debates as well. Don't ask for print copies or PDFs of books, however; most authors will consider this rude.

Editors. If you did your best and still couldn't get many relevant sources, state your limited access in the submission form (or cover letter) when you submit your article to the journal you've chosen. Tell the editors that you think you have good data, but you don't have access to the related literature. If the editors like the article, they may want to be of assistance. Some are aware of the difficulties that scholars at resource-poor institutions labor under and sometimes want to help. Just do your best to cite at least two articles published in their journal in the previous two years.

STRATEGIES FOR CITING YOUR READING

Ensuring that you cite your reading accurately, completely, and fairly is one of the biggest challenges of writing an article. It's extremely tough to cite properly, and incredibly easy to do it wrong. That's because this process is not just a matter of, say, typing in the correct year of a publication; it's ensuring that all aspects of how you address texts are correct. Here are some steps you can take to ensure that you use these sources properly.

Common Mistakes in Citing Texts

Don't misattribute big ideas. If you attribute general beliefs or entire systems of thought to one person, peer reviewers can dismiss your article as unscholarly. For instance, you cannot state in passing that "Howard Winant discovered that race is a socially constructed phenomenon." Thousands have argued for the social construction of identity. At most you could write, "Sociologists since Durkheim have argued that social interaction makes reality; Howard Winant was instrumental in calling attention to the constructed nature of race."

Don't misattribute small ideas. If you cite one scholar's articulation of another scholar's idea, peer reviewers can dismiss your article as unscholarly. If Brian Edwards writes that "the postcolonial has always been affected by the risks and potentialities of what Edward Said called 'travelling theory'" (2007, 289), you don't cite Brian Edwards on "traveling theory." That is, just because you found out in Brian Edwards's article that this idea belongs to Said, it doesn't mean that you cite Edwards. It means that you must read and cite Said.

Don't cite asides. If you cite as related literature those articles that do not fully address the debate in which you are engaging, peer reviewers can dismiss your article as unscholarly. For instance, several articles have been written about "the age of circulation." If you're writing on that topic, don't cite an article that has only a pertinent sentence or two; cite those that discuss the topic at length. Students who have read only classroom-assigned works often make the mistake of citing only what professors have assigned them. Take the time to find articles and books that are devoted to your topic.

Don't cite the derivative. As noted, if you cite websites or newspapers as the source of your information about important scholarly arguments and debates, peer reviewers will dismiss your article as unscholarly. For instance, don't arrange your article about modernism around theoretical definitions explained in an online site about a Tate Gallery exhibit in London. Don't cite US demographic data from any text other than that obtained from the US Census Bureau (it's easy to find online).

Don't cite irrelevant literature. If you cite literature unrelated to your topic, peer reviewers can dismiss your article as digressive. For instance, if you're analyzing an educational experiment in which undergraduates conduct real field research, don't spend half the article discussing various theories of field research.

Don't cite one secondary text too much. If you cite one related-literature text throughout your article or repeatedly in reference to your argument, peer reviewers may suspect that your work is derivative. Don't depend on one secondary text for more than one or two paragraphs at most. This includes not overciting the theorist whose theory you're deploying—that individual's work can appear near the beginning and the end of your article, but your perspective should dominate.

Don't overcite definitions. Classroom essays can devote pages to scholars' or even dictionaries' definitions of various terms. Publishable articles do not. You must efficiently address the challenges of defining your terms—define each in a sentence or maybe a note. Few articles get published that simply dispute other scholars' definitions.

Don't quote too much. Your job is to summarize, evaluate, and/or analyze the secondary literature, not reproduce it. If your article contains too many quotations, especially block quotes, you're probably not digesting the secondary literature enough. Do not fatten your writing with others' works.

Don't omit citations. If you use the phrases "scholars argue that" or "research shows that," always include citations after them. Most journal editors won't accept references to scholarly trends without citations of actual publications.

Don't fail to update. If you cite related-literature articles that were published five to ten years ago, you need to not only check which articles have cited them since then but also give a sense of how the conversation has evolved. This is easy to do. Search for the article in Google Scholar and then, in the search results, click on the "Cited by" and/or "Related to" links beneath each result. This will give you a list of articles and books that have cited your source. Then restrict those results to the last year or two. This procedure works best in the social, health, behavioral, and natural sciences, as citations in humanities articles are rarely tracked well.

Don't cite too little. The more you cite, the more you get cited. The scholar Gregory Webster researched psychology journals and the journal *Science* (Webster, Jonason, and Schember 2009), finding that, as he told a reporter, "there is a ridiculously strong relationship between the number of citations a paper receives and its number of references. . . . If you want to get more cited, the answer could be to cite more people" (Corbyn 2010). Other research has confirmed this (Wang et al. 2012; van Wesel, Wyatt, and ten Haaf 2014). However, thoughtful citing is still important for creating this effect; the least cited articles were those that randomly cited sources across disciplines, linking many sources rarely cited together (Shi, Leskovec, and McFarland 2010). So artificially inflating the number of your citations won't help you much (e.g., by copying strings of citations from other articles). Rather, this statistic shows that articles solidly built on previously published research are more persuasive (van Wesel, Wyatt, and ten Haaf 2014).

Don't fail to check for retractions. If you're in the biomedical sciences, it's wise to check the articles that you've cited at Retractionwatch.com, to see whether any of them have been retracted (i.e., the authors or editors had to withdraw the article from publication because of fraudulent or incorrect data). A growing problem is that people continue to cite articles that have been retracted. To check your citations, just type the last names of the authors or a distinctive string of words from each title into Retractionwatch.

Don't forget to cite yourself. If your previous articles or books are on the same topic, cite them. One study found that 10 percent of all citations are self-citations, but that men cite themselves 70 percent more than women do (M. King et al. 2016). Being cited matters for hiring and promotion, so if you're a humble person, don't be shy. Cite yourself.

Don't fail to cite the journal. Some obsess about citing many articles from the journal to which they intend to send their article or citing the work of its editor, and I don't agree with that. But if the journal has published an article on your exact topic, you must cite it. One journal editor wrote that upon receiving a submission, "we scan the references, and if there are no citations to [our] journals, then the paper is probably not aligned with our discourse," and the journal rejects it (Hall 2015, 61). An editor at a top humanities journal recently told me that they automatically reject any submission that has fewer than two citations to articles in the journal. Another way of putting this is that if you can't find any related literature in the journal to which you're sending your article, it probably isn't the right journal for your article.

> Am I making any of these common mistakes in this article? What two things can I do to avoid making these mistakes?

Establishing Your "Citation Values"

All scholars should be working to ensure that biases do not prevent them from citing strong work. Research on the "politics of citation" (Delgado 1984) shows that academia privileges some scholarly voices while marginalizing others, even when their work is directly relevant or even superior. Research even demonstrates that "women produce higher quality research than men" (Rivera Leon 2017, par. 8; Rivera Leon, Mairesse, and Cowan 2016, 24, 25, 28, 33, 44, 45). Moreover, research shows that disciplines fail to cite even strong work by women and scholars of color (Delgado 1984; Morris 2015; Ahmed 2017). In all fields, a diversity of authors produces good scholarship. Nevertheless, replicating the biases of scholarship is all too easy. All you have to do is cite only whomever everyone else is citing. Good scholars create innovative research precisely because they do not follow well-trodden paths, whether in terms of topic, approach, or citation.

So take the opportunity to expand the scope of your article beyond the biases of your field's intellectual tradition. To do so, you'll need to think about your "citation values," a term the scholar Brian Herrera coined when we were discussing this issue. What do you want your citations to say about you? Do your past citation practices accurately reflect your priorities as a member of particular scholarly communities? Do you want to work toward avoiding the biases of your discipline and including those most unjustly excluded? What types of authorship do you want to be sure not to ignore?

Establishing your citation values is not just about being a good person. It's about avoiding embarrassing, even humiliating errors. If the editors of a philosophy journal's special issue had done so, they wouldn't have had to apologize for publishing an entire issue on the Black Lives Matter movement without a single black author (Jaschik 2017). African Americans have done the most important work on the topic; to ignore them is a failure of scholarship, not just an ethical failure. So be especially careful that you don't exclude women and people of color when writing on a topic that affects those scholars or in which those scholars predominate (Delgado 1984; Ahmed 2012).

Of course, your article's citations don't have to eradicate all injustice. For instance, an importance citation value of mine is citing women and black authors, but I don't have a citation value of ensuring that I cite Latinx or Asian authors, because there are so few of them in my field of African studies. I also don't have the great citation value of my colleague Karen Emmerich in comparative literature, who prioritizes citing sources written in non-English languages, thereby encouraging the reading, circulation, and translation of scholarly work from linguistic elsewheres. But all scholarship should make the world a more just place, and one way to do that is establishing your citation values. I will discuss this in more detail later in this chapter.

Avoiding Improper Borrowing (Don't Skip This!)

Many of us would benefit from frank conversations with other scholars about improper borrowing, otherwise known as plagiarism, but the topic is so hot that most professors avoid discussing it, except in warnings to their undergraduates. Unfortunately, however, the advice we give to undergraduates isn't enough to guide scholars embarking on publication. Even more unfortunately, most scholars think, "I'm a good person; I couldn't possibly be committing a sin as bad as plagiarism." Therefore, I'm going to say something aggressive to you: if you have only *heard* about plagiarism and never *studied* what plagiarism is in scholarship, you're a plagiarist. That is, I guarantee that you're making the mistakes in your writing that constitute plagiarism. I'll explain in a moment.

If you refuse to read the rest of this section, just make sure you read this paragraph. You should not plagiarize for five reasons. First, we're now living in a brave new world where advances in technology are exposing authors past and present for their borrowing of others' work (Citron and Ginsparg 2015; Kolowich 2016; Gehrke et al. 2006; Watson 2016). Plagiarizing is no longer a lottery in which it's unlikely that your name will ever be picked. It's now an absolute that a plagiarized article will be caught—maybe not this year, maybe not next year, but some year it will happen. Don't do something today that may be caught in five years and ruin your reputation with the mistake of a younger self. Second, many journals now run all submissions through plagiarism-detection software like iThenticate or CrossCheck. If they find "overlap" with another author's work, they will send your article to that author, with your name revealed. And the journal editors have a scorched-earth policy: they'll make a point of contacting everyone possible about your violation, including your advisors, chair, department, and university. Third, representing others' work as your own is morally wrong. It's theft. Fourth, research shows that articles filled with borrowing are less likely to be frequently cited (Citron and Ginsparg 2015). Fifth, plagiarism will cost you everything. Someone I know recently lost the opportunity to file his dissertation, earn a PhD, go on a fellowship, and ever obtain an academic job, all because of the kind of plagiarism many don't know they're doing.

If you think that you'll be able to defend your borrowing practices, be warned that editors and deans aren't impressed with the following defenses: "I have an excellent memory; I had no idea that I was repeating that work verbatim"; "I feel so bad; I'm such a sloppy note-taker!"; "The pastiche approach is an acceptable postmodern methodology"; "I had such a heavy workload that it was justified"; or "In my culture, this is accepted practice." Authorities have heard all the excuses before—it seems that, perhaps unsurprisingly, excuses for plagiarism are themselves plagiarized.

What Is Improper Borrowing?

Part of the reason that plagiarism persists is that scholars' understandings of what constitutes "really bad plagiarism" differ. No scholars anywhere think that taking another scholar's entire article, word for word, and publishing it as their own original work is right. Everyone agrees that such a practice is theft. Where things get murkier is with any type of borrowing less egregious than that. For some, cobbling others' writing into a whole piece that reads coherently feels so satisfying, even fun, that it doesn't feel like stealing— it feels like taming chaos. For others, cultural norms of writing are quite different (Ehrich et al. 2016; Doss et al. 2016). Borrowing is perceived differently in educational systems that focus on memorizing and imitating classics (Hu and Lei 2012), perceive texts as belonging to the community, not the individual (Mundava and Chaudhuri 2007), or view articles as repositories for collected knowledge, not for constructing knowledge (Hayes and Introna 2005). In other words, it's not that some cultures approve of stealing; it's that views of what constitutes stealing vary. As a result, a study about overlap in the arXiv repository found that authors from certain countries outside the Americas and Europe are about twice as likely to reuse text as authors from the United States and the United Kingdom are (Citron and Ginsparg 2015). Such rates of reuse don't mean that people from these countries are lacking in moral fiber; they mean that norms of reuse vary.

Even those who have attended US schools their entire life can have different views of what constitutes plagiarism. I know, because one drawback to the success of this workbook is how many articles and chapters online have plagiarized from it. The authors may have thought they weren't plagiarizing, because they cited the workbook frequently; but they didn't put quotation marks around many phrases taken directly from the workbook, and the structure and thrust of their article followed the workbook too closely. And these same authors ostensibly had read this very section on plagiarism! How is that possible? Maybe they weren't careful, or they just didn't think it was a "big deal." For instance, I often think that undergraduates perceive our forbidding plagiarism as akin to our forbidding cell phone use in class—both are things professors don't want you to do, but everyone does anyway.

Undergraduates don't understand that professors perceive a massive difference between cell phone use in class and plagiarizing—the first is breaking a rule, the second is criminal theft.

If you're a conscientious scholar, all these warnings will make you anxious. They make me anxious! I wrote this workbook over a very long period—what if I incorrectly copied something fifteen years ago and, thinking it was my own wording, dumped it into my manuscript without placing it within quotation marks? What if I so liked how a scholar phrased something that I regularly quoted it aloud to people and gradually forgot that the words weren't my own? Both seem quite possible. The story that truly terrifies me is the one where the scholar warning against plagiarism "plagiarized the definition of plagiarism" (Thomason 2014). Every time I think of it, I keep returning to this section, searching for any slipups! But honestly, such anxiety isn't helpful. The very fact that you bought this book, and have worked hard enough to reach this chapter, is an excellent sign that you're unlikely to commit plagiarism with any deliberateness. Still, you may wonder, are you unknowingly committing some academic sin? It's possible. Let's turn to a gray area rarely covered in undergraduate courses.

What Is Paraphrase Plagiarism?

Some types of paraphrasing are plagiarism as well—slightly or even heavily varying sentences or paragraphs even when the source is cited. If your wording is too close to the author's, it may be problematic despite the citation. This issue of paraphrase plagiarism is covered in the excellent undergraduate text *The Craft of Research* (Booth et al. 2016), now in its fourth edition, which is a wonderful resource for conducting research and drafting papers. The authors reproduce a paragraph verbatim and then show various examples of paraphrasing it that are questionable. Here are the examples, themselves taken verbatim from *The Craft of Research* (2003). To indicate the problem more clearly, I have added underscore for unvaried words that appear in the same order in the original version, and underdots for words that have been slightly changed.

> **Original paragraph:** It is trickier to define plagiarism when you summarize and paraphrase. They are not the same, but they blend so seamlessly that you may not even be aware when you are drifting from summary into paraphrase, then across the line into plagiarism. No matter your intention, close paraphrase may count as plagiarism, even when you cite the source.

> **Plagiarized version:** It is harder to describe plagiarism when summary and paraphrase are involved, because they differ, their boundaries blur, and a writer may not know that she has crossed the boundary from summary to paraphrase and from paraphrase to plagiarism. Regardless of intention, a close paraphrase is plagiarism, even when the source is cited. This paragraph, for instance, would count as plagiarism of that one (Booth, Colomb, and Williams 169).

> **Borderline plagiarized version:** Because it is difficult to distinguish the border between summary and paraphrase, a writer can drift dangerously close to plagiarism without knowing it, even when the writer cites a source and never meant to plagiarize. Many might consider this paragraph a paraphrase that crosses the line (Booth, Colomb, and Williams 169).

Correctly summarized version: According to Booth, Colomb, and Williams, writers sometimes plagiarize unconsciously because they think they are summarizing, when in fact they are closely paraphrasing, an act that counts as plagiarism, even when done unintentionally and sources are cited (169).

When I present this example in workshops, half the audience exclaims in consternation, "Oh, my God, I've plagiarized!" Although it's a common practice to do what's been done in the plagiarized and borderline plagiarized versions above—take a couple sentences from someone else's work, then cut them a bit, vary a few of the words so there's no need for quotation marks, and then cite the original—it's plagiarism.

Why? you may ask. What's the problem if the source is cited? First, the way that the plagiarized and borderline plagiarized paragraphs put the citation at the end suggests that the ideas in only the last sentence are from another source, not the ideas of the entire paragraph. Second, the wording in the first two versions is just too close. That is, it's not just ideas that are the intellectual property of authors but their wording. For instance, the phrase "make writing social" appeared once on the internet before my first edition of the workbook was published in 2009, and it has appeared forty-seven times since. The previous instance was unrelated to academic writing in that it was used in a discussion of how wikis work (Mejias 2005). But all the appearances since my workbook came out have been in the context of academic writing, and most of the time the people using the phrase don't cite the workbook. And I don't call anyone on it, even though it took me a long time to come up with that pithy phrase, because (1) I'm pretty sure that most of them don't remember where they saw that phrase; (2) it's remotely possible that at least one of them came up with that phrase on their own; and (3) it's likely that I've done the exact same type of borrowing somewhere in this book! Like most everything else having to do with writing, none of us is perfect. But all of us should try to be better about acknowledging the work of others, including their wording.

Now, to be honest, if you improperly paraphrase one paragraph from one source in one article, no one will chase you out of the profession. However, if you do this repeatedly in one article for paragraphs from the same source or for many paragraphs from multiple sources, you're plagiarizing and could draw an editor's ire. (By the way, software developers are working hard to come up with antiplagiarism software that will be good at catching this type of plagiarism, so don't think that paraphrasing will avoid detection.)

So let's get to the practical details of avoiding plagiarism. What exactly should you do to avoid getting in trouble with editors and other authors?

Good Citation Habits

The best way to ensure that you cite sources accurately, completely, and fairly is to maintain good research and writing habits.

Always revise. Any author carefully going over every sentence in their piece—seeking for ways to improve diction, sentence structure, clarity, and flow—is unlikely to have chunks of others' work remaining in it. Even if a paragraph accidentally entered the article wholesale from somewhere else, its totality won't survive a true revision process.

Whenever I see cases of authors getting in trouble for publishing an article that includes word-for-word paragraphs from others' work, I always find it striking, because they clearly aren't revising their work. What kind of author would leave any paragraphs untouched?! The problem with such an author is deeper than merely borrowing.

Review others' work briefly rather than at length. As mentioned earlier and in previous chapters, you need to review the previous literature quickly and then move on firmly to your own ideas. If you're paraphrasing other sources heavily and repeatedly throughout your research article or summarizing entire articles or books in lengthy sections, your problem is not just possibly plagiarizing—it's being too derivative in a larger sense.

Focus on being persuasive rather than brilliant. Most of us know that we're not the smartest scholar out there—whether in our discipline or in our field. Fortunately, the point of article writing is not to prove that you're brilliant; it's to persuade your readers to believe something. If you focus on persuasion, the temptation to borrow someone else's smartness diminishes. Weirdly, narcissism (the obsessive desire to prove one's worth) is the very thing that leads people to be less themselves and more a borrowed version of others' selves. If you get over yourself, you won't plagiarize.

Don't worry about your English. Research suggests that nonnative speakers of English are more likely to reuse others' texts, because they're anxious about their English (Devlin and Gray 2007, 188). They insert others' writing into their articles because they think that others write better in English. But perfect English is not the reason that journal articles get published—they get published because they have a strong argument, robust evidence, and a clear structure, the very qualities this workbook helps you learn. If English is your second language, focus on argument, evidence, and structure, not phrasing, and your article will do fine.

Use an RMS program. Those who use a reference-management software (RMS) program are less likely to plagiarize. Without such programs, some authors fall into paraphrase plagiarism because they fail to note the source of a text and then try to change the wording enough so they don't feel the need to cite the source. It's shoddy methods, not immoral ones, causing the problem here. And then, when such authors get caught they protest, because they know their own heart and their purpose wasn't to steal. As some scholars put it, "There is a fine line between plagiarism and poor academic practice" (Burkill and Abbey 2004, 440). Using an RMS program is the best way to ensure true accuracy of citations across texts and time.

Develop systematic notes. Take notes that make absolutely clear the distinction between your comments on the text and your direct quotations from or paraphrases of the text. If words in your notes are a direct quote, always place them inside quotation marks. If they're a paraphrase, add a remark after the words stating that this is the case (e.g., "my paraphrase"). If they represent your own thoughts or commentary, place them inside brackets (or use all capitals, yellow highlight, or red font). Whatever you do, develop a method so that you'll know tomorrow or in ten years exactly what you copied directly from the text, what you paraphrased, and what your own commentary is.

Paraphrase without looking at the source. When reading something useful in another text, try setting that text down and typing what you remember it to have said. Taking notes from memory can be a good way to avoid putting things exactly as the original did. If you have an excellent memory, this technique may not work—be sure to check your notes against the original and confirm that your wording isn't too close.

Check your coauthors' work. Some coauthors have been surprised to learn that an article to which they contributed, but did not actually write out, contained plagiarized portions (Watson 2016). Be sure that your coauthors are also aware of the perils of lifting material from others' work. In addition, if you don't know them well, read their material carefully for variations in style or diction that might signal borrowing.

Check your translators' work. Some authors have also been surprised to discover that after commissioning a translation of their article (or parts of some source text), the translator plagiarized the translation, borrowing from previous publications (Watson 2016). Be sure that your translator is mindful of improper borrowing, and read the translation carefully for variations in style or diction that might signal that this has occurred.

Don't self-plagiarize. Rules of thumb vary, but using without attribution in a new article the exact phrases and sentences from one of your published articles won't endear you to editors. You can sometimes repeat three to four paragraphs verbatim, but only if you clearly state that you've done so in the text or in the notes. Even then, such paragraphs must be from background, context, or methods sections of an article, as these don't contain the argument or evidence. However, if you don't use the exact same sentences or paragraphs from your earlier article, you can write an article that has the same argument but different evidence (or the same evidence but a new argument) as your previously published work. If you're uncertain, write a brief email to get the opinion of the journal editor, providing a brief description of your article and its similarities to previous work.

Check that you correctly copied your quotations. If you make mistakes in citing and quoting others' work, that's a form of plagiarism. If you misspell an author's name or give a wrong publication date, scholars may not be able to find that work and algorithms may not count citations, affecting their impact factor. Research shows that many authors make mistakes such as these (Tfelt-Hansen 2015; Jergas and Baethge 2015). In some cases, "unreliable, inapplicable or misquoted citations" may even lead to "dangerous consequences" in the real world (Smith and Banks 2016, 408).

Do I need to develop any better citation habits? If so, what are two steps I can take toward that?

Post-borrowing Solutions

Good citation habits prevent you from plagiarizing. But what if you haven't had such good habits? What if you suspect that your article has some problems as a result? As I wrote in the introduction, this workbook is not intended for academic purists or those who do everything right the first time. It's for those scholars trying to do better. Here are some solutions for improper borrowing after the fact.

Spot-check wording. All of us have some sense of our own writing style. If you're starting to revise a document that you drafted awhile ago and you come across a phrase that doesn't sound like you, spot-check. It takes just a second to copy the phrase, paste it into Google, and view the results to see whether that phrase originated with someone else. Try checking the phrase with and without quotation marks around it. Most of the time, the words will be your words, but on some occasions they may not be, and you can correct the mistake by giving proper attribution. If you continue to have a nagging sense that the words come from someone else, try eliminating them. The trend is toward shorter and shorter articles.

Rework sentences based on another source. Starting at the beginning of your article, review each sentence. When you come to a sentence based on another source, stop and do three things. First, if you don't provide a citation, add one. Second, go back to the source, find the material, and check to see how close your phrasing is to it. If it's too close, change your phrasing to the source's and put quotation marks around it. Or change your phrasing so that it's truly paraphrasing. Third, if you have a whole paragraph paraphrasing another source, don't bury its author in a citation at the end of the paragraph; give credit in the body of the text. Start the paragraph's first sentence with something like "[Author's name] makes an intriguing argument regarding this object. She suggests that . . ."

Delete sentences whose sources have been lost. Often, the easiest solution is to cut what's not working. So if you find yourself with some good information or a great quote for which you've lost the source, try cutting it from your article. If your article won't work without it, you need to spend as long as it takes to relocate that source.

Ask authors. If you suspect that your article weighs too heavily on the work of one or more scholars, you can always send the article to those authors and ask them what they think.

Cite yourself to avoid self-plagiarism. If you insert a chunk from your published article into your unpublished article, you must cite it. Always note any such reuse directly—either in a footnote or, if the journal forbids footnotes, in the text itself. Some formulations people use are "This Methods section is slightly revised from my previously published article [name date]" or "This paragraph and the next two are adapted from those I previously published [name date]."

Do I need to take any of these steps to ensure that my article is not borrowing improperly?

STRATEGIES FOR GETTING READING DONE

If scholars rarely discuss their process of writing, they almost never talk about their process of reading. It seems useful to share some strategies for finding, limiting, and reading research literature for your journal article.

Reading Theoretical Literature

For some in the humanities and interpretive social sciences, reading theoretical texts is a reason for living. They find the texts' complexity delicious.

Many others, however, decide that they "don't do theory." Indeed, much theory is so obfuscating that it seems deliberately designed to make us feel stupid. Or annoyed at the arcane musings of elites. Unfortunately, however, you can't decide not to do theory—everything is theoretical. Everything you write is influenced by some theory, whether you know it or not. As John Maynard Keynes said some time ago, "Practical men, who believe themselves to be quite exempt from any intellectual influences, are usually the slave of some defunct economist" (Keynes 1936, 383). In other words, either you use theory deliberately or it uses you.

So don't get intimidated. Trust your instinct that quite a bit of theorizing is nothing masquerading as something. But also develop a tolerance for not understanding things and not feeling in control. Students can demonize incomprehension, uncertainty, and struggle. But you must spend time not understanding theory before you can start to get a feel for it.

Finally, you don't have to pack your article with theoretical references; you just need to articulate your theoretical approach to your topic. And you must do so in a way that displays a grasp of that approach. For instance, if you declare that you are writing a gender analysis of prisoners' writing but do little more than say, "Hey, some of the authors were women!" or "Hey, some of the authors wrote about women!" you haven't displayed a grasp of that approach. A gender analysis is more than pointing out that women exist. You must claim how gender makes a difference in our analysis of prisoners' writing, showing how, for instance, women authors describe their prison experiences more positively than male authors, or male authors represent women as long-suffering and passive rather than radical and active.

So if you're in the humanities or interpretive social sciences and feel that you don't have a sufficient grasp of the relevant theories for your article, try some of the following steps:

Take theory courses. It's easier to learn the basics in a classroom than to read such texts on your own. Although theory courses can seem intimidating and frustrating, use them to focus on the theories that would be helpful to you in thinking about your interests.

Read with an expert. If you're a graduate student, ask to do an independent study with a professor in your field. That way you can read the seminal theoretical works and then discuss them with someone knowledgeable. This will further your understanding of their import.

Read book reviews. A great way to keep abreast of scholarship is to read book reviews. As one author put it, "Book reviews, not books, [are] the principal engines of change in the history of thought," precisely because they reduce and summarize, thus contributing the "distortions" that are essential to the "forward flow" of scholarship (Baker 1991, 64). Free online book reviews appear on the H-Net Humanities and Social Sciences website.

Read biographies of theoreticians. It can be easier to grasp a thinker's ideas in the context of his or her life. Excellent biographies have been written about a number of the important twentieth-century thinkers, including Michel Foucault (J. Miller 1993), Hannah Arendt (Young-Bruehl 2004), and Frantz Fanon (Cherki and Benabid 2006). Many of these individuals had fascinating lives, so their biography can make for easier reading, a break from your other types of reading. Film documentaries can be another good source, such as the one about Derrida (Dick and Ziering 2002).

Use reference books. Books that give brief, helpful descriptions of important concepts, theories, and terms are essential to have at hand. They help you not only identify theoreticians whose thoughts might be useful to your argument, but also understand those theoreticians' writings more readily and thoroughly when you read them. Also, it's just as important to know what scholars now think about, for example Émile Durkheim, than what Durkheim actually said or, realistically, what you think Durkheim said (unless Durkheim's thought is the primary text that you're analyzing in your article, in which case your views are essential). Some of these reference books may be found online, such as the *Stanford Encyclopedia of Philosophy* (Zalta 2016).

Read public-intellectual newspapers. One of the best ways to learn theory is to follow or subscribe to newspapers that publish the work of public intellectuals. In such forums, scholars often present their theory in shorter form and in more accessible language. They also tend to be more open about their feuds with other scholars. One of the best of these publications is the *Times Literary Supplement*, a famous British weekly often called the *TLS*, which reviews significant scholarly books. Comparable US publications are the *New York Review of Books* (not to be confused with the *New York Times Book Review*) and the online *Los Angeles Review of Books*. The best, in my opinion, is the *Chronicle of Higher Education*, a weekly newspaper about academia that includes accessible articles by scholars about their work. I think it's the most interesting periodical published in the United States today.

> Do I need to get a better grasp of theory in my field for this article? If so, what are two steps I can take toward that?

Reading Related Secondary Literature

Slightly different skills are required for reading the related literature, typically in peer-reviewed journals, than for reading the theoretical literature. Here are some steps or techniques for doing so.

Set up your RMS program. Yes, this is the fourth time I've nagged you about this. Do it!

Winnow your reading list. It would be easy to drown in the related research, so you must have a strategy for limiting your reading in this area. It's terrifying to do this, because we fear missing something, but the alternative—reading forever and never writing—is of course worse. Just remember that your article is not your last statement on the subject, and hence should not be comprehensive. Many articles are published that reference just five to ten related-literature articles (for a total of twenty sources in the Works Cited section). But what strategy should you have for winnowing your reading list? One is to eliminate certain categories of materials. Some limiters that scholars use include setting aside most materials written

- some time ago (e.g., read nothing written over ten years ago, or five or two, depending on your field)
- in another language (e.g., read articles in English and French, not Spanish)
- in non-peer-reviewed publications (e.g., don't read conference proceedings or dissertations)
- for journals outside your discipline (e.g., read anthropology journals, not sociology journals)
- by certain kinds of authors (e.g., read authors in your discipline, not outside it)
- about a different geographic area (e.g., read articles about West Africa, not southern Africa)
- in a different context (e.g., read articles about public hospitals, not private hospitals)
- about a different time period (e.g., read articles about the nineteenth century, not the eighteenth century)
- about different kinds of experiments (e.g., read quantitative studies, not qualitative studies)
- about different kinds of participants (e.g., read studies of the elderly, not teenagers)
- using different variables (e.g., read studies of age and gender, not age and race)
- without your keyword in the title or abstract (e.g., read only those articles with your keyword in the title and abstract, not just in the body of the article)
- without your argument (e.g., read only those articles about labor organizing for commercial berry pickers, not the environmental degradation of commercial berry cultivation)
- in nonelectronic formats (e.g., read only those articles electronically accessible in full from your home computer)

Please don't get me wrong; I am not insisting on any of these winnowing methods. They all come with real costs. In particular, if you don't read print resources or articles in other languages, you'll miss important innovations. Further, more than one scholar became famous by ignoring such limits and deciding to review a category of related literature that no one else had looked at closely, such as old publications or the so-called gray literature (e.g., government or market research reports, memos, technical documentation, and conference abstracts). However, you simply can't read hundreds of articles. So decide which winnowing methods are least problematic for your particular article and use them insofar as you feel comfortable.

Start a journal club. Initiated in the 1830s by medical students (Linzer 1987, 475–76), journal clubs consist of a university department or laboratory that meets weekly or monthly, as organized by a senior faculty member, during which the graduate students and postdocs each deliver a critical review of a very recent article in the field. This is a way to crowdsource keeping abreast of the exponentially increasing literature—attendees enter the meeting having read only one article, but leave as if they've read seven or eight. So make reading social and start a journal club. An excellent guide, with a very useful breakdown of how to critically review an article, is "How to Prepare for and Present at a Journal Club" (Bowles et al. 2013). Some journal clubs are now successfully held virtually, including on Twitter or at PubPeer, an online journal club hosting site.

Schedule journal reading. In scientific disciplines, graduate students used to be advised to spend Friday afternoons in the periodical section of their university library. Adding journal reading to your weekly schedule is an excellent idea, whether you physically go the library or not. I knew a graduate student who did this, and he told me that it not only kept him up-to-date on trends and names but enabled him to impress job interviewers by mentioning their research.

Receive journal tables of contents by email. Sign up to receive the publishers' emailed announcements of the tables of contents of relevant journals so you can easily learn of articles germane to your research. All the large journal publishers, including Elsevier, Taylor and Francis, Springer-Verlag, John Wiley, SAGE, Hindawi, Cambridge, and Oxford, have TOC alerts. The easiest way to sign up is to go to the free site JournalTOCs, where you can select any number of peer-reviewed journals and get their TOC alerts. In addition, your university library often sends out alerts about its purchases.

Subscribe to print journals. If you can afford it, subscribe to the main journals in your field and get them delivered in print to your house. You may be more likely to read them if they're right at hand.

Read the newest material first. It's frustrating to take notes on several older books on a topic and then read the newest book, because the most recent book often summarizes the previous ones, reviews them, and offers the best way forward. You can always go back to the older books, but it's best to start with the newest.

Limit note taking. When novice authors start out on their related literature reading, they find themselves using their notes to reproduce the articles they read. They copy down every sentence that seems particularly well put, or they highlight most of the article's points. By the time they're finished, they could give a lecture on each article! But you won't have space in your article for more than one quotation from or summarizing sentence about any one related-literature article. Further, having dozens of great quotes will hinder your writing an article about what *you* think. When reading, don't look for quotations but instead seek out debates, arguments, and "organizing ideas" (Giroux 2003, 102). If you find a beautifully expressed idea in someone else's article, post it on Twitter or Facebook so that you can let go of it. However, if you love taking notes or want to improve your note taking, check out Katherine Firth's popular blog *Research Degree*

Voodoo at researchvoodoo.wordpress.com, where she presents her adaptation of the Cornell method for taking notes.

Highlight sparingly. One trick I use on myself is to put one check mark next to material that I find interesting, two next to material that would be useful for my article, and three next to material I absolutely must include in it (or, if reading electronically, I use different text highlight colors). When finished reading the article or book and placing the check marks, I take notes only on the material where I put three check marks. I find that when I am reading, all sorts of things interest me and get check marks, but when I go back through, only the three check marks really matter. It's a way of tricking my perfectionist impulses. If you decide to use this technique, be sure to type up your notes within a day or two of reading the material so that you can remember why you marked what you did.

Don't wait to write. A student once confessed in my class that she had spent a year reading intensively, for hours every day, and taking copious notes for her dissertation. At the end of the year she sat down to write, picking up the notes from her first text, only to realize that she couldn't make heads or tails of them. She said, "I wish that I had started writing my dissertation at the same time as I began my reading, and then inserted material where it seemed relevant. If I had written up just a paragraph on each text—something about what I found important about the text, and how it related to my argument—I would be a lot farther ahead. I have enough for ten books here."

It's best to read a bit, write up what's relevant, and then read some more and write some more. A fellow graduate student taught me this lesson early on: I came across her typing her classroom essay with a stack of print articles and books next to her. I could see that these sources had no sticky notes, no underscored passages, and no marginalia, so I could tell that she was reading them for the first time. Occasionally, she stopped reading and typed something into her paper. I asked her what she was doing and she replied, "I don't believe in notes." This made a huge impression on me, and I started practicing this technique myself. As I'm writing, if I need related literature, evidence, a definition, or an explanation, I look for the relevant source, read it online, insert what's needed into my article, download the citation into Endnote, insert the citation into Microsoft Word, and move on. This method doesn't work for primary or theoretical literature, but it works perfectly for the related literature. Others use the Corkboard feature in Scrivener software to keep track of material. Whichever method you choose, you should still focus on writing items up in full sentences, not just taking notes.

Learn to skim. We all need to read some materials carefully, but many of us read *all* materials carefully. You can't afford the time to do that. You need to train yourself to read not word for word or for the elegant language and general information of the text but for the text's significance and argument. One social scientist told me that he regularly read, in order, only the title, abstract, references, and conclusion of any article. Rarely did he read an entire article. In my experience, it takes a long time to learn to skim effectively, so don't chastise yourself for being a slow reader. Just practice. One technique for teaching yourself to skim is by opening a PDF and typing Ctrl + Shift + H to initiate autoscroll. Read at its pace all the way through, write up what you understood the article to say, and then check to see whether you were right. You will likely be surprised by how much you got. Another technique is to go the library and skim articles and books while standing in the stacks where you find them. In this position, you simply can't fall into the habit of reading the article in full.

Do I need to cite more related literature in this article? If so, what are two of the techniques above that I can take toward that?

Reading Original, Primary, or Exhibit Literature

Reading your primary or exhibit sources—be they archived material, literary texts, or qualitative studies—takes time and care. Because you read primary sources over months and even years, it's easy to lose track of relevant material. Highlighting phrases in texts and adding sticky notes here and there are all well and good, but the main work of writing remains undone. So spend half an hour writing summaries of your reading at the end of any day in the archive or any afternoon or evening of reading sources. If you do that, you'll find you've already written whole passages of your article.

STRATEGIES FOR WRITING YOUR RELATED-LITERATURE REVIEW

A big part of any publishable article is your review of the related literature, the previously published research on your exact topic. Once you've read the prior scholarship, how do you go about citing it? You start by identifying your general relationship to the related literature, called your "entry point," and then continue by evaluating the literature in that light.

What's Your Entry Point?

All journal articles exist in relation to other journal articles. You need new ideas to get published, but the "authority" of your work (i.e., your "air of confidence, reliability, and trustworthiness") also lies in your ability to relate your arguments to others' arguments (Gaipa 2004, 419). Long ago, the literary critic Kenneth Burke described scholarly writing as akin to entering a parlor full of people engaged in an "unending conversation" that started long before you and will continue long after you (Burke 1974, 110). Two scholars have usefully called authors' relationship to that parlor conversation their "entry point," their argument's relationship to previous scholarly arguments (Parker and Riley 1995, 87). If you imagine your article as entering into a conversation, it makes perfect sense that you wouldn't just walk into a room and start talking about your own ideas. If people were already in the room, you'd listen to them for a while first. If you decided to speak, you would do so because you agreed or disagreed with something someone said. If the conversation went on for a long time without addressing some topic dear to you, you might say, "I notice that we haven't talked about such-and-such yet." In all cases, you'd acknowledge the conversation and then make your point. A frequent error of novice authors is a failure to do just that. As one editor complained, "Lots of submissions [to my journal] are from people unaware of the conversation. They think they are finding something for the first time that's been around for a million years or [they inadvertently] put a new spin on something that's been dead" and cannot be revived (interview in Vandenberg 1993, 80).

A useful aspect of this conversation analogy is that it focuses your mind on the necessity of argument. You wouldn't walk into a room of your field and portentously announce descriptive information (e.g., *Midnight's Children* was published in 1981" or "South African apartheid formally ended in 1994"). Everyone in that room already knows this basic information. You enter into the related-literature conversation by supporting an argument they're making, debating an argument they're making, or announcing that an argument no one is making needs to be made. Therefore, your entry point is how your argument enters the debate occurring in the previous research on the topic.

Types of Entry Points

To aid undergraduates in the humanities, the composition scholar Mark Gaipa (2004, 426–32) has identified "eight strategies for relating to the critics," which he summarizes as "picking a fight with an individual critic," "riding a critic's coattails," "standing on the shoulders of giants," "biting the hand that feeds you," "settl[ing] a dispute between two critics," "tak[ing] on the critical establishment," "redefin[ing] what is central to the conversation," and "injecting really new material into the debate." For those writing journal articles, these map well onto the three broader entry points into the related literature that I articulate:

1. finding the previous research inadequate or nonexistent and filling the gap
2. finding it sound and supporting it or extending it
3. finding it unsound and correcting it

Since articles often depend on several bodies of research, sometimes all three of these positions coexist in the same article. Let's look at these three positions more closely.

Entry Point Type 1: Addressing a Gap in Previous Research.
Identifying a gap (or gaps) in the related scholarly literature and setting out to fill it is one of the most common entry points in journal articles. In the humanities, gap claims often relate to sources, with scholars claiming that there is a gap in attention given to certain authors or texts, or to particular types of authors, texts, or textual themes. In the professions, social sciences, or health sciences, gap claims often relate to problems—many scholars claim that there is a gap in attention given to certain equality challenges in politics, economics, society, health, and so on. Filling gaps is a strong claim for significance. However, the success of this claim rests on having a good grasp of the research. I have seen peer reviewers send more than one submission back to an author with the article's literature gap claim crossed through and a list of published works penned next to it. "Nonsense," one reviewer wrote. "Lots has been published on this topic." The best way to avoid this is to hedge if you're not certain. Rather than making your gap claim absolute by saying, "No one has published about *x*" or "Nothing has been written about *x*," you can limit the gap claim by saying, "*X* is understudied," or "Little research has been conducted on *x*," or "Few scholars have addressed *x*." Also, if no one has written on the topic before or written on it in quite your way, you may have to prove to the reader that the topic or approach

is important. That is, the reader may suspect that the gap is there because it's not vital knowledge.

Here is an example from a published article of an author announcing a *gap entry point* into previous research. I have added underscore.

> **Filling a gap in the related literature.** "Listening is surprisingly and problematically underlined{overlooked} in the large body of literature on organization-public communication including government, political, corporate, and marketing communication. Based on critical analysis of relevant literature and primary research among 36 organizations in three countries, this analysis identifies a 'crisis of listening' in organization-public communication and proposes strategies to address gaps in theory and practice including attention to the work of listening and the creation of an architecture of listening in organizations, which can offer significant stakeholder, societal, and organizational benefits." [from Macnamara 2016, 133]

Entry Point Type 2: Supporting Previous Research.
Approving of and using other scholars' theories to analyze new subjects is another common scholarly entry point. Thus, naming authors or articles you find useful is part of positioning your article vis-à-vis the previous research. This can be as simple as identifying the school, camp, movement, or tradition your research participates in. For instance, stating that your work is "psychoanalytic" or using the word *postcolonial* positions your article as part of a stream of research. In all disciplines, supporting or extending previous research often relates to theorists, with scholars claiming that a particular theorist's work, idea(s), or definition is especially helpful in understanding the subject at hand (or that a group of theorists or a school of theory is helpful). Supporting or extending previous research often relates to data as well, with scholars claiming that they have found confirming evidence or data for another scholar's claim.

Bridging two discussions in the related literature is another way of supporting or extending research. Interestingly, articles that created bridges between fields by citing two or more bodies of literature were often the most highly cited; that is, such articles were "more likely to be an interdisciplinary paper that explores connections between dense but distant fields" (Shi, Leskovec, and McFarland 2010, 56). Other articles that did well tended "to cluster their citations in a narrow, well defined and connected field," citing sources that cite each other (50).

Here are examples from published articles of authors announcing *supportive entry points* into previous research. I have added underscore.

> **Extending the related literature.** "Although some evidence indicates that personality characteristics, such as extroversion and proactivity, are related to career success, scholars have called for research to understand how such effects occur. . . . Consistent with prior research . . ., we theorize that personality traits, specifically extroversion and proactivity, influence mentoring received, which in turn influences career success." [from Turban et al. 2016, 21]

> **Bridging two bodies of related literature.** "We bring together two long-standing rural sociological traditions to address debates framed at the national level and for Appalachian

communities facing the throes of transition from the coal industry. From rural sociology's 'poverty and place' tradition and from natural resources sociology, we examine the relationship between coal employment and communities' economic well-being as indicated by poverty, household income, and unemployment. Our findings extend the poverty and place literature and the natural resources literature and underscore why a just transition away from coal should focus on moving communities toward sectors offering better future livelihoods." [from Lobao et al. 2016, 343]

Bridging a debate in the related literature. "Recent statistics on African American readers outline distinct trends that are difficult to reconcile with each other: . . . trailing in proficiency yet thriving in general book reading. . . . A roiling debate . . . focuses on whether readers' preoccupation with urban fiction is symbolic of black literacy's triumph or downfall in the twenty-first century. . . . I examine the motivating factors . . . of these positions in the debate. First I discuss democratizers who . . . advocate . . . bringing urban fiction into the classroom. I then consider cultural gatekeepers who bemoan mass book reading as a kind of rampant false consciousness. . . . I turn, finally, to a position between them that values urban fiction in those spaces and situations that are friendly to its consumption. . . . I characterize the position as *merely reading* . . . adjustable to its surroundings and supple in its execution, it is compatible with serious reading and other literate behaviors." [from Nishikawa 2015, 697, 698, 702]

Entry Point Type 3: Correcting Previous Research.
The most common entry point into the previous research is stating that previous scholarly approaches to a subject are erroneous, and that your article will overturn these misconceptions. Such corrections of the related literature take many forms, from weighing in on a debate (whether choosing one side or saying both are wrong); questioning a policy, practice, or interpretation; addressing a contradiction; or offering a solution.

For novice authors, correcting previous research is often the most tempting entry point. And it can even be the right one. Just be sure to give credit where credit is due, keep your tone collegial, and acknowledge how others' work enables yours. Stating that you're offering a contrasting or alternate opinion rather than asserting an outright rebuttal is often wise. Scholars who have published extensively rarely attack others' research directly—they are all too aware of how any scholarship, including their own, is always flawed. So they don't write that things are "wrong," but rather say things like "I am reading against the consensus," "While interesting, these approaches have not been helpful enough," or "Although many argue for *x*, little evidence suggests that this is the whole story."

Here are examples from published articles of authors announcing a *correcting entry point* into previous research. I have added underscore.

Criticizing a theorist. "Giorgio Agamben's formulations of 'the state of exception' and 'bare life' have become touchstones for analyses of sovereign violence and biopolitics, yet it seems to have escaped note that Agamben's use of these terms is marked by a peculiar oversight. While Agamben's Eurocentrism has been redressed by scholars such as . . . , even his most careful readers do not comment on Agamben's treatment of a word that he takes from Primo Levi as the key to understanding politics and ethics after World War II . . . 'der Muselmann.' . . . I track this bizarre omission in order to raise questions about the <u>institutionalized blindnesses</u> that continue to determine the priorities and periodizations that frame critical and literary studies concerned with modern forms of state violence." [from Jarvis 2014, 707, 710]

Questioning a policy or practice named in the related literature. "We argue that sexism conceals itself through its continual movement, and that sexual <u>harassment is</u> <u>perpetuated</u> within universities through tactics that relocate the problem away from the individual and the institution. . . . <u>Mechanisms within the institution</u> set up to address sexual harassment work not only to distance the institution from responsibility for the harassment, but also to hide the harassment even in the moment when women and their allies are insistently working to try to make it appear." [from Whitley and Page 2015, 34]

Addressing a contradiction in the related literature. "The <u>contradictory positions</u> that reading digitally is not very different from reading print texts, and that today's students are increasingly conditioned by digital technologies to be unable to read well are mistaken: aspects of reading digitally are quite different from reading print texts, and today's students are developing new forms of literacy to cope with environments of pervasive ambient information." [from M. Edwards 2016, 138]

Offering a solution to a problem named in the related literature. "This research examines whether culture influences the extent to which people's attitudes <u>tune toward</u> <u>others' egalitarian</u> beliefs. . . . Americans and Hong Kong Chinese who were primed with a collectivist mind-set showed less explicit and implicit prejudice when the experimenter was thought to endorse egalitarian views than when no views were conveyed. Such differences were not found when both cultural groups were primed with an individualist mind-set. These findings suggest that cultural value orientations can <u>help mitigate</u> <u>prejudice</u>." (from Skorinko et al. 2015, 363)

Articulating Your Current Entry Point

Considering the foregoing, what do you think your entry point into the related literature is? It's possible that you have multiple entry points—you're addressing a gap in one body of literature, correcting some assumptions of another body of literature, and agreeing with a third. You'll be working more on this later; if you aren't sure what your entry point is now, make a guess and keep going.

> What are my bodies of literature, and what's my entry point into them? Do I show how my argument relates to previous arguments?

What Is a Related-Literature Review?

In the preceding section, I asserted the importance of positioning your article vis-à-vis the previous research, of articulating your entry point into the scholarly conversation.

This can sometimes be done quite briefly, such as by stating something as simple as "No research has been done on Chicana labor in Boyle Heights factories in Los Angeles; this article fills that gap." But sometimes it can't be done briefly if there's a lot of related literature on your topic, you disagree with what little has been written, or you think that another body of research entirely can help. Then you must write what I prefer to call a *related-literature review*, frequently called just a literature review.

So what is it exactly? A related-literature review is an evaluation (not a summary) of the existing scholarship on your topic. That is, if your entry point is stating how your argument relates to previous arguments, a related-literature review is an evaluation of those previous arguments. Such a review documents the previous research's relationships, limitations, problematic interpretations, inadequate approaches, and so on. In it, you establish the significance and origin of your argument, defend your approach or methodology, and show the relationship of your research to what has come before.

For many novice authors, the related-literature review is one of the most difficult parts of the article to write. It's easy to air our own ideas; it's not always easy to summarize and evaluate others' usefully. Further, related-literature reviews vary so much from published article to published article that it can be difficult to determine their common elements. Sometimes a literature review is only a paragraph long; sometimes it makes up the entire content of the article, in which case the article is called a review essay. Usually, the related-literature review appears in the introduction or right after it; but in the humanities and interpretive social sciences, citations to the related literature don't form a discrete section but rather weave in and out throughout the article. For whichever form your related-literature review takes, here are some guidelines.

Be selective. In a dissertation and in many books, the related-literature review is often exhaustive. No related secondary text is left unturned. In an article, however, you must be more efficient. Don't summarize every article and book written on the topic. Instead, choose only the most relevant, most representative, and most informative sources. Then be sure not to list all the information you gleaned from them, only that which is relevant to your argument.

Organize sources as a debate. One of the best ways to think about writing a related-literature review is to imagine yourself telling a colleague about a debate you overheard. You report who participated in the debate (and sometimes who didn't), who took what side, who was the most convincing to you, who was the least. Then you note what would have made an argument more convincing—points the author didn't make or could have made better with other evidence.

Group literature according to sides taken in the debate. Many novice scholars read the related literature in order to arrive at an argument, but then don't use that argument to arrange their related-literature review. If you hope to keep readers interested, don't give a he-said-she-said version of the debate, reproducing verbatim and chronologically all the statements made in two dozen recent articles on the topic. You must focus on evaluating the existing literature with your argument firmly in mind. This means selecting and grouping the related research into sides of a debate, its camps, and then reviewing each side rather than working your way through each piece. Alternately, you can select and group the related research into approaches toward clarifying a problem. For instance, you could address the proposals of each of three groups of literature that approach the problem in differing ways, and then show how you are proposing a fourth way. Alternately, if you're writing about race and the 1847 novel *Wuthering Heights*, you would note which of the most famous scholarly articles and books about that novel do not address race, and then summarize the strengths and weaknesses of the racial analysis of those that do. You might divide the latter into two groups: those that address gender in addition to race, and those that don't.

Consider multiple related-literature reviews. Two types of articles may require more than one related-literature review—those SciQua articles having a formal Discussion section, and those articles integrating information from various fields. In other words, different sections may contain different literature reviews. For instance, the focus of the related-literature review in your introduction is situating your article in the larger conversation, showing how it contributes to that conversation. By contrast, the focus of the literature review in your Discussion section is clarifying the limits and strengths of your findings. Or you may need more than one review because your article is addressing more than one scholarly conversation. For instance, if you're writing about Vietnamese immigration to the United States, you may need to review *political science* research about Vietnamese national politics, *historical* research about US immigration policy, and *anthropological* research about Vietnamese immigrants' living situation in the United States. If you're writing about Latinx educational attainment in Los Angeles, you might review both the research explaining attainment in general and the research on Latinx in Los Angeles specifically. If you're in anthropology, you commonly review three bodies of literature in your article.

> Do I have a related-literature review in this article? If not, what debates should I use to organize my sources? Do I need more than one review?

How Do You Write a Methodological- or Theoretical-Literature Review?

I do not directly address how to write a review of the methodological or the theoretical literature. Most articles don't include such a review, because their methodological or theoretical approach is standard and needs no defense. But if you ever need to write methodological- or theoretical-literature reviews, the principles for related-literature reviews apply for them as well, except that they tend to be even briefer.

WRITING ABOUT OTHERS' RESEARCH

Day 1 Tasks: Reading the Workbook

On the first day of your fifth writing week, read this week 5 chapter all the way through the next two paragraphs, answering all the questions posed. Write directly in the boxes provided or in your own document. These tasks will take awhile. If you're working with coauthors who are writing up the review separately from you, you'll need only to skim the following.

Schedule a Meeting for Next Week

Next week, on day 2, you'll meet with another scholar to exchange articles (or parts of them). If you're not going through the workbook with a writing group, class, friend, or coauthor, today is a good day to email that person and arrange the day, time, and (virtual) place you'll meet to do that. It will be a self-contained event, not a read-in-advance meeting. You will meet, read, and give feedback all at once, in about three hours. You'll need to allot time to discuss your thoughts, not just give written feedback.

Tracking Writing Time

Each day, use the Calendar for Actual Time Spent Writing This Week form (or digital time-tracking software) to keep track of the time you spent writing this week. Then, at the end of the week, evaluate how you spent your time.

If busy, at least mark the check boxes with how long you wrote today. ☐ 15+ min. ☐ 30+ ☐ 60 + ☐ 120+

WEEK 5, DAYS 2–5: READING AND TASKS

Day 2 Tasks: Evaluating Your Current Works Cited List

Today you'll identify how much reading you have left to do by evaluating your existing citations. If you feel confident that your Works Cited list is accurate and sufficient, you can skim this day's tasks and move on to the next day's or the next week's. But don't skip today's tasks just because you lack time—problems with citations are the third main reason why journals reject articles.

Evaluate Types of Citations

Count citations. Print out or view your article's current Works Cited list and count how many citations you have. Note that the average number of citations per article in 2010 was 42 in the social sciences, 34 in the medical and health sciences, and 32 in the humanities (Marx and Bornmann 2015, 1825). You can cite many more works or a few less; the numbers are just to give you a sense of norms. However, if your SciQua article has fewer than 15 citations, chances are good that you're not citing enough texts. Even in the humanities, fewer than 10 citations could indicate a problem. Conversely, if you have more than 60 citations and aren't in the discipline of history, you may want to pare your citations down.

The total number of my citations   ◯ Might be too high   ◯ Might be too low   ☐ Is good

Code sources by category. Using the codes from the Belcher Citation Evaluation Form on the next page, code each citation in your Works Cited list, whether by hand on paper or digitally in an electronic document. Then total your citations in the column on that form titled "Number of Citations."

Belcher Citation Evaluation Form

	Number of citations?	More (or fewer) citations needed?	Topics needing more citations
Original sources (OC) (often less than 5)			
Derivative documents (DC) (should be 0)			
Contextual literature (CC)(often less than 5			
Methodological literature (MC) (often less than 5)			
Theoretical literature (TC)(often less than 5)			
Related literature (RLC) (should be at least 5, up to 30; should be mostly recent)			
Multicategory literature (MCC) (any amount)			
Target journal literature (TJC)(2)			
Other types of texts			
_____			
Total (often between 32 and 42)			

Evaluate by text category. Review this citation total against the norms in the first column, and make a note to yourself in the column titled "More (or Fewer) Citations Needed" about what the discrepancies suggest. Regarding *primary/exhibit* sources, if you're in the humanities and analyze only one primary source, perhaps you need to think about adding another source. As for *derivative* documents, you shouldn't have any. Regarding *contextual* literature, make sure you haven't overdone the background information. For *methodological* literature, make sure that your article contains at least one citation to it if your method is unusual or controversial in your field. Regarding *theoretical* literature, if you have many citations to it, make sure you haven't spent too much time in your article summarizing others' ideas. If you have no citations of this nature, perhaps consider whether you need any. Regarding *related literature*, make sure you have some citations to it. For *multicategory literature*, if you have too many citations in this category, recode them into the other categories so that you can ensure that you haven't missed anything. As for *target journal literature*, it's wise for your article to have at least two citations to articles published in the journal to which you intend to send your work. And check that a majority of your citations are *recent literature*, not too dated.

In the humanities, many novice authors need to increase the number of related-literature citations. In the other disciplines, related-literature reviews can get too long, so if you have a high number of related literature citations, ask yourself how much of your article is taken up by the literature review. Is it too long?

Evaluate Authorship of Citations

Now let's turn to authorship, another aspect of your citations to consider.

Articulate your citation values. What do you want your citations to say about you? Do your past citation practices accurately reflect your priorities as a member of particular scholarly communities? Do you want to work toward avoiding the biases of your discipline and including those most unjustly excluded? What types of authors do you want to be sure to include in your cited works? Using the first column of the Belcher Citation Values Form that appears later in this chapter as a prompt, identify your citation values and arrive at your codes. I put suggested codes in this form, but of course you can create your own.

Set your baselines for citation. Now that you have your citation values, how are you going to decide whether a certain article of yours has achieved them? That is, what are your goals for the number of citations per author category that you give? Let's take the case of women, which, frankly, should be a citation value for everyone (including women, who often demonstrate the same biases as men against citing women). How many citations of women authors are enough? One measure might be their percentage of the article's total citations, perhaps based on rates of women faculty in your discipline or overall. In the United States in 2015, 42 percent of all US faculty were white men (McFarland et al. 2017). That suggests that if more than half your citations are to scholarship by white men, you're probably following the biases of your field. But if men are publishing more often than women in your field, perhaps you should use rates of authorship instead. In medicine, for instance, 37 percent of first-time authors in major medical journals were women in 2014 (Filardo et al. 2016, 1). That means that if you're in medicine and citing fewer than 30 percent women authors in your article, you're not even *rising* to the level of bias in your field. In the United States in 2015, 6 percent of all faculty were African American, 4 percent were Latino, and 10 percent were Asian or Pacific Islander (McFarland et al. 2017). So if less than 10 percent of your citations are to people of color, you have a problem. To be a good scholar, you always need to be mindful of your biases.

By the way, I'm not saying all this at some safe remove—a rough check of my citations for this book shows that only about 40 percent are to works authored by women. And it was often tough to tell whether an author was a woman or a person of color—I had to check some university web pages and author websites, and even then wasn't always successful. So the aim of your citation check is to become conscious of the issue and to strive to do better, not to be perfect. If you can't correct your article at this late date, aim to do better on your next one.

Consider the Gray Test. If all this math is too tough, we need an equivalent of the Bechdel-Wallace test for film representations of women (Bechdel 1985). Let's call it "the Gray test." To pass the #GrayTest, which I named for the scholar Kishonna Gray, who invented the hashtag #citeherwork in 2015, a journal article must not only cite the scholarship of at least two women and two nonwhite authors but also mention it meaningfully in the body of the text. Examples of meaningful mentions would be sentences such as "Ruha Benjamin's book on this technology is illustrative," "Marina Warner's book on the Virgin Mary argues . . . ," or "Richard Delgado coined the term *politics of citation* in 1984." That is, you can't pass the test by putting four in-text citations at the end of one sentence that otherwise lacks author names. If your article fails this bare-minimum test, it's biased and should be improved. If you can't find such scholars to cite, it's time for you to do something about the pipeline of scholars entering your field.

Now use the Belcher Citation Values Form as a prompt to quantify your citation values.

Code your article citations by authorship. Using the codes from the Belcher Citation Values Form as a guide, code the citations in your current Works Cited list, and then calculate how many of your sources are written, edited, or translated by those in your citation values categories. In general, it's easier to identify women (by name) than it is to identify authors from other categories, so you may need to do extra research to see whether any of your sources are by authors of color. To code all citations, including those from dominant groups, you can use codes such as M (male), W (white), AM (American), and so on. If you're marking these in the margin of a printout of your Works Cited list, you may find it useful to indicate gender in one column and race in another. It's not essential to be extremely precise in your counting; you're trying to arrive at a general picture of your citation rates and biases. For instance, if more than three people regularly coauthor articles in your field, you may want to count just the lead author.

Evaluate your article citations by authorship. Does your article reflect your citation values? If it doesn't, consider doing extra research to find at least two other sources that do reflect those values. You may also need to decide, if you're in a field that tends to bor-

Belcher Citation Values Form

Who do I want to be sure to cite, and by how much? (Below are prompts, not requirements.)

	50%	___%	At least 2	Not a value
Author gender: women/females (code F) or _____	☐ 50%	☐ ___%	☐ At least 2	☐ Not a value
Author race: African American (code B)	☐ 50%	☐ ___%	☐ At least 2	☐ Not a value
Author race: Latinx/Chicanx etc. (code L, CH)	☐ 50%	☐ ___%	☐ At least 2	☐ Not a value
Author race: Asian American/Hapa etc. (code A)	☐ 50%	☐ ___%	☐ At least 2	☐ Not a value
Author nationality: Middle Eastern (code ME) (or specific country: _____)	☐ 50%	☐ ___%	☐ At least 2	☐ Not a value
Author nationality: Asian (code AS) (or specific country: _____)	☐ 50%	☐ ___%	☐ At least 2	☐ Not a value
Author nationality: African (code AF) (or specific country: _____)	☐ 50%	☐ ___%	☐ At least 2	☐ Not a value
Author nationality: European (code EU) (or specific country: _____)	☐ 50%	☐ ___%	☐ At least 2	☐ Not a value
Author status: junior scholars (J)	☐ 50%	☐ ___%	☐ At least 2	☐ Not a value
Queer authors or: _____	☐ 50%	☐ ___%	☐ At least 2	☐ Not a value
Authors with a disability: _____	☐ 50%	☐ ___%	☐ At least 2	☐ Not a value
Article language: _____	☐ 50%	☐ ___%	☐ At least 2	☐ Not a value
Author religion: _____	☐ 50%	☐ ___%	☐ At least 2	☐ Not a value
Other: _____	☐ 50%	☐ ___%	☐ At least 2	☐ Not a value
Other: _____	☐ 50%	☐ ___%	☐ At least 2	☐ Not a value
Other: _____	☐ 50%	☐ ___%	☐ At least 2	☐ Not a value

row other articles' strings of citations about a topic, to stop that practice if it just reproduces bias. If you want to be part of changing citation values, you can use social media to post links to articles by women and people of color with the hashtags that scholars have invented to encourage others to attend to these issues, such as #CiteHerWork (Gray 2015). Or, as the literature professor Koritha Mitchell innovated, you can regularly post this challenge on social media: "Have you cited a woman of color today?" Finally, if you're interested in promulgating the theories of African American women but aren't sure who they are, check out the great list of theorists and articles at www.blackfeminisms.com/theory-black-women/.

Tracking Writing Time

Mark your electronic calendar, the Calendar for Actual Time Spent Writing This Week form, and/or the check boxes here with how long you wrote today. ☐15+ min. ☐30+ ☐60+ ☐120+

Day 3 Tasks: Identifying and Reading Any Additional Works

Today you'll read any additional works if needed. (If you have already read everything that you need to, you can skip to the next section.) Your main aim with writing your article is to attempt to be thorough without bogging down. Many of us find that starting to read the literature in preparation for this writing is like entering the forest of no return. We just keep going deeper and deeper, getting more and more lost, and eventually forget the destination we were trying to reach in the first place. Two methods can help you in dipping into the related literature without getting lost in it: one method is to read while writing, the other is to read and then write later.

Read while Writing

The easiest way to update your citations is to open your article, read the first paragraph, and ask yourself whether it needs additional citations—not "Could it use some?" but "Does it *need* some?" If yes, find them, read them, and insert them. Then read the next paragraph, repeating the process until you reach the end of your article. It's best to read a bit, write up what's relevant, and then read some more and write some more.

Read Then Write

The other method is more expansive, so I provide an exercise for skimming materials rather than reading them. You should still end up with a manageable final reading list of about a dozen texts in the related literature. It's extremely important to be realistic about how much you can read.

Ask. Ask those in your field what they recommend you read on the topic. You can also ask a reference librarian.

Search. Since material is always being added to databases, you might want to do an online search using the keywords most closely related to your article. This search is especially important if it's been awhile since you've last done so—more than six months ago for SciQua or more than twelve months for HumInt.

Draft a reading list. Once you've completed these tasks, collate a list of materials you intend to skim for their usefulness. Don't spend a lot of time typing up this list, organizing it alphabetically, or otherwise massaging it. It's only a step, not a destination. You can use some of the online software for this organizing, such as Pocket (which lets you shelve items to read later), LibraryThing (for cataloging the print books you own), and CiteULike and Mendeley (for organizing scholarly articles).

Stay alert to your citation values. If your article wasn't meeting your citation values, ensure that you find works by some authors that help you attain those values, and add these sources to your reading list.

Winnow your reading list. If you ended up with a list of more than twenty-four articles and books, keep paring it down.

Don't panic! Many scholars find that they have to spend extra days on reading additional sources for their article. That's okay. Slow and steady still wins the race to publication.

Finalize your reading list. Organize the reading list in order from the most important to the least important source so that, if interrupted, you have been reading to effect.

Skim the identified materials. Since most of us can perseverate on research, try to limit this task. At this point, you're merely trying to identify whether the materials you've chosen to review are going to be helpful in revising your article.

Get copies. If while skimming you find some articles or books that are going to be helpful to you in revising the article, download the article or scan/photocopy the relevant sections. Always make sure to include the copyright page from each source so you have all the bibliographic data you need for proper citations.

Start reading. Read the few related sources you have selected and write full sentences about the text: "This article argues that . . . The author takes the side of . . . A weakness of this article is . . ." If you can write miniature book reviews of the book, evaluating but not summarizing its content, you're on your way to improving your related-literature review.

Winnow further. If it's clear that a source is less relevant than you thought, stop reading it and move on to the next, using your reading list to note why in five or six words.

Tracking Writing Time

Mark your electronic calendar, the Calendar for Actual Time Spent Writing This Week form, and/or the check boxes here with how long you wrote today. ☐15+ min. ☐30+ ☐60+ ☐120+

Day 4 Tasks: Identifying Your Entry Point into the Related Secondary Literature

Today you'll work on identifying your entry point into the related literature. If you already know what your entry point is, you can skip today and move to the next day. If you're not sure, revisit the "What's Your Entry Point?" section above and consider the questions below. If possible, have someone else ask you these questions; it is through the relation of conversation that we can arrive at our best insights about our relation to the literature.

- What have you found about the relationships among various articles and scholars? Are they speaking to one another, engaged in some debate? Or speaking to others you haven't read yet?
- How are previous scholars justifying their argument, claiming novelty, acknowledging debts, displaying allegiances, and signaling disciplinary community?
- How are these arguments similar to yours? Where do they differ?
- How are key concepts or theories getting defined or used?
- What are the limitations of this related literature?
- Can you identify a unified story in this related literature?

Using these questions, start grouping the texts by argument and debate, always keeping in mind how your argument relates to it and making decisions about your entry point.

Tracking Writing Time

Mark your electronic calendar, the Calendar for Actual Time Spent Writing This Week form, and/or the check boxes here with how long you wrote today. ☐ 15+ min. ☐ 30 + ☐ 60+ ☐ 120+

Day 5 Tasks: Writing or Revising Your Related-Literature Review

Today you'll write or revise your related-literature review or reviews using your answers to questions from days 1 through 4. Remember, your argument should be organizing your related-literature review; don't let the literature take over. As Howard Becker warns in his chapter titled "Terrorized by the Literature" (in what's still one of the best works about citing scholarly literature), "Use the literature, don't let it use you" (Becker and Richards 2008, 149).

When finished, you can ask a friend or colleague to read it and let you know whether you have been clear about the debate, the related literature, and your entry point.

Again, if this takes you longer than you hoped (in hours or days), don't worry—it's essential.

Tracking Writing Time

Mark your electronic calendar, the Calendar for Actual Time Spent Writing This Week form, and/or the check boxes here with how long you wrote today. ☐ 15+ min. ☐ 30 + ☐ 60+ ☐ 120+

Then, here at the end of your workweek, take pride in your accomplishments and evaluate whether any patterns need changing.

DOCUMENTING YOUR WRITING TIME AND TASKS

Calendar for Actual Time Spent Writing This Week

Time	Day 1	Day 2	Day 3	Day 4	Day 5	Day 6	Day 7
5:00 a.m.							
6:00							
7:00							
8:00							
9:00							
10:00							
11:00							
12:00 p.m.							
1:00							
2:00							
3:00							
4:00							
5:00							
6:00							
7:00							
8:00							
9:00							
10:00							
11:00							
12:00 a.m.							
1:00							
2:00							
3:00							
4:00							
Total minutes							
Tasks completed							

WEEK 6
Crafting Your Claims for Significance

Task Day	Week 6 Daily Writing Tasks	Estimated Task Time in Minutes	
		HumInt	SciQua
Day 1 (Monday?)	Read from here until you reach the week 6, day 2 tasks, filling in any boxes, checking off any forms, and answering any questions as you read.	90	60
Day 2 (Tuesday?)	Exchange your article with another scholarly author and do the "So What?" exercise.	120	90
Day 3 (Wednesday?)	Write and insert your claims for significance.	90	30
Day 4 (Thursday?)	Revise your article according to the results of the article exchange exercise.	90+	60
Day 5 (Friday?)	Revise your article according to the results of the article exchange exercise.	90+	60
Total estimated time for reading the workbook, completing the tasks, and writing your article		**8+ hours**	**5+ hours**

Above are the tasks for your sixth week. Make sure to start this week by scheduling when you will write, and then tracking the time you actually spend writing (using the Calendar for Actual Time Spent Writing This Week form or online software).

Group work. You can do the article exchange and the "So What?" exercise on the same day, whenever your group meets this week.

Individual work. If last week you didn't schedule a time this week to meet with another scholar to exchange your article, email someone today to set up that meeting (preferably for the second day of your writing week). Schedule it for a two-hour time block so that you have enough time to read and discuss each other's articles. If you don't feel ready to exchange your writing with someone else, still arrange a time to talk with someone about your claims for significance. If you don't feel ready to do that either, move this task to one of the following weeks and use this week for catch-up. Then come back and read this chapter the week that you do the exchange, as parts of it contain guidelines for exchanging writing. Just remember that being willing to share your writing is an essential step in the publication process. Frequent exchange helps you cope better with peer reviewers' negative comments when they come, which they inevitably will. It will also sharpen your ability to explain your work, which helps you interpret critical feedback usefully and craft better claims for significance.

WEEK 6, DAY 1: READING AND TASKS

FIFTH WEEK IN REVIEW

You have now spent five weeks working on establishing a writing schedule, revising your argument, selecting the right journal for publishing your article, and refining your Works Cited list. By this week, you should be in the groove, making progress and getting closer to completing your article. But that may not be happening. Instead, you may be doubting yourself, wondering why you can't seem to convert my writing advice to better writing, more writing, or consistent habits.

To be honest, the problem may be this very workbook! It divides an organic process into steps. The workbook posits a rigid, linear structure, unlike real writing, with its flexible, recursive structure. You can't really complete work on your argument one week and then leave it behind to develop your abstract the next. Rather, you may have to go back and forth. As the sociologist Peter Elbow comments, in his typically generous and radically vulnerable way:

> The common model of writing I grew up with preaches control. It tells me to think first, make up my mind what I really mean, figure out ahead of time where I am going, have a plan, an outline, don't dither, don't be ambiguous, be stern with myself, don't let things get out of hand. As I begin to try to follow this advice, I experience a sense of satisfaction and control: "I'm going to be in charge of this thing and keep out of any swamps!" Yet almost always my main experience ends up one of *not* being in control, feeling stuck, feeling lost, trying to write something and never succeeding. Helplessness and passivity. The developmental model, on the other hand, preaches, in a sense, *lack* of control: don't worry about knowing what you mean or what you intend ahead of time; you don't need a plan or an outline, let things get out of hand, let things wander and digress. Though this approach makes for initial panic, my overall experience with it is increased control. (Elbow 1998, 32–33; emphasis in the original)

If you haven't been getting much done and Elbow's words truly speak to you, maybe it's time for you to do something different. Instead of following this week's tasks, try reading and revising your article from start to finish, working on whatever attracts your attention. Then you can return to this chapter next week, or to whichever chapter seems most relevant for you right now. Changing the plan to suit your process is not self-deceit but self-knowledge. So long as you're working on your article, however slowly, you're doing fine.

In the previous weeks, we covered the three most important reasons why journal articles don't succeed—because they lack an argument, get sent to the wrong journal, or don't cite the right bodies of literature. This week, we turn to the next most common reason why journal articles don't succeed—they fail to articulate a claim for significance. So this week, you'll focus on crafting that claim.

MOTIVATING READERS

On the Difference Between Arguments and Claims for Significance

In the first edition of this workbook, I didn't include a chapter about asserting a journal article's significance. That's because it took me awhile to realize that an article's argument is not the same thing as what I call its "claim for significance," which is a statement in the article's introduction about the article's worthiness or value, emerging from its object of study, approach, argument, or solution. That is, a claim for significance states why the article's argument matters. Making vivid claims for significance is part of how you demonstrate your authority to speak on the topic. I realized the importance of claims for significance because I saw that a decently written article, with an acceptable argument, structure, and evidence, could still fail in the peer-review process if it didn't have a claim for significance. I also saw that the better the journal, the more likely its articles were to contain an aggressively strong statement about the significance of the article. Research confirms that over the last forty years, the frequency of aggressive wording in claims for significance, incorporating terms such as such as *robust*, *novel*, *innovative*, and *unprecedented*, has skyrocketed (Vinkers, Tijdink, and Otte 2015, 1–2).

The other reason that the difference between argument and claim for significance became clear to me was my discussions of article drafts with authors. An author and I might have a "blah" feeling in response to the article's stated argument. We knew it was an argument, and we knew that it had good evidence, but we didn't feel excited about it. And the author and I would find ourselves saying something like, "But why should readers care about that?" If we came up with a reason why readers should care, then we got excited again. Even well-published authors would plaintively ask me how to "sell," as they often put it, the article they had written. They would say things like, "Many scholars don't read articles further than the abstract; how do I get them to read at least the introduction of this article?" Or "I think this is fascinating; how do I convince other people to see it that way?" Or even "We proved *x* and I know it matters, but I'm not sure why." And as we searched together for reasons why the article was significant, our conversations would range over many aspects of the article—its argument, literature review, findings, implications, or recommendations—in search of this point that would compel readers to dig in. Frequently, we'd find multiple possible claims for significance and would have to decide whether to include all of them or just the best one for the most desired audience.

What Is a Claim for Significance?

Now, as with the term *argument*, we could get lost in defining and bracketing off what a journal article's claim for significance is. Let's try to make this simple instead. Almost every US book about academic writing published since 1980 advises that an author convincingly answer readers' questions of "So what?" That is, "What will reading this article do for me? Why does/should your article matter to readers like me?" Other variations include "Why are you telling me this?" or "Will it solve my/our/their problem?" All that writing advice about answering the "So what?" question is advice about making a claim for significance.

A more complicated way to define this term is Gordon Harvey's (1994; 2009) concept of *motive*; that is, what will motivate your potential readers to read your journal article? As developed for his teaching in the Harvard College Writing Program, Harvey articulates a motive as the reason your journal article "should interest a real person" (1994, 650). That is, reasons why your argument "isn't simply obvious, why there's a mystery to unfold, how the matter is different from what one might expect or some have said" (650). Later, Harvey clarified that he wasn't talking about what motivated *the author* to write the article—"which could be private and idiosyncratic"—but what would motivate scholars to read it: "a misapprehension or puzzle that an intelligent reader (not a straw dummy) would really have, a point that such a reader would really overlook" (2009, 1). Harvey's emphasis on the qualities of being interesting and somewhat surprising are helpful reminders about the nature of claims for significance. I am not a fan of the single word *motive*, because it doesn't make clear, in and of itself, whose motive we're taking about, authors' or readers'; but in my head I always say "readerly motivation," and then it works for me. Also helpful is Pat Thomson and Barbara Kamler's book about writing (2013), which provides a series of excellent examples of and advice about writing up the contribution and significance of an article.

Let me just reiterate that we're not trying to lock down a definition of the claim for significance, especially since any particular claim for significance can easily blend with your entry point and your argument. That's fine—you don't need to categorize and divide these up for them to work in your article. Rather, just make sure that in your article's introduction you do three things: take a stand (argument), relate that stand to the previous scholarship (entry point), and point out how that stand matters to those in your field or discipline (claim for significance). If those all happen to be in the same sentence, that's fine. If you have more than one claim for significance per article, that's also fine.

Types of Claims for Significance

As mentioned, claims for significance emerge from different elements of your article. For convenience, I identify ten types of claims, but as prompts for your thinking rather than strict categories. Types can easily overlap in one article—findings, implications, and recommendations, for instance. Your article should have at least one of the following:

Subject-based claim. A claim that is subject-based states the importance of the person, text, group, question, approach, or problem that you have taken as your subject. This is a typical, and good, claim for significance, especially when the subject has received little attention. But what makes a subject significant? In the United States, being at an extreme—the first or the last, the best or the worst, the largest or the smallest—is a time-honored mark of significance. Another is that the subject makes an important, overlooked difference in the world. Don't assume that your readers know why or how your subject is important. Even if they do know, part of your task of pulling readers into your article is stating the claim for significance in a particularly clear or powerful way.

> Do I have a subject-based claim for significance? If so, what is it, and is it stated clearly in my article?

Audience-based claim. A claim that is audience-based states that a specific audience has a previous and demonstrated interest in your subject, approach, problem, or solution. Such an audience often comprises scholars in a discipline or field and the specific journal in which you aim to publish, but it also may include policy makers, activists, teachers, and other particular publics. You need to articulate what it is about your article that would interest them.

> Do I have an audience-based claim for significance? If so, what is it, and is it stated clearly in my article?

Literature-based claim. A claim that is literature-based states that your article fills a gap, extends previous research, or corrects previous research. It is also known as your article's entry point, which was covered in "Week 5: Refining Your Works Cited." Stating that you're challenging, developing, or clarifying arguments in the related literature is a very typical claim for significance.

> Do I have a literature-based claim for significance? If so, what is it, and is it stated clearly in my article?

Practice-based claim. A claim that is practice-based states that your article extends or corrects common practices, views, assumptions, or perceptions of nonscholars, who are often practitioners of the discipline's knowledge area (e.g., teachers in education; business owners in business administration).

> Do I have a practice-based claim for significance? If so, what is it, and is it stated clearly in my article?

Method-based claim. A claim that is method-based states that your model or methodology has strong explanatory value: it's new, you invented it; it reveals something useful that can solve problems that people care about; it illuminates a previously unknown or little-understood subject; and/or it reshapes larger frameworks of understanding. The expansion, clarification, or introduction of key terms also constitutes a methods-based claim.

> Do I have a method-based claim for significance? If so, what is it, and is it stated clearly in my article?

Findings-based claim. A claim that is findings-based states that your findings, results, or interpretations have a strong advantage, because they shed new light on the subject, they reveal a new subject, or they will change how people view the subject. Some claims of this type assert that the findings contribute in important ways to our knowledge, particularly our understandings of social inequalities, how institutions work, and how human beings act. Such claims may also include defenses of what readers might assume are minor findings.

> Do I have a findings-based claim for significance? If so, what is it, and is it stated clearly in my article?

Disciplinary/field-based claim. A claim that is disciplinary or field-based states that your article will help your field or discipline become stronger or better. Disciplinary or field claims must match the journal to which you plan to submit your article. That is, a cultural anthropology journal may not care about how the article advances the field of, say, prehistoric archaeology; your claim would need to relate to cultural anthropology.

> Do I have a disciplinary/field-based claim for significance? If so, what is it, and is it stated clearly in my article?

Theory-based claim. A claim that is theory-based states that your article develops better ways of theorizing. Some such claims are that the article improves or shifts ways of thinking about the world or human relations; challenges systems of ideas; or reshapes general principles. Theory-based and method-based claims may be identical in some articles.

> Do I have a theory-based claim for significance? If so, what is it, and is it stated clearly in my article?

Implications-based claim. A claim that is implications-based states that your article demonstrates a phenomenon's problematic and unjust effects or positive and helpful effects in the world.

> Do I have an implications-based claim for significance? If so, what is it, and is it stated clearly in my article?

Recommendation-based claim. A claim that is recommendation-based states that your article will help others act powerfully on the issue at hand by giving them particular recommendations. The claim can also take the form of recommendations for future research.

> Do I have a recommendation-based claim for significance? If so, what is it, and is it stated clearly in my article?

Finally, if you have claims for significance, at least one of those claims needs to appear early in the article, in the introduction. Many authors place their claims for significance in the conclusion, which is fine, but the best motivating reasons for reading the article should appear early.

> Where do my claims for significance appear in the article? Do I need to move any to the introduction?

Examples of Claims for Significance

The examples I give below are of big, aggressive claims, but most articles have limited ones. So don't worry if none of your claims are monumental. Modest ones will do the trick at the clear majority of journals, just not at the top disciplinary ones.

HumInt claims. A published example of a claim for significance in the humanities is in an article by the literary critic John Kucich. In it, he argues that the writing of three nineteenth-century authors constitutes a "masochistic discourse" that might seem like an expression of powerlessness but is in fact a form of power (Kucich 2011, 89). This article appeared in the top journal in literature, *PMLA*, in part because of its strong claims for significance regarding history and gender activism. Kucich articulates seven of the types of claims for significance named above: stating the importance of his *subject*; addressing the *audience* of scholars and activists directly; correcting the *literature*; stating that his *findings* shed new light on more than literature; aiming to change *common views* of masochism; challenging scholarly *theories* of masochism; demonstrating the positive *implications* of masochism; and making *recommendations* for activism. Major, multiple claims for significance such as this, in combination with strong arguments and evidence, make a real difference in one's chances of publication, especially in a top journal. A less self-assured writer might have settled for saying that few have conducted research on these three authors, who have interesting relations to masochism. Kucich's aggressive claims for significance about how history itself works is the way to get into a top journal. Kucich also claims that his article can change how scholars and activists view masochism (seeing it no longer as a weakness but as a potent form of political power), and change how gender and sexuality scholars and activists view female suffering in the context of oppression (by "making visible feminism's historical debts" [99] to the harnessing of "intractable pain" [97] into "a source of empowerment" [97]). You can see how a top journal might not be interested in an article that claims only to document traces of masochism in a few nineteenth-century letters, but might be quite interested in an article claiming to change radically how we view masochism itself.

SciQua claims. In the social, health, behavioral, and natural sciences, claims for significance are less about interpretation, as in the humanities, and more about the article's role in illuminating human problems. For instance, a frequently downloaded article examines pharmaceutical firms' costs in developing new drugs (DiMasi, Grabowski, and Hansen 2016). The article, one in a series on the topic by its authors since the 1990s, shows that the firms' costs have increased in tandem with their drug development failure rates.

A substantial part of the article's introduction consists of claims about the significance of the article and its findings. First, the authors directly state which *audience* will find the article valuable: "drug developers, drug regulators, policy makers, and scholars interested in the structure and productivity of the pharmaceutical industry and its contributions to social welfare" (31). They substantiate this claim for significance by pointing to citations by this audience of the authors' prior studies on the topic. In other words, the series has already proved its value and has an eager audience. Second, the authors claim that their research is important because of its *implications* that past costs affect how firms behave in the future. They state why that matters in compelling language: "The costs required to develop these new products clearly play a role in [firms'] incentives to invest in the innovative activities that can generate medical innovation" (20). In other words, the authors' research is relevant to the fate of medicine as a whole. Third, they make claims about the rigor and reliability of their *findings*, based on their consistent methodology used over thirty years of studying the subject. You can see how a top journal might not be interested in an article that claims only to document increases in new drug costs, but might be quite interested in an article that suggests how medical innovation may best proceed in the future.

Making Claims for Significance

Including claims for significance in your article is essential; fortunately, they don't take up much space. They're often just three or four sentences in the introduction and a few in the conclusion, and may even go unmentioned in the rest of the article. Unlike argument, the claims for significance do not organize the material in an article (although they can organize the introduction and conclusion). However, although claims are among the shortest parts of the article, they're among the toughest parts to write.

Having multiple claims for significance is fine; many articles do. However, you must be sure to articulate them so that they seem organized. If you arrive at more than four, try to figure out how you can combine them or nest them. One graduate student's advisor told her that her article contained too many claims for significance. Their solution was to clearly state that there was more than one, then list them in consecutive sentences as distinct subject-based, discipline-based, theory-based, and implication-based claims.

The political theorist Desmond D. Jagmohan told me how he organized claims for significance in an article he has been writing (in progress) on the African American intellectual W. E. B. Du Bois. Jagmohan has organized his claims by the very different audiences who would be interested in them: either scholars of African American thought or scholars of political theory. That is, political theorists, faced with a claim about how the article enhances our understanding of Du Bois, might ask, "Why should I care what an early twentieth-century historian thought?" So Jagmohan has articulated different claims for the two sets of readers. Jagmohan could have written his entire article about Du Bois's perspective on racial uplift politics without ever mentioning the *value* to scholars of understanding what Du Bois thought. But he has articulated such claims for significance, and has done so with a keen understanding of his audiences.

The "So What?" Exercise

As a graduate student once said to me, "The 'So what?' question is the easiest question in the world to ask and the toughest question to answer." How do you know whether something is interesting, especially if you're in a field that doesn't produce practical solutions to real-world problems? Inventing your claim(s) for significance for a particular article can be a difficult task.

Certainly, it's so difficult that most scholars need other people to help them identify their claims for significance. That's for several reasons, I suspect. Most of us have only a limited sense of what other people want to hear. Novice scholars in particular may be unaware of the scholars and questions their work might aid, needing advisors to help them frame their contribution in light of those questions. Another challenge is that claims for significance require us to get out of our own heads and articulate precisely what is self-evident to us, and thus seems in no need of saying. Thus, the perplexity of our friends helps us see what isn't self-evident. Finally, as authors, we sometimes really don't know what our work is about. I remember complaining to my undergraduate advisor John Lemly that I had no idea what the real subject of my creative writing senior thesis was. He replied, "I know exactly what it's about. It's about death." Like magic, that one word coalesced the whole project for me. With some distance from my work, my advisor could see what I could not. So don't be shy about asking others to identify what interests them in your work and to help you articulate your claims for significance.

If you're struggling to craft your claims for significance, I recommend what I call the "So What?" exercise. It is adapted from one developed by a management expert, who identified the "So what?" question as an effective tool for applying pressure to topics in order to find the "ultimate benefit for your particular audience" (Aubuchon 1997, 87). If you have someone ask you a string of "So what" questions, it will help you get to your article's broader benefits, or claims for significance. This exercise can help you move from the concrete particulars of your article to the abstractions about its value. If it causes you to arrive at multiple values or benefits, that's fine. The exercise can be teeth-gnashingly frustrating, as I'll discuss later—but it's remarkably effective.

Examples of the "So What?" Exercise in Action
Here's an imagined example of the exercise, based on information in a literature review about lobbying (Craig and Madland 2014). In other words, with apologies to the authors, I devised this skit, inspired by their article but not reflecting it.

SciQua "So What?" Exercise, Skit 1
AUTHOR: My article is about the important effect on the US economy of lobbying by businesses. [*subject-based claim*]
READER: What effect?
AUTHOR: Well, the practice of business lobbying is a form of rent-seeking behavior.
READER: I have no idea what rent-seeking behavior is, but okay, so what?
AUTHOR: Rent-seeking behavior is trying to gain a benefit without actually producing anything. So rent-seeking behavior redirects government money to projects that are unnecessary or inefficient. [*findings-based claim*]
READER: That seems pretty clear. But so what?
AUTHOR: Well, that means that rent seeking redistributes money from productive parts of society to unproductive parts of society. [*implications-based claim*]
READER: I like what you did there; you scaled up to a big claim. So what?

AUTHOR: Well, rent seeking harms the economy. [*implications-based claim*]

READER: I'm still kind of unclear on what rent seeking is. Can you clarify?

AUTHOR: Okay, let me put it this way: lobbying harms the economy. [*implications-based claim*]

READER: Good, I understand that. But wait, didn't we already know that lobbying is bad?

AUTHOR: We suspected, but economists didn't have a way of measuring it. [*disciplinary-based claim*] My new economic model shows what is actually happening. [*approach-based claim*]

READER: Cool. So what?

AUTHOR: My model shows that lobbying produces inequities in access to jobs and goods. [*approach-based and implications-based claim*]

READER: So what?

AUTHOR: Why do inequities matter? Isn't that obvious?!

READER: Hey, don't shoot the messenger. This is your exercise!

AUTHOR: Okay, fine. Well, the production of inequities means that lobbying harms not just the economy but democracy. [*implications-based claim*]

READER: That seems good too. So what?

AUTHOR: Well, it's kind of a chicken-or-egg thing: without democracy, capitalism weakens. [*implications-based claim*]

READER: Okay, I'm not an economist, but I think you're getting too general now.

AUTHOR: Maybe the harm to democracy was the time to stop?

READER: Yes, but I kept thinking you were going to say, "Something should be done about lobbying." [*recommendation-based claim*]

AUTHOR: Oh, right. Yeah, that *is* the point.

READER: So who cares about that?

AUTHOR: Scholars, policy makers; really, any citizen. [*audience-based claim*]

[*Conversation ensues between reader and author; author drafts while reader suggests some language, resulting in a crafted claim for significance as follows:*]

AUTHOR: Many are concerned about the effects of lobbying in the United States, but they have not had adequate ways of evaluating that impact. This article provides a new economic model of value to economists, workers, and policy makers, as it demonstrates that lobbying harms the economy, creating social inequities, and as a result damages democracy. With the evidence from this model, reforms of the US system of lobbying can be more precisely designed. (Inspired by Craig and Madland 2014)

SciQua "So What?" *Exercise, Skit 2*

Here's another imagined example of the exercise, inspired by the work of Norwegian criminologist Heidi Mork Lomell (2002, 2010), but not reflecting it.

AUTHOR: My article is about urban video surveillance of the public by the police using closed-circuit television.

READER: I heard that every street downtown has cameras, which is super creepy; but so what?

AUTHOR: Urban video surveillance used to be rare, but now it's common. [*subject-based claim*]

READER: Makes sense. But so what?

AUTHOR: Urban video surveillance is sold as a good way to keep some populations safe. [*practice-based claim*]

READER: Why do you say "some populations"?

AUTHOR: Because they don't use it to protect everyone. Police use it to keep some populations safe by excluding other populations. [*findings-based claim*]

READER: Which ones?

AUTHOR: Police use video surveillance to exclude homeless people from urban centers. [*findings-based claim*]

READER: Really?! Wow. Okay, that's bad, so I feel weird asking—but so what?

AUTHOR: Urban video surveillance actually doesn't work well in keeping some populations safe; it just works really well in excluding homeless people. [*implications-based claim*]

READER: That's super clear; I like that. But since I'm supposed to keep asking, so what?

AUTHOR: Urban video surveillance is an expensive, ineffective tool for public safety. [*implications-based claim*]

READER: Even clearer. But where did your point go about the practice having increased? Can you put it all together?

AUTHOR: I think so. Despite its being ineffective and an incursion on civil liberties, cities and police departments keep expanding urban video surveillance programs. [*findings- and implications-based claims*]

READER: Great! So what?

AUTHOR: We should stop using urban video surveillance programs. [*recommendation-based claim*]

READER: Really? You see no value whatsoever in them? You don't think they should just be used differently?

AUTHOR: Honestly? I think they are pernicious and should be abolished.

[*Conversation ensues between reader and author; author drafts while reader suggests some language, resulting in a crafted claim for significance as follows:*]

AUTHOR: Over the past ten years, cities and police departments have expanded urban video surveillance programs, touting their role in ensuring public safety, despite concerns about privacy and equity. I argue that such programs work better at excluding certain publics than in protecting all publics, and recommend that policy makers retrench such programs, not simply because they restrict civil liberties but because they don't work. (Inspired by the work of Heidi Mork Lomell [2002, 2010])

HumInt "So What?" *Exercise Skit*

Here's one more example of the "So What?" exercise in action, this one in the humanities. It's adapted from a conversation I had with a scholar of German literature; I have changed the subject and import, however.

AUTHOR: My article is about this obscure German journalist [Name], who wrote an eclectic critique of modernity. [*subject-based claim*]

READER: So what?

AUTHOR: Well, no one knows her now, but she was renowned in her time. [*subject-based claim*]

READER: So what?

AUTHOR: She is unjustly overlooked in scholarship on German history. [*literature-based claim*]

READER: Okay, but you keep on focusing on her. You already know that scholars conducting research on her will read your article no matter what. But don't you want additional readers?

AUTHOR: Yes, I would like it to appeal more broadly, say, to historians of Germany or scholars of modernity.

READER: Okay, so why should they read your article?

AUTHOR: Well, historians and modernists should care because her critique of modernity anticipated those of the now more famous male German authors Theodor W. Adorno and Max Horkheimer. [*literature-based and audience-based claims*]

READER: Wow; really? That finding would definitely be interesting to many people. So what?

AUTHOR: That finding forces us to rewrite twentieth-century intellectual history. [*findings-based and disciplinary-based claims*]

READER: Nice! You really scaled up with that claim. That would interest a range of academic readers, including those in other disciplines, because it might change how they write their own article. But just to keep going: so what?

AUTHOR: My article is part of a larger trend to reinsert important women into a history that forgot them. [*literature-based claim*]

READER: Sounds good. You kind of pulled back, though, made a more modest claim there. Okay, that sounds wrong to say that inserting women back into history is modest, but you know what I mean.

AUTHOR: Yeah. But I'm going back to her because I don't want to lose her. Although, I should be sure to say, she was a horrible person. Like, her politics were terrible.

READER: Yikes. Why is that, anyway? Why do so many thinkers in the twentieth century have terrible politics?

AUTHOR: I've been thinking about that myself.

READER: Do you think she helps us understand that phenomenon?

AUTHOR: Hmm. Yeah, I think I could claim that.

READER: Okay, how does that claim go?

AUTHOR: Maybe, the author's critique of modernity helps us answer one of the haunting questions of the twentieth century: how could so many great thinkers do such terrible things politically? [*literature-based and implications-based claims*]

READER: Wow! That's terrific. Who wouldn't want to read that article? Although, actually... hmm. I guess you would have to say *how* her critique answers that question.

AUTHOR: Aargh. Yeah, I can pose the question, but I'm not sure I can answer it.

READER: Okay, so maybe that isn't a claim of yours but a question posed at the very end of the article, opening things up.

AUTHOR: Yeah, I'll have to think about it.

[*Conversation ensues between reader and author; author drafts while reader suggests some language, resulting in a crafted claim for significance as follows:*]

AUTHOR: Intellectual historians often overlook the contributions of women, and perhaps no case better demonstrates that than [Name], a now undeservedly obscure German journalist who anticipated Theodor W. Adorno's and Max Horkheimer's critiques of modernity. In this article, I will lay out for scholars of Germany and modernity how the work of [Name] changes our understanding of German history and even our genealogies of theories of modernity.

You can see how a top journal might not be interested in an article that claims only to introduce us to an obscure journalist, but might be quite interested in an article that claims to rewrite history or answer huge philosophical questions. The body of the article might be nearly the same, but the claims for significance position it very differently. The takeaway here is that depending on which claims you select, your introduction will shape up quite differently.

TYPES OF FEEDBACK

Let's switch gears. This week, you are to exchange your article with another person, so in this section I provide some instructions on how to give and receive feedback. I want to be sure that you receive the most constructive feedback possible.

Learning to interpret and use feedback in your writing is an essential part of becoming a good writer. Unfortunately, one of the occupational hazards of being in academia is that our critical faculties wax and our supportive faculties wane. By the time we get out of graduate school, we are a lot better at pointing out what people are doing wrong than in enabling people to do better. While there is a place for pure critique, the informal activities of this chapter are about changing that dynamic and getting you feedback that can help you improve your article, not abandon it.

In the following section, then, are instructions for *giving* feedback; in the section after that are instructions for *receiving* it (including how to deal with bad feedback).

What to Do When Giving Feedback

One of the best ways to improve your own writing is to learn to give good feedback and thus be supportive of others' struggles. Certainly, studying this topic helped my writing a lot! So how do we learn to use our critical faculties to enable others to write better and, eventually, help ourselves do so? By embracing the practices of good readers and avoiding the obsessions of bad readers, as follows:

Start with the positive. A little bit of sugar makes the medicine go down. A student once told the class that she had two advisors. One advisor she liked and did everything she recommended; the other she disliked and resisted everything she recommended. Why? The student commented,

> I realized that the reason I liked the one and disliked the other had nothing to do with the criticism itself. In fact, the one I disliked tended to have fewer critical things to say than the other one. But the advisor I liked always started off enthusiastically—she always

loved the paper, thought it was a great project, was sure it would be published, and then would give me a long list of what was wrong with it. But because she had "bought in," because I felt like she had signaled she was on my side, I listened to her and I walked away feeling encouraged. The other advisor always started with the problems. It just felt so discouraging: "Well, you've really got to work on your structure, and you didn't cite these three people I told you to cite, and you really should learn APA style better." At the end she would say, "But it's a very solid project, and I think you are doing good work." By then, it just seemed like a kiss-off, like bribery, like I was a little kid who could be bought off. And what's funny is that even realizing that she was actually less critical didn't help; I just never could quite hear the second advisor as well as I could the first.

I have found this to be true for many people. One of the biggest steps you can make toward being a useful reader is to start with the positive when you give feedback.

Be specific. However, when starting with the positive, make sure it's specific. Vague praise such as "Good article!" is not enough. Most authors in the position of receiving feedback are like patients waiting for their doctor to give them the results of their health test. As soon as the doctor walks into the room, they're trying to read her expression and her words for catastrophic news. For some reason, generalities inspire fear: "She just said that I'm looking good—that means I have something fatal!" Starting with a specific positive—I really like your argument about x, I thought your conclusion was especially strong—lets the author know that you're being sincere, not just placating him or her until you get around to delivering critical feedback.

If you feel that you do have a solution, that you do know something specific that would improve the article, be clear about it. Nothing is worse than someone who reads your work and tells you something is wrong with it, but he or she isn't sure what that flaw is: "I mean, it's a really good article, but I don't know, something about it doesn't quite hang together, you know?" By the same token, don't tell someone, "Your writing style needs a lot of work, like, you keep using the same words over and over," as this is vague and unhelpful. Say instead, "You might think about working on making your sentences more active and less passive; also, I thought you overused some words, like *interesting*."

Focus on giving a response. The writing research says that the most helpful review you can give authors is to tell them what you understood their article to say (Elbow 1998; McMurry 2005). You don't have to tell them what's wrong with it or how they should change it. You only have to tell them, "I understood this article to be about . . .; it seemed like your argument was . . .; you seemed to say that your article is a contribution because of . . ." If you focus on giving a response rather than on offering solutions, it will help you be respectful of authors and their intent. They're not you; they don't put things the way you would. And they don't have to agree with you or accept what you're saying to them.

Continuing on this theme, I believe that what is helpful for authors is not so much telling them what is wrong with their article and how to fix it as marking what made you stop. In other words, ideally, what you as a reader offer is a marker of what you noticed, what stood out. What you say about what you noticed is often less important than that you identified a section to be addressed. Where did you have to reread the sentence or paragraph several times? Or where did you stop because you thought, "Wow, that's really good!"? Just letting the author know these moments is helpful. Sometimes you mark where you stumbled, and the author will realize that actually nothing is wrong there; it's the preceding paragraph that's the problem. In summary, this is the response approach to feedback: you're not attempting to solve problems but merely to identify where you as a reader had problems.

Always suggest. If you feel that you do have a solution, that you do know something specific that would improve the article, something that goes beyond response, frame it as a suggestion. Again, the work is not your own, you aren't the expert on it, so all you can do is make suggestions. Admit your limitations and don't invent advice on material that's beyond your knowledge.

Well-trained copy editors know how to give suggestions to authors, because they are trained to ask questions instead of give orders. The difference between a comment bubble that says "Redundant." and one that says "Redundant?" may not seem like much, but that question mark prevents criticisms from denting authors' egos. The period places you as the authority; the question mark places the author as the authority. "Sentence fragment. Rewrite?" or "Relevance?" suggests that it's possible this isn't an error but a choice on the part of the author, which it may well be. All we can offer is our opinion.

Focus on the large-scale writing issues. Most readers get distracted by the small stuff. You'll become known as a good reviewer if you can stay focused on the big stuff. Does the article have an argument? Is that threaded throughout? Are the sections of the article the right size, or are some unusually long? Three solid observations about the article's large-scale writing aspects—its argument, evidence, structure, findings, or methods—are worth any number of smaller observations. In these early stages, try to think about the totality and the logical flow of the piece. Most people can't absorb many comments at one time.

Use a form. To keep yourself on task when reading someone else's work, you may find it helpful to use the Belcher Journal Article Review Feedback Form that appears later in this chapter. Filling it out as you read will keep you focused on the large-scale writing aspects of the article.

What *Not* to Do When Giving Feedback

The following obsessions prevent us from providing useful feedback to our friends and colleagues:

Don't obsess over the author's bibliographic sources. A good reader does not simply name five, ten, or fifty additional articles that the author should have consulted and cited. Your job is to focus on what the author does with what he or she has read. In a thirty-page article, no one can possibly cite everything on a topic. An article is not meant to be exhaustive.

Often, people use reading recommendations as a substitute for actually engaging with the content of the article, how the author has gone about putting his or her ideas together. If you read a thirty-page article with twenty to sixty citations, don't let your only feedback be a long list of titles. And don't develop the nervous tic of academia to rattle off only loosely related titles. People have written amazing articles without citing many texts.

"But, but, but," you say, "are you really saying we should never recommend texts? What if the author really has left out an important text? What if I just happen to know a text that would provide him or her with a perfect proof? I love it when my professor tells me what to read!" Yes, you can recommend reading, but don't gild the lily. Ask yourself whether, given the size of the article, the author has a fair number of references to literature in the field. If that's the case, actively resist the impulse to recommend texts. But if the author doesn't seem to engage with his or her field—remember that the work must say something new about something old—then you can make some kind of blanket comment about this: "I don't think you cite enough of the other scholarship about dating apps" or "There's a fair amount of scholarship on Ngugi wa Thiong'o's theory; you might want to cite some of it."

And if you read someone's article and get this excited feeling that you can truly help that person by recommending a particular text, go for it. Or if you get this sinking feeling the longer you read and you find yourself repeatedly thinking, "How can this person possibly write on black feminism without mentioning Brittany Cooper?!" then try to articulate what such a text could do for the author's argument. If you feel that the author needs certain sources to back an argument, say that. You don't have to suggest which ones unless you really know which ones and why they're necessary. In other words, watch this impulse in yourself.

Don't obsess over what's *not* in the article. It's your job to focus on the article's content, not to insist that the author include what isn't there. Don't ask for additional research or experimentation; instead, comment on what the author managed to do with the data collected. If it isn't convincing, then say it isn't convincing. A thirty-page article can only do so much; by definition, it will have huge gaps. It's perfectly acceptable to write an article quantifying racism in middle schools without addressing gender at length; to write about nineteenth-century Chinese thought without mentioning eighteenth-century Chinese thought; to write about southern India without mentioning northern India; to write about African authors without mentioning Nadine Gordimer; to write about German art without mentioning surrealism. For you to make a general comment that the omission of, say, race or classical thought raises serious questions is okay—but again, it shouldn't be the lion's share of your comments. Good readers pay attention to what is there.

Don't obsess over fixing the article. Because most of us have more experience writing than reviewing, we tend to approach other people's articles as writers, that is, as if the article were our own writing. We don't separate ourselves enough from the text in front of us, and so we think it's our job to rewrite it.

Two problems arise from not setting enough distance from others' work. First, we often start to feel overwhelmed. It's a huge job to go into someone else's writing and solve its problems. We start to experience mistakes in an author's work as an offense: "How dare this person ask me to read something that's so confused? How am I supposed to help when so much help is needed?" We feel anxious, because we're not sure how to fix the writing. This leads to the second problem. Since we don't feel adequate to the job and since this feeling of inadequacy is unbearable, we sometimes take it out on the author. We then deliver our review in anger and frustration, which is useless to the author, who can't hear the advice because of the emotional way that we delivered it, which sparks his or her own anxieties. It's not your job to fix other people's articles; it's your job to give them a constructive response to their work.

Don't obsess over judging the work. You need not consider yourself an expert on anyone else's writing. You're simply a reader. One subjective, slightly tired, slightly distracted reader. So don't regard your own position as all-knowing.

In practice, what this means specifically is, don't be harsh. Be kind when reading others' work and your own. You shouldn't praise everything, of course, but avoid phrasing your criticisms in ways that are harsh and unhelpful. I mean such words as *sloppy*, *incoherent*, *nonsense*, *ridiculous*, and *boring*—and those are just a few of the words I have seen on the margins of my own papers over the years! Students have told me that on their paper, professors have written "hackneyed," "rubbish," "tedious," "hokey," "fake," and (I don't know why I find this so shocking after all the rest) "shit." Such comments are counterproductive. Remember not to judge the article (it isn't a contest) but to give feedback according to your own subjective views.

It can be particularly difficult to avoid being a judge when you disagree politically with the article's content. If you find someone else's work disturbing and don't want to get into it, you can always excuse yourself: "I just don't think I would be a good reader for your article about deconstructing the poetry of this openly racist writer." That's all you need to say, and there is no reason for either side to feel bad. You aren't obligated to read disturbing things. If you can't give feedback on an article at this initial stage without prejudice or emotion, it's best to leave it to others. If, however, you strongly disagree with the author's topic or approach and want to take it on, make a concerted effort to remember that you're not a judge, and it's your job to provide a response. Every argument has flaws; point out where the argument is not working on the author's own terms. Lee Bowie, a logic professor of mine at Mount Holyoke College, used to say, "It is difficult to convince individuals that their premises are wrong. It is easier to show them how their premises do not lead to their conclusions." If you can do that, you're more likely to help authors see the error of their political position as well.

Don't obsess over the work's relation to yours. Don't use others' research as a leaping-off point to think through your own ideas. Stay engaged with the author's project and aims. If you find that most of your comments are about making over this person's work into something more like yours, stop. Go do some of your own writing to get over that impulse!

Work on improving, and forgive your failures. It's tough giving constructive feedback. Even as the author of this section and the rest of this workbook, I can find myself giving an author a stream of criticisms with few positive comments. If I feel that I've given some assistance and the author doesn't follow it, I can start to feel punitive. I have more than once had to send an apologetic email after a feedback session saying, "I'm sorry I pushed so hard." None of us are perfect, and giving feedback is arduous. Staying open and transparent about the process helps.

What to Do When Receiving Feedback

Now let's leap over to the other side. How do we go about being a good recipient of feedback? How do we survive the process?

Give instructions. When you hand your article to others, let those readers know what kind of feedback you need. If you're about to send the article to a journal, you can say that you're just looking for a last check for typos or egregious errors; you aren't in a place where you can absorb much else. If you're still writing your first draft, feel free to say that you're currently looking for input about large-scale writing issues, not line editing of spelling and grammatical errors.

Listen and don't talk. A good practice when receiving criticism of your writing is to be silent. Just listen and take careful notes. Later, you can decide which criticisms are useful and which are not; for now, just make sure that you understand what the criticisms are. It's easy to get swept up in defending your work orally instead of listening to its critique. But even if you orally convince others of your point, your defense still isn't on the page, which is where it needs to be. In my writing groups, we have a rule that those being critiqued cannot speak until all readers have given their opinion. That way, your focus is on listening, not defending. It also allows you to have the wonderful experience of hearing others defending your work for you.

Allow your feelings. As Lisa Munro (2015b) says, "It is okay to feel vulnerable, scared, angry, or hurt when receiving feedback." She adds, "It's important to validate our own feelings. We do ourselves no favors when we try to tell ourselves that we shouldn't feel a certain way." She is exactly right.

Separate the delivery from the message. Many people are bad at giving criticism— they don't start their critique with the article's positive aspects; rather, they get angry, they get frustrated. If possible, you should separate the content of their criticism from the emotions with which it gets delivered. If you can stay calm, you'll be better able to evaluate the criticism on its own merits. Criticism delivered in a hostile manner can still be correct; criticism delivered in a kind manner can still be wrong. You need to learn to sift the useful from the useless feedback regardless of its delivery method.

Take advantage of primitive readings. Every criticism provides an opportunity for you to explain your ideas more clearly in the article. So even if you rightly think, "What an idiot! Anyone smart would get that sentence," you should try to make that sentence clearer. If your reader stumbles, help.

You are the final authority on your own writing. You don't have to do anything anyone tells you to do, no matter how hard he or she pushes. Make only the changes that you understand and that make sense to you. Once you firmly believe that you're the final judge of your writing, you can be more open to others' comments and suggestions. Graduate students often feel that they must do what their advisors say, no matter what; but even advisors who seem very insistent can be merely brainstorming about your work rather than providing you with a required to-do list. Most want you to attend to their critique, but not unquestioningly. My amazing dissertation advisor Felicity Nussbaum—widely agreed to be the best advisor of her generation—did me the honor of telling me early on in my dissertation writing process that she didn't like my theory of "discursive possession." Her repeated objections upped my game, forcing me again and again to refine the idea until, in the end, I overcame her objections and convinced her of its utility. I never ignored her feedback; I used it for my purposes.

Be grateful. Interestingly, the more famous you get, the less feedback you get. A student in one of my classes told us a story about her participation in a graduate student journal. The journal's editorial board, composed entirely of graduate students, reviewed submissions individually and as a group. Each board member read all the articles; then the board debated their strengths and weaknesses, and drafted a letter to each author containing the board's various recommendations for that author's article. Only after doing so would the board learn the author's identity. On one occasion, it found that a submission was from an extremely famous scholar, Benedict Anderson. The article was quite problematic, however, clearly a first draft. The students debated what to do and then decided, courageously, to proceed as they normally would as an editorial board and send off the recommendations. Anderson wrote back almost immediately, saying that it had been years since he had received detailed feedback, and he was very grateful to the board! He revised the article as suggested and resubmitted it. So be glad that you're in a place where people still critique your work!

CLAIMING SIGNIFICANCE

Day 1 Tasks: Reading the Workbook

On the first day of your sixth writing week, read this week 6 chapter all the way through the next paragraph, answering all the questions posed. Write directly in the boxes provided or in your own document, being sure to articulate some claims for significance.

Tracking Writing Time

Each day, use the Calendar for Actual Time Spent Writing This Week form (or digital time-tracking software) to keep track of the time you spent writing this week. Then, at the end of the week, evaluate how you spent your time.

If busy, at least mark the check boxes with how long you wrote today. ☐ 15+ min. ☐ 30+ ☐ 60+ ☐ 120+

WEEK 6, DAYS 2-5: READING AND TASKS

Day 2 Tasks: Exchanging Writing and Doing the "So What?" Exercise

Today you'll focus on giving and receiving feedback. It's important to complete both tasks this week, because in the process of giving feedback you learn something about revising your own work. When you exchange your article with another scholarly author, have your partner read the "Types of Feedback" section above and the instructions for completing the exercise below so that your partner approaches your writing in the same spirit with which you will approach that person's. As noted in previous weeks, meeting in person (whether in a group or in pairs) and exchanging your writing, so you're both giving and receiving critique, is best.

Also, reading in the moment is best. When you give an article to someone to read while alone later, it can be difficult for that person to get around to reading it. Most people experience reading others' work as yet another task on their long to-do list, so making this activity social helps them complete it. So when I lead this exercise in class, we spend forty-five to sixty minutes of class time reading, and give feedback immediately afterward.

Exchange Writing Exercise

Once you and your partner have handed your articles to each other, follow the reading process below. The reason for this process is to train you to maintain some distance from your partner's article, thereby avoiding getting wrapped up in it. As noted earlier, the reader's job is to identify problems, not try to solve them.

1. Tell each other what kind of feedback you each need at this point in the writing process (and/or agree to use the Belcher Journal Article Review Feedback Form on the next page). Do *not* say anything about the content of your article. You want your reader to be responding to what's there on the page, not what you said about it. (5 minutes)
2. Taking up your partner's article, skim through it once *without* a pen (or mouse) in your hand. Don't make any marks on the article—just familiarize yourself with it. Don't get distracted by the small stuff; you're trying to keep the entire article in mind. Then turn over the article and on the back page write a summary of what you understood the article to be about. It's okay if you're not clear yet; that's part of the point of doing the summary now. Peer reviewers skim; you want to communicate what a peer reviewer might understand about the article by skimming yourself. (30 minutes)
3. Return to the beginning of the article and pick up your pen. Go through the whole article, putting a check mark (☑) next to whatever is good, clear, vivid, or compelling. You can put a check next to an entire paragraph, a sentence, a word, an example, a heading, whatever you think is good. If you want, next to the check write down what you liked about that part. (30 minutes)
4. Go back to the beginning and circle (O) what's unclear, what you don't fully understand, what you'd like to know more about, and what could be improved. (30 minutes)
5. Fill out the Journal Article Review Feedback Form, which will help you give comments on large-scale writing issues. (10 minutes)
6. Take turns going over reader's marks and the feedback form with the other author. Starting with the positive aspects of the article is essential during feedback. (20 minutes each)
7. Go on to the "So What?" exercise below. (Or you can do this exercise with someone else.) (20 minutes each)

If your partner wants to work through possible writing solutions with you, that's fine, but don't feel you need to have all the answers. If your partner starts explaining aspects of the article to you, try to take notes. These notes can help the author later, when revising. Be sure to return your marked-up copy of your partner's article.

Belcher Journal Article Review Feedback Form

The following questions will help you comment on the article you are reviewing. Your answers should guide the author in revising his or her work. You may not find all the questions relevant to reviewing the article that you're reading, especially if you're not in the same field; use what is useful.

General

What are the strengths of this article?

Content

Does the author state the argument of the article early and clearly? If not, where might this be done?

What is the argument of the article (so far as you understand it)?

Does the author make claims for significance in the article? If not, where might they be added?

What are the claims for significance of the article (so far as you understand them)?

Does the author situate the article well within the scholarly literature? If not, how might this be done?

Which scholarly debates is the author addressing (so far as you understand them)?

Does the author describe the methods comprehensively and concisely? If not, what needs to be added?

Could the author's argument be better supported with evidence? If so, specify where and how.

Did you notice any errors in sources, dates, quotations, facts, or proper names? If so, note them.

Organization

Do the article's first few paragraphs draw the reader in? If not, what might make them more compelling?

Does the article need more or better subheads? If so, which ones need to be revised, and where should additional ones be placed?

Does the author raise questions that go unanswered? If so, specify where.

Were any parts of the article repetitive or digressive? If so, specify where.

Are there any unclear or missing transitions? If so, specify where.

Was there any section in which you lost interest? If so, specify where, and what might have held your interest better.

Did any sections go on too long? If so, specify which ones.

Does the conclusion summarize the article? If not, specify what might tie it together.

Is the argument organizing the article (or is the evidence problematically running the show)?

Contribution (if reviewer and author are in the same field/discipline)

Does the article add new and valuable information and insight to scholarship?

Will the article appeal to the general readers of a journal?

Is the argument justified, given the findings and evidence?

Are the claims for significance justified, given the findings and evidence? If not, how might they be improved?

General

What did you find most intriguing about this article?

Doing the "So What?" Exercise

On day 1 this week, I explained the rationale behind the "So What?" exercise and gave some examples. You can do this exercise with a range of people. It can work well with someone who has just read your article (after the feedback exercise). But you can still do the exercise with someone who hasn't read it if you feel that your article isn't ready for exchange with another author. People who have a deep knowledge of your discipline can be helpful in crafting disciplinary-oriented claims for significance. But having to explain your work to interlocutors outside your discipline can help you craft broad claims for significance. You can also do this exercise with more than one person. Alternately, if you don't have a partner for this exercise, you can try it out on yourself, although it works best with an audience.

Here are some caveats about how the "So What?" exercise works. It brings up many feelings, as it can be frustrating, annoying, and even scary. In the middle of it, you might begin to think, "There's no there there!" But I promise you, there is value in what you write, and part of the point of this exercise is to force you to acknowledge and articulate that value. So once you've started the "So What?" exercise, keep forcing yourself to articulate both the obvious and what you didn't know you knew.

Next, this exercise has a lot to do with breaking open your thinking about the article, so use it to experiment. If you feel like you've reached a roadblock, try being speculative or even arrogant. Have some fun and try out ridiculous or outrageous claims for significance; sometimes one of the toned-down versions of those is the right claim for significance. Or try articulating your assumptions and see whether that gets you somewhere. Being playful can help.

Most important, the structure of the exercise makes it feel like you should be evolving to better and better answers, but that's not necessarily the case. The best "So what?" might be one in the middle. Finally, even if you can't come up with a good claim in the moment, don't worry. You may find that it comes to you while falling asleep that night or talking with someone the next day.

Here are the instructions for the "So What?" exercise.

1. Be prepared to document what you learn. Both writing and tape-recording are wise, because you often come up with oral formulations that you won't remember well later. Both of you should have a pen and a piece of paper to capture remarks. I like to do this exercise while walking, in which case we don't write but only record our conversation.

2. Next, have your interlocutor read the earlier section about how to do the "So What?" exercise, including the examples.

3. Then urge your interlocutor to leap in with questions, pose alternate answers, or attempt formulations as you describe your article.

4. Tell your interlocutor in a sentence or less what your article is about.

5. Then have your interlocutor ask, "So what?"—in an interested tone of voice, never a sarcastic one—after which you give your answer. Once more, have the interlocutor ask, "So what?" and answer. I recommend trying at least six rounds. It's fine, although not essential, to talk about each answer before going on to the next "So what?"

6. When finished with the exercise, spend a few minutes silently writing down possible claims for significance. You can use the box on the next page for this purpose. Avoid excessive formulations. Claiming that something has been true "for all time" or "for

all of human history" or "in all cultures" or "for all peoples" or "around the globe" will mark your article as unsophisticated. Almost nothing has been true always or everywhere.

My Claims for Significance	
Reasons that would motivate scholars to read my article:	**Which audience(s) would be interested in that claim?**

Tracking Writing Time

Mark your electronic calendar, the Calendar for Actual Time Spent Writing This Week form, and/or the check boxes here with how long you wrote today. ☐ 15+ min. ☐ 30+ ☐ 60+ ☐ 120+

Day 3 Tasks: Writing and Inserting Your Claims for Significance

Today you'll revisit your answers in the "Types of Claims" section and the "My Claims for Significance" box. Then reread your article with an eye for claims for significance.

Are they there? If not, add them. Do you clearly articulate them in a few sentences in the introduction and conclusion? If not, clarify them.

Tracking Writing Time

Mark your electronic calendar, the Calendar for Actual Time Spent Writing This Week form, and/or the check boxes here with how long you wrote today. ☐ 15+ min. ☐ 30+ ☐ 60+ ☐ 120+

Days 4-5 Tasks: Revising Your Article according to Feedback Received

Today and tomorrow, you will revise your article according to the feedback you received this week, especially that which pertains to argument, citations, or claims for significance. If you received feedback regarding evidence, structure, titles, introductions, or conclusions, you may want to put notes into your article about those suggestions, but not incorporate them fully until you have read the upcoming chapters on those topics. Just be sure not to lose those suggestions; note them in the electronic version of your article.

The last day of this week is also a good day to do a status check, on your own or with any writing partners or groups. To identify this status, fill out the Current Status of My Article form below. You don't need to spend a lot of time on this activity—just jot down what you know, and leave out what you don't.

Current Status of My Article

Working title:	
Readers' motivation to read my article:	
Working argument:	
Evidence for my argument (e.g., particular book, data set):	
Possible journals for my article:	
Daily writing schedule:	

Tracking Writing Time

Mark your electronic calendar, the Calendar for Actual Time Spent Writing This Week form, and/or the check boxes here with how long you wrote both days. ☐ 15+ min. ☐ 30+ ☐ 60+ ☐ 120+

Then, here at the end of your workweek, take pride in your accomplishments and evaluate whether any patterns need changing.

DOCUMENTING YOUR WRITING TIME AND TASKS

Calendar for Actual Time Spent Writing This Week

Time	Day 1	Day 2	Day 3	Day 4	Day 5	Day 6	Day 7
5:00 a.m.							
6:00							
7:00							
8:00							
9:00							
10:00							
11:00							
12:00 p.m.							
1:00							
2:00							
3:00							
4:00							
5:00							
6:00							
7:00							
8:00							
9:00							
10:00							
11:00							
12:00 a.m.							
1:00							
2:00							
3:00							
4:00							
Total minutes							
Tasks completed							

WEEK 7
Analyzing Your Evidence

Task Day	Week 7 Daily Writing Tasks	Estimated Task Time in Minutes	
		HumInt	SciQua
Day 1 (Monday?)	Read from here until you reach the week 7, day 2 tasks, filling in any boxes, checking off any forms, and answering any questions as you read.	60	60
Day 2 (Tuesday?)	Highlight and analyze the evidence in your article.	60+	30+
Day 3 (Wednesday?)	Analyze the quality and relevance of the evidence in your article.	120+	90+
Day 4 (Thursday?)	Analyze the interpretation of the evidence in your article.	120+	90+
Day 5 (Friday?)	Collect any needed additional evidence.	120+	90+
Total estimated time for reading the workbook, completing the tasks, and writing your article		**8+ hours**	**6+ hours**

Above are the tasks for your seventh week. Start this week by scheduling when you will write, and then tracking the time you actually spend writing (using the Calendar for Actual Time Spent Writing This Week form or online software).

Today starts two weeks of focusing on your evidence. This week, you'll consider the strength of your evidence; next week you will examine your presentation of that evidence. That is, you won't make any revisions to the actual writing in your article this week; you're focusing entirely on analyzing your evidence. You will work on revising the evidence in the article itself next week.

WEEK 7, DAY 1: READING AND TASKS

SIXTH WEEK IN REVIEW

You have now spent six weeks working on some of the most important tasks involved in revising an article for publication: designing a plan, creating an argument, selecting a journal, writing up the scholarly literature, and making claims for significance. You now turn to spending two weeks on your biggest task: improving your presentation and interpretation of your evidence.

The good news is that you're past the halfway mark with your article! It isn't easy doing such concentrated work, so congratulate yourself! Especially since, as Arthur L. Stinchcombe (1966, 25) noted years ago, we academics must motivate ourselves to write by believing in the results of our research goals, which, unfortunately, is "a weak reed to sustain . . . drudgery." In response to this drudgery, one of the readers of this workbook's first edition came up with an incentive system she called the "dress fund." She often wore sweats while writing, so she decided that buying a dress would be something nice she could do for herself. She broke down her writing tasks for the day into thirty- to sixty-minute chunks. If she completed a task within the amount of time she had estimated, she put a dollar into a box until she had enough to buy the dress. A side benefit of such an incentive system was that it forced this reader to get a better understanding of how long it took her to complete tasks. Previously, she would castigate herself for being slow. And then her anxiety about her slowness made her even slower. Over time, however, she realized that writing slowly still got the article finished and sent off to a journal. So she decided to accept that she was a slow writer. The benefit of that acceptance was surprising: "I think that by accepting my slowness, I have actually become quicker!" So if you're still searching for your incentive, now may be the time to think up a fund for fun that might help in keeping you on track.

ANALYZING EVIDENCE

The most damning comment to receive from an editor or reviewer of your article is that your analysis was found to be problematic. In fact, "inadequate theory" and "methodological problems" are among the most frequent reasons given by journals for rejecting an article (Weller 2001, 50, 52; Paltridge 2017, 62), followed by "poor analysis" and "inadequate interpretation" (Weller 2001, 53; Paltridge 2017, 62, 50). "Limited or misused data" as well as unacknowledged "bias," exaggerated claims, and ethical issues (Woods 2006, 94, 147) are other typical reasons for rejection. Negative comments about methods, research design and questions, and analysis of findings make up the greater part of rejection peer-review reports (Paltridge 2017, 61). Unfortunately, a theoretically or methodologically flawed article with weak findings has little chance of surviving peer review, and the journal editor may even tell you that it's not revisable. Generally, editors don't see such problems as being correctable (Weller 2001, 52–53). It's best, then, to work hard not to get a judgment of "hopelessly flawed" from an editor or reviewer.

Yet this critique might not be right. Regrettably, a few editors are unethical and will block from peer review any work with which they disagree. A student received a desk rejection stating that the article was neither sufficiently theoretical nor rooted in the main methodology of the discipline, both of which were patently untrue. The student was quite puzzled, until one of the assistant editors wrote privately to say that the article was rejected because of its radical politics, not because of any inadequacies. On a more optimistic note, two graduate students conducted fascinating interviews with leading economists, asking them to discuss "instances in which journals rejected their papers" (Gans and Shepherd 1994, 165). The students' survey revealed that "many papers that have become classics were rejected initially by at least one journal—and often by more than one" (166). Rejections of articles that went on to be cited in thousands of other articles were often made for theoretical reasons—that is, "too general" a hypothesis, "preposterous" predictions, "uninteresting" conclusions, "inappropriate" models, and "trivial" substance (171, 168). Editors can fail to recognize articles that represent an advancement in the field and hence mislabel them, especially if they contain some unusual features.

Before turning to what you can do to improve your analysis of evidence, let's consider what constitutes evidence. Forms of evidence in different disciplines vary so much as to be almost impossible to discuss together. We select, present, and interpret the four types of evidence—textual, qualitative, quantitative, and experimental—quite differently. For instance, if you asked scholars to write an article about animal language, those in the humanities might use as evidence *representations* of animals communicating in creative works like paintings and poems, while anthropologists and sociologists might use ethnographic *observations* of humans and animals interacting indoors and outdoors; economists and political scientists might use government financial *data* about zoos and national polls about pets; and psychologists and zoologists might set up laboratory *experiments* testing whether what we think of as animal language is actually communication. Now that we're all so interdisciplinary, the types of evidence we use have become even more complicated, as many scholars use a variety of evidence in combination. In Donna J. Haraway's influential book about animal communication, *When Species Meet* (2008), she uses everything from ancient philosophical texts and biology experiments to her experiences in agility training with her dogs Cayenne and Roland. In other words, you may have to do some extrapolating in this chapter to arrive at the right questions for evaluating your evidence.

When analyzing the pertinence and quality of your evidence in this article, the biggest temptation you'll face is the desire to search for and produce lots of new evidence. Resist! It's scary to make arguments. and piling up evidence makes it feel less scary. But piles of evidence aren't how you make convincing arguments. A few pieces of well-analyzed and well-interpreted evidence will beat out piles of badly analyzed evidence any day. The point of this chapter is not to urge you to question your evidence. It is to urge you to think about what the evidence you have tells you, and how best to explain that. Once you've done a full analysis, you may decide that you simply must acquire more evidence, and that's fine. But don't start there.

So let's move to analyzing the pertinence and quality of your evidence. (If you're writing a SciQua article, my assumption is that you've already conducted your study or experiment and are trying to find the best way to interpret and present your data. If you're still conducting your study or have yet to conduct it, you'll need to use the following sections as a prompt to writing your article rather than analyzing it.)

TYPES OF EVIDENCE

Let's consider four types of evidence. Most articles have just one of these types, but some articles have two or more (called combined-methods articles).

Textual Evidence

In the humanities, the most common form of evidence is textual evidence. A "text" is any object that humans create to communicate meaning. Therefore, a text might be written—for example, a poem—but it might also be a photograph or even a car. For instance, sports utility vehicles are designed to communicate "dominance" (Olsen 2002, 184–85) and therefore can be "read." Owing to this broad definition, texts are in fact the most common type of evidence in any discipline—from the humanities to the sciences. While some disciplines don't use evidence from primary-source texts (like novels or field notes), all scholars use evidence from secondary-source texts (evidence collected by other scholars and presented in books and journal articles). However, scholars generally think of the humanities and interpretive social sciences as depending on textual evidence, while the social, health, behavioral, and natural sciences depend on data evidence.

Example. One example of the use of textual evidence from both primary and secondary sources is an article of mine (Belcher 2016). I used as my *primary source* a seventeenth-century hagiography of an Ethiopian female saint (Gälawdewos 2015), and as *textual evidence* from that primary source I used two scenes from the hagiography along with some short passages from other parts of the hagiography. Near the end, I also used as *textual evidence* quotations from three other *primary sources*: a recent Ethiopian newspaper article, two ancient Egyptian letters, and a short fourteenth-century Ethiopian tale. In addition, I used about ten *secondary sources* on marriage and sexuality in the ancient world and Africa as *textual evidence*.

Either through consulting your article or just from memory, answer the following:

> Do I use textual evidence? If so, from what sources? What passages constitute my textual evidence?

Qualitative Evidence

If field observation appears in your article, it is qualitative evidence. Qualitative evidence is typically that collected either during lengthy open-ended or structured interviews with a few individuals or during observations of real-life situations (in person or through recordings). Many books provide useful instructions for writing up qualitative evidence (Denzin and Lincoln 2011; Little 2013; Salkind 2013; Leavy 2014; Tavory and Timmermans 2014; Beuving and de Vries 2015; Marshall and Rossman 2016). If you regularly conduct field research, own some of these guides. I still find Howard Becker's the most stimulating; his way of conceptualizing issues with evidence is so original that it continually prompts scholars to view their article from new angles and generate new solutions. Every social scientist should own his *Tricks of the Trade* (Becker 2008).

Example. An example of the use of qualitative evidence is a cultural anthropology article about Islamic women's agency (Mahmood 2001). The author used as *primary sources* her fieldwork with pious Muslim women in Cairo, and as *qualitative evidence* from that primary source, her brief conversations with two of these women about the pressures they experienced about being single in a society where marriage was the norm. (Note that in the humanities, such conversations constitute *textual evidence*, as the record of the conversations is textual.) Most of the *secondary sources* the author used were in extended related-literature reviews about theories of agency vis-à-vis gender, religion, and Islam. Using this qualitative data, the author argued that Western theories of agency are flawed because, in part, they cannot account for the agency of religious women dedicated to reducing the self.

Either through consulting your article or just from memory, answer the following:

> Do I use qualitative evidence?
> If so, what is it?

Quantitative Evidence

If numerical data appear in your article, you are using quantitative evidence. This data might result from a study you conducted observing or surveying human behavior, or it might result from a study conducted by someone else (or by an organization, such as the US Census Bureau). Typical quantitative evidence includes government data, publicly available survey data, or your own independent surveys, polls, and interviews (whether online, over the phone, in person, or on paper) with many people. Quantitative evidence is useful for speculating about the characteristics of large groups of human beings or social processes. Many books provide helpful instructions for writing up quantitative evidence, but one of the most helpful is not about writing at all but about how to catch out other scholars' evidence errors. Scott R. Harris's (2013) excellent book *How to Critique Journal Articles in the Social Sciences* provides a wealth of examples of common errors in evidence presentation and analysis. I've used his insights frequently in what follows.

Example. One example of the use of quantitative evidence is a political science article about social media and US elections (DiGrazia et al. 2013). It used as a *primary source* tweets posted on Twitter and as *secondary sources* reports from the US Census Bureau and the Federal Election Commission. The article's *quantitative evidence* was a random sample of the 3.5 billion tweets posted in the fall of 2010 and 2012, a sample totaling around half a million, as well as congressional election results in those years. Using this big data, the authors argued that social media can accurately forecast elections: "The amount of attention received by a candidate on Twitter, relative to his or her opponent, is a statistically significant indicator of vote share" (4).

Either through consulting your article or just from memory, answer the following:

> Do I use quantitative evidence? If so, what is it?

Experimental Evidence

If you collected your evidence in a laboratory, you are using experimental evidence. A laboratory most often is a room in a building, but it may also be in the field (and many now conduct field experiments online). To be an experiment, the study must *manipulate* something (e.g., the subjects or the setting). If you simply observe the subjects or setting, that constitutes a qualitative study.

Example. An example of the use of experimental evidence is a psychology article about implicit bias (Jacoby-Senghor, Sinclair, and Shelton 2016). The article reports on an experiment the authors conducted using simulated teacher-student interactions in which a white undergraduate instructor taught a black or a white undergraduate learner. The experimental evidence was collected using videotapes of the interactions, instructors' performance on an assigned task, and learners' performance on a test of what they learned. These tape, task, and test texts were transformed into statistical *quantitative evidence* by coding the videotapes and running linear regression analysis on the results. Using these experimental data findings, that instructors' implicit bias predicted diminished test performance among black learners, the authors argued that "underperformance by minorities in academic domains may be driven by the effect implicit racial biases have on educators' pedagogical effectiveness" (Jacoby-Senghor, Sinclair, and Shelton 2016, 50).

Either through consulting your article or just from memory, answer the following:

> Do I use experimental evidence? If so, what is it?

REVISING YOUR EVIDENCE

Day 1 Tasks: Reading the Workbook

On the first day of your seventh writing week, read this week 7 chapter all the way through the next two paragraphs, answering all the questions posed. Write directly in the boxes provided or in your own document.

Since the reading is relatively short, and the tasks for the week are time-consuming, consider starting the tasks for day 2 today.

Alternately, contact a colleague to discuss what constitutes worthy evidence in your field. Thinking about such meta-aspects of writing is helpful. To prepare for that conversation, you may want to study some of your favorite articles or journals for how those in your field present evidence. Afterward, consider writing up your notes about what you have found and ask others what they think, either by sending the notes to colleagues by email or by posting them on social media.

Tracking Writing Time

Each day, use the Calendar for Actual Time Spent Writing This Week form (or digital time-tracking software) to keep track of the time you spent writing this week. Then, at the end of the week, evaluate how you spent your time.

If busy, at least mark the check boxes with how long you wrote today. ☐ 15+ min. ☐ 30+ ☐ 60+ ☐ 120+

WEEK 7, DAYS 2-5: READING AND TASKS

Day 2 Tasks: Highlighting and Analyzing Your Evidence

Today you'll determine whether your evidence is worthy and, just as important, perceived as worthy. If the value is in doubt, you need to decide what you can do about it. To help you with these tasks, first highlight the evidence you use in your article and then proceed to evaluate it. The following will help you review each paragraph of the body of your article to determine whether your evidence is clear, and whether your interpretation of that evidence progresses logically and has explanatory power.

Instructions for the highlighting exercise. Today works best if your article is in a locked form, where you can mark it but not change it. This setup aids you in stepping back from your article, giving you a broader perspective from which to focus on broader solutions, not edit line by line. For me, that procedure involves printing the article out on paper and using pens or highlighters in various colors. For you, that procedure might be converting the article into a PDF and marking it up with a stylus on a tablet. If neither of those methods is an option, you can mark your electronic document using your computer's Text Highlight Color and Comments tools, but try to defamiliarize your article by viewing it at 50 percent size or in a different font than usual. Once you have your article in locked form, complete the following steps.

Task One: Highlighting Your Evidence

Highlighting your presentation of evidence. Highlight in GREEN any sentences in which you present or describe your evidence. (You'll be highlighting interpretation of your evidence in the next step; here, just focus on the presentation of your evidence.) This presentation could be a summary of the plot of the novel you're analyzing or quotations from the novel; a description or images of an art object or artifact; a depiction of the village or classroom where you collected the evidence or quotations from interviews with villagers or students; observations at or photographs of a festival or other human behavior; a biography of your subject; an account of an epoch; and all charts, tables, graphs, or quantitative data. Highlight in GREEN any place where you present information about what you studied.

Recall that a journal article is not an editorial in which your own opinions count as evidence. If your article simply lambastes a theory, discipline, or general view, you have no evidence. In my workshops, more than one novice author has reached this point, only to discover that they don't have any GREEN in their article. If that's you, don't panic! Just use the exercises below to think about what evidence might best serve your purposes.

Highlighting your interpretation of evidence. Highlight in BLUE any sentences in which you analyze your evidence. This interpretation could be as follows, continuing with the preceding examples: close readings of the quotes from the novel you are analyzing; explicating the cultural aesthetics revealed by the art object; comparing and contrasting villagers' access to health care delivery in the village you studied; sketching out how other scholars' interpretations of the festival are wrong and yours are right; revealing the impact of familial relations on the subject of your biography; explaining how one epoch disrupts the legacies of the previous one; or laying out the meaning of your statistics. Highlight with BLUE any place where you analyzed what you studied. Most SciQua articles separate into different sections the presentation of evidence (Results) and the interpretation of evidence (Discussion), while humanities articles tend to group them together. If you have separate Results and Discussion sections, make sure that no BLUE (interpretation) appears in your Results, and no GREEN (presentation) appears in your Discussion. If you find such, move it to the proper section.

Task Two: Analyzing the Proportion, Amount, and Presentation of Your Evidence
Now that you have highlighted your article's presentation and interpretation of evidence, you will proceed with analyzing that presentation and interpretation. The information and sections that follow are prompts, reminders of some of the issues regarding evidence. They aren't requirements. So if a category doesn't speak to you, skip it, and move to the next one.

Proportion of evidence to interpretation. In most disciplines, interpretation takes up the biggest proportion of published articles' content. If less than a third of your article is BLUE (interpretation), perhaps you aren't spending enough time interpreting your evidence. Evidence can't speak for itself; you must speak for it. If more than half your article is GREEN (presentation), perhaps you're spending too much time presenting your evidence. To address such issues, do the following. First, roughly estimate how much of your article is presentation and how much interpretation. At this point, your answer may be more of a guess, but that's okay. Second, review the article to ensure that for every GREEN highlight, there is a BLUE highlight. That is, make sure that you interpret all the evidence you present, and that you present all the evidence that you interpret. On his academic writing blog *N = 1*, the anthropologist Matthew Wolf-Meyer (2014) astutely observes, "My general rule is that for every line of evidence, there should be two lines of analysis. So, if you have a quote from someone or a text that runs four lines, you should spend at least eight lines discussing its relevance to your argument." Third, make sure that you interpret the evidence evenly. If you have three pieces of evidence and spend ten pages interpreting the first two, and then half a page interpreting the last one, your article may be out of proportion. Sometimes this is justified, but if so, explicitly state why in the article. Otherwise, work to balance the article. In the box that follows, note your impressions of that balance (as before, checking off a round check box indicates you have work to do), and speculate on some solutions. You can also note imbalances, lacks, or unevenness in the relevant margin of the article so that you know where to concentrate your work when revising.

My Proportion of Evidence to Interpretation

My presentation of evidence	☐ Is enough ◯ Is too little ◯ Is too much	One solution might be
My interpretation of evidence	☐ Is enough ◯ Is too little ◯ Is too much	One solution might be
Is all evidence accompanied by interpretation, and vice versa?	☐ Yes ◯ No ◯ I'm not sure	One solution might be
Do I interpret all evidence evenly?	☐ Yes ◯ No ◯ I'm not sure	One solution might be

Amount of evidence. In addition to the number of pages devoted to evidence in your article, you need to attend to the amount of evidence itself. Almost any evidence if well interpreted can be enough to carry an argument; so if you tend to add, add, add, this question may not be the best one on which to focus. Be careful that you're checking your evidence, not derailing it. In the margins of your article, place *insertion marks* (the caret ^) next to sentences, paragraphs, or sections where you suspect that you need more evidence to support your argument. For instance, it's tough to make a convincing argument about the entire oeuvre of a composer if you analyze just one of his or her compositions. At the very least, you must prove why that composition is exemplary by comparing it, even if briefly, to the artist's other compositions.

If you decide that you don't have enough evidence, you have some options for adding more. One possibility would be including more *objects* of analysis (e.g., not just one poem but two; not just three sculptures but ten; not just twelve institutions but fifty; not just fifty patients but one hundred). Another possibility would be adding evidence that is more *diverse* (e.g., not just poems but also novels; not just male CEOs but also female CEOs; not just white addicts but also older addicts; not just Pakistan but also Afghanistan). Another would be adding more *details* (e.g., examining ten passages in the novel or ten quotations from the interview, not just two). Another would be adding *sites* (e.g., not just one hospital but two, not just two classrooms but four). By contrast, place *deletion marks* (the letter X) next to those sentences, paragraphs, or sections where you need less evidence to be more convincing. Having too much evidence to interpret well is almost as much of a problem as having too little. Note in the margin what you might cut. In the box that follows, note any issues with your amount of evidence, and speculate on some solutions.

| My amount of evidence | ☐ Is enough
◯ Is too little
◯ Is too much | One solution might be |

Visual presentation of evidence. Next, attend to the visual presentation of your evidence: charts, tables, maps, drawings, photographs, musical notations, and so on. If you have none, should you have some? Most humanities and interpretive social science articles have no visual presentations of evidence, so it's perfectly acceptable to have none. Nonetheless, visuals can help draw readers in, so you might think about whether a photograph of the subject(s), a manuscript page, or a cover of the first edition might add something valuable to your article. If you're in one of the quantitative fields, visual presentation of statistical evidence is essential. A senior social scientist told me that he no longer reads the bodies of articles, only the tables and charts. So ensure that you present the most important parts of your data visually. (Next week, you will focus on actually formatting such visual presentations; this week, just focus on whether you present enough of your data visually and what you would consider adding.) In the box that follows, note any issues with your visual presentation of evidence, and speculate on some solutions.

| My visual presentation of evidence | ☐ Is enough
◯ Is too little
◯ Is too much | One solution might be |

Tracking Writing Time

Mark your electronic calendar, the Calendar for Actual Time Spent Writing This Week form, and/or the check boxes here with how long you wrote today. ☐ 15+ min. ☐ 30+ ☐ 60+ ☐ 120+

Day 3 Tasks: Analyzing the Quality, Relevance, and Placement of Your Evidence

Today you'll continue with analyzing your article's evidence. As with yesterday's tasks, some prompts follow; if a category doesn't speak to you, move on to the next one.

Quality of Evidence

In addition to the amount of evidence, you need to attend to the quality of that evidence. Put *check marks* (☑) in the margin next to evidence that you consider particularly strong. Put *circles* (◯) in the margin next to evidence that you think could be stronger. If you know you've been careful in collecting your evidence, resist doubting that now. Questions about quality can be tough to answer if you're a novice author. If you're in doubt, ask experts in your field what they think about the quality of your evidence. If they think it could be stronger, ask them what you can do at this point to improve it. If you identify a problem with the quality of your evidence, you proceed differently according to that problem. You can work on finding better evidence; you can pare down your evidence and focus only on its strongest parts; or you can articulate why the evidence, even if not quite as strong as you wish, nevertheless is relevant and useful. Here are some problems and their solutions.

Addressing Evidence Limitations

If your article evidence is generally fine but is lacking in some areas, you have several options. Does that lack matter to your argument, or do you just need to state it as a limit of your evidence? All evidence is limited in some way; stating that yours is limited is one solution to issues with quality. Alternately, aim for a lower-ranked journal or an inter-disciplinary journal, either of which is likely to care more about intriguing ideas than bulletproof evidence. Or scale back your argument or claims for significance. Examples of limitations are a partial archive (e.g., you have only two grave markings from that period) and respondents who aren't entirely representative of the population from which their sample was drawn (e.g., sample is missing those of a certain age, gender, religion, race, ethnicity, class, education level, marital status, health status, work status, living situation, familial background, organization membership, belief system, historical period, environment). In the box that follows, note any issues with evidence limitations, and speculate on some solutions.

Does my evidence have some limitations?	◯ Yes ☐ No ◯ I'm not sure	One solution might be

Solving Evidence Problems

Sometimes your evidence is not merely limited but also problematic. In this case, you can't resolve it in the rhetorical ways listed above. You may need to start over and collect new evidence. But short of that, you do have some options. Below are a few typical evidence problems and potential solutions. Note any issues with the quality of your evidence in the boxes that follow, and speculate on some solutions. What can you do about that problem? Should you discard it as evidence? (If so, what will you use as evidence instead? Or was that evidence not that necessary?) It may be wise to place time limits on finding evidence solutions so that you don't get carried away.

Dated. If your *qualitative evidence* is dated (collected five or more years ago), you could update it by redoing the interviews with the same people (or some of the same people) and adding a longitudinal element. Alternately, if the qualitative evidence was collected long ago, decades ago, a few journals might be interested in a historical article. In general, however, journals automatically reject articles containing dated qualitative evidence.

Is my qualitative evidence dated?	◯ Yes ☐ No ◯ I'm not sure ☐ N/A	One solution might be

Statistically insignificant. If your *quantitative evidence* does not achieve statistical significance, you could use it to critique published articles that have found a significant correlation between your variables. Or you could publish an article of null results, which are not common. In general, journals automatically reject articles with statistically insignificant quantitative evidence.

Is my quantitative evidence statistically insignificant?	◯ Yes ☐ No ◯ I'm not sure ☐ N/A	One solution might be

Poor method. If your qualitative or quantitative study has been improperly designed and your data incorrectly sampled, collected, or measured, you don't have many options. For instance, if the characteristics of those in your sample are "significantly different than the population that researchers want to generalize about" (Harris 2013, 69), you have a problem with sampling. You will need to make your generalizations from that evidence more modest. Especially watch the tendency to generalize from studies conducted on US populations alone (69). You can't generalize about all adoptees if you've studied only US adoptees. European and US citizens tend to be highly unrepresentative samples of world populations.

Does my study use poor methods?	◯ Yes ☐ No ◯ I'm not sure ☐ N/A	One solution might be

Incorrect causal order claims. If your quantitative study claims a causal relationship between two variables, it's wise to ponder which variable is affecting which. Perhaps your independent variable is actually your dependent variable and vice versa. For instance, in an example that Harris gives, does the number of a police officer's arrests (variable X) increase the number of complaints about excessive force (variable Y), or does the number of complaints about excessive force (Y) increase the number of arrests (X) "in an attempt to justify [excessive force] or cover it up?" (Harris 2013, 82).

Does my study make incorrect causal claims?	◯ Yes ☐ No ◯ I'm not sure ☐ N/A	One solution might be

Proxy errors. If your *quantitative evidence* depends on treating one variable as a proxy for another, check it twice. For instance, peer reviewers may criticize using marital status as a proxy for class status, or office building architecture as a proxy for all buildings. This may be just a limitation of your evidence, or it may be an active problem. The solution may be to cite articles that defend using that variable as a proxy for the other. If you're interpreting *textual evidence*, make sure that you don't slip into treating one aspect of the text as a proxy for the whole text. If you're arguing that a novel's character is idealistic, for example, don't assume that the text itself is idealistic. Maybe it is, but you would have to demonstrate that, not treat the part as equivalent to the whole.

Does my evidence have proxy errors?	○ Yes	One solution might be
	☐ No	
	○ I'm not sure	
	☐ N/A	

Comparability. Does your interpretation use the same texts, types, strategies, or measures as the related literature you're critiquing or updating? New approaches are great, but they can foreshorten your ability to critique other work if you're comparing apples and they're comparing oranges. That is, "if scholars frequently use inconsistent measures, then is their research comparable and cumulative? Are different scholars studying the same thing, and can their research findings be combined into a coherent set of implications, facts, or lessons about the social world?" (Harris 2013, 54). If your article lacks comparability because of an improved method, how can you explain that? If it just lacks comparability, how can you fix that?

Is my evidence or method not comparable with that of my related literature?	○ Yes	One solution might be
	☐ No	
	○ I'm not sure	
	☐ N/A	

Unreliable authorship. If your *textual evidence* is suspect owing to its authorship (the author's reputation, perspective, or identity affect the perceived reliability of the text's evidence), find sources proving that the author/text is reliable, or at least more reliable than previously thought, and address the issue directly. Alternately, explain why the text's particular form of unreliability doesn't matter that much to your argument. Or make its unreliability an interesting part of your argument. Failing all that, search for an analogous text for your purposes. Some authorship problems: the authors were exposed as unethical and their work retracted, were not scholars but members of the public who may not have done careful research, were biased dominant-culture scholars doing research on subjugated cultures.

Does my textual evidence have unreliable authors?	○ Yes	One solution might be
	☐ No	
	○ I'm not sure	
	☐ N/A	

Unreliable texts. If your *textual evidence* is suspect for reasons other than authorship, you may need to select other evidence. Perhaps your medieval manuscript has missing sections or material inserted by another. Perhaps the artist painted the image very late or very early in his career and it is not representative. One solution is to challenge those who have suggested that the texts you use are problematic. Or if your own analysis has revealed that the text has weaknesses, you might pair it with other texts to strengthen your argument.

| Is my textual evidence from unreliable texts? | ○ Yes
☐ No
○ I'm not sure
☐ N/A | One solution might be |

Category errors. If you analyze things together as if they were in the same category but they aren't, you may have a problem. If you analyze one autobiographical short story with a folktale, or four ethnic groups with one religious group, you may encounter peer reviewer resistance. Think through your evidence to make sure that you're comparing apples with apples and not with oranges (or bicycles).

| Is my evidence not all in the same category? | ○ Yes
☐ No
○ I'm not sure
☐ N/A | One solution might be |

Poor translation. Collecting *textual evidence* from texts in other languages is great. But you need to make sure that you properly translate the material and are basing your analysis on a clear understanding of the original. Working with texts translated from languages that you don't understand can be a problem if you're relying on them heavily.

| Do translation problems affect the validity of my textual evidence? | ○ Yes
☐ No
○ I'm not sure
☐ N/A | One solution might be |

Other. The above are a few prompts regarding the quality of your evidence. Many other problems with quality exist. Spend a moment thinking about the quality of your evidence and any other problems that you might face.

| Do I have any other challenges regarding the quality of my evidence? | ○ Yes
☐ No
○ I'm not sure
☐ N/A | One solution might be |

Keeping in mind any round checkboxes you checked off above, make a note regarding the overall quality of your evidence in the box on the next page and plan your next steps accordingly.

| The quality of my evidence | ☐ Is solid
○ Needs to be improved in part
○ Needs to be replaced in part | Some solutions might be |

Relevance of Evidence

In addition to the amount and quality of your evidence, you need to attend to its relevance. Mark an X in the margin next to evidence that you now suspect is not entirely relevant to your argument, or even weakens it. For instance, if your article is about sexuality and you find yourself presenting evidence on gender, you are likely off topic. If your article is about colonial literature but you include discussion of postcolonial novels, you are likely off topic. You can cut that evidence, move it to another potential article, or reframe your article as being about both topics. If you don't have the evidence to prove the argument you started with, what argument can it prove? If you can't prove that declines in real estate prices caused antiunionism, maybe you can prove that antiunionists used claims about "home" to attack labor unions. In the box that follows, note any issues with the relevance of your evidence, and speculate on some solutions.

The relevance of my evidence	☐ Is solid ◯ Needs to be improved in part ◯ Needs to be replaced in part	Some solutions might be

Placement of Evidence

In addition to the amount, quality, and relevance of your evidence, you need to attend to its placement. If you find any problems, place *move* marks (the arrow ↑) in the margin to indicate what evidence presentation or interpretation needs to be moved and to where. One problem is analyzing your evidence before you have fully presented it. Check that you haven't described your evidence *after* you analyze it. Be sure to track whether presentation appears in the Discussion section or interpretation in the Results/Findings section, and then move them to the correct section if necessary. In HumInt articles, the presentation and interpretation of evidence usually appear close to each other or woven together. If you have entire sections that proceed without any interpretation, that is a problem. Contextual background sections may include presentations of evidence, but in general they should be providing context, not evidence. In the box that follows, note any issues with the placement of your evidence, and speculate on some solutions.

The placement of my evidence	☐ Is good ◯ Needs to be improved	Some solutions might be

Tracking Writing Time

Mark your electronic calendar, the Calendar for Actual Time Spent Writing This Week form, and/or the check boxes here with how long you wrote today. ☐ 15+ min. ☐ 30+ ☐ 60+ ☐ 120+

Day 4 Tasks: Analyzing Your Interpretation of Your Evidence

Today you'll continue with analyzing your article's evidence. As before, the information and sections below are prompts, not requirements. If a category doesn't speak to you, simply move to the next one.

Quality of Interpretation

Finally, we reach the most important aspect of your article: you need to ensure the quality of your *interpretation* of your evidence. While you must address problems with evidence as evidence, what can matter most is the richness with which you interpret that evidence. And you can spend many fruitful hours refining the interpretation in your article. Put *check marks* (☑) in the margin next to interpretations that you are think are particularly strong. That is, mark where you make the most of the evidence for your argument, express it in the most compelling manner, draw out the significance or implications of the evidence especially well, and link it clearly to your argument. Put *circles* (O) in the margin next to interpretations that you think could be stronger or clearer.

Quality of Interpretation Questions
Taking advantage of Howard Becker's genius at articulating issues with the quality of interpretation, here are some questions you can ask about your article's interpretation. If any of them don't speak to you, that's fine—just go to the next one. If you find yourself regularly checking "I'm not sure" in the boxes that follow, it's time to discuss your article with someone in your field.

Coherence. Does your interpretation tell a coherent story? That is, will the reader, reaching the end of your article, feel that all your interpretation adds up to something (Becker 2008, 18)? And that nothing was missing? If your article's interpretation is not coherent, how can you fix that?

Is my interpretation coherent?	☐ Yes ○ No ○ I'm not sure	One solution might be

Congruity. Does your interpretation align with the evidence, is it congruous with any related facts, or does it ignore or violate some of these? In some cases, that might be okay. Indeed, some interesting interpretations can have unaccounted-for data. But the best interpretations account for what's inconvenient, enriched with the "real world" (Becker 2008, 19). Alternately, if something is throwing off your analysis or argument, perhaps it's not actually a case of what you're exploring (58). If your article's interpretation is not congruous, how can you fix that?

Is my interpretation congruous?	☐ Yes ○ No ○ I'm not sure	One solution might be

Connection. Does your interpretation assume that objects, texts, people, and processes are connected and therefore always organically shaping and altering one another? Good. Becker calls this treating "society as an organism" and objects as "congealed social agreements" (Becker 2008, 42, 50). He insists that we focus not on typing people and objects as immutable and permanent but on understanding changing activities and relationships. If your article's interpretation is typing things as unchanging, how can you fix that?

| Does my inter-pretation assume connectedness? | ☐ Yes ◯ No ◯ I'm not sure | One solution might be |

Grounding. Does your interpretation take into account the environment or milieu of what you are studying? As Becker points out, everything "is taking place somewhere specific," so don't ignore that local variation, but rather account for it in your interpretation (Becker 2008, 56). If your article's interpretation isn't grounded, how can you fix that?

| Is my interpretation grounded? | ☐ Yes ◯ No ◯ I'm not sure | One solution might be |

Theory. Does your interpretation depend on scholarly theories? Most articles are linked not just to the related literature but also to theories, such as feminist, Marxist, queer, or behavioral theory. If your article's interpretation isn't theoretical, how can you fix that?

| Is my interpretation theoretical? | ☐ Yes ◯ No ◯ I'm not sure | One solution might be |

Newness. Does your interpretation bring new insights into the conversation or simply rehearse what others have already said? If your article's interpretation is not new, how can you fix that?

| Is my interpretation new? | ☐ Yes ◯ No ◯ I'm not sure | One solution might be |

Implications. Does your interpretation conclude with implications or recommendations? It's not essential, but many of the best articles suggest the positive consequences of taking the article seriously. If you haven't made such a suggestion, how can you do so?

Does my interpretation express implications or recommendations?	☐ Yes ◯ No ◯ I'm not sure	One solution might be

Foregrounding. Does your interpretation foreground your most important insights? Or have you mixed them all up together without signaling value? Sections should conclude by summarizing the most important points. If you haven't foregrounded your article's interpretation, how can you fix that?

Does my interpretation foreground the most important insights?	☐ Yes ◯ No ◯ I'm not sure	One solution might be

Definitions. Does your interpretation use the best keywords and terms? It's easy to get so used to a term that you stop seeing that it's not quite apt. In early iterations of this workbook, for some reason I talked about "academic articles" (only half a million hits on Google) instead of "journal articles" (33 million hits). It wasn't until someone asked me what I meant by "academic articles" that I realized the problem. Do you define your terms explicitly, succinctly, and early? Have you cited how any of your definitions vary from or align with those of others? Have you checked whether someone else has already invented one of your terms (or one like it)? Do your definitions arise from your data? Or have you failed to add nuance to your definitions as you refine your understanding of the data? If one or more of your keywords haven't been defined well, how can you fix that?

Does my interpretation use the right key terms and define them clearly?	☐ Yes ◯ No ◯ I'm not sure	One solution might be

Statistics. If you have quantitative data, do you use the best statistical method for analyzing your evidence? If you aren't sure, consult books like *The Chicago Guide to Writing about Numbers* (Jane Miller 2015) or use the "Which Stats Test," a simple online tool developed to help scholars determine the most appropriate statistical method for their evidence, at methods.sagepub.com/which-stats-test. Note that the best method isn't always the most complicated one.

Does my interpretation use the best statistics?	☐ Yes ◯ No ◯ I'm not sure	One solution might be

Ethics. Does your interpretation protect the identities of the vulnerable, give credit where credit is due, anticipate the negative results of publishing some ideas, and avoid bias? Did you get human subjects approval from an institutional review board if you're studying human beings? Americans failing to obtain such permission for studies abroad is a problem, especially in Africa, as is failing to obtain informed consent from study participants. If ethics is an issue in your interpretation, how can you fix that? A terrific source for information about ethical issues is the Committee on Publication Ethics (COPE) website. See its guidelines and flowcharts to understand what editors consider to be ethical violations (COPE 2015).

Is my interpretation ethical?	☐ Yes ○ No ○ I'm not sure	One solution might be

In the box that follows, note any issues with the quality of your interpretation (keeping in mind any checked circle boxes above), and speculate on some solutions.

The quality of my interpretation	☐ Is good ○ Needs to be improved	Some solutions might be

Quality of Interpretation Tests

The questions above are great prompts for evaluating your article's interpretation. But sometimes it helps to think about approaching your evidence entirely differently. Howard Becker recommends many of the following tests to get at alternative and perhaps better ways of interpreting your evidence:

Contrary test. One way to check your interpretation is to spend a few minutes thinking about what would happen if you made the opposite argument, if you argued something you don't believe to be true. Considering the opposite argument may help you anticipate counterarguments and nuance your interpretation.

Insignificant test. Becker calls this test the "null hypothesis trick," spending some time assuming that your variables "are related only by chance" or coincidence (Becker 2008, 20, 28). It might enable you to "formalize your thinking and perhaps see some connections you might not have noticed or taken seriously" (23).

Designed test. Another way to check your interpretation is to assume that any phenomena you're treating as broken, incoherent, problematic, or flawed are in fact designed exactly and perfectly as they should be. Becker calls this test the "machine trick," assuming that something is "what some omniscient and omnipotent Creator intended" (Becker 2008, 39). What happens if you imagine the social machine that would produce, say, the contradictions of a poem or the harm done by a cultural practice?

Explanation test. You can assess your interpretation by asking whether it answers one or both of these questions: *"why* something was or became *necessary"* or *"how* something was or became *possible"* (Becker 2008, 63, citing von Wright 1971, 58). In general, Becker argues, focusing on "why" doesn't get you far; focusing on "how" is the better option.

In the box that follows, note any issues with the quality of your interpretation, and speculate on some solutions.

> Do any of these tests provide me with new interpretive insights? If so, what are they?

Final Decisions about Evidence and Interpretation

Now, using the box below, make some final decisions about the status of your evidence and its interpretation.

My article's evidence	☐ Great, good, acceptable	◯ Needs a little or some work	◯ Needs a lot of work	◯ Needs a total overhaul
Time needed	☐ A few days	☐ 1 week	☐ 2–4 weeks	☐ 4–8 weeks
My article's interpretation of that evidence	☐ Great, good, acceptable	◯ Needs a little or some work	◯ Needs a lot of work	◯ Needs a total overhaul
Time needed	☐ A few days	☐ 1 week	☐ 2–4 weeks	☐ 4–8 weeks

Finally, jot down for tomorrow some notes about whether you need additional evidence and/or better interpretation, along with a plan for collecting that evidence or improving its interpretation.

Tracking Writing Time

Mark your electronic calendar, the Calendar for Actual Time Spent Writing This Week form, and/or the check boxes here with how long you wrote today. ☐ 15+ min. ☐ 30+ ☐ 60+ ☐ 120+

Day 5 Tasks: Collecting Additional Evidence

Today you'll work on collecting additional evidence if your analysis of your evidence over the past few days suggests you should. Next week, you're going to focus on revising the write-up of evidence in your article; this week, you focus entirely on the evidence itself. Depending on how much evidence you need, this task may take a few hours or several weeks. If you need to take quite a bit of time for this task, you're joining a lot of other workbook users. It's perfectly normal!

Tracking Writing Time

Mark your electronic calendar, the Calendar for Actual Time Spent Writing This Week form, and/or the check boxes here with how long you wrote today. □15+ min. □30+ □60+ □120+

Then, here at the end of your workweek, take pride in your accomplishments and evaluate whether any patterns need changing.

DOCUMENTING YOUR WRITING TIME AND TASKS

Calendar for Actual Time Spent Writing This Week

Time	Day 1	Day 2	Day 3	Day 4	Day 5	Day 6	Day 7
5:00 a.m.							
6:00							
7:00							
8:00							
9:00							
10:00							
11:00							
12:00 p.m.							
1:00							
2:00							
3:00							
4:00							
5:00							
6:00							
7:00							
8:00							
9:00							
10:00							
11:00							
12:00 a.m.							
1:00							
2:00							
3:00							
4:00							
Total minutes							
Tasks completed							

WEEK 8
Presenting Your Evidence

Task Day	Week 8 Daily Writing Tasks	Estimated Task Time in Minutes	
		HumInt	SciQua
Day 1 (Monday?)	Read from here until you reach the week 8, day 2 tasks, filling in any boxes, checking off any forms, and answering any questions as you read.	60	30
Day 2 (Tuesday?)	Revise your presentation of evidence.	60	60
Day 3 (Wednesday?)	Revise your presentation of evidence.	120+	60
Day 4 (Thursday?)	Revise your presentation of evidence.	120+	60
Day 5 (Friday?)	Check your presentation of evidence section by section.	120+	60
Total estimated time for reading the workbook, completing the tasks, and writing your article		**8+ hours**	**4.5+ hours**

Above are the tasks for your eighth week. Start this week by scheduling when you will write, and then tracking the time you actually spend writing (using the Calendar for Actual Time Spent Writing This Week form or online software).

This week, you'll receive the least amount of advice of any week, even though presenting and interpreting evidence take up most of your article. This brevity isn't due to this week's work being less! Once you begin to revise the presentation and interpretation of your evidence, you may find yourself doing the most work of any week. Fortunately, you've already used the workbook to examine many other aspects of your article, so you've already started to think about presenting evidence.

WEEK 8, DAY 1: READING AND TASKS

SEVENTH WEEK IN REVIEW

You have now spent seven weeks working on your article. This week's work is a continuation of last week's, but moving from analyzing your evidence to presenting it in your article.

With all this work now behind you, you might think that basic questions about the article's worth would not arise, but something about being a little more than halfway through the article-writing project tends to inspire such questions. You begin to wonder: Is this article worth the time I'm spending on it? Should I keep working on it or switch to another article? If you haven't been asking yourself questions like these, skip to the next section.

If you have been wondering about the worth of your article, ask yourself whether the main reason for this is because you're scared, tired, or bored. If so, push on! These negative feelings will pass.

Sometimes, however, the reason you want to stop is because you believe you have slowly uncovered some fatal flaw in your article. Maybe you now think that your argument is unprovable or uninteresting to your field. Maybe you now think that your evidence is too slim to support any argument or that you can't shape a provocative argument from the largely descriptive piece you had. Maybe you no longer believe that what you were trying to prove is true. If so, don't abandon the article right away. Rather, ask a trusted reader whether he or she agrees with your assessment. You can show the whole article to this person or, since experienced academics can give good advice without even reading an article, describe the article, telling your reader what you think the problem is. Perhaps you've missed an easy fix.

On a few occasions, however, the best thing to do is to walk away from the article. If you make that decision, don't feel that you've wasted your time. Nothing confirms that you're a true writer more than having the courage to set writing aside and begin again. Indeed, you've learned essential skills through the revising process. In my article-writing course, quite a few novice authors make significant revisions and then decide that the paper they chose to work on was too flawed to revise into publishable quality. But I've learned not to treat that as a failure: many of these students email me later to say that the process of revising their own work taught them more about how to write than drafting articles from scratch ever had. They found that subsequent writing flowed more quickly and much more easily as a result.

If you decide that you're not going to work on this article, which one will you work on? Go back to the texts you revisited when you started using the workbook and reconsider them. If you want to revise one of these, work on reorienting yourself to the new article by returning to the chapter "Week 2: Advancing Your Argument." Alternately, if you want to write an article from scratch, go now to "Week 0: Writing Your Article from Scratch." It can help to read the scholarship published in top journals over the last year to get a sense of the discussions and to generate ideas. Whatever you do, don't simply stop writing; you must always be working toward publication. Moreover, the longer you leave off writing, the more difficult it will be to restart.

PRESENTING EVIDENCE

Reviewers at journals frequently reject submitted articles because of how authors presented their evidence, not because of any lack in the evidence itself. Indeed, one scholar's study of peer reviewers' reports found that two-thirds of their comments were about problems with "the effectiveness of the writer's interaction with the reader (*interpersonal*)" (Gosden 2003, 95). Most editors are looking for articles written in a clear way that is legible across fields.

How you present evidence depends on your discipline and field of study. If you're in the social, health, behavioral, or natural sciences, whether experimental, quantitative, or qualitative, you are fortunate to have standard forms, with sections clearly delineated and the presentation of evidence formulaic. If you're in the humanities, you are fortunate to have greater freedom in presenting your evidence, determining sections and the manner of presenting the evidence yourself.

At times, we envy each other—the social scientists wishing for more freedom, the humanities scholars wishing for more guidance. If you're among them, don't hesitate to use my advice for the other side as a prompt. As a humanities scholar, I often find SciQua formulas useful. For instance, no social scientists would omit discussing how they arrived at their sample, their selection of subjects. And yet many of us in the humanities never explain our samples; we never discuss why we chose the texts we chose. We simply get on with interpreting them. Explaining our sampling procedure is a good idea that we can borrow from the social scientists. Conversely, social scientists can borrow useful methods from the humanities. For instance, no humanities scholars would present a text without close-reading it—unpacking its subtleties, what isn't obvious on the surface. Yet many social scientists assume that their findings are transparent, and so fail to interpret them in their article. So if it interests you, in the following sections use as prompts not just the advice addressed to those in your discipline but also the recommendations for others.

Presenting Evidence in SciQua Articles

Standard SciQua articles have three formulaic sections for the presentation and interpretation of evidence: Methods, Results (or Findings), and Discussion. We will go into specifics later; for now, here are some general points.

In the *Methods* section, you detail the procedures you used to obtain your data. In some ways, this is an easy section to write—you just describe what you did. Do so in enough detail that someone else could repeat your experiment and test your results. At the same time, although this section seems straightforward, typical problems plague it, such as describing your statistical approach in too much detail or mixing in your results and discussion.

In the *Results* or *Findings* section, you describe what you found, the data you collected, and the new information you have to offer. In some ways, this, too, is an easy section to write—you just describe what you found. However, be sure you don't present every single piece of data you found; don't replicate in the text what you've thoroughly presented in the tables and charts; and don't organize your findings by your discovery of them but instead organize them by theme. Identifying themes in the data and then creating and presenting a typology of themes are helpful in organizing a Results or Discussion section. For instance, the author of an article about undocumented immigrant young adults in the United States organized the Results section thematically by the three determinants of the participants' mental health and well-being (Siemons et al. 2017).

The *Discussion* section is the most difficult section to write and yet the most important. How you write this section can determine your article's rejection or acceptance at a journal. Even if you have great data, your article can get rejected for poor or incorrect interpretation. Structuring your discussion around your argument will best enable readers to understand the significance of your study for their own research and for the field. Use the instructions in the relevant section below to best interpret your findings in this section.

Presenting Evidence in HumInt Articles

The bodies of humanities, interpretive social science, and even some qualitative science articles consist of interpreting or analyzing texts, whether novels, historical chronicles, or interviews with patients. Such presentation and interpretation does not easily break down as in the preceding section. Rather, the format depends heavily on the author's discipline, field, theoretical approach, style, and even temperament. Therefore, instead of trying to cover a range of disciplines, I have chosen to cover just one below.

In literary criticism, two theoretical modes are common: interpretive new criticism (also called close reading) and analytical cultural studies. In the 1990s, scholars infrequently paired these two modes; now they are commonly paired. I continue to separate them out here so as to discuss the strengths and pitfalls of each.

In literary criticism articles that focus on "close reading"—an interpretive practice forwarded in the early twentieth century by the New Critics—scholars focus on discrete parts of texts, digging into the meanings of individual words and tropes to reveal the text's truths and beauties. They interpret the text's poetic or aesthetic meaning, rather than analyzing its cultural context or complicity. Many wonderful articles have been published using this mode, but it can pose certain challenges. As a graduate student once said to me, "It's a lot more fun to write close readings than it is to read them." Use the instructions in the relevant section below to best present your close readings.

In literary criticism articles that focus instead on analyzing texts as a symptom of society, the evidence lies not in close-reading the themes, imagery, or diction of a text but in asking questions of the social and political location of the text. These articles still interpret primary sources as documents from the period, but not toward understanding the text as a text; instead, the interpretation is done with the aim of understanding the society or context from which the text arises. The evidence in such articles will consist of exploring how the text reproduces the conflicts of its period or culture, participates in constructing particular knowledge systems, or highlights social or political contradictions. For instance, which characters get to speak when, and to whom? How does the rhetoric, narrative, or language of the text enable relationships of power? How can understanding this text better help us create a more just society? Use the instructions in the relevant section below to best present your cultural interpretation.

Presenting Evidence in Illustrations

Many articles contain images. If your article has no photographs, line drawings, maps, tables, diagrams, charts (pie, line, scatter plot, etc.), or graphs (bar, line, circle, histogram), you can skip this section. If you do have illustrations, you need to ensure that your images are in the proper format and that you have permission to reproduce them if they are the work of others. Some journals have very strict instructions for publishing illustrations, so be sure to check their guidelines before submitting your article.

Presenting your data in clear, powerful images is not easy. If you regularly must create charts, tables, or maps, own one of the books on "data visualization" (Tufte 1992; Cairo 2012, 2016; Kirk 2012; Monmonier 2015). Some journals are now publishing articles about how they want authors to present data in tables and charts (Duquia et al. 2014). For advice on how to create compelling graphics for your article, you can consult one of the posters that have been popping up online, including the "Graphic Continuum" by Jon Schwabish and Severino Ribecca or the "Visual Vocabulary" guide by Alan Smith and others. Designed as wall charts, they show you at a glance the best ways to present various aspects of data, including deviations, correlations, rankings, distributions, changes over time, magnitude, part-to-whole, space, and flow. Books like Andy Kirk's *Data Visualization* (2012) are designed the same way—starting from the aspect of your data you're trying to show—but they provide more options and explanations. Note that it defeats the purpose of a journal graphic if it contains only three or four bits of information. Use a graphic only if the complexity of your data merits it.

Even if you can conceive of a great image, being able to draw it electronically is difficult. Graphic design programs like Adobe Illustrator are complicated, and natural science journals require professional-quality images. If you have funding, you might consider hiring a professional graphic designer. If you don't, you could find out whether your institution has a designer on staff, usually in the library. If you have neither, keep your images simple. Most inexperienced illustrators use easy systems like Microsoft PowerPoint, Microsoft Paint, or Microsoft Excel; but some journals won't allow you to crop the image from those programs, because the image can't then be altered as needed for publication. For this reason, some journals require authors to create tables in Microsoft Word, so that in-house staff can modify them to fit their journal's format. Use the instructions in the relevant section below to ensure that your illustrations are suitable.

Obtaining Permissions for Using Others' Images or Texts

If you plan to reproduce a significant portion of someone else's creation in your article, you'll need to provide the journal publishers with permission from the work's copyright owner. A word to the wise: the permissions process is so complicated that many authors decide not to include any material in their article that requires permissions. The University of Chicago Press has good templates for requesting permission, at www .press.uchicago.edu/infoServices/permissions.html. Below is a quick explanation of some of the most important considerations.

Materials requiring permission. Any photograph, map, cartoon, table, graph, chart, or other form of visual illustration created by someone other than you (and your coauthors) requires that you obtain permission from its creator to reproduce it in your article. The only visual material that you don't have to ask permission to reproduce are advertisements (such as publicity movie stills) or images marked as open access with the Creative Commons licensing system (such as those at Wikimedia Commons). Some try to get around this rule by redrawing a table, graph, or chart that's not open access, but that's unethical. You must ask for permission to publish any close adaptation of a previously published image. As a side note, you also need to ask permission to reproduce song lyrics or poems if you're quoting a significant portion of that song or poem in one place. For more advice about what is under copyright, see the helpful Copyright Information Center at Cornell University.

Time line for permissions. It is your responsibility, not the journal's, to arrange all copyright permissions and to pay any permissions fees, so it's best to start this process even before your article is accepted for publication—it can take many months for permissions documents to come through. Copyright owners often require six to eight weeks to process requests. You don't have to ask for permissions at this early stage, before you have submitted your article to a journal, but I mention it now so that you can decide whether reproducing someone else's work in your article is worth the time and effort required of you.

Images of people. You must submit any photographs of living people, especially children, with signed releases indicating that they have agreed to let their image be used in the context of your article. The ethnocentric exception: photographs of people from outside Europe or North America, which, questionably, many journals accept without requiring signed releases.

Images of texts. Copyright law strongly protects unpublished texts, sometimes called manuscripts. You will need to ask permission of the creator or owner (usually an archive or museum) to reproduce correspondence (including emails), diaries, memos, interviews, and so on.

Owner of the image. Authors and artists often sign over the copyright to their work in order to get it published. Thus, the copyright owner is often a publisher. One of your first tasks, then, is to find out who owns the copyright to the image you wish to use. The sources of illustrations sometimes appear in the figure caption or in the acknowledgments of the work in which it was published previously. If you aren't sure who owns the copyright, it's easiest to start with the publisher, since it can forward you to the artist if needed.

Cost of reproduction. Museums and publishers can charge stiff fees to reproduce original artworks. A museum owner told an art history student that it would cost two thousand dollars in fees for each of the dozens of paintings she discussed in her dissertation. As a result, her dissertation included not one of the paintings that were its subject! You can beg the copyright owner to reduce its fees, but you can do little more. Some academic institutions have funds set aside for the costs of photography and permissions, so if the cost won't come down, find out whether your institution will subsidize it. Most journals will not subsidize this expense.

Do I need to obtain permission for using others' images or texts? If so, what is the name and address of each copyright owner that I need to ask for that permission?

REVISING YOUR PRESENTATION OF EVIDENCE

Day 1 Tasks: Reading the Workbook

On the first day of your eighth writing week, read this week 8 chapter all the way through the next two paragraphs, answering all the questions posed. Write directly in the boxes provided or in your own document.

Tracking Writing Time

Each day, use the Calendar for Actual Time Spent Writing This Week form (or digital time-tracking software) to keep track of the time you spent writing this week. Then, at the end of the week, evaluate how you spent your time.

If busy, at least mark the check boxes with how long you wrote today. ☐ 15+ min. ☐ 30+ ☐ 60+ ☐ 120+

WEEK 8, DAYS 2–5: READING AND TASKS

Days 2–4 Tasks: Revising Your Presentation of Evidence

Today, tomorrow, and the next day, revise your article using last week's analysis of your article's presentation and interpretation of evidence, including the marked-up draft, filled-out boxes, and notes to yourself, all the while attending to the amount, quality, relevance, and placement of your evidence as well as the quality of your interpretation. It may take some time to make these revisions—that's because evidence takes up the biggest part of your article, everything between the introduction and conclusion.

You have two paths you can take this week. Path one is to use the workbook as organized, completing the days 2–4 task (revising your article using last week's work) and then the day 5 task (using the checklist to confirm that you have done what you need to do). Path two is to start with the day 5 checklist, further clarifying how you need to revise your presentation of evidence—and only then go on to revising your article using last week's work. Either way works well. Path two is for those who like to collect all their information before revising; path one is for those who like to revise with what they know so far and then check whether they have covered all the bases.

Tracking Writing Time

Mark your electronic calendar, the Calendar for Actual Time Spent Writing This Week form, and/or the check boxes here with how long you wrote these three days. ☐ 15+ min. ☐ 30+ ☐ 60+ ☐ 120+

Day 5 Tasks: Checking Your Presentation of Evidence by Section

Today you'll go through the evidence checklist on the following pages to confirm that you've revised your evidence well and haven't forgotten anything.

Revising Your SciQua Presentation of Evidence

As noted earlier, strict SciQua articles have three formulaic sections for the presentation and interpretation of evidence. Even if you don't use such sections in your article, you can use the questions below as a prompt to make sure that you have covered everything.

Revising Your SciQua Methods

Here are some issues to check when revising your Methods section.

Describe your sample and sampling procedure. Who or what did you study? How did you pick your subjects? How many did you study? What were their characteristics? Are there any possible problems with your sample or procedures (e.g., not random, no control group)? ☐ Done ☐ Not applicable ○ To do

Describe your measurement instrument. What did you do to measure the findings (e.g., unstructured interview, closed questionnaire)? What did you measure? Who did the measuring? How long did you measure? Are there any possible problems with your instrument (e.g., observer effects, statistical problems)? ☐ Done ☐ Not applicable ○ To do

Describe your research context. Where did you do the study? Which people and events were key? Are there any possible problems with your setting (e.g., contextual effects)? ☐ Done ☐ Not applicable ○ To do

Describe your variables. What are your independent variables? What are your dependent variables? What are your control variables? ☐ Done ☐ Not applicable ○ To do

Write in the past tense. The study has been completed; therefore, you report on it in the past tense. This isn't difficult to remember if you did the study in the past, but if you're still conducting research, you may have to work to describe the study as if it were over. Alternately, if you're using your study or grant proposal to draft the Methods section, don't let any future tense creep in (e.g., "this study will"). ☐ Done ☐ Not applicable ○ To do

Don't give a statistics tutorial. Your aim is to describe the statistics you used, not to teach others how to do statistical analysis. Most statistical methods can be described very briefly. It's true that you may need to defend some statistical approaches, but that can usually be done quickly with citations to studies that defend those approaches. ☐ Done ☐ Not applicable ○ To do

Don't mix in your results. The Methods section is for describing *how* you did the study, not *what* you found. Be sure to check the last paragraph of your Methods section for any results that have crept in, as this is a common mistake. ☐ Done ☐ Not applicable ○ To do

Match Methods subheads to Results subheads. Some debate this advice; others think it's useful to structure your Methods section similarly to your Results and Discussion sections to help your readers keep track of the findings. Often, the methods will be too short for subheads, but if you do include them, it's worth correlating them with those in the Results section or ordering them similarly. ☐ Done ☐ Not applicable ◯ To do

Watch repetition. If you order your Methods section chronologically—first you did x, then you did y—you may find yourself repeating a lot of information. Try to find a sequence that keeps repetition at a minimum. ☐ Done ☐ Not applicable ◯ To do

Check with your journal for instructions. Some journals prefer that you write the Methods section in a particular way; that information is good to find out early. ☐ Done ☐ Not applicable ◯ To do

Keep it short. You must give all the detail needed to describe your methodology, and yet be brief. Study examples of short Methods sections in journal articles in your field. Note that in some fields, a separate Methods section has been eliminated. Rather, the methods are covered in two or three sentences in the article's introduction. ☐ Done ☐ Not applicable ◯ To do

If you haven't already done so while reading the items above, revise your article to complete all the tasks that you've marked with a "To do" check.

Revising Your SciQua Results
Here are some issues to check when revising your Results or Findings section.

Be choosy. Any study has more results than can be presented in one article. Don't use the Results section as a data dump. Present only those results that relate to your argument or hypothesis. ☐ Done ☐ Not applicable ◯ To do

Use tables and graphs. Information that's difficult to read in paragraph form becomes easily readable once it's arranged in a table or graph. Use only as many as necessary—remembering the point above about not dumping data. The purpose of a table or graph is to present information that would be difficult to grasp in prose. If readers can easily understand the evidence in text form, there's no need for a table or graph. ☐ Done ☐ Not applicable ◯ To do

Standardize tables and graphs. Your tables and graphs should appear the same way throughout your article—in the same font, with similarly worded labels and titles, and using the same type of symbols. Otherwise, they'll look sloppy to peer reviewers. ☐ Done ☐ Not applicable ◯ To do

Design tables and graphs properly. Poorly executed tables or graphs are worse than none. If you lack expertise in designing and creating these, consult with your institution's librarian or a gifted friend. ☐ Done ☐ Not applicable ◯ To do

Title and label tables and graphs properly. The title should describe the variables that appear in the table or graph as well as the type of data presented. If your title is only three or four words long, it probably isn't comprehensive enough. ☐ Done ☐ Not applicable ◯ To do

Don't repeat the tables in your text. Another frequent problem that novice authors have is repeating in their text the information that appears in their tables. Use the text to point out trends in the tables or to highlight the significance of some of the most interesting data; just don't repeat the data. If you have a sentence that lists three or more percentages, you're probably duplicating the information that's already in one of your tables. Let the tables work to free up your prose for analysis. At the same time, make sure to mention all the tables in the text. Peer reviewers will flag as irrelevant any table that goes undiscussed in your article. ☐ Done ☐ Not applicable ◯ To do

Don't organize your results by discovery. Remember the earlier advice to write like a lawyer, not a detective. We don't want to know how you came across each result. We're reading your article precisely because we want to save the time that you devoted to the study—so organize your results efficiently. ☐ Done ☐ Not applicable ◯ To do

Organize your results around your variables. If you're asking whether some effect is a function of variable a, variable b, or variable c, organize your Results section around variable a, then b, then c. For instance, if you're asking how homeless women's coursework is benefiting them, organize your Results section by the types of benefits the women are receiving. If you're investigating the progression of political campaigns, organize your Results section by the stages of that progression. If you're examining how socialites participate in charitable organizations, organize your Results section by types of participation. ☐ Done ☐ Not applicable ◯ To do

Identify respondents. If you're quoting study participants, it may be helpful to include identifying information in your text at the end of block quotes (e.g., male, 43, fourth-grade teacher). ☐ Done ☐ Not applicable ◯ To do

Don't mix in your methods. A frequent mistake of novice authors is letting their methodology mingle with their results. Be sure to check the first paragraph of your Results section for any methods that may have crept into it. If you find them, move them back to the Methods section. ☐ Done ☐ Not applicable ◯ To do

Write in the past tense. You found your results in the past; describe the process as completed. ☐ Done ☐ Not applicable ◯ To do

Keep it short. Unless you're combining your Results section with your Discussion section, this section should be brief. ☐ Done ☐ Not applicable ◯ To do

If you haven't already done so while reading the items above, revise your article to complete all the tasks that you've marked with a "To do" check.

Revising Your SciQua Discussion
Here are some issues to check when revising your Discussion section.

State whether you confirmed your hypothesis. Start your discussion by stating your argument or conclusion: what you thought would happen, what did happen, and why you think it happened. Many will have skipped reading your methodology and your results, so it's good to reiterate your findings and hypothesis here, in no more than two sentences. ☐ Done ☐ Not applicable ◯ To do

Link results. Identify the relationships among your results. That is, show which variables correlated and which didn't. ☐ Done ☐ Not applicable ◯ To do

Relate results to previous research. State whether your findings confirmed or contradicted those in other studies. Discuss why contradictions might exist. ☐ Done ☐ Not applicable ◯ To do

List some implications. What do your findings suggest? What can we conjecture about the world based on your results? Should policy change? ☐ Done ☐ Not applicable ◯ To do

Claim significance. Don't let readers walk away thinking, "So what?" Spell out the significance of the results for them. Just be careful in stating your claims about causality, as they are the trickiest to prove. What is novel about the findings? ☐ Done ☐ Not applicable ◯ To do

Question the findings. Evaluate the evidence for your hypothesis: its relevance, contradictions, mechanisms, explanatory power. What degree of certainty does the evidence enable? Is causality shown, or just correlation? Are there alternative explanations for the findings? Are there anomalies in the data? What could explain the differences in findings (e.g., gender)? Anticipate rebuttals, and note unresolved questions and possible biases. ☐ Done ☐ Not applicable ◯ To do

Note the limitations. All studies have certain limitations. It's best to acknowledge the more important of these. Sometimes you can mention how you would do the study differently next time. Just be careful not to overemphasize or apologize for your study's limitations. ☐ Done ☐ Not applicable ◯ To do

Suggest future research. You don't need to suggest future research, and some experts even advise against it as clichéd, but it used to be a typical part of many articles. If you have some suggestions, give them. ☐ Done ☐ Not applicable ◯ To do

Discuss the results; don't repeat them. Since the discussion depends on the results, it can be tough to keep them separate. But do what you can not to list the results in your Discussion section. ☐ Done ☐ Not applicable ◯ To do

Be thorough. You must discuss every result that you mentioned in the Results section. If you don't discuss a particular result, then perhaps that finding shouldn't be included under Results. It must be in both the Results and the Discussions sections or else in neither. ☐ Done ☐ Not applicable ◯ To do

Focus. Although the Discussion section is often the longest section, be careful that it's not too long. It's easy to use this section to brainstorm about all the possible meanings of the data. Don't overanalyze. Before writing the discussion, spend some time categorizing your data, then linking it in different ways, so that you don't use the Discussion section to brainstorm. ☐ Done ☐ Not applicable ◯ To do

Develop examples proportionately. Each of your case studies doesn't need to be the same length as the others in your article, but you do need to develop all of them in the same manner. Your examples aren't evenly developed if, for instance, in an article about drug use among homeless teenagers, you (1) address heroin use at length, detailing its use among homeless teens, its impact, and their comments about heroin, and then (2) include very little about marijuana, but (3) proceed to discuss at length the history of opioids in the United States. You've covered the first example more carefully, more in depth than the second, and the third isn't about drug use among homeless teens at all. The sections are uneven in multiple ways. Now, imbalance in length can be justified if for instance it takes less evidence to convince your readers of your first case, or if it takes more space to explain the complexity of your last case. Maybe the section on heroin will be longer, but if your sections on opiods and marijuana don't also discuss the youths' use of, impact on, and comments about these drugs, you haven't developed them proportionately. Check your examples and sections to make sure that you have developed all examples evenly. You may need to cut some sections entirely if you can't develop them to the same level as the others. If you find it tough to cut, put those deleted sections in another file as a possible beginning of another piece. Or save the file before you remove a large portion of text, and then use Save As to give the file a slightly different filename, so you keep the version with that eliminated material. ☐ Done ☐ Not applicable ◯ To do

If you haven't already done so while reading the items above, revise your article to complete all the tasks that you've marked with a "To do" check.

Revising Your Presentation of Evidence in Illustrations
Here are some issues to check when reviewing your illustrations.

Don't use murky photographs. Photographs work only if they're in focus, their subject is prominent without distracting background, and they're directly related to your subject. If you need to explain what the photo is about (e.g., "See there in the corner of the photo, that little blob, behind the dancing bears, that's the author I'm discussing"), don't use it. Are all your photographs clear? ☐ Done ☐ Not applicable ◯ To do

Don't use web-quality photographs. You will need to provide the journal publisher with print-quality versions of any photographs you want printed with your article. If you took the photographs yourself using a good camera, they'll likely be of print quality. But a scanned image or an image downloaded from the web probably won't be. A frequent mistake that novice authors make is assuming that they can use an image that works on the web or a newspaper in a print journal or book. That can't be done.

The amount of detail in a print image is thousands of times more than that needed for the web. For instance, a web image is often 70 to 700 KB, while a print image is often 3,000 to 30,000 KB. Almost never will an image taken from an ordinary website work for print. Do you have print-quality scans of your photographs? ☐ Done ☐ Not applicable ◯ To do

Don't scan images at low resolution. If you're scanning someone else's work—from a book, archive, or photograph—be aware that the standard settings on most scanners won't be set high enough; a minimum of 300 DPI is usually required. Journals will not accept poor scans from books or photocopies of newspaper articles. Plan to procure good versions of your images early, since they may not be available for photographing when you want them. Archival items in particular are sometimes in process, moving, lost, or lent out, and so cannot be photographed. Are your scans high resolution? ☐ Done ☐ Not applicable ◯ To do

Design powerful graphics. Are any graphics you created clear and compelling in presentation? Do you present your data in the best visual format? Do your graphics contain more than a few bits of information? ☐ Done ☐ Not applicable ◯ To do

Label and title your illustrations well. All photographs, drawings, and maps must have captions, and all graphs, tables, charts, and diagrams must have labels and titles. That wording must appear the same way throughout—in the same font, with similar phrasing, and using the same type of symbols. Titles of tables should describe the variables that appear in the tabular matter as well as the type of data the table presents. For example, "Attitudes about Integration" isn't a descriptive-enough title, but "Attitudes toward Racial Integration by Residential Neighborhood by Race" is. If you have dates, those are excellent to give in the titles as well. If your table title is only three or four words long, it probably isn't comprehensive enough. For graphics you may also need a legend, which explains the symbols used in the chart or labels. Are your illustrations well labeled and titled? ☐ Done ☐ Not applicable ◯ To do

Give correct credit lines for illustrations. If you obtained your image or the data in your graph from another scholar or source, you must provide information about that source in a credit line. Journals have their own style for credit lines, but one standard is, "From [full citation]. Copyright [year] by [copyright owner name]. Reprinted with permission." Do you have the information you need to write proper credit lines? ☐ Done ☐ Not applicable ◯ To do

If you haven't already done so while reading the items above, revise your article to complete all the tasks that you've marked with a "To do" check.

Revising Your Presentation of Evidence in the Humanities

In the humanities, instruction abounds on such microrevising issues as shortening your sentences, improving your diction, and correcting your grammar. Much rarer is instruction on macrorevising issues such as marshaling and presenting evidence. Few sources say much beyond noting that you should have evidence to support an argument. Here are a few general instructions.

Describe primary sources briefly. Classroom essays often devote many pages to summarizing the plot of novels and dramas or describing texts. Ensure that you haven't summarized at length. At the same time, make sure that you do describe your primary sources and their context, rather than assuming your readers have in mind at that moment all the pertinent details. ☐ Done ☐ Not applicable ◯ To do

Quote meaningfully. Don't pack your article with dozens of beautiful quotations from your primary or secondary sources. You are to interpret them, not replicate them. Be selective. Don't quote when you can paraphrase, don't quote material irrelevant to your argument, and don't quote at length unless your argument fails without that quotation. The more famous the text, the less you should quote it and the more you should paraphrase. In skimming your article, do you see many quotation marks or block quotes? If so, how will you reduce them? ☐ Done ☐ Not applicable ◯ To do

Introduce quotations. Always introduce quotes and interpret them, rather than letting them stand as ciphers. ☐ Done ☐ Not applicable ◯ To do

Select what to analyze carefully. Don't try to analyze every part of your primary source. Select only a few parts for analysis. To help you do this, ask "why" or "how" of the text, not "what." For instance, ask yourself, "Why is this particular rhyme scheme used?" rather than "What is the rhyme scheme?" ☐ Done ☐ Not applicable ◯ To do

Read toward an end. You examine a primary source passage not so much to identify what the passage says as to uncover what the passage says about other things. ☐ Done ☐ Not applicable ◯ To do

Reference the larger picture. Classroom essays often stop at simply discovering a particular theme, symbol, or fact in a primary source. You must go beyond discovery and use what you discover to make an argument. Further, you must make that argument in the context of your critical approach, whether feminist, psychoanalytic, postcolonial, queer theory, cultural studies, or otherwise. Make sure to make the connections. ☐ Done ☐ Not applicable ◯ To do

Limit footnotes. Most journals outside the humanities have dispensed with notes entirely, and more humanities journals are limiting the number and type of footnotes or endnotes. Some allow notes only for source citations (documentary notes), and some allow only a few notes for defenses or explanations (substantive notes). Almost none but history journals allow them for digressions. What does your journal expect? ☐ Done ☐ Not applicable ◯ To do

Deploy theory; don't replicate it. Classroom essays often bog down in presenting theory rather than deploying it. Don't spend long sections of your article explaining feminist theory, for instance; rather, make a feminist analysis of your primary source. At the same time, do make sure to mention what theory or approach you are using. ☐ Done ☐ Not applicable ◯ To do

Write in the correct tense. When analyzing literature in a literary discipline, use present tense for discussing primary sources. That is, you write, "In his novel *The Secret History of Las Vegas* (2014), Chris Abani treats the conjoined twins, who are called Fire and Water, as something other than carnivalesque." When writing history, use past tense when discussing primary sources. ☐ Done ☐ Not applicable ◯ To do

Point first, evidence second. The scholar of Chicanx literature and *corridos* Guillermo E. Hernández used to say about writing, "You don't eat a cake the way you make a cake." When you make a cake, you apply the frosting last; when you eat a cake, you taste the frosting first. Likewise, when we authors write an article, we often state our idea most richly at the end of a paragraph or section, when we have written our way toward understanding. But when revising, we need to move that richness to an earlier location, because readers need the richest part first. The principle here is point first, evidence second. Your readers should encounter no evidence without first being told for what purpose they are reading that evidence. One signal that you may not be putting the point first is if a paragraph's first sentence contains statistics or a quotation and its last sentence has a phrase like "Thus, we see that . . ." or "Therefore, it becomes clear that . . ." or "As this evidence shows . . ." It's nice to have a summation at the end of the paragraph, but if it started with data, you may need to add something at the beginning. Sometimes, of course, you will have several paragraphs in a row analyzing the same piece of evidence. In that case, stating the point at the beginning of the first paragraph only is okay. But if you're regularly putting your evidence first, you need to work on that. Check the beginnings and ends of two paragraphs and two sections. Do they have a point first, evidence second structure? If not, is there a reason for that? If you find this problem when you're spot-checking, you would be wise to check the beginnings of all paragraphs and sections. ☐ Done ☐ Not applicable ◯ To do

Don't give too much evidence. It's tempting to include everything in your article that you found. However, this is a mistake. As the historian James McPherson recommends to his graduate students, think of your article as an iceberg: "only one-seventh of the data, quotations, and other information one finds in one's research should make it into the text" (quoted in Toor 2016). Check your article for streams of data, and ensure that they haven't taken over. ☐ Done ☐ Not applicable ◯ To do

Develop examples proportionately. Each text under discussion does not have to take up the same length in the article, but you do need to develop all of them in the same way. If you've covered the first text more carefully, more in depth than the second text, then you've developed them unevenly. Now, sometimes imbalance in length is justified—for instance, if it takes less evidence to convince your readers of your analysis of the first text, or if it takes more space to explain the complexity of your last text. ☐ Done ☐ Not applicable ◯ To do

If you haven't already done so while reading the items above, revise your article to complete all the tasks you've marked with a "To do" check.

Of course, each discipline and approach has certain ways of discussing evidence. As an example, I give you a few issues to check when revising the body of a literary article containing cultural analysis.

Avoid discussing intentionality. Classroom essays often focus on what the author or creator intended or might have intended. In cultural analysis, focus on the text and your reading of it, not the author. If you want to discuss intentionality, find a recent article in your field that does so, and study how the author successfully makes this analysis. ☐ Done ☐ Not applicable ◯ To do

Avoid biography. Classroom essays often focus on how the life experiences of authors or creators shaped their work. Again, in the cultural analysis mode, focus on the text itself. If you feel that biography is important, find a recent article in your field that does such analysis well, and study it. ☐ Done ☐ Not applicable ◯ To do

Avoid simple politicizing. Classroom essays often vulgarize cultural studies arguments by misusing the discipline's terms to bludgeon texts or peoples. The essence of sophisticated cultural studies criticism is an acknowledgment that it's difficult to know anything for certain, and that we all (strong and weak) participate in creating the world we live in, whether we are perpetuating its injustices or resisting them. Be careful to nuance your argument; that's how you will best persuade readers, whether sympathetic or wary. ☐ Done ☐ Not applicable ◯ To do

If you haven't already done so while reading the items above, revise your article to complete all the tasks that you've marked with a "To do" check.

Revising Evidence in Your Discipline

If your article fits none of the disciplinary categories above, you might want to write a few notes here about what you have observed about the presentation of evidence in your discipline or field.

Principles for Presenting Evidence in My Field

Tracking Writing Time

Mark your electronic calendar, the Calendar for Actual Time Spent Writing This Week form, and/or the check boxes here with how long you wrote today. ☐ 15+ min. ☐ 30+ ☐ 60+ ☐ 120+

Then, here at the end of your workweek, take pride in your accomplishments and evaluate whether any patterns need changing.

DOCUMENTING YOUR WRITING TIME AND TASKS

Calendar for Actual Time Spent Writing This Week

Time	Day 1	Day 2	Day 3	Day 4	Day 5	Day 6	Day 7
5:00 a.m.							
6:00							
7:00							
8:00							
9:00							
10:00							
11:00							
12:00 p.m.							
1:00							
2:00							
3:00							
4:00							
5:00							
6:00							
7:00							
8:00							
9:00							
10:00							
11:00							
12:00 a.m.							
1:00							
2:00							
3:00							
4:00							
Total minutes							
Tasks completed							

WEEK 9
Strengthening Your Structure

Task Day	Week 9 Daily Writing Tasks	Estimated Task Time in Minutes	
		HumInt	SciQua
Day 1 (Monday?)	Read from here until you reach the week 9, day 2 tasks, filling in any boxes, checking off any forms, and answering any questions as you read.	90	90
Day 2 (Tuesday?)	Outline a good published article.	60	30
Day 3 (Wednesday?)	Make a postdraft outline of your article.	90	60
Day 4 (Thursday?)	Restructure your article.	120+	90+
Day 5 (Friday?)	Restructure your article.	120+	90+
Total estimated time for reading the workbook, completing the tasks, and writing your article		**8+ hours**	**6+ hours**

Above are the tasks for your eighth week. Start this week by scheduling when you will write, and then tracking the time you actually spend writing (using the Calendar for Actual Time Spent Writing This Week form or online software).

Some articles need a lot of restructuring; others need only a little. If you find yourself making dramatic changes this week—moving paragraphs, cutting cases, tossing or adding whole sections—that's a good sign. It means you're gaining clarity about your article and getting closer to submitting it to a journal. If, after thinking carefully about the logical flow of your article, you make few to no changes, that's good too. You're making your last checks.

EIGHTH WEEK IN REVIEW

You have now spent eight weeks on vital article publishing tasks: designing a plan, selecting a text for revision, writing an abstract, organizing your article around your argument, picking the right journal, reviewing the scholarship, crafting your claims for significance, and presenting and analyzing your evidence. Congratulations! If you made it this far in the workbook, feel free to tweet me using the hashtag #WYJA8W (*Writing Your Journal Article* 8 Weeks in) so that I can congratulate you.

ON THE IMPORTANCE OF STRUCTURE

Journal articles are a specialized form of writing governed by highly standardized conventions. While these conventions vary a bit by discipline and field, they are for the most part surprisingly uniform.

One of the most standardized conventions is structure—that is, the organization of your argument and the evidence for your argument. A well-structured article is one in which ideas are organized hierarchically, based on their importance, and their organization is apparent. Without a strong structure, your article lacks a skeleton and its ideas collapse into a morass. With the skeleton of a strong structure, your article comes to life, supporting the weight of its own ideas. That's because regular patterns aid readability. Research indicates that people read a well-structured article more quickly and retain more of it (B. Meyer 2003, 208, 212, 214). Strong structure also enables readers to grasp content more readily, converting them from distracted observers to intrigued fellow travelers. Perhaps even more important, regular patterns aid *you*, the author. Organizing your ideas helps you better understand them and their connections to each other.

Arriving at a strong structure isn't easy, however. Frequently, we write down ideas in the order they come to us, perhaps rearranging them a bit in ways that are intuitive to us but not to others. Also, most of us write on computers, where we can see only a few paragraphs at a time; this makes it easy for us to lose the thread of the entire article. Finally, uncovering the best order for our articles "often cannot be done until the work is well underway" (Willis 1993, 156). So learning how to structure your article is essential if you want it to survive the peer-review process. This chapter offers techniques to help you understand the structure of your article and properly link its parts.

ARTICLE-STRUCTURING PRINCIPLES

The structure of articles can be categorized in a variety of ways. Studying some of these approaches may aid you in identifying the best structure for your article. In what follows, you'll find information about an article's macrostructure and microstructure, the five organizational structures of writing, and the best ways to structure information rhetorically and to signal structure to the reader. You'll also find information about how your familiarity with structures for other genres of writing may be interfering with your ability to structure your journal article as a journal article.

Macrostructure and Microstructure

You need to attend to two levels of your article's structure: macrostructure and microstructure. The macrostructure can be articulated in the outline of the article; the microstructure can be articulated in diagrams of the article's paragraphs and sentences. Some scholars alternately describe these as "coherence" and "cohesion," with coherence representing the overall organization of the article and cohesion representing "how smaller units of texts fit together, such as neighboring sentences" (McTigue and Slough 2010, 221; see also B. Meyer 1975; Halliday and Hasan 1976). During week 10, you'll be completing exercises to ensure that your microstructure is strong; this week is focused entirely on macrostructure.

In other words, then, macrostructure is the superstructure, the overarching meaning working down through the entire article to organize it, with argument being the main organizing principle. You have a coherent macrostructure when each section, subsection, and paragraph of your article is organized argumentatively into an overall logical structure—with everything in the right place, nothing missing, and nothing extraneous. The best description of journal article macrostructure is also one of the shortest, written by an anonymous senior scholar in a writing forum on July 26, 2012, at the *Chronicle of Higher Education*. "Marigolds" stated that an article does not have an "inductive shape." That is, he or she writes, it does not take the form of "*A*, thus *B*, then *C*, therefore *D*." Rather, it has an argumentative shape, which Marigolds described as "*D*! And the reasons for *D* are *A*, *B*, and *C*. And here's why you should care about *D*." This scholar gets it exactly right.

By contrast, microstructure is the focused meaning working *up* from the paragraph and sentence level, with clarity as the organizing principle. You have a cohesive microstructure when each sentence is clear and grammatical, leads logically to the next sentence, and adds up to a paragraph that has a unifying concept and hangs together. Too often, paragraphs consist of sentences that seem related, but lack logical, argumentative connections with each other.

As you may have guessed, distinguishing microstructure from macrostructure isn't always possible. The main aim of describing these two levels, however, is to aid you in avoiding a common problem. A frequent error of novice authors is spending all their time on the microstructural task of word phrasing and ignoring the macrostructural task of arranging. The heuristic of microstructure and macrostructure is just another way of saying, don't always stay down in the grass, in the details of the work, but get up into the trees, viewing the whole. This week, you'll be working on exercises to ensure that you're viewing your article as a whole and building a strong macrostructure.

Structural Building Blocks

Scholars maintain that there are five basic organizational structures in texts (B. Meyer, Brandt, and Bluth 1980; B. Meyer, Young, and Bartlett 1989). When teachers train students to recognize these basic structures, their reading and retention improve. By the same token, these strategies can aid us scholars not only to read better but to write more clearly and understand our own structures better. Journal articles use these structures at both the macrostructural and the microstructural level.

Description. The description structure is organized by information about a topic in which characteristics are described. This structure is commonly found in journal articles' introductory and/or background sections as well as in Methods sections; it is organized around the who, what, where, and when of the topic. A macrostructural example of the description structure would be an essay about gender-based violence that describes what it is, who it affects, and when and where it most often happens. All journal articles contain descriptive (also called expository) paragraphs, but an article that has only descriptive paragraphs and a description macrostructure can't be published in a peer-reviewed journal; it's not argumentative. Signals that description structure is in use include words and phrases such as *for example, such as, that is,* or *some features are.*

Sequence. The sequence structure is organized by sequential order, most often chronological or procedural, such that readers learn about events in order of their occurrence or learn how to make something. This structure is commonly found in journal articles' background, Methods, or Results sections. A macrostructural example of the sequence structure would be an article about gender-based violence that provides a history of scholarship on the problem or gives step-by-step instructions for training nurses to both recognize the signs of and report on such violence. An article that has only sequence (also called narrative) paragraphs and a sequence macrostructure can't be published; it's not argumentative. Signals that sequence structure is in use include words and phrases like *first, second, next, before,* or *more recently.*

Causation. The causation structure is organized by cause-and-effect relationships: why (cause) and what (effect) happened? This structure is commonly found in Results or Discussion sections of journal articles. A macrostructural example of the causation structure would be an article about gender-based violence that discusses theories of why men commit violence against women and the consequences of this violence for both. Causation structure is common in published journal articles. Signals that causation structure is in use include words and phrases such as *because, thus, as a result,* and *therefore.*

Problem-solution. The problem-solution structure is organized by a problem and its solution: it asks a question and answers it, defining the problem, unpacking its implications, thinking through it, and then addressing what is being done or what could be done to solve the problem. This structure is commonly found in Discussion sections of journal articles. A macrostructural example of the problem-solution structure would be an article about the problem of gender-based violence that lays out the efficacy of three attempted solutions. By contrast, an article about the problems that arose from certain solutions to gender-based violence, without proposing other solutions, would exhibit the causation structure. Problem-solution structure is common in published journal articles. Signals that a problem-solution structure is in use are words or phrases like *the question is, the puzzle facing, proposes,* or *responds.*

Comparison. The comparison structure is organized by the differences and similarities among things: in what ways are things alike; in what ways are they different? This structure commonly appears in literature reviews. A macrostructural example of the comparison structure would be an article that discusses how gender-based violence among those in opposite-sex relationships differs from that in same-sex relationships. Comparison structure is common in published journal articles. Signals that a comparison structure is in use are words or phrases like *in contrast, instead, on the other hand, both,* or *similar.*

Either through consulting your article or just from memory, answer the following:

> Does my article contain more than descriptive or sequence macrostructure? If not, what can I do to improve that?

The Rhetorical Orders of Structure

Scholars also maintain that whatever structural building blocks a writer uses, readers understand information more easily when it appears in particular orders. What those sequences are can be mysterious to novice authors, however. Some of the excellent advice they learned in high school or college for structuring essays, such as the BEAM method (Background, Evidence, Analysis, Method) (Bizup 2008) and the MEAL plan (Main idea, Evidence, Analysis, Lead out) (Duke University 2012), may not seem perfectly apt for writing journal articles. So I want to focus on just two ordering methods: reader-knowledge-oriented order and Eric Hayot's "Uneven U" order.

Reader-Knowledge-Oriented Order

One principle that scholars recommend when structuring information in an article is to start where your readers are and bring them along. To orient your article toward readers, start with

- **The familiar.** Begin with what you assume your readers know and proceed to what they don't know.
- **The easy.** Proceed from the simple to the complex. Get your readers comfortable before introducing the difficult information.
- **The accepted.** Proceed from the uncontested to the more contested. Readers who have been convinced to believe one thing may more readily believe the next.
- **The overview.** Proceed from the general to the specific. Start with the big picture and then focus in on the details.
- **The few.** Proceed from discussing the fewest items to discussing the most. In other words, if you're analyzing a number of texts, objects, or studies, you might treat just a few in the first section of the article, more in the second section, and the most in the last section. This technique has argumentative weight, as you're laying out the argument with just a few pieces of evidence, but later piling up lots of evidence.
- **The historical.** Proceed chronologically from the past to the present. (This common sequence isn't always the best one; it tends toward a data-organized article rather than an argument-organized one.)
- **The visual.** Proceed spatially through a succession of linked objects, as if on a guided tour. This technique works particularly well for articles addressing a topic in art history and geography, for instance.

Either through consulting your article or just from memory, answer the following:

Would my article benefit from using more of one of these orders? Where?

Hayot's "Uneven U" Order

Although designed for the humanities, any scholarly writers interested in improving their writing can benefit from Eric Hayot's useful theory of the "Uneven U," described in his book *The Elements of Academic Style* (2014). In chapter 8 of that text, Hayot breaks all writing down into five levels, from the most abstract to plain data, and advises how to organize them for rhetorical effect. The Uneven U is his theory of how academic prose moves—starting with abstract ideas, moving down into the details, and then traveling back up into the abstract. It does this within paragraphs, but also in the article overall. For example, one type of Uneven U paragraph "starts with a general statement of the problem, introduces evidence, provides evidence more fully, summarizes and interprets that evidence, and finally connects to a new idea whose endpoint lies beyond the paragraph itself" (Hayot 2014, 63).

You may have started to sense the Uneven U structure in previous weeks when you highlighted the presentation of evidence with green and its interpretation in blue, and saw that the beginnings of strong paragraphs tended to be blue. I have given only the bare bones of Hayot's sophisticated theory here; to take full advantage, you must read his chapter 8. Among the gems in this chapter is his point that scholarly paragraphs rarely have topic sentences of the high school type (which "tell the reader exactly what will happen in the paragraph") but rather have *opening* sentences (which make "thematic, argumentative, and structural promises") (Hayot 2014, 62). As he notes, authors shouldn't use his theory to draft all paragraphs, but knowing its principles can help you strengthen your prose. Study the beginnings and endings of your paragraphs—if they're not regularly more abstract than the middles of your paragraphs, you might need to make some changes. The same advice goes for the article as a whole.

Either through consulting your article or just from memory, answer the following:

Would my article benefit from attending more to Hayot's Uneven U structure? Where?

Structure Signals

Moreover, scholars point out that whatever building blocks and rhetorical order writers use, readers understand information more easily when the text clearly signals the structure being used, rather than assuming that readers will intuitively grasp it. Fortunately, such signals aid not just your readers but also you the author, keeping you alert to logical sequence. Some stylebooks advise against obvious "signposting" (or, in a memorable phrase, "outside plumbing"). So do some scholars. As one senior scholar complained to me, authors should help readers to "smell the steak" and therefore should not "yell the steak." Nonetheless, I still recommend that you include structure signals to get your article through peer review. Then, if you're dedicated to a more literary style and really hate such signaling, delete it in the copyediting phase of your writing process. At the peer-review stage, the benefits of signaling your structure outweigh any inelegance.

Subheadings. Research shows that people read material containing subheadings more quickly and understand more of it (B. Meyer 2003; Moore 2006; McCabe et al. 2006). Visible cues to structure are particularly helpful in getting reviewers to look on your article favorably. Even if you failed to do what you set out to do, your subheadings make your general project come across more clearly, and the peer reviewers can push you to accomplish what you intended for your article rather than rejecting your article outright. Subheadings help not just the reader but also you the author. One study showed that teaching college students to use descriptive headings in their writing resulted in a "marked improvement" in their article's organization, use of sources, and argument (Murphy 1998, 233). If you're writing a SciQua article, subheadings are uniform and required, but you may still find that additional subheadings aid your readers. For instance, some authors provide subheadings in their Methods section (e.g., Participants, Data Collection, Measures, and Analysis).

Either through consulting your article or just from memory, answer the following:

> Would my article benefit from more subheadings? Where?

Synopsis. In HumInt articles, authors are wise to provide a summary at the end of the introduction about the order of information in the rest of their article. This overview serves as a road map, aiding readers in choosing to keep reading the article, as they have a clear view of what's ahead, which sections they need to read, and which they can skim. Even in fields where synopses haven't been common, such as literary studies, they are becoming commonplace. Just remember to keep yours brief—two to three sentences are generally sufficient.

Either through consulting your article or just from memory, answer the following:

> Does my article have a synopsis? If not, might it benefit from one?

Summing-up sentences. Peter Elbow advises writers to make "lots of summings up" (Elbow 1998, 35). Providing a summing-up sentence or two at the end of sections or even some paragraphs aids the reader in seeing how the analyzed evidence has shaped the argument to that point in the article. The strongest articles move forward and sum up at the same time, regularly reminding readers of what's at stake and what they've learned so far. When exchanging articles, you may have found that the most frequent request of a reader was for more summation—whether of your argument up to that point, of the interpretation of that paragraph, of the answer to the main question so far, or of the articulation of conceptual connections. Just note that good summing up isn't verbatim restatement but argumentative nuancing or forceful clarity. For example, in an article about representations of Native Americans, the author powerfully summed up her previous five pages discussing US history textbooks by three different authors, using just one sentence: "In Miller, Indians had been simply beneath notice; in Vaughn, they belonged to an inferior culture; and in Jennings, they were the more or less innocent prey of power-hungry whites" (Tompkins 1986, 107–8). Previews, indicating at the beginning of a section the argumentative destination of that section, can also be effective.

Either through consulting your article or just from memory, answer the following:

> Would my article benefit from more summing up? Where?

Switch-signaling words. Words that signal rhetorical switches are useful; examples include *nevertheless*, *however*, *by contrast*, and *on the one hand*. So are words that differentiate items in a sequence: *first*, *second*, *then*, *before*, and *after*. But don't use them except where they actually apply. Sometimes novice authors just sprinkle them at the beginning of sentences, which doesn't work. An actual switch in logic must follow a switch word.

Either through consulting your article or just from memory, answer the following:

> Would my article benefit from more switch-signaling words? Fewer? Where?

Questions. At the beginning and end of sections, "questions that guide readers" can be helpful (McTigue and Slough 2010, 221). Posing the question that's in the reader's mind at that point is a challenge, however. So is asking focused argumentative questions. Novice authors often pose a series of unrelated questions, what occurs to them in the moment, and then fail to answer or even address those questions. Your aim in posing questions should be to further the forward movement of your article and its argument, not just list unsolvable problems.

Either through consulting your article or just from memory, answer the following:

> Would my article benefit from more questions? Fewer? Where?

Common Genres' Structures

Whatever structural building blocks, rhetorical order, and signals authors may use, many macrostructural problems are caused by their writing in the wrong genre. Most academics read many different genres of text, so they are steeped in many different macrostructures. The macrostructure of a mystery novel is different from the macrostructure of a newspaper article, which is different from the macrostructure of a cookbook. Since you're in the habit of reading a variety of genres, their conventions may cause some confusion for you when you work on structuring articles. A frequent mistake of novice authors is using macrostructures that are unsuitable for journal articles. Nothing is wrong with these other structures—indeed, accomplished writers may even consciously select aspects of other genres' structures to vary the structure of their journal articles. The problem arises when these other macrostructures unconsciously influence you. Having a better understanding of them will help you avoid that.

Newspaper article structure. Many academics read newspapers and unconsciously absorb their style, which causes problems for their journal article writing. For one thing, newspaper articles are supposed to be objective, just reporting on facts and offering no interpretations. That is, most aren't organized argumentatively, so they aren't good models for journal articles. Second, these articles have an inverted-pyramid structure, in which the most important information appears first and the least important information last. Such an article doesn't circle round or even wrap up, working quite differently than a journal article. (By the way, this inverted-pyramid structure arose because of the technological limitations of print. Before publishers had computers, fitting all the articles into the allotted space was difficult, so editors needed to be able to trim articles if they ran out of space. The inverted-pyramid structure of news stories allowed for them to be cut from the bottom up if necessary without editors fearing they might be removing crucial information.) You can't write your journal article using the newspaper article structure, as you need to interpret, not just document, a variety of information (important and less so) throughout your article, not just at the beginning. And you need a solid conclusion.

Newspaper editorial structure. Many academics also read editorials in newspapers. Editorials explain a current issue, note opinions from various sides of the debate about that issue, and propose a solution or an action. Although they're persuasive and argumentative, they aren't evidence based—it's impossible to fit more than a few statistics into the five hundred words allowed for most editorials. This genre represents pure rhetoric. By contrast, journal articles are longer and thoroughly examine much evidence.

Magazine article structure. Many academics also read magazines and their "feature" articles (which also can appear in newspapers). Such articles start with a "billboard," an anecdotal narrative that captures the reader's attention and is about one to three paragraphs long. This anecdote is followed by a "lede," a sentence that announces the article's point. The lede is the pivotal part of the article, guiding readers in reading the rest of the article. The conclusion then returns the article to the narrative of the billboard. For instance, a feature might start with a billboard about Dwayne, whose mother noticed that he was gaining weight and urinating more frequently than usual. When she took him to the doctor, she found out that he had juvenile diabetes. The next sentence, the lede, might then state the point of the article that the anecdote illustrates: millions of children have undiagnosed juvenile diabetes. Often, the feature will conclude with an update to the anecdote, such as Dwayne feeling better. While journal articles in the humanities can sometimes successfully imitate the magazine article opening by starting with an anecdote, many journal articles do not and cannot start in such a way. Further, the journal article conclusion is different, moving out to broader implications, not narrowing to the individual.

Blog post structure. Many academics read or write blogs, which can be terrific for developing thoughts and getting feedback. However, blogs are informal and highly individualized; journal articles are formal and conventional. Although it's good to develop a voice for your journal articles, that voice is more formal than that of a blog; it's as if you're speaking to the Nobel Prize committee, not your best friend. Also, blogs post ideas in process and speculate on causes and consequences; journal articles report on refined and finalized ideas based on solid research.

Mystery novel structure. Many academics read mysteries or watch them on television. Unfortunately, some unconsciously imitate mystery structure in their journal article writing, which leads to twisted structures. Many novice authors believe that readers will stop reading their article if told the argument or findings too early, so they withhold these until the end of the article, where they reveal the surprise, the equivalent of "The butler did it!" But academics don't read journal articles the way that they read mystery novels. Indeed, readers are far more likely to read your article if they have a good sense of where it is going. Further, an article that announces the argument early and summarizes what is coming is more democratic, enabling the reader to be a fellow investigator instead of a passive observer waiting for the mystery to be solved. Most of all, articles that withhold their purpose, import, or conclusions until their end often have warped microstructures and distorted macrostructures. They must actively avoid being clear so that the mystery is sustained. In the humanities, some gifted authors can pull off a mystery format, but in those few cases they provide so many clues along the way that the reader is pleased but not entirely surprised upon reaching the end.

Non-Western text structures. Many academics grew up in non-Western contexts. If you're one of them, it's vital to know that the macrostructure of articles in peer-reviewed journals is not "natural," not better than other structures—it's simply the most dominant one. As the research on "cross-cultural contrastive rhetoric" has shown, different intellectual traditions organize written knowledge in different ways, many of which yield structures that are rhetorically impressive and compelling (Connor 2002; Liu 2015). In some West African traditions, for instance, knowledge is formulated in extremely dense and allusive patterns that must be unpacked, as Karin Barber's extraordinary work on Yoruba oral verbal art demonstrates (Barber 2013). By comparison, journal articles seem boorishly direct and simplistic. Traditional Chinese texts sometimes took advantage of what was called the four-part structure or eight-legged structure, organized around successive arguments and quoting the classics (Kirkpatrick 1997; Z. Wu 2014). By comparison, journal articles seem boringly reductive and obvious. Researchers have even generalized about such cultural differences, claiming that "English academic writing is 'linear,' Chinese 'circular,' Romance languages 'digressive,' Middle Eastern languages 'parallel,' and Russian and German 'a variable of parallel'" (Straker 2016, 302, summarizing the work of McLean and Ransom 2005, 57, who were summarizing the work of Kaplan 1966). As a result, nonnative speakers of English can find their journal articles criticized for repetition, indirectness, and too broad a scope (Kourilova-Urbanczik 2012).

Although such generalizations can be problematic, international scholars often feel relieved to learn that their struggles with journal article structure aren't caused by an innate quality of theirs, but instead arose from the different cultural rhetorics they were exposed to while growing up. The research confirms my impression, as graduate students taught about cross-cultural contrastive rhetoric showed increased recognition of the forms of academic writing (Zhou 2016). Of course, one may be "international" at home too; many in the United States grew up with different modes of knowledge production. Be aware of any non-Western writing structures that may be influencing you, and study how journal articles differ from them.

Greek oration structure. The journal article has certain rhetorical features that have persisted for thousands of years. The ancient Greeks contended that a public speech should begin with an introduction that attracts the audience (called an *exordium* in Latin) and is followed by background on the topic or issue (*narratio*). The speaker then should propose a claim or argument (*partitio*), provide evidence for the argument (*confirmatio*), and refute potential criticisms of the argument (*refutatio*). Finally, the speaker should articulate a moving conclusion, often a call to arms of some sort (*peroratio*). This ancient structure persists in the topic, thesis, evidence, and conclusion structure of most scientific articles. It also persists in the essay that many high school students learn to write: set the context (who, what, where, when); introduce the argument (why, how); provide three pieces of evidence; and conclude and/or recommend. Of course, few are listening to Greek orations these days, but it wouldn't do much harm if they were, because the orations' macrostructure is an antecedent of the journal article structure discussed in this chapter.

Report structure. Many academics are also practitioners, particularly those in international development, and must write reports on their field projects. The structure of these reports often influences their journal article drafts. But reports tend to present everything found, all the results, not a selection of evidence. These unfiltered data are why reports as reports are so valuable; but this feature also makes them bad models for journal articles, which must select the best evidence. Also, reports tend not to include arguments and can be very long and speculative, proposing untested solutions. Consequently, reports are great bases for developing journal articles, but avoiding their macrostructure is essential.

Dissertations, books, and book chapters. All academics read other scholarly genres, and even these can cause problems. A journal article is not a book or a dissertation, either of which is hundreds of pages long to explore many ideas; rather, it's twenty to forty pages on a single significant idea. Nor is a journal article a book or dissertation chapter, which can depend on the chapters before and after it to give background information and theory. Rather, it stands alone, entire and complete. Structuring a journal article as if it were a dissertation chapter is one of the most common errors.

Knowing the multiplicity of writing structures can help you write better journal articles, preventing unsuitable macrostructures from creeping into your academic writing.

Either through consulting your article or just from memory, answer the following:

Which other genre structures may have crept into my article? For instance, does it end with the least important information, lack a conclusion, insufficiently analyze evidence, lack formality, withhold findings, lack an argument, or run too long?

TYPES OF JOURNAL ARTICLE MACROSTRUCTURES

Returning to journal article structure, some disciplines use more standardized structures than others do. The sciences have absolute formulas; the humanities have looser ones; the social sciences vary along a spectrum. Those in the sciences sometimes wish that their structures were less rigid; those in the humanities sometimes wish that they had simple formulaic structures they could follow. The good news is that you can improve your writing by knowing the structuring principles of other disciplines.

SciQua Macrostructure

Quantitative, experimental, and many qualitative articles follow what is called an IMRD (sometimes IMRaD) structure, an acronym for the order of the articles' sections: Introduction, Methods, Results, and Discussion. This type of article moves from why and how the scholars obtained the results to what the results mean. Each section has a specific format organized around the research question. The IMRD structure has an hourglass shape, because it starts out with a broad focus in the introduction, proceeds to a narrow focus in the methods and results, and then opens back out to a broad view in the discussion. (This movement of prose is also reflected in Hayot's Uneven U order.)

Here is a bit more detail about SciQua macrostructure, provided in outline form.

1. Section I—Inverted-pyramid structure, moving from general to specific
   a. Introduction—general subject of investigation (often a social problem)
   b. Review of the literature—literature on the subject of investigation (gaps and lacks)
   c. Statement of the hypothesis—your argument in the context of other work
2. Section M—Specific description of study, all information needed to replicate study
   a. Methods
   b. Procedures
   c. Materials and instruments
   d. Experiment
   e. Context and setting
   f. Population or sample
3. Section R—Specific description of results
   a. Results—report on findings (often with tables and graphs)
4. Section D—Pyramid structure, moving from the specific of results to the general
   a. Discussion—comment on validity of methods and findings
   b. Conclusions—place research in the context of the scholarly literature

Notably, some scientific disciplines don't use IMRD macrostructures. Mathematics articles, for instance, only have an introduction and a Results section because their methods are established, and discussion isn't necessary to interpret the results (Graves, Moghaddasi, and Hashim 2013).

Either through consulting your article or just from memory, answer the following:

> Do I use this SciQua macrostructure? And/or does it spark any ideas about how to structure my article?

HumInt Macrostructure

Humanities and interpretive social science articles usually have an essayistic macrostructure. Like SciQua articles, HumInt articles have introductions, but these vary. For instance, the HumInt macrostructure lacks an hourglass shape; the author doesn't separate the evidence (results) from the interpretation (discussion). Rather, interpretation occurs continuously in HumInt macrostructure, as the author walks the reader through multiple layers of thinking through a question. The author presents evidence, interprets that evidence, suggests how that evidence supports the argument, and repeats this process until satisfied that the argument is convincing. To put it another way, as the literature scholar Rachel Bergmann astutely said to me, "Social science articles *report* on their experiment, while humanities articles *stage* their experiment."

Although HumInt macrostructure can differ quite a bit internally, many HumInt articles look something like this:

I. Introduction
    A. Vivid example/problem/anecdote/text, often communicating who, what, why, where, when
    B. Review of the scholarly debate and/or general perception of the subject
    C. Statement of author's argument relevant to context, debate, and perceptions
    D. Claim for the significance of the subject, approach, or argument
    E. Synopsis of article structure and points
II. Body
    A. Background (e.g., subject context, including history, region, period, group)
    B. Analysis of something
        1. Describes the thing under analysis (e.g., text[s]/passage[s], individual[s]/group[s], artwork[s], case[s], theme[s], event[s], proposition[s], principle[s])
        2. States the subargument about that thing
        3. Analyzes that thing, plus any other relevant things
        4. Often considers any relevant insights about that thing in the work of other scholars
        5. Sometimes addresses possible counterarguments
        6. Sums up what was discovered, found, concluded, and inferred so far, and sets up the next section
    C. Analysis of something else (i.e., section B above repeats once, twice, up to five or six times)
III. Summing up (how all the things, scholarship, discoveries, and argument relate)

IV. Conclusion
 A. Why these discoveries are fascinating
 B. Why this article is a contribution to the scholarly debate and/or field

Because HumInt macrostructure varies so much, it's wise to study the structure of articles in your discipline.

Either through consulting your article or just from memory, answer the following:

> Do I use a HumInt macro-structure? And/or does it spark any ideas about how to structure my article?

Disciplinary Macrostructures

Dedicated study of articles in your discipline or field can help you detect their article structure formulas. Some participants in my workshops have sent me their findings (and you are welcome to do the same!). Scholars have also published their research on disciplinary macrostructures. Here's information about three of these.

Linguistics. One author in my workshop found some standardization among articles in her discipline of linguistics. The articles tended to be thirty to thirty-five pages in length with abstracts of 150–250 words. They had short introductions followed by literature reviews of three to five pages that reviewed approximately forty to fifty citations. After a short Methods section, they proceeded to the analysis or discussion, which typically took up about 75 percent of the article and was organized around the debate announced in the literature review. Most articles had a summarizing conclusion.

Applied linguistics. Two scholars have formally studied articles in applied linguistics, finding that they often strayed from the IMRD structure. For instance, these articles often included the theoretical background, the related literature, or background information in sections *after* the introduction, in the body of the article (Ruiying and Allison 2003, 2004). Frequently, applied linguistics articles also had a section before the conclusion about the pedagogical implications of the research. In addition, the body of the articles consisted of argumentation, but of three different types. One body type was oriented toward theory, pursuing a series of subarguments. Another type had a problem-solution format. The last type had a problem-solution format but added a component on the application of the solution. I mention these variations in applied linguistics as an example of how disciplines can vary from the ostensibly universal rules for structuring articles.

Anthropology. One author studied articles in her discipline of anthropology and found that they devoted half their space to reviewing the literature and related theories, contrary to my advice not to spend too much time on others' ideas. Most had literature reviews at least eight pages long and reviewed three different bodies of literature. Many of the articles also had, near the beginning, about two paragraphs of background on the field site and population. Just as this author had, test my advice by studying the norms of articles in your discipline. If they differ from what I said, follow your disciplinary norms, not my advice!

Synaptic Macrostructure

Over the years that I have taught my writing workshop, a contingent of humanities students has argued against rigid article structures. They insist that some published articles are not so argument driven but instead pose a question, move poetically and nonlinearly through a process of discovery, and reveal an answer only in the conclusion (if then). Such articles proceed with merely the promise of an answer or with only a provisional argument that cannot be understood until the piece has been read through. Argument is not a structure but a plot, these students say, a seductive puzzle that foments critical desire and depends on a deferred closure. I call such articles "synaptic," since they proceed by sparking readers' imaginations, lighting up synapses like fireworks with a series of epiphanies, which are only loosely related.

In my warning to authors against stringing together insights without any organizing principle, perhaps I *am* prohibiting the development of more sophisticated, intuitive, and open articles. If it's your heart's desire to write such articles, go for it. But let me give a few warnings that may help you be successful with the form. First, many readers resist reading such articles because they're more difficult to read or skim, and readers have only so much time. As one workshop participant wittily put it, "I find it tough to read them because I'm constantly debating if the author is a genius or just confused." Even if you're dedicated to the synaptic style, still attempt to provide some of the structure that aids readers. Increasingly, I see synaptic articles that still have extremely clear, nonsynaptic introductions. Fred Moten's much-cited article "Blackness and Nothingness (Mysticism in the Flesh)" is a good example (Moten 2013). Another is Jeff Dolven's article "Panic's Castle," which has all the pleasures of an allusive, elliptical, and lyrical prose style, yet a rock-solid structure and an admirably brief statement of the argument on the second page: "Panic, and the fear of panic, are the generative principles of *The Faerie Queene*" (Dolven 2012, 2). Second, many novice authors are attracted to writing high theory because that's what they read most in graduate school. And it seems like writing theory is what the smartest do. Yet in fact, the clear majority of what is published is not high theory. Again, if you truly love reading and writing theory, and others tell you that you do it well, absolutely do it. But don't misunderstand the profession. It's not mostly about pure theory. Third, you face an uphill battle in getting published, as the journals that publish synaptic articles are getting rarer. Make sure the journal to which you're sending your material publishes them. Also, if you're not tenured, consider writing some conventionally structured articles as well so that your odds of getting published are better.

Either through consulting your article or just from memory, answer the following:

> Do I use the synaptic macrostructure? If so, should I write a less synaptic introduction or conclusion?

TYPES OF PRE- AND POSTDRAFT OUTLINING

While most of us think about article outlining as a task authors perform *before* they start writing, creating an outline *after* you've written a draft is perhaps the most valuable step you can take to improve your structure. Outlining something already written is called a postdraft outline. (Note that some incorrectly call this reverse outlining, which is a different technique, according to Crabbs, Allan, and Crabbs [1985].) Any time you feel like you're beginning to lose control of the article is a good time to make a postdraft outline. Many of us discover through this exercise that the article isn't doing what we thought it was doing. Outlining it can then help us feel calmer, more certain about the way forward. This week, you'll be required to outline a published article and your own. Many novice authors have found making a postdraft outline to be the most useful exercise in the whole workbook, so don't skip it.

Most of us learned the traditional method of outlining, which is linear, using numbers and letters to indicate primary and secondary ideas, and often including subheadings and parts of topic sentences, as demonstrated in the outlines of the SciQua and HumInt macrostructures given earlier. The traditional method works great for many people, but if you feel like it's boxing you in, you can use one of the methods that follow for either your pre- or your postdraft outlining.

Map outline. If you're visually oriented, you might want to draw a map of your article. You can use words or symbols to represent the article's ideas and their relationships to one another. This process can help you identify your topic or narrow it, especially if you feel like language sometimes confines you. A map outline can be more flexible, as it enables you to see in more directions and notice omitted material. Its drawback is that it doesn't always make clear any breaks in structure or logical progression.

Flowchart outline. If you're visually oriented, a flowchart may work better than a map, as it forces you to indicate relationships between all items with arrows and hierarchy. Argument-mapping software often aids in making flowchart outlines. Some use different shapes for different elements of the chart, such as circles for evidence and triangles for argument.

Storyboard outline. If you're visually oriented, another technique, one used in producing movies and television programs, is a storyboard, which resembles a cartoon panel. If your journal article is describing objects or telling a story, you may find it helpful to sketch key moments in your article, including captions and imagined reader responses.

Make-it-social outline. Narrate the story of your article to someone else. For instance, "I start here, I go there, and I'm a little confused on where I go next. I need to get there." See whether articulating your postdraft outline aloud gives you clarity.

Herrera Motivation Outline. The popular-performance scholar Brian Herrera proposes what he calls a Motivation Outline. Inspired by Konstantin Stanislavski's system for training actors, which requires actors to think deeply about what motivates the character they are portraying, Herrera's outline method tracks the author's own motivations in writing. Herrera told me that focusing exclusively on the reader's motivations for reading doesn't help him structure his articles. Rather, he also needs to articulate his own motivations, in part because he can't always state them directly in the article, for the sake of politeness (e.g., "This critic is doing active harm in the world with this theory and needs to be stopped"). So his outline has two columns. In the left column is a traditional outline; in the right column he lists his motivations, or what he calls "big ideas," for each section of the article. In the workshop where he presented this outlining method, authors who perceived academic readers as different from themselves—as largely white, straight, and male US readers—found that this dual way of thinking about both the readers' and the author's motivations was incredibly useful. They believed that it would help them avoid losing themselves in the demands of their profession.

As an example, below is a postdraft Motivation Outline Herrera produced for an article he published after attending many college performances of the Latinx drama *In the Heights* (Herrera 2017). I added the material in brackets to indicate the number of paragraphs in that section of the article.

Brian Herrera's Motivation Outline
for "'But Do We Have the Actors for That?': Some Principles of Practice for Staging Latinx Plays in a University Theatre Context" (Herrera 2017)

Opening: [7 paragraphs] Provocation [3] Lit Review [2] Guidepost/Thesis [2]	Motivation/Big Idea: Must think through these enduring questions about staging in emphatically different ways
Method: [8 paragraphs] What I did When I did it Where I did it How I did it Why I did it	Motivation/Big Idea: University theater departments' largely unacknowledged and paradoxical status as simultaneously professional and amateur
Material: [7 paragraphs] Why *In the Heights* is so well suited for this experiment	Motivation/Big Idea: Uninterrogated presumptions underlying the tradition of pan-Latinx casting often collapses in the university context
Proposal—3 principles of staging practice [12 paragraphs] First proposed principle (short) [3] Second proposed principle (medium length) [3] Third proposed principle (longest, most complex) [6]	Motivation/Big Idea: Clear leadership is required to create and maximize opportunity for all
Closing: [3 paragraphs] Reflective summary of Big Ideas/ Motivations	Motivation/Big Idea: College theater can be a transformative site for diversity in theater if leaders embrace opportunity

Klima Question Outline. On his website, the academic writing coach Alan Klima proposes what he calls a Question Outline method (Klima 2016). Unlike a conventional outline, which is organized around statements and information, the Question Outline includes only questions. Klima points out that readers read an article to find answers to questions, so organizing your outline around questions keeps you focused on the readers. Also, asking questions helps you think more clearly about the logical order of your ideas. That is, if you ask a question and answer it, then you must ask what question follows from that answer. So instead of writing your outline with items like "1A. Definition of *branding*," you would write, "1A. What is your definition of *branding*?" Watch Klima's video about this method to learn his advice about which types of questions work best; for instance, he recommends that you not ask "how" questions but instead ask "in what ways" questions.

> Which of these outlining techniques speak to me? Which one will I try this week?

REVISING YOUR STRUCTURE

Day 1 Tasks: Reading the Workbook

On the first day of your ninth writing week, read this week 9 chapter all the way through the next paragraph, answering all the questions posed. Write directly in the boxes provided or in your own document.

Tracking Writing Time

Each day, use the Calendar for Actual Time Spent Writing This Week form (or digital time-tracking software) to keep track of the time you spent writing this week. Then, at the end of the week, evaluate how you spent your time.

If busy, at least mark the check boxes with how long you wrote today. ☐ 15+ min. ☐ 30+ ☐ 60+ ☐ 120+

WEEK 9, DAYS 2-5: READING AND TASKS

Day 2 Tasks: Outlining Someone Else's Published Article

Today you'll outline a good published article as a step toward outlining your own. Select an article you admire that was published in the last year (perhaps the good article you examined in week 3), one that does well what you want to do in your article.

Then, using one of the techniques from the "Types of Pre- and Postdraft Outlining" section above, outline that article in no more than one page. On the outline, next to each bullet point, subheading, or image, note how many paragraphs, pages, and/or words are in each section. Are there parts in that other person's article that surprised you by being shorter or longer than you thought they would be? Does the article use subheadings? Does it use charts, tables, or other illustrations? Where are they, and how long? Study when the argument appears. How early is it? Calculate how many citations the article has. Are there more or fewer citations than you thought there would be? In general, what are the implications of this article as a model for yours? Note that the article may do some things well and other things badly, and that's okay—study it all. Identifying what you don't want to do is also helpful.

If interested, outline other articles in your field, perhaps going back to articles you already read in previous weeks. If you do enough of these exercises, you'll begin to see what is typical in your discipline or field, which will help you immensely when writing.

Tracking Writing Time

Mark your electronic calendar, the Calendar for Actual Time Spent Writing This Week form, and/or the check boxes here with how long you wrote today. ☐ 15+ min. ☐ 30+ ☐ 60+ ☐ 120+

Day 3 Tasks: Making a Postdraft Outline of Your Article

Today you'll create a postdraft outline of your article as it stands; then you'll study its structure. This will help you determine whether your article is coherent and cohesive. If it isn't, then you'll create a new outline of the structure of your article as you would like it to be. This process has four steps, using a printout or other locked form of your article.

1. Highlight Your Article's Current Structure

A couple of weeks ago, you went through your article, highlighting your evidence in green and your interpretation in blue. This week, you'll go through your article highlighting structure and terms.

Structure. Every time you find structure signals, such as summing-up sentences or subheadings, highlight them in PURPLE.

Subject terms. Then, every time you find your key terms and subject of study, highlight them in GREEN. Thus, if your article is an argument that the plant-based paints used in some well-known Byzantine religious icons suggest that these works date to the seventh century, earlier than previously thought, then the words *paint*, *icon*, *seventh century*, and perhaps *plant* should be appearing regularly and together, not just one per paragraph.

Argument. Every time you find statements of the argument, highlight them in BLUE. It's okay if you highlight argument hints and subarguments.

2. Analyze the Article's Current Structure

Now, flip through the print version of the article, or change your screen view to 50 percent so that you can see the entire page at one time, to answer the following questions:

Purple: Structure

Does my article use (enough) subheadings? As mentioned, subheadings help you as the author as well as your readers. Subheadings should consist of informative words, but even three asterisks standing alone between sections help signal a new section to the reader. Many word-processing programs, including Microsoft Word and Scrivener, now boost the effect of subheadings by providing authors with ways to see them in a sidebar onscreen, helping writers keep their whole work in mind. (If you use Microsoft Word, always use the Styles feature to code heads so that they'll appear in the navigation sidebar.) Check to ensure that you have subheadings at least every five to seven pages or more frequently, depending on standards in your field or discipline.

> Could my article use more subheadings? If so, mark where.   ☐ No   ☐ I'm not sure   ◯ Yes (to do)

Does my article have a synopsis? If you're using the SciQua macrostructure discussed earlier, you don't need a synopsis of your article. If you're using the HumInt macrostructure, consider including a short one at the end of the introduction.

> Could my article use a synopsis? If so, mark where.   ☐ No   ☐ I'm not sure   ◯ Yes (to do)

Does my article use (enough) summing up? As mentioned, summing up aids the reader. Good summing up at the ends of sections and even some paragraphs moves the article forward by articulating your argument and providing strong links between what has been said and what will be said. Note that *summary* and *summing up* aren't the same thing. An example of a *summary* is, "I covered *x*, *y*, and *z* in the last section and will now move to consider *a*, *b*, and *c*." An example of *summing up* is, "In other words, while we cannot claim that *x* causes *y*, because the evidence simply doesn't support it, we can say that *x* and *y* are correlated in an intriguing way. The meaning of that correlation is what I turn to next." Check your article to ensure that purple summings-up are appearing regularly at the ends of sections. If they're missing, write a note about what summing up there would look like.

> Could my article use more summing up? If so, mark where.   ☐ No ☐ I'm not sure ◯ Yes (to do)

Are my article sections about the right length? One trick to keep any one section from being too long is to calculate the number of pages you have for each section, using your subheadings. If your HumInt article is twenty-four pages long, that means you have one or two pages available for your introduction, one or two pages for your conclusion, one or two pages for a background section (if you have one), and four or five pages for each of your four sections (or eight pages for each of your two sections, etc.). If your SciQua article is twenty-four pages long, you have one or two pages available for your introduction, one to three pages for your Methods, four to seven pages for your Results, and ten to fifteen pages for your Discussion. Of course, your article doesn't have to be exactly even, but if your Methods section is ten pages and your Discussion is two pages, you have a structural problem.

> How long are my sections? Does their page length suggest that some are too long or too short?   ☐ No ☐ I'm not sure ◯ Yes (to do)

Green: Subject Terms

Do my subject terms appear regularly? If important subject terms are disappearing for pages at a time, you have a structure problem. So for instance, if your article is a gender analysis of credit card use, *gender* and *credit card* should be appearing in nearly every paragraph. Also, "the repeating of key or thesis concepts is especially helpful at points of transition from one section to another, to show how the new section fits in" (Harvey 2009, 1). Do you rightly see green subject terms appearing in every section, especially at the end? Or, do you go many paragraphs without those green terms appearing?

> Could my article use more appearances of my key terms? If so, mark where.   ☐ No ☐ I'm not sure ◯ Yes (to do)

Does my article digress? Everyone knows that they shouldn't digress, but not everyone is ruthless about identifying what is relevant and what isn't. For instance, an article about drug use among homeless teenagers should not have long passages about teen pregnancy. Teen pregnancy is related indirectly, not directly. If a paragraph has no green terms, maybe it's a digression you should cut. One easy check is to ask yourself whether you could drop that paragraph wholesale without disrupting the argument or creating a visible absence in the text. If so, you should probably drop it.

| Does the lack of green terms in any paragraph suggest that I should cut it? | ☐ No ☐ I'm not sure ◯ Yes (to do) |

Blue: Argument

Is my argument appearing regularly? Unlike a book or chapter, you must carefully organize your article around a single significant idea, your argument. You worked on this before, in week 2, but it's time to look at argument again, now that you've worked on the evidence. Many problems with structure arise from the author's failure to relate the specific, usually evidence, to the general, usually the theory or argument. Make sure each section and paragraph relates to your single significant idea. Now, check everywhere you highlighted your article in blue (argument). Do you see blue in the introduction and not after? Does the argument fall out of the entire middle of your article? We should get a sense of your argument in the title, see it clearly in the abstract, again in the introduction, at least once in each section of the article, and clearly in the conclusion. If you can do this organically, simply by logical flow, great. If not, feel free to provide signposting.

| Is my argument appearing regularly? If not, mark where it should. | ☐ No ☐ I'm not sure ◯ Yes (to do) |

Other Structure Issues

Does my article wrongly have a discovery structure? It's perfectly acceptable to mention in your article the origins of your idea or how you came to notice something elusive, that is, to provide a narrative of the discovery process. What isn't acceptable is to structure your article according to that process. Only rarely will an article structured by the order in which you discovered the evidence provide a strong and satisfying structure. (An order derived from the order in which you retrieved evidence from memory is unlikely to work well either.) Organize your notes, evidence, and article by theme and topic instead. Elements learned during the discovery process should emerge in the article, but rarely in the order in which you discovered them. Check the order of sections and evidence in your article, ensuring that they are organized by your ideas about them, not your discovery of them. Remember, write like a lawyer, not like a detective.

| Should my article use less discovery-process structure? If so, how might it be differently structured? | ☐ No ☐ I'm not sure ◯ Yes (to do) |

Does my article wrongly have a mystery novel structure? As mentioned earlier, don't withhold the purpose, import, or conclusions until the end of the article. Nothing is more likely to help you structure your article properly than to avoid mystery. If you're committed to the mystery structure, much like the synaptic structure, remember that the best mysteries give many clues, so that the revelation isn't a true surprise. Check your last section and conclusion to ensure that you aren't withholding information the readers needed earlier.

| Should my article use less mystery novel structure? If so, what should I move up? | ☐ No   ☐ I'm not sure   ○ Yes (to do) |

Does my article repeat itself? When you outline your article as a whole, you often find that you repeat the same information in different places. Reading your article in one sitting helps you detect such repetition, even if it's widely spaced in the article.

| Do some paragraphs repeat information that appeared earlier? If so, where will I cut that repetition? | ☐ No   ☐ I'm not sure   ○ Yes (to do) |

Does my article ask questions it does not answer? Do a search for every question mark in your article. Especially note anywhere you have a series of questions together. Are they on point? Do you answer them? If you pose questions, be sure to track through the article whether you address and answer them.

| Do I answer the questions posed? If not, should I delete them or add answers? | ☐ No   ☐ I'm not sure   ○ Yes (to do) |

Does material from one section creep into another section? In a SciQua article, methods, results, and discussion should be quite separate. Methods shouldn't wander into the Results section; discussion shouldn't wander into the Results section. Check your article to ensure that this creep hasn't happened.

| Are my Methods, Results, and Discussion sections suitably separate? If not, what should be moved? | ☐ No   ☐ I'm not sure   ○ Yes (to do) |

3. Outline Your Article's Current Structure

Using the instructions for outlining given on day 1 this week, create an outline of your article as it stands. If you find the task of outlining tough, it may be because your article lacks a strong enough structure. Poorly constructed paragraphs with discordant ideas are difficult to outline. If you're tempted to stop outlining the current structure and start drafting your article's future structure, resist. Instead, complete both tasks. It's essential that you outline the whole article as it stands, not just through the part where you decide you don't like the current structure.

4. Outline a New Structure for Your Article

If you found your structure to be solid, you can skip this step. But if you found structure problems, start a new outline of your article, creating the structure you'd like the article to have. Indicate where you would add summing up, subtract digressions, or move statements of your argument to a more prominent position. You can use the outline of the published article you made earlier this week to aid in your restructuring.

Tracking Writing Time

Mark your electronic calendar, the Calendar for Actual Time Spent Writing This Week form, and/or the check boxes here with how long you wrote today. ☐ 15+ min. ☐ 30+ ☐ 60+ ☐ 120+

Days 4–5 Tasks: Restructuring Your Article

Today and tomorrow, you will start correcting any structural problems you found and, if necessary, restructuring your article around that new outline.

This task of restructuring poses several challenges, as noted by Rachel Cawley, a writing expert who also recommends outlining drafts in her blog *Explorations of Style*. In her instructions, she acknowledges that the process of restructuring is often "scary," as authors fear that they "might take away existing coherence and flow without being able to replace it with something better." Indeed, if you just move the paragraphs around without revising them, you'll find that your article will "bear too many traces of its earlier self" (Cawley 2011). But if you follow your plan, and carefully review the new draft for cohesion, editing where necessary for logical flow, you'll witness the article coming together in a much stronger way. Even after all these years of writing, I still end up regularly restructuring my prose. While I'm in the middle of that restructuring, I always feel profound doubt; but when I'm done, I'm glad I did it. A couple of times I decided that something about the original order was better, but the solution to its problems became clear only through the restructuring, so I'm still glad to have done all that work.

Once finished, you may find it helpful to return to the questions I asked you to answer without reading your article in the sections "Article-Structuring Principles" and "Types of Journal Article Macrostructures." Check whether you have now solved those problems.

Checking Progress

If you have a little extra time, you have three tasks you could consider. First, this might be a good moment to make a list of remaining tasks, taking stock of where you are in the process of revising the article and what tasks remain. Second, if you haven't sent out your query letter yet (see the advice in week 4), now is a good week to do so. Third, in week 6, you had a chance to exchange your article with someone else. If you didn't feel ready then, this is an excellent week to get others' responses to your article. If you still have doubts about your article's worth or the time you're spending on it, sharing it with someone can reinvigorate your commitment to it. If you do have an exchange, use the instructions in week 6 for giving and getting feedback.

Tracking Writing Time

Mark your electronic calendar, the Calendar for Actual Time Spent Writing This Week form, and/or the check boxes here with how long you wrote both days. ☐ 15+ min. ☐ 30+ ☐ 60+ ☐ 120+

Then, here at the end of your workweek, take pride in your accomplishments and evaluate whether any patterns need changing.

DOCUMENTING YOUR WRITING TIME AND TASKS

Calendar for Actual Time Spent Writing This Week

Time	Day 1	Day 2	Day 3	Day 4	Day 5	Day 6	Day 7
5:00 a.m.							
6:00							
7:00							
8:00							
9:00							
10:00							
11:00							
12:00 p.m.							
1:00							
2:00							
3:00							
4:00							
5:00							
6:00							
7:00							
8:00							
9:00							
10:00							
11:00							
12:00 a.m.							
1:00							
2:00							
3:00							
4:00							
Total minutes							
Tasks completed							

WEEK 10
Opening and Concluding Your Article

Task Day	Week 10 Daily Writing Tasks	Estimated Task Time in Minutes	
		HumInt	SciQua
Day 1 (Monday?)	Read from here until you reach the week 10, day 2 tasks, filling in any boxes, checking off any forms, and answering any questions as you read. Revise your title.	90	60
Day 2 (Tuesday?)	Mold your introduction.	120+	60
Day 3 (Wednesday?)	Mold your introduction and choose your name.	150+	90
Day 4 (Thursday?)	Revisit your abstract and author order.	60	90
Day 5 (Friday?)	Construct your conclusion.	60	60
Total estimated time for reading the workbook, completing the tasks, and writing your article		**8+ hours**	**6+ hours**

Above are the tasks for your tenth week. Start this week by scheduling when you will write, and then tracking the time you actually spend writing (using the Calendar for Actual Time Spent Writing This Week form or online software).

This week, for the first time, you will work on your title, which includes the most important words in your entire article. If possible, gather two or three academics together to workshop your title and theirs so that everyone benefits.

This week may take less time than allotted, because an opening consists of what you've already worked on in previous weeks: stating the argument (week 2), writing the abstract (week 3), considering the journal (week 4), articulating the entry point (week 5), and claiming significance (week 6). However, finalizing all these moving parts into a convincing introduction and elegant conclusion may take more time, as finalizing them sometimes results in changes to the body of the article.

NINTH WEEK IN REVIEW

You have now spent nine weeks working on your article. You have sharpened your argument and structured your article around your argument, analyzed and presented your evidence, and are now nearing the finish line. Congratulations! Just be careful. Sometimes, the closer we get to sending our articles to a journal, the more issues with our articles we dream up. Remember that sending is not the last step in the article-writing process—you'll have a chance to improve it when it comes back from peer review. So don't fixate on perfection now. Focus instead on a final few strengthening exercises.

ON THE IMPORTANCE OF OPENINGS

First impressions are vital. We live each day confronted by a barrage of media in which loud, bright, sexy, or violent images work constantly to capture our attention as consumers. Sophisticated delivery systems, which depend on consumers' ever more refined ability to read content in fractions of a second, remain the context of our writing. The expectation created by tweets, text messages, search results, and banner advertisements is that meaning can be communicated with tremendous brevity. Although the journal article is not competing with infomercials or reality television for attention, the dense commercial context of the United States does shape readers' expectations. However quiet and unassuming, the twenty-first-century journal article is under pressure to prove its value quickly. And not just once, but twice—to reviewers and to readers.

Prepublication reviewers. To get published, your article must prove its value to editors and peer reviewers at the journal you've selected. Busy scholars can find an article frustrating if it fails to communicate its worth up front. If the worth of your article becomes apparent only on page 5, or page 25, it will fare poorly with editors or peer reviewers. Indeed, how little of your article is read before a decision is made can be shocking. As one observer put it, "Many years ago, I observed a referee, under pressure, open a manuscript, glance at it for a few seconds, and reject it out of hand" (Hauptman 2011, 12).

So here's the terrible news: most people will never read your entire article. Analysis of journal publishers' log files reveals that scholars spend very little time reading published articles online: session times are short, and they look at an average of one to three pages. Some scholars download articles for future reading, but admit that they read no more than half the articles they download. Around 40 percent admit to not reading all of the last "important" article they read (Nicholas and Clark 2012, 93). This might be a product of our multitasking age, but it's more likely that better analytical tools have revealed what has always been the case: scholars tend to read in snippets and to skim (Ware and Mabe 2015, 52–53).

So when reviewers get your article, the first thing they do is skim it in order to decide whether to read it now or set it aside for later. When the article's value is immediately clear, this is a big incentive to reviewers, who now anticipate that the review process will be uncomplicated and that their labor will result in a published article. If the article's value is unclear, this is a big disincentive for reviewers, who now anticipate that the review process is going to be arduous and a waste of their valuable time, in that they will be doing the author's work for the author. So clearly stating your project, argument, approach, sources, contribution, and relevance in the first two or three pages will dramatically aid your chances with peer reviewers. As the writing advisor Matt Might tweeted on July 12, 2015, your "abstract, intro and conclusion are 80% of your paper from the perspective of a referee."

Postpublication readers. To get cited, your article must gain the notice of readers. Any article you publish is competing for scholars' attention with the multitude of other academic articles published in each field every year. With about two million articles published annually, according to Scopus, skimming has become a way of life. Busy scholars conducting research read past the first page only if the value of the article has made itself apparent. And unfortunately, only two things establish an article's value quickly: the reputation of its author(s) and its opening (i.e., the title, abstract, and introduction). Since none of us are famous (yet!), we must focus on the openings of our articles, because articles with strong titles, solid abstracts, and compelling introductions are more likely to be accepted for publication, more likely to be read, and more likely to be cited.

Most of us need no convincing that starting strong is smart. The only question is, how is that accomplished? How do authors quickly establish the value of their article? The following pages give the main ingredients for starting and ending strong. You can certainly cook without some of these ingredients, but you'll have a poor concoction if you use none of them.

Fashioning Your Title

Your title is the highway billboard of your article, the only part of it most scholars will ever read, and even that only briefly as they whip by on their way to other destinations. Indeed, your title—including your subtitle—will be read more than your article by a factor of at least one thousand to one, more likely ten thousand to one, because it lives an independent life on your curriculum vitae and department websites as well as in electronic databases, others' bibliographies, and tables of contents. Like an advertisement, your title will most frequently appear without its product, without any supporting material. Editors often send potential peer reviewers only the title of an article when asking them to review. In such cases, peer reviewers decide whether to review your article based on the title's descriptive strength alone.

As a result, the title of your journal article must be the most carefully crafted part of the article. It must serve as an announcement that draws readers to your work and invites them into a particular conversation. It must clearly describe your article and communicate your article's topic. It must assist scholars using online search engines in finding your work easily by employing common keywords. If possible, it should suggest your argument and hint at policy implications. It must avoid creative or allusive phrases if they're distracting or unclear.

Fascinating research has been conducted on titles, including which aspects of titles correlate with the frequency with which their articles are cited. First, longer titles are cited more often in many disciplines (Jacques and Sebire 2010, 2–3; van Wesel, Wyatt, and ten Haaf 2014, 1606; Habibzadeh and Yadollahie 2010, 167). Although some studies have found "a small negative effect" for longer titles in the pure sciences (van Wesel, Wyatt, and ten Haaf 2014, 1602, 1606, other studies have found short titles to be not as "rich in content" (Kerans, Murray, and Sabatè 2016, 18). Titles of medical articles have an average of fifteen words, which probably holds for many disciplines (17). Owing to the research, I advise you to use longer titles, as they give more opportunities for searchable keywords. Second, titles that contain a colon are more likely to be cited in most disciplines (Jacques and Sebire 2010, 2; Buter and van Raan 2011, 611; van Wesel, Wyatt, and ten Haaf 2014, 1611). Third, titles that contain question marks had poorer citation rates (Paiva, Lima, and Paiva 2012, 512). Finally, "articles with results-describing titles were cited more often than those with methods-describing titles" (512).

Keeping all that in mind, use the advice that follows about key terms, coherence, and argument to consider whether your current title could be improved. To aid you in seeing more easily the changes in the examples—from the draft titles to the revised titles—I highlighted with underscore the most important additions and changes in revised titles.

Start by writing your current title (or different versions of it) below.

My current title:

Get Your Title Terms Right

Avoid broad titles that would better serve entire books or series. It's always tempting to suggest the importance of your article by giving it an all-encompassing title. But you only annoy your readers if the article's title doesn't match the article's content. It's no fun to track down "Twentieth-Century American Cultural Dynamics," only to find that the author should have titled the article "Inventing Northern California Counterculture in 1968." While you don't want your title to suggest that your article is narrower in scope than it is, you also don't want to overpromise. One possible sign of an overly broad title is one that's short, under seven words. Here are examples of titles that authors revised to make them specific.

Humint Titles

Original: The Mystery of the Missing Letters
Revision (<u>underscore</u> **signals vital revisions**): Forging the <u>Armenian</u> Past: Questionable <u>Translations</u> of Abstract <u>Expressionist</u> Arshile <u>Gorky's</u> Missing Letters (Abbamontian 2003) [*The new title specified nation, topic, discipline, and artist subject.*]

Original: Constructing West Hollywood
Revision: Performing an Un-<u>Queer</u> City: West Hollywood's <u>Image Marketing Campaign</u> in the <u>1980s</u> [*specified the method, discipline, and period*]

Sciqua Titles

Original: The Challenges of Housing the Poor
Revision: <u>Mitigating Apprehension</u> about <u>Section 8 Vouchers</u>: The <u>Positive Role</u> of <u>Housing Specialists</u> in <u>Search and Placement</u> (Marr 2005) [*specified the subject, population studied, method, and argument*]

Original: Tradition and the Spread of AIDS

Revision: <u>Risky</u> Traditional <u>Practices</u> associated with the Spread of HIV/AIDS among <u>Pregnant Women</u> in <u>Malawi</u> (based on the work of Lily Kumbani) [*specified the subject, population studied, nation, and argument*]

If you're worried that using specifics will reduce citations, study examples of highly cited articles that use specifics in combination with broader terms. The following is a title that communicates both its localized context and its wider implications:

Published: Green Violence: Rhino Poaching and the War to Save Southern Africa's Peace Parks (Büscher and Ramutsindela 2015)

> Is my title too broad? If so, what specifics might I add to correct that problem?

Avoid strings of vague abstractions. First drafts of titles often start with three or four abstractions strung together to signal the broad import of the article. No article is going to measure up to such immense concepts, however, so it's better to pare them down. Not only are they unsearchable, but they also mean more to you than the average reader will understand on a quick read anyway.

Humint Titles

Original: Revolution, Change, and Transition: Television in the Twenty-First Century

Revision: <u>Primetime</u> Television Challenges to the <u>Movie Industry</u>: The Rise of <u>Reality Programming</u> in the <u>2000s</u>

Original: Gender, Women, and Twitter

Revision: <u>Girl Code: Performing</u> Gender in Women's Twitter <u>Profiles</u>

Sciqua Titles

Original: Booms, Busts, Prices, and Rates: Predicting the Dynamics of Housing Markets

Revision: <u>The Predictive Role of Interest Rates in the Cyclical</u> Dynamic of Housing Markets

Original: The Politics of Space: Environment and Conflict in Nigeria

Revision: The Consequences for <u>Civil Society</u> of Struggles over <u>Natural Resources</u>: Lessons from the <u>Oil</u>-Rich <u>Niger Delta</u> of Nigeria

The point here is to avoid vague abstractions. But strings of specific *variables* can work well, as in this review of the literature on psychological adjustment:

Published: Mothers, Fathers, Families, and Circumstances: Factors Affecting Children's Adjustment (Lamb 2012).

> Do I use too many vague abstractions in my title? If so, which can I take out?

Name your subjects. It's odd how many times quite specific articles have titles that don't name those specifics. If your article is about a particular author or text, name that author or text in the title. If it's about a city, region, or country, name that geography. If it's about a population—women, Latinos, students—name the group. If it's about particular variables, think about naming them. It may seem obvious to you, but nothing is obvious to a search engine. Now, some research shows that articles with nations or regions in their title are cited less (Jacques and Sebire 2010), but I think that's because the content is narrower, not the title. (We need a more focused study to find out, one that identifies whether articles about specific nations that mention those nations in their title are cited more often than articles about those nations that don't.) Below are some novice authors' revisions to titles.

Humint Titles

Original: Reinterpreting the Cidian Cycle
Revision: <u>Gendering</u> the <u>Spanish</u> Cidian Cycle: <u>Nineteenth-Century British</u> Writer <u>Felicia Hemans's</u> *The* Siege *of Valencia* [*specified approach, nation, period, author subject*]

Original: The Electoral Ethnic Bandwagon in New Democracies
Revision: <u>Getting on</u> the Ethnic Bandwagon in New Democracies: Electoral Relationships between <u>Political Elites</u> and <u>Voters of Their Ethnicity</u> [*specified populations studied*]

Sciqua Titles

Original: Socially Organized Initiations, Responses, and Evaluations in a Classroom
Revision: Socially Organized <u>Questions</u> and <u>Answers</u>: <u>Student-Teacher Interaction</u> in an <u>Elementary</u> School Science Classroom [*specified approach, populations studied, and site*]

Original: Effect of Social Support on Pain and Depression
Revision: Effect of Social Support on Pain and Depression among <u>Rheumatoid Arthritis Patients in the United States</u> [*specified population studied, disease subject, and site*]

Original: Khartoum Urban Violence: Can It Happen Again?
Revision: The Role of <u>Wealth Distribution, Social Inequality, and Ethnicity</u> in Urban Group Violence in Khartoum, <u>Sudan</u> (based on the work of Idris Salim ElHassan) [*specified variables, nation*]

> What are my subjects? Have I named them in the title? If not, what might I add?

Embed your title with searchable keywords. Around 60 percent of articles are found through a Google search (Ware and Mabe 2015, 53). So because most articles read or cited were found through an online search, keywords are essential to your title. You may have added keywords above, in naming your subjects; but you also need to ensure that those keywords are searchable. Here are some principles for creating searchable keywords (part of a process called "search engine optimization"). First, it sometimes pays to be slightly repetitive. Using seemingly redundant keywords like "gender" and "women" enables researchers using either word to find your article. Second, avoid using keywords that mean multiple things and return too many results. If you use the keyword "African American," scholars searching for that term will easily find your article. If you use the term "black," scholars searching for that term will get too many results, because "black" appears in many titles that have nothing to do with race (all the articles where the author is named "Black," or that mention "black box," "black bear," "black hole," and so on). Likewise, use the keyword "drama," not "play," because a search for "play" returns too many low-quality results. Third, use the most common keyword. A search on Google Scholar will help you identify which formulation is more common. For instance, the keyword "college athletes" retrieves over 39,000 results on Google Scholar, while "college student athletes" retrieves only 5,500 results. So use the former in your title. Make sure to search with both the singular and the plural versions of your keywords, as the results can differ dramatically. Perhaps even more effective is using a site like Academia.edu, which lists documents with author-provided keywords along with the number of documents with that keyword and the number of scholars following that keyword. Fourth, be specific about region, pairing cities with states, and provinces with nations. Such pairings increase scholars' chances of finding your article. So, as in the last title revision example above, include both "Khartoum" and "Sudan." Sometimes it may even be useful to include both nations and their region (e.g., "India" and "South Asia").

Let's look at some examples of how authors improved titles:

Original: Black Faculty Salary Differentials
Revision: The Black <u>Professoriate</u>: Explaining the Salary <u>Gap</u> for <u>African American Female</u> Faculty (Guillory 2001) [*specified gender, used both "black" and "African American"*]

Original: The Boundaries of Achebe's Africa
Revision: <u>Converting Chinua</u> Achebe's Africa for the New <u>Tanzanian</u>: *Things Fall Apart* in Swahili Translation (Arenberg 2015) [*specified text, used both "Tanzania" and "Swahili"*]

> What are my keywords?
> Have I given all the most
> searchable keywords
> in the title? If not, what
> should I change?

Make Your Title Coherent

Put keywords in relation. Since my advice about keywords usually results in quite long and even dense titles, make sure you put those words in relation with each other through prepositions and possessives. That is, avoid creating titles that are nothing more than strings of keywords, which make little sense to the reader. One easy way to revise a title with this problem is to rework it until it no longer has commas. Sometimes that reworking will push the title too far, and you'll need to pull some of it back; but at least some of what you do to get rid of the commas will be useful. Below are examples of revisions to titles to make them less dense and more readable.

Humint Titles

Original: Degas's Modistes, Chic Consumers, and Fashionable Commodities
Revision: Fashionable Consumption: Women <u>as</u> Consumers and Clerks <u>in</u> the French

Impressionist Painting of Degas (based on the work of Iskin 2014) [*added three prepositions, added six words, dropped three words*]

Original: John Powell, Somatic Acoustics, Racial Difference, and Symphonic Music
Revision: Unequal Temperament: The Somatic Acoustics of Racial Difference in the Symphonic Music of John Powell (Feder 2008) [*added three prepositions, added two words*]

Original: Sirak, Amharic Translation, the Postcolonial Subject, and Johnson's *Rasselas*
Revision: The Melancholy Translator: Sirak Ḥəruy's Amharic Translation of Samuel Johnson's *Rasselas* (Belcher and Bekure Herouy 2015) [*added one preposition, added five words, including one possessive, dropped two words*]

Sciqua Titles

Original: Elites and the Dinka-Mundari-Bari Conflict
Revision: The Overlooked Role of Elites in African Grassroots Conflicts: A Case Study of the Dinka-Mundari-Bari Conflict in Southern Sudan (based on the work of Paul Wani Gore) [*added four prepositions, added twelve words*]

Original: FDI, Economic Growth, Carbon Emissions
Revision: The Role of Foreign Direct Investment in Increasing Economic Growth and Lowering Carbon Emissions [*added two prepositions, added four words, including two verbal forms*]

> Is my title too dense? If so, how can I use prepositions and possessives to put my keywords in relation?

Include a verb if possible. As noted above, long titles that include only nouns and adjectives are difficult to absorb. In addition to prepositions and possessives, you can use verbs and verbal forms to put your keywords in relation and make your titles easier to read. Here are some examples of revised titles.

Humint Titles

Original: The Central American Exposition of 1897: German Popular Anthropology in the Americas
Revision: A German Scientist Visits a World's Fair: (Mis)reading Race and Science at the Central American Exposition of 1897 in Guatemala (Munro 2015a) [*added twelve words, including two verbal forms*]

Original: Resistance, Women, and the Portuguese in Seventeenth-Century Ethiopia
Revision: Sisters Debating the Jesuits: The Role of African Women in Defeating Portuguese Proto-Colonialism in Seventeenth-Century Abyssinia (Belcher 2013) [*added eleven words, including two verbal forms*]

Sciqua Titles

Original: Political Parties in Sudan: Organized Forces or Social Networks
Revision: Unstable Political Parties in Sudan: Oscillating between Traditional Social

Networks and Professional Elite Organizations (based on the work of Atta El-Battahani) [*added eight words, including one verbal form*]

One of the easiest ways to use a verb in a title is a verbal form ending in *-ing*:

Published: Recovering Performance in the Short Term after Coach Succession in Spanish Basketball Organisations (Gómez-Haro and Salmerón-Gómez 2016)

Published: Tracing the Origins of Relapse in Acute Myeloid Leukaemia to Stem Cells (Shlush et al. 2017)

Is my title too dense? If so, how can I use a verb or a verbal form to put my keywords in relation?

Don't start your title with non-English words. When I was publishing books, we published an English-language book whose title began with three words from another language. Everyone assumed that the book itself was in that non-English language, including bookstores, who constantly placed it in their foreign language section. The book never got the attention it deserved as a result. Scholars are reading quickly; if they see words that they don't understand, they move on. So place English-language words first in your title. It's totally fine, however, to use non-English terms as keywords somewhere else in the title.

Does my title start with non-English terms? If so, how can I move them to later in the title?

Avoid using your title to prove how witty or well-read you are. This rule is a matter of some debate in my workshops and does depend a bit on your field. Using quotations, puns, double entendres, or allusions in titles is a time-honored tradition in the humanities, and most editors won't stop you; but such titles must also communicate clearly if they are to serve you well in our digital age. If your title is an obscure, exclusionary in-joke not entirely related to your topic and understood by readers only after reading the whole article word for word, reconsider. If, when questioned about the title, you find yourself saying, "Get it?!" reconsider. Remember that what seems clever is often just clichéd. Search for titles riffing on Blake's quote "burning bright" or Melville's quote "call me Ishmael" to see how quickly literary gymnastics start to seem hollow. One study of literary allusions found that in biomedical articles published from 1950 to 2005, more than fourteen hundred contained allusions to Shakespeare, most of them to "What's in a name?" and "To be or not to be" (Goodman 2005, 1540–41). Also, scholars found no association between the catchiness of an article's title and the impact of that article in the discipline of psychology (Haslam 2008, 178). Now, in the disciplines of literature, some of the most cited articles have very catchy titles. But make sure that yours communicates. Failed cute titles are why some scholars mistakenly hate colons; don't hate the innocent colon just because of the sins of authors! And be sure that your clever title is not exclusionary. If your title is a play on "demolition derby," for instance, non-US readers won't get the cultural reference.

Below is an example of a title so generic, it's impossible to find electronically. But the author loved the musical pun in it (a "note" is both a musical pitch and a textual apparatus) and refused to relinquish it. The revised title would have been a wiser choice:

Published: Research Note

Proposed Revision: A Song for My Father: Honoring the Family Roots of Research

Here is an example of a title revised to remove an intriguing but unclear proverb:

Original: Money Has No Name: Unemployment, Informalization, and Gender in Accra, Ghana

Revision: When Men Do Women's Work: Structural Adjustment, Unemployment, and Changing Gender Relations in the Informal Economy of Accra, Ghana (Overå 2007)

If you remain unconvinced, and still really want to use a pun or quotation in your title, let's look at some examples that work.

In the following title, the first part is an allusion to a folktale and a metaphor for the article's argument, one that makes sense when you read the subtitle, suggesting that social media is no fail-safe protector of democracy:

Published: The Dictator's New Clothes: The Relationship between E-participation and Quality of Government in Non-democratic Regimes (Linde and Karlsson 2013)

In the next title, the quotations are two full phrases, not unreadable fragments. In addition, they directly relate to the rest of the title, so they communicate clearly:

Published: "Nowhere Has Anyone Attempted . . . in This Article I Aim to Do Just That": A Corpus-Based Study of Self-Promotional *I* and *We* in Academic Writing across Four Disciplines (Harwood 2005)

Highlighting "an inconsistency, an irony, a contradiction, or an illogicality" can be an effective technique to draw readers in (Woodside 2015, 22). Just make sure that it works for readers, not just you.

> Does my title have an unclear quote, pun, or allusion? If so, how might I revise it?

Have an Argumentative Title

Suggest your argument and/or findings if possible. To be honest, it's tough to give a sense of your argument in your article's title. That's why I left this advice to the end. But if you can, you should. Including some of your variables, some implications, or words with a negative or positive valence can also be ways of signaling your argument.

Below are examples of novice authors' revisions to good titles, made even stronger by suggesting the article's argument.

Humint Titles

> **Original:** Grave Matters: The Representation of Women in Funerary Offerings in Pre-Columbian West Mexico
>
> **Revision:** Mournful Mothers: Representing Infant Mortality in Funerary Offerings in Pre-Columbian West Mexico [*added variables and words with valence*]

Sciqua Titles

> **Original:** Thou Shalt Have Children: Families and Income in Bangladesh
>
> **Revision:** Thou Shalt Have Dependents: Fertility's Lack of Impact on Household Composition and Poverty in Bangladesh [*added variables and findings*]

Here are some much-cited articles that do a good job of suggesting the argument and findings:

> **Published:** The Negative Association between Religiousness and Children's Altruism across the World (Decety et al. 2015)

> **Published:** Improved Skeletal Muscle Mass and Strength after Heavy Strength Training in Very Old Individuals (Bechshøft et al. 2017)

> **Published:** The Brain Adapts to Dishonesty (Garrett et al. 2016)

Have I suggested my argument and/or findings in the title? If not, could I suggest it/them?

Last Few Aspects of Strong Titles

In the third paragraph of this section, I mentioned some aspects of titles that research shows correlate with citation frequency. First, long titles generally are cited more often, so your title should avoid being too short. However, there are diminishing returns after twenty-one words. Second, titles with colons generally have a higher citation rate. A colon is not a requirement for your title, but don't avoid one out of some misguided attempt to be different. Third, titles with questions generally are cited less often. If you have a question in your title, turn it into a statement of your argument. Instead of "Does *X* affect *Y*?" have "*X* Affects *Y*." Finally, does the title make sense on its own? Few titles can, but the best titles do.

Deciding on a Title

Later today, you will work on finalizing your title. But if you feel that you've already gained clarity about it, you can write it below.

My new title:

Molding Your Introduction

If you have a strong title and a solid abstract, you're off to a great start. Now turn to your article introduction, which must accomplish much in a short space. Spending time on your introduction repays your investment. Given two versions of the same article, one version with a strong introduction and the other without, readers evaluated the *entire* article more highly with the first version (Townsend et al. 1993, 674).

Research indicates that introductions have some standard features in common, called "moves" (Swales 1990; Bhatia 2013; Henry and Roseberry 1997; Kanoksilapatham 2012), and that studying them improves introductions (G. Brown and Marshall 2012). John Swales (1990) identified three moves in article introductions across disciplines, each with three steps, which he summarized in the CARS (Creating a Research Space) model. The first move is "Establishing a Territory," or the *situation*, usually by claiming that a subject of research is worthwhile and that previous research on the subject is inadequate. The second move is "Establishing a Niche," or the *problem*, usually by stating that your article fills a gap, corrects previous interpretations, or extends knowledge—that is, articulating the entry point. The third move is "Occupying the Niche," or the *solution*, usually by making an argument, announcing findings, and giving an article synopsis. Thus, the three moves of an introduction are identifying a context, a problem, and a solution.

To say this in a more familiar way, your introduction must articulate the article's entry point, argument, and claim(s) for significance, and (often) provide a synopsis. So let's get down to specifics.

What to Include in Your Introduction

Start with a gripping first sentence. A vivid first sentence gets your introduction off to a good start. Unfortunately, many journal articles do not start strong. For instance, a very typical humanities opening analyzes a quotation by someone else, which I have yet to find compelling. Others start with a series of unanswered questions, which I find frustrating. I have enough unanswered questions of my own! Of course, this is my taste, so when you read articles, identify what you find compelling in others' writing so you can construct compelling first sentences yourself.

You can strengthen your introduction by starting with a telling anecdote, a striking depiction of your subject, an aggressive summary of the literature, a dire social problem, an intriguing thought puzzle, or a solid claim about the significance of your topic. Below are some strong first sentences of published articles, demonstrating the variations possible.

Subject opening. Since the identification of the Zika virus in Brazil in early 2015, the virus has spread rapidly throughout the Americas.

> (Rasmussen et al. 2016) (For an article about the relationship between the virus and birth defects)

Anecdotal opening. When I was growing up in New York City, my parents used to take me to an event in Inwood Park at which Indians—real American Indians dressed in feathers and blankets—could be seen and touched by children like me. This event was always a disappointment.

> (Tompkins 1986) (For an article analyzing US textbooks' presentation of indigenous peoples' role in US history)

Critical opening. Historians have been much more concerned with explaining questions surrounding how Africans produced, transported, and sold captives than with exploring African strategies against the slave trade.

> (Diouf 2003) (For an article about Guinea Bissauans' strategies for resisting the slave trade)

Significance opening. Few children's movies can rival the success of *The Lion King* or the controversy that has surrounded it since it was first shown commercially in 1994. (Martin-Rodriguez 2000) (For an article about Latina/o immigration to the United States as the anxious subtext of a Disney film)

Historical opening. In the 1970s and 1980s, amid concerns over the negative effects of concentrated urban poverty and suburban resistance to the encroachment of public housing, the U.S. Department of Housing and Urban Development (HUD) slowed the construction of new large-scale public housing projects and increased the use of Section 8 certificates and vouchers to subsidize low-income households in the private rental market.

> (Marr 2005) (For an article about tactics that community workers used to help low-income families gain housing when landlords were suspicious of Section 8 vouchers)

Argumentative opening. Civic education is important.

> (Blair 2003) (For an article arguing that civic education is essential to a functioning democracy)

> Could the introduction's first sentence be more gripping? If so, how could I accomplish that?

Give basic information about your subject. As is the case with titles, introductions frequently don't introduce the subject properly. If you haven't given the who, what, why, where, and how of your topic, you haven't introduced it. Keep in mind two truths. When you're writing for publication, you're usually writing for people who know less than you do about the topic. And they may be reading your article long after you wrote it or in a different context. For example, what came to US readers' minds when they read the word *Harvey* in 2018 was very different from what came to their mind when reading it in 2017. So explain with a sentence such as "Harvey, the Atlantic hurricane of 2017 that caused seventy deaths and over $100 billion in property damage, was the wettest in US history." If you're discussing an event, give the dates; a place, give its geopolitical context; a new term, define it; a noncanonical text, give the author, date of publication, a summary, and its claim to importance.

Basic information doesn't have to be given in full sentences or long paragraphs. It can often be given quite quickly, in clauses. Indeed, when introducing case studies for which you have hundreds of pages of detail, you need to avoid giving too much information. Below are some examples of briefly giving basic information in published articles.

Text information. Among Europe's experimental films from the 1920s and 30s, perhaps none offers a more fascinating conjunction of psychoanalysis and representations of race than *Borderline*, the expressionist, interracial melodrama produced by the POOL group and directed by Kenneth Macpherson. (Walton 1997)

Movement information. The New Journalism—that genre-blurred mélange of ethnography, investigative reportage, and fiction—is widely and rightly considered to be *the* characteristic genre of the sixties. (Staub 1997)

Theory information. I focus here on Herman Witkin... the first researcher to extend the study of psychological sex differences into the area of human perception. (Haaken 1988)

Term information. In this article, prosody refers collectively to variations in pitch, tempo, and rhythm. (Hardison 2004)

In the introduction, do I give basic information about my subject? What else is needed?

State your entry point (i.e., identify your position vis-à-vis the previous research). As discussed in week 5, your research must be demonstrably related to what has been written previously in the related literature. An important part of an introduction is announcing how your argument relates to previous arguments about your topic. In some introductions, a full review of the related literature also appears. Below is an example of the statement of an entry point in an introduction:

Example of entry point: People with more friends and more social ties in their community tend to live longer. Many researchers interpret this association as evidence that greater social support and social network integration lead to better health outcomes. For example, social integration is thought to improve health by motivating engagement in healthy behaviors, improving immunity, and reducing inflammation. However, nearly all of this work has been conducted in the context of real-world, face-to-face social interactions. As more and more people use online social media to maintain friendships (as of June 2016, about 1.1 billion people use Facebook daily), an open question is whether or not this new context can be used to measure real world social activity and, distinctly, whether online social interactions are similarly associated with better health and increased human longevity. (Hobbs et al. 2016)

Do I state my entry point in the introduction? If not, where can I do that?

State your argument and, if possible, your findings. An article introduction is not an introduction until it clearly states your single significant idea (what I am calling the argument). See week 2 of this workbook for information about crafting an argument and stating it concisely. Note how the published introduction below weaves the argument together with claims for significance, basic information, and findings.

Example of argument and findings: Driven by technological progress, human life expectancy has increased greatly since the nineteenth century. Demographic evidence has revealed an ongoing reduction in old-age mortality and a rise of the maximum age at death, which may gradually extend human longevity. Together with observations that lifespan in various animal species is flexible and can be increased by genetic or pharmaceutical intervention, these results have led to suggestions that longevity may not be subject to strict, species-specific genetic constraints. Here, by analysing global demographic data, we show that improvements in survival with age tend to decline after age 100, and that the age at death of the world's oldest person has not increased since the 1990s. Our results strongly suggest that the maximum lifespan of humans is fixed and subject to natural constraints. (Dong, Milholland, and Vijg 2016)

Do I state my argument clearly in the introduction? If not, where can I add it?

Articulate the significance of your subject. Make sure that your readers know the importance of the person, text, group, question, or problem you have taken as your subject. Don't assume that they know why your subject is important or how important it is. Even if the readers do know the significance, one aspect of pulling them into reading your article is your stating the case in a particularly clear or powerful way. This is part of how you demonstrate your authority to speak on the topic and what the reader will gain from reading your article. In the opening sentences of the published articles excerpted below, the authors effectively claim the significance of their topic by establishing the tremendous impact of their subjects or the events associated with them. In this way, they also quickly contextualize their subjects, painting the larger picture that makes their question and argument important.

Example of significance: The terrorist attacks of September 11, 2001, on New York City (NYC) were the largest human-made intentional disaster in U.S. history. The sheer scope of the attacks, the level of property destruction, the financial repercussions, and the continuing level of anxiety suggested that these attacks might have mental health consequences both for direct victims of the attacks and for the population at large. (Fairbrother et al. 2004) (For an article about children's poor access to mental health services after 9/11)

Another traditional claim for significance is stating that the popular understandings of a subject are erroneous.

Example of significance: Enshrined in the Bill of Rights in 1789, the grand jury has been praised as the greatest instrument of freedom known to democratic government and a bulwark against oppression. At the same time, the grand jury remains one of the most controversial and least understood aspects of the criminal justice system, and has been abolished in many states and in England. (Fukurai 2001) (For an article about Latino participation on US grand juries)

Do I state my claims for significance in the introduction? If not, where will I do that?

Provide a synopsis of your article. If your article does not use the IMRD structure described in the week 9 chapter, summarizing your article's structure in your introduction makes it easier for the reader to follow your progress.

Do I provide an
article synopsis in the
introduction? If not,
should I?

Have a pull quote. This step is quite tough to accomplish, but if possible, your introduction should include a sentence that a hiring or promotion committee could pull and use alone to discuss the meaning and value of your article. Or if you prefer to think about the scholarly community, what is the one sentence that most everyone citing your article would quote? It might be your statement of the argument, but it might also be a definition or a claim for significance. It's often the sentence at the end of the introduction or right before the article synopsis. So for instance, in Judith Butler's much-cited article "Performativity, Precarity, and Sexual Politics," one sentence in her introduction is cited hundreds of times in the literature. It's her definition of the term *precarity*, which has gained increasing importance in theory.

> **Example of pull quote:** "Precarity" designates that politically induced condition in which certain populations suffer from failing social and economic networks of support and become differentially exposed to injury, violence, and death. (Butler 2009) (For an article updating Butler's theory of gender performativity)

Do I have one sentence
in the introduction that
might get pulled and
quoted by scholars?

What to Avoid in Your Introduction

But your introduction also must avoid subtle mistakes in tone and substance. That is, it must start the process of convincing your readers of your argument by providing the argument's context, enticing continued reading, and establishing your authority (G. Brown and Marshall 2012, 654). Mismatches or imbalances among these three factors (of scholarly context, readers, and author) lead to problems. You need to get all three aligned, as follows:

Don't Mismatch Context and Readers

Having a keen understanding of your readers is essential to a strong introduction. You must properly perceive what your readers already know and don't know for effectively communicating what they will get to know in the article. An introduction is a form of relation, one that draws on "readers' knowledge, beliefs, and assumptions" (Arrington and Rose 1987, 307). Three mistakes are common when matching context to readers.

Don't assume too little knowledge. One mistake of novice authors is assuming that readers know little about the topic, and thus introducing contexts that scholars in their field already know, as if readers were their former undergraduate self. The introduction to an article about *Hamlet* in a theater journal should not introduce basic disciplinary knowledge, such concepts as "drama," "literature," "England," "language," "character," "plot," "foreshadowing," "desire," "early modern," and so on.

Don't assume too much knowledge. Another mistake is assuming that potential readers will intuit what the author is writing about and will automatically be interested. Novice authors are often "surprised that their writing didn't convey the whole" to readers (Willis 1993, 64). If you're publishing a small article in a small journal for a small sub-sub-field audience, you can get away with a short introduction that does little. In other words, "the more abbreviated the introduction, the more the writer assumes the reader will know, the more the writer takes the reader's interest for granted" (Arrington and Rose 1987, 308). But a strong introduction for a broader audience should not read like a personal letter, one you wrote yesterday to a dear friend who doesn't need to be told what city you live in, how you vote, or who your Auntie Abena is. Finding this perfect position, between telling your readers too much and telling your readers too little, is for novice authors the great trick of a well-crafted introduction.

Don't give irrelevant information. Another common mistake is giving the wrong contextual information—that unrelated to the argument or situation. The introduction to an article about substance-induced psychosis in Uruguayan college students should not have, without explanation, information about pregnancy-induced psychosis in the United States. That's irrelevant.

> Have I given too much, too little, or the wrong contextual information in the introduction? What needs to be deleted or added?

Don't Fail to Establish Yourself as the Author

Establishing a bond of trust between you and your readers is also important. To do so, your presentation of yourself as the author must strike the right balance between indirect and direct, formal and informal, distant and personal, all-knowing and ignorant. The strategies with which you stage yourself and your strengths depend a great deal on your field—that is, on what's typical in your field's journals and with your field's readers. In literary studies and anthropology, articles can have personal openings based in anecdotes; in economics, authors are expected to be more impersonal. Here are some general rules.

Don't cite your credentials, prove them. Establishing yourself as an authority doesn't mean citing your credentials—you rarely see references to titles or degrees in introductions (in part because most journals now publish bios with articles, so readers know your institution, career stage, and previous work). Rather, authors establish themselves as authorities through the style of their prose, their stance on field debates, their use of cutting-edge or traditional theories, the depth of their research, the aggression of their argumentation, the rigor of their method, their mastery of material in other languages, their self-reflexivity, or their humor. It's wise to study conventions in your field for establishing the authority of an author. In general, demonstrated knowledge of the field and the literature on the topic is the strongest element for establishing authority.

Don't belabor your motivations.　Briefly indicating your passion for a topic or your reasons for writing is an effective way of establishing a relation with your readers. However, a mistake some novice authors make is spending too much time describing their private motivations, their personal experience with the subject, or their affective stance toward the material. An introduction is not a diary entry in which you expend few words about context and lots of words about feelings. An important exception is anthropology, in which describing the self may be a valuable rhetorical strategy.

Don't fail to claim your ideas.　Perhaps the biggest mistake that novice authors make in creating their authorial persona is failing to state ownership of their ideas—especially their argument or coined terms. I often read drafts in which the author's hard-won observations seem ownerless, mere statements of fact. For instance, a novice author will write, "Revenge tragedies began in England in the 1550s" instead of "I argue that revenge tragedies began in England in the 1550s, a decade earlier than previously thought." Coined terms simply appear in passing, as if they existed before the publication of the article, and aren't indicated as the author's. Preface your unique ideas with "My term for this is . . ." or "A neologism I propose for this phenomena is . . ." Finally, never denigrate your contributions, such as stating, "This is just my opinion" or "I'm not an authority on this subject, but . . ." (Arrington and Rose 1987, 315).

> Do I establish myself as an authority in the introduction? If I could do more in this regard, what would it be?

Avoid Clichés

Some undergraduate writing practices can creep into your introduction. First, don't start with a dictionary definition. Indeed, don't devote whole paragraphs anywhere in your article to various dictionary definitions of your main terms, unless your article is etymologically driven. Dictionaries aren't sacred objects to be consulted as oracles. Second, don't start with Wikipedia or any other encyclopedia. Third, don't start with sweeping claims about humanity, time, or the world. Almost nothing has always or everywhere been true.

> Do I avoid the above clichés in the introduction?

Later this week, you'll work on finalizing your introduction. For now, let's turn to one last issue in the article opening.

Choosing Your Name

You get to choose the name under which you publish. Owing to biases against their name, many academics have been forced to think about the implications of names since grade school. Yet everyone can benefit from careful consideration of this issue. Will you use your middle name or omit it? Will you use initials? Will you use your birth name or your married name? Will you hyphenate your double-barreled last name? Or will you change your name altogether? You are not obligated to publish under your legal name. When making your choice of name, you must balance extrinsic factors (how the world perceives names) and intrinsic motivations (who you want to be) to arrive at a name with which you'll be happy.

Let's visit some of the naming challenges and solutions.

Extrinsic: consistency. The more consistent your name is throughout your career, the easier it is to build a reputation. If you've never published, choosing a name you can use over a lifetime is valuable. Of course, consistency isn't always possible. Maybe you have already published under a name you don't like, or you have experienced life changes that dictate some alteration—such as gender transitioning. In that case, consistency isn't everything. More than one important scholar has published first with initials, then with full birth name, then with married name, and then back to birth name upon divorce. You always have options. Further, sometimes you don't want to be consistent. You may want to use informal versions of your name for social media identities and formal ones for academic publishing so that your rants don't come up in the same internet searches as your research.

Extrinsic: legality. You are not obligated to publish under your legal name. If you want to use a nickname instead of your first name, or add a middle name because you don't have one, it's up to you. When signing the legal contract, you need to use your legal name, but you don't need to put it on your article. However, please note that your name as it appears in an article byline will almost always appear with your academic affiliation, so there's not much point in using a pen name.

Extrinsic: author disambiguation. One of the biggest challenges facing librarians today is distinguishing authors from one another. Not only are there more and more authors but some names are extremely common, such as John Smith, Kim Lee, and Zhang Wei. If organizations and algorithms can't figure out which articles belong to whom, they can't properly compile citation statistics. The problem is so serious that an entire research field has arisen to develop methods for distinguishing authors with similar names. Why does this matter to you? It affects your citation rate if you receive no credit for your articles. And scholars interested in reading your work can't find it. Insofar as it is possible, using a unique name for your publications is desirable. If even one other scholarly author shares both your first and last names, especially if that author is in the same discipline or field as yours, you need to think about what you're going to do to differentiate yourself. Setting up a Google Scholar Profile, unique ORCiD identifier, Academia.edu, or ResearchGate account and listing your work there will help, but nothing will help as much as having a unique name.

Your first step is to go to Google Scholar and search for your own full name, searching both with and without quotation marks, and with and without your middle initial or middle name. If you already have a unique name, you're all set. However, I do urge people with unique names to use a middle initial or name anyway if they have one, because even if a name is currently uncommon, soon it may not be. If you have a very common last name such as Smith, Garcia, Lee, Nguyen, or Wong, to name just five among the most common US names, do what you can to distinguish it. If you can't arrive at a unique version of your real name, identify how similar your research is to those scholars who share your name. If these individuals are biologists and chemists and you're an anthropologist whose focus is Argentina, then you can expect that your work probably won't turn up in the same searches. But if they do similar work, you might consider taking more drastic measures. If you're among the tens of thousands of Americans with very common first- and last-name combinations like James Johnson or Maria Hernandez, you probably need to do more than add a middle name. You might substitute a nickname for your first name (so long as the nickname isn't infantilizing) or add a second middle name (perhaps your mother's birth name).

> Do one or more scholars in my field share my name? If so, how might I differentiate my name from theirs?

Extrinsic: bias. Here's the depressing news. Names that come across as female, African American, Muslim, or "foreign" are evaluated more negatively. Scholars—both men and women—still evaluate publications with a male name in their byline as of higher quality than those with a female name (Cikara, Rudman, and Fiske 2012, 264; West et al. 2013, 5; Knobloch-Westerwick, Glynn, and Huge 2013, 619). Immigrants to the United States who Americanized their name obtained better jobs over time (Biavaschi, Giulietti, and Siddique 2017, 1114). Resumes with "African American–sounding" names or "Asian American–sounding" names receive fewer interview requests (Lavergne and Mullainathan 2004, 1006; Banerjee, Reitz, and Oreopoulos 2018, 10). However, on the other side of the equation, children given a more African-sounding name by their African American mother were shown to have higher self-esteem (Anderson-Clark and Green 2017, 73). And South Asians are the Asian Americans least likely to Americanize their name, and yet they have the highest income among Asian Americans in the United States. So giving up identities may incur costs.

If your name is not a typical white American–seeming name, I hope that you keep it. After all, a man with the visibly non-English and Muslim name Barack Hussein Obama became president of the United States. And he went by "Barry" in his family, so he could have chosen to erase part of his identity when campaigning for the nation's highest office, but instead he chose to claim it. The only way that real change will come is if people insist on publishing their brilliant work under their own name. As one person said in a Facebook discussion with me on the topic, "If we all become Tom Smith, Ed Lang or Sam Young, don't we inadvertently reinforce the stereotype of the researcher as being 'naturally' whitish, normcore, potentially male, and Anglo-Saxon?" Absolutely we do. However, my job is to give you all the information you need to succeed. And I don't believe that the very people the system is biased against are the ones most obligated to fight that system. I would urge my white U.S. readers to change their name to Jamal and Ximena as a way of trying to change the system, but none of us relinquish privilege easily, including me. So I hate that we live in the kind of world where your name may affect the fate of your article. But we do, and it's your absolute right to counter the bias against you individually rather than systemically.

To avoid gender bias, you could change your first name. A businesswoman changed hers to a male-sounding nickname—and as "Mack McKelvey," Erin McKelvey found more success (Cohn 2016). A friend of hers shortened her feminine name from Alexandra to the gender-neutral Alex; she, too, felt that she had more success. Another time-honored way of disguising gender is using initials. Many believe that J. K. Rowling would not have achieved the success she did if she had used her first name, Joanne. Or you could change your last name. This is just speculation on my part, but my instinct is that women whose last names are typical male first names get a little boost from that association (e.g., Jane Stanley, Laura James, Susan Richards). Finally, you could choose to use a man's name in print, as did the nineteenth-century author George Eliot (born Mary Anne Evans) to great success.

To avoid ethnic or racial bias, you could shorten your first name, since there is less bias against shortened names like Sri than Srinivasan. Many immigrants choose to keep their last name but Americanize their first name, which also can work. Or you can legally change your name entirely. When I was in graduate school, an African American classmate legally changed the Muslim name his mother had given him to a non-Muslim name, in part because he had never been Muslim.

> Is my name subject to bias? If so, do I want to change my name? If so, to what?

Extrinsic: alphabetizing errors. Often, US editors and authors don't properly alphabetize authors in their bibliographies because they've mistaken last names for middle names or first names or vice versa. For instance, in the Spanish language tradition, authors use both fathers' and mothers' last names to form their surname. So US editors and authors will mistakenly alphabetize Raul Pacheco Vega under *V*, not *P*. Therefore, Pacheco Vega, like many other Latinx, decided to hyphenate his last name, making it Pacheco-Vega, to prevent incorrect alphabetizing, and also to prevent the incorrect shortening of Pacheco to *P.* as if it were a middle name. In Semitic languages, many last names are compound, such as Walatta Petros (Daughter of [St.] Peter), ʿAbd el-Raʾūf (Servant of the Compassionate), and Ben Gurion (Son of the Lion), which people mistakenly shorten—rather like calling someone "Son" because he has the name Johnson. If you have a compound first or last name, you may find that adding a hyphen will prevent alphabetizing errors. Of course, some erroneous alphabetizing can't be prevented. In Ethiopia and across the Middle East, people have individual names and then add their father's and grandfathers' names. That means that every generation of a family has a different last name. Thus, in Ethiopian publications the MacArthur Foundation Fellowship recipient Getatchew Haile would be alphabetized under *G*, not *H*.

> Is my last name subject to erroneous alphabetizing? If so, do I want to add a hyphen?

Intrinsic: life change. You may want to change your name owing to a life change. Perhaps you got married, and you and your spouse decided to join your last names with a hyphen. Perhaps you want to return to using your birth name after a divorce. Perhaps you are gender nonconforming, or are beginning to think that you might transition genders in the future; you may want to chose a different name now. One novice author, whose father had not accepted him when he came out, legally changed his last name to that of his mother's side of the family right before his first publication.

> Have I experienced any life changes that suggest I should change my name? If so, what do I want my name to be?

I hope you keep your name and become part of the change we hope to see in the world, but no one has the right to tell you what to do on this issue. How you want to represent your name is entirely up to you.

ON THE IMPORTANCE OF CONCLUSIONS

Conclusions aren't anywhere near as important as introductions, but authors who elegantly wrap up their articles with a rephrasing of their argument and a gesture toward their argument's implications go a long way toward making their articles memorable and cited. Research demonstrates that article conclusions share some common features (Henry and Roseberry 1997; Paltridge 2002; Ruiying and Allison 2003; Bunton 2005). Two moves were generally present: (1) the authors made a claim about the strength of the argument and its supporting evidence and then (2) linked that argument to the wider context (Henry and Roseberry 1997, 485). That is, they stated how (1) the *internal* outcome of the article (the success of the argument) could lead to (2) an *external* outcome (a change in the world or how we think about the world). Thus, conclusions were usually marked by an expansion from the argument through its evaluation and implications. The research also found that article conclusions tended to evaluate or reaffirm the argument, but also could include predictions, admonishments, consequences, solutions, or personal reactions (491–93).

So a good conclusion is one that summarizes your argument and its significance in a powerful way. It also should restate the article's relevance to the scholarly literature and debate. Although the conclusion does not introduce new arguments, it does point beyond the article to the larger context or the more general case. It doesn't merely repeat the introduction but takes a step outward to the larger picture by stating why the argument matters in the larger scheme of things, what its implications are. In other words, as the scholar Brian Herrera said to me, "Say what you said in your introduction, but bigger."

Occasionally, SciQua conclusions also include remarks about the limitations of the research and (therefore) possible directions for future research. Humanities conclusions are often more eloquent than the rest of the article, with an elevation in language and lyricism. As the scholars Stevens and Stewart observed, humanities scholars tend to begin their articles by declaring the significance of their argument, and conclude them by declaring the significance of their text (e.g., the poem, score, or painting they analyzed) (Stevens and Stewart 1987, 110).

> Is my conclusion doing a good job of summing up and moving outward? How could I improve it?

FINALIZING YOUR OPENING AND CONCLUSION DAY 1 TASKS:

Day 1 Tasks: Reading the Workbook and Revising Your Title

On the first day of your tenth writing week, read this week 10 chapter all the way through the next few paragraphs, answering all the questions posed. Write directly in the boxes provided or in your own document. Then work on finalizing your title, following the instructions given earlier in the chapter and using the checklist below.

Title Checklist

Not all the boxes below must, or even should, be checked. Some won't be right for your title. But you should have most of these aspects of good titles checked. If not, revise your title to improve it.

My Title Checklist

My title

- [ ] Avoids being too broad
- [ ] Doesn't have strings of vague and unsearchable abstractions
- [ ] Names the article's subjects and topic (e.g., author, text, nation, region, population)
- [ ] Includes two to five relevant keywords
- [ ] Includes the most searchable versions of keywords
- [ ] Has keywords in relation, not just strung together
- [ ] Has a verb
- [ ] Doesn't start with non-English words
- [ ] If quotations, puns, double entendres, or allusions are used, they aren't muddy, exclusionary, or clichéd
- [ ] Hints at the argument and/or findings and/or implications
- [ ] Includes variables
- [ ] Isn't over twenty-one words long, and isn't under seven words
- [ ] Has a colon
- [ ] Doesn't have a question
- [ ] Suggests an inconsistency, an irony, a contradiction, or an illogicality
- [ ] Makes sense to readers without their having read the article

My new and improved title:

Title Workshopping Exercise

If you feel that your work could use some polish, find a room where you can work, and gather a group of scholarly friends together with a blackboard or whiteboard to brainstorm a better title. You can often see quite spectacular improvements with this exercise—it's one of my favorites. After summarizing my points about what makes a good title, put your title up on the board, and have your friends ask you questions or make suggestions about it. If a suggestion seems right to you, cross out the old words and insert the new ones. If a suggestion doesn't seem right, explain why. Often, you can find better wording through dialogue.

It usually takes ten to twenty minutes per title to do this brainstorming. This exercise is especially helpful if you've gotten stuck on a title that you like but no one understands. It also works well if all participants have a title they're workshopping—whether of an article, a dissertation, or a book.

Tracking Writing Time

Each day, use the Calendar for Actual Time Spent Writing This Week form (or digital time-tracking software) to keep track of the time you spent writing this week. Then, at the end of the week, evaluate how you spent your time.

If busy, at least mark the check boxes with how long you wrote today. ☐ 15+ min. ☐ 30+ ☐ 60+ ☐ 120+

WEEK 10, DAYS 2–5: READING AND TASKS

Day 2 Tasks: Molding Your Introduction

Today, following the instructions given earlier in the chapter and the checklist below, you will work on finalizing your introduction. This may or may not include working on your related literature review.

Introduction Checklist

Not all the boxes below must, or even should, be checked. Some won't be right for your introduction. But you should have most of these aspects of good introductions checked. If not, go back and revise your introduction to improve it.

My Introduction Checklist

My introduction

☐ Starts with a gripping first sentence

☐ Gives basic information about my subject

☐ States my entry point

☐ States my argument and, if possible, my findings

☐ States my claim(s) for significance

☐ Has an article synopsis (in the humanities)

☐ Has at least one sentence that might be pulled and regularly cited by scholars

☐ Doesn't provide too much, too little, or the wrong contextual information

☐ Establishes my authority as the author through style, stance, assertiveness, and claims

☐ Avoids dictionary definitions, encyclopedia material, and sweeping claims

My new and improved first line for my article:

Tracking Writing Time

Mark your electronic calendar, the Calendar for Actual Time Spent Writing This Week form, and/or the check boxes here with how long you wrote today. ☐ 15+ min. ☐ 30+ ☐ 60+ ☐ 120+

Day 3 Tasks: Molding Your Introduction and Choosing Your Name

Today you'll continue to mold your introduction, using yesterday's checklist.

Deciding about Your Name

If you haven't already, make a final decision about how you want your name to appear in the byline of this article.

My name will appear as

Tracking Writing Time

Mark your electronic calendar, the Calendar for Actual Time Spent Writing This Week form, and/or the check boxes here with how long you wrote today. ☐ 15+ min. ☐ 30+ ☐ 60+ ☐ 120+

Day 4 Tasks: Revisiting Your Abstract and Author Order

Today you'll work on finalizing other aspects of your opening, following the instructions given in previous chapters.

Abstract. Most journals will require you to provide an abstract when you submit your article. Keep in mind that if your title serves as the highway billboard for your article, your abstract is the full-page magazine ad. So if you haven't had a chance to finalize your abstract, do so now. Follow the advice in "Week 2: Advancing Your Argument," keeping in mind the changes you've made to the argument, related literature review, evidence, and structure. Also, make sure to optimize your abstract for search engines by repeating any keywords. An article that repeats the keyword "Ellen Johnson Sirleaf" each time, rather than using "she" in sentences after its first mention, will turn up higher in search results for her. Some research suggests that longer, denser abstracts are correlated with a higher citation rate, so use up your entire word count and pack in your key terms (Weinberger, Evans, and Allesina 2015, 3). Also correlated with citation frequency are abstracts that signal novelty and importance, use superlatives, and bring images to mind (3).

Author order. A final issue to resolve regarding your opening is relevant only to those of you writing with coauthors. It's time to make a final decision about the order of appearance of everyone's name in the article's byline. I addressed this vital issue in "Week 1: Designing Your Plan for Writing." If you had dealt with the issue earlier but no longer believe that the arrangement is fair, you have your work cut out for you now. Just remember that in the social, health, behavioral, and natural sciences, many graduate students never get their name listed first on coauthored articles, and many scholars in their field wouldn't expect it. Even if a student had written every draft of an article, many fields will view it as fair for the student not to appear as first author if he or she did not collect the data or arrive at the hypothesis. If it's any comfort, the more authors that are listed in a byline, the greater the article's chances of being accepted for publication by a journal and of being cited subsequently (Weller 2001, 128–29).

> What is my author order currently? Do I have any coauthor issues? If so, how should I proceed?

Tracking Writing Time

Mark your electronic calendar, the Calendar for Actual Time Spent Writing This Week form, and/or the check boxes here with how long you wrote today. ☐ 15+ min. ☐ 30+ ☐ 60+ ☐ 120+

Day 5 Tasks: Constructing Your Conclusion

Today you'll follow the instructions below to finalize your article's conclusion.

Conclusion Checklist

Not all the boxes below must, or even should, be checked. Some won't be right for your conclusion. But you should have most of these aspects of good conclusions checked. If not, go back and revise your conclusion to improve it.

My Conclusion Checklist

My conclusion

☐ Rearticulates the argument

☐ Affirms that the argument and evidence are strong

☐ States the argument's relevance to the scholarly literature and debate

☐ Suggests how the argument's success changes how we think

☐ Gives the implications of the argument, why it matters (predictions, consequences, solutions)

☐ Expresses directions for future research (sometimes)

☐ Names limits of the argument and evidence (sometimes)

☐ Declares the significance of the subject

What additional work do I need to do on the conclusion?

Conclusion Workshopping Exercise

By the time you reach the conclusion, you may feel that you have no language left. If you're finding the conclusion difficult to write, ask one or two colleagues to read your article (or even just skim the introduction) and tell you what they understand the article to be about and why it is important. They can often suggest new language and slightly different ways of saying the same thing.

> What are some useful sentences or words from my reviewers' summary of my article?

Tracking Writing Time

Mark your electronic calendar, the Calendar for Actual Time Spent Writing This Week form, and/or the check boxes here with how long you wrote today. ☐ 15+ min. ☐ 30+ ☐ 60+ ☐ 120+

Then, here at the end of your workweek, take pride in your accomplishments and evaluate whether any patterns need changing.

DOCUMENTING YOUR WRITING TIME AND TASKS

Calendar for Actual Time Spent Writing This Week

Time	Day 1	Day 2	Day 3	Day 4	Day 5	Day 6	Day 7
5:00 a.m.							
6:00							
7:00							
8:00							
9:00							
10:00							
11:00							
12:00 p.m.							
1:00							
2:00							
3:00							
4:00							
5:00							
6:00							
7:00							
8:00							
9:00							
10:00							
11:00							
12:00 a.m.							
1:00							
2:00							
3:00							
4:00							
Total minutes							
Tasks completed							

WEEK 11
Editing Your Sentences

Task Day	Week 11 Daily Writing Tasks	Estimated Task Time in Minutes	
		HumInt	SciQua
Day 1 (Monday?)	Read from here until you reach the week 11, day 2 tasks, filling in any boxes, checking off any forms, and answering any questions as you read. Run the Belcher Editing Diagnostic Test.	150+	90
Day 2 (Tuesday?)	Revise your article using the diagnostic test.	90+	90+
Day 3 (Wednesday?)	Revise your article using the diagnostic test.	90+	90+
Day 4 (Thursday?)	Revise your article using the diagnostic test.	90+	60+
Day 5 (Friday?)	Revise your article using the diagnostic test.	60+	60+
Total estimated time for reading the workbook, completing the tasks, and writing your article		**8+ hours**	**6.5+ hours**

Above are the tasks for your eleventh week. Start this week by scheduling when you will write, and then tracking the time you actually spend writing (using the Calendar for Actual Time Spent Writing This Week form or online software).

When I wrote this chapter, I wondered whether anyone would take the time to complete its complicated revising exercise, but many authors wrote me to say that this chapter was their favorite. While it took significant time to finish, they said, it was well worth the effort, as it permanently improved their writing. If you don't have time to run the exercise on your entire article, run it on your introduction. If your introduction is smooth, it helps readers through the whole article.

TENTH WEEK IN REVIEW

You have now completed all the large-scale macrorevising tasks of writing an article, in particular organizing your article's evidence around your argument and giving the article a strong title and introduction. You will now turn to small-scale microrevising tasks—the little changes that will give your article the polish it needs to satisfy peer reviewers. You're nearing the article submission point, so keep moving!

THE NATURE OF MICROREVISING

You spent all ten of the previous weeks on large-scale macrorevising of your article. Now, in week 11, you will finally turn to small-scale microrevising. As noted in week 8, macrorevising involves major changes to organization and content—moving paragraphs, adding examples, deleting sections, and rewriting pages. Such changes happen when you properly organize your article around your argument, add a literature review or background section, ensure a solid structure, and so on. By contrast, microrevising involves minor changes to mechanical, grammatical, and lexical matters—such as correcting grammar and spelling, adding punctuation, standardizing capitalization, and changing layout.

We spend only one week on small-scale microrevising, because the writing research shows that large-scale macrorevising is the far more important activity. Unfortunately, however, macrorevising is the most difficult kind of revising to do; therefore, it's the least likely to get done and the most difficult to teach. That's why novice authors tend to focus too much on microrevising (Barkaoui 2016, 333; Chanquoy 2009, 93). According to one frequently cited study, most inexperienced writers' changes to their essay were little edits that did not affect the meaning of the piece (Faigley and Witte 1981, 406–7). By contrast, experienced writers' changes to their essay were three times as likely to cause large changes to meaning (Faigley and Witte 1981, 407). Surprising, isn't it? You would think that better writers would produce flawless drafts the first time around, that better writers would make fewer major changes to their prose, but in fact the opposite is true—good writers make more and greater revisions. They know that they may not have hit on the best way of expressing an idea at first. So if you've been making many large changes to your article, that's a sign of your skill, not your lack of it! Just know that many novice authors avoid macrorevising, and many experienced authors find it an ongoing challenge—that's why I spend most of the book giving you macrorevising tasks.

But the time has come, here in the eleventh week, to turn to small-scale microrevising. Many people call this kind of revising editing or even proofreading, in which individual words and sentences are examined by the writer for opportunities to address grammar, punctuation, spelling, style, and diction. When people say that a piece demonstrates "good writing," they often mean that it's working at the micro level, without grammatical errors or infelicities of style.

Although I spend only one week on small-scale microrevising, you would be wise to learn to do it well. For one thing, the quality of your article's prose can make a difference in the acceptability of your article. Good writing can (unfortunately) cover up bad research and bad ideas—but good research usually can't carry a badly written article into publication. Second, it's a peculiar fact that effective microrevising can lead to effective macrorevising. Sometimes improving your diction can help you better articulate your argument and lead you back into macrorevising, reorganizing text for a sturdier argument. Or sometimes you pull on the thread of a single word and realize that you need to reshape an entire paragraph. Fortunately, once you've completed the microrevising proposed in this chapter, your article will be ready for submission. Yes, you could hire an editor to do this work for you if you have the funding, but learning how to edit your own work will help you be a better writer in the future. Nobody is born with this skill; like a violinist, you must practice a lot of microrevising before you become good at it.

At this point in the article revision process, you may be tired and just want to send your article to a journal as quickly as possible! You may not be interested in learning all the fine points of grammar. Therefore, I've designed this week's exercises with speed in mind. I identify some common academic writing errors and then give you a tool for diagnosing where your writing could be briefer, clearer, or stronger. Once you have diagnosed your writing for simple problems, you can work toward making simple changes that improve your word choice and sentence structure.

US academic style has, I would argue, eight main principles:

1. **Brevity.** Don't use two words where one will do.
2. **Vigor.** Don't use a noun when you can use a verb.
3. **Potency.** Don't use a weak verb when you can use a strong verb.
4. **Dynamism.** Don't use the passive voice unless the subject is unknown or unimportant.
5. **Lucidity.** Don't use a pronoun when a noun would be clearer.
6. **Efficiency.** Don't use a preposition when you can use a noun or verb.
7. **Leanness.** Don't use an adjective or adverb unless you must.
8. **Specificity.** Don't use a general word when you can use a specific one.

For most of human history, the more flowery, indirect, and elaborate your language, the more admired you were as a wordsmith. But in the United States, with the exponential increase in print, value has come to inhere in brevity. Modern people want not just fast cars and fast food but fast texts.

THE BELCHER EDITING DIAGNOSTIC TEST AND ITS PRINCIPLES

In 1995, I came up with a diagnostic test that used colored pencils to help participants in my first writing workshop improve their writing. I'm not sure what inspired the idea, but using different colors to correct different writing errors has a long history (for examples of such recommendations, see Fisher 1975; J. Day 1980). I invented the Belcher Editing Diagnostic Test because many novice authors know that they should do something to improve their prose, but feel exhausted by the very idea of such revision: where to start, what to focus on, and how to do it? My test makes the task of line editing less daunting by identifying straightforward problems and giving simple solutions. It provides a method for entering sentences and fixing problems. Those of you familiar with Strunk and White's *Elements of Style* (1999) will notice that this book has inspired quite a few of the test's instructions.

The main principle of the Belcher Editing Diagnostic Test is that certain words signal certain prose problems, and thus the opportunity for you to take certain microrevising steps. If authors focus their revising attention on these signal words and the words around them, they can improve their writing without having to memorize many rules. If the test seems overwhelming at first, remember that linguistic theory posits only four categories of transformation: deletion, addition, substitution, and rearrangement. In other words, you can make only four kinds of changes to your prose. That seems manageable, right?

Before we proceed, here are some caveats about this test. First, seeing any of these signal words in your prose does not automatically indicate a problem. Many instances of signal words will be perfectly acceptable. But clusters of these do indicate places for you to *consider* revising. Second, if you hate grammar or your knowledge of grammatical terms like *nominalization* or *gerund* is weak, don't worry—just study the examples. They show you everything you need to know. Third, this test is best at capturing the tics of native speakers of English trained to write in North American or British schools. For instance, overuse of the passive voice is a common error of native speakers of English, but not of nonnative speakers. For nonnative speakers, I instead recommend any of the books by John M. Swales and Christine B. Feak (Swales and Feak 2000, 2012). Finally, this diagnostic test can't identify all the places where you could improve your prose. You'll need to study a book about grammar if you have problems with verb tense, subject-verb agreement (or any other kind of agreement), possessives, conjunctions, sentence construction, and dangling or misplaced modifiers. Reading in your field or taking composition classes can also give you the tools you need to identify poor prose and write better prose. But what this test can do is help you identify the places in your writing where little changes can have the biggest impact.

Below, read the five principles of the Belcher Editing Diagnostic Test. Then I will give you instructions on how to run the test, which will highlight various signal words in red, green, blue, purple, or orange.

You'll probably find it easiest only to skim the revision principles here in the instruction section and proceed to the day 1 task of running the diagnostic on your writing. After you've finished, return here for instructions on how to edit particular sentences.

1. Reduce Your Lists (Red)

Much that is wrong with poor academic writing involves lists—that is, items strung together with little more than a conjunction to support them. Sometimes journal articles seem to be nothing *but* lists! Yet tracking just two signal words in your writing can help you identify and edit the lists in your writing. After you run the diagnostic, start at the beginning of your article and evaluate the words immediately on either side of every instance of the signal words in RED, which are the conjunctions *and* and *or*, to determine whether any instance signals a problematic list. If so, revise that list. These two signal words will help you identify the following types of lists that vex academic writing:

False lists (or doublings). Don't use two synonyms where one will do. Such pairings are called "doublings" (RSA 1985, 18; NASA 2000, 12). One example of a doubling is the phrase "blocked and obstructed." The reader needs only one of the two synonyms to get the author's meaning. The author should use one and delete the other. If you're unsure whether a list is a doubling, use your word-processing program's thesaurus to check whether the words appear as synonyms. Even when the two (or three or four) words in a list aren't exact synonyms, ask yourself whether they differ enough to justify using more than one. It's better to be concise.

Action: If synonyms appear on either side of the signal words **and** or **or**, delete one of the synonyms.

    Doublings: The patient was dizzy **and** lightheaded, disoriented **and** confused.

    ☆ **No doublings:** The patient was disoriented.

    Doubling: Yang **and** Yu argued that emotion is necessary **and** essential.

    ☆ **No doubling:** Yang **and** Yu argued that emotion is necessary.

      Note: "Yang and Yu" is not a doubling—the two words do not mean the same thing—so you cannot cut either word. But "necessary and essential" is a doubling; delete one of the synonyms.

All-inclusive lists. Replace lists that include (nearly) every subcategory in a category. That is, if you've named all the items in a category, delete the list and use the category. For instance, replace "American army, navy, and air force" with "US armed forces" (which includes the United States Coast Guard and the National Guard).

Action: If an all-inclusive list appears around the signal words **and** or **or**, replace the subcategories with their category.

    List of subcategories: The medical interns, residents, fellows, **and** attendings gathered for the lecture.

    ☆ **No list of subcategories:** The physicians gathered for the lecture.

      Note: However, you wouldn't change a sentence that stated, "Response rates differed among medical interns, residents, fellows, **and** attendings," because each item in the list is a population under study in the article.

Noninclusive lists. Replace lists that seem inclusive but lack many items. Lists that string together abstractions often have this problem. Common lists of this type are formulations like "social, cultural, political, and economic" or "race, gender, sexuality, and class." The problem is that we could add dozens of items to each of these lists without ever becoming comprehensive. For instance, the formulations just given should really include "geographic," "religious," "national," and so on. If the items in the list are actual variables of your study or items that you treat carefully in turn, then go ahead and use them. But if you're just listing them to seem comprehensive, cut them. Lists of abstractions make your writing seem more diffuse, not more precise.

Action: If a noninclusive list appears around the signal words **and** or **or** and its items aren't your variables, cut the list entirely.

    Noninclusive list: Some of the drugs that have been withdrawn from the US market include Aldoril, Cytoxan, Hibitane, Navane, Rifadin, Thorazine, **and** Vagitrol, among hundreds of others, **and** for a variety of cultural, economic, **or** health reasons. Auto manufacturers have also had to recall car parts for a variety of cultural, economic, **or** health reasons.

☆ **Noninclusive list dropped:** Pharmaceutical companies and auto manufacturers have had to withdraw <u>their products</u> from the US market <u>for similar reasons</u>.

Flipped lists. Present the list concept first and the list second in a sentence. That is, don't present a list with the unifying concept at the end of the sentence, which is tough for readers to follow. Always introduce lists.

<u>Action</u>: If a flipped list appears around the signal words *and* or *or*, move the list concept up front.

> **List concept last:** The predominant sounds of the steel guitar <u>and</u> fiddle, vocal timbres of strain in their higher register, regional accents, comparable ranges, <u>and</u> lyrics that address the pains of romance demonstrate that Wells <u>and</u> Williams sung about similar topics, such as infidelity, **in** comparable manners.

> ☆ **List concept first and more parallel:** The <u>music of Wells and Williams</u> has in common the predominance of the steel guitar and fiddle, a strain in the higher vocal registers, distinct regional accents, and heart-wrenching lyrics about infidelity and the other pains of romance.

Disordered lists. Present your list items in a sequence. In US English, items generally appear in order of increasing importance (e.g., peasants, nobles, and monarchs) or size (e.g., centimeters, meters, and kilometers). Reading items in a random order (e.g., kings, servants, and queens) slows readers down. Ross-Larson also argues that words with few syllables should appear before those with many syllables (e.g., "arts and letters," not "letters and arts"), and that phrases with few words should appear before phrases with many words (e.g., "*Beowulf, Pilgrim's Progress,* and *Pride and Prejudice*") (Ross-Larson 1996, 17).

<u>Action</u>: If a disordered list appears around the signal words *and* or *or*, reorder the list.

> **List concept last and disordered list:** When each section, paragraph, **and** subsection of your article proceeds logically from the previous one, you have a coherent structure.

> ☆ **List concept first and ordered list:** You have a <u>coherent structure</u> when <u>each paragraph, subsection, and section</u> of your article proceeds logically from the previous one.

Nonparallel lists. Present list items in parallel with one another. Items in a list that start with different parts of speech are not parallel. You can't have one item in a list start with a verb, another with a noun, another with an adjective, and another with a preposition (which is what happened in the example below). The easiest way to make a nonparallel list parallel is to start by placing the same word before each item, often the word that appeared right before the entire list. If any item then reads ungrammatically or awkwardly, improve its phrasing. Once every item starts with the same part of speech, you can remove the repeated word.

<u>Action</u>: If a nonparallel list appears around the signal words *and* or *or*, revise until each item in the list starts with the same part of speech and is parallel with the other items.

> **Not parallel:** During the weeklong demonstration, students did all sorts of things, including act as security, van driving, administrative liaisons, **and** by cooking and serving food.

Parallel but awkward: During the weeklong demonstration, students did all sorts of tasks, including acting as security, ~~including~~ driving vans, ~~including~~ liaising with administrators, and ~~including~~ cooking and serving meals.

☆ **Parallel:** During the weeklong demonstration, students took on multiple tasks as security officers, ~~as~~ van drivers, ~~as~~ administrative liaisons, ~~as~~ cooks, and ~~as~~ servers.

Note: In the first sentence, the items begin with different parts of speech: a verb (*act*), a noun modifier (*van*), an adjective (*administrative*), and a preposition (*by*). In the second, all items begin with gerunds, but the first item is awkward. In the third sentence, all the items begin with nouns that follow naturally from *as*. Then *as* is dropped.

2. Strengthen Your Verbs (Green)

Much of what else is wrong with poor academic writing involves the overuse of weak verbs and the underuse of strong verbs. Tracking the signal words below, you can identify where you bury verbs as nouns or employ vague verbs instead of vivid verbs. After you run the diagnostic, start at the beginning of your article and evaluate the signal words highlighted in GREEN, which include the endings *-ent*, *-ence*, and *-ion* and the signal verbs *to be*, *to do*, *to make*, *to provide*, *to perform*, *to get*, *to seem*, and *to serve*, to determine whether you can replace them with a stronger verb. These signal words will help you identify three types of verb problems that vex academic writing.

Buried verbs (nominalizations). Don't use a noun when you can use a verb. Burying your verbs as nouns is a process called nominalization. If you can, dig those verbs out. Why write the wordy "she gave the explanation for" when you can write the vigorous "she explained"? The endings *-ent*, *-ence*, and *-ion* often signal verbs buried as nouns. Indeed, you can convert almost any noun ending in them when bracketed by *the* and *of*. Some add searches for *-ance*, *-ing*, *-ity*, *-ness*, *-ure*, *-acy*, and *-al*, but don't drive yourself crazy. If you just unbury *-ence*, you'll have done a lot. Free those verbs from the noun cage! Of course, not all words ending in *-ent* or *-ence* are buried verbs (e.g., *sentence*, *percent*, *science*), so not all instances need to be changed.

Action: If any word ending in *-ent*, *-ence*, or *-ion* appears, especially with a preposition right after it or in association with the verb *to be*, consider converting it back into a verb.

Buried verbs: The state's improvem**ent** *was* due to *the* establishm**ent** *of* an impartial judiciary.

Unburied verb: The state's improvement was due to establishing an impartial judiciary.

☆ **Unburied verbs:** The state improved upon establishing an impartial judiciary.

Buried verbs: One considerat**ion** *is* whether the confer**ence** *will be* any good for those who *are* presenting papers.

☆ **Unburied verbs:** We must consider whether the conference will be rewarding for presenters.

Note: The nominalization *consideration* becomes the verb *consider*; the nominalization *conference* remains the same.

Weak verbs. Avoid overused verbs. As has often been observed, the verb *to be* is the workhorse of the English language—essential for the progressive tense (e.g., the dog was running), for use as a linking verb (e.g., Abena is tall), and for the passive voice. The verb *to be* will always be common in your writing; just make sure you haven't used it when another verb or sentence construction would be stronger. The verb *to have* is also essential, for the perfect tense (e.g., they have waited, they will have waited). But *to have* sometimes buries another verb as a noun, especially when paired with an article such as *a* or *an*. The verb *to do* is essential for questions about actions (e.g., do you intend to go?), but *to do* can bury a verb as a noun, especially when paired with an article such as *a* or *an* or the word *not*. Other weak verbs are *to make*, *to provide*, *to perform*, *to get*, *to seem*, and *to serve*. These verbs, too, can bury a strong verb, especially when paired with an article such as *a* or *an* and prepositions. You don't have to get rid of all instances of these, but improving some of them will strengthen your writing.

Action: If the signal word *to be* appears (i.e., *is*, *are*, *was*, *were*, *am*, *be*, *being*, and *been*), especially when followed by *a* or *an* and a nominalization, try to replace it with a stronger verb (unless *to be* is part of the progressive tense).

> **Weak verb:** In the early twentieth century, "the Mexican Problem" **was** the phrase most often used in reference to Mexican American culture.
> ☆ **Strong verb:** In the early twentieth century, scholars' frequent comments about of "the Mexican Problem" denigrated Mexican American culture.
> **Note:** A stronger verb replaces the verb *was* and the nominalization *reference*.

> **Weak verb:** Hakami **is** a student of patient narratives on disease blogs and the designer of health curricula.
> ☆ **Strong verb:** Hakami studies disease blog narratives and designs health curricula.
> **Note:** A stronger verb replaces the verb *is* that was immediately followed by the article *a* and the nominalization *student*.

> **Weak verb:** Humankind **is** a part of nature and shares in the phenomenon that applies to other animals.
> ☆ **Strong verb:** Humankind, a part of nature, shares in the phenomenon that applies to other animals.
> **Note:** You can often delete the verb *to be* when followed closely by *and*.

Action: If the signal word *to have* appears (i.e., *have*, *has*, *had*), especially when followed by *a* or *an* and a nominalization, try to unbury the verb nearby (unless *to have* is part of the perfect tense).

> **Buried verb:** The candidates **have** a tendency to exaggerate their accomplishments, which is indicative of their insecurity.
> **Unburied verb:** The candidates tend to exaggerate their accomplishments, a sign of their insecurity.
> ☆ **Best sentence:** The candidates' insecurities led them to exaggerate their accomplishments.

> **Weak verb:** Poor scholarly articles also **have** problems with adequate research.
> ☆ **Strong verb:** Poor scholarly articles also suffer from inadequate research.

<u>Action:</u> If the signal word ***to do*** appears (i.e., *do*, *does*, *did*), especially when followed by *a*, *an*, or *not*, try to replace it with a stronger verb (unless *to do* is part of an action question).

Buried verb: We would like **to do** a study on animal husbandry.

Unburied verb: We would like <u>to study</u> animal husbandry.

☆ **Strengthened verb:** We <u>intend</u> to study animal husbandry.

Cluttered: It is clear that the experiment that they **did did** <u>not</u> succeed.

Better: Their experiment <u>did</u> not succeed.

☆ **Best sentence:** Their experiment <u>failed</u>.

<u>Action:</u> If any of the signal words ***to make***, ***to provide***, ***to perform***, ***to get***, ***to seem***, or ***to serve*** appear, especially when followed by *a*, *an*, a preposition, or a nominalization, try to replace them with stronger verbs.

Buried verb: This course will **provide** an <u>introduction</u> to Judaic studies to undergraduates.

☆ **Better:** This course will <u>introduce</u> undergraduates to Judaic studies.

Passive voice. Don't overuse passive voice. Let's return to the verb *to be*, which often signals passive construction (e.g., a sentence that buries the subject). If the subject of the sentence is delivering the action, it is in the *active* voice (e.g., "She [subject] kicked the ball [object]"). If the subject is receiving the action, the sentence is in the *passive* voice (e.g., "The ball [object] was kicked by her [subject]").

Although some misguided instructors insist that authors eliminate all passive voice from their writing, sometimes passive voice is justified. How can you tell when passive voice is appropriate? Passive sentences come in two forms: with the subject and without the subject. If your passive sentence is missing its subject entirely, this absence may suggest that the subject is irrelevant, in which case you can leave the sentence in passive voice. If your sentence has a named subject, however, you often can convert it into active voice, which is stronger. Don't restructure a passive sentence to emphasize an unimportant or unknown subject.

The easiest way to check your sentences for passive voice is by using a grammar-checker. Not everything the grammar-checker identifies as passive voice is passive, and not everything it skips isn't; but most of the time, it's right. Some checkers, including the one in Microsoft Word, can also let you know the percentage of your article that's in passive voice (just select "Show readability statistics" after selecting the "Check grammar with spelling" check box). If you see your proportion of passive sentences drifting over 18 percent, consider converting some of the passive-voice sentences in your article into active voice.

<u>Action:</u> If the signal word ***to be*** appears (i.e., *is*, *are*, *was*, *were*, *am*, *be*, *being*, and *been*), followed by a verb in the past tense (often ending in -*ed*) and/or the preposition *by*, try to move the subject up to the front of the sentence.

Passive: The difficulties that translators faced when translating for the first time **shall** always **be** remember**ed by** them.

Active: <u>Translators</u> remember the difficulties that they faced when translating for the first time.

☆ **Best:** <u>Translators</u> remember the difficulties that they faced when first translating.

Passive: The new museum **was** design**ed by** the award-winning French architect Odile Decq.

☆ **Active:** <u>Odile Decq</u>, the award-winning French architect, designed the new museum.

You do *not* have to improve a sentence containing passive voice if the subject is unknown or unimportant or when the object has been the subject of the paragraph. Passive voice also may be appropriate if it helps you avoid putting a long list at the beginning of the sentence.

Passive: The paint **must be** carefully prepared before it **can be** <u>used in</u> the restoration process.

☆ **Active:** [Leaving this sentence in the passive voice may be appropriate. If the section in which the sentence appears is instructional, it may not be possible to introduce an anonymous subject like "the art restoration expert" or "you." The context may not support either an invented actor or the repetition of the subject.]

Passive: The new bridge **was** complet**ed** in April, reducing traffic bottlenecks by 27 percent.

☆ **Active:** [We do not need to know that the Los Angeles Department of Public Works completed the work. The sentence is about traffic, not the bridge.]

Passive: The activist **was** trampl**ed** during the demonstration and suffer**ed** a knee injury.

☆ **Active:** [The impact of the action on the known "object," the activist, may be more important than the unknown "subjects" who trampled him.]

Passive: The Alaska Supreme Court ruled that same-sex couples are eligible to receive survivor benefits. It has not yet **been** ask**ed** to rule on whether the state's ban on same-sex marriage violates the federal equal protection clause.

☆ **Active:** [The passive voice in the second sentence is fine because the court is the subject of the first sentence.]

3. Clarify Your Pronouns (Blue)

Poor academic writing also suffers from unclear pronouns, which are words used in place of nouns. Sometimes, which noun the pronoun is replacing is unclear, so the reader must reread the sentence to understand it. The farther the pronoun is from its noun, the more likely that you need to clarify it or add a noun. After you run the diagnostic, start at the beginning of your article and evaluate the signal words highlighted in BLUE, which are the pronouns *it, there; that, which, who; this, these, those;* and if you want, *they, them, their, its, she, he,* or *we,* to determine whether you need to replace the pronoun with a noun or add a noun to it. These signal words will help you identify five types of pronoun problems that vex academic writing.

Empty pronouns. Don't use pronouns where you can use a verb. The pronouns *there* and *it* can signal the use of filler subjects instead of real subjects, particularly when paired with the verb *to be* and the relative pronouns *that, which,* or *who.* You can often delete such pronouns and transform some words around them into modifiers or verbs. Note that "there are" and "it was" are common even in good writing; so you don't have to delete them all, just don't overuse them. The Microsoft Word grammar-checker does a good job of marking this problem with *there* and *it*. Also, note that sometimes *that* and *which* are essential to the meaning of the sentence (especially right after a comma), so don't just delete them automatically.

Action: If either of the signal words **there** or **it** appears, followed by the verb *to be* and the words **that**, **which**, or **who**, try to bring in a stronger verb and move the subject up to the front of the sentence.

Cluttered: **It was** obvious from the high participation **that there are** many who find writing retreats valuable.

Better: The high participation obviously <u>showed</u> that many find writing retreats valuable.

☆ Best: The high participation <u>demonstrated</u> that many <u>value</u> writing retreats.

Wordy: It **should be** noted **that there are** several **who** did not agree with the verdict.
Better: Several did not agree with the verdict.
☆ Concise: Several disagreed with the verdict.

Wordy: Their fundamental belief is **that there is** a conflict between Sartre's philosophy and his ethics.
☆ Concise: They believe that Sartre's philosophy conflicts with his ethics.

Action: If any of the signal words **that**, **which**, or **who** appear, especially followed by the verb *to be*, bring in a stronger verb and move the subject up to the front of the sentence.

Cluttered: The mathematician **who was** well known for giving a new proof of Witten's conjecture is Maryam Mirzakhani.

☆ Better: The mathematician Maryam Mirzakhani <u>famously gave</u> a new proof of Witten's conjecture.

Wordy: Poor households pay more for the food **that** they buy, because local merchants exploit them.

☆ Concise: Poor households pay more for their food, <u>because</u> local merchants exploit them.

Wordy: Government facilities can only spend funds **that are** available.
☆ Concise: Government facilities can only spend available funds.

Unclear antecedents. Don't use a pronoun when its antecedent would be clearer. The antecedent (the noun to which a pronoun refers) can be lost if more than one pronoun appears in a sentence, the pronoun appears too distant from its correct antecedent, or the pronoun appears too close to other nouns. Make sure that the noun to which the pronoun refers is clear.

Action: If any of the signal pronouns *it*, *there*, *they*, *them*, *their*, or *its* appear after a noun that is not that pronoun's antecedent or appear more than twenty words after that pronoun's antecedent, replace it with the noun.

Unclear pronouns: The experiment survived the power failure because of the university's backup generator, but <u>it</u> soon grew overheated and then <u>it</u> was ruined.

Clear pronouns: The experiment survived the power failure because of the university's backup generator, but the <u>generator</u> soon overheated and the <u>experiment</u> was ruined.

☆ **Best sentence:** The university's backup <u>generator</u> saved the <u>experiment</u> when the power failed, but the <u>generator</u> soon overheated and the <u>experiment</u> was ruined.

Note: The first *it* referred to the last noun, *generator*, but the second *it* referred not to its nearest noun but to one much earlier in the sentence, *experiment*.

Unclear antecedent: The students were supposed to compete against their lecturers in football, but **they** waited in vain for them to show up.

Clear antecedent: The students were supposed to compete against their lecturers in football, but the <u>students</u> waited in vain for the <u>lecturers</u> to show up.

Better sentence: The students were supposed to compete against their lecturers in football, but the <u>lecturers never showed</u> up.

☆ **Best sentence:** The <u>lecturers</u> never showed up to compete against their <u>students</u>, who waited in vain <u>to play</u> football.

Unclear antecedent: <u>It</u> was not always efficacious for all the patients, **they** told **them**.

Clear antecedent: The drug was not always efficacious for all the patients, the <u>researchers</u> told the <u>company</u>.

☆ **Best sentence:** The drug <u>failed to help</u> all the patients, the <u>researchers</u> told the <u>company</u>.

Dangling constructions. Make sure that clauses and pronouns are working together, not dangling. In a dangling construction, the pronoun does not refer to the subject of the clause before it. Pronouns can signal a dangling construction if they appear with the verb *to be* and after an introductory clause. Passive voice after an introductory clause often leads to dangling constructions. If the pronoun does not refer to the subject of the clause, it needs to be moved.

<u>Action</u>: If the signal words *there, it, them, this, these,* or *those* appear immediately after a comma and with a form of the verb *to be*, evaluate whether that pronoun refers to the subject of the clause before it. If not, replace it with a noun.

Dangling: Having completed the experiment, **there was** no reason for the students to stay.

☆ **Attached:** Having completed the experiment, the <u>students</u> had no reason to stay.

Note: "There" didn't conduct the experiment, "the students" did.

Dangling: Although <u>it</u> seems too aggressive at first, <u>it</u> turned out that **it is** argued really well.

Attached: Although seeming too aggressive at first, the <u>introduction</u> is well argued.

☆ **Attached and active:** Although the <u>author's introduction</u> seems too aggressive at first, <u>she</u> argues her case well in it.

Note: "It turned out" is not what is well written, the "introduction" is.

Dangling and passive: Using the multiple-choice tests and essay questions, **these were** prepared for the registrar.

Better: Using the multiple-choice tests and essay questions, these <u>class grades</u> were prepared for the registrar.

☆ **Attached and active:** Using the multiple-choice tests and essay questions, teaching assistants prepared class grades for the registrar.

> **Note:** The "class grades" or the "registrar" didn't prepare the "tests and essay questions," the "teaching assistants" did.

Absent nouns. Avoid using demonstrative pronouns like *this*, *these*, and *those* alone. They often appear without nouns after them. If the antecedent appears shortly before, it's sometimes acceptable; but if it's far, include the noun. Additionally, when attempting to place an absent noun after a solitary *this*, *these*, or *those*, you often find that the antecedent isn't what you thought it was, and you can solve that problem as well.

Action: If the signal pronouns *this*, *these*, or *those* appear without a noun immediately after them, consider adding the antecedent.

> **Unclear pronoun:** This demonstrates the ways in which syntax is tied to public and visible processes of projection.

> **Clear noun:** This study demonstrates how syntax is tied to public and visible projection processes.

> ☆ **Best sentence:** This study demonstrates how syntax interacts with visible projection processes.

> **Unclear pronoun:** Those in which the variables were left undecided were few.

> **Clear noun:** Those studies in which the variables were left undecided were few.

> **Better noun:** Those studies that left the variables undecided were few.

> ☆ **Best sentence:** Few studies left the variables undecided.

Premature pronouns. Use pronouns after their antecedent, not before it. We need to know what the pronoun means first, not wait until dozens of words later. If the pronoun appears before its noun antecedent, switch them so that the pronoun is not premature.

Action: If the signal words *it*, *they*, *she*, *he*, or *we* appear before their antecedent, move them to *follow* their antecedent.

> **Premature pronoun:** If she had taken to heart all the criticism of her research, Margaret Mead might never have published.

> ☆ **Punctual pronoun:** If Margaret Mead had taken to heart all the criticism of her research, she might never have published.

4. Decrease Your Prepositions (Purple)

Another characteristic of poor academic writing is an overabundance of prepositions. When prepositions start piling up in one sentence, clustering, they can signal unneeded phrases. Strings of prepositional phrases often signal buried verbs, as noted earlier, but also awkward sentence constructions. After you run the diagnostic, start at the beginning of your article and evaluate the signal words highlighted in PURPLE, which are the prepositions *by*, *of*, *to*, *for*, *toward*, *on*, *at*, *from*, *in*, *with*, and *as*, to determine whether you need to replace some prepositional phrases. You can accomplish this task by turning some of the nouns into adjectives and some of the nouns into verbs. These signal words will help you identify two types of preposition problems that vex academic writing.

Preposition clustering. Delete unnecessary prepositional phrases. You don't have to get rid of all of them, but try to unload some of them if they cluster in one sentence.

Action: If three or more of the signal words *by, of, to, for, toward, on, at, from, in, with,* and *as* appear in one sentence, try to delete prepositions by replacing pronouns with nouns and changing nouns into modifiers and verbs.

> **Wordy:** In the case of a great number of developing countries, the volume of production rose over the course of the year far higher than the predictions of the economists.
>
> **Better:** The yearly production of many developing countries rose higher than economists predicted.
>
> ☆ **Best:** The yearly production of many developing countries exceeded economists' predictions.
>
> **Concise:** Many developing countries' yearly production exceeded economists' predictions.
>
> > **Note:** Some will feel that the third revision is going too far, as the subject is now a string of adjectives and nouns. You can stay with the second revision to avoid that problem.

> **Cluttered:** There had been major changes in the presentation related to the data accumulated as a consequence of exhaustive study of the results of treatment in cancers of the head and neck, breast, and gynecological tract.
>
> ☆ **Clean:** The author changed her presentation after exhaustively studying the results of treated cancers of the head and neck, breast, and gynecological tract.
>
> > **Note:** Not all prepositions were removed; some were needed.

> **Wordy:** It is a question of some importance how Russians remember Stalin.
>
> ☆ **Strong:** An important question is how Russians remember Stalin.
>
> > **Note:** The noun *importance* becomes the adjective *important*.

Wordy phrases. Avoid clichéd noun and preposition compounds like "the fact that" or "on account of." By attending to clustering pronouns and prepositions, as you did earlier, you'll most likely catch such compounds. Also, the grammar-checker in Microsoft Word is good about noting these. But just in case you didn't address the problem earlier, let's look at how these wordy phrases are formulated. They often appear in this order: an article, a noun indicating a group or category, and a preposition. Some formulations are "the [noun] that," "a [noun] of," "the [noun] of," and "the [noun] in which"; such as *the type of thing that*, a *variety of*, *the ways in which*, and so on. You can often replace such phrases with one word. For instance, you can usually replace the very common "the ways that/in which" with "how"; or "the fact that" with "because." Look online to see lists of such phrases and their replacements.

Action: If you find a noun sandwiched between *a/an/the* and *that/of/in*, try replacing it with one word.

> **Wordy:** The way in which the candidates conducted themselves was observed by the election observers.
>
> **Better:** The election observers observed how the candidates conducted themselves.
>
> ☆ **Concise:** The election observers monitored the candidates' conduct.
>
> > **Note:** Sometimes switching the sentence around can solve the problem.

5. Cut Unnecessary Words (Orange)

Finally, poor academic writing suffers from wordiness. Now, all writing instructors tell you to cut. If you cut as often as they told you to cut, you would have nothing left! Nevertheless, you can eliminate certain consistent phrases and constructions without losing the meaning of your text. Indeed, cutting will help you be more specific. After you run the diagnostic, start at the beginning of your article and evaluate the signal words highlighted in ORANGE, including the adverbs *not* and *very*; adverbial participles like *in, out, up, on, off,* and *away*; and words ending in *-ly*, as well as nouns like *fact, type,* and *way*, especially when paired with prepositions and pronouns. (Sometimes you'll need them—I myself use "type of" in the next sentence!—but sometimes you can cut them without causing problems.) These signal words will help you identify three types of wordiness that vex academic writing.

Negatives. Avoid using *not* to hide your real thoughts or arguments. Writers afraid of their argument embrace *not* because it seems safer, but bland writing receives less attention. It's better to be attacked for assertiveness than to be dismissed as wimpy. The word *not* can signal a weak noun, a weak adjective, a problem with multiple negatives, or insipid language instead of argumentative language.

Action: If the signal word **not** appears, try to rewrite the sentence with stronger nouns, verbs, and adjectives, and without double negatives.

Multiple negatives: Not only does Bosey's novel **not** have a well-defined plot, but it also does **not** have strong character development or interesting writing.

Better but weak adjectives: Bosey's novel does <u>not</u> have a well-defined plot, strong character development, or interesting writing.

☆ **Best sentence:** A <u>murky</u> plot, <u>poor</u> character development, and <u>dreary</u> writing <u>mar</u> Bosey's novel.

Note: The writer veils the criticism in the first version and displays it in the third version.

Negative: Industrial progress depended **not** only on improving the nation's infrastructure, they said, but also on improving the nation's racial stock.

☆ **Best sentence:** Economic progress depended on <u>whitening</u> the nation's native peoples, they said. (Munro 2015c)

Note: The writer unveils the argument in the second version, a much more compelling sentence.

Weak adjectives/adverbs. Avoid weak adjectives, adverbs like *very*, and adverbs ending in *-ly*. They represent lost opportunities to be more specific. As the experts say, "The adjective hasn't been built that can pull a weak or inaccurate noun out of a tight place" (Strunk and White 1972, 64). Adverbs ending in *-ly* that you can often take out include *really, basically, certainly,* and *extremely*.

Action: If the signal word **very** or the signal ending *-ly* appears, try to replace it with a stronger verb or adjective.

Cluttered: The project participants were **very** tired.

☆ **Best:** The project participants were <u>exhausted</u>.

Weak adjective: Memory is selective: it represses (or forgets) incidents that are of less interest or that reflect bad<u>ly</u> on the individual.

☆ **Strong:** Memory is selective: individuals repress <u>uninteresting</u> or <u>unflattering</u> incidents.

Wordy: Universalists might argue that what society accepts is not necessari<u>ly</u> that which is most ethical.

☆ **Strong:** Universalists might argue that the practices society accepts are sometimes <u>unethical</u>.

Particles. Avoid adverb particles, which can signal weak verbs. For instance, "put on" can become "wore"; "take off" can become "fled"; "put out" can become "extinguished"; and so on.

<u>Action</u>: If the signal words *in*, *out*, *up*, *on*, *off*, or *away* appear with a verb, try to use a stronger verb.

Wordy: She was brought <u>up</u> by her aunt.

Better: She was raised by her aunt.

☆ **Concise and active:** Her aunt raised her.

All this has been a lot to absorb in one day; much of it will become clearer when you start editing your own article. Let's turn to that now.

EDITING YOUR ARTICLE

Day 1 Tasks: Reading the Workbook and Running the Belcher Editing Diagnostic Test

On the first day of your eleventh writing week, read this week 11 chapter all the way to this page.

Next, run the Belcher Editing Diagnostic Test on your writing, following the instructions below for running it either by hand on paper or digitally in an electronic document.

Running the test by hand takes hours longer, so I advise you to run it electronically. Microsoft Word has the most powerful Find and Replace feature of any existing word processor, so the Belcher Editing Diagnostic Test works best in Word. It will also work in LaTeX (see below). Setting up the process will take about ten minutes, but then you'll have it permanently, for every article. If you're using a word-processing program with a weak Find and Replace feature, such as Google Docs or Pages for Mac, it's tough to run this test electronically. If you want to try, you must be very knowledgeable about Find and Replace procedures, or else you'll create a mess of your article.

If you run the test electronically and find that you have time today, move on to the day 2 task of revising your article using the Belcher Editing Diagnostic Test.

Running the Belcher Editing Diagnostic Test by Hand

If you aren't running this test electronically, buy pencils, pens, or highlighters in a variety of colors, print out your article, and start at the beginning to mark up the signal words as instructed. If you feel that your introduction is solid, you could start instead with a section that you already suspect is sluggish and unclear. If you don't have coloring utensils, use symbols to mark the signal words (e.g., brackets, underscores, slashes, plus signs). Use the instructions below to move methodically through your article, highlighting the signal words you find with the appropriate color or symbol.

Reduce Your Lists

- Search for the conjunctions *and* and *or* and highlight with RED (or put double plus signs on either side of them; e.g., ++and++).

Strengthen Your Verbs

- Search for words ending in *-ent*, *-ence*, or *-ion*, and highlight with GREEN (or underscore the ending; e.g., <u>ence</u>).
- Search for forms of the verb *to be* (i.e., *is*, *are*, *was*, *were*, *am*, *be*, *being*, and *been*), and highlight with GREEN (or underscore them).
- Search for forms of the verb *to have* (i.e., *have*, *has*, *had*), and highlight with GREEN (or underscore them).
- Search for forms of the verb *to do* (i.e., *do*, *does*, *did*), and highlight with GREEN (or underscore them).
- Search for forms of the verb *to make* and highlight with GREEN (or underscore them).
- Search for forms of the verb *to provide* and highlight with GREEN (or underscore them).
- Search for forms of the verb *to perform* and highlight with GREEN (or underscore them).
- Search for forms of the verb *to get* and highlight with GREEN (or underscore them).
- Search for forms of the verb *to seem* and highlight with GREEN (or underscore them).
- Search for forms of the verb *to serve* and highlight with GREEN (or underscore them).

Clarify Your Pronouns

- Search for *there* and *it* and highlight with BLUE (or put double forward slashes on either side of them; e.g., //there//).
- Search for *that*, *which*, and *who* and highlight with BLUE (or //).
- Search for *they*, *them*, *their*, and *its* and highlight with BLUE (or //).
- Search for *this*, *these*, and *those* and highlight with BLUE (or //).
- Search for *she*, *he*, and *we* and highlight with BLUE (or //).

Decrease Your Prepositions

- Search for prepositions like *by*, *of*, *to*, *for*, *toward*, *on*, *at*, *from*, *in*, *with*, and *as* and highlight with PURPLE (or put double brackets on either side of them; e.g., [[by]]).

Cut Unnecessary Words

- Search for *not* and *n't* and highlight with ORANGE (or put double tildes on either side of them; e.g., ~~not~~).
- Search for *very* and highlight with ORANGE (or ~~).
- Search for words ending in *-ly* and highlight with ORANGE (or ~~).
- Search for *in*, *out*, *up*, *on*, *off*, and *away* and highlight with ORANGE (or ~~).
- Search words sandwiched with *a/an/the* and *that/of/in* and highlight with ORANGE (or ~~).

Then, over the next few days, use the principles and examples introduced earlier to move through your highlighted article and improve it.

Running the Belcher Editing Diagnostic Test in MS Word

John T. Sherrill coded a free Microsoft Word macro to automate the Belcher Editing Diagnostic Test so that it colors signal words in just a few seconds. Just copy the text of the macro and load it into your MS Word program using either my instructions below or Sherrill's three-minute video at johntsherrill.com/belcher-diagnostic-word-macro. If you don't find the instructions there for some reason, go to my website and search for "Belcher Editing Diagnostic Test."

1. Open the MS Word document for your article. Copy the file and save it as a backup in case anything goes wrong.
2. Go to johntsherrill.com/belcher-diagnostic-word-macro.
3. Copy the coding for the macro (it's quite long) at http://johntsherrill.com//wp-content /uploads/2017/05/belcher_diagnostic_macro.txt.
4. In your article, go to View in your toolbar and click on Macros; then click on View Macros.
5. In the Macro dialogue box, click on Create.
6. Paste the coding for the macro into the dialogue box that pops up, pasting over everything that's in the box already. Don't worry if it doesn't give you a chance to give the macro a title; that will happen automatically.
7. Then close the dialogue boxes until you see your document again.
8. Once again, go to View in your toolbar and click on Macros; then click on View Macros.
9. Select the Belcher Diagnostic macro and then click on Run.
10. The macro will highlight all the signal words, which might take awhile if your article is long.
11. Edit your article.
12. When finished editing and you want to get rid of the highlights that the macro inserted, click on Select in your toolbar and then on Select All.
13. In the Font toolbar, select the Highlight icon and then No Color, and it will remove all the colors.
14. If the Belcher Editing Diagnostic Test doesn't run properly for some reason, go to my website and search for updated instructions.

Running the Belcher Editing Diagnostic Test in LaTeX

Carlos Alfredo Barreto Suárez created a free program that automates the Belcher Editing Diagnostic Test for documents in LaTeX, a document preparation system used in the disciplines of computer science, engineering, chemistry, physics, and sometimes in economics, psychology, and political science. Called BDT_latex (Belcher Diagnostic Test for LaTeX), the program implements the test on projects that use multiple files, such as TeX files or images. You can find it at github.com/carlobar/BDT_latex.

Running the Belcher Editing Diagnostic Test in Other Word-Processing Programs

If you're using a word-processing program with a strong Find and Replace feature, such as WordPerfect, you can use the instructions above as a template for running the test by hand or adapting the MS Word macro for your use. If you're using a word-processing program with a weak Find and Replace feature, such as Google Docs or Pages for Mac, you can try using the symbols I laid out earlier, when describing how to run the test by hand. That is, when replacing the signal words, replace them with an extra character instead of with a font-color change. So for instance, change "and" to "++and++" so that you can easily see the signal words. It doesn't work nearly as well as highlighting, but it is a work-around.

Tracking Writing Time

Each day, use the Calendar for Actual Time Spent Writing This Week form (or digital time-tracking software) to keep track of the time you spent writing this week. Then, at the end of the week, evaluate how you spent your time.

If busy, at least mark the check boxes with how long you wrote today. ☐ 15+ min. ☐ 30+ ☐ 60+ ☐ 120+

WEEK 11, DAYS 2-5: READING AND TASKS

Days 2-5 Tasks: Revising Your Article Using the Belcher Editing Diagnostic Test

Today, tomorrow, and the next day, you'll revise your now quite colorful article! Skim it and look for color (or symbol) clusters. The more red, blue, green, purple, and orange words that cluster in a sentence or paragraph, the more likely the prose there needs to be improved. Below are the instructions for how to address the color clusters. Use the day 1 reading for examples of how to edit using the highlighting. Please keep in mind that some instances of the signal words won't signal problems—but each signal word provides you with a possible opportunity to improve your prose after close examination.

Belcher Editing Diagnostic Test Principles Summarized

Red words: doublings and lists. Starting from the beginning of your article, pick the first sentence containing several RED words (or ++). Look carefully at the black words on either side of the RED. If they are a doubling, could you delete one of them? If they are a list, could you use a summarizing category word instead? If you need the list, does it appear in the right place in the sentence, after being introduced? If it appears in the right place, do the items in the list appear in the correct order? If the items are in the correct order, are they parallel? Proceed through your article asking whether you can delete, replace, rearrange, or make parallel the words before or after the RED. Reducing your lists will declutter your writing.

Green words: weak verbs and passive voice. Go back to the beginning of your article and start looking at sentences containing GREEN words (or <u>underscore</u>), especially when they appear close to BLUE words. If a verb is buried close by as a noun (words with GREEN endings, like *-ence*), can you unbury that verb? Or can you replace the GREEN verbs with stronger verbs? If your sentence is passive, with GREEN *to be* and maybe a "by" nearby, but has a named subject, can you convert it into active voice? Strengthening your verbs will invigorate your prose.

Blue words: unneeded pronouns, floating pronouns. Examine sentences that have several BLUE words (or //), especially when they appear near GREEN words. Could you delete the BLUE words (vague pronouns)? Phrases with the GREEN verb *to be* near BLUE pronouns *there/it* or *that/which/who* can often be cut. Also, how distant are your BLUE pronouns from their noun antecedent? If any are far, can you replace the pronoun with that antecedent? If a BLUE pronoun appears right after a comma, is the antecedent actually the subject of the clause before it? If not, clarify it. If the BLUE pronouns *this*, *these*, and *those* appear alone, would it be a good idea to add a noun after them? If a BLUE pronoun appears before its antecedent, would it be a good idea to switch them? Clarifying your pronouns will make your article easier to read.

Purple words: unneeded prepositional phrases. Examine sentences that have several PURPLE words (or [[]]), especially when they appear near ORANGE or BLUE words. Can you delete some of those PURPLE words and convert those nearby BLUE words into verbs or adjectives? PURPLE words often appear as part of empty phrases like "due to the fact that" and "a variety of." Sometimes you need them, but delete all that you can. Deleting unneeded prepositional phrases will energize your writing.

Orange words: empty words. Examine sentences containing several ORANGE words (or ~~), which often are doing little but cluttering up the sentence. Are you using *not* to avoid writing something assertive? Does a sentence have several negatives? Replace the negatives with strong words instead. Are you using *very* to intensify a weak adverb instead of choosing the right adverb? Use the strong adverb instead. Are words ending in *-ly* (e.g., *really, actually, definitely*) weakening your prose? Delete them and replace them with stronger verbs or adjectives. Are you using weak adverb particles instead of strong verbs? You can change such weak formulations as "started on" to the stronger verbs *commenced* or *launched*. Deleting empty words will strengthen your writing.

Running this test will take awhile, but doing so will not only improve this article but also teach you much about your writing that will serve you for years to come.

Belcher Editing Diagnostic Test Quick Reference
You may find this quick reference chart useful.

Belcher Editing Diagnostic Test Quick Reference				
Signal words	Part of speech	Color/ symbol	Problem	Action
and, or	conjunctions	red	Lists: false, all-inclusive, noninclusive, flipped, disordered, nonparallel	Replace the subcategories with the category, cut the list, move the list concept up front, reorder the list, make parallel
be, have, do, make, provide, perform, seem, serve	verbs	green	buried verbs, weak verbs, passive voice	Convert noun back into verb, replace weak verb with strong verb, convert passive voice into active voice
it, there; that, which, who; this, these, those; they, them, their, its; she, he, we	pronouns	blue	empty pronouns, unclear antecedents, dangling constructions, absent nouns, premature pronouns	replace pronoun with stronger verb and move subject up front, replace pronoun with noun antecedent, add noun to demonstrative pronouns, move pronouns to follow antecedents

Belcher Editing Diagnostic Test Quick Reference *(continued)*

Signal words	Part of speech	Color/symbol	Problem	Action
by, of, to, toward, on, at, from, with, as	prepositions	purple	prepositional clustering	replace preposition with modifiers and verbs
not	negative	orange	weak adjectives	replace with strong adjectives
-ly, very	adverbs	orange	empty words	replace with strong verb or adjective
in, out, up, on, off, away	particles	orange	weak verbs	replace with strong verbs

From *Writing Your Journal Article in Twelve Weeks: A Guide to Academic Publishing Success* by Wendy Laura Belcher. Chicago, IL: University of Chicago Press. Copyright 2019 by Belcher. All rights reserved.

Editing Each Other's Writing

Exchange. If you're struggling with revising your own writing, you might try meeting with a colleague and exchanging paragraphs: each of you works on revising a paragraph of the other person's text. Focus on adding, deleting, substituting, and rearranging the words, whatever makes the text sound better to you. Then discuss the paragraph revisions with each other. Don't insist that your way is better—it's up to the original author to decide what he or she wants to do—but this exercise can help you see the many ways of saying the same thing, and the kinds of changes that tend to improve a sentence. It can also help you be a better editor: by dialoguing with the author, you learn the article's possibilities and can expand them.

Workshopping. When I'm teaching my writing workshop, we work on this editing exercise as a group. Gather a group of people who have run the diagnostic test on their writing. Have each person select a particularly problematic sentence and either write it on the board or project it on a screen. Then work together out loud to improve the sentence, with the author of the sentence making the possible edits on the draft. We've often found that together we could do a much better job of improving the sentence than working alone. Having seen the technique in action, everyone can edit their own work more easily.

Tracking Writing Time

Mark your electronic calendar, the Calendar for Actual Time Spent Writing This Week form, and/or the check boxes here with how long you wrote today. ☐ 15+ min. ☐ 30+ ☐ 60+ ☐ 120+

Then, here at the end of your workweek, take pride in your accomplishments and evaluate whether any patterns need changing.

DOCUMENTING YOUR WRITING TIME AND TASKS

Calendar for Actual Time Spent Writing This Week

Time	Day 1	Day 2	Day 3	Day 4	Day 5	Day 6	Day 7
5:00 a.m.							
6:00							
7:00							
8:00							
9:00							
10:00							
11:00							
12:00 p.m.							
1:00							
2:00							
3:00							
4:00							
5:00							
6:00							
7:00							
8:00							
9:00							
10:00							
11:00							
12:00 a.m.							
1:00							
2:00							
3:00							
4:00							
Total minutes							
Tasks completed							

WEEK 12
Sending Your Article!

Task Day	Week 12 Daily Writing Tasks	Estimated Task Time in Minutes	
		HumInt	SciQua
Day 1 (Monday?)	Read from here until you reach the week 12, day 2 tasks, filling in any boxes, checking off any forms, and answering any questions as you read. Identify what remains to be done.	90	30
Day 2 (Tuesday?)	Put your article into the journal's style.	90+	30
Day 3 (Wednesday?)	Wrap up any remaining issues.	90+	60+
Day 4 (Thursday?)	Wrap up any remaining issues.	90+	60
Day 5 (Friday?)	Send and celebrate!	Freedom!	Freedom!
Total estimated time for reading the workbook, completing the tasks, and writing your article		**6+ hours**	**3+ hours**

Above are the final tasks for your twelfth week. It's time to send! Make sure to start this week by scheduling when you'll complete these final tasks, and then tracking the time you actually spend doing them. This week might take you no more than an hour, but it might take many hours if you haven't been using reference management software. Knowing how long it takes to send your article will be useful for future submissions.

Also, if you want, tweet me #12WeekArticleSent when you submit your article so I can congratulate you!

WEEK 12, DAY 1: READING AND TASKS

ELEVENTH WEEK IN REVIEW

Last week, you worked on editing your writing, making the small changes that increase reader comprehension. Everyone's writing can improve at this level, including people who've been writing for decades. Fortunately, if the large-scale aspects of your article are strong, its small-scale aspects matter less.

ON THE IMPORTANCE OF FINISHING

The primary goals of this workbook have been to aid you in revising an article and sending it to the editor of a suitable journal. I have designed this workbook as an end run around our common tendency both to procrastinate (by not writing) and to perfect (by endlessly revising). To get published, you must train yourself to get over both tendencies. Let me put this another way.

At a dinner party hosted by a fellow writer, I met an engineer who had published eight hundred articles. His publication list, in ten-point type, was thirty-two pages long.

"Eight hundred articles!" I exclaimed. I had never met anyone who'd published so much, although I knew that engineers tend to write more articles than their counterparts in other scientific disciplines, and far more than scholars in the humanities. "You've got to tell me—what's the secret of your success?"

He replied with a smile, "You know, I have one." I waited with bated breath until he declared, "It's six words: 'beyond the scope of this article.'"

"What?"

He beamed. "I do a little research, I do a little typing, and when I run through what I know and am up against something I don't know, I simply type that such-and-such is 'beyond the scope of this article,' and send it to a journal."

This may not seem like genius at first glimpse, but it is. This engineer had learned how to abandon the posture of mastery so that he could pursue the search for knowledge. This was the "secret" at the heart of his tremendous productivity: letting go. Like him, you need to decide what's beyond the scope of your article. Then you must take the most difficult step of all: sending.

FOLLOWING JOURNAL SUBMISSION GUIDELINES

Most journals have submission guidelines posted on their website, and you need to study them closely. Some even have Microsoft Word templates that you can download to facilitate putting your article in their style. Knowing the content your intended journal is expecting and having this information at hand will make your submission process go more smoothly. If any of that journal's guidelines contradict my advice in this chapter, follow the journal, not me! In the absence of clear instruction from the journal, follow the instructions I give below.

Understanding the Journal's Style Manual

All academic journals standardize the articles they publish by using one of the style manuals, reference books that give detailed instructions for preparing academic materials. Each manual represents its publishing organization's conventions for standardizing punctuation, spelling, non-English languages, capitalization, abbreviations, headings, quotations, numbers, names and terms, mathematics, tables, figures, notes, and reference citations in text. Since authors and editors from around the world and in various fields have different educational and training backgrounds and therefore present information in widely varied ways, style manuals aid in standardizing these presentations. By setting rules on matters of taste and choice, these reference works ensure that all the articles in a journal or book appear in a uniform manner. For instance, while everyone agrees that a period should appear at the end of a sentence, should a note reference number precede the period or follow it? What about a quotation mark? There's no right or wrong answer, but since regular patterns increase readability, editors use style manuals so that the works in their publication's pages are uniform.

Common Style Manuals

Every scholar should own at least one of the most common style manuals, which are as follows:

The Chicago Manual of Style. 17th ed. Chicago: University of Chicago Press, 2017. Commonly called *CMOS*, this manual is the standard for the preparation of books and articles across all fields in what's become known as "Chicago style." It also has an impressive website with advice for authors. *CMOS* provides two types of documentation systems—an author-date system and a notes and bibliography system. The first is applicable to any discipline, and calls for sources to be cited briefly in the text. The second is intended specifically for the humanities, with sources cited in footnotes or endnotes. *CMOS* is the most detailed of all the style manuals, and any author can benefit from its terrific section on grammar. Aspects of the *CMOS* author-date documentation style include using authors' full first and last names in entries in the reference list; including a place of publication for books in that list; organizing the reference list entries alphabetically; and using no comma between author and year of publication in in-text citations—for example (Van Cleve 2016) or (Blain 2015). See chicagomanualofstyle.org.

Publication Manual of the American Psychological Association. 6th ed. Washington, DC: American Psychological Association, 2010. Commonly called the APA, this manual is a standard for those across the social sciences, not just psychology. It focuses on the preparation of journal articles, not books. It provides more advice on writing than some style manuals, as it was originally designed for first-time authors. In addition to technical matters of style, it addresses designing and reporting on research, structuring articles, writing clearly, following ethical standards, avoiding bias in language, and converting the dissertation into a journal article. APA also has an excellent section on writing clear and useful abstracts. Aspects of APA's author-date documentation style include using initials for authors' first and middle names in entries in the reference list; organizing the reference list alphabetically; and using a comma between author and year of publication in in-text citations—for example (Van Cleve, 2016). See apastyle.org.

MLA Style Manual and Guide to Scholarly Publishing. 8th ed. New York: Modern Language Association of America, 2016. Commonly called the MLA, this manual is often used by those writing about literature or language. It can be used to prepare either articles or books. In addition to technical matters of style, it addresses selecting a journal or publisher, wading through the swamp of copyright issues, and writing for a particular audience. Aspects of MLA style include using authors' full first, middle, and last names in the bibliography, which it refers to as the Works Cited list; placing the year of publication last in these listings; and dispensing with year in in-text citations—for example (Van Cleve). See style.mla.org.

AMA Manual of Style: A Guide for Authors and Editors. 10th ed. New York: Oxford University Press; 2007. Commonly called the AMA, this manual is the standard in medicine, and was first published by the *Journal of the American Medical Association.* Many biomedical journals use this manual. Instead of including names and year in the text for citations, AMA uses numerals. Let's say that an article by Margaret Schwarze is the first citation in an article. Instead of seeing "(Schwarze 2017)" in the text, you would see the numeral 1. If you clicked on that numeral, it would take you to the full source citation. Then, for every subsequent citation of this Schwarze source in the article, you would see the numeral 1. So at the end of a sentence you could see a string of numerals, such as "1, 4, 15, 20." Some aspects of AMA style: using initials for authors' first and middle names in the list of citations, naming that list References, and ordering the sources in the list by order of appearance in the article, not alphabetically by last name. Another style very similar to AMA style is Vancouver style (by the International Committee of Medical Journal Editors), used by the Medline database and the search engine PubMed, except that it doesn't use italicization for any titles of works. See amamanualofstyle.com.

Using Journal Style Shortcuts

Many journals will tell you that it's essential for you to put your article in their style upon initial submission, not just upon acceptance. But how important is that requirement? After all, these style manuals are long and complicated. Some are over a thousand pages! No author is going to be able to standardize an article exactly according to such a manual. Indeed, given the high article rejection rates, I think it's unconscionable for editors to insist that authors first submitting articles put them in the journal's style. If a journal has a 90 percent rejection rate, I think it should be banned from making this requirement. Unfortunately, authors are stuck with these draconian rules for now, in part because they do seem to work. That is, as one journal editor told me, "When an article arrives in our style, it looks like something we would publish." Further, journals are familiar with related journals' styles, so they may decide that another journal had rejected your article if it's not in *their* style. Thus, it's to your benefit to have your article reflect the style of the journal you're sending it to.

Given the amount of work it can entail to conform your article to a particular journal's style, the astute question is this: what's the least effort you can expend and still make your article look like it's in the journal's style? One editor advised that "it is not necessary to follow every ingredient of house style for the initial submission . . ., but the fundamental issue of whether to use MLA, Chicago, or another system makes a huge difference in how articles present themselves, not only procedurally but sometimes even structurally" (Argersinger and CELJ 2006).

I would say that three aspects of style are essential to apply to your article before submitting it: documentation, punctuation, and spelling. If you address these three issues, most journals will assume that you have put the article in their style. Fortunately, the second two aspects of style tend to be uniform across style manuals.

Implementing the Journal's Documentation Style

Your number one task in putting your article in the journal's style is standardizing your documentation according to that style, both in the body of your text and in the list of works cited. This standardizing can be time consuming if you haven't been using reference management software like Zotero or EndNote. My assumption is that you have followed my advice and are using such software, so you won't need detailed advice from me. Such programs can do more than put citations in a general style; they can format documentation for specific journals, including the *American Economic Review*, *New England Journal of Medicine*, and *PLOS ONE*. If you haven't been using reference management software, you'll need to make these changes to your documentation yourself, as I will instruct you later.

To get a sense of the most common style manuals' differences in documenting citations, here are some highlights.

Examples of Citing a Book

CMOS author-date: Van Cleve, Nicole Gonzalez. 2016. *Crook County: Racism and Injustice in America's Largest Criminal Court.* Palo Alto, CA: Stanford University Press.

Note: Spelled-out author name, year of publication second, capitalized and italicized title, and place of publication. The in-text citation, including page reference, would be (Van Cleve 2016, 10).

MLA: Van Cleve, Nicole Gonzalez. *Crook County: Racism and Injustice in America's Largest Criminal Court.* Stanford UP, 2016. Print.

Note: Spelled-out author name, capitalized and italicized title, no place of publication, shortened publisher name, year of publication last. Then the medium of publication is given: print, web, email, and so on. The in-text citation, including page reference, would be (Van Cleve 10).

APA: Van Cleve, N. G. (2016). *Crook County: Racism and injustice in America's largest criminal court.* Palo Alto, CA: Stanford University Press.

Note: Initials with periods for first and middle author name; year of publication second and in parentheses; title not capitalized (except in the case of proper nouns) but italicized; place of publication. The in-text citation, including page reference, would be (Van Cleve, 2016, p. 10).

AMA: 1. Van Cleve NG. *Crook County: Racism and Injustice in America's Largest Criminal Court.* Palo Alto, CA: Stanford University Press; 2016.

Note: Associated citation numeral; initials without periods for first and middle author name; title capitalized and italicized; place of publication; semicolon preceding the year of publication, which comes last. The in-text citation would be the citation numeral.

Examples of Citing a Journal Article

CMOS **author-date:** Blain, Keisha N. "'We Want to Set the World on Fire': Black Nationalist Women and Diasporic Politics in the New Negro World, 1940–1944." *Journal of Social History* 49, no. 1 (2015): 194–212.

> **Note:** Spelled-out first author name, capitalized title in quotation marks, issue number preceded by "no.," year of publication in parentheses, colon preceding page range. The in-text citation, including page reference, would be (Blain 2015, 10).

MLA: Blain, Keisha N. "'We Want to Set the World on Fire': Black Nationalist Women and Diasporic Politics in the New Negro World, 1940–1944." *Journal of Social History* 49.1 (2015): 194–212. Web.

> **Note:** Spelled-out first author name, capitalized title in quotation marks, issue number preceded by a period, year of publication in parentheses, colon preceding page range. Then the medium of publication is given: print, web, email, and so on. The in-text citation, including page reference, would be (Blain 10).

APA: Blain, K. N. (2015). "We want to set the world on fire": Black nationalist women and diasporic politics in the New Negro world, 1940–1944. *Journal of Social History, 49*(1), 194–212. doi:10.1093/jsh/shv032

> **Note:** Initials with periods for first and middle author name; year of publication second in parentheses; title not capitalized and not in quotation marks; volume number italicized; issue number in parentheses; comma preceding page range; DOI. The in-text citation, including page reference, would be (Blain, 2015, p. 10).

AMA: 1. Blain KN. "We want to set the world on fire": black nationalist women and diasporic politics in the new negro world, 1940–1944. *J Soc Hist.* 2015;49(1):194–212. doi:10.1093/jsh/shv032

> **Note:** Associated citation numeral; initials without periods for first and middle author name; title not capitalized (including the first word of a subtitle) and not in quotation marks; journal title italicized and abbreviated but with period after; year of publication with semicolon before volume number; issue number in parentheses; colon preceding page range; DOI. The in-text citation would be the citation numeral.

Implementing the Journal's Punctuation Style

Punctuation style varies from journal to journal, but here are some general punctuation rules.

Serial commas. Academic style requires a serial comma, meaning a comma preceding the last item in a series. An example is the comma after the second name in the following list: "Alicia Garza, Opal Tometi, and Patrisse Cullors." Not using a serial comma in academic writing alerts an editor or reader to your status as a novice.

Double quotation marks. US academic journals use "double" quotation marks; British and commonwealth journals use 'single' quotation marks. US journals place punctuation inside the quotation marks; British journals place them outside.

Block quotation marks. Don't place quotation marks around material formatted in block quotes unless those quotation marks appeared in the original text. Separate into a block quote any quotation longer than four or five lines on a page.

Scare quotes. Think twice about using scare quotes—quotation marks indicating that single words or phrases are either problematic or being used in an ironic way. If the term is problematic, find another; don't reproduce the problem. If you are unable to resolve this issue, then place quotation marks around that word or phrase only at its first appearance, note the problem, and subsequently use the term without scare quotes; don't keep signaling that it's problematic.

Exclamation marks. In the humanities, you can use one exclamation mark somewhere in your journal article, but that's it. In the other disciplines, that's one exclamation mark too many. Let your sentence structure deliver the emphasis.

Hyphens and dashes. No editor would expect you to do this, but one easy thing you can do to make your writing look more professional is to use the appropriate mark of punctuation for hyphens and dashes. The well-known hyphen is used in compound words and end-of-line word breaks. It appears on your keyboard and is the shortest horizontal line available to you. A dash represents a break in thought—editors call it an em-dash. A less known type of dash appears in number ranges, such as page ranges (e.g., 35–45). Editors call it an en-dash. If you haven't been inserting em-dashes or en-dashes, I provide instructions on how to do so later in the chapter.

Implementing the Journal's Spelling Style

Spelling style varies little from US journal to US journal, but quite a bit between US journals and UK journals. For instance, the words spelled *labor, analyze, defense,* and *theater* in the United States are spelled *labour, analyse, defence,* and *theatre* in the United Kingdom. If you need to switch US spelling to UK spelling or vice versa, I give instructions on how to do that later in the chapter.

IMPLEMENTING OTHER ASPECTS OF THE JOURNAL'S STYLE

Here are some final general style rules.

"Down style" capitalization. Almost all US academic journals follow what's called a "down style"; they rarely capitalize anything but proper nouns. It depends on the journal, but most won't capitalize racial categories (e.g., white or black) or status titles standing alone (e.g., the professor or the president).

Italics and boldface for non-English words. Most journals prefer that you use italics only for non-English words or the titles of works. If you regularly use italics for emphasis, most editors will see this as a form of "shouting." If your sentence structure is clear, you shouldn't need to rely on italics for stressing certain words. The one exception is sentences occurring in block quotes, where you can't restructure the sentence but may want to draw attention to parts of it. If you add italics to a block quote, always add "(italics added)" to the end of the block quote. Never use boldface for emphasizing individual words; academic journals never allow this practice.

Acronyms. Always spell out an acronym at its first appearance in the body of your article, with the acronym immediately after it in parentheses; for instance, "United States Agency of International Development (USAID)." Thereafter, use the acronym, not the full version of the name.

Proper nouns. Give the full first name of any person at its first appearance in your article (e.g., Erich Auerbach, not just Auerbach).

Inclusive language. Using inclusive language is important not only for ethical reasons but also for practical ones—you have no idea who the peer reviewers will be, so avoid giving offense with language that is sexist, racist, homophobic, ableist, ageist, anti-Semitic, Islamophobic, classist, and so on. Many online guides provide information about what language to avoid. One overall point is that placing *the* in front of a word can lead to offense in certain instances. For example, instead of "the elderly," write "older people"; instead of "the blind," write "visually impaired people"; instead of "the wheelchair bound," write "wheelchair users." When it comes to gender, almost all sexist English words now have nonsexist equivalents that work quite well. So there's no need to refer to "firemen," "mankind," or "manpower" when you can refer just as easily to "firefighters," "humanity," and "workers." In terms of disability, avoid using *blind* or *deaf* in negative ways—such as "blind spot," "blinded by," or "turn a deaf ear to"—and demeaning words about intelligence, such as *dimwitted* or *imbecilic.* Finally, be careful not to refer to men and women differently; for example, calling men by their last name but women by their first name (e.g., Sanders and Hillary). Refer to all by their last name.

Singular *they*. To avoid using *he* or *she,* many now write to avoid singular verbs when discussing human beings. While the singular *they* is becoming increasingly common in written English (e.g., "many a poet writes their poem slowly"), a few senior faculty are touchy about it. If you prefer the singular *they,* you might note that in your article submission for the peer review round.

Collecting Journal Submission Information

Journal editors maintain that too many submissions contain errors revealing that the authors never looked at the publication's submission guidelines. You're not going to be among those people! Typical errors that editors grumble about are overlooking article length, title length, or abstract length requirements; failing to use the required font or line spacing; improperly formatting headings and tables; omitting keywords, and using a documentation style other than the journal's. Below are instructions on what information to collect before submitting your journal article. Don't worry; you won't need to memorize these lessons, because there will be a checklist later. For now, just become acquainted with them. Then, fill out the checklist at the end of this section to collect all the information you need to submit an article that won't annoy editors.

Method of submission. To process article submissions, almost all journals use online peer-review management systems, like ScholarOne Manuscripts, Editorial Manager, or EJPress. These systems automate much of the process, not just making editors' lives easier but also enabling authors to see what's happening. No longer do you have to write to the editor to learn the status of your article—just go to the submission site to find out whether it's under review or still with the editor. To submit an article electronically, go to your journal's website, click on the submission link there, and proceed to the journal's portal. Surprisingly, however, many journals in the humanities, even prestigious ones, still accept article submissions only by email, and a few still require them to be sent by post.

Submission cover letter. Most web-based submission portals don't provide an opportunity to submit a cover letter, instead having you fill out a form with the information you would have provided in that letter. But since web-based portal forms focus on what helps the journal process your submission, not what helps you get published, you may find it useful to read the instructions later in this chapter for writing a submission cover letter, and include some of that information in a comment or note in your submission form. A top journal editor recently told me that even a brief message in the note field of the web submission form makes a difference, because the forms are so sterile that a little bit of humanity registers. If the journal wants you to submit your article by email or post instead of through a web-based portal, you must accompany the article with a cover letter.

Final abstract. Ensure that your abstract is in the journal's format—meeting the stated word count, the required structure, and any required subheadings. Don't hesitate to use up all the words allotted, and to pack the abstract with keywords. But be aware that most web submission portals will reject abstracts that exceed the word count.

Keywords. Some journals require you to provide a list of keywords separately from the title, abstract, or article. Sometimes they expect you to invent these keywords yourself; sometimes you must use a specialized list, such as Library of Congress subject terms. Either way, try to use a standardized list, so that your keywords are terms for which scholars actually search. The website Academia.edu, which is organized by author-provided keywords, is a good place to search for terms that have many followers.

Article word count. If the journal has a minimum or maximum word count for its articles, you need to meet it. Journal editors don't check this closely, so if you're a hundred or even two hundred words over, that will be okay. But you can't be over by several pages.

Type of article. Some journals publish various types of articles, such as shorter research reports or review articles as well as research articles. Sometimes they list their requirements for each type. Ensure that your article meets those requirements.

Suggesting reviewers. Some journals will ask you to suggest potential reviewers. Never suggest any unless the editors or journal website specifically ask you to do so (although you can *offer* to provide names if they are interested). If you do recommend reviewers, the journal expects that each suggested reviewer is not from your institution, has not helped you develop the submission in any way, and has not recently collaborated with you or any of the other authors. It also expects suggested reviewers to have knowledge in your specific area or field of research and to be publishing themselves. If it asks you to recommend reviewers, do so—research shows that author-recommended reviewers are more likely than editor-chosen reviewers to recommend publication (Kowalczuk et al. 2015, 5).

Deprecating reviewers. Alternately, you may want to request that the journal not ask a particular individual to review your article. This is a very tough thing to pull off, however. Few editors will accept your naming someone as a "deprecated" or "nonpreferred" reviewer without your giving a good reason. And many editors believe that there are only two good reasons. One is that the potential reviewer is in direct research competition with you, such that the reviewer has a real incentive to delay reviewing your article or give it a negative review. The other is that this person deplores all research conducted using a certain methodology or theory, not just your work. Any other reason is likely to inspire the curious editor to ask that person for a review precisely because you named them. Knowing this, some scholars try tricks, little realizing that journal editors are on to those. One trick is sending the article to that potential peer reviewer in advance, and then mentioning that in the submission cover letter. The trick is based on the authors' thinking that editors assume authors send their work only to friendly readers. (They don't assume that.) Another trick is based on an old saying in political science, "Thank your enemies; cite your friends." That is, in the submission cover letter, you thank your enemies, but in the article itself you don't mention them. Ostensibly, this maneuver prevents editors from asking as reviewers those you've thanked, as editors assume them to be your friends. (Again, editors don't assume that.) Also, while frequently tendered as advice, it's not quite clear how this would work in practice. You can hardly omit citing someone whose work you use! To sum up, effective methods for deprecating peer reviewers are rare.

Anonymizing. If the journal to which you will submit your article has an anonymous peer-review process, you will need to strip the article of any information that would identify you as the author. This step is particularly important if you're not a full professor at a prestigious US university. Bias is real; the anonymous peer-review process exists to protect you from it. Anonymizing an article is not just removing your name at the beginning of the article. It means taking out any reference to yourself anywhere, including any direct reference to your own work, any thanks to well-known advisors, any mention of grants or institutions, and so on. If you cite your own work in a way that suggests that its author and the article's author are the same, put "[author]" in the text, and remove the citation entirely (don't leave the title, journal, and year in the Works Cited section). Most journals won't allow you to submit acknowledgments in the first round, which is wise, because it prevents such revealing statements as "I would like to thank my advisor [name omitted] in anthropology at Addis Ababa University." Leaving in the university and department is not anonymizing your article. Take out any running heads or running feet containing your name. Finally, and most important, strip your name from the properties of your Microsoft Word document or PDF, which registers who last modified a file.

Illustrations. If you don't have any illustrations in your article, you can skip this section. If you do use any maps, drawings, photographs, tables, or charts, journals may ask you, even upon original submission, to submit them in complicated ways. Journals often have strict instructions for illustration formats, sizes, naming, placement, captions, titles, and so on. Most of the time you don't need to provide high-quality versions of your illustrations in the first round, but sometimes you do. Note that if the journal wants you to send illustrations in a separate file, you'll need to indicate where each table, graph, and so on is to be inserted in the body of your article. For example, you would type "[Table 1 about here]" in the place where the table should appear in the published article. Also, make sure that you discuss any illustrations in the text. A common mistake is to have images go unreferenced. Always include a direct reference in the text, such as "(see table 1)." And remember to provide captions for all illustrations, and source lines for all tables and charts.

Permissions. At some point, you'll also need to obtain permission from the creator of any artwork you reproduce in your article but that you did not create yourself—including any maps or others' photographs of artwork. In addition, if you quote most of a poem or contemporary song lyric, you'll need to ask its creator for permission to use it. Further, you must have a signed release from an interviewee to publish a transcript of an interview you conducted with that person. Fortunately, most journals don't require original submissions to have already solicited permissions. But, as mentioned previously, obtaining permissions is a notoriously labor-intensive process. Finding the right address for the correct owner of the copyrighted material and extracting a signed permission are difficult, so start early.

Journal style. The better the journal, the more likely it is to require you to submit your article in its own documentation, spelling, and punctuation style, even for peer review.

Documenting sources. As noted, journals use different formats for citing sources, according to the style manual they use. If you have been using reference management software to produce your sources, standardizing your citations according to that style manual will be finished in a matter of a few minutes. If not, you have some work ahead of you.

Footnotes and endnotes. Some journals allow footnotes; most discourage them. Also, if you're in the humanities and using footnotes, convert them into endnotes. At first submission, it's standard practice to have notes at the end of the article, not at the bottom of pages.

File format. Some journals want your article already in PDF; some web submission sites automatically convert documents into PDF. Online submissions often require that you submit the parts of the article in separate documents, so separate them if needed.

Author information. Many journals are requiring authors to submit their ORCiD, a digital identifier that distinguishes them from every other researcher, with their article submission. So register with ORCiD if you haven't done so. If you have coauthors, be sure that you've represented each of their names exactly as they'd wish, with or without nicknames or middle names and so on. In addition, some journals will ask you to fill out a form describing each author's contribution to the article. The journal's website will make this clear, as it often provides the form.

Location information. Some journals are requiring authors to include geolocation information in a section within their article, but even if your journal doesn't require it, including Lthis information is wise. For instance, if your article is about Islamic banking in Tehran, Iran, you would include the geolocation information (the coordinates for a point location or bounding box) for Tehran somewhere in your article. Global positioning coordinates should appear in latitude and longitude format with decimal degrees (e.g., 35.719988°N, 51.364229°E; don't add the abbreviations "lat" or "long," because they may hamper search results). You can easily use Google Maps to find this information, just go to the location, right click on the spot, and select "What's here?"

My Journal Submission Checklist

Go to the journal's website and find the answers to the questions given in these boxes, making any decisions needed. If you haven't standardized your article according to the task in question, check "To do" in the relevant box and add that task to your to-do list.

Method of Submission

| How does the journal accept submissions? | ☐ Web-based portal ☐ By email ☐ By post |
| What is that address? | |

Submission Cover Letter

| Will I need a submission cover letter for this article? | ☐ Yes ☐ No ☐ Must find out (to do) |
| If I need one, have I written it yet? | ☐ Yes ☐ No (to do) |

Final Abstract

Will I need an abstract for this submission?	☐ Yes ☐ No ☐ Must find out (to do)
If needed, does the journal have an abstract word limit?	☐ Yes ☐ No ☐ Must find out (to do)
What is that word limit?	
Are particular subheadings required?	☐ Yes ☐ No ☐ Must find out (to do)
Is my abstract in compliance with the requirements?	☐ Yes ☐ No (to do)

Keywords

Will I need keywords?	☐ Yes ☐ No ☐ Must find out (to do)
If needed, must I use a specialized list?	☐ Yes ☐ No ☐ Must find out (to do)
What is the minimum/maximum number of keywords?	
Have I written the keywords yet?	☐ Yes ☐ No (to do)

Article Word Count

Does the journal have rules about article word count?	☐ Yes ☐ No
If yes, what are they?	
Does that count include the list of works cited and tables?	☐ Yes ☐ No
Is my article in compliance with the word limits?	☐ Yes ☐ No (to do)
Does the journal have rules about title word count?	☐ Yes ☐ No
If yes, does my title comply?	☐ Yes ☐ No (to do)

Type of Article

Does the journal list requirements for different types of articles?	☐ Yes ☐ No
If yes, what are those requirements for my type of article?	
If so, does my article meets those requirements?	☐ Yes ☐ No (to do)

Suggesting and Deprecating Reviewers

Does the journal ask me to recommend peer reviewers?	☐ No ☐ Yes ☐ Must find out (to do)
If so, whom will I recommend? (Do not name advisors or previous readers of the article.)	
Only if essential: Whom will I deprecate as a reviewer? What good reason will I give?	

Anonymizing

Does the journal have an anonymous review process?	☐ Yes ☐ No
If yes, have I removed from my article	
my name on the first page?	☐ Yes ☐ No (to do)
self-citations?	☐ Yes ☐ No (to do)
acknowledgments?	☐ Yes ☐ No (to do)
running heads or running feet containing my name?	
my name from the document properties?	☐ Yes ☐ No (to do)
Is my article anonymized?	☐ Yes ☐ No (to do)

Illustrations

Does my article contain images (including tables and graphs)?	☐ Yes ☐ No (skip this section)

Regarding illustrations, does the journal want me to

submit tables and charts in a separate file?	☐ No ☐ Yes
submit each image (e.g., photographs, graphs) in a separate file?	☐ No ☐ Yes
submit each image with a particular filename?	☐ No ☐ Yes
submit each image in a specified file format?	☐ No ☐ Yes
submit each image at a specified resolution?	☐ No ☐ Yes
submit captions for illustrations in a separate file?	☐ No ☐ Yes
If the journal wants the illustrations in a separate file, have I indicated where in my main file those illustrations are to be placed (e.g., "[Table 1 about here]")?	☐ Yes ☐ No (to do)
Do I call out (mention) each one of the illustrations by name in the body of the article (e.g., "see table 1")?	☐ Yes ☐ No (to do)
Do my tables, charts, and graphs have clear titles and source lines that accurately describe their contents?	☐ Yes ☐ No (to do)
Do my images have clear captions and acknowledgment of permissions granted?	☐ Yes ☐ No (to do)
Have I prepared my illustrations to meet all the requirements above?	☐ Yes ☐ No (to do)

Permissions

Are any of my illustrations produced and owned by anyone else (e.g., are they from someone else's book or an original artwork)?	☐ No ☐ Yes
If yes, does this journal require me to have that permission documentation finished upon original submission?	☐ Yes ☐ No
If yes, have I asked the owner of the copyrighted material for permission to reproduce it?	☐ Yes ☐ No (to do)
If yes, have I collected the contact information I will need?	☐ Yes ☐ No (to do)

Journal Style

Does my article use the serial comma?	☐ Yes	☐ No (to do)
Does my article avoid exclamation marks?	☐ Yes	☐ No (to do)
Does my article spell out acronyms at their first appearance?	☐ Yes	☐ No (to do)
Does my article give full first and last names at first appearance?	☐ Yes	☐ No (to do)
Does my article use inclusive language?	☐ Yes	☐ No (to do)
Does the journal use British spelling and punctuation?	☐ Yes	☐ No
If yes, does my article use single quotation marks?	☐ Yes	☐ No (to do)
If yes, does my article use inside punctuation?	☐ Yes	☐ No (to do)
Does the journal use US spelling and punctuation?	☐ Yes	☐ No
If yes, does my article use double quotation marks?	☐ Yes	☐ No (to do)
If yes, does my article use outside punctuation?	☐ Yes	☐ No (to do)
If yes, does my article avoid scare quotes?	☐ Yes	☐ No (to do)
Does the journal require that I submit my article in a specified font and font size? (12-point font is standard.)	☐ Yes	☐ No
Is my article in the correct font (and font size)?	☐ Yes	☐ No (to do)
Does the journal require that I submit my article with particular line spacing (single, double)?	☐ Yes	☐ No
Does the journal require double line spacing even for block quotations, tables, and the Works Cited section?	☐ Yes	☐ No
Does my article have the required line spacing?	☐ Yes	☐ No (to do)
Does the journal require that I submit my article with particular margins? (One-inch margins are standard.)	☐ Yes	☐ No
Does my article have the required margins?	☐ Yes	☐ No (to do)
Does my article use many diacritics or a special language font?	☐ Yes	☐ No
Am I ready to give information about laying out those diacritics or special language font?	☐ Yes	☐ No (to do)
Does my article use many non-English words, and does the journal have any instructions for the presentation of such words?	☐ Yes	☐ No
Does my article present those non-English words as instructed?	☐ Yes	☐ No (to do)
Does the journal require that I format subheads in specified ways?	☐ Yes	☐ No
Have I formatted the subheads in those ways?	☐ Yes	☐ No (to do)
What other style instructions appear on the journal's website (e.g., capitalization, citing social media)?		
Does my article follow those additional instructions?	☐ Yes	☐ No (to do)

Documenting Sources

What style manual does the journal use?	☐ Chicago/*CMOS*, author-date ☐ Chicago/*CMOS*, note-bibliography ☐ APA ☐ MLA ☐ AMA ☐ Other:
Does the journal expect me to cite sources author-date style (by listing the author and publication year in the text)?	☐ Yes ☐ No
If no, does it expect me to cite sources in footnotes or endnotes?	☐ Yes ☐ No
Either way, is my article in that documentation style?	☐ Yes ☐ No (to do)
Does each quotation in my article appear with a source citation after it?	☐ Yes ☐ Must find out (to do)
Does each quotation in my article that's longer than one hundred words or four to five lines on a page appear as a block quote?	☐ Yes ☐ Must find out (to do)
Was I careful when typing quotations from other sources to get them exactly right?	☐ Yes ☐ No
If not, have I checked all quotes against the original?	☐ Yes ☐ No (to do)
Did I use reference management software to format my citations?	☐ Yes ☐ No
If not, does each source's author name and publication year match throughout? (i.e., "Mihret 2019" in the text is correct, but "Mirhet 2015" in the Works Cited section is wrong)	☐ Yes ☐ Must find out (to do)
Do all the sources cited in the text appear in my Works Cited section?	☐ Yes ☐ Must find out (to do)

Footnotes and Endnotes

Does the journal have rules about notes?	☐ Yes ☐ No
If my article has notes, do they follow those rules?	☐ Yes ☐ No (to do)
Do they appear as endnotes, not footnotes?	☐ Yes ☐ No (to do)

File Format

Does the journal specify the file format in which they want the article (e.g., PDF, MS Word)?	☐ Yes ☐ No ☐ Must find out (to to)	
What is that file format?		
If so, is my article in that file format?	☐ Yes ☐ No (to do)	
Will I need to submit a separate title page?	☐ Yes ☐ No ☐ Must find out (to do)	
Do I include page numbers on every page?	☐ Yes ☐ No (to do)	

Author Information

Does the journal want a postal address for author(s)?	☐ Yes ☐ No
If yes, do I have the best addresses given travel schedules?	☐ Yes ☐ No (to do)
Have I registered at orcid.org for an ORCID, a digital identifier that distinguishes me from every other researcher?	☐ Yes ☐ No (to do)
Did I coauthor this article?	☐ No ☐ Yes
If yes, am I the "corresponding author," the one who must submit the article and be the point person for all information?	☐ No ☐ Yes
If yes, do I have my coauthors' preferred version of their name for publication?	☐ Yes ☐ No (to do)
If yes, does the journal require me to define the role of each author?	☐ Yes ☐ No
If yes, do I have those definitions ready to go?	☐ Yes ☐ No (to do)
If yes, have all the coauthors agreed to the wording?	☐ Yes ☐ No (to do)

Location Information

Is my article about a specific place?	☐ Yes ☐ No
If so, what are the coordinates?	
Have I inserted them?	☐ Yes ☐ No (To Do)

Giving Warrants

Many journals now require authors to assure the editor that they've produced their article ethically. A journal will ask you to make a series of warrants, or vows, about the originality, authorship, status, and ethics of your article, either in your submission cover letter or through the journal's online submission system. They are as follows:

Authorship warrant. You must be able to state that you are the "sole author" or, if you have coauthors, "we are the sole authors." If you are not the author of the article, you should not be sending it to a publisher.

Can I/we honestly state that I am/we are the sole authors?	☐ Yes ◯ No (then don't send)

Copyright ownership warrant. You must be able to state that you "own the copyright" to the work. All authors own their work from the time of its inception, so the only reason you would not own the copyright to your own work is if you had published the work previously and, therefore, signed over the copyright to a publisher. If you do not own the copyright, you should not be sending the article to a publisher.

| Can I/we honestly state that I/we own the copyright? | ☐ Yes   ○ No (then don't send) |

Previous publication warrant. You must be able to state that you have not published the article previously. Editors want new work. Here are your options for asserting that your work is new enough to secure their consideration.

- **No part published.** If no part of the article has been published online or in print in any country or in any language, state that "this article has not been published before in any form." It's perfectly acceptable, even desirable, for you to have presented the article orally as a paper at a conference, so having done so does not preclude you from saying that no part has been published. It's also acceptable if you have published articles with similar arguments or evidence (but not both).

- **Small part published.** If a small section of the article proceeds exactly like a published article of yours—the same background information or methodology section, for instance—state that "this article has not been published before." Leave off the words "in any form." Also, be sure to note that overlap in the article at the relevant place. If more than 10 percent of the article has been published previously, you must ask the editor in advance by email for permission to submit the article. Most editors will accept the article for consideration if the argument and/or data are different.

- **Conference paper posting.** Some conferences ask authors to submit their entire article for discussion. Before participating in such a conference, ask the organizers whether they will make the articles available only to conference participants, and won't post them online where anyone can view them. If the latter is the case, refuse to participate in the conference. If your article has already been posted, tell the journal editor, "This article has not been published in a peer-reviewed journal, but was posted openly online for [the name of conference] and is still available online" or "is no longer available online." If it's still available online, email the editor in advance to ask permission to submit it.

- **Translation publication.** Some journals will be interested in publishing an article of yours that you translated from another language, particularly if the original journal is obscure. If that describes your article, state, "This article of mine has not been published in English before, but was published in [language] in [journal], and I have translated it into English for republication." In addition, you should email the editor before submitting the article to ask whether it's okay for you to submit it.

- **Working paper publication.** If the article appeared previously as a working paper, you can state, "This article has not been published in a peer-reviewed journal, but previously appeared as a working paper with [the name of the institute]." If that paper is still available online, email the editor in advance to ask whether it's okay for you to submit the article.

| I can honestly state, regarding previous publication, that this article [fill in wording] | |
| If the forgoing advised me to contact the editor, have I done so? | ☐ Yes   ○ No (to do) |

Not currently under submission warrant. You must be able to state that the article "is not currently under submission at any other journal or publisher." If your article is under submission elsewhere, you should not be sending it to another publisher. Academia considers simultaneous submission unethical, and editors will ban you from their journal if they find out that you did it.

Can I honestly state that this article is not currently under submission elsewhere?	☐ Yes ◯ No (then don't send)

Human subjects research warrant. Outside the humanities, you may have had to get Institutional Review Board (IRB) approval to research human subjects. If so, some journals require you to submit a copy of the approval letter, fill out a form, or check a box asserting that "this article has IRB approval." Even if your journal hasn't asked for information about your IRB approval, always include a sentence mentioning it in your article.

Can I honestly state that this article meets ethical requirements for research on human subjects?	☐ Yes ◯ No (then don't send)
If I have received IRB approval, have I mentioned it in the article somewhere?	☐ Yes ◯ No (to do)

Conflicts of interest warrant. You must also be able to state that you have no conflicts of interest, financial or otherwise, regarding the content or data in your article. If you received any corporate funding for the research, consult the journal's procedures for reporting potential conflicts of interest. Some journals require all authors to make a statement about any potential conflicts of interest.

Can I honestly state that this article meets ethical requirements for funding?	☐ Yes ◯ No (then don't send)

Plagiarism warrant. Don't copy sentences from other works without citing their author, and don't change those sentences slightly so as not to place them within quotation marks. Your article needs to quote and cite others' ideas properly. Also, don't copy others' work wholesale and present it as your own.

Can I honestly state that this article properly cites other sources and does not plagiarize?	☐ Yes ◯ No (then don't send)

You now have all the information you need to start the final preparation of your article.

Writing a Submission Cover Letter

Most journals' electronic submission systems use forms to collect all the information formerly included in a submission cover letter. If your journal uses such a form, you don't need to write a cover letter. However, if you're submitting your article directly to the editor of a special or themed issue, or to one of the few small journals that accept submissions only by email or even post, you'll need to write that letter. You can also read the following for information you might include in the Comments field of a web-based submission form, since the form prioritizes the journal's needs, not yours.

Format. If submitting your article by post, use university letterhead if possible for your cover letter; if submitting by email, use your university email if possible and place the cover letter in the body of the email (never as an attachment) (Gump 2004, 94–95).

Name the editor. Address the cover letter to a specific person, not just "Editor." Usually, this information is available online. Using the editor's name shows that you've done your research and aren't randomly sending your work to just any journal.

State your interests. Begin by stating your interests (e.g., "I am a scholar of settler colony modernisms" or "I conduct research on racial inequality and social networks").

Provide the title. Include the title of your article so that the editor has all the needed information in the letter.

Note if requested. If the article was solicited in any way, include the editor's positive email response to your query letter, thank the editor for requesting that you submit the article, and remind the editor of when this request was made. If you discussed the article with the editor by phone or email, remind them of any advice they gave (Day 2003, 208).

Mention any related awards. Note any awards you received for the article itself (e.g., best graduate student article, best paper in conference) or any prestigious awards to fund its research (e.g., Fulbright fellowship).

Mention any related buzz. Mention any attention that the article has drawn, such as sparking a heated debate at a recent conference or on social media.

Articulate the contribution. State the significance of the work to the field. This should be clear but not too self-aggrandizing. In other words, you don't need to state that the article is going to change the field, just that it contributes to our knowledge or fills a gap in the literature.

Describe the appeal to the readers. If possible, declare why you think this particular journal's subscribers might be interested in reading the article (Gump 2004, 96). For instance, you could state that the article fits the journal's mandate or that the journal has published previous articles on the topic, particularly if your article launches from those articles. If you can't think of why these readers would be interested in your article, that may be a sign that you're sending it to the wrong journal. At this point the appropriate question is not "Where would I like my article to appear?" but "Which journal's subscribers would be interested in reading my article?"

Mention the journal's scholarship. State your reason for wanting your article to appear in this journal. Without being obsequious, you can state that you would like to see your article published in the journal because it's the journal of record in the field or has been publishing innovative scholarship on your topic. If it recently published an important article on your topic, mention it.

Offer warrants. Provide statements about your article's authorship, copyright, previous publication, submission history, human subjects research, and potential conflicts of interest.

Give the word count. Provide the article's total word count, including notes and works cited. This is particularly important if you've worked to meet the journal's word limit.

Mention any permissions. State whether you are reproducing in your article any illustrations or texts still under copyright. If you are, state whether you are currently requesting permission to reproduce this material.

Mention any funding. State any public or corporate funding sources for your project. (Editors will want to know of any possible conflicts of interest.)

Mention any related publications in good journals. If you have previously published an article on a similar topic in a prestigious journal, some scholars recommend that you mention that place of publication (e.g., "I published a different article about Shakespeare in *PMLA* a few years ago").

Omit status. If you are a graduate student or an independent scholar, you don't need to state that. Your status should be irrelevant to the editor, but if the editor is unethical, it's better that you protect yourself by not including it.

Be meticulous. As with any formal document, your cover letter should not be sloppy. Ensure that it contains no typos, weird fonts, mixture of fonts, or differently aligned paragraphs. If addressed to a specific editor, check the spelling of the editor's name twice.

Don't be too long. Your cover letter should never be more than a page long; if it's no more than half a page, all the better.

Sample Submission Cover Letter

Dear Dr. [First and Last Name of Faculty Editor]:

Thank you for encouraging me, at the [Conference Name], to submit the enclosed article, [Article Title], for possible publication in [Journal Name]. I am a scholar of [broad research interest], and I believe that this research will interest your readers because you regularly publish important scholarship on [Your Topic]. I have been reading your journal with great interest, and found [Author Name]'s article on [Topic] relevant and useful.

I am the sole author of this 7,012-word article, which has not been published before in any form and is not under submission to any other journal or publisher.

An ongoing issue in [Discipline or Field] has been [problem]. In this article, I argue that . . . After discussing these issues . . . , I suggest how . . . These findings will reshape our understanding of . . .

I have included a possible illustration, which would be the only material for which I would need permission.

Sincerely,

[Your Name]
[Your Address and Email]

What To Do After Sending

I want to note here, before you submit your article, what you'll need to do *after* you send. Regarding the stages that your article will go through after you send it, see the section "Some Publishing Terms and Processes" in this workbook's introduction.

Get ready to revise. In two or three weeks, read "Week X: Revising and Resubmitting Your Article" for detailed instructions on tracking the progress of your article at the journal to which you submitted it.

Keep writing. After submitting your article and while waiting for the journal's decision, continue working on other projects and preparing other material for submission. Some scholars say that you should always have three articles in progress at any given time: an article under development, an article under submission to a journal, and an article under revision for a journal. This is a good rule of thumb, because the writing and publication process can take such a long time, and one article can stall out or be repeatedly rejected while another sails through. Placing all your eggs in one article basket may lead to significant delays.

GETTING YOUR SUBMISSION READY

Getting your article ready to send requires several last steps.

Day 1 Tasks: Identifying What Remains to Be Done

On the first day of your final writing week, read this week 12 chapter all the way through the next two paragraphs, answering all the questions posed. Write directly in the boxes provided or in your own document.

Earlier in this chapter, you collected information about what the journal expects when you submit your article. It's best to have everything ready before you go online to start the submission process, because some websites will time you out if you take too long. Revisit the boxes you filled out earlier, identify which of the journal's requirements you still need to complete, and then complete them.

Tracking Writing Time

Each day, use the Calendar for Actual Time Spent Writing This Week form (or digital time-tracking software) to keep track of the time you spent writing this week.

If busy, at least mark the check boxes with how long you wrote today. □15+ min. □30+ □ 60+ □ 120+

WEEK 12, DAYS 2–5: READING AND TASKS

Day 2 Tasks: Putting Your Article in the Journal's Style

Today you'll start putting your article in the journal's style, now that you've collected all the information concerning the journal's submission requirements. As mentioned, standardizing documentation, punctuation, and spelling according to the publication's style manual covers most of what it wants from its authors at submission. Here are some specifics on accomplishing these three essential tasks.

Put documentation in its style. If you have used reference management software, the task of standardizing your documentation according to the journal's style manual is only a matter of a few minutes. If you haven't used reference management software and haven't followed the journal's style in documenting your article's sources, you have some work ahead of you that will need to be done by hand. Fortunately, you can use Google to help you. First, go into the Google Chrome browser (download it if you don't currently use it). Next, install the Google Scholar plug-in. Then search for each of your citations in Google Scholar. When you find one of your sources, highlight the title and click on the plug-in button. A dialogue box will pop up displaying one or more sources with those words in the title. The box should include the citation you were searching for, in which case click the button that's an image of a quotation mark. The citation will now appear in various documentation styles, including MLA, APA, Chicago, Harvard, and Vancouver. Copy the citation that's in the appropriate format and paste it into your document. Now, this method isn't anywhere near as efficient as using reference management software, in part because Google doesn't display all the styles with complete accuracy. But it will get you closer. Other online services can help you prepare your sources as well, such as Cite This for Me. If you have used the wrong title capitalization style for your intended journal (e.g., rendering all journal article titles in lowercase), you can use a website like Title Case Converter to convert them (one by one).

Put punctuation in its style. Don't try to standardize your punctuation by hand. Rather, use your word-processing program's grammar-checker. You do this by setting it to match the journal's style. If the journal is US based and thus uses US punctuation, set the grammar-checker to "Inside punctuation with quotes." If the journal is British based and thus uses British punctuation, set the checker to and "Outside punctuation." Then go through the article, right-clicking on any punctuation that the program highlights as wrong. If the journal requires a serial comma, set Microsoft Word's grammar-checker on "Comma required before last list item" to "Always," and it will prompt you to add a comma where needed.

If you haven't been inserting em-dashes and en-dashes as you go along, you can do so now. You create each by clicking on Insert in your toolbar, then Symbol, followed by Special Characters, then Em Dash or En Dash. If you have been using a hyphen instead of an en dash between number ranges, you can globally change them in MS Word. Open the Find and Replace dialogue box; in the Find What field, type ([0-9])-([0-9]); then in the Replace With field, type \1–\2 (note the en-dash). Then check the box "Use wildcards" and click Replace All. That will insert an en-dash in all page ranges.

Put spelling in its style. Don't try to standardize your spelling by hand. Rather, use your word-processing program's spell-checker. You do this as follows: if the journal uses US spelling, set your spell-checker's proofreading language to "English (United States)"; if it uses British spelling, set proofreading language to "English (United

Kingdom)." Then go through your article, right-clicking on any word that the program highlights as misspelled. The dialogue box that pops up will usually give you the correct spelling, and you can simply accept it. You can quickly correct your entire document in this manner. Most spell-checkers do not automatically check notes, so to check these properly you must place a cursor in one of your notes before launching the spell-check program.

If you want, you can use Microsoft Word's Add to Dictionary spelling feature to catch errors in proper nouns, especially authors' names. Go through your article; right-click on correct spellings of scholars' names and then on Add to Dictionary. Then go back through the article to see whether any scholars' names are flagged as misspelled. For instance, if you added the correct spelling "Mazeika" to your dictionary, then the incorrect spelling "Mazieka" will stand out by appearing with a red squiggly line beneath it.

Check grammar. Grammar is standard across journals, so you don't need to consult your journal's style manual about it, but you may want to run a grammar-check on your article now. Unfortunately, your grasp of grammar must be strong to use an electronic grammar-checker. That's because some of the program's suggestions will be wrong (e.g., telling you to use the singular form when in fact your referent is plural), so you must carefully evaluate all suggested corrections. Currently, Google Docs does not have an electronic grammar-checker, although many online grammar-check programs now exist, such as Grammarly. Yet none is as effective as Microsoft Word's grammar-checker, perhaps because it's been under development much longer. If you're using Microsoft Word, make sure that the grammar-checker is turned on (go to the Review tab, and under Spelling and Grammar select the "Check grammar" box). If you're not sure whether a suggestion is correct, click Word's Explain button for help in making the correct choice. Although it takes a little effort, a grammar-check can help anyone identify misused words, sentence fragments, punctuation errors (especially with semicolons), passive voice, overuse of prepositional phrases, capitalization problems, and subject-verb agreement issues. Even if you run a grammar-check for passive voice and subject-verb agreement alone, it will prove useful. When running the grammar-checker, you can also select Capitalization as something to be checked and Gender-specific language, which will recommend gender neutral alternative words.

Use today to complete the task of putting your article in the journal's style.

Tracking Writing Time

Mark your electronic calendar, the Calendar for Actual Time Spent Writing This Week form, and/or the check boxes here with how long you wrote today. ☐ 15+ min. ☐ 30+ ☐ 60+ ☐ 120+

Days 3–4 Tasks: Wrapping Up Any Remaining Issues

Today and tomorrow, write your submission cover letter, finalize your abstract and keywords, format any illustrations, prepare the final version of your article in the required format (whether in MS Word, PDF, or printed out), and complete any other remaining tasks. As a last check, use the My Final Checklist for Sending form on the next page.

My Final Checklist for Sending

Submission cover letter	☐ Completed	☐ To do
Abstract meets journal's requirements	☐ Completed	☐ To do
Keywords meet journal's word count and other requirements	☐ Completed	☐ To do
Article meets word count limits	☐ Completed	☐ To do
Article meets article type requirements	☐ Completed	☐ To do
Potential reviewers' names and contact information, if required, compiled	☐ Completed	☐ To do
Article anonymized for peer reviewers	☐ Completed	☐ To do
Illustrations, if any, meet requirements for submission, including file format, separate files, naming, resolution, captions, titles, and callouts	☐ Completed	☐ To do
Permissions, if any required, solicited	☐ Completed	☐ To do
Article meets style requirements in terms of format, including spelling, punctuation, font, line spacing, subheads, and non-English words	☐ Completed	☐ To do
Article meets style requirements regarding documentation, including all citations' title wording, spelling of author names, and publication year matching their entry in the Works Cited list	☐ Completed	☐ To do
Article meets style requirements for quotations, including documenting all quotations and quoting them correctly from their source	☐ Completed	☐ To do
Article meets style requirements in terms of notes	☐ Completed	☐ To do
Article meets document file format requirements (e.g., PDF, MS Word)	☐ Completed	☐ To do
Author and coauthor (if any) information collected, including postal and/or email addresses, ORCiDs, preferred names, and description of coauthor roles	☐ Completed	☐ To do
Geolocation, if appropriate, provided	☐ Completed	☐ To do
Warrants meet standards about authorship, copyright, previous publication, review elsewhere, human subjects, and conflicts of interest	☐ Completed	☐ To do
Final spell-check of article performed	☐ Completed	☐ To do
Electronic reminder set for three weeks (SciQua) or three months (HumInt) from date of submission (for checking in with the editor about its progress)	☐ Completed	☐ To do
Backup file of the article saved, the exact version submitted	☐ Completed	☐ To do
Electronic document file started for listing any changes that come to mind before the article comes back	☐ Completed	☐ To do

Web-based submission. Once you've completed those remaining tasks, enter the journal's website, register, and start the submission process.

Postal submission. If you're submitting your article by post, don't staple the pages together, print on both sides, send poor photocopies, or include original art. Generally, you send at least two print copies; some journals require three or four.

Record keeping. Try to get a sense of how long the review process will take at this particular journal. The journal's website should say something about this, but if it doesn't, good SciQua journals aim for a two- to three-week review process and deliver their decision within a month; good HumInt journals aim to deliver their decision within three months. Record the exact day that you sent the article to the journal, and set a reminder to check in with the editor in three weeks (SciQua) or three months (HumInt). Also, preserve a backup of the electronic document exactly as you sent it (which should remain untouched, so you'll have a version that's identical to the editor's), keep a file of changes you think of before the article comes back to you, and save all email or postal communication from the editor (every single one).

Lessons Learned

If you have a moment, write down what you've learned through the process of revising this article. What do you know better now than when you started the workbook?

Lessons Learned from Revising My Article

Tracking Writing Time

Mark your electronic calendar, the Calendar for Actual Time Spent Writing This Week form, and/or the check boxes here with how long you wrote both days. ☐ 15+ min. ☐ 30+ ☐ 60+ ☐ 120+

Day 5 Tasks: Send and Celebrate!

Today you'll send your article to the journal—if you haven't already.

If you're having trouble letting go because you're worried about your article's imperfections, consider the hairy-arm story. This apocryphal tale has many versions in many industries, but they're all about the same thing—managing those who have power over you by leaving errors in your work. The first print version appeared in a blog (San 2001), but here's a great later version:

> One of Joe's clients was forever ruining projects by insisting on stupid changes. Then something odd started happening: each time the client was presented with a newly photographed layout, he'd encounter the image of Joe's own arm at one edge of the frame, partly obscuring the ad.
>
> "The guy would look at it," Joe recalled, "and he'd say, 'What the hell is that hairy arm doing in there?'" Joe would apologize for the slip-up. And then, "as [the client] was stalking self-righteously away," Joe said, "I'd call after him: 'When I remove the arm, can we go into production?' And he'd call over his shoulder, 'Yes, but get that arm out of there first!' Then I'd hear him muttering, 'These people! You've got to watch them like a hawk.'"
>
> That arm, of course, was no error: it was introduced so the client could object, and feel he was making his mark—and justifying his salary—while leaving the ad untouched. (Burkeman 2013, par. 5)

The moral of the story: don't perfect your article! All peer reviewers feel they must say at least one critical thing, so give them grist for their mill. Then they won't touch what's good about your article.

If that doesn't convince you, remember that your article will take so long to come back to you that by then you'll have gained some distance concerning it and will more easily identify what needs to be improved. You're going to have to make revisions at that time anyway in response to the peer reviewers' requests. Don't perfect now.

So what are you waiting for? Submit that article!

Then go celebrate. You deserve it. You've just accomplished something many people dream of and never accomplish. You have joined the ranks of those brave souls who've had the courage to send their writing to an actual publisher. Well done!

DOCUMENTING YOUR WRITING TIME AND TASKS

Calendar for Actual Time Spent Writing This Week

Time	Monday	Tuesday	Wednesday	Thursday	Friday	Saturday	Sunday
5:00 a.m.							
6:00							
7:00							
8:00							
9:00							
10:00							
11:00							
12:00 p.m.							
1:00							
2:00							
3:00							
4:00							
5:00							
6:00							
7:00							
8:00							
9:00							
10:00							
11:00							
12:00 a.m.							
1:00							
2:00							
3:00							
4:00							
Total minutes							
Tasks completed							

WEEK X
Revising and Resubmitting Your Article

Task Day	Week X Daily Writing Tasks	Estimated Task Time in Minutes	
		HumInt	SciQua
Day 1	Read from here through to the end of juncture 3, and identify which journal decision was made.	120	100
Day 2	Read junctures 4 and 5 on responding to journal decisions.	60	60
Day 3	Read juncture 6 on setting up for revising your article, and complete the tasks.	60	60
Day 4 to Day ?	Read juncture 7 on revising your article. Complete the tasks, following the reviewers' recommendations and workbook instructions.	120–1600+	120–960+
Day ?	Read juncture 8 on drafting your revision cover letter, and junction 9 on sending your article out again.	60	60
Day ?	Read juncture 10 on reviewing someone else's article and review one.	120+	100+
		8–30+ hours	**6.5–20+ hours**

Above are the tasks you'll need to complete once a journal gives you a decision about publishing your article. These tasks aren't part of the twelve-week schedule for submitting an article to a journal (which is why this week has no number), but they are the necessary last steps to achieving academic publishing success.

Depending on the readers' reports, these tasks may take longer than a week to complete. In the humanities, they may even take months. But don't worry. As someone wrote to me, "The best article I ever wrote was a substantive revision, which took me an entire year! I needed that much time to rethink my approach to not just the topic but the audience. So some revisions may not be swift, but nevertheless highly successful." You're nearing the finish line either way.

Since working with editors and peer reviewers is interactive in that you're responding to others' responses to your work, you'll have a range of choices to make about revision. Next, I give you the information you need to make the right decisions for you.

NAVIGATING THE REVIEW PROCESS

How you respond to journal decisions about the articles you submit will determine your success as an academic. That may seem to be a strong statement, but it's true. If you take negative journal decisions as accurate assessments of your aptitude for scholarship, if you fail to revise when advised to do so, or if you abandon an article just because it was rejected, you won't do well in your chosen profession. Those who persevere despite outright abuse, blithe dismissals, and cruel rejections are those who succeed. Persistence and hard work, not necessarily brilliance, are what garner publication.

So what are the specifics of how to proceed through the postsubmission process?

JUNCTURES 1–3: RECEIVING THE JOURNAL'S DECISION

JUNCTURE 1: TRACKING THE JOURNAL'S TIME TO DECISION

As soon as you send your article to the journal, start tracking the journal's response time. Although waiting to hear about your article is tough, the good news is that a bit of a wait is a good sign. Rejections often come very quickly: in as little as one day (if you submitted your article electronically and the journal has such a large backlog that it's temporarily rejecting all submissions), or one or two weeks (if the journal editors decide that the article is unworthy of peer review).

A well-run journal should send you a receipt of submission immediately, then let you know within a week to a month whether the article has been sent to peer reviewers. If the article passed the first cut with the editors and proceeded to peer review, a decision might come in a few weeks (from a SciQua journal) or in three to six months (from a HumInt journal). Many humanities journals continue to take six to nine months to return decisions, and some very slow journals (like *Social Text*) take eighteen months or more from submission to decision letter. Therefore, do *not* write to an editor a week after sending your article, asking whether the journal has accepted your article for publication. Journals don't work that quickly.

But when is the process taking too long? A frequent complaint of authors is the failure of editors to stay in touch (Huisman and Smits 2017, 647), so you need to keep on top of what's happening. Let's go through the various scenarios.

Branch 1: You receive no acknowledgement within a week after submission that the journal received your article. If you submitted your article through an online submission website, you should have received an immediate email notice that your article arrived. If not, something went wrong, and you need to contact the journal to find out what happened. If you're one of the few who submitted their article by email or post and you don't get a notice within a week that the journal received it, you need to email the managing editor and ask whether your article is in-house. Don't wait longer than that. If matters aren't resolved quickly, withdraw your article from that journal (more on this later in the chapter) and move on to another one.

Branch 2: You receive no notification within a month that the journal has sent your article to peer reviewers. If you submitted your article through an online submission website and have heard nothing further after a month, check your article's status there. If the journal has neither rejected the article nor sent it to peer reviewers, email the managing editor. It shouldn't be taking this long. If you submitted your article by another method, you should have heard about its status from the editor. If you haven't heard back by the end of a month, email that editor, politely inquiring about the status of your article. Your message should be brief: "I am writing to inquire whether you intend to send my article titled [Title] to peer reviewers. I submitted it to your journal on [date.]" If you don't hear back, send the email again in a week, cc'ing one or two other journal staff members. If you don't hear back even then, withdraw your article from that journal and move on to another one. Any journal too disorganized to respond to repeated emails is not a good bet.

Branch 3: You receive no notification within three to six months that the journal has reached a decision about publication. The amount of time for the first review round, from when you submitted the article to when you receive a decision, varies greatly by discipline. In the humanities and social sciences, only half the authors receive a decision within three months (Huisman and Smits 2017, 640). By contrast, in public health, three-quarters of authors receive a decision within three months (640). Better-ranked journals do tend to give decisions more quickly (641). If your article has been with peer reviewers for longer than the journal stated it would take, start sending polite emails to the managing editor, asking about your article's status. In other words, if you were told that the review would take three months, start emailing at three months and one day. Editors know that authors deserve a timely decision, and they accept that it's your right to be persistent. If the editor doesn't respond to your initial email, make your email inquiries more frequent: once a month and then once a week. The emails should never escalate in tone, and they should use the exact same wording as the first: "I'm writing to inquire about the status of my article titled [Title], which I submitted to your journal on [date] and which you sent to review on [date]." If other parties have expressed interest (e.g., if someone asked whether he or she could include your article in a special issue), include that information in the email. If you don't hear back after three emails, withdraw your article from that journal and move on to another one. Your marker for the viability of a journal's review process must be its editors' responsiveness to your email inquiries.

Branch 4: Editors state that the peer reviewers are taking longer than expected. If in response to your inquiries the editors say that they are working to extract reviews from the reviewers, that's a good sign. Just keep waiting. It's not the editors' fault that they've been unable to give a decision—it's the recalcitrant reviewers' fault. In fact, the editors may be as frustrated as you are with the slow review process. They can even appreciate repeated emails from you, because these remind them to send a reminder email in turn to the reviewers, asking them to submit their reviews. This is the nag chain.

Branch 5: No publication decision seems imminent after months of waiting. Some well-run journals give an automatic out. That is, they ask authors to promise that their editors have exclusive consideration of the article for four months. If the editors have not delivered a decision to an author in that period, they allow the author automatically to submit the article to another journal. It's one way that some journals help authors, by not making them guess about what to do next. If your article is not at such a journal, but the editors regularly respond to your inquiries and say that they're working to get the reviews, I recommend that you stick it out. Many a HumInt author has published an article after waiting a year or more at the encouragement of the journal's editors. And if you withdraw and resubmit to another journal you could experience the same delays there! However, I should note that statistically, your chances of receiving a positive decision after six to nine months of waiting are dwindling. Most peer reviewers take more months to reject an article than to accept it (Weller 2001, 157; D. King, McDonald, and Roderer 1981, 112; Huisman and Smits 2017, 640). In a study of peer reviewer types, one type is the "procrastinator," the reviewer who takes the most time to review a piece. Such a reviewer, the scholar claimed, always has only negative comments, so you can anticipate little reward for hanging in there (Fagan 1990, 110). Therefore, if you withdraw the article even when editors are telling you they're trying to extract reviews, no one can criticize you.

JUNCTURE 2: EMOTIONALLY MANAGING THE JOURNAL'S DECISION

When you see a new message in your email in-box from a journal to which you've submitted your work, I recommend that you avoid opening it if you're on your way to class or a meeting. Try to save the email for when you have the time to emotionally absorb its contents on your own. If reading the body of the email is unavoidable, wait to read the reviewers' reports, which often come as attachments, until you have some real time. Even positive decisions usually arrive with critical comments, so it's better to wait until you have the emotional space to cope.

Once you are in a place where you can process the contents, take a deep breath. Then remind yourself that all reviews are subjective, and that academic reviewers see their purpose not as affirming your brilliance but as critiquing your imperfections.

Next, open the email and read the attached readers' reports. Some scholars prefer to skim the editors' decision letter as quickly as possible to get the general gist, and then set it aside for a day or two. When they return to reading it, they're better able to absorb the recommendations or the decision. Letting the decision settle for a few days helps them take on the specifics of the news more easily.

Giving yourself time and space to absorb the readers' reports is vital, because you won't have enough evidence to evaluate the reviewers' recommendations clearly until you've completed the actual revision process. Many authors have ranted about their journal's decision and reviewers' comments until they began revising their article. Then these same authors tended to realize that despite the wisdom or idiocy of the comments themselves, the very process of revising always produces a stronger article. Studies have repeatedly shown that peer review improved the quality of articles, especially as pertains to the discussion of the study's limitations, the generalization of the findings, the tone of the conclusion, general readability, statistical content, missing citations, and presentation (Roberts, Fletcher, and Fletcher 1994, 121; Weller 2001, chap. 4; Ware 2011, 26; Casnici 2017, 544). Although many authors feel that peer reviewers made some recommendations based on personal quirks or bias, almost all also felt that the process of peer review improved their articles (Bradley 1981, 32; Ware 2011, 26; Nicholas et al. 2015, 16). It seems, then, that authors must live with two contradictory truths: peer review is a subjective, biased process rife with problems, *and* peer review is a process that improves articles.

Years ago, an author humorously explained why it's so important for authors to give themselves time, over several days, to absorb the journal's decision:

> The rejection of my own manuscripts has a sordid aftermath: (a) one day of depression; (b) one day of utter contempt for the editor and his accomplices; (c) one day of decrying the conspiracy against letting Truth be published; (d) one day of fretful ideas about changing my profession; (e) one day of re-evaluating the manuscript in view of the editors' comments followed by the conclusion that I was lucky it wasn't accepted! (Underwood 1957, 87)

This emotional journey from despair to acceptance is one with which published authors are very familiar. Do allow yourself the time and the space for the entire process.

So how should you cope with the feelings that arise upon reading various types of reviewer comments?

Branch 1: The editors' letter does not give instructions for interpreting the reviewers' reports. A good editor will write a *revise-and-resubmit notice*, advising you on how to read the reports and improve your article. This notice is necessary, because editors and peer reviewers are often at cross-purposes—editors want authors to trim their article, while peer reviewers want authors to expand their article by adding citations, explanations, and related material. So a helpful editor will differentiate between reviewer recommendations the editor takes seriously and those the author can safely ignore as nonessential or even wrong. An unhelpful editor will send the author a formulaic letter with the readers' reports attached, leaving the author to adjudicate reviewer disagreements. The best way to regard such negligence is that it allows you to make your own decisions. If you need help, write to the editor and ask for guidance.

Branch 2: The reviewers' reports are long and detailed. Research shows that the lengthier the peer reviewers' comments, the more likely the article is to be cited in the future (Laband 1990, 348). Detailed reviewers' reports aren't just rare but complimentary—few scholars take the time to pore over an article they don't consider worthwhile. So if your reviewers give you lots of advice, it's a good sign—don't get discouraged.

Branch 3: The reviewers are negative and rude. Studies have demonstrated that peer reviewers always have more negative comments than positive ones (Bakanic, McPhail, and Simon 1989, 643; Paltridge 2017, 64). Further, peer reviewer reports, perhaps because they're anonymous, have little of the politeness and tact common in other arenas of academia such as books, lectures, and conferences (Kourilova-Urbanczik 2012, 114; Paltridge 2017, 72). Thus, how blunt and even rude reviewers can be shocks novice authors. However, if you've ever yelled at other drivers from the safety of your car, saying things you'd never say to their face, remember that reviewers are rather like that. You're not real to them—don't take their remarks personally.

Branch 4: The reviewers' reports are problematic and/or biased. Reviewers' comments do have a high probability of being problematic (García, Rodriguez-Sánchez, and Fdez-Valdivia 2015, pp. 2020, 2027, 2028). For instance, one study found that 25 percent of reviews were very poor in quality (McKenzie 1995, 539). Another study found that over 40 percent of reviews had comments indicating bias and prejudice (Spencer, Hartnett, and Mahoney 1986, 21, 32). Many studies have shown that given the identical article to review, reviewers will have a range of responses: some rejecting it, some accepting it, with agreement among the reviewers ranging from a low of 40 percent to only as high as 70 percent (Weller 2001, chap. 6; Casati et al. 2009, fig. 11, par. 3, sec. 3.5). What kind of subjective process is peer review if reviewers agree in their judgments only about half the time?! Yet some studies suggest, again, that this is not to be taken personally. That is, while some studies have found that editors were biased toward former graduate students, friends, and prestigious institutions, many other studies found no significant correlation between higher acceptance rates and editors' relationships with authors or authors' institutional affiliations (Weller 2001, chap. 3). So don't dismiss the peer-review process and insist that it's all about whom you know. You're in control of your own article, you get to decide how you respond to reviewers' comments, and you can make excellent revisions in response to even biased reviews. You need to leap from them, not bow down to them. I'll have more to say about this later in the chapter.

Branch 5: The reviewers are unclear. Peer reviewers often phrase their criticism poorly. That's because almost none have had any official training in peer review (Paltridge 2017, 148). Rather, three-fourths learned how to conduct peer reviews "by reading reports on their own submissions to academic journals" and through "trial and error" (148). As a result, reviewers make criticism personal, saying "I'm lost" or "I'm not buying it" instead of describing what's happening in the text or what would improve it. They also make it personal by directly addressing the author as "you" instead of "author." The formulation of "you are . . ." is at the core of many poor reviews, problematically conflating the writing and the author. Although many faculty members remember how devastating even single words were in their undergraduate career, over time they lose the ability to detect when they themselves are devastating others with similar terms. I don't exempt myself from this failure! But setting aside the reports for a few days will help you interpret their problematic criticisms in constructive ways.

Branch 6: The reviewers didn't understand the article. When many of us first read reviewers' comments, we feel depressed, because so many of these seem based in the most vulgar reading of our articles, the least nuanced. A plaintive response that I've frequently heard authors give is, "But did they even read my article?!" The answer is no—they probably did *not* carefully read your article all the way through. According to self-report, the average amount of time peer reviewers spend reading an article is five hours (Ware and Mabe 2015, 50), but others spend only two to three hours (McNutt et al. 1990, 1373; Nylenna, Riis, and Karlsson 1994, 150; Weller 2001, 157). Thus, you simply can't assume that anyone is carefully reading your article. The good news is that if you assume that people won't be reading your manuscript carefully, then you become a better writer. In other words, don't write for the genius readers who spend eleven hours poring over your article. Write for the slightly distracted scholars who skim parts of your article. It's your job to prevent people from reading your article in stupid ways. In my experience, that means articulating your assumptions, which always makes the article stronger. (I've certainly found misreadings tremendously beneficial to my own revision process. They enable me to make explicit what I had buried in my article, or to add a paragraph about the bias that led to such misreadings.)

Branch 7: The reviewers give conflicting advice. This is a frequent problem (Nicholas et al. 2015, 16). One peer reviewer will praise the article; another will attack the very thing the other peer reviewer praised—making it difficult to know whose advice to follow. Editors fail to note that the reviewers are in conflict, or to give guidance on how to weigh the reviewers' advice (Huisman and Smits 2017, 647). Moreover, even individual peer reviewers give conflicting signals—on the one hand praising the article as "carefully researched," on the other hand criticizing the literature review. The "good news-bad news" structure of peer-review reports can make them confusing, particularly for novice authors (Gosden 2003, 92, 99). Fortunately, you get to pick which parts of this conflicting advice you follow.

Branch 8: The reviewers phrase everything as suggestions. The nationality and temperament of reviewers shape how they communicate their concerns (Kourilova-Urbanczik 2012, 105–6, 114). Take the report comment "I suggest that the author do . . ." If written by a Dutch reviewer, this might actually *be* a suggestion, so the author might not have to make the change; but if written by a British reviewer, this is probably a directive, and the author should make the change (Rottier, Ripmeester, and Bush 2011, 410). When reports are phrased as suggestions, not directives, out of reviewers' desire to be "kind" and "supportive," then "interpreting what changes need to be made in order to achieve success can be . . . difficult" (Paltridge 2017, 78). My advice? Assume that any suggestions are directives, but that you still have choices.

What's the upshot? One scholar formulated what he calls the golden rule: "No reviewer is ever wrong" (Starbuck 2014, 85). This assertion is "patently ludicrous," he notes, but when faced with rude or ignorant reviewer comments, the rule reminds authors that "editors and reviewers are only reporting what they thought when they read your paper and every editor and every reviewer is a potentially useful example from the population of potential readers" (85). As another academic adds, "Like everyone, at first, I'm quite offended by some of the remarks made by reviewers. . . . But when I think it over, I usually get what they're saying" (Cloutier 2015, 74). So when first reading the reviewers' reports, always remind yourself that the peer-review process has a proven record of enabling authors to produce stronger articles. It will help you too if you use the information I give next.

JUNCTURE 3: INTERPRETING THE JOURNAL'S DECISION

Once you've absorbed the editors' decision letter emotionally, your first task is to interpret the journal's decision. Surprisingly, it can be difficult to determine just what the journal is telling you! Sometimes this is due to poor wording or editorial inexperience, but most often it's due to editorial avoidance. The editors are unclear because they don't want to be devastating. Unfortunately, there's no standard language and no agreed-on formula for delivering the verdict on publication. Therefore, sometimes only experience helps. One student of mine, upon receiving two negative reviews from a journal, assumed that the journal had rejected her article. When she forwarded the reviews without comment to her advisor, however, he surprised her by writing back "Wonderful news!" In fact, the journal was asking for a revision.

To aid you in parsing the editors' decision letter, keep the following in mind: editorial decisions fall into three broad categories. Editors can accept your article, ask you to revise and resubmit your article, or reject your article. The most room for interpretation comes with the revision and rejection decisions. That's why you need to decide which of the seven decisions listed below has been made about your article before you proceed. If you aren't sure which decision it is, ask the editors to clarify their remarks. Later, I will address how to respond to each of these decisions.

Forms of Editorial Acceptance

1. Accepted unconditionally. It almost never happens that a journal accepts an article as is. In my eleven years as managing editor of a peer-reviewed journal, we never once did so. An editor at another journal likewise states that "for the more than 250 manuscripts received while I have been assisting with *JLR*, not one first draft has been accepted unconditionally, and very few have been conditionally accepted pending minor revisions" (Holschuh 1998, 6). A study of over 3,500 review experiences found that only 1.2 percent of the articles received unconditional acceptance (Huisman and Smits 2017, 638). Over the thousands of articles my students have submitted, I have seen them receive such decisions only twice, and both editors expressed astonishment, noting that it was the first time they had ever sent an email stating that the reviewers loved the piece and had only a few grammatical or style recommendations to make. In other words, don't expect any journal to accept your initial submission as is; this isn't the reality of how journals work. The best-case scenario is one of the following two decisions:

2. Revise minor problems and resubmit. Receiving a decision that your article needs only minor work, sometimes called a "warm R&R," is cause for celebration. Articles in this category have been conditionally accepted, pending minor revisions specified by the peer reviewers in their reports attached to the journal's decision letter. Although many novice authors assume that any criticism is a bad sign, it's not. You can receive this kind of decision only if all the peer reviewers and editors liked your article, which is somewhat miraculous. Therefore, your chances of publication are now very good.

So if you've received such a decision, drop everything, make the revisions, and resubmit your article. Fortunately, with minor revisions your article isn't routed back to the reviewers but instead goes straight to the editors, who check to make sure that you've made the changes recommended. If you have, the journal publishes your article. When novice authors tell me that they've been sitting on a warm R&R for a year or two, I can't help but start chiding them. Such a journal decision should be treated as merely a stage, like copyediting, in the publishing process. You must make the revisions, but then the journal will publish your article. Should the editors sending the decision letter ask you to make minor revisions, make them! And right away!

Signs of minor R&R. The only problem with this journal decision is detecting it. Some signs that the article has been conditionally accepted are that the editors are either urging you to resubmit the article by a certain date or suggesting that it will appear in a certain issue if you resubmit by a certain date. Another sign is the recommended changes are all minor, such as rewriting the abstract, expanding the methodology section, adding a few references, developing the conclusion, or defining some terms.

3. Revise major problems and resubmit. Receiving a decision that your article requires major revisions is also an excellent decision to receive, as it's still considered a "warm" response. Articles in this category have a strong chance of getting published, should the author be able to accomplish the work specified by the reviewers. You usually receive this kind of decision when the reviewers and editors liked the piece, but at least one had substantial suggestions for improvement. Sometimes you'll receive this decision even if one or more of the reviewers had major reservations—but only if the editors believe that the identified problems are fixable.

The "major R&R" decision often results in a different review process for your article than the minor or warm R&R. At some journals, all articles that have undergone major revisions must return to their original reviewers for vetting. Then the reviewers conduct a second review to see whether the author has responded to their recommendations. If they believe that an author has appropriately corrected the problems, then the editors will publish that article. However, some journals hate to trouble their reviewers with this task, so the editors (or editorial assistants) review these revised articles to see whether the reviewers' recommended changes have been made. Thus, it's important for you to know before you start revising whether the same reviewers will be reading your resubmitted article, since they will care more about how closely you followed each of their suggestions. You can search the journal's website for information about the process; but if this information isn't posted, ask the editors for it.

The chances of rejection after revising and resubmitting an article originally deemed major R&R are greater than with those deemed minor R&R. Everyone agrees about how to make minor revisions, but there can be a wide disparity of opinions concerning how to make major changes. If you don't revise your article sufficiently or in the ways that the editors had hoped, then you may receive a journal decision letter stating that the article was not revised appropriately. In such a case, sometimes editors will the reject the article, but sometimes they'll give the author another chance at revision. Indeed, I hate to tell you that the norm these days is for scholars to go through at least two rounds of revision with peer reviewers (Huisman and Smits 2017, 641), with each resubmission triggering additional revision requests in further rounds. I have frequently talked with authors gnashing their teeth because the peer reviewers kept asking for new changes in subsequent rounds. The authors didn't feel they could refuse, since they'd already spent so much time doing what these reviewers wanted that they didn't want to start over at another journal. Most of those writing SciQua articles have gone many rounds with peer reviewers before their work is accepted for publication; that's just how the process works, unfortunately. You can refuse the reviewers' requests, but so long as their requested revisions don't affect anything central, do what they want. As one scholar put it to me, "Don't argue if you don't have to."

Another problem with interpreting this decision is that sometimes editors imply that revisions are major when in fact they're minor or vice versa. To me, major revisions are rewriting sections of the article, restructurin7g the article, reviewing a whole new body of literature, refining the argument throughout, significantly shortening or lengthening the article, interpreting the evidence differently, adding case studies, or (the most difficult task) repairing theoretical or methodological flaws. Draw your own conclusions about how difficult and substantive the changes must be.

If your article receives a major R&R ruling, you're not obligated to revise and resubmit it to the journal that gave this verdict, but it's always in your interest to do so. Your chances of publication are much greater upon resubmission to the same journal than upon initial submission to another. Unless you can't stomach the changes the reviewers are recommending, revise and resubmit to that publication.

Signs of major R&R. The decision of major R&R is the most difficult to detect of all the editorial rulings. Editors delivering this decision never use the term "major R&R", but instead will make confusingly discouraging or encouraging remarks. What follows are four real editors' letters that reveal the language the editors might use for articles that need major revisions:

Editors' letter 1. I am happy to inform you that your article has been accepted pending major revisions. You will note that the reviewers seem to feel that the revisions they recommend will be too major to accomplish, but frankly, I think they are wrong. I see these revisions as quite doable, and I do encourage you to revise and resubmit your article. Should you revise as instructed, within reason, and quickly (within the month), I will be glad to accept this article on such a timely and important topic.

Editors' letter 2. Enclosed please find the reviewers' reports on your article. One reviewer has minor recommendations for revision; the other has substantial recommendations. Although their reports are very positive about your article, they also include helpful suggestions for improving the article, especially regarding [some revisable element: most often the argument or the related literature]. Given the reviewers' concerns, I cannot accept the article in its present form. I can offer, however, to send a revised version of the article back to the second reviewer, should you wish to rework your argument substantially in line with these reports and resubmit the article to us. I am sorry to have to convey what I know must be disappointing news, but I do feel strongly that with careful revision this article could be accepted for publication in our journal.

Editors' letter 3. I am sorry to have to return your manuscript, because it falls outside our guidelines. However, we would like to invite you to resubmit your article. In order to conform to our guidelines, you would need to reformulate your article to clarify your thesis and resituate the piece within a more scholarly background. Thank you for considering our journal, and we look forward to hearing from you.

Editors' letter 4. Given the seriousness of the reviewers' critiques, I am not certain whether they can be addressed with a revision. Nevertheless, I am inviting you to revise and resubmit your manuscript. You will need to do a substantial revision, focusing on articulating your contribution and developing your concept of [concept]. Please know that I view this as a high-risk revision [i.e., one with only a slim chance of attaining the standards the editors would require].

Forms of Editorial Rejection

4. Desk rejection. If your article rejection arrives quickly and unaccompanied by reviewers' reports, you're most likely getting a desk rejection: the editor has turned down your article without sending it on to peer reviewers. This practice is about three times more common than it used to be (Lewin 2014, 170), and many journals now give a desk rejection to over half the articles they receive (S. Brown and Petitt 2016, 5–6; Antonakis 2017, 3). Editors give desk rejections for a variety of reasons. Sometimes it's because they don't believe the article is strong enough to survive peer review—they believe that any peer reviewer would reject it. Peer reviewers' time is valuable, and they get cranky if they regularly receive articles that are unpublishable.

But editors also often reject articles for not fitting their journal's mandate. One survey found that the most common reason that editors gave for rejecting an article immediately, without sending it through peer review, was that it was off topic (Floyd et al. 2011, 628). Rejection in such cases has nothing to do with the quality of the article, just its aptness for a particular journal. For instance, when I managed a journal on Chicanx, we frequently received articles about Brazilians in Brazil or Mexicans in Mexico or Cubans in Miami. That wasn't our mandate—our mandate was Mexican Americans in the United States. So those articles were off topic for us, and the authors had wasted not only our time but also, and more important, their own.

Alternately, the editors may have recently accepted an article about your artist, period, theory, population, country, and so may need to return yours without reading it. For instance, our journal had to reject a good article because we had just published one on that very topic. Unfortunately, the second article was better than the published one, but we were hardly going to say as much in the rejection letter. You can't know what article topics journals frequently receive, so don't worry about it. What's great about a desk rejection is that it usually comes quickly, within ten to seventeen days, although sometimes up to thirty days, especially lower-ranked journals (Huisman and Smits 2017, 642–43). That means that you can move on to another journal instead of wasting months waiting for what turns out to be a rejection.

5. Rejected but will entertain a resubmission. This editorial verdict may surprise you, but it still counts as a win. It's not as good as an acceptance, of course, but it's still good. It means that you still have a chance of getting your article published with the journal. When the rejection decision letter indicates a willingness to see a revision of the article, this decision is still a form of "revise and resubmit," in this case a "cool R&R." Reviewers' reports always accompany this form of rejection, and usually all the reviewers have substantial suggestions for improving the article. If they don't, you can assume that they sent private comments to the editor, separate from the report sent to you, detailing their concerns. In such asides, reviewers are typically franker, which is why you sometimes get kind remarks in the reviewers' reports, but the editor tells you that your article is being rejected.

If you decide to revise and resubmit this article, it will go through the review process again. Depending on the journal, it may go back to the original reviewers or to completely different ones. Some editors will even helpfully specify that they'll treat the revised article as a new submission. It's a better sign for you if the editors say that the article will go back to its original reviewers.

Most of the time, editors give a cool R&R because they thought the article was strong but had major flaws that would be tough to overcome. Since they found the article interesting, they don't want to close off the unlikely possibility that the author will come up with some brilliant solution for its problems. Other times, they don't think the article is redeemable, but they don't have the heart to say that they've rejected it; so this is their attempt to be encouraging. At my journal, I know we were sometimes surprised to see an article resubmitted that we thought we had rejected, but when we reread our decision letter, we saw how the (hopeful) author might have read into it more than we had intended. The editor must tread a fine line between clarity and cruelty. Finally, and unfortunately, some journals trying to increase their rejection rates reject almost all articles in the first round. Then, along with the rejection, they give clear instructions for revising the article, so that an author feels encouraged to resubmit anyway.

It's up to you whether you revise and resubmit your article to the same journal that gave it a cool R&R. Most journal editors don't really expect to see a resubmission of an article that received this decision, believing that the author will probably move on to another journal for a more positive response. However, if you feel that the reviewers were helpful and you're happy to follow their suggestions, then by all means revise and resubmit it to that journal.

Signs of equivocal rejection. The difference between this decision and the acceptance decisions described earlier can be extremely difficult to detect. The decision may even be delivered in identical language. If the editors' letter says they are rejecting your article, but it has such phrases as "not publishable *in its current form*" or "not *yet* ready," these qualifiers suggest that they might welcome it in another form. Here are three real editors' letters that reveal the language editors might use to reject articles that an author can resubmit.

Editors' letter 5. Enclosed please find the reviewers' reports on your article. They agree that you have a very promising idea, but that serious revision is necessary. In particular, they would like to see [some major improvement like a better grasp of the chosen theoretical approach or a deeper analysis of evidence, etc.]. Given their concerns, I cannot accept the article for publication in its current form. Should you feel able to address their concerns and submit a substantially revised version of the article, I would be glad to ask the reviewers to read the article again.

Editors' letter 6. Given the reviewers' reports, we cannot accept your article for publication. Should you choose to revise the article thoroughly according to the reviewers' substantial recommendations and submit it again to us, we will send it to new reviewers.

Editors' letter 7. Although the reviewers thought the article was [some positive word like *strong* or *thought-provoking*], they have noted some serious flaws that must be addressed before the article is publishable. Please see the attached for the reviewers' suggestions.

6. Rejected and dismissed. This rejection is absolute, usually with reviewers' reports attached to the email notification to back up the editors' decision that the article is not revisable. Some authors are deceived into thinking that the mere presence of reviewers' reports with concrete suggestions is a positive sign. This is not the case if the decision letter itself mentions nothing about resubmission. As one editor explained to me, "When I send along a reader's report saying that the central premise is flawed, I think it's pretty clear that the article probably needs to be gutted, with maybe a few parts recycled into a brand-new article—not that it should be prettied up and sent back." Thus, the editors attach the reviewers' reports because you might find their remarks helpful in knowing where you went wrong or simply because the reports exist and should not go to waste. These don't signal an expectation of resubmission.

If you can use the reports to revise your article for another journal, do it. Sometimes the editors will even suggest that you consider submitting the article elsewhere, because that other journal is better suited to your topic or argument. (You'll sometimes receive this suggestion after the peer-review process as a kind of consolation, but it's not a good practice: a good editor should never have allowed an article inappropriate for that editor's journal to go through that process.) So if the comments aren't helpful, just move on.

Surprisingly, this decision is not the worst you can receive. Any time an article of yours makes it to peer review, consider it a triumph (since so many editors now reject articles without sending them to peer review). The opposite of love is not hate but indifference. If the reviewers really hated what you were doing, maybe you are onto something! Don't get discouraged; most articles were rejected two to five times before being published (Azar 2004, 269), and low peer-reviewer opinion was not correlated with low citation rates (Casati et al. 2009, par. 1, sec. 4).

Signs of rejection. When giving an outright rejection, the editors sending the decision notification will often say that the article "is not publishable," "is not ready for publication," "cannot be published," "does not meet our standards for publication," or "is not right for us." Other language editors might use:

> **Editors' letter 8.** I am sorry to return your article, but our submissions guidelines require that articles reveal something new and demonstrate a thorough grasp of previous criticism on the topic. Your submission lacks this dimension, and therefore we cannot consider it further at this time.

> **Editors' letter 9.** Thank you for offering us your manuscript. We have read it with interest, and regret that we cannot accept it for publication. We hope that the attached readers' reports prove helpful to you as you revise the article for publication in another journal.

> **Editors' letter 10.** The reviewers appreciated your line of thought. We hope that you will find the reviewers' reports helpful as you continue to work on these interesting ideas.

No editors will directly say, "We have rejected your article" or "Please don't resubmit this article." Indeed, editorial politeness causes problems for the recipients of such editors' letters, especially if they aren't native speakers of English. Can the journal's editors be rejecting the article if their letter is encouraging and includes suggestions for improving the article? Yes. Although the editors may include some positive language and may even seem to suggest that you continue working on the article, the letter is not a revise-and-resubmit notice unless they mention resubmission. If you can't tell whether your article has been rejected, email the editor and ask, "Thank you for sending me your decision on my article. I just wanted to make sure that I understand it properly: are you requesting that I revise and resubmit this article, or do you not expect to see it again?"

7. Rejected after a long time and without reviewers' reports. This rejection comes after several months, perhaps even after the editor told you the article was going to reviewers, yet the notification includes neither reports nor a detailed editorial decision letter. Several different things might have happened. At a poorly run journal, this may actually be a desk rejection—that is, it took this long for the editor to even look at your article and decide it was unsuitable (Huisman and Smits 2017, 634). (Editors also give this decision because they never got peer reviewers, and they prefer to reject your article than to confess that they couldn't get anyone to review it.) Or the editors sent your article to reviewers, but none of the reviewers ever sent in a report. Alternately, perhaps the editors received the reports and the reviewers made mild criticisms, but the editors consider those same flaws very serious. Instead of sending you the mild reports, which might give you the wrong impression, the editors reject your article and don't send them along. Or the reviewers' reports made compelling points, but were too hostile or rude to be passed along. Or instead of receiving a report, the editor got a brief email saying, in effect, "Why did you bother me with this article? I'm too busy to write a detailed report listing all the many reasons it should be rejected!"

Thus, your main problem interpreting this decision is that it can mean either that your article is truly terrible or that no one took the time to find out whether it was good or bad. If the editors mention the reports and yet don't attach them to their email message, you can ask for them but I don't generally recommend it. The editors are usually trying to protect you from unhelpful reports or they don't exist. Many scholars get this kind of unexplained rejection; just move on to your second-choice journal.

Signs of editorial rejection. The lack of reports is one of the clearest signs of rejection, as is the appearance anywhere in the decision letter of the phrase "best of luck!" That phrase means that the journal's editors considers your exchange now closed, and are expecting you to move on to try your luck elsewhere.

JUNCTURES 4–9: RESPONDING TO THE JOURNAL'S DECISION

Whether the editorial decision letter was generally positive or overwhelmingly negative, you still have control over the fate of your own work, and you have decisions to make. Let's start with the worst-case scenario first.

JUNCTURE 4: RESPONDING TO A JOURNAL'S DECISION TO REJECT YOUR ARTICLE

Let's say that your article gets rejected. First, remember that almost all scholars have had their work rejected at one point or another—85 percent of prominent scholars admit this (Gans and Shepherd 1994, 166). So you're in excellent company. Second, allow yourself to feel angry and depressed. You're only human! Third, after allowing yourself to feel down for a week or two, revisit the decision letter and its recommendations if any. It's time to decide about how you're going to proceed. Your options upon rejection are to (1) abandon the article, (2) send the article without a single change to another journal, (3) revise the article and send it to another journal, or (4) protest or appeal the decision and try to resubmit the article to the rejecting journal. Let's go through these choices.

Should I abandon the article? No! Studies conducted several decades ago on the publication experiences of those in the physical and social sciences found that of the authors who had an article rejected, one-third abandoned not only the article but also the entire line of research on which it was based (Garvey, Lin, and Tomita 1972, 214). Don't let that be you! Be among the 85 percent of scholars who now send their rejected articles to another journal (Rotton et al. 1995, 9). In fact, several studies suggest that 20 to 50 percent of published articles were first rejected by another journal (Weller 2001, 66). One study found that between 5 and 10 percent were accepted at the third to the sixth journal to which they were sent (Dirk 1996, 3, 9, 11). An older study found that about 1 percent of published articles were rejected by four or more journals before being accepted (Garvey, Lin, and Tomita 1972, 213–14). As the librarian Ann C. Weller concludes in her review of this research, "Studies have shown that indeed, a good percentage of rejected manuscripts do become a part of the published literature" (Weller 2001, 70). That's because many articles are rejected that have solvable problems.

If your article is rejected the first time you submit it, definitely send it to a second journal. If three or more journals have rejected the article, it may be time to think about giving up on it, but a political science professor told a colleague that an article of his had been rejected *eight* times before being published. And a scholar admitted that one of his articles had been rejected *fifteen* times before being published (Martin 2013). The main reason to abandon your article, then, is if reviewers raise objections to your methodology, theoretical approach, or argument so serious that you believe they are unsolvable. Another reason is if the peer reviewers at different journals regularly agree on the article's weaknesses. Research shows that peer reviewers tend to agree with each other when an article is poor, but tend to disagree when an article is strong (Weller 2001, 193–97). So if you've been getting split reviews, that's a good sign.

Should I resubmit the article elsewhere without revising it? One older study shows that about half of rejected articles that were resubmitted to other journals were not revised (Yankauer 1985, 7). Indeed, I know well-published scholars who insist that they never revise an article until three different journals have rejected it. As one author put it, he doesn't revise unless the editor is strongly encouraging him to resubmit the article: "Once it's clear the editor is not interested, I'm not that interested in what the reviewers had to say, [because] . . . one reviewer may argue strongly that you change *x* to *y*, another may argue equally strongly that you change *y* to *x*. Authors should be wary of being drawn into this morass until they find an interested editor. When that happens, then you pay extremely close attention to the reviewers' comments" (Welch 2006, 8). However, among peer reviewers who review often, they do sometimes see the same article come back to them, unrevised, and get angry that the author ignored them entirely. And getting the same reviewer is more likely if your field is small. So if you really hate the reviewers' recommendations, don't act on them, but take advantage of having had a few months' distance from your article to revise it in ways that make the article stronger in your own eyes.

Should I revise and resubmit the article elsewhere? Most scholars try to use the reviewers' recommendations to revise their article each time it's rejected so that they can send an improved article to the next journal. You can't go wrong with this practice, so long as you don't spend too much time revising and respond only to those critiques with which you agree. If you're feeling discouraged, start a writing group. One experiment found that when five faculty members began a group to work on previously rejected manuscripts, they got four rejected articles accepted for publication (Brandon et al. 2015, 535).

Should I resubmit my article to a better journal? Choosing the journal to send your article to next is an important decision. A question novice authors frequently ask me is, Should I send my rejected but revised article to a journal of higher rank than the one that rejected it, or to a lower-ranked one?

According to several studies, scholars traditionally send their rejected articles to less prestigious journals, because they think that their chances for publication are better in doing so (Calcagno et al. 2012, 1067; Weller 2001, chap. 2). But other studies show that many scholars send those articles to equivalent journals, and some send them to better journals (Weller 2001, chap. 2). That's because some authors start by submitting their article to their second-choice journal first. If their article isn't accepted there, but they get useful reviewers' reports that lead them to make a strong revision, they then move up the chain and send the improved article to a better journal. (Yes, you're under no obligation to send your work to the journal that led to that improvement. You haven't signed any agreement.)

However, other authors start by sending the article to a tough disciplinary journal known for rejecting articles but giving useful reviewers' reports, which they can use to improve their article. If this process leads to the article getting into the first, highly ranked journal, all the better; if it doesn't, such authors feel that the first journal's reviewers' reports are improving their chances of getting into their second-choice publication. Given the subjectivity of reviewing, I'm not sure this is a brilliant strategy. Reviewers at disciplinary journals may ask for the kinds of changes that would not improve your chances at an interdisciplinary journal. As Robert Heinlein said years ago, "Don't rewrite unless someone who can buy it tells you to" (quoted in Pournelle and Pournelle 1996, 102). If the journal isn't going to "buy" it, why revise for that publication? But there is some evidence for this start-at-the-top strategy: studies suggest that a high percentage of articles rejected by prestigious journals are published elsewhere (Weller 2001, 66). For instance, 72 percent of the articles rejected by the *American Journal of Public Health* were subsequently published in other journals (Koch-Weser and Yankauer 1993, 1619). What's the upshot? If you revise and resubmit your article to another journal, you increase your chances of getting published.

Should I practice cascade review? In the sciences, some journals allow "cascade review," in which authors submit their rejected article, along with the peer reviewers' reports, to a second journal. This practice is to your benefit if the reviewers liked your article but thought it didn't have enough scope or significance (Ware 2011, 35). Even if you don't have access to that type of review, you can mimic it. Some years ago, *PMLA* rejected a student's article about an African author, saying that it had never published anything on that author and so wanted its first published piece to be an overview of that author's work. Since the article had been very positively reviewed at *PMLA*, the student wrote to the editor of a related journal, stated what had happened, and asked whether the editor was interested. The editor was, and once the student had submitted the article and reviewers' reports, the article made its way quickly into print at that second journal.

Should I protest the decision? Sometimes, even after allowing yourself time and space, you perceive the reviewers' or editors' comments as cruel, unfair, ignorant, outrageous, or biased. And you may be right. Some articles are rejected because editors and peer reviewers have a bias against certain methods, theories, or results, especially unorthodox or groundbreaking research (Luukkonen 2012, 49–50; Lee et al. 2013, 9; Weller 2001, 223–24).

In these situations, is it worthwhile or effective to complain to the journal editors, the very people who delivered the decision?

Everyone has the right to speak truth to power, and if you want to exercise that right, you should. Later, I will address the chances of its being effective. For now, start by deciding what you want out of protesting. Do you just want to register your complaints? Do you want the editor to allow you to revise and resubmit the article while ignoring one reviewer's comments? Do you want the editor to submit the article to a third reviewer? Of the last two options, getting an additional reviewer is the most likely. What you want affects the kind of protest you make.

You're most likely to succeed in changing the decision if the reviewers were grossly negligent. An example is if a reviewer says that your article is missing an important type of data, but you not only had that data, you discussed it. You can also be successful if you can demonstrate that the reviewers are proffering dated or biased criticisms or seem to be against all articles detailing a certain method or theory, not just yours. Another example of negligence: if one of the reviewers rejected the article after spending the entire review obsessing about a minor methodological point and commented on nothing else.

You can sometimes persuade an editor who has rejected your article to send it to new reviewers, especially if you received a split review (Martin 2008, 308). Editors are aware that the reviewers they select may not be quite apt. They sometimes send interdisciplinary work to disciplinary reviewers, or regional work to scholars who don't work on that region. But only the most dispassionate of appeals, based on evidence, not rhetoric, will win the day. A professor in one of my courses explained how he persuaded an editor to give his article another chance. When this author received the editor's negative decision with the reviewers' reports, he wrote to the editor, commenting that both reviewers had paid no attention to the content of his article, only its methodology. He said that he thought he could solve the methodological problems they identified, and asked the editor, "If I revise the article as the reviewers suggest, would you be able to send it to new reviewers who would comment on the content?" The editor responded that he would do so if the author truly addressed the first reviewers' comments. The professor revised the article; the editor agreed that he had solved the methodological problems, and sent the revised version to two new reviewers. They liked the article, and it was published. An important key to this author's success was the very professional tone that he maintained throughout, never insulting the reviewers, accepting that their concerns were valid, and being willing to go through a second review process. Persistence was key.

On very rare occasions, editors may change their decision. At our interdisciplinary journal, we once gave a negative decision to an author whose subject matter wasn't familiar to us. He had received one favorable report and one very negative report. In response to the negative reviewer's report, the author sent an eight-page, single-spaced defense. The tone of the defense was never insulting but very focused, providing a swathe of data to disprove the reviewer's objections and laying out how the author's and the reviewer's differences reflected a much larger debate going on in the field. The author insisted that the reviewer had not given the article a fair hearing. Since we liked controversial work and found the defense convincing, we asked the author to include much of that defense in the article itself, and then we published it. So although protests can't carry the day, professional responses directly addressing the reviewers' critiques sometimes can. Of course, I don't recommend that you spend time writing eight-page defenses, especially to journals that have sent unkind or unhelpful remarks. If you receive a definitive rejection, it's best to move on to the next journal.

You're unlikely to change the editor's decision if you're protesting only a reviewer's cruel wording. If the editor agrees that it was cruel, the journal may ban using that reviewer in the future, in which case you have done a good deed for others and nothing for yourself. But most editors are well aware of the delivery style of individual reviewers, and have decided that the value of their acumen in identifying real problems outweighs their unfortunate wording of those criticisms. Finally, you're also unlikely to change the decision if you insist that you know who the unkind reviewer was, and explain why that person has a personal vendetta against you. Some authors find it difficult to refrain from trying to guess their reviewers' identity. They'll tell everyone that their field is small, and so they can always figure out who their reviewers are. All I can say is that your chances of being right are low. In my years as an editor, I've never had an author guess correctly. Not once. Another editor commented publicly, "Never assume you know who is reviewing your article—as I've heard from nearly every editor, likely, you are wrong even if you are sure you're right" (Fargot-stein 2013). And I have seen more than one relationship destroyed because the author was wrongly convinced about the identity of a negative reviewer. Don't waste time on this game.

If you decide to protest, you can email or phone about your objections. If you email, make sure that your protest letter does not commit the same sins that inspired it: be courteous. Since we often lose impartiality in such situations, have someone edit your protest letter before you send it. You don't want to have sent the kind of unprofessional letter that makes you feel awkward about submitting work to that journal in the future. Alternately, one editor advised that disgruntled authors not send angry emails but make a polite phone call to the editor. In that call, "tell [the editor] that the reviewer comments seem a bit off. Don't be angry and defensive. Ask them to help you navigate the comments. Maybe you weren't clear about something in your paper. Maybe the reviewer was not an appropriate person to review the paper. The editor may not know that. Before wasting your time yanking the paper, reformatting the paper for another journal, and waiting for a first round of peer review elsewhere, take a few minutes to have a conversation with the editor" (Cochran 2016). Another option, if you ever deign to submit work to that journal again, is to mention in your cover letter that with your previous submission you thought you had received an "unhelpful" review (use that exact word, nothing stronger) and would prefer, if possible, to have a different reviewer this time.

However, the plain truth is that writing such letters is a time-consuming task with only a slim chance of return. An interviewer asked a well-published faculty member whether he had ever protested journal decisions. The author answered with one word: "Yes." The interviewer then asked whether the protesting ever worked. The author again answered with one word: "No" (Welch 2006, 2). Your chances are better if you send your work to another, more receptive journal. Fortunately, the desire to protest journal decisions tends to wane as you gain more experience with submitting articles. You come to understand that plenty of successfully published articles once received harsh treatment at the hands of others, and you learn to move on. So if you feel like protesting your first or second journal decision, resist the impulse. You don't know enough yet about how it all works. Get some more experience under your belt before protesting.

If it's any comfort, in eleven years as an editor reading reports by reviewers I knew, I began to sense a correlation between niceness and productivity. I can't prove it, but it seemed to me that the kinder and more constructive reviewers were more likely to be productive writers themselves. The harsher and less helpful reviewers were more likely to be unproductive writers. We give others the messages we give ourselves.

Should I formally appeal the decision? Most good US-based journals belong to the Council of Editors of Learned Journals, which has a mediation board for resolving disputes between authors and editors. Some large disciplinary journals have their own formal appeal processes, with independent boards. Over the years, many scholars have recommended that more journals institute better appeal processes and provide authors and reviewers with more opportunities to dialogue (Epstein 1995)—but this sea change doesn't seem to be coming anytime soon. A study of author appeals to the *American Sociological Review* found that only 13 percent of appeals were successful (Bakanic, McPhail, and Simon 1987, 632). Your chances of publication are greater, I think, if you move on to another journal.

JUNCTURE 5: RESPONDING TO A JOURNAL'S REVISE-AND-RESUBMIT NOTICE

Let's say, alternately, that your article receives good news—a revise-and-resubmit notice. What do you do?

Should I revise and resubmit my article? Yes, yes, a thousand times yes! You must revise and resubmit your article. Don't debate whether to do it, don't doubt whether you should do it, don't wait to do it—just do it. Remember that your chances of publication increase substantially on a revised and resubmitted article—by some estimates, up to 75 percent (Henson 2007, 785).

Should I revise and resubmit my article to the same journal? A minority of authors, upon receiving a warm revise-and-resubmit notice from a journal, choose not to revise their article for that journal but to try their chances elsewhere. They use the peer reviewers' comments and, if they think the revisions have substantially improved the article, send the article to a better journal. Editors don't consider this fair, since you've taken their labor yet not given them a product. Some journals are rumored to ban authors from ever publishing in their pages if they find that another journal published the article that they had reviewed positively. To be sure, you haven't signed a contract with the journal, and your intellectual property is yours to dispense as you please. Please note, however, that all the research shows that your chances of publication double when you resubmit an article to the same journal (Henson 2007, 785), while your chances at other journals remain lower, the same as for all first-time submissions. If you want to be on the safe side, therefore, it's better to dance with the one that brought you good feedback first.

Should I wait to revise my article? Upon receiving a recommendation to revise, at first it's easy to feel that the revision is going to take a long time, and that you should wait until you have more time to complete the task. Resist this impulse! Often, a revision will take less time than you anticipate. The article will seem to be at a distance, since you last worked on it several months ago, but it will become familiar again within a few hours of your working on it. So within two weeks of receiving a revise-and-resubmit notice, make sure to at least open the article, reread it, and make one change. This returns the article to the front burner of your mind, gets your unconscious working on it. Aim for getting the article back to the journal within a month or two, unless the journal requests that you send it sooner. On average, scholars revise and resubmit articles within thirty-nine days; about 90 percent resubmit within three months (Huisman and Smits 2017, 644). Although most editors won't give you a deadline for returning the article, new articles are always coming through and you don't want to be scooped. Also, the longer you wait, the more likely it is that you'll need to redo your related literature review. So get on it!

JUNCTURE 6: SETTING UP FOR REVISING YOUR ARTICLE

Once you've decided that you're going to revise and resubmit your article, you must take several steps: collect and evaluate the editorial and peer reviewer recommendations, ask the editor for any needed clarifications, start your revision cover letter, and decide how you'll address the recommended changes in your revised article.

Get centered. One of the biggest mistakes that novice authors make is assuming that they must do everything the reviewers tell them to do. Yet no editor expects authors to make all the recommended changes. What they do expect is that you take all recommendations seriously, and that you do something to your article in response to each criticism. But doing something and doing what the reviewers told you to do are two very different things. I'll have more to say about this later. For now, don't get discouraged if you see that some of the recommended revisions are untenable. Remember, you're in control of your article.

Collect the recommendations for revision. Some of the recommendations for revising your article may be in the editorial decision letter, others may be in the reviewers' reports, others may be in emails, and still others may be ideas that occurred to you while awaiting the journal's decision. You need to keep track of all recommended revisions so that you won't forget any of them and can respond to all of them (even if your response is "I won't do that").

Categorize the recommendations. Unfortunately, peer reviewers and editors don't organize or classify recommendations for you. This may seem like a small matter, but it can be quite confusing figuring out what they're recommending or whether they're recommending the same thing. For instance, several sentences in a report may contain no real recommendations, and then the next short sentence will contain three. Or a reviewer will say something vague like "You need to strengthen this sentence, and the ones like it throughout," and you slowly realize that this recommendation isn't about your grammar but about enhancing the thread of your argument. Or one reviewer will say, "You need to cite x and y," and another reviewer will say, "You need to cite the literature on z," but they both mean the same thing.

You can use any method you like to organize the recommendations. Many SciQua scholars use an Excel spreadsheet. This spreadsheet can be quite simple, with one column for reviewer criticisms, one column for noting the relevant line and page, and another for your response. If you find it helpful, you can adapt the table on the next page about the

Recommendations for Revising My Article					
(Use the codes R1, R2, and Ed. after a comment to indicate which reviewer made the comment.)					
Text features evaluated	Positive comments	Negative comments	Valid comment? Difficulty of revision?	Line/ page/ section?	Done?
Relation to audience (e.g., clarity)					
Argument					
Literature review, relation to previous research					
Methods					
Presentation of evidence					
Interpretation of evidence					
Claim for significance					
Implications					
Style					
Technical, factual errors					
Typos, spelling errors (with line, page number)					
Other					

Source: Adapted from Paltridge 2017, 176.

types of recommendations editors and peer reviewers make (partly based on an excellent one in Paltridge 2017, 176). Use it to collect and categorize all the recommendations. If there are many, it may be better to create a more complex document with a line for each reviewer-recommended change, along with information about which reviewer made the recommendation; the validity of the recommendation; the level of revision it requires (none, small, medium, large); the revisions planned to address the recommendation; and the line, page, or section where that change needs to be made. Some scholars use the spreadsheet to rewrite any negative comments in a positive, more constructive way. For instance, if the reviewer writes, "This piece has no argument," rewrite it as "Develop and clarify my argument." If you don't want to be so formal, print the reviewers' reports and mark them up. Whatever you do, don't treat their comments lightly. Also, be sure that you cross-reference the editors' decision letter with the reviewers' reports in case the editor has disagreed with or underscored any reviewer recommendations.

Get any needed clarifications from the editor. It's not always clear how the editor wants you to revise. For instance, if the reviewers make opposing recommendations, which do you act on? If the editor says that you need to shorten the article, and both reviewers make recommendations that lengthen it, whose directions should you follow? If you aren't sure, email the editor asking for clarification on which changes to make. If you know the changes you want to make, then don't ask the editor, just make the changes that make the most sense to you. In other words, don't ask for advice you're unwilling to take.

Start a revision cover letter. Standard practice in the SciQua fields, and increasingly in HumInt ones, is for authors to submit, along with their revised article, a letter stating exactly how they revised the article according to the reviewers' recommendations. Nothing will increase your chances of a successful resubmission as writing such a letter, one that guides the editor in interpreting your responsiveness. With it, you signal your compliance with the editors' requests, but also explain any choices you made not to follow reviewers' recommendations for revising. Don't wait to start this letter after you've completed the revisions—you'll find it tough to remember what you did. Instead, create an electronic document for the revision cover letter that allows you to keep track of improvements. Some scholars use their Excel spreadsheet to categorize the recommended changes, but I find it helpful to have both documents running: I often will talk myself out of something in the letter. I will start by explaining why I am not going to make a change, but as I'm defending my position, I will slowly see how I might address the critique and yet maintain my own voice and views. So constantly drafting this letter helps me with the revision process.

Perform triage on the reviewers' recommendations. Once you have collected and categorized the recommendations and started your revision cover letter, you may find it useful to make some decisions about what you will actually do before starting your revision. Use a column of the spreadsheet to think about whether you want to make the change, its level of difficulty, and perhaps the place or places where the change will be made. Don't spend a lot of time on this—much becomes clearer during the revision process itself. But some initial thinking can help. For instance, an editor advised, "Those changes that seem reasonable, that appear to strengthen the article's argument and to extend its implications, and that deepen and broaden the context, should be attempted. Those that seem to the author to misread the purpose of the article or to require a kind of research or revision that would turn the essay into something quite different may not be worth attempting" (CELJ 2007). In general, stay focused on two questions: What exactly does this reviewer want me to do? (so that you don't exaggerate beyond that) and If I do what they want, will I like my article more? (so that you remain true to your vision). According to one study, "nearly 25% of the respondents admitted to revising their manuscripts to placate a referee or editor and as a result actually making changes they as authors felt were incorrect" (Bedeian 2004, 209). You want to avoid that situation.

Open a new copy of the article with Track Changes on. Most editors will ask you to edit your article with Track Changes on so that they can easily see how you altered your article in response to the reviewers' recommendations. Even if you haven't been asked to do this, think about doing it, as it makes your case for publication clear to the editor. If you don't like editing with all the changes visible, in Microsoft Word simply select "Simple markup" under Track Changes and it will hide them.

Start the revision. You can now proceed thoughtfully with your revision, following the instructions below.

JUNCTURE 7: REVISING YOUR ARTICLE

Now that you have categorized the recommendations, what exactly do you do in response? How do you approach the various recommendations for revision? Different types of recommended revisions require different approaches. Some instructions to get you started follow; remember that you can always consult previous chapters in the workbook for advice on improving arguments, structure, literature reviews, prose, and so on. Even if you don't agree with a recommendation, try to do something small to the article so that you can say that you did something in response, such as adding a footnote or citing someone who defended that methodology. In the process, you may find that you better understand the problem the reviewer was having.

Starting Small

One of the biggest mistakes authors make when asked to revise and resubmit an article is planning to do too much in response to the reviewers' recommendations. You can often resolve even serious objections to your work in straightforward ways. So don't make the mistake of thinking that the more serious the objection, the more time, effort, and suffering you must invest. Start by making the smallest possible changes to address the largest objections. If making small changes leads you to make larger, substantive changes, good for you. Any article can be improved. But it's best to start with targeted revisions. That way you won't get overwhelmed, and you'll be more likely to resubmit the article. This approach doesn't prevent you from doing more, but it does prevent you from doing too much. A colleague once told me that if she thinks that it will take two weeks to solve a problem the reviewers identified, she tries working on it for thirty minutes. If she can't fix it in that amount of time, she cuts that part of the article entirely.

Revising Minor Errors

If the recommended changes aren't substantial, start by fixing the minor problems: spelling, syntax, typos, missing information. It's a great way to get back into the article.

Revising Citations

The reviewer's report that does not recommend additional citations is rare. Almost all recommend that authors cite one to twenty additional sources. In my experience as an editor, however, recommended citations are rarely essential to an article. They're the books that popped into the reviewers' heads—because they recently read them or wrote them. If your initial response to the reviewers' recommendations is planning on reading ten new books and incorporating a paragraph about each of them into your article, the editor isn't going to be happy with how bloated your article has become. You're doing too much in response to the recommendation. You can, of course, go ahead and read this important literature. That makes you a good scholar. But it doesn't necessarily make you a published author. So, shockingly, I recommend that you first try to write the suggested citations into your article *before* reading them.

Revising an article for publication does not require that you know those books and articles by heart. In fact, reading them may make completing your revision more difficult. Novice authors in particular imagine that other authors have put their concepts more cogently and so begin to lard their article with quotations that cause more problems than they solve. Instead, start by identifying where you would discuss those citations in your article, and quickly draft a sentence or two referring to those citations based on what you already know. Then, and only then, skim the recommended literature. If it's truly relevant, then you can read it. You already have twenty to fifty solid citations—be wary of spending a lot of time carefully reading new material and adding whole paragraphs about new citations. A sentence here and there will usually suffice.

There's one exception to my advice. Sometimes reviewers will state that it's odd that you haven't cited so-and-so's article on your topic, since you seem to be making very similar arguments or directly contradictory arguments. You'll need to read that work carefully, particularly if that scholar has done seminal work in your field. It will be important to differentiate what you're doing from that scholar's research. Otherwise, most reviewers aren't expecting to see you engage their recommended citations at length. For more advice, see the section "Strategies for Citing Your Reading" in "Week 5: Refining Your Works Cited."

Revising Literature Reviews

Sometimes the reviewers will state that you haven't discussed an entire body of scholarship or the relationship of your argument to it. If this literature isn't on your topic, you may not need to address the objection. That is, it may not be necessary to cite recent work on the biostatistics of snakebites in North Carolina if you're addressing it in Bangladesh. But if the reviewers' recommendations cite a body of scholarship that's relevant, you must take such a comment seriously. This is particularly true if a reviewer suggests that you're unaware of a new stream in the research on your exact topic, or if a reviewer notes that you haven't cited anything published in the last five to ten years. Not engaging the previous literature is a frequent error of novice authors, and you should be grateful to a reviewer who merely asks you to revise an article that contains this mistake. Recommendations such as these enable you both to seem better versed than you are and to make your article stronger and smarter.

As you revise your article in light of that scholarship, remember that no publishable article can include many pages summarizing new research. Try to find a review article that helps you think about that body of scholarship as a whole and your argument vis-à-vis that scholarship. Likewise, as you read the most useful works, think carefully about how your argument relates to their arguments. It's vastly more important for you to state how your work relates to that scholarship than to summarize it in any detail. For more advice, see the section "Strategies for Writing Your Literature Review" in the week 5 chapter.

A case of light revision may be illustrative here. In an article our journal once received, the author had stated that there was no published research on the topic of her article and that her work filled this gap. One of the reviewers scribbled "nonsense" next to that claim, then penciled in five titles published in the last few years that dealt with precisely that topic. Since the article was based on careful fieldwork and strong findings, we didn't reject it, but we did ask that it be better situated in the related literature. When the article came back, the author had simply switched her claim for significance, taking out the sentence about the gap in research and inserting a single sentence stating that there was exciting new research on the topic. She then placed a footnote at the end of the new sentence and listed the five recommended books. Two of these books came up briefly later in the discussion, but she hadn't significantly revised her article based on that literature. Some editors would have rejected such a revision as insufficient. Others would have concentrated on whether the article was an original contribution. We thought that hers was, and so we published it. My own instinct as an author would have been to take more advantage of that previous research. But my point here is to convince you that briefly addressing the shortcoming can work.

Revising Terms and Definitions

Many reviewers ask authors to define their terms more carefully. Often, this request is lazy reviewing, but it certainly can't hurt your article for you to be clearer. Just don't take up too much time or space adding definitions. It's easy to go overboard. Usually, adding five to ten words of description upon the first mention of the term can clarify matters perfectly. If you think further clarification is truly necessary and you have endnotes, give a one- or two-sentence definition, either your own or someone else's.

If your reviewers have major objections to a term you've used, citing someone else's definition can be a good tack. For instance, let's say that your reference to an "Irish diaspora" enraged one respondent, who insisted that the term *diaspora* could not be used to refer to the Irish and that the entire piece was vitiated by your regular reference to it. Yet despite this reviewer's strong response, the other reviewers don't even mention the term. You could attempt an overhaul, but if you believe in the term, your best response would be to include a footnote the first time you use it. In the note, cite the term's use by other academics: "My use of the term 'Irish diaspora' follows that of [author names with citation date] and should be understood as referring to . . ." Remember that in academia, as in law, the best defense is precedence.

Revising to Shorten

Editors tend to ask authors to shorten their work. Brevity can work for research that doesn't challenge the status quo, but it poses problems for research that does. But let's say that your editor insists. Which of your precious jewels should you remove?

If you need to reduce the word count significantly, start by cutting out block quotes, footnotes, long summaries of others' research, and additional cases. In the humanities, it's usually safer to delete evidence—some close readings, some historical analysis—than articulations of your argument or contribution. Then start at the beginning of the article and examine each sentence for ways to make it shorter. If you work your way through your article taking out the deadwood of unnecessary words, you'll improve it as a piece of prose (reread "Week 11: Editing Your Sentences" for advice on how to do this). If you remove just two words per sentence in a 7,500-word article, you can reduce your count by over 600 words. If your article is far too long, say, twice the allowed length, perhaps it's time to think about how you could split it into two different articles. Splitting one article into two is especially successful if you can revise so that each would appeal to a different type of journal.

Revising to Lengthen

Reviewers tend to ask authors to expand and elucidate. I heard about a professor whose review of others' work consisted entirely of scrawling "More!" next to sentences and paragraphs. Unfortunately, editors usually want "Less!" Since many journals are run by corporations, which impose exact page limits to keep paper costs down, editors wanting to have enough articles in each issue to make the journal interesting must limit their authors to fewer words each.

These contradictory instructions—shorten! lengthen!—create one of the main dilemmas facing authors. Whose instructions to follow? Fortunately, you can use this contradiction to your advantage. If the reviewers have asked for more content about an issue that you either know little about or view as irrelevant, you can use the word limit to explain why you're not addressing their concerns. If the editor agrees that the recommendations weren't essential, this will work. But if the editor thinks they're important, it won't work. Thus, you can't use the word limit to defend your failure to make your work clearer, more theoretically sophisticated, or more significant. You can use it only as a polite way to decline a recommendation to add more content on tangential topics. If the reviewers have asked for more on a topic that you do think is relevant, then you can ask the editor whether you could go past the word limit to insert that new material. You might mention that some research shows that longer articles tend to be more frequently cited (Thelwall, Kousha, and Abdoli 2017, 517).

Revising Theoretical or Methodological Approaches

If the reviewers have major objections to your theory or method, there are no shortcuts. If you believe that the reviewers are wrong, move on to a new journal. If you think they're right, embark on a serious overhaul. Sometimes you can address the objection directly and effectively by stating in the article that the problem is a limitation or shortcoming of your research and that further research is needed.

Revising Argument

A frequent comment of both reviewers and editors is that the author's argument could be clearer or better defended. One easy fix is bringing material from your conclusion to your introduction (since we tend to get clearer as we go along). Make sure that you announce your argument clearly and early, and thread it throughout your article. You can also add subheads to direct the reader. Another fix is to make sure that you're not varying your main terms too much. Avoid repetition when it comes to adjectives and verbs; increase it for your main nouns. See "Week 2: Advancing Your Argument" for additional information.

Revising Grammar and Style

If the editor says that your writing needs dramatic improvement (especially for ESL-related problems), consider hiring a copy editor. It's not cheap—in the United States, a copy editor charges $35 to $75 an hour and can copyedit only one to four pages an hour. But if lack of a published article is preventing you from obtaining a tenure-track position or tenure itself, hiring a copy editor can be an important investment in your future earnings. Many scholars can't afford this, but if you can, you should. You can find copy editors at the Editorial Freelancers Association website. Retired professors are sometimes interested in helping junior scholars as well, so you might ask for such assistance. See "Week 11: Editing Your Sentences" for instructions.

Revising Documentation Style

Editors will generally ask that you ensure that your source documentation is both accurate and in their journal's style. Even if the editors don't ask for this, do it. Follow the journal's directions and be meticulous. If you've been sloppy about this, it can get your article returned to you.

Completing the Final Steps

Once you have made your changes, you might consider sharing your revised article with a writing group. You can let the group know the reviewers' concerns and ask participants whether they think you've addressed the concerns adequately. Also, if you have coauthors but are responsible for making the changes, don't forget to run the revised version of the article by them.

JUNCTURE 8: DRAFTING YOUR REVISION COVER LETTER

Since editors and peer reviewers tend not to read revised articles carefully, a detailed revision cover letter is your best weapon in getting a revised article accepted. If the letter is professional and indicates a deep commitment to revision, the editor may take you at your word and do little more than skim the article to see whether you've made the recommended changes.

Use bullet points. It's best to arrange the cover letter as a series of bulleted items, with the reviewers' critiques grouped by category and followed by each alteration you made to solve the problem. This format is easier for the editor to follow.

Order rhetorically. Organize the letter's content from compliance to noncompliance. That is, start with all the changes you made obediently in response to the reviewers' recommendations, and only at the end get to the recommended changes you didn't make and your reasons for not addressing them. This arrangement is more convincing than beginning the letter with your objections.

Use page references. Some scholars suggest that you list page locations for each change you made. I think that's fussy (given documents' sophisticated find and search functions), and if you have Track Changes on, your revisions will be clear. But you may find it useful to include page references in your letter, and some editors may require it.

Assume that reviewers will read it. If the editors send your article back to the original reviewers, undoubtedly your revision cover letter will be sent along as well. Remember to thank the reviewers in the letter, and praise their suggestions as helpful.

List independent improvements. If you do make additional changes to the article, beyond what the reviewers suggested, do mention this in the cover letter. That you spent extra time to improve the article will usually impress the editors, but they will want to check to make sure that you haven't worsened the article.

Give good reasons for noncompliance. You must be able to offer an academic reason for disregarding recommendations. And no matter how accurately expressed, the given reason can't be "The reviewer is an idiot!" Below are examples for defenses you can give in your revision cover letter. Note the even tone of these responses. Don't attack the reviewers; rather, explain how their recommendations have enabled you to improve the article, even if you haven't done what they told you to do.

Dates. Reviewer 1 has disputed my dating of [some event]. I stand by my dating, but I have added a footnote explaining how I arrived at the dates, backed by two additional sources.

Analysis. Reviewer 2 disagrees with my list of the causes of [some crisis]. Although I think that my list is correct, there is a debate in the literature on the causes, so I have briefly discussed that debate in the text.

Argument. Reviewer 1 seems to have misread the premise of my article, which was [premise]. I thought I was clear, but I have taken the opportunity to clarify this premise so it is less easily misread.

Data. Although Reviewer 1's comment about the relevance of my argument about child psychiatry to pet therapy was intriguing, I could not add material on that topic and still meet the word limit.

Data. I thought that the second reviewer's comment regarding the relevance of [such-and-such] was astute, but after several attempts, I could not frame this in the text in a brief enough space. Instead, I have inserted a general note.

Data. Reviewer 2 says that my statement of the limitations of my evidence prompts the question of why I didn't collect more evidence of this type. As explained there, I did not set out to collect such evidence because [reason] would have made it near impossible. I think that the statement of limitations is sufficient as it stands.

Data. Reviewer 2 asks whether there are works in [another genre] on the topic, when the article is explicitly about [genre]; I consider addressing a different genre to be beyond the scope of the current article.

Cases. Since the reviewers were in conflict on the treatment of the second case (one recommending that I say more about it and the other recommending that I eliminate it), I have chosen to follow the second reviewer and eliminate that discussion.

Title. I did keep more of the title than Reviewer 1 wanted, as I think it better suggests the argument; but I have added more specificity so that it will more accurately show up in online searches.

Citation. The second reviewer recommended that I address [such-and-such], but there just wasn't space for it and [famous author] addresses this at length, so I just added a sentence citing that work.

Term. One reviewer thought my use of the word [word] was too obscure, but I have found it used in this way more than a dozen times in academic texts in the field, so I have chosen to keep it. I can provide you with those citations if you wish.

Additional. Once I started revising in response to the peer reviewers' helpful comments, I saw some other problems and revised several sections so that they were tighter and more to the point. I also changed my text/case in the second section from [text/case 1] to [text/case 2], since it supports my point better.

Editors assume that the reviewers stumble over something in an article for a reason. If reviewers say that there's a problem, editors believe them. Where you create a space for yourself, however, is that editors also assume that reviewers' proffered solutions to that problem may be wrong. You have control over your article—so seize opportunities to clarify and defend your meaning. As one editor advises, "If a reader misinterprets something you wrote, there must be an improvement that will help" (Rothman 1998, 333).

Examples of Revision Cover Letters

Sample Revision Cover Letter 1

Dear [Editor's Name]:

Enclosed please find the revised version of my article titled [title]. I am grateful for the thorough reading of the reviewers, and I have addressed their concerns in the following ways:

Errors. I added the missing . . . and corrected the . . .

Significance. One of the reviewers thought I should make my contribution clearer, so I have . . .

Introduction. I have tightened the introduction but have also provided examples of . . . so my subject is clearer and clarified the meaning of my main term . . .

Theoretical framework. I shortened the theoretical section but also added material on so-and-so's work, as the second reviewer requested, so it is now a bit longer. The recommendation meant I was also able to address the first reviewer's concern about . . . , so the increased length seems justified.

Terms. I have abandoned the problematic classification of . . .

Section 1. In the section on . . . , I have incorporated the texts that the second reviewer recommended.

Section 2. For reasons of length, I have eliminated much of . . .

Section 3. I have developed the section as recommended . . .

Conclusion. I have focused on arguing more strongly for the rest of the article, providing better, more provocative conclusions from my analysis.

Length. By adding the recommended texts, defining my subject more clearly, expanding the readings with references to one another and the theoretical texts, and threading my argument throughout, the article expanded beyond the word limit. To reduce the word count, I radically cut the notes, works cited, block quotes, and textual examples. This meant that many careful notes had to be dropped. It also meant that any secondary literature not directly related to the texts had to be sacrificed, such as all the references in the introduction and theoretical section. Moreover, I could not cite the five additional texts that the second reviewer suggested; as he/she was not insistent about adding those, I assume that this is acceptable. The article is now just under the word limit.

I believe that these revisions have radically improved the article's argument and clarity—thanks to the editors' and reviewers' thoughtful recommendations. Please let me know whether there is anything further I can do; in particular, I can return deleted material to the text for clarity.

Sincerely,

[Your Name]

Sample Revision Cover Letter 2

Dear [Editor's Name]:

Thank you for considering my article [give title and journal's number for the article] for [journal title]. I appreciate the comments I received and am resubmitting this manuscript for your consideration. In this letter, I detail how I addressed the reviewers' comments.

The first reviewer's comments and my revisions were as follows:

Comment: "I would be curious to know whether gender affected . . ."

My Revisions:

• While, as this reviewer noted, the effect of gender is tough to determine because of the size of my sample ($n = 9$), I revisited and reanalyzed the data. There appeared to be no significant differences in how men and women viewed . . .

• At the beginning of the Results section, I added a phrase noting that there were few differences in responses across gender and socioeconomic status.

• When addressing the limitations of this study in the Implications section, I added a sentence suggesting that the small sample size limits my ability to determine whether there are differences between men and women in . . .

Comment: "It would have been nice to have seen a longitudinal element."

My Revision:

• On page 26, I highlighted as a limitation of this study that it is not longitudinal.

Thank you very much for your time and consideration. If you have any questions about the manuscript or changes that I have made, please do not hesitate to be in touch.

Sincerely,

[Your Name]

JUNCTURE 9: RESUBMITTING YOUR ARTICLE

Resubmit your article to the journal editors, along with your revision cover letter. Congratulations, you're one step closer to publication!

JUNCTURES 10–11: AFTER THE JOURNAL PUBLISHES YOUR ARTICLE

JUNCTURE 10: BRINGING ATTENTION TO YOUR ARTICLE

I once asked a recently tenured professor whether she had any advice about getting tenure. She looked at me sideways and then asked, "Do you really want to know?" When I said I did, she replied, "Well, some would consider this tacky or too aggressive, but whenever I published an article, I sent it individually by email to fifty faculty." She shrugged. "So when it came time for tenure, people in my field knew who I was." If you aren't doing the equivalent, you aren't completing the last step of publication in the modern world: bringing attention to your article. Many articles go uncited; you need to do what you can to ensure that yours is. Announce your article on social media like Twitter and Facebook, list the title on scholarly networks like Academia.edu and ResearchGate, include it as a link at the bottom of your emails, and send it to relevant faculty in your field. Finally, set up a Google Alert for your name and your article title so that you can track whether the article is being cited. You can find excellent resources online for increasing the visibility of your research, such as the book *Communicating Your Research with Social Media* (Mollett et al. 2017), the research article "Effective Strategies for Increasing Citation Frequency" (Ale Ebrahim et al. 2013), or the web application Kudos for Researchers. As a side note, when the time comes, authors are expected to follow the *text recycling rule*: they aren't supposed to lecture on or present material they have already published. Presenting it before publication is, of course, encouraged.

JUNCTURE 11: REVIEWING SOMEONE ELSE'S ARTICLE

Since an editor and two or three reviewers spent time helping you get into print, you owe it to academia to help others get published by accepting invitations to peer-review articles. As one observer put it, "Researchers are becoming increasingly vociferous about turnaround times and the robustness of the peer review system for their own papers, while at the same time abrogating their reviewer responsibilities in droves" (Didham, Leather, and Basset 2017, 1). So if you're an author, you should be agreeing to review others' articles. The standard practice for authors is "to do at least two reviews for every one paper . . . published" (1). Just remember that what makes a report valuable are "specific comments and advice" and not abstract evaluations of quality (Casati et al. 2009, par. 1, sec. 4).

WEEK 0
Writing Your Article from Scratch

Task Week	Daily Writing Tasks	Estimated Task Time
Week 1	Steps 1–7: Read workbook chapters 1, 2, 5, and 6; name and match up your interests; identify journals using chapter 4; and set up RMS	12+ hours
Week 2	Step 8: Read relevant journals and articles	12+ hours
Week 3	Steps 9–13: Brainstorm ideas and arguments, ask others about and take stock of your arguments, and check the scholarly literature and method	12+ hours
Week 4–Week ?	Step 14–16: Imagine the study, select an appropriate journal, and do the study	1–20+ weeks
Week 5–Week ?	Step 17–20: Outline the article, write an abstract using chapter 3, and write a three- to five-page draft	5–30+ hours
Week 6–Week 12	Step 21: Read and do assignments in chapters 7–12. Send!	6+ weeks

This workbook aids you in *revising* a piece of academic writing into a journal article. Most graduate students and junior faculty do have a classroom essay, conference paper, BA or MA thesis, dissertation chapter, talk, or unpublished article that can serve as a draft to revise for publication, even if it's very rough and just a few pages. However, a few readers may have merely an idea for an article, without any draft, and a few may not have even an idea. This week 0 chapter assists such readers, those who are *drafting* an article from scratch, not revising one, and who have neither completed nor started their study, data collection, data analysis, or experiment. Creating a draft from scratch will take at least three weeks and most often much longer. Many of the steps in this chapter require you to read and do tasks from other chapters of the writing workbook, but in a different order than those revising..

A few principles guide this chapter. Many people are taught not to start writing until they know what they want to say (Richardson and St. Pierre 2005, 960). Frequently, though, it's not ideas that generate writing but writing that generates ideas. Writing is not a task to be completed after you figure everything out, it *itself* is thinking. To imagine otherwise causes writing dysfunction. One study found that students who saw "a strict demarcation between collecting data, or doing research, and the writing up of this material as a thesis" were more likely to experience problems with completing writing projects (Torrance and Thomas 1994, 107). You'll write more easily if you understand that "data is produced in writing, it is not found" (Kamler and Thomson 2014, 3). We write to find out what we think, so be sure to write as you go through the tasks below in search of ideas.

WRITING YOUR ARTICLE FROM SCRATCH WITHOUT AN IDEA

Some readers come to this book very early in their academic career, as an undergraduate or beginning graduate student, without an acceptable piece of prose to revise or without knowledge of how to arrive at publishable ideas. This section is for you.

The tasks that follow should help you generate ideas, whether for several articles or longer works.

SETTING UP

Step 1: Start a document. Before doing anything else, set up a print or electronic document titled "Ideas for Articles." Use it to write down your ideas as you go through the steps below. In other words, don't just read the steps; actually follow their instructions to write. Alternately, you could post, blog, or tweet about this process, which some use to pitch ideas and get responses to them (Daniels 2013). *Time*: 5 minutes.

Step 2: Create a writing schedule. Read the workbook's introduction and first chapter, "Week 1: Designing Your Plan for Writing," and complete the assignments in those pages. The readings and activities will aid you in understanding the keys to being a successful academic writer, including writing regularly, and guide you in designing an article-drafting process given your particular time constraints. *Time*: 3–8 hours.

Step 3: Learn what it takes to get published. To get published, you must have an argument related to a current debate in your field. I discuss these aspects of writing at length in the chapters "Week 2: Advancing Your Argument"; "Week 5: Refining Your Works Cited"; and "Week 6: Crafting Your Claims for Significance." Skimming the instruction in these chapters without doing the exercises will aid you in understanding the qualities of an article that journals are looking for. You'll also receive information about what a publishable argument is and how to review the literature, identify current debates, and make claims for significance related to those debates. *Time*: 3–8 hours.

GETTING AN IDEA

Step 4: Name your interests. Having learned what journals are looking for, write up a list of your own interests following the instructions that follow. Write this list of seven items with as much detail as possible—it will provide a foundation for years to come.

More than one person has left academia because they couldn't find a way to write about things that genuinely interested them. Research anchored in your own interests will sustain you, not drain you. If you're attending graduate school in midlife, this is all the more important and useful a step because of your range of life and work experiences. You may not get to write about any of the things you name, but identifying them will help you recognize areas of interest. As you go through the writing tasks here and find yourself starting to write an idea or an argument for an article, don't stop yourself from doing so. That's the point, to use your life as a prompt. *Time*: 1-6 hours.

- Start with what you consider to be your nonacademic interests: hobbies (e.g., knitting or dirt biking), passions (e.g., fashion design or fostering dogs), political commitments (e.g., ending transphobia or protecting free speech), sports (e.g., yoga or watching soccer), and so on. After each, put a short reason as to why it interests you. That is, don't explain why you *enjoy* it—explain why it *interests* you.
- List your areas of expertise, your skills or knowledge in various fields, such as cooking, speaking Swahili, sculpting, and carpentry, or accounting, horror movies, disability law, and so on. Include anything that you know deeply or well.
- List your disciplines, those branches of knowledge in which you have training, whether at the undergraduate or the graduate student level. You may have just one, or you may be interdisciplinary. For instance, you might list philosophy and literature, or architecture and film, or just anthropology. Provide one or two reasons why that discipline interests you, but also what about that discipline drives you nuts or falls short.
- List your academic fields or academic interests, trying to use standardized, searchable academic terms, like "implicit bias," "seventeenth-century Chinese literature," "natural resource wars," "medieval women's hagiography," and so on. List as many as possible. Again, include after each item a short reason why it interests you. If you find that the same reason motivates your interest in different topics, all the better.
- List from memory the academic scholarship that made a lasting impression on you, that shaped how you think about the world. You don't need to do online searches for it or get the title or any quotations exactly right; the point is to write down a little bit about what made it formative. For example, "*Guns, Germs, and Steel* by Diamond (1999) (an antiracist biological argument for why some regions and peoples are now poorer than others)" or "'Sitting on a Man' by Van Allen (1972) (about how British colonialism reduced Igbo women's autonomy and power rather than freeing them from 'barbarous' traditional sexism)."
- List from memory the academic theories that you found compelling. For instance, "Janice Radway's (1984) theory of genre reading as a paradoxical social event that both provides an escape from repressive gender roles and reinscribes those gender roles."
- List from memory recent media activity that struck you as particularly interesting or true, such as newspaper articles, blog posts, or Twitter comments.

Step 5: Match up your interests. Once you've compiled your list of interests, examine it to see whether any of your interests are starting to match up, such as a discipline overlapping with a skill set overlapping with recent reading. One of the reasons to do this is to find research topics that would interest you. For example, perhaps you're a graduate student in history who is an expert cook of Ghanaian food who recently read a newspaper article about how coffee, okra, and watermelon are native to Africa. Since you frequently cook okra, you begin to wonder whether through the years there has been a change in how it is cooked in Ghana, in which dishes it appears. As a historian, you could follow this question and see whether it got you anywhere interesting. You might end up not writing about okra at all but writing about, say, traditional healing plants.

Another reason to match up your interests is to find suitable research topics. Sometimes novice authors try to write about topics that interest them, but for which they don't have the disciplinary training or research skills. It's true that academia is becoming more interdisciplinary, but journals reject many, many, many articles for not following disciplinary conventions in approach, argument, method, or evidence. It's tough to get published in another discipline. For instance, if you're a political scientist who is passionate about melodrama in Nollywood films, you're probably not going to be successful in writing about genre in such films. Your discipline is in the social sciences and your passion is in the humanities, so you don't have the right tool set. You would be wiser to write about how Nollywood films influence Nigerian elections or vice versa. Alternately, find a coauthor with complementary disciplinary skills. Similarly, if you're an anthropologist interested in demonstrating large-scale trends in Nigerian voting, you may not have the statistical training to collect and analyze such data.

Finally, let's say you're an English literature graduate student who works on early modern British drama but who attends the Comic-Con convention every year in Tharja cosplay, reads lots of Japanese anime in translation, and has begun to track the metaphors for sexuality in them. If your skill set doesn't include the Japanese language, you may find it tough to pursue this interest productively. Your lack of fluency in the texts' original language will cause peer reviewers to question the quality of your research. Maybe you're willing to spend the time to learn Japanese (which can't be done in twelve weeks!) or to find a coauthor who's fluent, but even so, your English department faculty may still question why you're pursuing a doctorate in English if your research is now on Japanese literature. In addition, its members won't be able to provide you with strong guidance, since your research area lies outside their area of expertise. And later, should you try to find a job in an English department with just one publication, which isn't even on an Anglophone text, its faculty may question your commitment to the field and hire someone else.

A strong alignment among discipline, skills, and interests is important for those seeking publication and eventually jobs. Of course, prejudice may lead some scholars to see your topic as unsuitable. They may assume that a Chinese national can't do justice to the French author Proust or that a woman can't properly study soccer culture. Don't let such prejudices stop you. But attend to your own real limits when selecting topics. *Time*: 1 hour.

Step 6: Identify influential journals. To get published, you need to have an understanding of current debates in your field. To gain this understanding, you need to read journals. Lots of them. To get started, read the instructions in "Week 4: Selecting a Journal." Then identify up to four top journals in your discipline and four top journals in your field (e.g., if you're interested in Japanese and British theater, your top disciplinary journals are *PMLA* and *Comparative Literature*, and your top field journals are *Theater Journal* and *Comparative Drama*). You may also want to consider journals that may not be directly in your field but that drive conversations. In the humanities, these would include *Social Text*, *Public Culture*, *New Literary History*, *Boundary 2*, and *Men and Masculinities*. *Time*: 3–8 hours.

Step 7: Set up a citation database. If you're new to academic writing and/or haven't started using a citation database, this is the time to start. Many scholars like the free online tools Zotero, RefWorks, or Mendeley, while others like paid software such as Endnote. Endnote is still the most sophisticated, the most adaptable to different uses, and the best for handling many citations. *Time*: 1–8 hours.

Step 8: Read relevant journals and articles. Once you have selected your journals, go online or to the library to obtain access to the last five years of publication in each journal, up to the most current issue. If your library doesn't subscribe to the journals, you'll still have free access online to their article titles and abstracts, so you can do the initial research. But try to find journals to which you have complete access. You may find returning to "Week 4: Selecting a Journal" and "Week 5: Refining Your Works Cited" helpful. For each journal you've selected, either with the print version at hand or by viewing the articles online, do the following, noting what you find in writing:

- Read the titles of all articles published in the past five years, taking notes on trends. Based on titles alone, what subjects are scholars in that journal interested in? Do any approaches predominate? Make a list of five typical subjects you see in the journal. *Time*: 30 minutes.
- Read the abstracts of all articles published in the past five years, taking notes on trends. Based on abstracts and titles alone, what are the most common topics or problems addressed? What methodologies or approaches appear repeatedly? Do scholars in the journal seem to be engaged in a particular debate? List the five most common topics, approaches, or arguments. If you can identity a debate in the journal, write that down. *Time*: 3 hours.
- Write down how your interests might match up with the concerns of the journal. Do any of your interests intersect with the common subjects, problems, or methods found within its pages? For instance, if you're interested in the environment, did the journal publish articles in environmental studies? If so, did any of the approaches used resonate with you, because they seemed either particularly sound or particularly wrongheaded? Do you happen to have any research or analysis that relates to the abstracts' concerns? List any of your research interests that match up with the concerns of the journal. *Time*: 1 hour.
- Attend carefully to hot topics. As Springer's advice website for journal authors recommends, "One good method for finding hot topics is to look for issues that cause problems for other researchers." If you find a hot topic of interest to you, consider reaching out to some of the authors. You can email them or look for them at conferences. Most scholars will be flattered to be approached about an article of theirs

that you've actually read. Most of us rarely meet people who can talk knowledgeably about something we've published, so go for it. *Time*: 1 hour.

- Read five to ten <u>articles</u> of the most interest to you that were published in the past five years in the journal. One way to identify influential articles to read is by using the journal's online features "Most Read Articles," "Most Downloaded Articles," or "Most Cited Articles." Once selected, read them attending not so much to content as to argument. What are scholars in the journal concerned about? What are they debating? When you read each argument, do you find yourself agreeing or disagreeing? Do you feel as though you bring a fresh perspective, one that enables you to see how the article's argument could be strengthened or attacked? If you start reading an article and find that it doesn't interest you, stop and go on to the next one. Your aim here is not to educate yourself in general, or even to be well read, but to find arguments about which you have an opinion and perhaps something to say. Write down, in complete sentences, any inspiration you received in relation to this reading. *Time*: 5 hours.
- When you've read the titles, abstracts, and articles, <u>write</u> an email to a friend about what you found out by working on this task. Report on the journals, their trends, and some of the arguments. In particular, identify whether you have anything to say that relates to the journal's content. It's fine to say that the journal ignored a certain topic or approach, and you would like to write about that. It's also fine to say that a journal was boring; just explain why. *Time*: 1 hour.

Step 9: Brainstorm ideas and arguments. Thinking back over what you did during the last five steps, write down twenty ideas for articles—not just one, not just five, not just ten, but twenty (as the chemistry professor Michael Schmidt recommends in his forthcoming book for students). Don't do this in consultation with anyone; instead, do it on your own, as brainstorming first with others can encourage groupthink. If possible, try to write up these ideas as questions or even arguments. That is, don't write "torture and male Roman Catholic saints" but "Are male Roman Catholic saints as pierced or tortured as Roman Catholic female saints? If not, why? Does it suggest something about masochism's relation to gender liberation? (inspired by Kucich 2011 argument)." Don't worry at this point whether your idea or argument is provable or already published by someone else. And don't worry if the process is slow. As the scholar Kevin Corley admits, "It's never an 'Ah-ha.' It's gradual. So you're reading, and you have an idea. You capture that idea, you read some more, and then you have another idea. I'm beginning to get a sense that this might be connected to that. Okay. Now I need to set the reading aside and get back to my writing because I've just figured out something important" (quoted in Cloutier 2015, 75). When asked about how he gets ideas for research, the prolific historian Anthony Grafton responded, "In the strangest possible ways. My favorites are the ones I find by falling down rabbit holes, which is how I found one of my current topics, connecting *The Last Supper* and the Passover seder in the Renaissance. I like to pull a string, and suddenly find that enough stuff has fallen in my head. That's my preeminent method: let stuff fall on my head and then try to crawl out and put some order to it" (Grafton and Charney 2013). *Time*: 1–3 hours.

TESTING YOUR IDEA

Step 10: Ask professors about your ideas and arguments. Set up individual fifteen-minute meetings with two or three professors you trust, telling them by email that you have some ideas for articles that you would like to discuss. When you meet, say that these ideas are just embryos, not remotely developed, and you want to get his or her impressions of your ideas. Most professors are used to hearing fully developed ideas, so you need to make sure that they understand that yours are speculative. Emphasize that their answers can be brief: from "Interesting!" to "Sorry, boring," to "That's been done already," to "Not sure/Don't know/Not my area of expertise." It can also be wise to give them three or four ideas and ask which one they find interesting. I wrote my dissertation on one of three ideas that I had asked many people about, surprised to find that everyone agreed on which was the most interesting. Be sure to take notes, and if possible ask each professor to take notes as well for you, because you can forget to while you're talking. Once you've finished the exercise and if the professor still has some time, ask for thoughts on the main trends and burning arguments in the field. If a professor tells you to research a specific topic or hypothesis, that's fine, but attend to how you feel about it. If the prospect perplexes you without inspiring you, don't do it. I know of more than one dissertation that was never completed because the student studied what an advisor said to study, and the student never could generate passion for the topic. *Time*: 1 hour.

Step 11: Take stock of your arguments. Write up what you've learned so far about the arguments you could attempt, hypotheses you could test, or leads you could pursue. If you feel as though your ideas still haven't cohered into something that would drive an article, try playing with the ones that most interest you. One way to play with them is to press on them with metaphor (Richardson and St. Pierre 2005, 973). Do you use a metaphor when explaining the idea? If so, if you think about how that metaphor serves as an analogy, does it tell you something you didn't know about your idea? Alternately, what if you think of the idea itself as a metaphor? For instance, what if the metaphor for the problem you study were an illness: how would it work? What if the metaphor for your idea were a movie or comic strip: who are the characters, and what are they doing to each other? Another way to encourage your ideas to gain cohesion is to discuss them while taking a walk outside with a friend. Research shows that creativity more than doubles during and after walking (Oppezzo and Schwartz 2014, 1147–48). Finally, you can try drawing your arguments, seeing whether visualizing the ideas in images, storyboards, or a map helps you. Returning to the advice in "Week 2: Advancing Your Argument" may be helpful as well. *Time*: 1–3 hours.

Step 12: Check the scholarly literature. No argument can be published if someone has already presented it. So identify what other people have said about your argument or even your topic. If you find little written about it or it's not written as you would, you can keep going with your argument. If you find that someone has said something close to what you've said but not quite, don't abandon your idea. It's fine to extend others' research; and the more you think about your idea, you'll often find that it develops differently from the published research. You can also use this search to find out whether scholars state that your topic itself is passé. The point of this search is not to be exhaustive but to identify any obvious overlaps with your argument that would make it untenable. If you do find it untenable, return to the previous step and see what argument you want to pursue now. Returning to "Week 5: Refining Your Works Cited" may be helpful. *Time*: 1–3 hours.

Step 13: Check the method. No argument can be published if you don't have the right method of analysis. When you read the scholarly literature, did it seem like the methods were ones you knew? For instance, if most of the articles use quantitative approaches and you've never taken statistics, you may not be able to pursue this interest. If you need to learn a new method or theoretical approach to write about the idea that most interests you, then take a course in it now. (Alternately, you can find a syllabus online and read up on it on your own.) Reading the advice in "Week 7: Analyzing Your Evidence" may be helpful. *Time*: 30 minutes (or longer).

COLLECTING EVIDENCE FOR YOUR IDEA

Step 14: Imagine the study. No argument can be published if you don't have evidence for it. Now, you need to do some trial analysis to find out whether your argument is provable. For instance, start reading primary texts (such as poems, field notes, archival notes, paintings) and writing up your thoughts in full sentences about what will serve as strong evidence for your argument. Or start looking at extant data sources (such as government records or archival manuscript handlists). Or start to imagine what type of study or experiment would provide you with evidence for your argument (such as a field study at a nursing home or exit poll interviews). The point of this examination is not to be exhaustive but to get a general sense of what you can use as evidence. If you find that no evidence exists for your argument or only very suspect evidence, or you have no way of collecting evidence, choose another argument. Keep doing this until you find a solid argument or hypothesis that you can prove. Reading the advice in the week 7 chapter may be helpful. Or you may need to read a book like *The Craft of Research* (Booth et al. 2016). *Time*: 1 to 10 weeks.

Step 15: Select an appropriate journal. Revisit "Week 4: Selecting a Journal" to identify a journal that might be interested in publishing that argument. You have the huge benefit of studying journals in advance of fully formulating your article idea, so the exercises will help you the most of anyone. *Time*: 1–3 hours.

Step 16: Do the study. Depending on your discipline, you may need to take some time to develop instruments and conduct studies. The amount of time for this step varies a great deal. It could be a day in an archive, a week reading, a month surveying, or two years on a Fulbright in a country overseas. Of course, you may find upon further analysis that the study you imagined leads to weak evidence. Or that your argument falls apart. This has happened to all of us. Be sure to read the week 7 chapter before giving up. *Time*: 1 to 10 weeks.

DRAFTING YOUR ARTICLE

Step 17: Outline. You can produce a traditional outline of your article if you feel you know enough now to do that. If you don't like traditional outlining, try one of the alternate ways of outlining presented in "Week 9: Strengthening Your Structure," such as question outlining or motivation outlining. Many scholars now use Microsoft Power-Point to outline books and articles (Toor 2013), since it's easy to move slides around, add images, and keep the whole in mind. Another option is to write one sentence in response to each of the questions in the form on the next page. *Time*: 1–3 hours.

Step 18: Write an abstract. Read and use "Week 3: Abstracting Your Article" to write a 250-word abstract of your article. *Time*: 1–3 hours.

Step 19: Write a three- to five-page draft. Now that you have some ideas, try to frame them out briefly. And yes, it will likely be terrifying and/or frustrating. As the scholar Bob Hinings has said, "Sometimes I can sit in front of the computer for a couple of hours and end up with two sentences. The ideas are kind of all there, but it's getting them onto the page that is a challenge. But once I've got those first couple of pages done, then I can go on, you know? Those first pages are really crucial, because they're saying, 'Here's what I'm going to do'" (quoted in Cloutier 2015, 77). The scholar Sarah Kaplan agrees: "For the first round, you kind of just have to get words on a paper, so I do try to just chug away . . . I try to get stuff down because I'm much better once there's at least some amount of text on paper. Then I go back and edit and rewrite section by section" (77).

If you're writing a quantitative article and are unsure about the order in which to write sections, consider the following advice from the scholar Kevin Corley:

> The easiest part of the paper to start writing is the methods, right? Because as you're collecting data, you write what you're doing. Then I'll write an intro that basically frames what it is I think I'm going to be writing about. Then I typically work on the findings section and discussion section. Once I have a good draft of that discussion section, I'll go back and write the literature review around what it now needs to be, based on the discussion. Because again, doing inductive research, you can't write your literature review beforehand. (quoted in Cloutier 2015, 77)

If you need help drafting sections, consult "Week 9: Strengthening Your Structure." *Time*: 1–20 hours.

REVISING YOUR DRAFT USING THE WORKBOOK

Step 20: Return to week 2 on argument. Now that you have a draft, you can use the workbook as everyone else does. Return to "Week 2: Advancing Your Argument" to see whether your argument, now that you've written it, is doing what you need it to. *Time*: 1–2 hours.

Step 21: Continue with the rest of the workbook. Now that you have a draft, abstract, and argument, revisit and complete any necessary tasks in "Week 5: Refining Your Works Cited," "Week 6: Crafting Your Claims for Significance," and "Week 7: Analyzing Your Evidence." Then read and complete the tasks in "Week 8: Presenting Your Evidence,"

My Article Drafting Outline

What is my subject of investigation?

What is my approach, methodology, and/or theory? (methods)

Whose research is mine in dialogue with, and/or how does it motivate my research? (literature review)

What question, problem, and/or puzzle am I trying to answer?

What have I found (or hope to find) through my research? (results)

What do my findings help us understand?

Why are my findings important, and/or how do they solve a problem? (significance)

What is my argument (as I understand it right now)?

"Week 9: Strengthening Your Structure," and "Week 10: Opening and Concluding Your Article." When you have a strong draft, read and complete the tasks in "Week 11: Editing Your Article" and "Week 12: Sending Your Article." *Time*: 8 weeks.

Step 22: Read "One Story of Arriving at Publishable Ideas." If you're interested, you're welcome to read the narrative on my website about how I arrived at my arguments that African thought has powerfully shaped the world, as published in such works as *Abyssinia's Samuel Johnson: Ethiopian Thought in the Making of an English Author* (2012), "Same-Sex Intimacies in the Early African Text the *Gädlä Wälättä Peṭros* (1672): Queer Reading an Ethiopian Female Saint" (2016), and my book in progress, *The Black Queen of Sheba: A Global History of an African Idea*.

WRITING YOUR ARTICLE FROM SCRATCH WITH AN IDEA

Some readers come to this book with an idea for an article, but no draft. If you are one of them, use the preceding section, "Writing Your Article from Scratch without an Idea," but adapted as instructed below.

Those with ideas have two potential paths through the workbook. First, if you haven't published an article before or want to ensure that you're not skipping anything, complete the steps listed in the previous section, but in the following sequence:

- Do step 1 (starting a document), step 2 (create a writing schedule), and step 3 (learning what it takes to get published).
- Skip steps 4 and 5.
- Do step 6 (identify influential journals) and step 7 (setting up a citation database if you haven't done so already).
- Do step 8 (reading relevant journals and articles in your field), but instead of focusing on how your *interests* match with the journal, focus on how your article idea or protoargument matches.
- Skip steps 9 and 10.
- Do step 11 (writing up your argument), step 12 (checking the scholarly literature), step 13 (checking the method), step 14 (imagining the study), step 15 (selecting a journal), and step 16 (doing the study).
- Do step 17 (outlining your article), step 18 (abstracting your article), and step 19 (writing a three- to five-page draft).
- Do step 20 (rereading "Week 2: Advancing Your Argument") and step 21 (moving through the rest of the workbook week by week until you've reached the end).

Second, if you've published journal articles before, follow the steps listed in the previous section, but in the following sequence:

- Skip steps 1–16.
- Do step 17 (outlining your article), then step 18 (abstracting your article), and then step 19 (writing a three- to five-page draft).
- Do step 20 (reading the week 2 chapter) and step 21 (moving through the rest of the workbook week by week until you've reached the end).

Good luck!

References

AAAS (American Academy of the Arts) and Stephen Bosch. 2015. "Trends in Academic Books Published in the Humanities and Other Fields." *Humanities Indicators*, December 2015. http://www.humanitiesindi cators.org/content/indicatordoc.aspx?i=88.

Abani, Chris. 2014. *The Secret History of Las Vegas*. New York: Penguin.

Abbamontian, Ramela Grigorian. 2003. "Forging the Armenian Past: Questionable Translations of Abstract Expressionist Arshile Gorky's Missing Letters." Paper presented at the Graduate Student Colloquium in Armenian Studies, University of California, Los Angeles, February.

Abbott, Andrew. 2004. *Methods of Discovery: Heuristics for the Social Sciences*. New York: Norton.

Acharya, Anurag, Alex Verstak, Helder Suzuki, Sean Henderson, Mikhail Iakhiaev, Cliff Chiung Yu Lin, and Namit Shetty. 2014. "Rise of the Rest: The Growing Impact of Non-elite Journals." http://arxiv .org/abs/1410.2217.

Adichie, Chimamanda Ngozi. 2006. *Half of a Yellow Sun*. New York: Alfred A. Knopf.

Agamben, Giorgio. 1998. *Homo Sacer: Sovereign Power and Bare Life*. Translated by Daniel Heller Roazen. Palo Alto, CA: Stanford University Press.

Agarwal, Ashok, Damayanthi Durairajanayagam, Sindhuja Tatagari, Sandro C. Esteves, Avi Harlev, Ralf Henkel, Shubhadeep Roychoudhury, Sheryl Homa, Nicolás Garrido Puchalt, and Ranjith Ramasamy. 2016. "Bibliometrics: Tracking Research Impact by Selecting the Appropriate Metrics." *Asian Journal of Andrology* 18:296–309.

Ahmed, Sara. 2008. "Open Forum Imaginary Prohibitions: Some Preliminary Remarks on the Founding Gestures of the 'New Materialism.'" *European Journal of Women's Studies* 15 (1): 23–39.

Ahmed, Sara. 2012. *On Being Included: Racism and Diversity in Institutional Life*. Durham, NC: Duke University Press.

Ahmed, Sara. 2013. "Making Feminist Points." *Feminist Killjoys*. September 11, 2013. https://feministkilljoys .com/2013/09/11/making-feminist-points/.

Ahmed, Sara. 2017. *Living a Feminist Life*. Durham, NC: Duke University Press.

Albert, Tim, and Liz Wager. *How to Handle Authorship Disputes: A Guide for New Researchers*. Hampshire, UK: Committee on Publication Ethics. http://publicationethics.org/resources/guidelines-new/how -handle-authorship-disputesa-guide-new-researchers.

Ale Ebrahim, Nader, Hadi Salehi, Mohamed Amin Embi, Farid Habibi, Hossein Gholizadeh, Seyed Moham-mad Motahar, and Ali Ordi. 2013. "Effective Strategies for Increasing Citation Frequency." *International Education Studies* 6 (11): 93–99.

Altmetric. 2016. "The Altmetric Top 100: What Academic Research Caught the Public Imagination in 2015?" https://www.altmetric.com/top100/2015/.

Anderson-Clark, Tracy N., and Raymond J. Green. 2017. "Basking in Reflected Glory: The Election of President Obama and Naming Behaviour." *Ethnic and Racial Studies* 40 (1): 63–76.

Antonakis, John. 2017. "Editorial: The Future of *The Leadership Quarterly*." *Leadership Quarterly* 28 (1): 1–4.

APA (American Psychological Association). 2010. *Publication Manual of the American Psychological Association*. Washington, DC: American Psychological Association.

Archambault, E., D. Amyot, P. Deschamps, A. Nicol, F. Provencher, R. Rebout, and G. Roberge. 2014. "Proportion of Open Access Papers Published in Peer-Reviewed Journals at the European and World Levels 1996–2013." *Science-Metrix*, October 22, 2014. http://science-metrix.com/en/publications/reports /proportion-of-open-access-papers-published-in-peer-reviewed-journals-at-the.

Arefin, Ahmed Shamsul, Renato Vimieiro, Carlos Riveros, Hugh Craig, and Pablo Moscato. 2014. "An Information Theoretic Clustering Approach for Unveiling Authorship Affinities in Shakespearean Era Plays and Poems." *PLOS ONE* 9 (10): e111445.

Arenberg, Meg. 2015. "Converting Achebe's Africa for the New Tanzanian: *Things Fall Apart* in Swahili Translation." *Eastern African Literary and Cultural Studies* 2 (3–4): 124–35.

Argersinger, Jana, and CELJ (Council of Editors of Learned Journals). 2006. *Getting Your Articles Published: A Compendium of Tips from CELJ Member Editors.* Pullman, WA: Council of Editors of Learned Journals. http://www.celj.org/downloads/Tips%20on%20Publishing.pdf.

ARL (Association of Research Libraries). 2000. Foreword to *ARL Directory of Scholarly Electronic Journals and Academic Discussion Lists.* Washington, DC: ARL. http://web.archive.org/web/20010302174815/http://dsej.arl.org/dsej/2000/foreword.html.

Arrington, Phillip, and Shirley K. Rose. 1987. "Prologues to What Is Possible: Introductions as Metadiscourse." *College Composition and Communication* 38 (3): 306–18.

Arthur, Craig. 2015. "Predatory Publishing: How Not to Fall Prey." *Virginia Libraries Journal* 61 (1).

Aubuchon, Norbert. 1997. *The Anatomy of Persuasion: How to Persuade Others to—Act on Your Ideas, Accept Your Proposals, Buy Your Products or Services, Hire You, Promote You.* New York: AMACOM (American Management Association).

Autorino, Riccardo, Giuseppe Quarto, Giuseppe Di Lorenzo, Marco De Sio, and Rocco Damiano. 2007. "Are Abstracts Presented at the EAU Meeting Followed by Publication in Peer-Reviewed Journals? A Critical Analysis." *European Urology* 51 (3): 833–40.

Avila, Eric R. 1998. "The Folklore of the Freeway: Space, Culture, and Identity in Postwar Los Angeles." *Aztlán: A Journal of Chicano Studies* 23 (1): 13–31.

Azar, Ofer H. 2004. "Rejections and the Importance of First Response Times." *International Journal of Social Economics* 31 (3): 259–74.

Bakanic, Von, Clark McPhail, and Rita J. Simon. 1987. "The Manuscript Review and Decision-Making Process." *American Sociological Review* 52 (5): 631–42.

Bakanic, Von, Clark McPhail, and Rita J. Simon. 1989. "Mixed Messages: Referees' Comments on the Manuscripts They Review." *Sociological Quarterly* 30 (4): 639–54.

Baker, Nicholson. 1991. *U and I: A True Story.* New York: Knopf Doubleday Publishing Group.

Bakhtin, Mikhail. 1984. *Problems of Dostoevsky's Poetics.* Translated by Caryl Emerson. Minneapolis: University of Minnesota Press.

Ballenger, Bruce P. 2003. *The Curious Writer.* New York: Pearson Custom Publishing.

Banerjee, Rupa, Jeffrey G. Reitz, and Phil Oreopoulos. 2018. "Do Large Employers Treat Racial Minorities More Fairly? A New Analysis of Canadian Field Experiment Data." *Canadian Public Policy* 44 (1): 1–12.

Barber, Karin Àjíké. 2013. "Yoruba at Home and Abroad: A Translation of 'Yorùbá nílé àti ní ìlú òkèèrè.'" *Journal of African Cultural Studies* 25 (2): 167–69.

Barkaoui, Khaled. 2016. "What and When Second-Language Learners Revise When Responding to Timed Writing Tasks on the Computer: The Roles of Task Type, Second Language Proficiency, and Keyboarding Skills." *Modern Language Journal* 100 (1): 320–40.

Basken, Paul. 2013. "Researchers and Scientific Groups Make New Push against Impact Factors." News, May 16, 2013, *Chronicle of Higher Education*, https://www.chronicle.com/article/ResearchersScientific/139337.

Bay-Cheng, Sara, J. Ellen Gainor, D. J. Hopkins, David Z. Saltz, Henry Bial, and Heather Nathans. 2013. "The Value of Electronic Publishing for Scholars in Theatre and Performance: A White Paper Prepared by the ATHE-ASTR Joint Subcommittee on Non-Print Book Publishing Presented to the ATHE Research and Publications Committee August, 2013, Orlando, Florida." American Society for Theatre Research, Association for Theatre in Higher Education.

Bechdel, Allison. 1985. *Dykes to Watch Out For.* Ithaca, NY: Firebrand Books.

Bechshøft, Rasmus Leidesdorff, Nikolaj Mølkjær Malmgaard-Clausen, Bjørn Gliese, Nina Beyer, Abigail L Mackey, Jesper Løvind Andersen, Michael Kjær, and Lars Holm. 2017. "Improved Skeletal Muscle Mass and Strength after Heavy Strength Training in Very Old Individuals." *Experimental Gerontology* 92 (June): 96–105.

Becker, H. S., and P. Richards. 2008. *Writing for Social Scientists: How to Start and Finish Your Thesis, Book, or Article.* 2nd ed. Chicago: University of Chicago Press.

Becker, Howard S. 2008. *Tricks of the Trade: How to Think about Your Research while You're Doing It.* Chicago: University of Chicago Press.

Bedeian, Arthur G. 2004. "Peer Review and the Social Construction of Knowledge in the Management Discipline." *Academy of Management Learning and Education* 3 (2): 198–216.

Belcher, Wendy Laura. 1987. *Street Beat: The Art of the Street.* Washington, DC: Potter's House Press.

Belcher, Wendy Laura. 2009. "Reflections on Ten Years of Teaching Writing for Publication to Graduate Students and Junior Faculty." *Journal of Scholarly Publishing* 40 (2): 184–200.

Belcher, Wendy Laura. 2012. *Abyssinia's Samuel Johnson: Ethiopian Thought in the Making of an English Author.* New York: Oxford University Press.

Belcher, Wendy Laura. 2013. "Sisters Debating the Jesuits: The Role of African Women in Defeating Portuguese Cultural Colonialism in Seventeenth-Century Abyssinia." *Northeast African Studies* 12:121–66.

Belcher, Wendy Laura. 2016. "Same-Sex Intimacies in the Early African Text the *Gädlä Wälättä P̣eṭros* (1672): Queer Reading an Ethiopian Female Saint." *Research in African Literatures* 47 (2): 20–45.

Belcher, Wendy Laura. In progress. The *Black Queen of Sheba: A Global History of an African Idea*. Princeton: Princeton University Press.

Belcher, Wendy Laura, and Bekure Heṛouy. 2015. "The Melancholy Translator: Sirak Ḥeṛuy's Amharic Translation of Samuel Johnson's *Rasselas*." *Age of Johnson* 23:160–203.

Beuving, Joost, and Geert de Vries. 2015. *Doing Qualitative Research: The Craft of Naturalistic Inquiry.* Amsterdam: Amsterdam University Press.

Bhatia, Vijay Kumar. (1993) 2013. *Analysing Genre: Language Use in Professional Settings*. London: Pearson Education. Reprint, Abingdon, UK: Routledge.

Biavaschi, Costanza, Corrado Giulietti, and Zahra Siddique. 2017. "The Economic Payoff of Name Americanization." *Journal of Labor Economics* 35 (4): 1089–1116.

Bishop, Dorothy. 2012. "How to Bury Your Academic Writing." *Impact of Social Sciences Blog*. August 26, 2012. http://deevybee.blogspot.com/2012/08/how-to-bury-your-academic-writing.html.

Bizup, Joseph. 2008. "BEAM: A Rhetorical Vocabulary for Teaching Research-Based Writing." *Rhetoric Review* 27 (1): 72–86.

Blain, Keisha N. 2015. "'We Want to Set the World on Fire': Black Nationalist Women and Diasporic Politics in the New Negro World, 1940–1944." *Journal of Social History* 49 (1): 194–212.

Blair, Harry. 2003. "Jump-Starting Democracy: Adult Civic Education and Democratic Participation in Three Countries." *Democratization* 10 (1): 53–76.

Bloom, Lynn Z. 1984. *The Essay Connection: Readings for Writers*. Lexington, MA: D. C. Heath.

Bohannon, John. 2013. "Who's Afraid of Peer Review?" *Science* 342 (6154): 60–65.

Boice, Robert. 1982. "Increasing the Writing Productivity of 'Blocked' Academicians." *Behaviour Research and Therapy* 20 (3): 197–207.

Boice, Robert. 1989. "Procrastination, Busyness, and Bingeing." *Behaviour Research and Therapy* 27 (6): 605–11.

Boice, Robert. 1990. *Professors as Writers: A Self-Help Guide to Productive Writing*. Stillwater, OK: New Forums Press.

Boice, Robert. 1992. *The New Faculty Member: Supporting and Fostering Professional Development*. San Francisco: Jossey-Bass.

Boice, Robert. 1997a. "Strategies for Enhancing Scholarly Productivity." In *Writing and Publishing for Academic Authors*, edited by Joseph M. Moxley and Todd Taylor, 19–34. Lanham, MD: Rowman and Littlefield.

Boice, Robert. 1997b. "Which Is More Productive, Writing in Binge Patterns of Creative Illness or in Moderation?" *Written Communication* 14 (4): 435–59.

Booth, Wayne C., Gregory G. Colomb, and Joseph M. Williams. 2009. *The Craft of Research*. 3rd ed. Chicago: University of Chicago Press.

Booth, Wayne C., Gregory G. Colomb, Joseph M. Williams, Joseph Bizup, and William T. FitzGerald. 2016. *The Craft of Research*. 4th ed. Chicago: University of Chicago Press.

Bowen, Glenn A. 2010. "From Qualitative Dissertation to Quality Articles: Seven Lessons Learned." *Qualitative Report* 15 (4): 864.

Bowles, P. F. D., K. Marenah, D. M. Ricketts, and B. A. Rogers. 2013. "How to Prepare for and Present at a Journal Club." *British Journal of Hospital Medicine* 74 (10): C150–C152.

Bradley, James V. 1981. "Pernicious Publication Practices." *Bulletin of the Psychonomic Society* 18 (1): 31–34.

Brandon, Catherine, David Jamadar, Gandikota Girish, Qian Dong, Yoav Morag, and Patricia Mullan. 2015. "Peer Support of a Faculty 'Writers' Circle' Increases Confidence and Productivity in Generating Scholarship." *Academic Radiology* 22 (4): 534–38.

Bronfen, Elisabeth. 2004. "Femme Fatale—Negotiations of Tragic Desire." *New Literary History* 35 (1): 103–16.

Brown, Gavin T. L., and Jennifer C. Marshall. 2012. "The Impact of Training Students How to Write Introductions for Academic Essays: An Exploratory, Longitudinal Study." *Assessment and Evaluation in Higher Education* 37 (6): 653–70.

Brown, Stephen J., and Barbara S. Petitt. 2016. "2015 Report to Readers." *Financial Analysts Journal* 72 (3): 5–6.

Brownstein, Michael, and Jennifer Saul, eds. 2016. *Implicit Bias and Philosophy*. Oxford: Oxford University Press.

Buckley, Charles A., and Michael J. Waring. 2013. "Using Diagrams to Support the Research Process: Examples from Grounded Theory." *Qualitative Research* 13 (2): 148–72.

Bunton, David. 2005. "The Structure of PhD Conclusion Chapters." *Journal of English for Academic Purposes* 4 (3): 207–24.

Burke, Kenneth. 1974. *The Philosophy of Literary Form: Studies in Symbolic Action*. Berkeley: University of California Press.

Burkeman, Oliver. 2013. "How to Use the 'Hairy Arm' Technique to Manage Your Boss." *Business Insider*, November 30, 2013. http://www.businessinsider.com/how-to-use-the-hairy-arm-technique-to-manage -your-boss-2013-11.

Burkill, Sue, and Caroline Abbey. 2004. "Avoiding Plagiarism." *Journal of Geography in Higher Education* 28 (3): 439–46.

Büscher, Bram, and Maano Ramutsindela. 2015. "Green Violence: Rhino Poaching and the War to Save Southern Africa's Peace Parks." *African Affairs* 115 (458): 1–22.

Buter, R. K., and Anthony F. J. van Raan. 2011. "Non-alphanumeric Characters in Titles of Scientific Publications: An Analysis of Their Occurrence and Correlation with Citation Impact." *Journal of Informetrics* 5 (4): 608–17.

Butler, Judith. 2009. "Performativity, Precarity and Sexual Politics." *AIBR. Revista de Antropología Iberoamericana* 4 (3): i–xiii.

Cairo, Alberto. 2012. *The Functional Art: An Introduction to Information Graphics and Visualization*. San Francisco: New Riders Press.

Cairo, Alberto. 2016. *The Truthful Art: Data, Charts, and Maps for Communication*. San Francisco: New Riders Press.

Calcagno, Vincent, Emilie Demoinet, K. Gollner, Lionel Guidi, Derek Ruths, and Claire de Mazancourt. 2012. "Flows of Research Manuscripts among Scientific Journals Reveal Hidden Submission Patterns." *Science* 338 (6110): 1065–69.

Campanario, Juan Miguel. 1995. "Commentary on Influential Books and Journal Articles Initially Rejected Because of Negative Referees' Evaluations." *Science Communication* 16 (3): 304–25.

Campanario, Juan Miguel. 1996. "Have Referees Rejected Some of the Most-Cited Articles of All Times?" *Journal of the American Society for Information Science* 47 (4): 302–10.

Campanario, Juan Miguel. 2009. "Rejecting and Resisting Nobel Class Discoveries: Accounts by Nobel Laureates." *Scientometrics* 81 (2): 549–65.

Carpenter, Julie. 2012. "Researchers of Tomorrow: The Research Behaviour of Generation Y Doctoral Students." *Information Services and Use* 32 (1–2): 3–17.

Caruso, Eugene, Nicholas Epley, and Max H. Bazerman. 2006. "The Costs and Benefits of Undoing Egocentric Responsibility Assessments in Groups." *Journal of Personality and Social Psychology* 91 (5): 857.

Casati, Fabio, Maurizio Marchese, Azzurra Ragone, and Matteo Turrini. 2009. *Is Peer Review Any Good? A Quantitative Analysis of Peer Review*. Trento, Italy: Departmental Technical Report, University of Trento.

Casnici, Niccolò, Francisco Grimaldo, Nigel Gilbert, Pierpaolo Dondio, and Flaminio Squazzoni. 2017. "Assessing Peer Review by Gauging the Fate of Rejected Manuscripts: The Case of the *Journal of Artificial Societies and Social Simulation*." *Scientometrics* 113 (1): 533–46.

Cassuto, Leonard. 2011. "From Dissertation to Book." *Chronicle of Higher Education*, May 30, 2011. http:// chronicle.com/article/From-Dissertation-to-Book/127677/.

Cawley, Rachel. 2011. "Reverse Outlines." *Explorations of Style: A Blog about Academic Writing*. February 9, 2011. https://explorationsofstyle.com/2011/02/09/reverse-outlines/.

Chanquoy, Lucile. 2009. "Revision Processes." In *The SAGE Handbook of Writing Development*, edited by R. Beard, D. Myhill, J. Riley, and M. Nystrand, 80–97. Thousand Oaks, CA: SAGE Publications.

Cherki, Alice, and Nadia Benabid. 2006. *Frantz Fanon: A Portrait*. Ithaca, NY: Cornell University Press.

Chung, Haeng-ja. 2004. "Performing Sex, Selling Heart: Korean Nightclub Hostesses in Japan." PhD diss., Department of Anthropology, University of California, Los Angeles.

Cikara, Mina, Laurie Rudman, and Susan Fiske. 2012. "Dearth by a Thousand Cuts? Accounting for Gender Differences in Top-Ranked Publication Rates in Social Psychology." *Journal of Social Issues* 68 (2): 263–85.

Citron, Daniel T., and Paul Ginsparg. 2015. "Patterns of Text Reuse in a Scientific Corpus." *Proceedings of the National Academy of Sciences* 112 (1): 25–30.

Cloutier, Charlotte. 2015. "How I Write: An Inquiry into the Writing Practices of Academics." *Journal of Management Inquiry* 25 (1): 69–84.

Cochran, Angela. 2016. "Should You 'Revise and Resubmit'?" The Scholarly Kitchen, October 20, 2016. https://scholarlykitchen.sspnet.org/2016/10/20/should-you-revise-and-resubmit/.

Cohn, Laura. 2016. "Name Bias: This Female Exec Changed Her Name to a Man's to Get a Job. Should You?" *Fortune Magazine*, June 7, 2016. http://fortune.com/2016/06/08/name-bias-in-hiring/.

Committee on Information Technology. 2003. "Statement on Electronic Publication." New York: Modern Language Association. https://www.mla.org/About-Us/Governance/Committees/Committee-Listings /Professional-Issues/Committee-on-Information-Technology/Statement-on-Electronic-Publication.

Committee on Information Technology. 2015. "Statement on Electronic Publication." New York: Modern Language Association. https://www.mla.org/About-Us/Governance/Committees/Committee-Listings /Professional-Issues/Committee-on-Information-Technology/Statement-on-Electronic-Publication.

Connor, Ulla. 2002. "New Directions in Contrastive Rhetoric." *TESOL Quarterly* 36 (4): 493–510.

Cooper, Beth Belle. 2016. "How I Became a Morning Person, Read More Books, and Learned a Language in a Year." *Fast Company*, February 12, 2016. http://www.fastcompany.com/3056613/how-i-became-a-morning-person-read-more-books-and-learned-.

COPE (Committee on Publication Ethics). 2015. "Flowcharts on Journal Publication Ethics." Committee on Publication Ethics, April 9, 2015. http://publicationethics.org/resources/flowcharts.

CELJ (Council of Editors of Learned Journals). 2007. "Guidelines for Contributors." New York: Council of Editors of Learned Journals. http://www.celj.org/downloads/CELJ_Guidelines_For_Contributors.pdf.

Corbyn, Zoë. 2010. "An Easy Way to Boost a Paper's Citations." *Nature*, August 13, 2010. http://www.nature.com/news/2010/100813/full/news.2010.406.html.

Crabbs, Michael A., John Allan, and Susan K Crabbs. 1985. "Action Approaches for the Writing Process." *Elementary School Guidance and Counseling* 20 (1): 4–10.

Craig, John, and David Madland. 2014. "How Campaign Contributions and Lobbying Can Lead to Inefficient Economic Policy." Washington, DC: Center for American Progress.

Crowe, M., and D. Carlyle. 2015. "Is Open Access Sufficient? A Review of the Quality of Open-Access Nursing Journals." *International Journal of Mental Health Nursing* 24 (1): 59–64.

Daniels, Jessie. 2013. "From Tweet to Blog Post to Peer-Reviewed Article: How to Be a Scholar Now." *London School of Economics and Political Science Impact Blog*. September 25, 2013. http://blogs.lse.ac.uk/impactofsocialsciences/2013/09/25/how-to-be-a-scholar-daniels/.

Day, Abby. 1996. *How to Get Research Published in Journals*. Aldershot, UK: Gower.

Day, Jeanne D. 1980. "Teaching Summarization Skills: A Comparison of Training Methods." PhD diss., University of Illinois at Urbana-Champaign.

Davis, Noela. 2009. "New Materialism and Feminism's Anti-biologism: A Response to Sara Ahmed." *European Journal of Women's Studies* 16 (1): 67–80.

Davis, P. M., B. V. Lewenstein, D. H. Simon, J. G. Booth, and M. J. L. Connolly. 2008. "Open Access Publishing, Article Downloads, and Citations: Randomised Controlled Trial." *British Medical Journal* 337:a568.

Davis, Robert, and Mark Shadle. 2000. "'Building a Mystery': Alternative Research Writing and the Academic Act of Seeking." *College Composition and Communication* 51 (3): 417–46.

Decety, Jean, Jason M. Cowell, Kang Lee, Randa Mahasneh, Susan Malcolm-Smith, Bilge Selcuk, and Xinyue Zhou. 2015. "The Negative Association between Religiousness and Children's Altruism across the World." *Current Biology* 25 (22): 2951–55.

De Groote, Sandra L., Mary Shultz, and Deborah D. Blecic. 2014. "Information-Seeking Behavior and the Use of Online Resources: A Snapshot of Current Health Sciences Faculty." *Journal of the Medical Library Association: JMLA* 102 (3): 169.

Delgado, Richard. 1984. "The Imperial Scholar: Reflections on a Review of Civil Rights Literature." *University of Pennsylvania Law Review* 132 (3): 561–78.

Delgado-Lopez-Cozar, Emilio, and Álvaro Cabezas-Clavijio. 2013. "Ranking Journals: Could Google Scholar Metrics Be an Alternative to Journal Citation Reports and SCImago Journal Rank?" *Learned Publishing* 26 (2): 101–14.

Denzin, Norman K., and Yvonna S. Lincoln. 2011. *The SAGE Handbook of Qualitative Research*. 4th ed. Thousand Oaks, CA: SAGE Publications.

Derrida, Jacques. 1976. *Of Grammatology*. Translated by Gayatri Chakravorty Spivak. New York: Norton.

Derrida, Jacques. 1981. *Dissemination*. Translated by Barbara Johnson. Chicago: University of Chicago Press.

Devlin, Marcia, and Kathleen Gray. 2007. "In Their Own Words: A Qualitative Study of the Reasons Australian University Students Plagiarize." *Higher Education Research and Development* 26 (2): 181–98.

Diamond, Jared. 1999. *Guns, Germs, and Steel: The Fate of Human Societies*. New York: Norton.

Diaz-Morales, Juan Francisco. 2007. "Morning and Evening-Types: Exploring Their Personality Styles." *Personality and Individual Differences* 43 (4): 769–78.

Dick, Kirby, and Amy Ziering Kofman, directors; Amy Ziering Kofman, producer. 2002. *Derrida*. DVD, 85 min. New York: Zeitgeist Films.

Dickens, Charles. 1850. *The Personal History, Adventures, Experience, and Observation of David Copperfield the Younger of Blunderstone Rookery*. London: Bradbury and Evans.

Didham, Raphael K., Simon R. Leather, and Yves Basset. 2017. "Don't Be a Zero-Sum Reviewer." *Insect Conservation and Diversity* 10 (1): 1–4.

DiGrazia, Joseph, Karissa McKelvey, Johan Bollen, and Fabio Rojas. 2013. "More Tweets, More Votes: Social Media as a Quantitative Indicator of Political Behavior." *PLOS ONE* 8 (11): e79449.

DiMasi, Joseph A., Henry G. Grabowski, and Ronald W. Hansen. 2016. "Innovation in the Pharmaceutical Industry: New Estimates of R&D Costs." *Journal of Health Economics* 47:20–33.

Diouf, Sylviane A., ed. 2003. *Fighting the Slave Trade: West African Strategies*. Western African Studies. Athens: Ohio University Press; Oxford: James Currey.

Dirk, Lynn. 1996. "From Laboratory to Scientific Literature: The Life and Death of Biomedical Research Results." *Science Communication* 18 (1): 3–28.

Disraeli, Benjamin. 1870. *Lothair*. New York: D. Appleton.

DOAJ (Directory of Open-Access Journals). 2015. "Historical APC Data from before the April Upgrade." Directory of Open-Access Journals, May 11, 2015. https://doajournals.wordpress.com/2015/05/11/historical-apc-data-from-before-the-april-upgrade/.

Dolven, Jeff. 2012. "Panic's Castle." *Representations* 120 (1): 1–16.

Dong, Xiao, Brandon Milholland, and Jan Vijg. 2016. "Evidence for a Limit to Human Lifespan." *Nature* 538 (7624): 257–59.

Doss, Daniel Adrian, Russ Henley, Balakrishna Gokaraju, David McElreath, Hilliard Lackey, Qiuqi Hong, and Lauren Miller. 2016. "Assessing Domestic vs. International Student Perceptions and Attitudes of Plagiarism." *Journal of International Students* 6 (2): 542.

DrugMonkey [pseud.]. 2013. "Citing Review Articles Robs the Authors of Original Research Articles. So Stop It." *DrugMonkey* (blog). September 13, 2013. http://drugmonkey.scientopia.org/about-2/.

Duke University, Thompson Writing Program. 2012. "Paragraphing: The MEAL Plan." Writing Studio. https://twp.duke.edu/sites/twp.duke.edu/files/file-attachments/meal-plan.original.pdf.

Duquia, Rodrigo Pereira, João Luiz Bastos, Renan Rangel Bonamigo, David Alejandro González-Chica, and Jeovany Martínez-Mesa. 2014. "Presenting Data in Tables and Charts." *Anais brasileiros de dermatologia* 89 (2): 280–85.

Eagan, Kevin, Ellen Bara Stolzenberg, Jennifer Berdan Lozano, Melissa C. Aragon, Maria Ramirez Suchard, and Sylvia Hurtado. 2014. *Undergraduate Teaching Faculty: The 2013–2014 HERI Faculty Survey*. Los Angeles: Higher Education Research Institute, University of California, Los Angeles.

Edwards, Brian T. 2007. "Marock in Morocco: Reading Moroccan Films in the Age of Circulation." *Journal of North African Studies* 12 (3): 287–307.

Edwards, Mike. 2016. "Unpacking the Universal Library: Digital Reading and the Recirculation of Economic Value." *Pedagogy* 16 (1): 137–52.

Ehrich, John, Steven J. Howard, Congjun Mu, and Sahar Bokosmaty. 2016. "A Comparison of Chinese and Australian University Students' Attitudes towards Plagiarism." *Studies in Higher Education* 41 (2): 231–46.

Elbow, Peter. 1998. *Writing without Teachers*. 2nd ed. Oxford: Oxford University Press. Original ed., Oxford: Oxford University Press, 1973.

Elkins, Caroline. 2005. *Imperial Reckoning: The Untold Story of Britain's Gulag in Kenya*. New York: Macmillan.

Else, Holly. 2015. "Tell Us about Your Paper—and Make It Short and Tweet." *Times Higher Education*, July 9, 2015. https://www.timeshighereducation.co.uk/opinion/tell-us-about-your-paper-and-make-it-short-and-tweet.

Elsevier. 2016. "Research Elements: Publish Data, Software, and Methods in Brief, Citable Articles." Elsevier. https://www.elsevier.com/books-and-journals/research-elements.

Emanuel, Jenny. 2013. "Users and Citation Management Tools: Use and Support." *Reference Services Review* 41 (4): 639–59.

Epstein, Seymour. 1995. "What Can Be Done to Improve the Journal Review Process." *American Psychologist* 50 (10): 883.

Ericsson, Karl Anders. 2016. *Peak: Secrets from the New Science of Expertise*. Boston: Houghton Mifflin Harcourt.

Ericsson, K. Anders, Ralf T. Krampe, and Clemens Tesch-Römer. 1993. "The Role of Deliberate Practice in the Acquisition of Expert Performance." *Psychological Review* 100 (3): 363.

Fagan, William T. 1990. "To Accept or Reject: Peer Review." *Journal of Educational Thought (JET)/Revue de la Pensée Educative* 24 (2): 103–13.

Fagelson, Marc A., and Sherri L. Smith. 2016. "Tinnitus Self-Efficacy and Other Tinnitus Self-Report Variables in Patients with and without Post-traumatic Stress Disorder." *Ear and Hearing* 37 (5): 541–46.

Faigley, Lester, and Stephen Witte. 1981. "Analyzing Revision." *College Composition and Communication* 32 (4): 400–414.

Fairbrother, Gerry, Jennifer Stuber, Sandro Galea, Betty Pfefferbaum, and Alan R. Fleischman. 2004. "Unmet Need for Counseling Services by Children in New York City after the September 11th Attacks on the World Trade Center: Implications for Pediatricians." *Pediatrics* 113 (5): 1367–74.

Fargotstein, Leah. 2013. "Nine Publishing Basics for Anyone Submitting to a Scholarly Journal." *SAGE Connection: Insight* (blog). November 5, 2013. http://connection.sagepub.com/blog/sage-connection/2013/11/05/9-publishing-basics-for-anyone-submitting-to-a-scholarly-journal/.

Feder, J. Lester. 2008. "Unequal Temperament: The Somatic Acoustics of Racial Difference in the Symphonic Music of John Powell." *Black Music Research Journal* 28 (1): 17–56.

Feliciano, Cynthia. 2001. "The Benefits of Biculturalism: Exposure to Immigrant Culture and Dropping Out of School among Asian and Latino Youths." *Social Science Quarterly* 82 (4): 865–79.

Filardo, Giovanni, Briget da Graca, Danielle M. Sass, Benjamin D. Pollock, Emma B. Smith, and Melissa Ashley-Marie Martinez. 2016. "Trends and Comparison of Female First Authorship in High Impact Medical Journals: Observational Study (1994–2014)." *BMJ* 352:i847.

Firth, Katherine. 2017. "Turn Your Notes into Writing Using the Cornell Method Second Edition." *Research Degree Voodoo* (blog). April 27, 2017. http://researchvoodoo.wordpress.com/2017/04/27/turn-your-notes-into-writing-using-the-cornell-method-second-edition/.

Fisher, Lynn Visson. 1975. "Teaching Stylistics to Students of Russian." *Slavic and East European Journal* 19 (2): 239–45.

Floyd, Randy G., Kathryn M. Cooley, James E. Arnett, Thomas K. Fagan, Sterett H. Mercer, and Christine Hingle. 2011. "An Overview and Analysis of Journal Operations, Journal Publication Patterns, and Journal Impact in School Psychology and Related Fields." *Journal of School Psychology* 49 (6): 617–47.

Francese, Enrico. 2013. "Usage of Reference Management Software at the University of Torino." *JLIS.it (Italian Journal of Library, Archives and Information Science)* 4 (2): 145.

Fukurai, Hiroshi. 2001. "Critical Evaluations of Hispanic Participation on the Grand Jury: Key-Man Selection, Jurymandering Language, and Representative Quotas." *Texas Hispanic Journal of Law and Policy* 5:7–40.

Fulkerson, Richard. 1996. *Teaching the Argument in Writing*. Urbana, IL: National Council of Teachers of English.

Gaipa, Mark. 2004. "Breaking into the Conversation: How Students Can Acquire Authority for Their Writing." *Pedagogy* 4 (3): 419–37.

Gälawdewos. 2015. *The Life and Struggles of Our Mother Walatta Petros: A Seventeenth-Century African Biography of an Ethiopian Woman*. Translated and edited by Wendy Laura Belcher and Michael Kleiner. Princeton, NJ: Princeton University Press.

Galla, Brian M., and Angela L. Duckworth. 2015. "More Than Resisting Temptation: Beneficial Habits Mediate the Relationship between Self-Control and Positive Life Outcomes." *Journal of Personality and Social Psychology* 109 (3): S508.

Gans, Joshua S., and George B. Shepherd. 1994. "How Are the Mighty Fallen: Rejected Classic Articles by Leading Economists." *Journal of Economic Perspectives* 8 (1): 165–79.

Garbati, Jordana, and Boba Samuels. 2013. "Publishing in Educational Research Journals: Are Graduate Students Participating?" *Journal of Scholarly Publishing* 44 (4): 355–72.

García, Jose A., Rosa Rodriguez-Sánchez, and Joaquín Fdez-Valdivia. 2015. "Bias and Effort in Peer Review." *Journal of the Association for Information Science and Technology* 66 (10): 2020–30.

Garrett, Neil, Stephanie C. Lazzaro, Dan Ariely, and Tali Sharot. 2016. "The Brain Adapts to Dishonesty." *Nature Neuroscience* 19 (12): 1727–32.

Garvey, William D., Nan Lin, and Kazuo Tomita. 1972. "Research Studies in Patterns of Scientific Communication: III. Information-Exchange Processes Associated with the Production of Journal Articles." *Information Storage and Retrieval* 8 (5): 207–21.

Gastel, Barbara, and Robert A. Day. 2016. *How to Write and Publish a Scientific Paper*. 8th ed. Westport, CT: Greenwood.

Geertz, Clifford. 1973. "Thick Description: Toward an Interpretive Theory of Culture." In *The Interpretation of Cultures: Selected Essays*, 3–30. New York: Basic Books.

Gehrke, Johannes, Daria Sorokina, Paul Ginsparg, and Simeon Warner. 2006. "Plagiarism Detection in arXiv." Submitted February 1, 2007. https://arxiv.org/abs/cs/0702012.

Geller, Anne Ellen, and Michele Eodice. 2013. *Working with Faculty Writers*. Boulder: Utah State University Press, an imprint of University Press of Colorado.

Gibbons, Jean D. 1990. "U.S. Institutional Representation on Editorial Boards of U.S. Statistics Journals." *American Statistician* 44 (3): 210–13.

Gill, Rosalind. 2009. "Breaking the Silence: The Hidden Injuries of Neo-Liberal Academia." In *Secrecy and Silence in the Research Process: Feminist Reflections*, edited by Roisin Ryan-Flood and Rosalind Gill, 228–44. London: Routledge.

Giroux, Henry. 2003. "Interview." In *Critical Intellectuals on Writing*, edited by Gary A. Olson and Lynn Worsham, 99–102. Albany: State University of New York Press.

Golash-Boza, Tanya. 2012. "How to be Productive by Writing Two Hours a Day." *Get a Life, PhD* (blog). January 21, 2012. http://getalifephd.blogspot.com/2012/01/how-to-be-productive-by-writing-two.html.

Gómez-Haro, Samuel, and Román Salmerón-Gómez. 2016. "Recovering Performance in the Short Term after Coach Succession in Spanish Basketball Organisations." *Coaching: An International Journal of Theory, Research, and Practice* 9 (1): 24–37.

Goodman, Neville W. 2005. "From Shakespeare to Star Trek and Beyond: A Medline Search for Literary and Other Allusions in Biomedical Titles." *BMJ* 331 (7531): 1540–42.

Goodrich, Dorris West. 1945. "An Analysis of Manuscripts Received by the Editors of the *American Sociological Review* from May 1, 1944 to September 1, 1945." *American Sociological Review* 10 (6): 716–25.

Gosden, Hugh. 2003. "'Why Not Give Us the Full Story?': Functions of Referees' Comments in Peer Reviews of Scientific Research Papers." *Journal of English for Academic Purposes* 2 (2): 87–101.

Graff, Gerald, and Cathy Birkenstein. 2014. *They Say / I Say: The Moves That Matter in Academic Writing.* 3rd ed. New York: W. W. Norton.

Grafton, Anthony, and Noah Charney. 2013. "Anthony Grafton: How I Write." *Daily Beast*, August 17, 2013. http://www.thedailybeast.com/articles/2013/07/17/anthony-grafton-how-i-write.html.

Graves, Heather, Shahin Moghaddasi, and Azirah Hashim. 2013. "Mathematics Is the Method: Exploring the Macroorganizational Structure of Research Articles in Mathematics." *Discourse Studies* 15 (4): 421–38.

Gray, Kishonna L. 2015. "#CiteHerWork: Marginalizing Women in Academic and Journalistic Writing." Lachezbippy.kinja.com. December 17, 2015. http://lachezbippy.kinja.com/citeherwork-marginalizing-women-in-academic-and-journ-1748501738.

Green, Judith, and Nicki Thorogood. 2009. *Qualitative Methods for Health Research.* Thousand Oaks, CA: SAGE Publications.

Guillory, Elizabeth A. 2001. "The Black Professoriate: Explaining the Salary Gap for African American Female Professors." *Race, Ethnicity and Education* 4 (3): 225–44.

Gump, Steven E. 2004. "Writing Successful Covering Letters for Unsolicited Submissions to Academic Journals." *Journal of Scholarly Publishing* 35 (2): 92–102.

Haaken, Janice. 1988. "Field Dependence Research: A Historical Analysis of a Psychological Construct." *Signs* 13 (2): 311–30.

Habibzadeh, Farrokh, and Mahboobeh Yadollahie. 2010. "Are Shorter Article Titles More Attractive for Citations? Cross-sectional Study of 22 Scientific Journals." *Croatian Medical Journal* 51 (2): 165–70.

Hall, Jeremy. 2015. "Publishing Technology and Innovation Management Journals in Perspectives from Both Sides of the Fence." In *A Guide to Publishing for Academics: Inside the Publish or Perish Phenomenon*, edited by Jay Liebowitz, 39–50. Boca Raton, FL: CRC Press.

Halliday, Michael A. K., and Ruqaiya Hasan. 1976. *Cohesion in English.* London: Longman.

Haraway, Donna Jeanne. 2008. *When Species Meet.* Minneapolis: University of Minnesota Press.

Hardison, Debra M. 2004. "Generalization of Computer-Assisted Prosody Training: Quantitative and Qualitative Findings." *Language Learning and Technology* 8 (1): 34–52.

Harris, Scott R. 2013. *How to Critique Journal Articles in the Social Sciences.* Thousand Oaks, CA: SAGE Publications.

Hartley, James. 2014. "Current Findings from Research on Structured Abstracts: An Update." *Journal of the Medical Library Association* 102 (3): 146.

Harvey, Gordon. 1994. "Presence in the Essay." *College English* 56 (6): 642–54.

Harvey, Gordon. 2009. "A Brief Guide to the Elements of the Academic Essay." Harvard Writing Project Brief Guide Series. Cambridge, MA: Harvard College Writing Program. http://writingproject.fas.harvard.edu/files/hwp/files/hwp_brief_guides_elements.pdf.

Harwood, Nigel. 2005. "'Nowhere Has Anyone Attempted… in This Article I Aim to Do Just That': A Corpus-Based Study of Self-Promotional *I* and *We* in Academic Writing across Four Disciplines." *Journal of Pragmatics* 37 (8): 1207–31.

Haslam, Nick, Lauren Ban, Leah Kaufmann, Stephen Loughnan, Kim Peters, Jennifer Whelan, and Sam Wilson. 2008. "What Makes an Article Influential? Predicting Impact in Social and Personality Psychology." *Scientometrics* 76 (1): 169–185.

Hauptman, Robert. 2011. *Authorial Ethics: How Writers Abuse Their Calling.* Lanham, MD: Rowman and Littlefield.

Haveman, Heather A. 2015. *Magazines and the Making of America: Modernization, Community, and Print Culture, 1741–1860.* Princeton, NJ: Princeton University Press.

Hayes, Niall, and Lucas Introna. 2005. "Systems for the Production of Plagiarists? The Implications Arising from the Use of Plagiarism Detection Systems in UK Universities for Asian Learners." *Journal of Academic Ethics* 3 (1): 55–73.

Hayot, Eric. 2014. *The Elements of Academic Style: Writing for the Humanities.* New York: Columbia University Press.

Henderson, Bill. 2012. *Rotten Reviews Redux: A Literary Companion.* New York: Pushcart Press.

Henry, Alex, and Robert L. Roseberry. 1997. "An Investigation of the Functions, Strategies, and Linguistic Features of the Introductions and Conclusions of Essays." *System* 25 (4): 479–95.

Henson, Kenneth T. 1999. *Writing for Professional Publication: Keys to Academic and Business Success.* Boston: Allyn and Bacon.

Henson, Kenneth T. 2007. "Writing for Publication: Steps to Excellence." *Phi Delta Kappan* 88 (10): 781–86.

Herrera, Brian Eugenio. 2017. "'But Do We Have the Actors for That?': Some Principles of Practice for Staging Latinx Plays in a University Theatre Context." *Theatre Topics* 27 (1): 23–35.

Hitchcock, Steve. 2013. "The Effect of Open Access and Downloads ('Hits') on Citation Impact: A Bibliography of Studies." Open Citation Project—Reference Linking and Citation Analysis for Open Archives. July 5, 2013. http://opcit.eprints.org/oacitation-biblio.html.

Hobbs, William R., Moira Burke, Nicholas A. Christakis, and James H. Fowler. 2016. "Online Social Integration Is Associated with Reduced Mortality Risk." *Proceedings of the National Academy of Sciences* 113 (46): 12980–84.

Hofmann, Angelika H. 2016. *Scientific Writing and Communication: Papers, Proposals, and Presentations*. New York: Oxford University Press.

Holschuh, Jodi L. 1998. "Why Manuscripts Get Rejected and What Can Be Done about It: Understanding the Editorial Process from an Insider's Perspective." *Journal of Literacy Research* 30 (1): 1–7.

Hu, Guangwei, and Jun Lei. 2012. "Investigating Chinese University Students' Knowledge of and Attitudes toward Plagiarism from an Integrated Perspective." *Language Learning* 62 (3): 813–50.

Huckin, Thomas. 2001. "Abstracting from Abstracts." In *Academic Writing in Context: Implications and Applications: Papers in Honour of Tony Dudley-Evans*, edited by Tony Dudley-Evans and Martin Hewings, 93–103. Birmingham, England: University of Birmingham Press.

Huisman, Janine, and Jeroen Smits. 2017. "Duration and Quality of the Peer Review Process: The Author's Perspective." *Scientometrics* 113 (1): 633–50.

Hyland, Ken. 2004. *Disciplinary Discourses: Social Interactions in Academic Writing*. Ann Arbor: University of Michigan Press.

Ilakovac, Vesna, Kristina Fister, Matko Marusic, and Ana Marusic. 2007. "Reliability of Disclosure Forms of Authors' Contributions." *Canadian Medical Association Journal* 176 (1): 41–46.

Iskin, Ruth E. 2014. *Modern Women and Parisian Consumer Culture in Impressionist Painting*. Cambridge: Cambridge University Press.

Jacoby-Senghor, Drew S., Stacey Sinclair, and J. Nicole Shelton. 2016. "A Lesson in Bias: The Relationship between Implicit Racial Bias and Performance in Pedagogical Contexts." *Journal of Experimental Social Psychology* 63 (March): 50–55.

Jacques, Thomas S., and Neil J. Sebire. 2010. "The Impact of Article Titles on Citation Hits: An Analysis of General and Specialist Medical Journals." *JRSM Short Reports* 1 (1): 2.

Jagmohan, Desmond D. 2018. "W. E. B. Du Bois and the African American Intellectual Tradition." Unpublished manuscript.

Jamali, Hamid R., and Mahsa Nikzad. 2011. "Article Title Type and Its Relation with the Number of Downloads and Citations." *Scientometrics* 88 (2): 653–61.

Jameson, Frederic. 1986. "Third World Literature in the Era of Multinational Capitalism." *Social Text* 15 (Autumn): 65–88.

Jarvis, Jill. 2014. "Remnants of Muslims: Reading Agamben's Silence." *New Literary History* 45 (4): 707–28.

Jaschik, Scott. 2017. "Analyzing Black Lives Matter without Black People Involved." *Inside Higher Education*, May 30, 2017. https://www.insidehighered.com/news/2017/05/30/philosophy-journal-apologizes-symposium-black-lives-matter-written-without-black.

Jergas, Hannah, and Christopher Baethge. 2015. "Quotation Accuracy in Medical Journal Articles—a Systematic Review and Meta-Analysis." *PeerJ* 3:e1364.

Jinha, Arif E. 2010. "Article 50 Million: An Estimate of the Number of Scholarly Articles in Existence." *Learned Publishing* 23 (3): 258–63.

Johnston, J., S. Wilson, E. Rix, and S. W. Pit. 2014. "Publish or Perish: Strategies to Help Rural Early Career Researchers Increase Publication Output." *Rural and Remote Health* 14 (2870). http://www.rrh.org.au/journal/article/2870.

Jones, Gaynor, and Jay Rahn. 1977. "Definitions of Popular Music: Recycled." *Journal of Aesthetic Education* 11 (4): 79–92.

Kamler, Barbara, and Pat Thomson. 2014. *Helping Doctoral Students Write: Pedagogies for Supervision*. New York: Routledge.

Kanoksilapatham, Budsaba. 2012. "Research Article Structure of Research Article Introductions in Three Engineering Subdisciplines." *IEEE Transactions on Professional Communication* 55 (4): 294–309.

Kaplan, Robert B. 1966. "Cultural Thought Patterns in Inter-cultural Education." *Language Learning* 16 (1–2): 1–20.

Kellogg, Ronald T. 1999. *The Psychology of Writing*. Oxford: Oxford University Press.

Kerans, Mary Ellen, Anne Murray, and Sergi Sabatè. 2016. "Content and Phrasing in Titles of Original Research and Review Articles in 2015: Range of Practice in Four Clinical Journals." *Publications* 4 (2): 11.

Kershaw, Alex. 1999. *Jack London: A Life*. New York: St. Martin's Press.

Ketcham, Catherine M., and James M. Crawford. 2007. "The Impact of Review Articles." *Laboratory Investigation* 87 (12): 1174–85.

Keynes, John Maynard. 1936. *The General Theory of Employment Interest and Money*. New York: Macmillan.

King, Donald Ward, Dennis D. McDonald, and Nancy K. Roderer. 1981. *Scientific Journals in the United States.* Stroudsburg, PA: Dowden, Hutchinson, and Ross.

King, Molly M., Carl T. Bergstrom, Shelley J. Correll, Jennifer Jacquet, and Jevin D. West. 2016. "Men Set Their Own Cites High: Gender and Self-Citation across Fields and Over Time." Submitted June 30, 2016. Last revised December 12, 2017. http://arxiv.org/abs/1607.00376.

Kingman, Russ. 1979. *A Pictorial Life of Jack London.* New York: Crown.

Kirk, Andy. 2012. *Data Visualization: A Successful Design Process.* Birmingham, UK: Packt.

Kirkpatrick, Andy. 1997. "Traditional Chinese Text Structures and Their Influence on the Writing in Chinese and English of Contemporary Mainland Chinese Students." *Journal of Second Language Writing* 6 (3): 223–44.

Klima, Alan. 2016. "Inquiry-Based Outlines: How to Make Outlines that You Can Actually Follow So That You Feel Propelled Forward while Writing." Narrated slide show. AcademicMuse.org.

Knobloch-Westerwick, Silvia, Carroll J. Glynn, and Michael Huge. 2013. "The Matilda Effect in Science Communication: An Experiment on Gender Bias in Publication Quality Perceptions and Collaboration Interest." *Science Communication* 35 (5): 603–25.

Koch-Weser, Dieter, and Alfred Yankauer. 1993. "The Authorship and Fate of International Health Papers Submitted to the American Journal of Public Health in 1989." *American Journal of Public Health* 83 (11): 1618–20.

Kolowich, Steve. 2016. "Brandon Stell Is the Vigilante of Scientific Publishing." *Chronicle of Higher Education*, April 10, 2016. http://chronicle.com/article/Brandon-Stell-Is-the-Vigilante/236007.

Kourilova-Urbanczik, Magda. 2012. "Some Linguistic and Pragmatic Considerations Affecting Science Reporting in English by Non-native Speakers of the Language." *Interdisciplinary Toxicology* 5 (2): 105–15.

Kowalczuk, Maria K., Frank Dudbridge, Shreeya Nanda, Stephanie L. Harriman, Jigisha Patel, and Elizabeth C. Moylan. 2015. "Retrospective Analysis of the Quality of Reports by Author-Suggested and Non-author-suggested Reviewers in Journals Operating on Open or Single-Blind Peer Review Models." *BMJ Open* 5 (9): e008707.

Krashen, Stephen. 2002. "Optimal Levels of Writing Management: A Re-analysis of Boice (1983)." *Education* 122 (3): 605–8.

Kristensen, Peter Marcus. 2015. "Revisiting the 'American Social Science'—Mapping the Geography of International Relations." *International Studies Perspectives* 16 (3): 246–69.

Kucich, John. 2011. "Psychoanalytic Historicism: Shadow Discourse and the Gender Politics of Masochism in Ellis, Schreiner, and Haggard." *PMLA* 126 (1): 88–106.

Laband, David N. 1990. "Is There Value-Added from the Review Process in Economics? Preliminary Evidence from Authors." *Quarterly Journal of Economics* 105 (2): 341–52.

Laine, Christine, and Margaret A. Winker. 2017. "Identifying Predatory or Pseudo-Journals." *Biochemia Medica* 27 (2): 285–91.

Lamb, Michael E. 2012. "Mothers, Fathers, Families, and Circumstances: Factors Affecting Children's Adjustment." *Applied Developmental Science* 16 (2): 98–111.

Langdon-Neuner, Elise. 2008. "Hangings at the BMJ: What Editors Discuss When Deciding to Accept or Reject Research Papers." *Write Stuff* 17 (2): 84–86.

Larivière, Vincent, Benoit Macaluso, Éric Archambault, and Yves Gingras. 2010. "Which Scientific Elites? On the Concentration of Research Funds, Publications, and Citations." *Research Evaluation* 19 (1): 45–53.

Lauer-Busch, Ines-A. 2014. "Abstracts: Cross-Linguistic, Disciplinary, and Intercultural Perspectives." In *Abstracts in Academic Discourse: Variation and Change*, edited by Marina Bondi and Rosa Lorés Sanz, 43–63. Bern: Peter Lang.

Lavergne, Michael, and Sendhil Mullainathan. 2004. "Are Emily and Greg More Employable than Lakisha and Jamal? A Field Experiment on Labor Market Discrimination." *American Economic Review* 94 (4): 991–1013.

Leavy, Patricia. 2014. *The Oxford Handbook of Qualitative Research.* Oxford: Oxford University Press.

Lee, Carole J., Cassidy R. Sugimoto, Guo Zhang, and Blaise Cronin. 2013. "Bias in Peer Review." *Journal of the American Society for Information Science and Technology* 64 (1): 2–17.

Lewin, Arie Y. 2014. "The Peer-Review Process: The Good, the Bad, the Ugly, and the Extraordinary." *Management and Organization Review* 10 (2): 167–73.

Linde, Jonas, and Martin Karlsson. 2013. "The Dictator's New Clothes: The Relationship between E-participation and Quality of Government in Non-democratic Regimes." *International Journal of Public Administration* 36 (4): 269–81.

Linder, Kathryn E., Frank Rudy Cooper, Elizabeth M. McKenzie, Monika Raesch, and Patricia A. Reeve. 2014. "Intentional Teaching, Intentional Scholarship: Applying Backward Design Principles in a Faculty Writing Group." *Innovative Higher Education* 39 (3): 217–29.

Linzer, Mark. 1987. "The Journal Club and Medical Education: Over One Hundred Years of Unrecorded History." *Postgraduate Medical Journal* 63 (740): 475–78.

Little, Todd D. 2013. *The Oxford Handbook of Quantitative Methods.* Oxford: Oxford University Press.

Liu, Donghong. 2015. "Moves and Wrap-Up Sentences in Chinese Students' Essay Conclusions." *SAGE Open* 5 (2): 1–9. doi/10.1177/ 2158244015592681.

Lobao, Linda, Minyu Zhou, Mark Partridge, and Michael Betz. 2016. "Poverty, Place, and Coal Employment across Appalachia and the United States in a New Economic Era." *Rural Sociology* 81 (3): 343–86.

Lomell, Heidi Mork. 2002. "Targeting the Unwanted: Video Surveillance and Categorical Exclusion in Oslo, Norway." *Surveillance and Society* 2 (2/3): 346–60.

Lomell, Heidi Mork 2010. "Videoovervåking: Myter og realiteter, I." In *Overvåking i en rettsstat*, edited by Dag Wiese Schartum, 243–61. Oslo: Fagbokforlaget.

Love, Heather. 2010. "Close but Not Deep: Literary Ethics and the Descriptive Turn." *New Literary History* 41 (2): 371–91.

Luukkonen, Terttu. 2012. "Conservatism and Risk-Taking in Peer Review: Emerging ERC Practices." *Research Evaluation* 21 (1): 48–60.

Mabe, Michael. 2003. "The Growth and Number of Journals." *Serials* 16 (2): 191–97.

Mackin, Ellie. 2013. "Writing Your Journal Article in Twelve Weeks: Week 4." *PhD2Published.com* (blog). November 8, 2013. http://www.phd2published.com/2013/11/08/writing-your-journal-article-in-12-weeks-week-four/.

Macnamara, Jim. 2016. "The Work and 'Architecture of Listening': Addressing Gaps in Organization-Public Communication." *International Journal of Strategic Communication* 10 (2): 133–48.

Mahmood, Saba. 2001. "Feminist Theory, Embodiment, and the Docile Agent: Some Reflections on the Egyptian Islamic Revival." *Cultural Anthropology* 16 (2): 202–36.

Marr, Matthew D. 2005. "Mitigating Apprehension about Section 8 Vouchers: The Positive Role of Housing Specialists in Search and Placement." *Housing Policy Debate* 16 (1): 85–111.

Marshall, Catherine, and Gretchen B. Rossman. 2016. *Designing Qualitative Research*. 6th ed. Thousand Oaks, CA: SAGE Publications.

Martin, Brian. 2008. "Surviving Referees' Reports." *Journal of Scholarly Publishing* 39 (3): 307–11.

Martin, Brian. 2013. "Learning to Love Rejection." *Inside Higher Education*, July 17, 2013. http://www.inside highered.com/advice/2013/07/08/essay-importance-rejection-academic-careers.

Martin-Rodriguez, Manuel M. 2000. "Hyenas in the Pride Lands: Latinos/as and Immigration in Disney's *The Lion King*." *Aztlan: A Journal of Chicano Studies* 25 (1): 47–66.

Marx, Werner, and Lutz Bornmann. 2015. "On the Causes of Subject-Specific Citation Rates in Web of Science." *Scientometrics* 102 (2): 1823–27.

Mason, Mark. 2010. "Sample Size and Saturation in PhD Studies Using Qualitative Interviews." *Forum Qualitative Sozialforschung / Forum: Qualitative Social Research* 11 (3): art. 8. http://nbn-resolving.de /urn:nbn:de:0114-fqs100387.

McCabe, Patrick P., Linda A. Kraemer, Paul M. Miller, Rene S. Parmar, and Marybeth B. Ruscica. 2006. "The Effect of Text Format upon Underachieving First Year College Students' Self-Efficacy for Reading and Subsequent Reading Comprehension." *Journal of College Reading and Learning* 37 (1): 19–42.

McFarland, J., B. Hussar, C. de Brey, T. Snyder, X. Wang, S. Wilkinson-Flicker, S. Gebrekristos, J. Zhang, A. Rathbun, A. Barmer, F. Bullock Mann, S. Hinz, and National Center for Education Statistics. 2017. *The Condition of Education: Characteristics of Postsecondary Faculty*. Washington, DC: National Center for Education Statistics. https://nces.ed.gov/programs/coe/indicator_csc.asp.

McKenzie, Sheila. 1995. "Reviewing Scientific Papers." *Archives of Disease in Childhood* 72 (6): 539–40.

McLean, Patricia, and Laurie Ransom. 2005. "Building Intercultural Competencies." In *Teaching International Students—Improving Learning for All*, edited by J. Carroll and J. Ryan, 45–62. London: Routledge.

McMurry, Alison Irvine. 2005. "Preparing Students for Peer Review." MA thesis, Brigham Young University.

McNutt, Robert A., Arthur T. Evans, Robert H. Fletcher, and Suzanne W. Fletcher. 1990. "The Effects of Blinding on the Quality of Peer Review: A Randomized Trial." *Journal of the American Medical Association* 263 (10): 1371–76.

McTigue, Erin M., and Scott W. Slough. 2010. "Student-Accessible Science Texts: Elements of Design." *Reading Psychology* 31 (3): 213–27.

Mejias, Ulises A. 2005. "Social Literacies: Some Observations about Writing and Wikis." *Ulises A. Mejias Blog*. March 4, 2005. http://blog.ulisesmejias.com/tag/wikis/.

Melles, Anne, and Kathryn Unsworth. 2015. "Examining the Reference Management Practices of Humanities and Social Science Postgraduate Students and Academics." *Australian Academic and Research Libraries* 46 (4): 250–76.

Meyer, Bonnie J. F. 1975. *The Organization of Prose and Its Effects on Memory*. Amsterdam: North-Holland.

Meyer, Bonnie J. F. 2003. "Text Coherence and Readability." *Topics in Language Disorders* 23 (3): 204–24.

Meyer, Bonnie J. F., David M. Brandt, and George J. Bluth. 1980. "Use of Top-Level Structure in Text: Key for Reading Comprehension of Ninth-Grade Students." *Reading Research Quarterly* 16 (1): 72–103.

Meyer, Bonnie J. F., Carole J. Young, and Brendan J. Bartlett. 1989. *Memory Improved: Reading and Memory Enhancement across the Life Span through Strategic Text Structures*. Mahwah, NJ: Lawrence Erlbaum Associates.

Meyer, Holly S., Steven J. Durning, David Sklar, and Lauren A Maggio. 2018. "Making the First Cut: An Analysis of Academic Medicine Editors' Reasons for Not Sending Manuscripts Out for External Peer Review." *Academic Medicine* 93 (3): 464–70.

Miller, D. W. 1999. "Sociologists Debate How to Broaden Scholarship in Their Flagship Journal." *Chronicle of Higher Education* 46 (2): A24–A25.

Miller, James. 1993. *The Passion of Michel Foucault*. Cambridge, MA: Harvard University Press.

Miller, Jane E. 2015. *The Chicago Guide to Writing about Numbers*. Chicago: University of Chicago Press.

Mollett, Amy, Cheryl Brumley, Chris Gilson, and Sierra Williams. 2017. *Communicating Your Research with Social Media: A Practical Guide to Using Blogs, Podcasts, Data Visualisations and Video*. Thousand Oaks, CA: SAGE Publications.

Monmonier, Mark. 2015. *Mapping It Out: Expository Cartography for the Humanities and Social Sciences*. Chicago: University of Chicago Press.

Moore, N. A. J. 2006. "Aligning Theme and Information Structure to Improve the Readability of Technical Writing." *Journal of Technical Writing and Communication* 36 (1): 43–55.

Morison, Samuel Eliot. 1953. *By Land and by Sea: Essays and Addresses*. New York: Knopf.

Morris, Aldon. 2015. *The Scholar Denied: W E. B. Du Bois and the Birth of Modern Sociology*. Berkeley: University of California Press.

Morton, Timothy. 2010. *The Ecological Thought*. Cambridge, MA: Harvard University Press.

Moss, Beverly J., Nels P. Highberg, and Melissa Nicolas. 2014. *Writing Groups inside and outside the Classroom*. New York: Routledge.

Moten, Fred. 2013. "Blackness and Nothingness (Mysticism in the Flesh)." *South Atlantic Quarterly* 112 (4): 737–80.

Mundava, Maud, and Jayati Chaudhuri. 2007. "Understanding Plagiarism: The Role of Librarians at the University of Tennessee in Assisting Students to Practice Fair Use of Information." *College and Research Libraries News* 68 (3): 170–73.

Munro, Lisa. 2015a. "Twelve Week Article Writing: Week Eight Recap." *Lisa Munro Writing and Editing* (blog). October 11, 2015. https://lisa-munro.squarespace.com/blog-1/2015/10/11/twelve-week-article -writing-week-eight-recap.

Munro, Lisa. 2015b. "Twelve Week Article Writing: Week Nine Recap." *Lisa Munro Writing and Editing* (blog). October 18, 2015. https://lisa-munro.squarespace.com/blog-1/2015/10/18/twelve-week-article -writing-week-nine-recap.

Munro, Lisa. 2015c. "Twelve Week Article Writing: Week Ten Recap." *Lisa Munro Writing and Editing* (blog). October 27, 2015. https://lisa-munro.squarespace.com/blog-1/2015/10/27/twelve-week-article-writing -week-ten-recap.

Munro, Lisa. 2016. "Twelve Week Article." *Lisa Munro Writing and Editing* (blog). February 24, 2016. http:// www.lisamunro.net/blog-1?tag=12+week+article.

Murphy, Eamon. 1998. "Using Descriptive Headings to Improve First Year Student Writing." In *Teaching and Learning in Changing Times: Proceedings of the Seventh Annual Teaching Learning Forum, 4–5 February 1998*, edited by Barbara Black and Natalie Stanley, 233–36. Perth: University of Western Australia.

Nairn, Karen, Jenny Cameron, Megan Anakin, Adisorn Juntrasook, Rob Wass, Judith Sligo, and Catherine Morrison. 2014. "Negotiating the Challenge of Collaborative Writing: Learning from One Writing Group's Mutiny." *Higher Education Research and Development* 34 (3): 596–608.

NASA. 2000. "Chapter 2: NASA Writing Standards." In *NASA Correspondence Management and Communications Standards and Style*, 10–20. Washington, DC: NASA. E-version from NADIS Library (NASA Online Directives Information System) is available at https://nodis3.gsfc.nasa.gov/displayDir.cfm?Internal _ID=N_PR_1450_010D_&page_name=Chapter2.

NCB (*Nature Cell Biology*) editors. 2009. "Editorial: Credit Where Credit Is Due." *Nature Cell Biology* 11 (1): 1.

Nicholas, David, and David Clark. 2012. " 'Reading' in the Digital Environment." *Learned Publishing* 25 (2): 93–98.

Nicholas, David, Anthony Watkinson, Hamid R. Jamali, Eti Herman, Carol Tenopir, Rachel Volentine, Suzie Allard, and Kenneth Levine. 2015. "Peer Review: Still King in the Digital Age." *Learned Publishing* 28 (1): 15–21.

Nishikawa, Kinohi. 2015. "Merely Reading." *PMLA* 130 (3): 697–703.

NLM (National Library of Medicine). 2015. "Structured Abstracts in Medline: Updated Label List and NLM Category Mappings File." Washington, DC: U.S. National Library of Medicine. https://structuredab stracts.nlm.nih.gov/.

North, Michael. 1984. *Henry Green and the Writing of His Generation*. Charlottesville: University Press of Virginia.

North, Michael. 1985. *The Final Sculpture: Public Monuments and Modern Poets*. Ithaca, NY: Cornell University Press.

North, Michael. 1991. *The Political Aesthetic of Yeats, Eliot, and Pound*. Cambridge: Cambridge University Press.

North, Michael. 1994. *The Dialect of Modernism: Race, Language, and Twentieth-Century Literature*. Oxford: Oxford University Press.

North, Michael. 1999. *Reading 1922: A Return to the Scene of the Modern*. Oxford: Oxford University Press.

North, Michael, ed. 2001. *"The Waste Land": Authoritative Text, Contexts, Criticism*. New York: W. W. Norton.

North, Michael. 2005. *Camera Works: Photography and the Twentieth-Century Word*. Oxford: Oxford University Press, USA.

North, Michael. 2008. *Machine-Age Comedy*. Oxford: Oxford University Press.

North, Michael. 2013. *Novelty: A History of the New*. Chicago: University of Chicago Press.

Nylenna, Magne, Povl Riis, and Yngve Karlsson. 1994. "Multiple Blinded Reviews of the Same Two Manuscripts: Effects of Referee Characteristics and Publication Language." *Journal of the American Medical Association* 272 (2): 149–51.

Ollé, Candela, and Ángel Borrego. 2010. "A Qualitative Study of the Impact of Electronic Journals on Scholarly Information Behavior." *Library and Information Science Research* 32 (3): 221–28.

Olsen, Richard K., Jr. 2002. "Living above It All: The Liminal Fantasy of Sport Utility Vehicle Advertisements." In *Enviropop: Studies in Environmental Rhetoric and Popular Culture*, edited by Mark Meister and Phyllis M. Japp, 175–96. Westport, CT: Praeger.

Olson, Gary A. 1997. "Publishing Scholarship in Humanistic Disciplines: Joining the Conversation." In *Writing and Publishing for Academic Authors*, edited by Joseph Michael Moxley, 51–69. Lanham, MD: Rowman and Littlefield.

Oppezzo, Marily, and Daniel L. Schwartz. 2014. "Give Your Ideas Some Legs: The Positive Effect of Walking on Creative Thinking." *Journal of Experimental Psychology: Learning, Memory, and Cognition* 40 (4): 1142–52.

Overå, Ragnhild. 2007. "When Men Do Women's Work: Structural Adjustment, Unemployment, and Changing Gender Relations in the Informal Economy of Accra, Ghana." *Journal of Modern African Studies* 45 (4): 539–63.

Pacheco-Vega, Raul. 2016. "What Counts as Academic Writing? #AcWri." *Raul Pacheco-Vega, PhD: Understanding and Solving Intractable Resource Governance Problems* (blog). March 11, 2016. http://www.raulpacheco.org/2016/03/what-counts-as-academic-writing-acwri/.

Paiva, Carlos Eduardo, João Paulo da Silveira Nogueira Lima, and Bianca Sakamoto Ribeiro Paiva. 2012. "Articles with Short Titles Describing the Results Are Cited More Often." *Clinics* 67 (5): 509–13.

Paltridge, Brian. 2002. "Thesis and Dissertation Writing: An Examination of Published Advice and Actual Practice." *English for Specific Purposes* 21 (2): 125–43.

Paltridge, Brian. 2017. *The Discourse of Peer Review*. London: Palgrave Macmillan UK.

Pannell, David J. 2002. "Prose, Psychopaths, and Persistence: Personal Perspectives on Publishing." *Canadian Journal of Agricultural Economics/Revue canadienne d'agroeconomie* 50 (2): 101–15.

Parker, Frank, and Kathryn Louise Riley. 1995. *Writing for Academic Publication: A Guide to Getting Started*. Superior, WI: Parlay Press.

Peer, Kimberly S. 2016. "Maintaining Scholarly Integrity: A Worthwhile Endeavor." *Athletic Training Education Journal* 11 (1): 3–4.

Penrose, Ann M., and Steven B. Katz. 2010. *Writing in the Sciences: Exploring Conventions of Scientific Discourse*. New York: Longman.

Peplow, Mark. 2016. "No Time for Stodgy: Crusading Editor Aims to Shake Things Up in Science." STAT: Reporting from the Frontiers of Health and Medicine. January 4, 2016. https://www.statnews.com/2016/01/04/bmj-editor-fiona-godlee/.

Perry, Imani. 2018. *Vexy Thing: On Gender and Liberation*. Durham, NC: Duke University Press.

Petherbridge, Lee, and Christopher Anthony Cotropia. 2014. "Should Your Law Review Article Have an Abstract and Table of Contents?" Loyola Law School, Los Angeles, Legal Studies Research Paper no. 2016–39. Posted October 5, 2014. Last revised November 20, 2016.

Petrucci, Carrie J. 2002. "Apology in the Criminal Justice Setting: Evidence for Including Apology as an Additional Component in the Legal System." *Behavioral Sciences and the Law* 20 (4): 337–62.

Dimock, Wai Chee. 2018. "Report from the Editor of *PMLA* for 2016–17." New York: Modern Language Association. http://www.mla.org/content/download/76300/2159890/Report-PMLA-2018.pdf.

Pony, Kourtney. 2016. "Complicating the Narrative: Viewing Medicine through a Literary Lens in Brazilian Lupus Patient Testimonies." BA thesis, Department of Comparative Literature, Princeton University.

Posusta, Steven. 1996. *Don't Panic: The Procrastinator's Guide to Writing an Effective Term Paper (You Know Who You Are)*. Santa Barbara, CA: Bandanna Books.

Pournelle, Jerry, and Alex Pournelle. 1996. "Modern Letters." *Internet World* 7 (2): 102–3.

Radway, Janice A. 1984. *Reading the Romance: Women, Patriarchy, and Popular Literature.* Durham: University of North Carolina Press.

Ramirez, Marisa L., Joan T. Dalton, Gail McMillan, Max Read, and Nancy H. Seamans. 2013. "Do Open Access Electronic Theses and Dissertations Diminish Publishing Opportunities in the Social Sciences and Humanities? Findings from a 2011 Survey of Academic Publishers." *College and Research Libraries* 74 (4): 368–80.

Randolph, Justus J., George Julnes, Roman Bednarik, and Erkki Sutinen. 2007. "A Comparison of the Methodological Quality of Articles in Computer Science Education Journals and Conference Proceedings." *Computer Science Education* 17 (4): 263–74.

Rasmussen, Sonja A., Denise J. Jamieson, Margaret A. Honein, and Lyle R. Petersen. 2016. "Zika Virus and Birth Defects—Reviewing the Evidence for Causality." *New England Journal of Medicine* 2016 (374): 1981–87.

Reeves, Richard V., and Sarah Holmes. 2015. "Guns and Race: The Different Worlds of Black and White Americans." Brookings Institute Social Mobility Memos, March 4, 2015.

Richardson, Laurel, and Elizabeth Adams St. Pierre. 2005. "Writing: A Method of Inquiry." In *Handbook of Qualitative Research*, edited by Norman K. Denzin and Yvonna S. Lincoln, 959–78. Thousand Oaks, CA: SAGE Publications.

Ripple, Anna M., James G. Mork, Lou S. Knecht, and Betsy L. Humphreys. 2011. "A Retrospective Cohort Study of Structured Abstracts in Medline, 1992–2006." *Journal of the Medical Library Association* 99 (2): 160.

Ritchie, Jane, Jane Lewis, and Gillian Elam. 2003. "Designing and Selecting Samples." In *Qualitative Research Practice: A Guide for Social Science Students and Researchers*, edited by Jane Ritchie and Jane Lewis, 77–108. Thousand Oaks, CA: SAGE Publications.

Rivera Leon, Llorena. 2017. "Women Aren't Failing at Science—Science Is Failing Women." The Conversation: Academic Rigor, Journalistic Flair. May 27, 2017. http://theconversation.com/women-arent-failing-at-science-science-is-failing-women-71783.

Rivera Leon, Llorena, Jacques Mairesse, and Robin Cowan. 2016. "An Econometric Investigation of the Productivity Gender Gap in Mexican Research, and a Simulation Study of the Effects on Scientific Performance of Policy Scenarios to Promote Gender Equality." MERIT Working Papers 72, December 2016. United Nations University, Tokyo / Maastricht Economic and Social Research Institute on Innovation and Technology (MERIT), Maastricht, the Netherlands.

Roberts, John C., Robert H. Fletcher, and Suzanne W. Fletcher. 1994. "Effects of Peer Review and Editing on the Readability of Articles Published in *Annals of Internal Medicine*." *Journal of the American Medical Association* 272 (2): 119–21.

Rocha da Silva, Pascal. 2015. "Selecting for Impact: New Data Debunks Old Beliefs." *Frontiers Blog.* March 20, 2015. http://blog.frontiersin.org/2015/12/21/4782/.

Rodman, Hyman. 1978. "Some Practical Advice for Journal Contributors." *Scholarly Publishing* 9 (3): 235–41.

Rogers, Lee F. 1999. "Salami Slicing, Shotgunning, and the Ethics of Authorship." *American Journal of Roentgenology* 173 (2): 265.

Ross, Michael, and Fiore Sicoly. 1979. "Egocentric Biases in Availability and Attribution." *Journal of Personality and Social Psychology* 37 (3): 322.

Ross-Larson, Bruce. 1996. *Edit Yourself: A Manual for Everyone Who Works with Words.* Rev. ed. New York: W. W. Norton.

Rothman, Kenneth J. 1998. "Writing for *Epidemiology*." *Epidemiology* 9 (3): 333–37.

Rottier, Bart, Nannette Ripmeester, and Andrew Bush. 2011. "Separated by a Common Translation? How the British and the Dutch Communicate." *Pediatric Pulmonology* 46 (4): 409–11.

Rotton, James, Paul W. Foos, Luz Van Meek, and Mary Levitt. 1995. "Publication Practices and the File Drawer Problem: A Survey of Published Authors." *Journal of Social Behavior and Personality* 10 (1): 1–13.

RSA (Rehabilitation Services Administration). 1985. *American Rehabilitation.* Washington, DC: Rehabilitation Services Administration, U.S. Department of Health, Education, and Welfare.

Ruiying, Yang, and Desmond Allison. 2003. "Research Articles in Applied Linguistics: Moving from Results to Conclusions." *English for Specific Purposes* 22 (4): 365–85.

Ruiying, Yang, and Desmond Allison. 2004. "Research Articles in Applied Linguistics: Structures from a Functional Perspective." *English for Specific Purposes* 23 (3): 264–79.

Salkind, Neil J. 2013. *Statistics for People Who (Think They) Hate Statistics.* 3rd ed. Thousand Oaks, CA: SAGE Publications.

San, Lawrence. 2001. "The Theory of the Hairy Arm." *1099: The Magazine for Independent Professionals*, February 1, 2001. http://1099.com/c/co/in/insanity006.html.

Sarsons, Heather. 2015. "Gender Differences in Recognition for Group Work." Working Paper 254946, Harvard University OpenScholar. November 4, 2015. http://scholar.harvard.edu/files/sarsons/files/gender_groupwork.pdf?m=1449178759.

Schmidt, Michael. Forthcoming. *Being a Scientist: Tools for Science Students.* Toronto: University of Toronto Press.

Schwartz, Tony. 2013. "Relax! You'll Be More Productive." *New York Times*, February 9, 2013. http://www
.nytimes.com/2013/02/10/opinion/sunday/relax-youll-be-more-productive.html.

Schwartz, Tony, Jean Gomes, and Catherine McCarthy. 2010. *The Way We're Working Isn't Working: The Four
Forgotten Needs That Energize Great Performance*. New York: Simon and Schuster.

Shelley, Mack C., and John H. Schuh. 2001. "Are the Best Higher Education Journals Really the Best? A
Meta-Analysis of Writing Quality and Readability." *Journal of Scholarly Publishing* 33 (1): 11–22.

Shi, Xiaolin, Jure Leskovec, and Daniel A. McFarland. 2010. "Citing for High Impact." In *Proceedings of
the Tenth Annual Joint Conference on Digital Libraries*, ed. Jane Hunter, 49–58. Gold Coast, Queensland,
Australia: ACM Digital Library.

Shlush, Liran I., Amanda Mitchell, Lawrence Heisler, Sagi Abelson, Stanley W. K. Ng, Aaron Trotman-Grant,
Jessie J. F. Medeiros, Abilasha Rao-Bhatia, Ivana Jaciw-Zurakowsky, and Rene Marke. 2017. "Tracing the
Origins of Relapse in Acute Myeloid Leukaemia to Stem Cells." *Nature* 547:104–8.

Siemons, Rachel, Marissa Raymond-Flesh, Colette L. Auerswald, and Claire D. Brindis. 2017. "Coming of
Age on the Margins: Mental Health and Wellbeing among Latino Immigrant Young Adults Eligible for
Deferred Action for Childhood Arrivals (DACA)." *Journal of Immigrant and Minority Health* 19 (3): 543–51.

Simkin, Mikhail V., and Vwani P. Roychowdhury. 2002. "Read before You Cite!" arXiv:cond-mat/0212043.
Submitted December 3, 2002.

Simon, Rita J., Von Bakanic, and Clark McPhail. 1986. "Who Complains to Journal Editors and What Happens." *Sociological Inquiry* 56 (2): 259–71.

Simpson, Erik. 2013. "Five Ways of Looking at a Thesis." Connections: A Hypertext Resource for Literature.
http://www.math.grinnell.edu/~simpsone/Connections/Documents/fiveways.pdf.

Skorinko, Jeanine L. M., Janetta Lun, Stacey Sinclair, Satia A. Marotta, Jimmy Calanchini, and Melissa H.
Paris. 2015. "Reducing Prejudice across Cultures via Social Tuning." *Social Psychological and Personality
Science* 6 (4): 363–72.

Small, Mario Luis. 2009. "'How Many Cases Do I Need?' On Science and the Logic of Case Selection in
Field-Based Research." *Ethnography* 10 (1): 5–38.

Smith, Helen M., and Peter B. Banks. 2016. "How Dangerous Conservation Ideas Can Develop through
Citation Errors." *Australian Zoologist* 38 (3): 408–13.

Snipp, C. Matthew, and Sin Yi Cheung. 2016. "Changes in Racial and Gender Inequality since 1970." *The
ANNALS of the American Academy of Political and Social Science* 663 (1): 80–98.

Sparks, Sue. 2005. *JISC Disciplinary Differences Report*. London: Rightscom. http://www.jisc.ac.uk/media
/documents/themes/infoenvironment/disciplinarydifferencesneeds.pdf.

Spencer, N. J., Jack Hartnett, and John Mahoney. 1986. "Problems with Reviews in the Standard Editorial
Practice." *Journal of Social Behavior and Personality* 1 (1): 21–36.

Starbuck, William H. 2014. "Squeezing Lemons to Make Fresh Lemonade: How to Extract Useful Value
from Peer Reviews." In *How to Get Published in the Best Management Journals*, edited by Timothy Clark,
Mike Wright, and David J. Ketchen, 85–108. Cheltenham, UK: Edward Elgar.

Staub, Michael E. 1997. "Black Panthers, New Journalism, and the Rewriting of the Sixties." *Representations*
57 (Winter): 52–72.

Stevens, Bonnie Klomp, and Larry L. Stewart. 1987. *A Guide to Literary Criticism and Research*. New York:
Harcourt Brace College Publishers.

Stinchcombe, Arthur L. 1966. "On Getting 'Hung Up' and Other Assorted Illnesses." *Johns Hopkins Magazine*
(Winter): 25–30.

Straker, John. 2016. "International Student Participation in Higher Education Changing the Focus from
'International Students' to 'Participation.'" *Journal of Studies in International Education* 20 (4): 299–318.

Strunk, William, Jr. 1920. *The Elements of Style*. 1st ed. New York: Harcourt.

Strunk, William, Jr., and Edward A. Tenney. 1935. *The Elements and Practice of Composition*. Rev ed. New
York: Harcourt.

Strunk, William, Jr., and E. B. White. 1959. *The Elements of Style*. 1st ed. [*sic*]. New York: Macmillan.

Strunk, William, Jr., and E. B. White. 1972. *The Elements of Style*. 2nd ed. New York: Macmillan.

Strunk, William, Jr., and E. B. White. 1999. *The Elements of Style*. 4th ed. New York: Longman.

Sugimoto, Cassidy R., Vincent Larivière, Chaoqun Ni, and Blaise Cronin. 2013. "Journal Acceptance Rates:
A Cross-Disciplinary Analysis of Variability and Relationships with Journal Measures." *Journal of Informetrics* 7 (4): 897–906.

Swales, John M. 1990. *Genre Analysis: English in Academic and Research Settings*. Cambridge: Cambridge
University Press.

Swales, John M., and Christine B. Feak. 2000. *English in Today's Research World: A Writing Guide*. Ann Arbor:
University of Michigan Press.

Swales, John M., and Christine B. Feak. 2004. *Academic Writing for Graduate Students: Essential Tasks and
Skills*. 2nd ed. Ann Arbor: University of Michigan Press.

Swales, John M., and Christine B. Feak. 2009. *Abstracts and the Writing of Abstracts*. Ann Arbor: University of Michigan Press.

Swales, John M., and Christine B. Feak. 2010. "From Text to Task: Putting Research on Abstracts to Work." *Utrecht Studies in Language and Communication* 22: 167–80.

Swales, John M., and Christine B. Feak. 2012. *Academic Writing for Graduate Students: Essential Tasks and Skills*. 3rd ed. Ann Arbor: University of Michigan Press.

Sword, Helen. 2016. "'Write Every Day!': A Mantra Dismantled." *International Journal for Academic Development* 21 (4): 312–322.

Sword, Helen. 2017. *Air & Light & Time & Space: How Successful Academics Write*. Cambridge: Harvard University Press.

Tavory, Iddo, and Stefan Timmermans. 2014. *Abductive Analysis: Theorizing Qualitative Research*. Chicago: University of Chicago Press.

Taylor, Keeanga-Yamahtta. 2016. *From #BlackLivesMatter to Black Liberation*. New York: Haymarket Books.

Tennant, Jon. 2016. "The Relationship between Journal Rejections and Their Impact Factors." Blog section, *ScienceOpen: Research and Publishing Network*. January 18, 2016. http://blog.scienceopen.com/2016/01/the-relationship-between-journal-rejections-and-their-impact-factors/.

Tenopir, Carol, and Donald W. King. 2014. "The Growth of Journals Publishing." In *The Future of the Academic Journal*, edited by Bill Cope and Angus Phillips, 159–79. Oxford: Chandos. Original ed., 2009.

Tenopir, Carol, Donald W. King, Lisa Christian, and Rachel Volentine. 2015. "Scholarly Article Seeking, Reading, and Use: A Continuing Evolution from Print to Electronic in the Sciences and Social Sciences." *Learned Publishing* 28 (2): 93–105.

Tenopir, Carol, Kenneth Levine, Suzie Allard, Lisa Christian, Rachel Volentine, Reid Boehm, Frances Nichols, David Nicholas, Hamid R. Jamali, and Eti Herman. 2015. "Trustworthiness and Authority of Scholarly Information in a Digital Age: Results of an International Questionnaire." *Journal of the Association for Information Science and Technology* 67 (10): 2344–61.

Tfelt-Hansen, Peer. 2015. "The Qualitative Problem of Major Quotation Errors, as Illustrated by 10 Different Examples in the Headache Literature." *Headache: The Journal of Head and Face Pain* 55 (3): 419–26.

Thelwall, Mike, Kayvan Kousha, and Mahshid Abdoli. 2017. "Is Medical Research Informing Professional Practice More Highly Cited? Evidence from AHFS Di Essentials in Drugs.com." *Scientometrics* 112 (1): 509–27.

Thomason, Andy. 2014. "Professor Plagiarized 'Plagiarism' Definition in Textbook, Co-author Says." *Chronicle of Higher Education*, August 15, 2014. http://chronicle.com/blogs/ticker/professor-plagiarized-plagiarism-definition-in-textbook-co-author-says/84063.

Thomson, Pat. 2013. "Dr Jekyll Writes—Binge Writing as a Pathological Academic Condition." *Patter* (blog). January 3, 2013. http://patthomson.net/2013/01/03/dr-jekyll-writes-binge-writing-as-a-pathological-academic-condition/.

Thomson, Pat, and Barbara Kamler. 2013. *Writing for Peer Reviewed Journals: Strategies for Getting Published*. New York: Routledge.

Thomson, Pat, and Barbara Kamler. 2016. *Detox Your Writing: Strategies for Doctoral Researchers*. New York: Routledge.

Tompkins, Jane. 1986. "'Indians': Textualism, Morality, and the Problem of History." *Critical Inquiry* 13 (1): 101–19.

Toor, Rachel. 2013. "My Little Bag of Writing Tricks: How I Translate Grammar Directives into Moves I Can Use to Make My Sentences Better." *Chronicle of Higher Education*, September 3, 2013. https://www.chronicle.com/article/My-Little-Bag-of-Writing/141309.

Toor, Rachel. 2016. "Scholars Talk Writing: James M. McPherson." *Chronicle of Higher Education*, February 21, 2016. https://www.chronicle.com/article/Scholars-Talk-Writing-James/235383.

Torrance, Mark S., and Glyn V. Thomas. 1994. "The Development of Writing Skills in Doctoral Research Students." In *Postgraduate Education and Training in the Social Sciences*, edited by R. G. Burgess, 105–23. London: Jessica Kingsley.

Toulmin, Stephen. (1958) 2003. *The Uses of Argument*. Updated ed. Cambridge: Cambridge University Press.

Townsend, Michael A. R., Lynley Hicks, Jacquilyn D. M. Thompson, Keri M. Wilton, Bryan F. Tuck, and Dennis W. Moore. 1993. "Effects of introductions and conclusions in assessment of student essays." *Journal of Educational Psychology* 85 (4): 670–78.

Tufte, Edward R. 1992. *The Visual Display of Quantitative Information*. Cheshire, CT: Graphics Press.

Turban, Daniel B., Timothy R. Moake, Sharon Yu-Hsien Wu, and Yu Ha Cheung. 2016. "Linking Extroversion and Proactive Personality to Career Success the Role of Mentoring Received and Knowledge." *Journal of Career Development* 44 (1): 20–33.

Underwood, Benton J. 1957. *Psychological Research*. East Norwalk, CT: Appleton-Century-Crofts.

Van Allen, Judith. 1972. "'Sitting on a Man: Colonialism and the Lost Political Institutions of Igbo Women." *Canadian Journal of African Studies/La Revue canadienne des études africaines* 6 (2): 165–81.

Van Cleve, Nicole Gonzalez. 2016. *Crook County: Racism and Injustice in America's Largest Criminal Court.* Palo Alto, CA: Stanford University Press.

Vandenberg, Peter. 1993. "The Politics of Knowledge Dissemination: Academic Journals in Composition Studies." PhD diss., Texas Christian University.

VanEvery, Jo. 2013. "Be Careful How You Use the Term 'Binge Writing.'" *Jo VanEvery Transforming Academic Lives* (blog). March 12, 2013. http://jovanevery.ca/be-careful-how-you-use-the-term-binge-writing/.

Van Til, William. 1986. *Writing for Professional Publication.* Lanham, MD: Allyn and Bacon.

van Wesel, Maarten, Sally Wyatt, and Jeroen ten Haaf. 2014. "What a Difference a Colon Makes: How Superficial Factors Influence Subsequent Citation." *Scientometrics* 98 (3): 1601–15.

Vinkers, Christiaan H., Joeri K. Tijdink, and Willem M. Otte. 2015. "Use of Positive and Negative Words in Scientific PubMed Abstracts between 1974 and 2014: Retrospective Analysis." *BMJ* 351:h6467.

Volmer, Dietrich A., and Caroline S Stokes. 2016. "How to Prepare a Manuscript Fit-for-Purpose for Submission and Avoid Getting a 'Desk-Reject.'" *Rapid Communications in Mass Spectrometry* 30 (24): 2573–76.

von Wright, Georg Henrik. 1971. *Explanation and Understanding.* Ithaca, NY: Cornell University Press.

Walton, Jean. 1997. "'Nightmare of the Uncoordinated White-Folk': Race, Psychoanalysis, and *Borderline.*" *Discourse* 19 (2): 88–109.

Wang, Mingyang, Guang Yu, Shuang An, and Daren Yu. 2012. "Discovery of Factors Influencing Citation Impact Based on a Soft Fuzzy Rough Set Model." *Scientometrics* 93 (3): 635–44.

Ward, Jane. 2016. "Advice from an Outlaw Writer." *Inside Higher Education*, March 4, 2016. https://www.insidehighered.com/advice/2016/03/04/three-principles-effective-writing-system-essay.

Ware, Mark. 2011. "Peer Review: Recent Experience and Future Directions." *New Review of Information Networking* 16 (1): 23–53.

Ware, Mark, and Michael Mabe. 2015. *The STM Report: An Overview of Scientific and Scholarly Journal Publishing; Celebrating the 350th Anniversary of Journal Publishing.* 4th ed. The Hague, Netherlands: International Association of Scientific, Technical, and Medical Publishers.

Watson, Roger. 2016. "The Value of Trusting No One and Using Similarity Checkers." *Nurse Author and Editor* 26 (2): 3.

Webster, Gregory D., Peter K. Jonason, and Tatiana Orozco Schember. 2009. "Hot Topics and Popular Papers in Evolutionary Psychology: Analyses of Title Words and Citation Counts in Evolution and Human Behavior, 1979–2008." *Evolutionary Psychology* 7 (3): 348–62.

Weinberger, Cody J., James A. Evans, and Stefano Allesina. 2015. "Ten Simple (Empirical) Rules for Writing Science." *PLOS Computational Biology* 11 (4): e1004205.

Welch, H. Gilbert. 2006. "Ask the Expert: How to Handle Rejection." *Society of General Internal Medicine Forum* 29 (7): 2, 8.

Weller, Ann C. 2001. *Editorial Peer Review: Its Strengths and Weaknesses.* Medford, NJ: American Society for Information Science and Technology.

West, Jevin D., Jennifer Jacquet, Molly M. King, Shelley J. Correll, and Carl T. Bergstrom. 2013. "The Role of Gender in Scholarly Authorship." *PLOS ONE* 8 (7): e66212.

Whitley, Leila, and Tiffany Page. 2015. "Sexism at the Centre: Locating the Problem of Sexual Harassment." *New Formations: A Journal of Culture/Theory/Politics* 86 (1): 34–53.

Willis, Meredith Sue. 1993. *Deep Revision: A Guide for Teachers, Students, and Other Writers.* New York: Teachers and Writers Collaborative.

Wolf-Meyer, Matthew. 2014. "How to Write a Journal Article (in 6 steps): Step 4—The Evidence." *N=1* (blog). May 15, 2014. http://nequalsone.wordpress.com/2014/05/15/how-to-write-a-journal-article-in-6-steps-step-4-the-evidence/.

Woods, Peter. 2006. *Successful Writing for Qualitative Researchers.* London: Routledge.

Woodside, Arch. 2015. "Grabbing Readers: How to Focus Your Paper's Title and Contents on Its Major Theoretical Contribution Rather than the Local Context of the Study." In *A Guide to Publishing for Academics: Inside the Publish or Perish Phenomenon*, edited by Jay Liebowitz, 39–50. Boca Raton, FL: Taylor and Francis.

Wu, Ming-der, and Shih-chuan Chen. 2012. "How Graduate Students Perceive, Use, and Manage Electronic Resources." *Aslib Proceedings* 64 (6): 641–52.

Wu, Zongjie. 2014. "'Speak in the Place of the Sages': Rethinking the Sources of Pedagogic Meanings." *Journal of Curriculum Studies* 46 (3): 320–31.

Yankauer, Alfred. 1985. "Peering at Peer Review." *CBE Views* 8 (2): 7–10.

Young-Bruehl, Elisabeth. 2004. *Hannah Arendt: For Love of the World.* New Haven, CT: Yale University Press.

Zalta, Edward N., ed. 2016. *The Stanford Encyclopedia of Philosophy.* Stanford, CA: Metaphysics Research Lab, Center for the Study of Language and Information, Stanford University. https://plato.stanford.edu/.

Zhou, Lin. 2016. "Is There a Place for Cross-Cultural Contastive [*sic*] Rhetoric in English Academic Writing Courses?" *Bellaterra Journal of Teaching and Learning Language and Literature* 9 (1): 47–60.

Index

Made in the USA
Coppell, TX
03 November 2023

23765988R00240